TWEETALIGE SAKWOORDEBOEK

TWEETALIGE SAKWOORDEBOEK

Afrikaans-Engels   Engels-Afrikaans

Beknopte uitgawe van die Skoolwoordeboek van

PROF. DR. D. B. BOSMAN
PROF. I. W. v. d. MERWE

Bygewerk deur

DR. A. S. V. BARNES

PHAROS

ISBN 1 86890 007 X

Vierde uitgawe, eerste druk
in 1997 uitgegee deur
Pharos Woordeboeke,
'n afdeling van
Nasionale Boekhandel Beperk,
Heerengracht 40, Kaapstad

Tweede druk 1998

Voorheen uitgegee deur
Nasou Beperk, Kaapstad

Gelitografeer en gebind deur
Nasionale Boekdrukkery,
Drukkerystraat, Goodwood,
Wes-Kaap

Voorwoord

By die samestelling van hierdie *Tweetalige Sakwoordeboek* het ek my dit ten doel gestel om die volgende beginsels toe te pas:

a) Die aanwending van sowel die frekwensie- as die bruikbaarheidsprinsipe om die belangrikste woorde vas te stel. 'n Groot aantal woordelyste in verskillende tale is geraadpleeg en gekorreleer;

b) die uitskakeling, beknoptheidshalwe van (I) dié samestellinge waarvan die betekenisse maklik van die twee (of meer) afsonderlike lede of grondwoorde afgelei kan word, (II) die meeste internasionale woorde – veral dié wat sowel in Afrikaans as in Engels dieselfde spelvorm het, bv. *abattoir, camouflage, gentleman*, ens., en (III) idiomatiese e.a. uitdrukkinge, uitspraak en klemtoon.

c) die byvoeging van enkele belangrike eiename – veral persoons- en plekname wat moontlik spellingmoeilikhede kan oplewer.

A. S. V. BARNES

By die sestiende druk

Alle woorde wat aan een of ander deel van die bevolking aanstoot kan gee, is geskrap.

A. S. V. BARNES

Afkortinge en Verduidelikinge

n., (*Lat.* nomen), *Afr.* selfstandige naamwoord, *Eng.* noun.
a., (*Lat.* adjectivum), *Afr.* byvoeglike naamwoord, *Eng.* adjective.
adv., (*Lat.* adverbium), *Afr.* bywoord, *Eng.* adverb.
prep., (*Lat.* praepositio), *Afr.* voorsetsel, *Eng.* preposition.
conj., (*Lat.* conjunctio), *Afr.* voegwoord, *Eng.* conjunction.
interj., (*Lat.* interjectio), *Afr.* tussenwerpsel, *Eng.* interjection.
pron., (*Lat.* pronomen), *Afr.* voornaamwoord, *Eng.* pronoun.
v(ide), kyk.

Die verlede deelwoorde van werkwoorde word as volg aangedui:
  (i) **loop,** (ge-) = (het) **geloop;**
  (ii) **afkap,** (afge-) = (het) **afgekap;**
  (iii) **verstaan,** (het) of net (–) = het **verstaan.**

Die (*-e*) of (*-s*) na 'n selfstandige naamwoord dui die meervoudsuitgang aan, bv. **hoed, (-e)** = **hoede** en **voël, (-s)** = **voëls.** Ander meervoudsuitgange word vollediger aangegee.

Die verbuiging van 'n byvoeglike naamwoord word net na die hoofwoord tussen hakies aangegee, bv., **lelik, (-e)** = **lelike;** **vol, (–, -le)** = **vol, volle,** bv., 'n **vol** rivier, 'n **volle** uur.

Waar samestellinge en afleidinge, veral afleidinge op **-er, -heid, -ing, -nis, -skap,** nie aangegee word nie, kan die vertaling meestal gevind word deur die *hoofwoord te raadpleeg.*

Woorde wat met **ge-** begin, is dikwels verlede deelwoorde of afleidinge van werkwoorde. As sulke woorde nie onder **ge-** verskyn nie, soek dan onder die werkwoord sonder **ge-.**

AFRIKAANS – ENGELS

a, interj. ah!, oh!.
aaklig, a. & adv. awful, beastly, horrible.
aal, (ale), eel.
aalmoes, (-e), alms, charity; dole.
aalmoesenier, (-e, -s), almoner; chaplain.
aalwee, (-s), **aalwyn** (-e), aloe, bitter-aloe.
aam, (ame), aum; cf. **halfaam**.
aambeeld, anvil; incus (in ear).
aambei(e), haemorrhoids, piles.
aamborstig, (-e), asthmatic; husky.
aan, prep. at, against, by, by way of, for, in, in the way of, near, next to, on, of, upon, with, to, up to.
aan, adv. in, on, onwards, upon.
aanbetref, (het –), concern.
aanbeveel, (het –), recommend.
aanbevelenswaardig, (-e), commendable.
aanbeveling, (-e, -s), recommendation; reference.
aanbie(d), **aanbieë**, (aange-), offer, proffer; give, tender.
aanbieding, (-e, -s), offer, tender; presentation.
aanbind, (aange-), bind, fasten, tie.
aanblaas, (aange-), blow; fan, stir up.
aanblik, n. aspect; look; sight, view.
aanblik, (aange-), glance (look) at, cast one's eyes (up)on.
aanbly, (aange-), continue, remain; last.
aanbod, **aanbot**, (aanbiedinge, aanbiedings, aanbotte), offer, tender; supply.
aanbot, vide **aanbod**.
aanbou, n. annex(e); construction; erection.
aanbou,(aange-), build on to, add on (a new wing).
aanbrand, (aange-), burn, be (get) burnt; stick (to the pan).
aanbrandsel, (-s), crust, crustation.
aanbreek, (aange-), dawn (day); close in (night); broach; come, be at hand (time).
aanbring, (aange-), bring, bring on, bring with; construct (a wall), install; make (improvements).
aand, (-e), eve, evening, night.
aandadig, **handdadig**, (-e), – **aan**, implicated in.
aandag, attention, notice.
aandagstreep, dash.
aandagtig, (-e), a. attentive.
aandeel, part, portion, share.
aandenking, (-e, -s), memory, remembrance; keepsake.
aandoen, (aange-, aangedaan), cause, give; affect, move, touch; call (touch) at (a port).
aandoening, (-e, -s), emotion; touch (of fever).
aandoenlik, (-e), moving, touching.
aandra(e), **aandraag**, (aange-), bring, carry.
aandraai, (aange-), fasten, tighten; turn on, switch on.
aandrang, pressure; urge, insistence; urgency.
aandring, (aange-), press, push, urge.
aandryf, **aandrywe**, (aange-), float ashore; float along; incite.
aandui(e), (aange-), indicate, point out; describe, designate; signify.
aanduiding, (-e, -s), indication; sign.
aandurf, **aandurwe**, (aange-), dare, venture (upon).
aaneen, vide **aanmekaar**.
aaneenskakel, (aaneenge-), connect, couple.
aaneenskakeling, sequence, series, string.
aaneensluiting, closing, joining, uniting; rallying; joint; union.
aangaan, (aange-), continue, go on, proceed; commence; carry on, go on (like mad); conclude (a treaty), incur (debts), enter into (partnership), lay (a wager), negotiate (a loan); concern, regard.

aangaande, as for (to), as regards, regarding.
aangebore, inborn, innate.
aangedaan, (-dane), affected; agitated.
aangee, (aangeë), n. pass (in football).
aangee, (aange-), give, hand, pass (on); record, register; allege (as reason); state particulars, set (the fashion); report (a matter); pass (in football).
aangeklaagde, (-s), accused, defendant.
aangeklam, (-de), slightly tipsy, squiffy.
aangeleentheid, affair, matter; importance, moment.
aangenaam, (-name), agreeable, pleasant.
aangenome, a. accepted, assumed (name), adopted (child, country); taken on.
aangenome, conj. assuming, supposing.
aangesien, considering, since.
aangesig, (-te), countenance, face.
aangeslaan, (-slane), coated, tarnished.
aangeteken, (-de), noted; registered.
aangewese, (aangewys), dependent (up)on, obvious, right.
aangroei, (aange-), grow, increase.
aangryp, (aange-), catch (hold of), fasten upon (a pretext), grip; jump at (a chance); seize, take.
aangrypend, (-e), gripping, touching.
aanhaak, (aange-), couple, fasten, inspan.
aanhaal, (aange-), bring along, carry, fetch, draw tight(er); quote (passage).
aanhaling, (-e, -s), quotation.
aanhalingstekens, inverted commas.
aanhang, n. adherents, party; favour, support.
aanhang, (aange-), adhere (be attached, cling, stick) to; follow, support; attach.
aanhangig, (-e), under consideration, pending.
aanhangsel, (-s), addendum, annexure, appendage, appendix (of a book), codicil (of a will), supplement.
aanhef, n. beginning, opening remarks; preamble
aanhef, (aange-), begin, commence; raise, set up (a cry), strike up (a song).
aanheg, (aange-), affix, attach.
aanhegsel, (-s), addendum, enclosure.
aanhits, (aange-), egg on, incite.
aanhoor, (aange-), give a hearing, listen to.
aanhou, (aange-), continue, hold (on), insist, last, persevere, persist; arrest (a thief); hold up (a train), keep (dog).
aanhoudend, (-e), continuous, incessant.
aanja(ag), **aanjae**, (aange-), hurry (race, rush) on; drive (animals), urge on (a person).
aankla(ag), **aanklae**, (aange-), accuse (of), charge (with).
aanklaer, **-klaagster**, accuser; prosecutor.
aanklag, (-te), accusation, charge.
aankleef, **aanklewe**, (aange-), adhere (stick) to.
aanklop, (aange-), knock (beat, rap) at the door.
aanknoop, (aange-), fasten (to); establish (relations), open (negotiations), begin; enter into conversation.
aankom, (aange-), come, come along (on, home, in); arrive; begin; come on, improve; come round, call, drop in; matter.
aankomeling, (-e), freshman, newcomer.
aankomend, (-e), coming; next; prospective.
aankom(men)de, vide **aankomend**.
aankoms, arrival, coming (in).
aankondig, (aange-), announce, notify, advertise; foreshadow, herald, spell; review (a book).
aankondiger, (-s), announcer.
aankondiging, (-e, -s), announcement; notification; (press-) notice, review.
aankoop, (aange-), acquire, purchase.

aankweek, (aange-), cultivate, grow, raise, rear; foster.

aankyk, (aange-), look at.

aanland, (aange-), arrive, land.

aanlas, (aange-), add to; join to; join on, lash on to; exaggerate (a story).

aanlê, (aange-), aim, take aim; apply (a bandage, a standard); build; found, plan, fit up, install; draw up, make (a list); moor, berth (a vessel).

aanleer, (aange-), acquire, learn.

aanleg, n. plan; plant; ability.

aanlei, (aange-), lead on; lead to.

aanleiding, (-e, -s), cause, inducement, motive.

aanliggend, (-e), contiguous (angle), adjacent (side).

aanlok, (aange-), attract, tempt.

aanloklik, (-e), alluring, tempting.

aanloop, n. patronage.

aanloop, (aange-), run (walk) along (on); call, drop in.

aanloopplank, spring-board.

aanmaak, (aange-), mix, prepare.

aanmaning, (-e, -s), exhortation; warning; recurrence, touch.

aanmatigend, (-e), arrogant, presumptuous.

aanmatiging, (-e, -s), arrogance, presumption.

aanmekaar, together; consecutively.

aanmekaar- . . . vide aaneen- . . .

aanmekaarskryf, -skrywe, (aanmekaarge-), write as one word, join (letters).

aanmekaarspring, (aanmekaarge-), start fighting.

aanmeld(e), (aange-), announce, report.

aanmerklik, (-e), considerable.

aanmoedig, (aange-), encourage; give (moral) support to; tempt, lead on.

aanneem, (aange-, aangenome), accept, receive; adopt (name, child), assume, take on (a colour), embrace (a faith); admit, confirm (as a member); assume, suppose; agree to, carry (a motion), pass (a bill); undertake, contract for (a work); engage, take on (labourers).

aanneemlik, (-e), acceptable; plausible.

aannemer, (-s), contractor; undertaker.

aanneming, (-e, -s), acceptance; adoption; admission; confirmation (of church-members); passage (of a bill), carriage (of a motion).

aanpak, (aange-), seize (upon), catch hold of, grip; undertake; tackle, attack (an enemy); adhere to, form a crust.

aanpaksel, (-s), layer (of dirt, etc.), tartar (of teeth).

aanpas, (aange-), fit (try) on (shoes); adapt.

aanplak, (aange-), paste (post) up.

aanplakbiljet, placard, poster, bill.

aanplant, (aange-), plant, grow.

aanprys, (aange-), extol, recommend.

aanraai, (aange-), advise; recommend.

aanraak, (aange-), touch.

aanrand, (aange-), assault; hold up.

aanrander, (-s), assailant, assaulter.

aanranding, (-e, -s), assault; hold-up.

aanreik, (aange-), hand (on), pass, reach.

aanrig, (aange-), cause, bring about, do.

aanroep, (aange-), call, hail; invoke.

aanroer, (aange-), touch; mention, hurry.

aanruk, (aange-), advance.

aans, by and by, presently.

aansê, (aange-), announce, inform.

aansien, n. appearance; complexion; prestige, respect.

aansien, (aange-), look at; consider, regard.

aansienlik, (-e), considerable; notable; handsome.

aansies = aans.

aansit, (aange-), sit at table, sit down (to dinner); put on (a ring); add, join; set (dogs) on, incite; start (motor).

aansitter, (-s), self-starter; inciter.

aanskaf, (aange-), get, purchase, secure.

aanskou, (het –), behold, view.

aanskoulik, (-e), clear; graphic, visible.

aanskouing, (-e, -s), observation.

aanskryf, -skrywe, (aange-, aangeskrewe), demand payment; summon.

aanskrywing, (-e, -s), letter of demand; summons, writ.

aanslaan, (aange-), touch, strike (a note), overreach, click (of a horse); salute; start (of a motor); switch on (light); assess, rate (property, taxes); get blurred (steamy, thick) (of pane), get furred (of kettle, tongue), tarnish (of metal); knock-on (in football).

aanslag, touch (piano); stroke; click; attempt, (bomb-)outrage; assessment; sediment; fur, furring, scale (in kettle); fur (on tongue); knock-on (in football).

aansluit, (aange-), connect; join; unite.

aansluiting, joining, junction, connection, affiliation.

aansmeer, (aange-), smear (over); apply (ointment).

aansoek, (-e), application, request; proposal.

aanspoel, (aange-), drift (wash) ashore, wash up.

aanspoor, (aange-), spur on, urge on.

aansporing, (-e, -s), encouragement; incitement; incentive, stimulus.

aanspraak, claim, title; company.

aanspreek, (aange-), address; accost.

aanspreeklik, (-e), accountable, liable, responsible.

aanstaan, (aange-), please, like, suit.

aanstaande (-s), n. fiancé(e).

aanstaande, a. next (week); (forth)coming (elections), approaching (marriage), prospective (father-in-law).

aanstaar, (aange-), gaze (stare) at.

aanstalte(s), preparation(s).

aanstap, (aange-), walk on along.

aansteek, (aange-), pin on (a flower), put on (a ring); light (a lamp), kindle (a fire); set fire to; infect; get infection.

aansteeklik, (-e), catching, infectious.

aanstel, (aange-), appoint (to a post); pretend; give oneself airs.

aanstellerig, (-e), affected, full of airs.

aanstellings, airs.

aanstip, (aange-), jot down; touch (on).

aanstons, presently; vide aans.

aanstoot, n. offence.

aanstootlik, (-e), objectionable, offensive.

aanstorm, (aange-), charge (rush) on (along).

aanstryk, (aange-), walk along (on).

aanstuur, (aange-), pass (send) on.

aansuiwer, (aange-), pay (off), settle.

aansukkel, (aange-), struggle (jog) along.

aantal, (-le), number.

aantas, (aange-), touch; affect; attack.

aanteel, n. breed(ing); increase.

aanteel, (aange-), breed, rear; increase.

aanteken, (aange-), note down; mark; register (a letter); record, enter; score (a try).

aantekening, (-e, -s), note, annotation, record.

aantoon, (aange-), show; demonstrate, prove; indicate.

aantref, (aange-), meet (with), find, come across (upon).

aantrek, (aange-), pull; attract, appeal to; tighten, brace; dress.

aantrekkingskrag, pull, gravity; appeal.

aantreklik, (-e), attractive; sensitive.

aantyging, (-e, -s), imputation.
aanvaar, (het –), set out on, begin; enter upon; accept (a position).
aanval, n. attack, assault; fit, stroke (of paralysis), bout, touch (of malaria).
aanval, (aange-), attack, charge, assail.
aanvallig, (-e), charming, sweet.
aanvang, (aange-), begin, start.
aanvanklik, adv. at first, originally.
aanvat, (aange-), catch (get, lay, take) hold of, seize.
aanverwant, (-e), allied, related.
aanvoeg, (aange-), add, join.
aanvoer, (aange-), bring, convey; supply; allege (reasons); raise (objections); adduce (proof); cite (a case); lead (an army), captain (a team).
aanvoerder, (-s), commander, leader.
aanvoor, (aange-), begin, start.
aanvraag, n. demand; request, requisition.
aanvul, (aange-), replenish (one's stock); make good; complete, supplement.
aanvuur, (aange-), fire (the imagination), incite, inspire.
aanwakker, (aange-), animate, rouse; fan (a flame); stimulate.
aanwas, n. growth, increase; accretion.
aanwas, (aange-), grow, increase; rise.
aanwen, (aange-), contract (a habit), fall into the habit of; reclaim (land).
aanwend, (aange-), apply, employ; appropriate (money); bring into play.
aanwensel, (-s), habit.
aanwesig, (-e), present; on hand.
aanwins, asset; gain, profit.
aanwys, (aange-), point out; allocate.
aanwysend, (-e), demonstrative (pronoun).
aanwysing, direction, instruction; hint; indication; index.
aap, (ape), ape; monkey.
aapstuipe: die – kry, fly into a passion.
aar, (are), ear (of corn); vein (in body, etc.); underground-watercourse; seam (of ore).
aarbei, (-e), strawberry.
aard, n. character, nature; kind; sort.
aard, (ge-), thrive, get on well.
aardbewing, (-e, -s), earthquake.
aarde, earth, mould, soil.
aardig, (-e), pleasant; queer.
aardrykskunde, geography.
aards, (-e), earthly, worldly.
aardwolf, striped hyena.
aarsel, (ge-), hesitate, waver.
aartappel, ertappel, potato.
aartappelskyfies, potato chips.
aarts- . . ., arch-, consummate, regular.
aartsengel, archangel.
aas, (ase), n. ace (in cards).
aas, n. bait, carrion, prey.
aasvoël, vulture; glutton.
ab, (-te), abbot.
abba, (ge-), carry (a child) on one's back.
abdis, (-se), abbess.
abdy, (-e), abbey, monastery.
Abessinië, Abyssinia.
abnormaal, (-male), abnormal.
absoluut, (-lute), a. absolute.
absorbeer, (ge-), absorb.
abuis, error, mistake, slip.
acre, (-s), acre.
activa, (pl.) assets.
adamsappel, Adam's apple.
adamsvy(g), Adam's fig.
adder, (-s), adder, viper.
adel, n. nobility.
adelaar, (-s), eagle; vide **arend**.

adellik, (-e), high-born, noble; titled.
adelstand, nobility, peerage.
adem, n. vide **asem, n.**
adenoïed, (-e), adenoïde, (-s), adenoid.
adjektief, (-tiewe), adjective.
adjudant, (-e), adjudant, aide-de-camp.
adjunk, (-te), adjunct, deputy.
administrateur, (-s), administrator.
administreer, (ge-), administer, manage.
admiraal, (-s), admiral.
adoons, baboon, monkey, jacko; ugly.
adres, (-se), address; memorial.
adresboek, directory.
adverteer, (ge-), advertise.
advertensie, (-s), advertisement.
advies, advice; opinion.
adviseer, (ge-), advise.
advokaat, (-ate), advocate, barrister.
af, off; down; from.
afbaken, (afge-), mark (stake) out; delimit; define.
afbeeld, (afge-), depict, portray.
afbeen, cripple(d).
afbetaal, (het –), pay off; pay on account.
afbind, (afge-), tie up; underbind.
afbrand, (afge-), burn down; be burnt down.
afbreek, (afge-), break off, snap; interrupt (a story); sever connections); demolish (a building), take down (scaffolding), strike (tents); break off, stop (short).
afbreuk, damage, injury.
afbring, (afge-), bring down, lead off; reduce.
afbrokkel, (afge-), crumble away (off).
afdaal, (afge-), come (go) down, descend.
afdak, lean-to, pent-house, shed.
afdank, (afge-), dismiss, discharge.
afdeel, (afge-), divide; graduate.
afdek, (afge-), clear (the table).
afdeling, (-e, -s), division; portion, section; detachment; compartment; department; floor, ward.
afdoen, (afge-, afgedaan), take off (clothes); detract from; settle (a business), get through (an amount of work).
afdoende, conclusive, effective.
afdraai, (afge-), turn off (a tap); wring (neck); run off, show (a film); play (a record); branch off (a road).
afdraand, afdraans, adv. downhill.
afdraand(e), afdraande(s), decline, declivity, slope.
afdro(ë), -droog, (afge-), dry, wipe off.
afdruk, (afge-), print, reproduce; impress; press down.
afdrup(pel), (afge-), drip (trickle) down.
afdryf, -drywe, (afge-), drift (float) down (away, off).
afdwaal, (afge-), stray; wander from (one's subject), ramble, digress; go astray, err.
afdwing, (afge-), wring from; compel (admiration), command (respect); enforce (obedience).
affère, (-s), affair, business, matter.
affodil, (-le), daffodil.
affront, (-e), affront.
affronteer, (ge-), affront, insult.
afgaan, (afge-), go down; leave, separate.
Afgaan, (-ane), Afghan.
afgebroke, broken (words); intermittent.
afgedankste, confounded, severe.
afgee, (afge-), deliver, hand over; give out (a smell); give off (smoke); stain; come off (of a colour).
afgeleë, distant, far-off, remote.
afgeleef, (-de), decrepit, worn out.

afgelei, (-de), derived.
afgelope, finished; ended, past (year).
afgemat, (-te), tired (worn) out.
afgerond, (-e), rounded (narrative); round (sum, figure).
afgesaag, (-de), hackneyed, stale.
afgesant, (-e), ambassador, messenger.
afgesien: – van, notwithstanding.
afgeskeie, separate(d); secluded, private.
afgesloof, (-de), fagged (out), jaded.
afgesonder(d), (-de), isolated, remote.
afgestorwe, deceased, dead.
afgetob, (-de), weary, worn out.
afgetrokke, abstract; absent-minded.
afgevaardigde, (–, -s), delegate, deputy.
afgewerk, (-te), tired; finished.
afgly, (afge-), glide (slide, slip) down (off).
afgod, idol.
afgooi, (afge-), throw down (off); unseat.
afgrond, abyss, chasm, precipice.
afgryslik, (-e), hideous, horrible.
afguns, envy, jealousy, spite.
afgunstig, (-e), envious, jealous, spiteful.
afhaak, (afge-), unhook; uncouple, detach, dis-connect (railway-carriages); get married.
afhaal, (afge-), bring (fetch) down; call for, meet; insult (a person).
afhang, (afge-), hang down; depend (turn) on.
afhanklik, (-e), dependent.
afhou, (afge-), keep off (from).
afjak, (afge-), snub, insult.
afkap, (afge-), chop (cut, lop) off, cut (hew) down; abbreviate (a word).
afkappingsteken, apostrophe.
afkeer, n. dislike, aversion, repugnance.
afkeer, (afge-), avert, turn away; ward off (a blow); turn aside (water).
afkerig: – van, averse to.
afkeur, (afge-), disapprove; reject; scrap.
afkeurenswaardig, (-e), blameworthy, censurable, reprehensible.
afklim, (afge-), climb down, descend.
afklouter, (afge-), clamber (shin) down.
afknip, (afge-), cut (snip) off; cut, crop (hair).
afknou, (afge-), gnaw off; hurt, bully.
afkoel, (afge-), cool (down); refrigerate; calm down.
afkom, (afge-), come down.
afkoms, descent, origin.
afkomstig, descended from.
afkondig, (afge-), declare, proclaim.
afkoop, (afge-), buy off, redeem; ransom.
afkorting, abridg(e)ment, abbreviation, shor-tening.
afkrap, (afge-), scrape (scratch) off; scribble (down).
afkry, (afge-), get down (off, out); get (someone) away from; get free (a day).
afkyk, (afge-), look down; crib; spy.
aflaai, (afge-), discharge, off-load.
aflaat,(afge-), let down; leave away (off).
aflê, -leg, (afge-), lay down (arms); discard; cover, do (forty miles), come (a distance).
afleer, (afge-), unlearn; overcome.
aflei, (afge-), lead away (down); conduct (light-ning), distract (one's attention), avert (sus-picion); infer; derive (words).
afleiding, (-e, -s), diversion, distraction; deriva-tion; deduction.
aflewer, (afge-), deliver.
afloer, (afge-), watch, spy (out).
afloop, (afge-), flow (run) down; expire, termi-nate; slope, shelve; run down (clock); gutter (candle); conclude, end, result.

aflos, (afge-), relieve, take turns; redeem (a loan), discharge.
afluister, (afge-), overhear; eavesdrop.
afmaai, (afge-), mow; reap (corn); cut off.
afmaak, (afge-), finish, settle, dispatch; slate (a book).
afmaker, sheller.
afmat, (afge-), fatigue, exhaust.
afmeet, (afge-), measure off; proportion.
afmeting, dimension, measurement.
afname, decline, decrease.
afneem, (afge-), remove, take down (away, off); deprive of; diminish; abate; subside; decline; fall, sink; slacken.
afnemer, (-s), photographer.
afpak, (afge-), pack off, unload, unpack.
afpeil, (afge-), gauge, fathom, sound.
afpen, (afge-), peg (stake) off (claims).
afpers, (afge-), draw (tears); extort (money).
afpluk, (afge-), pick (off), gather.
afpraat, (afge-), talk over, arrange, settle.
afraai, (afge-), dissuade.
afraak, (afge-), get away (stray) from, get rid of.
aframmel, (afge-), reel off, gabble.
afransel, (afge-), lick, thrash, flog.
afreis, (afge-), depart, leave.
afreken, (afge-), settle accounts.
afrekening, settlement.
afrig, (afge-), coach; train.
afrigter, (-s), coach; trainer.
Afrika, Africa.
Afrikaan, (-kane), (native) African.
Afrikaans, (-e), n. & a. Afrikaans.
afrikaner, (-s), marigold.
Afrikaner, (-s), Africander.
Afrikanerbees, Africander (breed of cattle).
afrokkel, (afge-), entice away, wheedle out of.
afrol, (afge-), roll down; unwind.
afrolmasjien, copying-machine.
afrond, (afge-), finish, round off.
afroom, (afge-), cream, skim.
afdruk, (afge-), pluck (pull, tear) down (off), snatch away.
afry, (afge-), drive (ride) off (down); cover.
afsaag, afsae, (afge-), saw off.
afsaal, (afge-), off-saddle.
afsak, (afge-), come (slip) down, sag (down); subside; drop (float, sail) down; slide down.
afsaksel, deposit, sediment, silt.
afsê, (afge-), cancel, countermand; break off an engagement with.
afsend, (afge-), consign, dispatch, forward.
afsender, consigner, sender, remitter.
afset, n. sale, turnover, market.
afsetter, cheat, sharp(er), swindler.
afsien, (afge-): – van, abandon, give up (a plan); forgo, relinquish (a claim).
afsienbaar, (-bare), measurable.
afsigtelik, (-e), ghastly, hideous, ugly.
afsit, (afge-), dash off, start; remove, take off (from fire); amputate, cut off (a limb); down, drop (a passenger); trim (a dress); dismiss (from office).
afsitter, starter.
afskaaf, afskawe, (afge-), plane down; chafe (one's skin).
afskaf, (afge-), abolish, do away with; abrogate, repeal (laws).
afskaffer, (-s), teetotaller; abolitionist.
afskeep, (afge-), ship; fob off; neglect someone; botch (one's work).
afskeer, (afge-), shave off, shear off.
afskei(e), (afge-), separate; secrete; extract.
afskeid, departure, good-bye, leave.
afskeier, (-s), separator.

afskep, (afge-), skim (off), scoop off.
afskeur, (afge-), peel (tear) off; secede.
afskiet, (afge-), discharge, fire; send up (rockets); shoot down (a bird); shoot off (a limb).
afskil, (afge-), peel, pare; skin; scale off.
afskilfer, (afge-), peel (off), flake (off).
afskink, (afge-), pour off, decant.
afskop, n. kick-off.
afskop, (afge-), kick off, kick down.
afskort, (afge-), partition off.
afskram, (afge-), glance off.
afskrif, copy, duplicate.
afskrik, n. horror; deterrent; aversion.
afskrik, (afge-), deter; frighten, dishearten.
afskrikwekkend, (-e), deterrent; terrifying; prohibitive.
afskryf, afskrywe, (afge-), copy, transcribe; crib; finish; write off (debt).
afsku, abhorrence, horror.
afskud, (afge-), shake off.
afskuwelik, (-e), abominable, hideous, vile.
afslaan, (afge-), beat (dash, knock, strike) off; repel, repulse (an attack); knock down, reduce (the price).
afslaer, (-s), auctioneer.
afslag, n. reduction; auction.
afslag, (afge-), flay, skin.
afsloof, -slowe, (afge-), : sig –, drudge, slave.
afsluit, (afge-), cut (shut, turn) off; close (accounts); balance (books).
afslyt, (afge-), wear away (out, down).
afsmeer, (afge-), rub off; palm off.
afsmyt, (afge-), fling (throw, hurl) off.
afsny, (afge-), cut, cut off; intercept.
afsonder, (afge-), separate; segregate.
afsonderlik, (-e), a. separate, special.
afsonderlik, adv. separately, singly.
afspeel, (afge-), finish, play off; take place.
afspoel, (afge-), rinse; wash away.
afspons, (afge-), sponge down.
afspraak, appointment, arrangement.
afspreek, (afge-, afgesproke), agree upon, arrange.
afspring, (afge-), leap down; alight (from a horse); fly off; chip off; (negotiations) break down.
afstaan, (afge-), cede, give up, surrender.
afstam, (afge-); – van, be descended from, spring from.
afstammeling, (-e, -s), descendant.
afstamp, (afge-), bump (dash, knock) off.
afstand, (-e), distance, range; interval; cession (of territory); abdication (from throne); relinquishment, surrender (of rights).
afstap, (afge-), step off; dismount; walk.
afsteek, (afge-), cut (solds), mark out; deliver (a speech).
afstel, n. postponement, procrastination.
afstem, (afge-), reject, turn down (a proposal).
afsterf, afsterwe, (afge-), die; lose touch with.
afstof, (afge-), dust; wallop.
afstomp, (afge-), blunt; deaden, dull.
afstoot, (afge-), dash (knock, thrust) down (off); repulse, rebuff.
afstootlik, (-e), repelling, repulsive.
afstort, (afge-), tumble down; fling (hurl) down.
afstroom, (afge-), flow (stream) down.
afstroop, (afge-), flay, skin; ravage.
afstuur, (afge-); dispatch, send off.
afswaai, (afge-), turn aside.
afsweer, (afge-), abjure, renounce.
aftap, (afge-), draw off, tap; drain; trickle down.
afteken, (afge-), copy, sketch; portray; mark off.
aftel, (afge-), count off; subtract; lift down.
aftog, retreat.
aftrap, (afge-), wear down (heels); step down.

aftree, (afge-), step down; retire, abdicate; pace, step off.
aftrek, n. deduction; demand.
aftrek, (afge-), deduct, subtract; extract (in chem.); pull down (off); divert (someone's attention); fire, pull the trigger.
aftuig, aftuie, (afge-), outspan, unharness.
aftuimel, (afge-), tumble down.
afvaardig, (afge-), delegate, depute.
afval, n. refuse, waste; tripe.
afval, (afge-), fall off, drop, fall (tumble) down; lose weight.
afvallig, (-e), disloyal, unfaithful.
afvallige, (-s), deserter, renegade.
afvee(g), (afge-), wipe (off); sweep.
afvoer, n. conveyance; discharge, outlet.
afvra(ag), (afge-), ask (for), demand.
afvryf, -vrywe, (afge-), rub, polish.
afvuur, (afge-), discharge, fire (off).
afwaai, (afge-), blow off; be blown off.
afwaarts, downward(s), aside.
afwag, (afge-), await, wait (for).
afwagting, expectation.
afwater, (afge-), drain; pour off; water down.
afwee(g), -weë, (afge-), weigh out.
afweer, (afge-), avert; keep off.
afwen, (afge-); break (of a habit); wean from.
afwend, (afge-), avert, turn aside (away); ward off; divert (attention); stave off (defeat).
afwerk, (afge-), complete; finish (off), work off (a debt); get through (a programme).
afwerp, (afge-), throw off; shed; yield (profit); shake off (a feeling).
afwesig, (-e), absent.
afwissel, (afge-), alternate, vary.
afwisseling, alternation, succession; change, variation; diversity, variety.
afwit, (afge-), whitewash.
afwyk, (afge-), deviate, diverge; differ; disagree.
afwys, (afge-), turn away; reject; decline (an invitation), dismiss (a claim).
ag, n. attention, care; in – neem, observe, practise, use, consider.
ag, (ge-), esteem, respect; consider, count, regard.
ag(t), (ags, agte), n. eight.
ag, interj. ah!, alas!, oh!
agbaar, (-bare), honourable, respectable.
ageer, (ge-), act.
agie, (-s): nuuskierige –, inquisitive person.
agiteer, (ge-), agitate; fluster.
ag(t)ste, (-s), eighth.
agteloos, careless, inattentive.
agte(r)losig, (-e), careless.
agtenswaardig, (-e), estimable, respectable.
agter, prep. behind; at the back of.
agter, adv. at the back; behind.
agteraan, behind, at the back.
agteraf, adv. back, backward, in the rear; poor; out of the way; secretly.
agteraf, a. backward, out-of-the-way; poor.
agterbaks, (-e), a. sly, underhand(ed).
agterbaks, adv. secretly.
agterbly, (agterge-), remain (stay, drop) behind; survive.
agterbuurt(e), slum(s), backstreet.
agterdog, suspicion.
agterdogtig, (-e), suspicious.
agtereen, vide aaneen & agtermekaar.
agtereenvolgens, consecutively, successively.
agtergrond, background.
agterhaal, (het –), overtake.
agterhoede, rear(-guard).
agterhou, (agterge-), keep (hold) back (behind), withhold; conceal.

agterin, at the back.
agterkant, back; backside.
agterkleinkind, great-grandchild.
agterkom, (agterge-), discover, find out.
agterlaaier, breech-loader; frock-coat.
agterlaat, (agterge-), leave, leave behind.
agterlik, (-e), backward; behind the times.
agtermekaar, a. spick and span, up-to-date; spruce.
agtermekaar, adv. on end, at a stretch; spick and span; in order.
agtermiddag, afternoon.
agterna, after, behind; afterwards.
agternasit, (agternage-), pursue.
agterom, back, behind; round the back.
agteroor, back(wards).
agterop, behind, at the back, in the rear.
agteropskop, (agteropge-), kick up the heels.
agteros, hind-ox.
agterossambok, ox-sjambok.
agterplaas, back-yard.
agterraak, (agterge-), drop (fall, lag) behind.
agterryer, attendant, henchman.
agterskot, (payment of) balance.
agterstallig, (-e), in arrear.
agterstand, arrears, arrearage; backward position.
agterste, a. hind, hindmost, last.
agterstel, n. back, tail(-end) of wagon); rear-chassis (of motor).
agterstevoor, the wrong way about (round), upside down, topsy-turvy.
agterstewe, -sten, stern, poop.
agteruit, back, backward(s).
agteruitgaan, (agteruitge-), go back(wards), get worse; come down in the world; deteriorate (of goods); degenerate (of morals).
agtervoegsel, (-s), suffix.
agtervolg, (het –), pursue; persecute.
agterwaarts, adv. back, backwards.
agterwaarts, (-e), a. backward, retrograde.
agterweë, back; – bly, fail to turn up; remain in abeyance.
agt(t)ien, eighteen.
agting, esteem, estimation.
ag(t)uur, eight o'clock; breakfast.
ai, interj. ah!., o(h)!; ow!, ouch!
aikôna, haikôna, oh no!; not at all.
aits(a), my!, hallo!, look out!, sorry!
akademie, (-s), academy.
akasia, (-s), acacia.
akkedis, (-se), lizard; newt.
akker, (-s), 1. field, plot (of land).
akker, (-s), 2. acorn.
akkerboom, oak(-tree).
akkommodeer, (ge-), accommodate.
akkoord, (-e), agreement; chord (mus.)
akkordeer, (ge-), agree; get on with.
akkordeon, (-s), accordion.
akkuraat, (-ate), accurate, precise.
akkusatief, (-tiewe), accusative.
akoestiek, acoustics.
akrobaat, (-ate), acrobat.
aks, (-e), eighth (of an inch).
aksent, (-e), accent.
aksie, (-s), action; agitation.
aksioma, (-s), aksioom, (-iome), axiom.
aksyns, excise(-duty).
akte, (-s), deed; diploma; act.
akteur, (-s), actor, player.
aktief, (-iewe), active, energetic.
aktrise, (-s), actress.
aktuaris, (-se), actuary.
aktueel, (-uele), actual, topical.

akuut, (akute), acute.
akwarium, (-s), aquarium.
al, (-le), a. all, each, every.
al, adv. already, yet; -te waar, only too true; – te veel, overmuch.
al, conj. (al)though, even if, even though.
alarm, (-s), alarm; tumult, uproar.
Albanees, (-nese), n. & a. Albanian.
albaste, a. alabaster.
albaster, (-s), marble.
albei, both.
album, (-s), album; scrap-book.
aldaar, there, at that place (spot).
aldag, every day.
aldeur, all the time, all along.
aldus, so, thus, as follows.
aleer, before, ere.
alfaam, halfaam, (-ame), halfaum.
alfabet, (-te), alphabet.
algar, all, everybody, the whole lot.
algebra, (-s), algebra.
algeheel, (-hele), a. complete, utter.
algeheel, adv. completely, totally.
algemeen, n.: in (oor) die –, in general.
algemeen, (-mene), a. general; universal; common; public; vague.
alhier, here, locally.
alhoewel, (al)though.
alias, (-se), n. alias.
alias, adv. alias, otherwise.
alibi, (-'s), alibi.
aljimmers, always, repeatedly.
alkali, (-ë, -'s), alkali.
alkant, (on) all sides.
alklaps, every now and then.
alkohol, alcohol.
alkoholis, alcoholic.
alla, allamapstieks, -mastig, -matjies, -mintig, -wêreld, gracious!, goodness!
alledaags, (-e), daily, common(place).
alleen, alone, by oneself; lonely; single-handed; only; mere; in private.
alleenhandel, monopoly.
alleenlik, only, merely.
alleenspraak, monologue, soliloquy.
alleenstaande, detached, single.
allegorie, (-ë), allegory.
allemansvri(e)nd, hail-fellow-well-met.
allengs, gradually, insensibly.
allenig, alone, lonely; vide alleen.
aller-...., the very..., the... of all, most.
allerbes(te), best of all, very best.
allereers(te), first of all.
allerhande, of all sorts, sundry.
allerlaas(te), very last; the very latest.
allerlei, (of) all sorts, miscellaneous.
allernodigs(te), most necessary.
allersyds, allerweë, everywhere.
aller yl: in –, in hot haste.
alles, all, everything.
allesbehalwe, anything but, far from.
allesins, in every respect; fully.
allig, probably, perhaps.
alliterasie, (-s), alliteration.
allooi, alloy; quality, standard.
alluviaal, (-iale), alluvial.
almag, omnipotence.
almagtig, (-e), almighty, omnipotent.
almal, all, everybody; everything.
almanak, (-ke), almanac.
almaskie, all the same, nevertheless.
almelewe, always, for ever.
alom, everywhere, on all sides.
alou(e), ancient, time-honoured.
alreeds, already.

alsiende, all-seeing.
also, thus, in this manner.
alsydig, (-e), all-round, many-sided, universal; versatile (sportsman).
alt, (-e), contralto.
alte, (al te), (only) too.
altaar, (-are), altar.
altans, at least, anyhow; at any rate.
altemit(s), perhaps, maybe.
altesaam, altesame, (al)together, all told.
altoos, always, ever; **vir –,** for ever.
altwee, (al twee), both.
altyd, always, for ever.
altyddurend, (-e), everlasting.
aluin, (-e), alum, alumen.
aluminium, aluminium.
alvorens, before, until.
alwaar, where; wherever.
alweer, again, once more.
alwetend, (-e), omniscient.
alweter, know-all.
amandel, (-s), almond; tonsil.
amasone, (-s), amazon.
Amasone, (-s), Amazon.
Amasone(rivier): die –, the Amazon (River).
amateur, (-s), amateur, novice.
ambag, (-te), n. (handi)craft, trade, business, profession.
ambag, (ge-), do, be busy with.
ambagskool, technical school, trade-school.
ambagsman, (-ne), artisan.
ambassade, (-s), embassy.
ambassadeur, (-s), ambassador.
ambisie, ambition.
ambulans, (-e), ambulance, field hospital.
amegtig, (-e), breathless, out of breath.
amen, (-s), amen.
amendeer, (ge-), amend.
Amerikaner, (-s), American.
ametis, (-te), amethyst.
ameublement, (-e), (set, suite of) furniture.
ammoniak, ammonia.
ammunisie, (am)munition.
amok, amuck: – **maak,** run amuck.
amp, (-te), function, office, post, duty.
amper(tjies), almost, nearly.
ampsbekleër, incumbent (of office).
ampshalwe, officially, ex officio.
ampsweë: van –, vide **ampshalwe.**
amptelik, (-e), official; professional.
amptenaar, (-are), civil (public) servant, official.
amusant, (-e), amusing, entertaining.
amuseer, (ge-), amuse.
analise, analysis.
analiseer, (ge-), analyse.
analogie, (-ë), analogy.
anargie, anarchy.
anatomie, anatomy.
Andalusies, (-e), Andalusian.
ander, (-e), n. & a. another; other.
anderdagmore, (-môre), the next morning.
anderdeels: eensdeels, . . . –, partly, . . . partly.
anderhalf, (-halwe), one and a half.
anderkant, prep. across, beyond.
anderland, abroad.
andermaal, again, once more.
anderman, someone else, another.
anders, different; else, otherwise.
andersdenkend, (-e), different(ly)-minded; dissentient.
andersgesind(e), vide **andersdenkend(e).**
andersins, otherwise.
andersom, the other way about (round).
anderste(r), otherwise; different.
andersyds, on the other hand.

angel, (-s), sting (of bee); (fig.) barb.
angelier, (-e), carnation.
Anglikaans, (-e), Anglican.
Anglisisme, (-s), Anglicism.
angora, (-s), angora.
angs, (-te), terror, anxiety, dismay.
angstig, (-e), afraid, fearful.
angsvallig, (-e), conscientious, scrupulous.
angswekkend, (-e), alarming.
anker, (-s), n. anchor; brace, tie (of wall); armature (of magnet); anker (liquid-measure).
anker, (ge-), anchor; brace.
annale, (pl.) annals.
annekseer, (ge-), annex; take.
anomalie, (-ë), anomaly.
anoniem, (-e), anonymous.
ansjovis, anchovy; white bait.
Antarktika, Antartic.
antibioties, a. antibiotic.
antibiotikum, n. antibiotic.
antipatie, (-e), antipathy, dislike.
antraks, anthrax.
antrasiet, anthracite.
Antwerpen, Antwerp.
antwoord, n. answer, reply.
antwoord, (ge-), answer, reply.
anys, anise.
apart, (-e), apart, aside, separate.
apologie, (-ë), apology.
apostel, (-s), apostle.
apparaat, (-ate), apparatus.
appel, (-s), apple.
appèl, (-le, -s), appeal.
appelkoos, (-kose), apricot.
appelliefie, (-s), Cape gooseberry.
appelskimmel, dapple-grey.
appelwyn, cider.
appendisitis, appendicitis.
applikasie, (-s), application.
apploudisseer, (ge-), applaud.
applous, applause.
appresieer, (ge-), appreciate, value.
apteek, (-teke), pharmacy.
apteker, (-s), chemist, druggist.
aptyt, appetite.
Arabier, (-e), Arab.
arbei, (ge-), labour, toil, work.
arbeid, labour, toil, work.
Arbeidersparty, Labour Party.
arbeidsaam, (-same), diligent, industrious.
arbitreer, (ge-), arbitrate; umpire.
arbitrêr, (-e), arbitrary.
arend, (-e), eagle.
argeloos, (-lose), guileless; unsuspecting.
argeoloog, (-loë, -loge), archaeologist.
argief, (-iewe), archives; record-office.
argipel, (-le, -s), archipelago.
argitek, (-te), architect.
argivaris, (-se), archivist.
arglistig, (-e), cunning, crafty.
argument, (-e), argument, plea.
argumenteer, (ge-), argue, reason.
argwaan, mistrust, suspicion.
Ariër, (-s), Aryan.
arig, (-e), queer, strange, unwell.
aristokraat, (-rate), aristocrat.
aristokrasie, aristocracy.
Aristoteles, Aristotle.
arkade, (-s), arcade.
arm, (-s), n. arm; branch; lever.
arm, (-), a. poor; unfortunate.
armband, bracelet, bangle.
arm(e)blanke, (-s), poor-white.
armbuurt, poor quarter.
arme, (-s), n. the poor.

armlik, (-e), needy, poor, shabby.
armoede, poverty; paucity (of ideas).
armoedig, (-e), poor, shabby; humble.
armrig, (-e), rather poor.
armsalig, (-e), poor, pitiful; beggarly.
arm(e)sorg, poor-relief.
aroma, (-s), aroma, fragrance.
aronskelk, arum-lily, pig-lily.
arpuis, harpuis, resin (rosin).
arres, arrest; custody, detention.
arrestasie, arrest, apprehension.
arresteer, (ge-), arrest.
arrie, (I) say!, heigh!, lo!, my!
arriveer, (ge-), arrive.
arsenaal, (-ale), arsenal, armoury.
arsenikum, arsenik, arseen, arsenic.
artikel, (-s), article.
artikuleer, (ge-), articulate.
artisjok, (-ke), artichoke.
arts, (-e), doctor, physician.
as, (-se), n. ash, ashes; cinders.
as, (-se), n. axle; axle-tree (of wagon); axis (of figure, earth, etc.); shaft, spindle (of engine).
as, adv., conj. & prep, as, like, such as; in the capacity of; when; if; as if.
asalea, (-s), azalea.
asbak, ash-pan; ash-bin.
asbes, asbestos.
asblik, ash-bin.
asem, (-s), breath.
asem, (ge-), breathe.
asemhaal, (asemge-), breathe.
asemloos, (-lose), breathless.
asetileen, acetylene.
asfalt, asphalt, bitumen.
as(se)gaai, (-e), assegai.
Asiaat, (-ate), Asiatic.
asjas, good-for-nothing, nincompoop.
askar, dust-cart, rubbish-cart.
askoek, ash-scone; rogue, scamp.
asma, asthma.
asmede, as also, and also, as well as.
asnog, as yet.
asof, as if, as though; **maak –,** pretend.

asook, including.
aspaai, hide-and-seek.
aspek, (-te), aspect.
aspersie, (-s), asparagus.
aspirant, (-e), aspirant, applicant.
aspirien, (aspirine), aspirin(e).
Aspoester(tjie), (-s), Cinderella.
aspres, (aspris, ekspres), on purpose.
asseblief, (if you) please.
assegaai, vide **as(se)gaai.**
assimileer, (ge-), assimilate.
Assiriër, (-s), Assyrian.
assistent, (-e), assistant.
assosieer, (ge-), associate.
assuransie, assurance, insurance.
aster, (-s), aster, chrysanthemum.
astrant, (-e), cheeky, impudent.
astronoom, (-nome), astronomer.
asuur, azure, sky-blue.
asvaal, ashen pale; ashen grey (colour).
asyn, vinegar.
asynsuur, a. as sour as vinegar.
ateïs, (-te), atheist.
ateïsme, atheism.
ateljee, (-s), studio.
Athene, Athens.
atjar, pickles.
atlas, (-se), n. atlas.
atleet, (-lete), athlete.
atletiek, athletics.
atmosfeer, atmosphere.
atoom, (-tome), atom.
atoomkrag, atomic energy.
atoomstapel, atomic pile.
attensie, (-s), attention, thoughtfulness.
attent, (-e), attentive; considerate.
attributief, (-iewe), attributive.
Augustus, August.
Australiër, (-s), Australian.
Avondmaal, Awendmaal, vide **Nagmaal.**
avontuur, awentuur, (-ture), adventure.
aweregs, (-e), inverted; perverse; purl.
awery, average, damage.

ba!, pshaw!, bah!
baadjie, (-s), coat, jacket.
baadjiepak, coat and skirt, costume.
baai, (-e), n. 1. bay.
baai, n. 2. baize.
baai, (ge-), bathe.
baaikostuum, bathing-costume.
baal, (bale), n. bale.
baan, (bane), n. course, track; channel; orbit (of planet); trajectory (of projectile); panel (of skirt); width, breadth (of cloth); court (for tennis); floor (for dancing).
baan, (ge-), clear; pave (the way).
baanbreker, pioneer.
baantjie, (-s), job, billet.
baar, (bare), n: 1. wave, billow.
baar, (bare), n. 2. bier; stretcher.
baar, a. raw, inexperienced.
baar, (ge-), bring forth, bear; cause (anxiety).
baard, (-e), beard; whiskers.
baardkoring, bearded wheat.
baars, (-e), bass, perch.
baas, (base), master, boss; manager, chief; overseer; champion.
baasraak, (baasge-), overcome, defeat; master.
baasspeel, (baasge-), domineer, rule the roost.
baat, n. benefit, profit.
baat, (ge-), avail.
baatsugtig, (-e), selfish, egoistic.
baba(tjie), babetjie, (-s), baby, infant.
babbel, (ge-), chatter, prattle.
babbelbek, –kous, chatterbox, gossip.
baber, (-s), barbel, bagger.
bad, (-de, -dens), bath; (baaie), hot spring.
bad, (ge-), bath; have a bath.
bad(s)kamer, bathroom.
bagasie, luggage, baggage.
bagasiekamer, -kantoor, luggage-office, cloak-room.
bagasiewa, luggage-van.
bagatel, vide **bakatel.**
bagger, (ge-), dredge.
baie, (meer, meeste), a., much: many.
baie, adv. very; much; many; far; frequently.
baiekeer, -maal, frequently, often.
bajonet, (-te), bayonet.
bak, (-ke), n. bowl; dish, basin; cistern, tank; bucket; trough; container; body (of car); hood (of snake).
bak, (ge-), bake (bread); fry (egg, fish); bask (in the sun).
bakatel, (-le), bagatelle, trifle.
bakbene, bandy legs.
bakboord: van – na stuurboord, from pillar to post.
baken, (-s), beacon, landmark; buoy.
bakermat, cradle, birth-place.
bakker, (-s), baker.
bakkery, (-e), bakery; baking.
bakkies, (-e), phiz, mug.
bakkopslang, ringed cobra.
baklei, (ge-), fight, scuffle, scrap.
bakoond, oven.
bakore, protruding ears.
bakpoeier, baking-powder.
baksel, (-s), batch, baking.
baksteen, brick.
baksteenoond, brick-kiln.
bakvis(sie), flapper.
bal, (-le), n. 1. ball.
bal, (-s), n. 2. ball, dance.
bal, (ge-), clench (fist).
balans, balance; balance-sheet.
baldadig, (-e), rowdy, wanton; frisky.
balein, (-e), whale-bone; busk.

balhorig, (-e), refractory, stubborn.
balie, (-s), tub; bar.
baljaar, (ge-), gambol, romp; kick up a row.
balju, (-'s), sheriff.
balk, (-e), beam; rafter (for roof); (floor-) joist; staff, stave (mus.).
balkon, (-s, -ne), balcony; platform (train, tram); dress-circle (in theatre).
ballade, (-s), ballad.
ballasmandjie, bushel-basket.
ballet, (-te), ballet.
balling, (-e, -s), exile.
ballon, (-ne, -s), balloon.
balsem, n. balm, ointment.
balsem, (ge-), embalm (corpse).
balsturig, (e), refractory, obstinate.
bamboes, bamboo.
ban, n. excommunication, ban.
ban, (ge-), banish, exile, expel.
banaal, (-nale), banal, trite, trivial.
banana, (-s), banana.
band, (-s, -e), band (round arm, etc.); tyre (of bicycle, motorcar); hoop (round barrel); bandage; binding, cover (of book); volume (book); belt; strap; sling (for arm); bond; tie (of friendship, blood).
bandelier, (-e, -s), bandoleer.
bandeloos, (-lose), lawless; unrestrained.
bandiet, (-e), convict.
bandom, bantom, (-s), bantam.
bandopnemer, tape-recorder.
bandsaag, endless saw, belt-saw.
bandvat, (bandge-), hold tight; pull up short.
bang, (–, -e), afraid, frightened; anxious.
bangbroek, coward, "funk".
banier, (-e), banner, standard.
bank, (-e), n. bench, seat; settee; pew (in church); desk (in school); bank.
bank, (ge-), bank.
banket, (-te), banquet.
bankier, (-s), banker.
bankrot, bankrupt, insolvent.
banneling, vide **balling.**
bantamhoendertjie, bantam (-cock, -hen).
bantom, bandom, (-s), bantam (pebble); striped, banded ox (cow).
bar, (-re), a. barren; inclement, severe.
barak, (-ke), barracks; hovel.
barbaar, (-bare), barbarian, savage.
barbier, (-e, -s), barber, hairdresser.
barlewiet, barley-wheat.
barmhartig, (-e), merciful, charitable.
barnsteen, amber.
barometer, barometer.
baron, (-ne, -s), baron.
bars, (-te), n. crack; burst, split; (of skin).
bars, (–, -e), a. harsh, rough, gruff.
bars, (ge-), burst, crack, split; chap (of skin); explode, burst (of shell).
barstens: tot – toe, bursting.
bas, (-se), n. (1) bass.
bas, (-te), n. (2) bark (of tree); rind (of tree, plant); skin.
basaar, (-s), bazaar.
basboom, wattle.
baseer, (ge-): – op, base on.
basis, (-se), base; basis (fig.).
Basoeto, (-'s), Basuto.
basstem, bass (-voice).
basta, stop; that's enough!
baster, (-s), bastard; half-breed; hybrid; mongrel.
baster, adv. kind of; rather; quite.
baster, (ge-), hybridize; interbreed.
basterskaap, Persian sheep.

basuin, (-e), trumpet; trombone.
bataljon, (-ne, -s), battalion.
bate, asset.
batig, (-e), –e saldo, credit-balance.
battery, (-e), battery.
beaam, (–), assent to, approve of.
beampte, (-s), official, officer.
beangs, (-te), anxious, alarmed.
beangstig, (–), alarm.
beantwoord, (–), answer; reply to; acknowledge (greeting); get on; thrive.
bearbei, (–), work; cultivate (ground); canvass (constituency, etc.); minister to the spiritual needs of.
bebloed, (-e), blood-stained.
beboet, (–), fine.
bebos, (–), afforest.
bebou, (–), build (up)on; cultivate.
bebroei(d), (-de), hard-set (egg).
bebrou, (–), spoil, mess up.
bed, (-de, -dens), bed; bedside.
bedaar, (–), calm down; subside; drop (of wind); soothe, pacify.
bedaard, (-e), calm, tranquil.
bedag, mindful (of); prepared (for).
bedags, by day, during the day.
bedagsaam, (-same), thoughtful; considerate.
bedank, (–), thank; resign (post); discharge (employee); decline (honour).
beddegoed, bedding, bed-clothes.
bedding, (-s), bed (of river, of flowers), seam (of coal); stratum (geol.).
bede, (-s), prayer; supplication.
bedeel, (–), endow (with talents).
bedees, (-de), bashful, shy.
bedek, (-te), covered; concealed, disguised, veiled; covert (threat).
bedek, (–), cover (up); conceal.
bedektelik, covertly.
bedel, (ge-), beg; ask alms; cadge.
bedelaar, (-s), beggar.
bedenking, (-e, -s), consideration; objection.
bedenklik, (-e), critical (condition); dangerous; serious; suspicious.
bederf, n. decay, putrefaction, decomposition; rot (in wood); corruption; ruin.
bederf, bederwe, (–), go bad, rot, decay; spoil; ruin (health); corrupt (morals).
bederflik, (-e), perishable; corruptible.
bedien, (–), serve, wait upon; mind (machine); preach (the Gospel); make use of, avail oneself of.
bediende, (-s), servant (in house); assistant (in shop).
bedink, (–), remember; consider (matter); think out, invent (story), devise (ways and means).
bedlêend, bedlêerig, (-e), bedridden.
Bedoeïen, (-e), Bedouin.
bedoel, (–), mean; intend; purpose.
bedoeling, (-e, -s), meaning; purpose, aim.
bedompig, (-e), stuffy, close, sultry.
bedorwe, depraved; spoiled; corrupt.
bedra(ag), bedrae, (–), amount to.
bedreig, (–), threaten, menace.
bedrewe, skilled, skilful; expert.
bedrieë, bedrieg, (–), deceive, mislead.
bedrieglik, (-e), deceptive.
bedroë, deceived, taken in.
bedroef, (-de), a. sad, sorrowing.
bedroef, (–), grieve, distress.
bedrog, (-drieërye), deceit, fraud.
bedruk, (-te), a. printed; depressed.
bedryf, (-drywe), deed; trade, business, profession; industry; act (of play).
bedryf, -drywe, (–), commit, perpetrate.

bedrywende vorm, active voice.
bedrywig, (-e), busy, active.
bedsprei, coverlet, bedspread.
bedug, afraid, apprehensive.
bedui(e), (–), signify; portend; indicate; point out, gesticulate.
beduidenis, meaning.
beduiwel(d), (-de), mad, crazy, daft.
bedwang, control, restraint.
bedwelm, (–), stun (by a fall); intoxicate (by strong drink); drug.
bedwing, (–), control, suppress; keep (hold) back, keep down; quell (insurrection); restrain (passions); contain (anger).
beëdig, (–), swear in; swear to.
beëdigde, sworn.
beef, bewe, (–), tremble; shake (with fear); shudder (with cold, horror); shiver (with cold).
beëdig, (–), finish, end, conclude.
beeld, (-e), n. image; reflection; statue (moulded figure); picture; figure of speech; conception.
beeld, (ge-), form, shape; portray.
beeldende, plastic (art).
beeldhou, (ge-), sculpture, carve.
beeldhouer, (-s), sculptor.
beeldradio, television.
beeldsend, (ge-), televise, telecast.
beeldskoon, (-skone), of rare beauty.
beeldspraak, figurative (metaphorical) language, metaphor.
been, (bene), leg; bone (of skeleton); side (of triangle).
been-af, with a broken leg; in love.
beer, (bere); bear (wild animal); boar (male pig)
beërf, beërwe, (–), inherit.
beerwyfie, she-bear.
bees, (-te), beast; brute.
beeste, cattle.
beeswagter, cattle-herd.
beet, (bete), 1. beetroot.
beet, n. 2. bite, hold, grip.
beethê, (beetgehad), have, get hold of.
beetkry, (beetge-), get (take, seize) hold of.
beetneem, (beetge-), take in, deceive, make a fool of.
beetpak, (beetge-), lay hold of, seize.
befaamd, (-e), renowned; notorious.
befoeter, (–), muck up.
befoeter(d), (-de), crazy, mad, daft.
begaaf, (-de), gifted, talented.
begaan, (-gane), a. beaten (track); concerned.
begaan, (–), tread, go; make (mistake); commit (crime).
begaanbaar, (-bare), practicable, passable.
begeef, begewe, (–), forsake, fail.
begeer, (–), desire, want, covet.
begeerlik, (-e), desirable; tempting; greedy (eyes); covetous.
begelei, (–), accompany; escort.
begenadig, (–), pardon, reprieve; grace, favour.
begerig, (-e), desirous, covetous.
begin, n. beginning, start, outset.
begin, beginne, begint, (–), begin, start.
beginsel, (-s), principle.
beginselvas, (-te), of firm principles.
begoël, begogel, (–), bewitch; delude.
begraaf, begrawe, (–), bury, inter.
begrafnis, (-se), funeral, burial.
begrens, (–), limit, bound.
begrepe, understood.
begrip, (-pe), idea, conception, understanding.
begroei, (–), overgrow.
begroet, (–), greet, salute.
begroot, (–), estimate, rate.
begryp, (–), understand, grasp.

begunstig, (-), favour; patronize.
behaag, behae, (-), please.
behaaglik, (-e), pleasant; comfortable.
behaal, (-), gain, win, (prize, victory), score; obtain (degree).
behae, n. pleasure.
behalwe, except, but, save.
behandel, (-), treat; deal with (subject, case, person); do; manage; attend; discuss.
behang, (-), hang (decorate) with; paper.
behartig, (-), look after; manage.
beheer, (-), manage, administer.
beheers, (-), control; govern, rule (people).
beheks, (-), bewitch.
behelp, (-): sig -, manage.
behels, (-), embrace; contain.
behendig, (-e), dexterous, adroit.
behep; - met, possessed by (with) (idea).
behoed(e), (-), protect; preserve; save.
behoedsaam, (-same), cautious, wary.
behoef, (-), need, require, want.
behoefte, (-s), need, want.
behoeftig, (-e), needy, destitute.
behoewe: ten - van, on behalf of.
behoor(t), (-), belong (to); be proper.
behoorlik, adv. properly, thoroughly.
behore: na -, properly, respectably.
behou, (-), keep; maintain; save.
behoudens, except (but) for.
behoue, safe, unhurt.
behuising, housing.
behulp: met - van, with the aid of.
behulpsaam, (-same), helpful.
beide, both.
beïnvloed, (-), influence, affect.
beitel, (-s), n. chisel; cutter.
beitel, (ge-), chisel.
bejaard, (-e), elderly.
bejammer, (-), pity; bewail; deplore.
bejammerenswaardig, (-e), pitiable; deplorable.
bejeën, (-), treat, use.
bek, (-ke), mouth; beak, bill (of bird); snout (of animal); muzzle (of fire-arm), jaws (of vice); spout; opening.
bek-af, down-hearted; worn out.
bekamp, (-), fight (against); combat.
beken, (-), acknowledge, admit; make out.
bekend, (-e), known; familiar.
bekende, (-s), acquaintance.
bekendmaking, (-e, -s), announcement; notice; publication.
bekentenis, (-se), confession, admission.
beker, (-s), jug, mug; beaker; cup.
bekken, (-s), basin; catchment-area; (baptismal) font.
bekla(ag), beklae, (-), pity (person); deplore; bemoan (one's lot).
beklad, (-), blot; sully; slander.
bekla(g)enswaardig, (-e), pitiable; lamentable.
bekleding, covering; cover; upholstering; up-hostery; lining; tenure (of office).
beklee(d), (-), clothe; upholster; drape (with cloth); case; line; panel (walls); hold (post).
beklemming, oppression; heaviness.
beklemtoon, (-), accent, stress (point).
beklim, (-), climb; scale.
beklink, (-), settle; drink to.
beklonke, settled, fixed up.
beknop, (-te), a. concise (style); condensed; compact; poky (room); cramped.
bekom, (-), get, obtain.
bekommer: sig - oor (om), worry about.
bekoms: jou - eet, (hê), eat (have) one's fill.
bekonkel, (-de), a. muddled up: mad.
bekonkel, (-), manoeuvre, wangle.

bekoor, (-), charm, fascinate.
bekostig, (-), afford.
bekragtig, (-), ratify; confirm.
bekrap, bekras, (-), scratch (scribble) all over.
bekrompe, a. confined (space); narrow-minded.
bekroon, (-), crown; award a prize.
bekruip, (-), stalk, steal upon.
bekwaam, (-kwame), a. competent, efficient; ripe.
bekwaam, (-): sig -, qualify (for); retain, study.
bekyk, (-), look at, view (lit. & fig.).
bel, (-le), n. bell; ear-drop; wattle (of turkey).
bel, (ge-), ring; (tele)phone.
belaai, (-), load; burden.
belaglik, (-e), ridiculous, ludicrous.
beland, (-), land.
belang, (-e), interest; importance.
belangrik, (-e), important; considerable.
belangstellend, (-de), interested; sympathetic.
belangstelling, interest; sympathy.
belangwekkend, (-e), interesting.
belas, (-), load; burden; tax (the farmers); instruct, charge with.
belasbaar, (-bare), taxable; dutiable.
belaster, (-), slander, blacken.
belasting, (-s), taxation; tax; (local) rates; load, stress, strain.
belê, beleg, (-), invest (money); convene (meeting).
beledig, (-), offend, insluit.
beleef, belewe, (-), live to see; experience.
beleef, (-de), a. polite, courteous.
beleefdheidshalwe, out of politeness.
beleër, (-), besiege.
beleër, belegger, (-s), investor (of money); convener (of meeting).
beleg (-leëringe), n. siege.
beleid, management; tact; policy.
belemmer, (-), impede, hamper; obstruct (the way); stunt (growth).
belese, well-read.
belet, (-), prevent; stop; forbid.
beletsel, (-s), impediment, hindrance.
belg: ge- wees, be angry (offended).
Belg, (-e), Belgian.
belhamel, bell-wether; ringleader.
belieg, (-), lie to (person).
belig, (-), light; expose (photography), throw light on, illuminate.
beliggaam, (-), embody.
beloer, (-), watch, spy upon.
belofte, (-s), promise.
beloof, belowe, (-), promise.
beloon, (-), reward; recompense.
beloop, n. way, course.
beloop, (-), walk: amount to.
beluister, (-), listen to; overhear.
belus: - wees op, crave, be keen on.
bely, (-), profess; confess.
belydenis, (-se), confession; creed (religion).
bemaak, (-), bequeath, leave.
bemagtig, (-), take possession of; make oneself master of seize; obtain.
bemes, bemis, (-), fertilize, manure.
bemiddelaar(ster), (-s), mediator, intermediary.
bemiddeld, (-e), well-to-do, well-off.
bemiddeling, mediation, intercession.
bemin, (-), love, be fond of.
beminde, (-s), lover, sweetheart.
beminlik, (-e), lovable, amiable.
beminnenswaardig, (-e), lovable.
bemodder, (-), bemire, stain with mud.
bemoedig, (-), encourage, cheer up.
bemoei: sig - met, meddle with.
bemoeial, (-le), busy-body, meddler.
bemoeilik, (-), impede, hinder, obstruct.

bemoeisiek, (-e), meddlesome.
bemoeisug, meddlesome.
bemors, (-), dirty, soil; beslaver.
bemos, (-te), mossy, moss-grown.
benadeel, (-), injure; harm; wrong.
benader, (-), approach; approximate.
benadering, (-e, -s), approximation.
benaming, (-e, -s), name, appellation.
benard, (-e), critical; straitened.
bende, (-s), gang, band; troop.
benede, adv. down, below; downstairs.
benede, prep. below; beneath.
beneem, (-), deprive of; take (one's own life).
benepe, cramped; small; petty, mean.
beneuk, (-te), mad, crazy.
benewel, (-), fog; befog, cloud; stupefy.
benewens, besides, together with.
Bengaals, (-e), Bengal (light).
bengel, (-s), n. urchin, rascal.
benning, (-s), band.
benodig, (-de), wanted, required.
benodigdhede, requirements, accessories.
benoem, (-), nominate, appoint.
benoeming, (-e, -s), nomination, appointment.
benoorde, (to the) north of.
benoud, (-e), close, sultry; stuffy; stifling; tight in the chest; terrifying (dream); frightened.
benoudebors, asthma.
benseen, benzene, benzol.
bensien, bensine, benzine.
benul, notion.
benut(tig), (-), make use of, utilize.
beny, (-), envy.
benydenswaardig, (-e), enviable.
beoefen, (-), practise (profession); cultivate (an art); exercise (patience).
beoog, (-), judge (person); adjudicate; review (book).
bepaal, (-), fix; appoint; determine; stipulate; ascertain (value); define; qualify, modify (gram.).
bepaal(d), (-de), a. fixed; specified; appointed (time); stated (times); definite (reply, number); distinct.
bepaald, adv. decidedly, undoubtedly, unmistakably.
bepaaldelik, specifically, particularly.
bepak, (-), load, pack.
bepaling, (-e, -s), fixing; determination; (legal) provision.
bepeins, (-), ponder over, meditate on.
beperk, (-), limit, confine; reduce.
beplak, (-), paper (wall); paste over.
beplant, (-), plant.
bepleister, (-), plaster (over).
bepleit, (-), champion, advocate.
beproef, beproewe, (-), try; test; afflict, visit.
beproef, (-de), tried; staunch (supporter); efficacious (remedy).
beproewing, (-e, -s), trial; affliction.
beraad, deliberation.
beraadslaag, (-), deliberate.
beraam, (-), devise; plan; estimate.
berde: iets ie – tring, bring a matter up.
bêre, berg, (ge-), put aside (away), store; hide.
beredder, (-), put in order; administer.
berede, mounted (police).
beredeneer, (-), argue, reason out.
berei, (-), prepare; curry (leather).
bereidvaardig, -willig, (-e), willing.
bereid, prepared, ready, willing.
bereik, n. reach, range; grasp.
bereik, (-), reach; achieve (object).
bereis, (-), travel (over, through).
bereken, (-), calculate, compute.

bêreplek, bergplek, store-room, shed.
berg, (-e), n. mountain, mount.
berg, (ge-), salve (cargo); vide bêre.
bergagtig, (-e), mountainous.
berig, (-te), n. tidings, report; notice.
berig, (-), report; send word; notify.
beriggewer, correspondent; informant.
berisp(e), (-), reprimand, censure.
beroem, (-): sig – op, pride oneself on, glory in.
beroemd, (-e), famous, illustrious.
beroep, (-e), n. calling, occupation; profession, trade, vocation; call (to minister of religion).
beroep, (-), call (a minister of religion); sig – op, appeal to.
beroer, (-), stir, disturb, perturb.
beroerd, (-e), miserable, wretched.
beroering, (-e, -s), disturbance; commotion.
beroerte, apoplexy.
berokken, (-), cause, bring (upon).
beroof, berowe, (-), rob; deprive (of).
berook, (-), (blacken with) smoke; fumigate.
berou, n. repentance, remorse.
berou, (-), repent, regret; rue.
berug, (-te), notorious, ill-famed.
beruik, (-), smell at.
berus, (-): – by, rest with (the Lord); be vested in.
berusting, resignation, acquiescence.
bery, (-), ride (horse).
berym, (-), rhyme, put into verse.
bes, n. best.
bes, adv. very well; – moontlik, quite possible.
besaai, (-), sow; strew, cover.
besadig, (-de), cool(-headed); calm; moderate (politician); dispassionate.
beseer, (-), injure, hurt.
besef, n. idea, conception; realization.
besef, (-), realize.
beseil, (-), sail (the seas).
besem, (-s), broom; bosom (of twigs).
besembos, broom-bush.
besending, (-e, -s), consignment.
beset, a. engaged, occupied; set (with gems).
beset, (-), occupy; set (with gems); garrison (fort).
besete, possessed (by the devil).
besetene, (-s), one possessed.
besie, (-s), cicada; small beast.
besiel, (-), inspire, infuse (into).
besien, (-), look at, view.
besienswaardig, (-e), worth seeing.
besig, (-), use, make use of.
besigheid, (-hede), business; occupation.
besigtig, (-), view, inspect.
besin, (-), reflect.
besing, (-), sing (the praises of).
besinning, consciousness, senses, head.
besit, n. possession; asset(s).
besit, (-), possess, have, own.
besitlik, (-e), possessive (pronoun).
beskaaf, beskawe, (-), civilize.
beskaaf, (-de), civilized; cultured.
beskaam, (-), shame; disappoint.
beskaam(d), (-de), ashamed; shamefaced.
beskadig, (-), damage; injure.
beskawing, (-e, -s), civilization.
beskeid, – gee, give a reply.
beskeidenheid, modesty.
beskeie, modest; unassuming.
beskerm, (-), protect, patronize.
beskermling, (-e), protégé.
beskiet, (-), fire at, bombard.
beskik, (-), arrange; dispose.
beskikbaar, (-bare), available.
beskikking, (-e, -s), disposal; decree; dispensation.

beskinder, (–), slander, blacken.
beskonke, intoxicated, drunk.
beskore, dit (die lot) is my –, it is my fate (lot).
beskot, wainscoting; partition.
beskou, (–), look at, view, contemplate; regard, consider.
beskroomd, (-e), shy, bashful, timid.
beskryf, beskrywe, (–), describe; draw.
beskrywing, (-e, -s), description.
beskuit, (-e), rusk; biscuit.
beskuldig, (–), accuse, blame.
beskuldigde, (-s), accused.
beskut, (–), protect, shelter, screen.
beslaan, (–), shoe (horse); mount (with metal); extend over (fifty acres); take up (space); run to (many pages).
beslag, mounting, mount; fittings; clamps (of chest); clasps (of book); seizure (upon person, goods); embargo (on ship).
besleg, (–), settle (dispute).
beslis, adv. decidedly, positively.
beslis, (–), decide; arbitrate.
beslistheid, resoluteness, firmness.
beslommering, (-e, -s), trouble, care.
besluit, (-e), conclusion; decision.
besluit, (–), conclude; resolve; pass a resolution.
besluiteloos, (-lose), irresolute.
besmeer, (–), (be)smear, grease; dirty.
besmet, (–), infect; pollute; contaminate; defile.
besmetlik, (-e), contagious; infectious.
besnede, cut; chiselled.
besnoei, (–), prune, clip (hedge); curtail, retrench, cut down (expenses).
besnuffel, (–), sniff at; pry into.
besoedel, (–), soil, pollute, defile.
besoek, (-e), n. visit; call (of short duration); guests.
besoek, (–), pay a visit to, call on; attend (church).
besoeking, visitation, affliction.
besog, (-te), visited; attended.
besoldig, (–), pay, salary.
besonder, n.: in die –, in particular.
besonder, (-e), a. particular, special.
besonders, (-e), special, particular.
besonke, well-considered (opinion).
besonne, staid; well-considered.
besope, drunk, fuddled.
besorg(e), besôre, (–), attend to (horses); cause (sorrow, trouble); deliver; provide.
besorg, (-de), anxious, concerned (about).
bespaar, (–), save, economize; spare.
bespat, (–), bespatter, splash.
bespeel, (–), play (the organ), play on.
bespeur, (–), observe, notice.
bespied(e), (–), spy on; watch.
bespieëlend, bespiegelend, (-e), contemplative; speculative (philosophy).
bespoedig, (–), expedite, speed up.
bespoel, (–), wash.
bespot, (–), mock, deride.
bespotlik, (-e), ridiculous, ludicrous.
bespreek, (–), discuss; reserve (seats); review (book); exorcise (a toothache).
bespring, (–), jump upon; assail.
bessie, (-s), berry.
bestaan, n. being, existence; livelihood.
bestaan, (–), exist; make a living.
bestaanbaar, (-bare), possible; reasonable; living (wage); – met, compatible with.
bestaande, existing.
bestand, a: – teen, proof against.
bestanddeel, component, constituent.
beste, n. best.
beste, a. best; first class; dear (friend).
bestee, (–), spend.

besteel, (–), rob, steal from.
bestek, (-ke), space; scope; (builder's) specifications.
bestekopmaker, quantity-surveyor.
bestel, (–), order; deliver (letters).
bestelling, (-e, -s), order; appointment; delivery.
bestem, (–), destine; set apart; fix (a day).
bestemming, destination; destiny, lot.
bestempel, (–), stamp; describe (as).
bestendig, (-e), a. lasting; permanent; steady; settled.
bestendig, (–), perpetuate, continue.
bestier, (divine) guidance.
bestiering, dispensation (of Providence), act of Providence.
bestook, (–), pelt, bombard.
bestorm, (–), storm, rush at, charge.
bestraal, (–), shine upon; x-ray.
bestraat, (–), pave.
bestraf, -strawwe, (–), reprimand, punish.
bestrooi, (–), bestrew, sprinkle, powder.
bestry, (–), combat; oppose (motion); dispute (statement); defray (expenses).
bestudeer, (–), study.
bestuif, bestuiwe, (–), pollinate (bot.).
bestuur, (-sture), n. management; rule; committee; managing-board.
bestuur, (–), drive (motor-car); pilot (aeroplane); guide, direct; manage (business); control; rule, govern (country).
bestuurder, (-s), driver; manager, director.
besuinig, (–), economize.
beswaar, (-sware), n. objection; scruple.
beswaarlik, hardly, with difficulty.
beswadder, (–), besmirch.
besweer, (–), swear; charge; exorcise, lay (ghost, wind); call up (ghost).
beswil: vir jou eie –, for your own good.
beswyk, (–), succumb; yield; collapse.
beswym, (–), swoon, faint.
besyde, beside (the truth), alongside.
betaal, (–), pay; settle (account).
betaam, (–), behove, become.
betaamlik, (-e), proper, becoming.
betakel, (–), dirty, begrime; besmear.
betaling, (-e, -s), payment, settlement.
betas, (–), feel, handle, finger.
beteken, (–), mean, signify; represent, stand for; portend.
betekenis, (-se), meaning, sense; significance, importance, consequence.
beter, a. & adv., better.
beterskap, improvement; recovery.
beterwete: teen sy –, against his own better judgment.
beterweter, betweter, (-s), wiseacre.
beteuel, (–), restrain, curb; repress.
beteuter(d), (-de), taken aback, perplexed.
betoër, betoger, (-s), demonstrator.
beton, concrete.
betoog, (-toë), n. argument, demonstration.
betoom, (–), curb; repress.
betoon, (–), show.
betower, betoor, (–), bewitch, enchant.
betraan(d), wet with tears, tearful.
betrag, (–), do; ponder.
betrap, (–), catch, surprise, detect.
betree, (–), set foot on; mount.
betref, (–), concern, relate to.
betreffende, concerning, regarding.
betrek, (–), (1) move into (a house); become overcast; cloud over (of face).
betrek, (–), (2) stalk (game); catch (person) off his guard.
betrekking, (-e, -s), post, situation; relation.

betreklik, (-e), a. comparative; relative.
betreklik, (-e), a. comparatively, relatively.
betreur, (-), deplore, regret.
betreurenswaardig, (-e), deplorable, regrettable; pitiable.
betrokke, overcast, cloudy (sky); concerned.
betroubaar, (-bare), reliable, trustworthy.
Betsjoeana, Bechuana.
betuie, betuig, (-), testify; declare; express; profess (friendship).
betweter, vide beterweter.
betwis, (-), dispute; contest (seat in Parliament); deny.
betwyfel, (-), doubt.
betyds, in time, in good time.
beuel, (-s), bugle; trigger-guard.
beuk, (-e), n. beech.
beul, (-, -s), executioner; beast.
beur, (ge-), tug; lift; struggle, strive.
beurs, (-e), purse; scholarship; exchange.
beurt, (-e), turn; innings (in cricket).
beurtelings, in turn, alternately.
beuselagtig, (-e), trivial, paltry.
bevaarbaar, (-bare), navigable.
beval, (-), please.
bevallig, (-e), charming, graceful.
bevalling, (-e, -s), confinement, delivery.
bevange, overcome, seized (with, by); foundered; over-ridden (horse).
bevat, (-), contain, hold.
beveel, (-), command, charge.
beveg, (-), fight (against), oppose.
beveilig, (-), safeguard, guard, protect.
bevel, (-e), command, order.
bevelhebber, bevelvoerder, (-s), commander.
bevelvoerend, (-e), commanding.
bevestig, (-), fasten; confirm (statement); affirm; prove; induct (minister of religion).
bevestigend, (-e), affirmative.
bevind, n.: na – van sake, according to circumstances.
bevind, (-), find.
bevinding, (-e, -s), finding; experience.
bevlek, (-), stain, soil; defile.
bevlie(ë), bevlieg, (-), fly at, attack.
bevlieging, (-e, -s), whim, fancy; fit.
bevoeg, (-de), competent, qualified.
bevoel, (-), feel, finger, handle.
bevogtig, (-), moisten, wet, damp.
bevolk, (-te), a. populate; populous.
bevolk, (-), people.
bevolking, (-e, -s), population.
bevoordeel, (-), benefit.
bevooroordeel(d), (-de), prejudiced, biassed.
bevoorreg, (-), privilege, favour.
bevorder, (-), further, promote.
bevorderlik, beneficial, conducive (to).
bevredig, (-), satisfy, gratify; indulge.
bevredigend, (-e), satisfactory, gratifying.
bevreem(d), (-): dit – my, it surprises me.
bevrees, afraid (of), apprehensive (for).
bevries, (-), freeze; freeze to death.
bevrore, frozen, frost-bitten; frosted.
bevrug, (-), impregnate; fertilise (bot.).
bevry, (-), free, set free; rescue; deliver (from); liberate.
bevuil, (-), dirty, foul.
bewaak, (-), guard, keep watch over.
bewaar, (-), save (coupons); keep (secret commandments); maintain (one's self-possession); preserve; protect, save.
bewaarder, (-s), guardian; caretaker.
bewaarheid, (-), verify, confirm.
bewaarskool, infant-school.
bewandel, (-), walk in, walk upon.

bewapen, (-), arm.
bewaring, custody, safe-keeping; trust.
beweeg, (-), move; stir; budge; persuade.
beweegbaar, (-bare), movable; moving.
beweeglik, (-e), movable; mobile; active.
beweegrede, motive, ground.
beween, (-), mourn for, lament.
beweer, (-), allege, aver, contend.
beweging, (-e, -s), movement; motion; commotion.
bewer, (-s), beaver.
bewerasie, bibberasie, the shakes.
bewering, (-e), shaking, shaky.
bewering, (-e, -s), assertion, allegation.
bewerk, (-), work (mine); cultivate; treat (ore); shape; adapt play; revise; bring about; manipulate, manage.
bewerkstellig, (-), bring about, accomplish.
bewimpel, (-), gloss over, cloak.
bewind, government, administration.
bewing, trembling, shivering.
bewoë, moved, touched, affected.
bewolk, (-te), a. clouded, overcast.
bewonder, (-), admire.
bewonderenswaardig, (-e), admirable.
bewoon, (-), inhabit, occupy.
bewoord, (-), word, phrase.
bewus, (-te), conscious.
bewussyn, consciousness.
bewusteloos, (-lose), unconscious.
bewys, (-e), n. proof, evidence; token (of affection); promissory note; receipt.
bewys, (-), proof; demonstrate; substantiate (charge); do (a favour), render (a service); show (kindness).
bewysstuk, document; exhibit.
beywer, (-): sig –, exert oneself.
bibber, (ge-), shiver, tremble, quake.
bibberasie, vide bewerasie.
biblioteek, (-teke), library.
bibliotekaris, (-se), librarian.
bid(de), (ge-), pray, beseech, beg; say grace (at a meal).
bidstond, biduur, prayer-meeting.
bied, (ge-), (1) offer (help), present (difficulty).
bied, bie(ë), (ge-), (2) bid.
biefstuk, beefsteak.
bieg, (ge-), confess.
biegvader, confessor.
bier, beer.
bies(melk), beestings.
biesie, (-s), (bul)rush, reed; whip.
bietjie, (-s), n. little (bit); moment.
bietjie, adv. rather, slightly.
bietjie-bietjie, a little at a time.
biggel, (-), trickle.
biljart, n. billiards.
biljet, (-te), poster; handbill; note.
biljoen, (-e), billion.
billik, (-e), a. reasonable, fair; just.
billikerwys(e), in fairness.
billikheidshalwe, in (all) fairness.
biltong, (-e), biltong.
bind(e), (ge-), bind; tie (up); thicken (of soup).
binne, prep. within; inside.
binneband, tube.
binnebly (binnege-), stay (indoors) (down).
binnegoed, entrails, intestines; works.
binne-in, (right) inside, within.
binnekant, inside.
binnekort, ere (before) long, soon, shortly.
binneland, inland, interior; up-country.
binnelands, (-e), inland; internal, domestic.
binnensmonds: – praat, mumble.
binne(n)ste, n. inside, interior.

binne(n)ste, a. innermost, inmost.
binnetoe, in, inside.
binnewaarts, adv. inward(s).
biografie (-ë), biography.
biologie, biology.
bioloog, (-loë, -loge), biologist.
bioskoop, (-skope), bioscope.
Birma, Burma.
biskop, (-pe), bishop.
bison, (-s), bison.
bits(ig), (-e), biting, cutting.
bitter, (-, -e), a. bitter.
bitter, adv. bitterly; precious (little).
bittereinder, (-s), die-hard.
bitterlik, bitterly.
bivak, (-ke), bivouac.
blaadjie, (-s), leaflet; sheet (of paper); tract; paper; rag.
blaai, (ge-), turn over the pages (leaves).
blaam, blame; reproach, blemish.
blaar, (blare), 1. leaf (of tree).
blaar, (blare), 2. blister, bleb.
blaas, (blase), n. bag, bladder; bubble.
blaas, (ge-), blow (instrument); breathe; spit (of cat); hiss (of goose).
blaasbalk, bellows.
blaasorkes, brass band, windband.
blaaspyp, -roer, blow-pipe; peashooter.
blad, (blaaie), n. leaf (of book); sheet (of paper), (news)paper; shoulder (-blade); top (of table); surface (road); blade (of saw).
bladsak, knapsack.
bladstil: dit was –, not a leaf stirred.
bladsy, page.
bladwisselend, (-e), deciduous.
bladwys(t)er, book-mark; index.
blaf, n. bark.
blaf, (ge-), bark; cough.
blafon, vide **plafon**.
blakend, (-e), burning, ardent.
blaker, (-s), (flat) candlestick.
blaker, (ge-), burn, scorch, parch.
blanc-mange, blancmange.
blameer, (ge-), blame, put the blame on.
blank, (-, -e), white; fair, pure.
blanke, (-s), a. white; **die –s**, the whites.
blanketsel, rouge, cosmetic, paint.
blas, dark, sallow (complexion).
blatjang, chutney, ketchup.
bleek, bleik, n. bleaching; bleachfield.
bleek, a. pale, pallid.
bleek, (ge-), vide **bleik**.
bleik, bleek, (ge-), bleach, whiten.
blêr, (ge-), bleat, bellow, cry, howl.
blêrkas, juke-box.
bles, (-se), blaze; bald head.
bleshoender, moor-hen.
bleskop, bald head, baldpate.
blik, (-ke), n. 1. tin.
blik, (-ke), n. 2. look, glance, gaze.
blik, (ge-), look, glance.
blikkiesmelk, condensed (tinned) milk.
blikmes, -snyer, tin-opener.
bliksem, (-s), n. lightning.
bliksem, (ge-), lighten; flash; fulminate.
blikskêr, plate-shears.
blikskottel, (-s), tin-dish; blighter.
blikslaer, (-s), tin-smith; blighter.
blind, adv. blindly.
blinddoek, (ge-), blindfold; hoodwink.
blinde, (-s), blind person; dummy (at cards): vide **blinding**.
blindederm, appendix.
blindelings, blindly; (trust) implicitly.
blindemol(letjie), blindman's-buff.

blinder, (-s), stymie (golf). Vide **blinding**.
blindevlieg, blind fly, sting-fly.
blinding, (-s), blind, shutter.
blink, a. shining, glittering, bright.
blink, (ge-), shine, gleam, glitter.
blits, (-e), n. lightning.
blits, (ge-), lighten; flash (of eyes).
blitspatrollie, flying squad.
blitssnel, adv. quick as lightning.
blitsvinnig, (-e), a. lightning-like.
bloed, blood.
bloedbad, massacre, slaughter, carnage.
bloeddorstig, (-e), blood-thirsty.
bloedeie: my – suster, my own sister.
bloederig, (-e), bloody; bloodstained.
bloedig, (-e), a. bloody; blazing (sun).
bloedig, adv.: **ek was – kwaad**, I was furiously angry.
bloedjie, (-s), poor mite, little thing.
bloedjong, bloedjonk, very young.
bloedlaat, (bloedge-), bleed, let blood.
bloedmin, precious little (few).
bloedpersie, -parsie, dysentery.
bloedrooi, blood-red.
bloedvat, blood-vessel.
bloedvin, (-ne), -vint, (-e), boil, furuncle.
bloedweinig, vide **bloedmin**.
bloei, n. blossom, bloom; prosperity.
bloei, (ge-), 1. blossom, flower.
bloei, (ge-), 2. bleed.
bloeisel, (-s), blossom.
bloekom(boom), vide **blougom(boom)**.
bloem, vide **blom**.
bloemis, (-te), florist.
bloemryk, (-e), flowery, florid, ornate.
bloes, (-e), bloese, (-s), blouse.
bloesem, (-s), n. blossom, bloom.
bloesend, (-e), rosy, ruddy.
blok, (-ke), n. block; log (of wood).
blok, (ge-), cram, swot, grind (at).
blom, (-me), n. flower; blossom.
blom, (ge-), flower; bloom, blossom.
blomkool, cauliflower.
blomkweker, florist, floriculturist.
blommemeisie, flower-girl.
blompot, flower-pot.
blomryk, vide **bloemryk**.
blond, (-e), fair, blond(e).
blondine, (-s), blonde, fair-haired girl.
bloos, (ge-), blush, flush.
bloot, (blote) a. bare, naked; very, mere (thought); bald (facts).
bloot. adv. merely, only.
blootlê, (blootge-), expose; disclose.
bloots, a. unsaddled.
bloots, adv. bareback.
blootshoof(s), bare-headed.
blootstel, (blootge-), expose, subject (to).
blootsvoet(s), barefoot(ed), with bare feet.
blos, blush, flush, bloom.
blou, n. blue.
blou, a. blue.
blouapie, vervet.
blou-blou: iets – laat, leave the matter there.
blouboontjie, ounce of lead, blue pill.
blougom(boom), bluegum (-tree).
bloukopkoggelmander, blue-headed lizard.
blouoog- . . . ., blue-eyed.
bloureën, wistaria.
blousel, blue.
blouskimmel, grey, dapple-grey (horse).
blousuur, prussic acid.
bloutjie, (-s), 1. carbon-copy.
bloutjie, (-s), 2. **'n – loop, gee**, get, give the mitten.
bluf, n. big talk, boasting, bragging.

bluf, (ge-), brag, boast, talk big.
blus, n. **sy – is uit,** hc is finished (played out).
blus, (ge-), extinguish, put out; slake (lime).
bly, (–, -e), a. glad, pleased, happy.
bly, (ge-), remain, live; keep; keep on.
blydskap, joy, gladness.
blygeestig, (-e), cheerful, gay, merry.
blyk, (-e), n. token, proof, mark.
blyk, (ge-), appear, be obvious.
blykbaar, (-bare), a. apparent, evident.
blykbaar, adv. apparently, evidently.
blykens, as appears from.
blymoedig, (-e), cheerful, joyful.
blyspel, comedy.
blystaan, (–), stick, get stuck.
blywend, (-e), lasting (peace); enduring.
bo, bowe, prep. above; past; beyond.
bo, bowe, adv. above; upstairs; at the top.
bo-aan, at the top; at the head.
boaards, boweaards, (-e), supermundane; supernatural.
bo-af: van –, from the top; from above.
bobaas, champion, master; topdog.
bobbejaan, (-jane), baboon.
bobotie, curried minced meat.
bod, bot, (botte), bid, offer.
bode, (-s), messenger; servant.
bodem, (-s), bottom; soil; territory; ship.
bodryf, -arywe, (boge-), float on the surface;
  prevail.
Boedapest, Budapest.
Boeddhisme, Buddhism.
boedel, (-s), estate; property.
boef, (boewe), villain, rogue, knave.
boeg, (boeë), bow(s) (of ship); shoulder-joint (of
  horse).
boeglam, dead beat, exhausted.
boegoe, buchu.
boei, (-e), n. 1. handcuff(s); fetter.
boei, (-e), n. 2. buoy.
boei, (ge-), handcuff; fascinate.
boek, (-e), n. book; quire (of paper).
boek, (ge-), enter, book.
boekdeel, volume.
boekery, (-e), library.
boeket, (-te), bouquet (also of wine).
boekevat, (boekege-), hold family prayers.
boekhandel, book-trade; bookseller's shop.
boekhou, n. book-keeping.
boekhou, (boekge-), keep an account of; keep the
  books.
boekhouer, book-keeper.
boekjaar, financial year.
boe(k)pens, vide **boepens.**
boekstaaf, (ge-), put on record.
boel, lot, crowd, heaps, lots.
boemel, n. spree.
boemel, (ge-), spree; loaf about.
boemerang, (-s), boomerang.
bo-ent, head (of table) upper end.
boender, (ge-), chase (drive) away.
boepens, pot-belly.
Boer, (-e), Boer.
boer, (-e), farmer; jack (cards).
boer, (ge-), farm; stay, remain.
boerbok, boer-goat, Swiss goat.
boerboontjie, broad bean.
boerdery, (-e), farming; farm.
boer(e)matriek, confirmation (church).
boerplek, haunt; favourite spot.
boers, (-e), boorish, rustic.
boesel, (-s), bushel.
boesem, (-s), bosom, breast.
Boesman, (-s), Bushman.
boet, n. brother.

boet, (ge-), pay, suffer.
boeta, boetie, (-s), brother.
boete, (-s), fine, penalty; penance.
boetebossie, "boetebossie".
boeteling, (-e), penitent.
boetseer, (ge-), model.
boetvaardig, (-e), penitent, repentant.
bof, (bowwe), n. den, home (in catch-games); tee
  (golf); base (baseball).
bof, (ge-), tee (golf).
bofbal, baseball.
bog, (-te), n. (1) bend, windcurve; bight.
bog, n. (2) nonsense; litter; fool; bad sort.
bo(we)genoemde, above(-mentioned).
boggel, (-s), hump, hunch.
bogkind, a mere child.
bogpraatjies, twaddle, senseless talk.
bogronds, (-e), overhead (wires); elevated.
bogtery, nonsense; nuisance.
bohaai, pohaai, fuss, noise.
Boheems, (-e), Bohemian.
boikot, (ge-), boycott.
bok, (-ke), n. goat; (wild) buck; buck (of wagon);
  vaulting-buck (gymnastics); trestle, support;
  rest (billiards); best girl; blunder, bloomer.
bokaal, (-kale), goblet, beaker.
bokant, n. upper side, top (-side).
bokant, prep. above, over (the door).
bokbaard(jie), goatee (beard).
bokerf, top notch; top-gear.
bokhaar, mohair.
bokkapater, gelded goat.
bokkem, bokkom, (-s), mullet, Cape herring.
bokkesprong, caper; –e, antics.
bokkie, (-s), buggy.
bokleer, kid, buckskin.
bokmakierie, bokmakiri, bush-shrike.
bokom, (boge-), get to the top, get on top; come
  up.
bokram, he-goat, billy-goat.
boks, (ge-), box.
bokseil, bucksail, tarpaulin.
bokser, (-s), boxer.
bokskryt, boxing-ring.
bokspring, (ge-), caper, buckjump.
Bokveld, Bokkeveld: –toe gaan, go west.
bokwa, buck-wagon.
bokwiet, buckwheat.
hol, (-le), n. ball; globe; sphere; crown (of hat);
  bulb (of plant).
bol, (ge-), bulge; swell.
Boland, Western Province.
bolig, sky-light, fan-light.
bolla, (-s), bun (of hair), chignon.
bol(le)makiesie, head over heels.
bolpen, ball-point pen.
bolvormig, (-e), spherical; bulbshaped.
bolwerk, rampart; stronghold.
bolyf, upper part of the body.
bolyfie, (-s), bodice.
bom, (-me), bomb, shell.
bombardeer, (ge), bomb(ard), shell.
bombarie, bombalie, fuss, noise.
bombasties, (-e), bombastic.
bomenslik, (-e), superhuman.
bom(me)werper, bomber, bombing-plane.
bo(we)natuurlik, (-e), supernatural.
bond, (-e), bond, league, confederation.
bondel, (-s), bundle (of washing); sheaf (of
  papers); cluster.
bondel, (ge-), bundle.
bondeldraer, pedlar, tramp.
bondgenoot, (-note), ally, confederate.
bondig, (-e), concise, succinct, terse.
bonk, (-e), n. lump; thump.

bonkig, (-e), bony; square-built (chunky).
bons, (-e), n. thump, bump, thud.
bons, (ge-), bump; throb (of heart).
bont, n. fur.
bont, (–, -e), a. pied, piebald (horse), spotted; gay (colours); motley (gathering).
bontjas, fur-coat.
bontpraat, (bontge-), ramble; contradict oneself.
bontspring, (bontge-), jump about; vide **bontstaan.**
bontstaan, (bontge-), stir one's stumps; try different tacks.
boodskap, (-pe), n. message; errand.
boog, (boë), n. bow (and arrow); arch (archit.); arc (geom.); curve.
booglamp, arc-lamp.
boogskutter, archer.
bo-om, round the top.
boom, (bome), n. (1) tree; barrier; punting-pole.
boom, (bome), n. (2) bottom, seat (of trousers).
boomgaard, orchard.
boomryk, (-e), woody.
boomskraap(sel), n. scrapings.
boon, (bone), bean.
boonop, besides, in addition.
boonste, n. top, upper part.
boonste, a. top, topmost, upper.
boontoe, upstairs; higher up: up(wards).
bo-oor, over the top; right (clean) over.
bo-op, at the top, on (the) top.
boor, (bore), n. bit; drill; boring-machine; gimlet.
boor, (ge-), drill, bore.
boord, (-e), n. 1. orchard.
boord, (-e), n. 2. border, edge; board (ship).
boordjie, (-s), collar.
boordjieknoop, collar-stud.
boorsalf, boracic ointment.
boortjie, (-s), gimlet.
boos, (–, bose), angry, cross; evil (spirit); malignant (ulcer).
boosaardig, (-e), malicious; malignant.
boosdoener, evil-doer, malefactor.
booswig, (-te), criminal, villain.
boot, (bote), boat, steamer.
bootsman, boatswain.
bord, (-e), plate (at table); (black)board.
bordpapier, cardboard, pasteboard.
borduur, (ge-), embroider (lit. & fig.).
borg, (-e), n. surety, guarantee; security; guarantor; bail (law).
borgstaan, (borgge-), stand surety.
**borgtog, surety, bail.
borrel, (-s), n. bubble.
borrel, (ge-), bubble.
borrie, turmeric.
bors, (-te), breast; bosom; (weak) chest; brisket (meat); front (of shirt).
borsbeeld, bust; effigy (on coin).
borsel, (-s), n. brush; bristle (stiff hair).
borsel, (ge-), brush; give a whacking.
borshemp, dress-shirt.
borslap, bib (of child).
borsplaat, breast-plate; breast-piece.
bors(t)rok, corset, stays.
borsspeld, brooch.
borswering, parapet, breastwork.
bos, (-se), wood, forest; bush, shrub; bunch (of carrots); bundle, sheaf; shock (of hair).
bosapie, bush-baby.
bosagtig, (-e), woody.
bosbaadjie, lumber-jacket.
bosbok, bush-buck.
bosbou(kunde), forestry.
bosduif, speckled (rock-)pigeon.

bose: die B., the Evil One.
bosgasie, boskasie, (-s), thicket, underwood; shock (of hair), unkempt hair.
boskasie, vide **bosgasie.**
boskat, wild cat.
bosluis, (bush-)tick, tampan.
bosryk, (-e), woody, (well-) wooded.
bossiedokter, herbalist.
bostaande, bowestaande, abovementioned.
bosvark, bush-pig.
bosveld, bush-country.
boswagter, forester, ranger.
boswerker, lumberjack.
bot, (–, -te), a. blunt, dull.
bot, (ge-), bud, sprout.
bot-af, blunt(ly), curt(ly).
botanie, botany.
botoon, bowetoon, overtone; **die – voer,** dominate.
bots, (ge-), collide; clash, disagree.
botstil, stock-still, quite still.
bottel, (-s), n. bottle.
botter, butter.
botterblom, buttercup, Cape daisy.
botterbroodjie, scone.
botterham(metjie), sandwich.
botterkop, blockhead; hinny (mule).
botterpot(jie), butter-pot.
botvier, (botge-), give rein to, indulge.
botweg, bluntly, flatly.
bou, (ge-), build; erect, construct.
boud, (-e), n. buttock; leg (of mutton).
boukunde, architecture.
boukundige, (-s), architect.
boul, (ge-), bowl (cricket).
bouler, (-s), bowler.
bou-ondernemer, builder and contractor.
**boustof, (building-)materials.
bout, (-e), bolt, rivet; pin; (soldering-)iron.
bouval, ruin(s).
bouvallig, (-e), dilapidated; decrepit.
bovermeld, (-), vide **bogenoemde.**
bowendien, besides, in addition.
bra, really, very.
braaf, (brawe), virtuous, good; brave.
braai, (ge-), roast (in pot), grill (on gridiron), fry (in pan), broil (meat on fire); toast (bread).
braak, a. fallow.
braak, (ge-), 1. break up, fallow (land).
braak, (ge-), 2. vomit; emit, belch.
braam, (brame), blackberry; bramble.
brabbel, (ge-), jabber, chatter.
Brahmaan, (-mane), Brahman (Brahmin).
brak, (-ke), n. 1. pup; mongrel.
brak, n. 2. salt-lick, brackish spot.
brak, a. brackish, saltish, alkaline.
brakhond, brakkie, (-s), mongrel: vide **brak,** n.
brand, (-e), n. fire, conflagration; blight, smut (in wheat).
brand, (ge-), burn; be on fire; roast (coffee); scald (with hot water); brand (with hot iron).
brandarm, penniless.
brandbom, incendiary bomb.
brander, (-s), breaker, wave.
brandewyn, brandy.
branding, breakers, surf.
brandkas, safe.
brandmaer, skinny, scraggy, lean.
brandmerk, (ge-), brand; stigmatize.
brandnekel, (-netel), stinging-nettle.
brandsiekte, scab.
brandslang, fire-hose.
brandspiritus, methylated spirits.
brandstigting, arson.
brandstof, fuel.

brandwag, picket, sentry, sentinel.
brandweer, fire-brigade.
bras, (ge-), revel, carouse.
Brasiliaans, (-e), Brazilian.
bredie, ragout, stew, "bredie."
breed, (breë), broad (chest), wide (road).
breedsprakig, (e), verbose, longwinded.
breedte, (-s), breadth, width; latitude (geogr.).
breedtegraad, degree of latitude.
breedvoerig, (-e), a. full, detailed.
breedvoerig, adv. at length, fully.
breek, (ge-), break; be broken; shatter; crush (stone).
breekgoed, crockery.
breekyster, crowbar; jemmy (of burglar).
brei, (ge-), 1. knit.
brei, (ge-), 2. prepare, curry, dress (skin); knead (clay); coach (athletes), train; harden.
breidel, (-s), bridle.
breidel, (ge-), bridle, curb.
brein, (-e), brain, intellect.
breiwerk, knitting.
bres, (-se), breach.
breuk, (-e), break, breach; rupture; fracture (of skull); crack; fault (geol.); fraction (maths.).
brief, (briewe), letter.
briefwisseling, correspondence.
briek, (-e), n. brake.
briek, (ge-), apply the brakes.
bries, (-e), n. breeze.
briesend, (-e), roaring; furious, raging.
briewebesteller, postman.
bril, (-le), n. (pair of) spectacles (glasses); goggles (for motoring); seat (of W.C.).
bril (ge-), wear glasses.
briljant, (-e), brilliant.
bring, (gebring, gebrag), bring; take, convey.
brinjal, (-s), egg-plant.
Brit, (-te), Britisher, Briton.
Brittanje, Britain, Britannia.
broeder, (-s), brother.
broei, (ge-), hatch, incubate; get hot (heated); brew, gather.
broeimasjien, incubator, hatching-machine.
broeis, broody (hen).
broeisel, (-s), clutch (of eggs); brood (hatch) (of chickens).
broek, (-e), (pair of) trousers; drawers, bloomers (female); back part (of harness).
broekskeur: – **gaan**, have a rough time.
broer, (-s), brother.
broerskind, nephew, niece.
brok, (-ke), piece, lump, fragment.
brokkel, (ge-), crumble.
broksgewys(e), bit by bit, piecemeal.
brokstuk, fragment, piece.
brom, (ge-), hum, drone (of insect); grumble (of person); growl (of animal).
bromfiets, buzz-bike, autocycle.
brommer, (-s), blue-bottle, blowfly; grumbler.
bromponie, motor scooter.
brompot, grouser, grumbler.
bron, (-ne), (hot) spring; well; source (of the Nile); origin, source; cause (of the evil); means (of living).
brongitis, bronchitis.
bronkors, water-cress.
brons, n. bronze.
brood, (brode), bread; loaf.
broodnodig, (-e), absolutely (highly) necessary, badly needed, essential.
broos, (-, brose), a. brittle, fragile.
bros, a. brittle, crisp, crumbly.
brosjure, (-s), brochure, pamphlet.
brou, (ge-), brew; bungle.

brouery, (-e), brewery.
brousel, (-s), brewing, brew; concoction.
brug, (brûe(ns), brugge), bridge; gangway.
brug, (2). bridge (card-game).
bruid, (-e), bride.
bruidegom, (-s), bridegroom.
bruidskat, dowry.
bruidsmeisie, bridesmaid.
bruikbaar, (-bare), serviceable, useful.
bruikleen, loan; in – hê, have on loan.
bruilof, (-te), wedding.
bruin, a. brown; annoyed.
bruinkapel, brown cobra.
bruinvis, porpoise.
bruis, n. froth, foam.
bruis, (ge-), fizz, bubble; boil, seethe.
brul, (-le), n. roar; bellow (of cattle).
brul, (ge-), roar; bellow (of cattle).
brulpadda, bullfrog.
brunet, (-te), brunette.
Brussels, (-e), Brussels.
brutaal, (-tale), impudent, insolent.
bruto, gross (weight).
bruusk, (-e), brusque, blunt.
bruut, (brute), brute.
bry, (ge-), speak with a burr.
buffel, (-s), buffalo; boor, churl.
buffer, (-s), buffer, bumper.
buffet, (-te), sideboard; (refreshment) bar.
bui, (-e), shower (of rain); whim; mood, humour; fit (of coughing).
buidel, (-s), bag, pouch.
buierig, (-e), showery; fickle; moody.
buig, buie, (ge-), bend; curve; stoop.
buigbaar, (-bare), flexible, pliable; declinable.
buiging, (-e, -s), bending; bend, bow; declension.
buigsaam, (-same), flexible; compliant.
buik, (-e), belly; stomach; bottom (of wagon).
buikband, -gort, -gord, vide **buikriem.**
buikriem, girth (of horse).
buikspreker, ventriloquist.
buil, (-e), boil; swelling.
builepes, bubonic plague.
buis, (-e), tube, pipe; duct (anat.).
buit, n. booty, spoils, loot.
buite, (ge-), seize, capture, take.
buite, adv. outside; in the country.
buite, prep. outside; out of; beyond.
buiteband, tyre; casing.
buitekant, outside; vide **buite.**
buitekants(t)e, vide **buitenste.**
buitelands, (-e), foreign; exotic.
buitelug, fresh air; open air.
buiten, except, but; besides; beyond.
buitendien, besides, moreover.
buitengewoon, (-wone), unusual, extraordinary.
buitenissig, (-e), odd, eccentric, unusual.
buitensporig, (-e), exorbitant (price), extravagant, preposterous.
buitenste, a. outside, outer, exterior.
buiten(s)tyds, out of season; out of hours.
buite(n)toe, outside, out.
buite-om, round (the outside).
buitestaander, (-s), outsider.
buitewaards, adv. outwards.
buitewêreld, outside world, outer world.
buitewyk, outlying district, suburb.
buitmaak, (buitge-), capture, loot.
buk, (ge-), bend, stoop, bow.
buks, (-e), buksie, (-s), small rifle; little fellow.
bul, (-le), 1. (papal) bull; diploma.
bul, (-le), 2. bull; whopper, thumper.
bulder, (ge-), roar; boom (of gun).
Bulgaar, (-gare), Bulgaars, (-e), Bulgarian.

bulk, (ge-), bellow, low, moo.
bullebak, (-ke), bully, bear.
bulsak, feather-bed.
bult, (-e), n. bump, lump, hunch, hump (on back); hill, ridge.
bult, (ge-), dent, indent.
bundel, (-s), n. collection, volume.
bundel, (ge-), collect, publish in book-form.
burg, (-e), 1. hog, barrow.
burg, (-te), 2. castle, stronghold.
burgemeester, mayor, burgomaster.
burger, (-s), citizen; burg(h)er.
burgerlik, (-e), civil; civilian; bourgeois.
burgeroorlog, civil war.
burggraaf, viscount.
bus, (-se), 1. (omni)bus.
bus, (-se), 2. box, drum; tin.
bus, (-se), 3. bush; socket, box.
buskruit, gunpowder.
buur, buurman, (bure), neighbour.
buurt, (-e), (-s), neighbourhood; quarter.
by, (-e), n. bee.
by, prep. by, with, near, at.
by, adv. present, there.
bybedoeling, ulterior motive.
bybehore(ns), accessories.
Bybel, (-s), Bible.
byblad, supplement (of newspaper).
bybly, (byge-), keep pace with; stick in one's memory.
bybring, (byge-), bring forward; quote (examples); afford; bring (person) to (round); instil(l) (ideas).
bydam, (byge-), accost, tackle.
byderhand, at hand.
bydra, (byge-), contribute (to).
bydrae, (-s), contribution.
byeen, together.
byeenkom, (byeenge-), come together, meet.
byeengeroep, (byeenge-), call (meeting), call together, summon.
byekorf, by(e)nes, beehive.
bygaande, accompanying; attached.
bygeloof, superstition.
bygelowig, (-e), superstitious.
bygevolg, consequently, therefore.
bygooi, (byge-), add.
byhaal, (byge-), bring (drag) in.
byhou, (byge-), keep up (with).

bykans, nearly, almost.
bykant, on-side (in cricket).
bykom, (byge-), get at, reach; recover consciousness; be included (added); come up with.
bykomend, (-e), incidental (expenses); attendant (circumstances); additional.
bykomstig, (-e), subsidiary, accidental, minor.
byl, (-e), axe, (light) hatchet, chopper.
bylae, (-s), appendix, enclosure.
bylas, (byge-), add, append.
bylê, (byge-), make up, settle (dispute).
bymekaar, together.
bymekaarkom, (bymekaarge-), come together, assemble.
bymekaarmaak, (bymekaarge-), save (money); round up (cattle); collect (things).
bymekaarstaan, (bymekaarge-), stand together; unite forces.
bymeng, (byge-), mix with.
byna, almost, nearly.
bynaam, nickname; surname.
byreken, (byge-), reckon in, add.
bysaak, matter of minor importance, sideline.
bysiende, short-sighted.
bysin, subordinate clause.
bysit, (byge-), 1. contribute (R5); inter, lay to rest.
bysit, (byge-), 2. sit by (near).
bysleep, (byge-), drag in.
bysmaak, tinge (lit. & fig.), flavour.
byspring, (byge-), lend a hand.
bystaan, (byge-), help, assist, back up.
byster, a.; die spoor – wees, have lost one's way; be at a loss.
byt, (-e), n. bite.
byt, (ge-), bite.
bytel, (byge-), add, include; count in.
bytend, (-e), biting, caustic; corrosive.
bytsoda, caustic soda.
byval, n. approval; applause.
byval, (byge-), remember.
byvoeg, (byge-), add; enclose; append.
byvoeglik, (-e), adjectival.
byvoegsel, (-s), appendix; supplement.
byvoorbeeld, for example.
bywoner, (-s), bywoner; squatter.
bywoon, (byge-), attend; be present at.
bywoord, adverb.

C

Calvinis, (-te), Calvinist.
camouflage, camouflage.
Carthaags, (-e), Carthaginian.
chaos, chaos.
chemie, chemistry.
chemikalieë, (pl.) chemicals.
Chinees, Sjinees, n. Chinaman.
chirurg, (-e), surgeon.
chloor, chlorine.
chloroform, chloroform.

cholera, cholera.
Christelik, (-e), Christian(ly), Christianlike.
Christen, (-e), Christian.
Christin (-ne), Christian woman.
Christus, Christ.
chronies, (-e), chronic.
chronologies, (-e), chronological(ly).
Coliseum, Colosseum, Coliseum, (Colosseum).
confetti, (pl.), confetti.

daad, (dade), deed; act; exploit.
daadwerklik, (-e), actual, real.
daagliks, daeliks, (-e), daily, everyday.
daai, ta!, thank you!
daal, (ge-), descend; sink, go down, drop; fall, decline; slump.
daalder, (-s), one shilling and sixpence (15c).
daar, adv. there; then.
daar, conj. as, because, since.
daaraan, by that, to that.
daaragter, behind it (that).
daarbenewens, besides, in addition to (that).
daarby, besides, in addition; near it.
daardie, that: (pl.) those.
daarenbowe, besides, moreover.
daarenteë, -teen, on the contrary, on the other hand.
daargelate, leaving aside, apart from.
daarginds, -gunter, over there.
daarheen, there, thither, to that place.
daarlaat, (daarge-), leave (it) at that.
daarlang(e)s, along there; somewhere there.
daarmee, with that, therewith.
daarna, after that, afterwards, next, then.
daarnaas, next to that; besides that.
daarnatoe, there, thither, in that direction.
daarnewens, besides, over and above that.
daarom, therefore, on that account.
daaronder, under that; underneath; among them; thereby: down there.
daaroor, about (concerning) that; because of that; across (over) that.
daarop, (up)on that; thereupon.
daarso, there, at that place (spot).
daarstel, (daarge-), make, bring about; erect.
daarteë, -teen, against that.
daartoe, for that (purpose); to (as far as) that.
daaruit, out of that, from that, thence.
daarvan, of that, from that, thereof.
daarvandaan, from there, thence; hence.
daarvoor, for that (purpose), therefore; for it.
dadel, (-s), date.
dadelik, (-e), a. immediate, prompt.
dadelik, adv. directly, at once.
daeraad, vide dageraad.
daeliks, vide daagliks.
dag, (dae), day.
dagblad, daily paper.
dagboek, diary; day-book (in book-keeping).
dagbreker(tjie), (South African) stonechat.
dageraad, daeraad, (-rade), dawn.
dagga, dagga, wild hemp.
dagluimier, dawn, daybreak.
dagteken, (ge-), date.
dagvaar, (ge-), summon(s), cite.
dagverhaal, journal, diary.
dahlia, (-s), dahlia.
dak (-ke), roof.
dakpan, (roofing-) tile.
dal, (-e), valley, dale, glen.
dalk, perhaps, maybe, possibly.
dalkies, by-and-by; presently.
dam, (-me), n. dam; reservoir; weir.
dam, (ge-), dam (up); crowd together.
damas, damask.
dambord, draught-board.
dame, (-s), lady.
damesakkie, lady's (fancy-, vanity-) bag.
damp, (-e), n. fume, steam, vapour.
damp, (ge-), smoke, steam.
dampkring, atmosphere.
dampomp, outlet-pipe (of irrigation-dam).
dan, then; than.
danig, (-e), a. thorough, strong.
danig, adv. very much; intimate; awfully.

dank, n. thanks, acknowledgment.
dank, (ge-), thank.
dankbaar, (-bare), grateful, thankful.
danke: te – aan, due to.
dankfees, thanksgiving-feast.
dankie, thanks!, thank you!
dankiebly, very pleased.
dankoffer, thank-offering.
danksê, (dankge-), thank, return thanks.
dans, (-e), n. dance.
dansparty, dance, ball; hop.
dapper, n.: met – en stapper, on foot.
dapper, a. brave, gallant, valiant.
darem, after all, all the same, though.
dartel, a. frisky, playful; wanton.
dartel, (ge-), frisk, gambol, sport.
das, (-se), n. (neck-)tie; bow.
dat, that; so that, in order that.
dateer, (ge-), date.
datum, (-s), date.
dawer, (ge-), roar, rumble, thunder.
de, the.
dè, here you are!
dê, so there!
debat, (-te), debate, discussion.
debatteer, (ge-), debate, discuss.
debet, debit; vide debiet.
debiet, debit; sale, market.
debiteer, (ge-), debit, charge (with).
debiteur, (-e, -s), debtor.
debuteer, (ge-), make one's début.
deeg, dough.
deeglik, (-e), sound, thorough, solid.
deel, (dele), n. part, portion; division, section; share; volume (of book).
deel, (ge-), divide, share; split.
deelagtig: – word, participate in.
deelneem, (deelge-): – aan, take part in.
deelnemend, (-e), sympathetic.
deelnemer, participant, competitor.
deels, partly, in part.
deelsgewys(e), bit by bit.
deelteken, diaresis; division-sign.
deelwoord, participle.
deemoedig, (-e), meek, submissive.
Deen, (Dene), Dane.
deerlik, (-e), a. piteous, miserable.
deerlik, adv. badly, profoundly.
deernis, commiseration, compassion.
deesdae, adv. nowadays.
definisie, (-s), definition.
deftig, (-e), dignified; smart.
dein, (ge-), heave, surge, swell.
deins, (ge-), shrink (back), retreat.
dek, (-ke), n. cover, covering; deck.
dek, (ge-), cover; tile, slate, thatch (a house); shield (a person); lay (table).
dekaan, (-ane), dean.
dekade, (-s), decade.
dekagram, decagram(me).
dekaliter, decalitre.
dekameter, decametre.
deken, (-s), counterpane.
dekgras, thatch.
dekking, cover; shelter, protection, guard.
dekmantel, cloak; excuse, pretext.
dekor, (-s), scenery (stage).
dekreet, (-ete), decree, edict, enactment.
deksel, (s), cover, lid, tap.
deksels, (-e), a. blessed, confounded.
deksels, interj. by gum!, by Jove!
delf, delwe, (ge-), dig, mine.
delfstof, mineral.
delging, payment, redemption.
delikaat, (-ate), delicate, ticklish.

delwer, (-s), digger.
delwerye, diggings.
demagoog, (-goë, -goge), demagogue.
demobiliseer, (ge-), demobilize.
demokraties, (-e), democratic.
demonstreer, (ge-), demonstrate.
demp, (ge-), fill up (a ditch); quell (a rebellion); dim (a light); extinguish, quench (fires).
demper, (-s), damper, silencer.
denkbaar, (-bare), conceivable, imaginable.
denkbeeld, idea, notion; view (of art).
denkbeeldig, (-e), imaginary; hypothetical.
denklik, (-e), possible, probable.
dennebol, fir-cone.
denneboom, fir(-tree).
departement, (-e), department, office.
departementeel, (-tele), departmental.
deposito, ('s), deposit.
deporteer, (ge-), deport; transport.
deposito, (-'s), deposit.
depot, (-s), depot; dump.
depressie, (-s), depression.
deputasie, (-s), deputation.
derde, third.
derdemag, cube.
derdemannetjie, twos and threes.
derderangs, (-e), third-rate.
derduiwelse, severe, confounded.
dergelik, (-e), such(like), similar.
derhalwe, consequently, therefore.
derm, (-s), intestine; gut; (pl.) entrails.
dermate, to such a degree (extent).
dertien, thirteen.
dertig, thirty.
derwaarts, thither.
derwisj, (-e), dervish.
des, of the.
dese, this; **na –,** after this.
Desember(maand), December.
deser, of this; **10de –,** tenth instant.
desgelyks, likewise.
desgewens, if required (necessary).
desigram, decigram.
desiliter, decilitre.
desimaal, (-male), n. decimal place.
desimaal, (-male), a. decimal.
deskundig, (-e), expert.
desnieteenstaande, nevertheless.
desnietemin, for all that, nevertheless.
desnoods, if need be, in case of need.
desondanks, nevertheless.
desperaat, (-ate), desperate, despairing.
despoot, (-ote), despot.
destyds, at that time.
desverkiesend, if desired; if so inclined.
desweë, on that account, for that reason.
deug, (-de), n. virtue; excellence.
deug, (ge-), be good for, serve.
deugdelik, (-e), sound, reliable; solid.
deugniet, (-e), good-for-nothing, rascal.
deugsaam, (-same), honest, virtuous.
deuk, (-e), n. dent, dint, cavity.
deuk, (ge-), dent, indent.
deuntjie, (-s), air, ditty, tune.
deur, (-e), n. door.
deur, prep. through; throughout; by; on account of.
deur en deur, thoroughly.
deurblaai, (deurge-), turn over the leaves of, glance at, skim (a book).
deurboor, (deurge-), bore (drill) through, pierce.
deurboor, (het –), pierce, transfix, stab.
deurbring, (deurge-), squander (one's money), pass (the time).
deurdag, (-te), considered; well-planned.

deurdat, as, because.
deurdrink, (deurge-), consider fully; reflect on.
deurdring, (deurge-), penetrate, pierce.
deurbring, (het –), permeate, fill.
deurdringend, (-e), penetrating, searching (look), shrill (cry.)
deurdruk, (deurge-), press (push, squeeze) through; persist, persevere.
deurdryf, -drywe, (deurge-), force (push) through; persist.
deurentyd, always, all the time.
deurgaan, (deurge-), go (pass) on; go through.
deurgaans, commonly, usually; right through.
deurgang, passage; thoroughfare.
deurgestoke: 'n – kaart, a put-up job.
deurgrawing, (-s), cutting, tunnel.
deurgrond, (het –), fathom, see through.
deurhaal, (deurge-), cross out; pull (a patient) through.
deurknip, n. door-latch.
deurknip, (deurge-), cut (snip) (through).
deurkom, (deurge-), get through; pass; pull through (an illness), survive, escape.
deurkruis, (het –), cross; traverse.
deurleef, -lewe (het –), go (live, pass) through, experience; survive.
deurloop, n. passage; arcade.
deurloop, (deurge-), go (walk) on; wear out with walking; thrash.
deurlopend, (-e), continuous, uninterrupted.
deurlugtig, (-e), illustrious.
deurmaak, (deurge-), vide **deurleef.**
deurmekaar, confused, delirious; insane.
deurmekaarspul, confusion, chaos, mix-up.
deurploeg, (het –), furrow; wrinkle; score.
deurreis, (deurge-), pass (travel) through.
deurreis, (het –), travel all over.
deurry, (deurge-), ride (drive) on; wear out by riding.
deursettingsvermoë, perseverance.
deursien, (deurge-), see through, sum up.
deursig, insight, penetration.
deurskaaf, -skawe, (deurge-), plane through; chafe.
deurskemer, (deurge-), filter (glimmer) through.
deurskynend, (-e), transparent, translucent.
deurslaan, (deurge-), drive (knock) through; punch.
deurslag, punch; carbon-copy; boggy ground, decisive factor.
deurslagpapier, carbon-paper.
deursnede, deursnee, section; diameter.
deursnee- . . . ., average.
deursny, (het –), cross, intersect.
deurspek, (het –), lard; interlard.
deurstaan, (deurge-, het –), endure, stand weather.
deursteek, (deurge-), cut, pierce, prick.
deursteek, (het –), stab, pierce.
deursyfer, (deurge-), trickle (ooze) through.
deurtastend, (-e), drastic, thorough.
deurtel, (deurge-), lift through.
deurtintel, (het –), thrill.
deurtog, march-through; passage.
deurtrap, (-te), crafty, consummate.
deurtrek, (deurge-), pull through, extend (a line); trek on (through).
deurtrek, (het –), pervade, permeate, soak.
deurval, (deurge-), fall through.
deurvoer, (deurge-), convey (goods) in transit; carry (a plan) through.
deurwaarder, -wagter, (-s), doorkeeper.
deurweek, (het –), soak, moisten.
deurworstel, (deurge-), struggle through (on).
deuskant, duskant, on this side of.

devalueer, (ge-), depreciate.
dewyl, as, because, since.
diagnose, (-s), diagnosis.
diaken, (-s), deacon.
dialek, (-te), dialect.
dialoog, (-loë, -loge), dialogue.
diamant, (-e), diamond.
diarree, diarrhoea.
die, art., the.
dié, pron. (demon.), this (these); that (those).
diederdae: van – af, from days of yore.
diederik, (-e, -s), didric-cuckoo.
dieet, (diëte), diet, regimen.
dief, (diewe), thief.
diefstal, robbery; larceny.
diegene, he, she; those.
dien, (ge-), serve; wait on, attend to.
dienaar, (-are, -s), servant; valet.
diender, (-s), constable, policeman.
diener, (-s), waiter; server (at tennis).
dienlik, (-e), serviceable.
dienooreenkomstig, accordingly.
diens, (-te), duty; function.
diensbaar, (-bare): – aan, subservient to; – maak, subjugate.
diensbode, servant.
diensdoende, acting; officiating; on duty.
diensjaar, year of service; financial year.
dienskneg, (man-)servant.
diensmaag(d), (maid-)servant; hand-maid.
diensmeisie, maid, maid-servant.
dienstig, (-e), serviceable, useful.
diensvaardig (-e), obliging.
dientengevolge, in consequence, therefore.
diep, (–, -e), a. deep, profound (interest); low (bow); intense (scorn).
diep, adv. deeply, profoundly.
diep(e)bord, soup-plate.
diepgaande, thorough; deep-lying.
diepsinnig, (-e), abstruse, profound.
diepte, (-s), depth; profundity.
dier, (-e), animal, beast; brute.
dierasie, (-s), devil, monster.
dierbaar, (-bare), beloved, dear.
dieretuin, zoo(logical garden).
dierkunde, zoology.
dierkundige, (-s), zoologist.
dierlik, (-e), animal; bestial, brutal.
dies: wat – meer sy, so forth.
dieselfde, the same.
diesman, duusman, Dutchman; European.
diesulke, such(like).
Diets, Middle Dutch; Pan-Dutch.
diets: iemand iets – maak, make a person believe something.
diftong, (-e), diphthong.
dig, (-te), a. closed, shut; tight; dense (forest), compact (mass), thick (fog).
dig, (ge-), write poetry (verses).
dig(te)by, close by, close to, near.
digkuns, poetic art.
digter, (-s), poet.
digterlik, (-e), poetic(al).
digtheid, closeness, compactness, density.
dik, thick; bulky; dense (fog); stout; swollen.
dikbek, sulky.
dikderm, large intestine, colon.
dikhuid, pachyderm, thick-skinned person.
dikkerd, (-s), fatty; chubby child.
dikkop(voël), thick-kneed (plover).
dikmelk, curdled milk.
diksak, vide dikkerd.
diktaat, (-tate), dictation; notes.
diktator, (-s), dictator.
dikte, (-s), thickness.

diktee, (-s), dictation.
dikteer, (ge-), dictate.
dikwels, frequently, often.
dinamiet, dynamite.
dinee, (-s), dinner.
ding, (-e), n. thing, matter, object.
dinges, what-do-you-call-it, (Mr) So-and-So.
dink, (dag, dog; gedink, gedag, gedog), think.
Dinsdag, Tuesday.
dip, (ge-), dip.
dipbak, dipping-tank.
diplomaat, (-mate), diplomat(ist).
direk, (-te), prompt(ly); at once.
direksie, direction; management.
direkteur, (-e, -s), director; manager.
dirigeer, (ge-), direct; conduct (orchestra).
dirigent, (-e), conductor, choirmaster.
dis, n. table, board.
dis = dit is, it is, that is.
diskresie, discretion; secrecy.
disnis: – loop, speel, outdistance, outdo.
dispens, vide spens.
dispuut, (-ute), controversy, disputation.
dissel, distel, (-s), n. thistle.
disselboom, beam, pole shaft.
dissipel, (-s), disciple.
dissipline, discipline.
distrik, (-te), district.
dit, this (these), it.
di(t)to, ditto, do.
diverse, sundries; incidental expenses.
dobbel, (ge-), (play at) dice, gamble.
dobber, (-s), n. float; buoy.
dobber, (ge-), bob, drift; fluctuate.
dodeakker, cemetery, graveyard.
dodelik, (-e), mortal (fear), fatal (accident); deadly (poison), lethal (dose).
doeane, custom-house; customs.
doedelsak, bagpipe.
doedoe, (ge-), (go to) sleep.
doek, (-e), cloth, linen; canvas (of painter); painting; screen; napkin.
doel, (-eindes), goal, purpose.
doel, (-e), goal (football); target.
doelbewus, (-te), purposeful; unswerving.
doeleinde, object.
doelmatig, (-e), efficient, practical.
doeltreffend, (-e), effective, efficacious.
doelwit, vide doeleinde.
doem, (ge-), doom, condemn.
doen: sy – en late, his doings.
doen, (ge-, gedaan), do, make (a discovery), take (a step), ask (a question).
doenig, doing.
doening, act, deed; behaviour.
doenlik, (-e), feasible, practicable.
doepa, magic-potion, philtre.
dof, (dowwe), dull (colour), faint (sound), dim (light, eyes).
dogter, (-s), daughter; girl, girlie.
dok, (-ke), dock.
dokter, (-s), n. (medical) doctor.
dokter, (ge-), doctor; nurse; treat.
doktor, (-e, -s), doctor (of literature, etc.).
dokument, (-e), document.
dol, (-le), a. mad; wild; crazy.
dolbly, overjoyed.
dolfyn, (-e), dolphin.
dolgraag, very much, ever so much.
dolk, (-e), dagger, dirk, poniard, stiletto.
dolleeg, (-leë), absolutely empty.
dolos, knuckle-bone.
dolosgooier, witchdoctor.
dolsinnig, (-e), hare-brained, mad.
dolwe, dolf, (ge-), dig up (deeply), trench.

dom, (-me), n. cathedral (-church); dome.
dom, a. stupid, dense, silly.
domastrant, (-e), cheeky, impudent.
dominee, (-s), clergyman, minister.
domkop, blockhead, fathead.
domkrag, jack(-screw), lifting-jack.
dommel, (ge-), doze, drowse.
domoor, vide **domkop**.
dompel, (ge-), plunge.
domper, (-s), extinguisher.
donasie, (-s), donation.
donateur, (-s), donor; contributor.
Donau, Danube.
donder, n. thunder.
donder, (ge-), thunder; rave, storm.
donderbui, thunderstorm.
Donderdag, Thursday.
donker, donkerte, n. dark, darkness.
donker, a. dark.
donkie, (-s), donkey; dunce.
dons, (-e), down, fluff.
dons(er)ig, donsagtig, (-e), downy, fluffy.
dood, n. death, decease, demise.
dood, [dooi(e)], a. dead, defunct.
dood, (ge-), kill; slay.
doodbedaard, (-e), as cool as a cucumber.
doodblaas, (doodge-), extinguish, blow out.
doodbloei, (doodge-), bleed to death.
dooddruk, (doodge-), press (squeeze) to death.
doodeenvoudig, (-e), quite simple.
doodeerlik, (-e), downright honest.
doodgaan, (doodge-), die.
doodgegooi: – wees, be madly in love.
doodgerus, perfectly calm.
doodgewoon, (-gewone), quite common, usual.
doodgoed, (-goeie), good to a fault.
doodgooi, (doodge-), kill (by throwing); knock out, finish.
doodjammer, dit is –, it is a great pity.
doodkis, coffin.
doodloop, (doodge-), come to a dead end; **jou –**, walk oneself off one's legs.
doodlu(i)ters, -leuters, as innocent as a lamb.
doodmaak, (doodge-), kill.
doodmak, quite tame.
doodmoeg, dead-beat.
doodonskuldig, (-e), as innocent as a lamb.
doodry, (doodge-), ride (a horse) to death; run over and kill (a person).
doods, (-e), deathly, deathlike.
dood(s)benoud, (-e), mortally afraid.
dood(s)berig, death-notice, obituary notice.
doodsbleek, deathly pale.
doodsiek, dangerously ill.
doodskaam, (doodge-), jou –, die of shame.
doodskiet, (doodge-), shoot (dead).
doodskop, (doodge-), kick to death.
doodskrik, (doodge-), jou –, be frightened to death.
doodslaan, (doodge-), beat (batter) to death.
doodslag, homicide, manslaughter.
doodsteek, n. death-blow, finishing stroke.
doodsteek, (doodge-), stab to death.
doodstil, stock-still.
doodtevrede, quite content.
doodtrap, (doodge-), trample to death.
doodvonnis, sentence of death.
doof, (dowe), a. deaf.
doof, dowe, (ge-), put out; dim; deaden.
doofstom, deaf and dumb, deafmute.
doofstomme, (-s), deaf-mute.
dooi, (ge-), thaw.
dooier, (-s), door, (dore), yolk.
dooierig, (-e), lifeless, listless.

dooi(e)mansdeur: voor – kom, find nobody at home.
dool, (ge-), roam, wander (about).
doolhof, maze, labyrinth.
doop, n. baptism, christening.
doop, (ge-), baptize, christen; name (a ship); sop (bread in milk), dip (biscuit in tea); initiate (a student).
doopseel, baptismal certificate.
door, vide **dooier**.
doos, (dose), box, case.
dop, (-pe), n. shell (of egg); husk (of seeds); pod (of peas); cap, top (of pen); tot.
dop, (ge-), shell (peas); fail (an examination).
dopemmer, milking-pail.
dophou, (dopge-), keep an eye on, watch.
doppie, (-s), shell; cap, cover (of pipe); percussion-cap.
dor, (-re), a. dry, barren, arid.
doring, (-s), thorn, prickle, spine.
doringboom, thorn-tree, mimosa.
doringdraad, barbed wire.
dorp, (-e), village.
dorpenaar, (-are, -s), villager.
dors, n. thirst.
dors, a. thirsty.
dors, (ge-), thresh (thrash).
dorsmasjien, threshing-machine.
dorstig, (-e), thirsty.
dos, (ge-), attire, deck, dress.
doseer, (ge-), lecture, teach.
dosent, (-e), lecturer, instructor.
dosis, (-se), dose, quantity.
dosyn, (-e), dozen.
dou, n. dew.
dou, (ge-), dew.
douvoordag, before daybreak.
dowwerig, (-e), rather indistinct; vide **dof**.
dra(ag), drae, (ge-), carry, bear, wear (clothes); discharge (of a wound); have a range (of gun).
draad (drade), thread; fibre, filament; grain (of wood); string (of pod); strand (of wire); fence.
draadloos, n. radio, wireless.
draadskêr, wire-cutters.
draadtrekker, fence-strainer (lit.); wire-puller, schemer.
draadwerk, wire-work; filigree(-work); **vol – wees**, be full of fads and fancies.
draagbaar, n. bier; stretcher.
draagbaar, (-bare), a. bearable; portable; wearable (clothes).
draagband, sling (for arm).
draaglik, (-e), bearable, tolerable.
draai, (-e), n. turn; kink, twist (of rope), bend, turning (of road).
draai, (ge-), turn; spin, rotate, revolve, wind; veer round (of the wind); tarry, dawdle.
draaibank, lathe.
draaijakkals, long-eared fox.
draaikous, dawdler, loiterer.
draaiorrel, barrel-organ.
draak, (drake), dragon.
draderig, (-e), stringy; fibrous.
draf, n. trot.
draf, drawwe, (ge-), trot.
drag, (-te), costume, burden, load; litter; crop; pus (of a wound).
drama, (-s), drama, play.
dramaturg, (-e), dramatist.
drang, (-e), pressure, urgency; impulse, urge.
drank, (-e), drink, liquor, beverage.
dreef, op – kom, get into one's stride.
dreig, (ge-), threaten; intend.
dreigement, (-e), menace, threat.

dreigend, (-e), threatening, imminent.
dreineer, (ge-), drain.
drek, filth, muck.
drempel, (-s), threshold (fig.).
drenk, (ge-), soak, steep.
drenkeling, (-e), drowning (drowned) person.
drentel, (ge-), loiter, saunter.
dresseer, (ge-), train, break in.
dreun, n. boom, rumble; drone.
dreun, (ge-), boom, roar, rumble; drone.
dribbel, (ge-), dribble.
drie, (-ë, -s), three; try (football).
drieërlei, of three kinds (sorts).
driehoek, triangle; set-square.
driehoeksmeting, trigonometry.
driekwart, three-fourths; threequarter (rugby); three-quarters.
drieling, (-e), triplets.
drievoudig, (-e), threefold, triple, treble.
driewiel(er), tricycle.
drif, (-te), n. anger, temper; haste.
drif, (-te, driwwe), ford, drift.
driftig, (-e), quick-tempered; hasty.
dril, n. drill.
dril, (ge-), drill, coach; quiver, shake.
drilboor, drill, wimble.
drilvis, electric ray (skate).
dring, (ge-), crowd, hustle, jostle, push, throng; press, urge.
dringend, (-e), pressing, crying, urgent.
drink, (ge-), drink.
dro(ë), droog, (ge-), dry; become dry.
droef, (droewe), dejected, sad.
droef(e)nis, grief, sadness, sorrow.
droefgeestig, (-e), dejected, melancholy.
droëlewer, dry-throated.
droesem, dregs, lees.
droewig, (-e), pitiful, sad, sorrowful.
drogbeeld, illusion, phantom.
drogis, (-te), druggist.
drom, (-me), crowd, troop; drum.
dromedaris, (-se), dromedary.
dromerig, (-e), dreamy; faraway (look).
drommel, (-s), beggar, wretch; devil.
drommels, {-e), a. confounded, deuced.
dronk, a. drunken (attrib.), drunk (pred.).
dronkaard, (-s), drunkard, inebriate.
dronkenskap, drunkenness, intoxication.
dronklap, drunkard.
dronkslaan, (dronkge-), beat, dumbfound.
droog, (droë), a. dry, parched; dull.
drooglê, (drooge-), drain, reclaim; make dry.
droogloop, (drooge-), run dry.
droogmaak, (drooge-), dry.
droogsit, (drooge-), get the better of; oust.
droogte, (-s), drought, dryness.
droogvoets, dry-shod.
droogweg, drily (dryly).
droom, (drome), n. dream.
droom, (ge-), dream.
droombeeld, illusion, vision.
dros, (ge-), desert, run away.
drosdy, (-e), dros(t)dy.
droster, (-s), runaway, deserter.
druif, (druiwe), grape.
druip, (ge-), drip (with blood); gutter (of candle); fail.
druipeling, (-e), failure (in an examination).
druipnat, dripping(-wet), soaked, drenched.
druipstert, adv. sneaking.
druis, (ge-), roar, swirl, swish.
druk, (-ke), n. pressure; weight, squeeze (of the hand); print, type (of letter); edition.
druk, a. busy, lively; crowded.

druk, (ge-), press, squeeze; push; weigh heavy upon; print (a book).
drukkend, (-e), oppressive; sultry.
drukker, (-s), printer.
drukkery, (-e), printing-office, printing-works.
drukking, pressure, weight.
drukpot, pressure cooker.
drukspyker(tjie), thumb-tack.
drukte, bustle, fuss, stir, to-do.
drumpel, (-s), threshold, doorstep.
drup, drip; eaves.
drup, (ge-), drip, drop, trickle down.
druppel, (-s), drop.
dryf, drywe, (ge-), float, drift (ashore); drive; impel, hustle; conduct, run (a business).
dryfveer, spring; incentive, motive.
dubbel(d), duwwel(d), (-e), double, dual, twice.
dubbeldooier, -door, double-yolked egg.
dubbelganger, double, second self.
dubbelpunt, colon.
dubbelsinnig, (-s), ambiguous.
dubbeltjie, (-s), penny.
dubbelvorm, doublet.
dui(e), (ge-), – op, hint at, point to, suggest.
duidelik, (-e), clear, plain; distinct; obvious.
duideliksheidshalwe, for the sake of clearness.
duif, (duiwe), dove; pigeon.
duik, vide **deuk.**
duik, (ge-), dive, dip, duck, plunge.
duikboot, submarine.
duiker, (-s), diver; diving-bird; duiker (antelope); culvert; yorker (cricket).
duikklopper, panel-beater.
duikweg, subway.
duim, (-e), thumb.
duimbreedte, the thickness of an inch.
duimspyker, inch-nail; drawing-pin.
duimstok, footrule, inch-measure.
duin, (-e), dune, sand-hill.
duisel, (ge-), get (grow) dizzy (giddy).
duiseling, dizziness (giddiness).
duiselingwekkend, (-e), dizzy, giddy.
duisend, (-e), thousand.
duisendpoot, millipede, centipede.
duister, n. dark, darkness.
duister, a. dark (night, future); obscure (style); gloomy (prospects); abstruse.
duisternis, dark(ness); 'n – **van,** scores (a multitude) of.
duit, (-e), farthing.
Duitser, (-s), German.
duiwel, (-s), devil.
duiwelagtig, (-e), devilish, diabolical.
duiwels, (-e), devilish; diabolical.
duld, (ge-), bear, (pain), tolerate (a person); stand (a treatment).
dun, a. thin, slender (waist), rare (atmosphere), scanty (hair), sparse (population), clear (soup).
dun, (ge-), thin, deplete (the ranks).
dundoek, bunting.
dunk, idea, opinion.
duplikaat, (-kate), duplicate.
duplo: in –, in duplicate.
durf, n. pluck, daring, nerve.
durf, durwe, (ge-), dare; risk; venture.
dus, consequently, therefore.
dusdanig, (-e), such.
duskant, vide **deuskant.**
dusketyd: om –, about this time.
dusver: tot –, so far, thus far.
dut, (ge-), doze, snooze.
dutjie, (-s), doze, snap.
duur, n. duration; life.
duur (dure), a. dear; expensive; solemn (oath).
duur, (ge-), continue, last; endure; keep.

duursaam, (-same), durable, lasting.
duusman, vide **diesman.**
duwweltjie, devil's thorn.
dwaal, (ge-), roam, wander; err.
dwaallig, will-o'-the-wisp.
dwaalspoor, false (wrong) track.
dwaas, (dwase), n. fool, ass.
dwaas, (dwase), a. absurd, foolish, silly.
dwaling, (-e, -s), mistake, error.
dwang, compulsion, constraint.
dwarrel, (ge-), whirl (round); flutter about.
dwarrelwind, whirlwind, tornado.
dwars, transverse, diagonal; cross, athwart, cross-grained, perverse, pig-headed.
dwarsboom, (ge-), obstruct, thwart.
dwarsdeur, right through, straight across.
dwarshout, cross-beam, cross-bar.
dwarsoor, right (straight) across.

dwarspaal, cross-bar.
dwarste, in die –, across, athwart.
dwarstrek, (dwarsge-), quarrel, squabble.
dwarsweg: iemand – antwoord, give a person a surly answer.
dweep, (ge-), be fanatical, gush, enthuse.
dweepsiek, (-e), fanatic.
dweper, (-s), fanatic; enthusiasm.
dwerg, (-e), dwarf, pygmy, midget.
dwing, (ge-), force, compel, constrain; be on the point of.
dwingeland, (-e), tyrant.
dwingelandy, tyranny.
dy, (-e), n. thigh.
dy, (ge-), thrive, prosper, succeed.
dyk, (-e), dike, bank.
dynserig, (-e), cloudy, hazy, misty.

eb, n. ebb(-tide).
eb, (geëb), ebb, flow back.
ebbehout, ebony.
edel, (-e), noble; generous; precious (metals).
edelagbaar, (-bare), honourable, worshipful.
edelgesteente, gem, jewel, precious stone.
edelman, (-ne, edelliede, edellui), nobleman, noble.
edelmoedig, (-e), generous, magnanimous.
edik, n. vinegar.
edik, (-te), n. edict, decree.
edisie, (-s), edition; issue.
êe, vide eg.
eed, (ede), oath.
eekhorinkie, (-s), squirrel.
eeld, eelt, (-e), callosity, callus.
eeld, eeltsweer, bunion.
een, (ene, -s), n. & pro. one; someone; something.
een, ene, a. & adv. a, a certain one.
eenbeentjie: – speel, play hopscotch.
eend, (-e), duck.
eendag, once (upon a time), one day; some day.
eenders(te), eenderster, a. & adv. alike, similar.
eendrag, harmony, union, unity.
eenkant, on one side.
eenkeer, vide eendag.
eenlopend, (-e), single, unmarried.
eenmaal, once; one day.
eenparig, (-e), unanimous(ly), by common consent.
eens, a. & adv. once (upon a time), one day, just; even; unanimous, of the same opinion.
eensaam, (-same), solitary, lonely.
eensdeels, partly, on the one hand.
eensgesind, (-e), unanimous.
eensklaps, all of a sudden.
eenslag, once; one day.
eenstemmig, (-e), a. unanimous; for one voice.
eensydig, (-e), one-sided; unilateral; partial.
eentjie, op jou –, by oneself.
eentonig, (-e), monotonous; drab.
eenvormig, (-e), uniform.
eenvoud, simplicity.
eenvoudig, (-e), simple, plain, homely.
eenvoudig, adv. simply, plainly.
eenvoudigheidshalwe, for (the sake of) simplicity.
eer, n. credit, honour, repute.
eer, adv. & conj. before.
eer, (geëer), honour, respect, revere.
eerbaar, (-bare), good, honest, virtuous.
eerbetoon, -betuiging, -bewys, (mark of) honour, homage, tribute.
eerbied, respect, reverence.
eerbiedig, (-e), respectful, devout.
eerbiedig, (geëerbiedig), respect; defer to.
eerbiedwaardig, (-e), respectable, venerable.
eerbiedwekkend, (-e), imposing, impressive.
eerder, rather, sooner.
eergevoel, sense of honour; pride.
eergevoelig, (-e), proud, touchy.
eergierig, (-e), ambitious.
eergister, the day before yesterday.
eergisteraand, -middag, -môre, (-oggend), the night (afternoon, morning) before last.
eerlang, -lank, before (ere) long, shortly.
eerlik, (-e), a. & adv. honest, upright; honourable; fair, square.
eerloos, (-lose), dishonourable, infamous.
eers, first, formerly; once; only.
eersaam, (-same), respectable; virtuous.
eersdaags, one of these days, shortly.
eersgeborene, (-s), first-born (child).
eersgenoemde, first-mentioned; former.
eerskomende, following, next.

eerste, a. & adv. first; chief, foremost; prime (minister).
eerstehands, (-e), first-hand (information).
eersteklas, adv. first-class; first-rate.
eersteling, (-e), first-born; first work (of artist).
eerstens, first(ly), in the first place.
eersterangs, (-e), first-class, first-rate.
eersug, ambition.
eersvolgende, following, next.
eertyds, (-e), a. & adv. former(ly).
eervol, (-le), honourable.
eerwaarde, reverend.
eerwaardig, (-e), time-honoured; venerable.
eet, (geëet), eat; dine, take (have) one's meals.
eetgoed, eatables.
eetkamer, dining-room.
eetlepel, tablespoon.
eetlus, appetite.
eetmaal, meal; dinner, banquet.
eeu, (-e), century.
eeuelang, -lank, age-long, secular.
eeue-oud, (-oue), centuries old.
eeufees, centenary.
effe, level, flat, smooth; plain.
effekte, (pl.), shares, stocks, securities.
effektebeurs, stock-exchange, share-market.
effektief, (-tiewe), a. effective, real.
effens, just; a little, slightly; a moment.
effentjies, vide **effens**.
eg, (-ge, êe), n. harrow.
eg, n. marriage, matrimony, wedlock.
eg, (-te), a. genuine, real, thorough, regular, proper; legitimate.
eg, êe, (geëg, geëe), harrow.
ega, (-s), consort, spouse.
egaal, (egale), even, level, smooth.
egalig, eengalig, (-e), smooth; uniform.
eggenoot, (-note), husband, spouse.
eggenote, (-s), wife, spouse.
eggo, (-'s), echo.
Egiptenaar, (-nare, -s), Egyptian.
Egipties, (-e), Egyptian.
egpaar, married couple.
egskeiding, divorce.
egtelik, (-e), conjugal, connubial, matrimonial.
egter, however, nevertheless, yet.
egtheid, authenticity, genuineness, legality, legitimacy.
eie, own, private; innate, natural (gifts); peculiar; familiar, intimate.
eiebelang, self-interest.
eiedunk, self-conceit.
eiegeregtig, [-(d)e], self-righteous.
eiemagtig, (-e), arbitrary, highhanded.
eien, (geëien), appropriate; recognize (a person).
eienaam, proper name.
eienaar, (-nare, -s), owner, proprietor.
ei(g)enaardig, (-e), peculiar, singular.
eiendom, (-me), property, belongings, estate.
eienskap, (-pe), quality, property, attribute.
eier, (-s), egg.
eier-in-die-hoed, hat-ball (game).
eierkelkie, egg-cup.
eiesinnig, (-e), headstrong, self-willed.
eiewaan, conceitedness, self-conceit.
eiewaarde, self-esteem, self-respect.
eiewys, (self-) conceited, cocky; obstinate.
eik, (-e), oak(-tree).
eikel, (-s), acorn.
eiland, (-e), island; isle.
eiland(e)see, archipelago.
eina!, interj. oh!, oh-oh!, ow!
einddoel, ultimate object (aim).
einde, (-s), close, conclusion, end; ending.
eindelik, (-e), a. last, ultimate.

eindelik, adv. at last (length), finally.
eindig, (geëindig), (come to an) end, conclude, finish, stop, terminate.
eindpaal, goal, limit; winning-post.
einste, same.
eintlik, (-e), a. actual, proper, real.
eintlik, adv. actually, properly, really.
eis, (-e), n. claim, demand; requirement, requisite.
eis, (geëis), claim, demand; require.
eiser, (-s) eiseres, (-se), claimant, plaintiff.
eiwit, white of an egg, albumen.
ek, ekke, I.
ekkerig, (-e), egotistic, self-centred; subjective.
eklips, (-e), eclipse.
ekonomie, economy; economics.
ekonoom, (-nome), economist.
eksamen, (-s), examination.
eksaminator, (-e, -s), examiner.
eksamineer, (geëksamineer), examine.
eksekuteur, (-e, -s), executor.
eksellensie, (-s), excellency.
eksemplaar, (-plare), specimen, sample; copy.
eksie-perfeksie, perfect, smart; punctilious.
ekskuseer, (geëkskuseer), excuse, pardon.
ekskuus, (-kuse), apology; excuse, pardon.
ekspedisie, (-s), expedition.
eksperiment, (-e), experiment.
eksperimenteer, (geëksperimenteer), experiment.
eksporteer, (geëksporteer), export.
ekspres, adv. vide **aspres**.
ekstase, ecstasy, rapture.
ekstra, a. extra, additional, special.
ekstrak, (-te), extract; excerpt.
ekwator, equator; vide **ewenaar**.
ekwivalent, (-e), equivalent.
el, (-le), ell; yard.
eland, (-e), eland (S.A.); elk (Eur.).
elastiek, (-e), n. elastic.
elders, elsewhere.
eleksie, (-s), election.
elektries, (-e), electric.
elektrisiteit, electricity.
element, (-e), element; (electric) cell; constituent.
elementêr, (-e), elementary.
elf, (elwe), n. elf, fairy.
elf, (-e, -s, elwe), n. & a. eleven.
elf-en-dertigste: op sy –, at a snail's pace, in a kind of way.
elfuur, eleven o'clock.
elimineer, (geëlimineer), eliminate.
elk, (-e), each, every, any.
elkeen, each, everyone, anyone.
elkers, every now and then (again).
ellelang, -lank, long-drawn.
ellende, misery, wretchedness.
ellendeling, (-e), villain, wretch.
ellendig, (-e), miserable, wretched; rotten.
elmboog, (-boë), elbow.
els, (-e), awl.
els, (-e), alder(-tree).
Elsasser, (-s), Alsatian.
emalje, enamel.
emigreer, (geëmigreer), emigrate.
emmer, (-s), bucket, pail.
emoe, (-s), emu.
emosie, (-s), emotion.
en, and.
end, end, close, conclusion, termination; extremity; tail.
endosseer, (geëndosseer), endorse.
endossement, endorsement.
end-uit, right to the end.
ene, vide **een** a. & adv.; **ten ene male**, absolutely, altogether.

enemmel, vide **emalje**.
energiek, (-e), energetic, active, pushing.
enerlei, of the same kind (sort).
eng, (-e), narrow, tight; narrow-minded.
engel, (-e, -s), angel.
Engels, (-e), n. & a. English; Anglican (Church).
Engelsman, (Engelse) Englishman.
enghartig, (-e), narrow-minded.
engte, (-s), narrowness; defile (between mountains); strait (of the sea); isthmus.
enig, (-e), only, sole; unique.
enigeen, anyone.
enigermate, to some extent, somewhat.
eniggebore, only-begotten (Bib.)
enigsins, somewhat, slightly, remotely.
enigste, only, sole; vide **enig**.
enjin, engine.
enkel, (-s), n. ankle.
enkel(d), (-), a. single.
enkel, adv. only, merely, simply.
enkeling, (-e), individual.
enkelspel, single(s).
enkelvoud, singular (number).
enorm, (-e), enormous.
ensiklopedie, encyclopaedia.
ent, (-e), n. piece; length; distance.
ent, (-e), n. graft; inoculation; vaccination.
ent, (geënt), graft; inoculate; vaccinate.
entjie, end, stub, piece; short distance.
entoesiasme, enthusiasm.
entomologie, entomology.
epidemie, (-ë, -s), epidemic.
epiek, epic poetry.
epies, (-e), epic.
epos, (-se), epic(-poem).
erbarm, (het –): jou – oor, have (take) pity on.
erbarming, compassion, pity; mercy.
erbarmlik, (-e), lamentable, miserable, pitiful; rotten, wretched.
erd, n. earth; clay.
erd, (geërd), earth (hill) up.
erdeskottel, earthenware-dish.
erdvark, aardvark, ant-eater, antbear.
erdwurm, earth-worm.
ere, n. honour; glory; vide **eer**, n.
ereboog, triumphal arch.
eregas, guest of honour.
erelid, honorary member.
êrens, somewhere.
erewoord, word of honour; parole.
erf, erwe, (geërf geërwe), inherit, succeed to (a title).
erfdeel, heritage, (hereditary) portion.
erfnis, heritage, inheritance.
erfgeld, money inherited.
erfgenaam, (-name), heir.
erflik, (-e), a. & adv. hereditary.
erflikheid, heredity.
erfpag, quitrent-tenure; quitrent.
erfporsie, heritage, inheritance.
erg, n.; **sonder –**, unintentionally; unsuspectingly; without malice.
erg, (-e), a. bad; ill; severe.
erg, adv. badly, severely, very.
erg, (geërg), vide **erge(r), geërge(r)**.
erge(r), [geërge(r)], annoy, vex.
ergerlik, (-e), annoying; offensive, scandalous, shocking.
ergernis, (-se), offence, annoyance, nuisance, vexation.
erken, (het –), acknowledge, admit; confess (guilt).
erkenning, acknowledgment; admission; confession.
erkentenis, acknowledgment; confession.

erkentlik, (-e), grateful, thankful.
erlang, (het –), acquire, gain, obtain.
erns, earnest(ness), seriousness, gravity.
ernstig, (-e), a. & adv. earnest (endeavour)
 serious, grave (condition), severe (illness);
 grave (face).
ertappel, vide aartappel.
ertjie, (-s, erte), pea.
erts, (-e), ore.
ervaar, (het –), experience.
ervare, experienced, expert.
ervaring, (-e, -s), experience.
es, (-se), n. (1) fireplace, hearth.
es, (-se), n. (2) ash(-tree).
es, (-se), n. (3) sharp turn.
esel, (-s), donkey; blockhead; easel.
eskader, (-s), squadron (naval).
eskadrielje, (-s), squadron (air-force).
eskadron, (-s), squadron (mil.).
Eskimo, (-'s), Eskimo (Esquimau).
essa(a)i, (-e), assay.
essehout, Cape ash.
essensieel, (-siële), essential.
ete, food, fare; meal, dinner.
Ethiopies, (-e), Ethiopian.
etiket, (-te), etiquette; label.
etlike, several, some.
etmaal, twenty-four hours.
ets, (-e), n. etching.
ets, (geëts), etch.
etter, n. discharge, pus.
etter, (geëtter), fester, suppurate.
Europeaan, (-ane), European.
Europees, (-pese), European.

euwel, (-s), evil; defect, fault.
evangelie, (-s), gospel, evangel.
evangelis, (-te), evangelist.
eventueel, (-uele), a. & adv. possible, potential;
 by chance.
evolusie, ewolusie, evolution.
ewe, n., dis my om die –, it is all the same to me.
ewe, a. even; – of onewe, odd or even.
ewe, adv. as, even, just, equally, quite; – goed,
 alike, (just) as well; – min, just as little; –
 veel, as much, the same.
eweas, ewenas, (just) as (like).
ewebeeld, picture, counterpart, image.
ewe-eens, eweneens, also, likewise, too.
ewemens, fellow-man.
ewenaar, n. equator; tongue (of balance);
 swingle-beam (of wagon); differential.
ewenaar, (geëwenaar), equal.
ewenas, vide eweas.
eweneens, vide ewe-eens.
ewe(n)wel, however, nevertheless.
eweredig, (-e), proportional, proportionate,
 commensurate.
eweseer, as much; alike.
eweso, likewise; as.
ewewel, vide ewe(n)wel.
ewewig, balance, equilibrium, poise.
ewewigtig, (-e), evenly balanced; level-headed.
ewewydig, (-e), parallel.
ewig, (-e), a. & adv. eternal (life), perpetual
 (snow), perennial (youth), everlasting.
ewigdurend, (-e), everlasting, perpetual.
ewigheid, eternity.

faal, (ge-), fail, be unsuccessful.
faam, reputation, repute.
fabel, (-s), n. fable; fabrication, fiction.
fabelagtig, (-e), fabulous; incredible.
fabriek, (-e), factory, mill, works.
fabrikaat, (-kate), manufacture, make.
fabrikant, (-e), manufacturer, maker.
fabriseer, (ge-), manufacture; concoct.
fakkel, (-s), torch.
faktor, (-e), factor.
faktuur, (-ture), bill, invoice.
fakulteit, (-e), faculty; board.
familiaar, (-iare), familiar, chummy, free, intimate.
familie, (-s), family; relations; relatives.
familiebetrekking, relative, relationship.
fanatiek, (-e), fanatic(al).
fanatisme, fanaticism.
fantaseer, (ge-), indulge in fancies, imagine.
fantasie, (-ë), fancy, phantasy; fantasia (mus.).
fantasties, (-e), fantastic; wild (stories).
fariseër, (-s), hypocrite.
Fariseër, Pharisee.
Fascis, (-te), Fascist.
fase, (-s), phase, stage.
fasiliteit, (-e), faculty.
fat, (-te), dandy, fop.
fataal, (-ale), fatal.
fatalisties, (-e), fatalistic.
fatsoen, (-e), n. fashion, form, shape, cut (of clothes); decency; decorum, good breeding (manners).
fatsoeneer, (ge-), fashion, mould, shape.
fatsoenlik, (-e), a. decent, respectable.
fatsoenlik, adv. decently, respectably.
fatsoenshalwe, for decency's sake.
Februarie, February.
federasie, (-s), federation.
fee, (feë), fairy.
feeks, (-e), shrew, virago, vixen.
fees, (-te), feast, festival, fête, treat.
feesmaal, banquet.
feestelik, (-e), a. & adv. festal, festive.
feesviering, feasting; celebration.
feil, (-e), n. fault; error; mistake.
feil, (ge-), err, go wrong.
feilbaar, (-bare), fallible, liable to error.
feilloos, (-lose), faultless.
feit, (-e), fact.
feitlik, (-e), a. actual, real.
feitlik, adv. practically, as a matter of fact.
fel, (-, -le), fierce, sharp, violent.
felisiteer, (ge-), congratulate.
Fenicies, (-e), n. & a. Phoenician.
ferm, (-, -e), firm, steady, solid.
ferweel, corduroy; velvet.
fes, (-se), fez.
festoeneer, (ge-), festoon.
fetisj, (-e), fetish.
fiemies, nonsense, whims.
fier, (-, -e), high-spirited, proud.
fieterjasies, superfluous ornaments, flourishes.
fiets, (-e), n. (bi)cycle.
figuur, (-ure), figure; character (in drama).
figuurlik, (-e), a. & adv. figurative(ly).
fiks, (-, -e), healthy, quick, robust.
fikseer, (ge-), fix (a photo); stare at (a person).
fiktief, (-tiewe), fictitious, imaginary.
filantroop, (-trope) philanthropist.
filantropies, (-e), philanthropist.
Filistyn, (-e), Philistine.
films, (-s), n. film; screen.
film, (ge-), film.
filosofeer, (ge-), philosophize.
filosoof, (-sowe), philosopher.

filtreer, (ge-), filter, filtrate, strain.
Fin, (-ne), Finn, Fin(lander).
finaal, (-ale), final, total, complete.
finansieel, (-siële), a. & adv. financial.
finansier, (-s), n. financier.
Fingo, (-'s), Fingo.
firma, (-s), firm, house, concern.
fisant, (-e), pheasant.
fisies, (-e), physical.
fisika, physics.
fisiologie, physiology.
fiskaal, (-ale, -s), fiscal; butcherbird.
fladder, (ge-), flutter, flap; flow.
flamink, (-e), flamingo.
flanelet, flannelette.
flank, (-e), flank, side.
flans, (ge-): inmekaar –, knock together.
flap, (-pe), n. iris; flap (of cart).
flap, (ge-), flap.
flard, (-e), rag, tatter.
flater, (-s), blunder, mistake.
fleim, vide **fluim**.
fleksie, (-s), flection (flexion).
flennie, flannel.
flens, (-e), flange.
flenter, (-s), n. rag, small piece, splinter.
flenter, (ge-), gad (idle) about.
flenters, adv. in rags (shreds, tatters); in pieces (splinters).
flerrie, (-s), n. flirt, gadabout.
flerrie, (ge-), flirt, gad (idle) about.
fles, (-se), bottle; flask.
fleur, bloom, flower, prime.
fliek, (-e), bioscope.
flikflooi, (ge-), cajole, coax, flatter.
flikker, (ge-), glitter, sparkle; flicker; twinkle.
flikkers, capers.
flink, (-, -e), a. fine, robust; spirited; energetic, pushing; considerable.
flink, adv. energetically, soundly, thoroughly; pluckily; firmly.
flirt, (-e, -s), n. flirt.
flirt, (ge-), flirt.
flits, (-e), flash(light).
flits, (ge-), flash.
flitslig, flashlight.
flodder, (ge-), flounder, splash.
flodderig, (-e), baggy, floppy; dowdy.
flodderkous, dowdy, frump, slattern.
flonker, (ge-), sparkle, twinkle.
floreer, (ge-), flourish, prosper, thrive.
floryn, (-e), florin.
flottielje, (-s), flotilla.
flou, (-, -e), tasteless (food); feeble (joke); dim (light); faint; remote (idea); weak (tea).
flouhartig, (-e), faint-hearted.
flouiteit, (-e), poor (silly) joke.
flous, (ge-), deceive, let down.
floute, (-s), fainting-fit, swoon.
fluim, mucus, phlegm.
fluister, (ge-), whisper.
fluit, n. whistle; flute (instr.).
fluit, (ge-), whistle; play on the flute; whiz, zip (of bullets); pipe (of birds).
fluit-fluit, easily.
fluks, (-, -e), a. & adv. hardworking, willing; quick, smart; quickly.
flus(sies), just now.
fluweel, velvet.
fnuik, (ge-), cripple, put down, break.
foefie, (-s), dodge, trick; pretext.
foei!, fie!, for shame!
foelie, n. mace; (tin-)foil.
foeter, (ge-), bother, trouble; thrash.
foliopapier, foolscap(-paper).

folter, (ge-), torment, torture.
folterbank, rack.
fondament, (-e), foundation; bottom.
fondeer, (ge-), found, lay the foundation.
fonds, (-e), fund; (pl.) funds; stocks.
fontein, (-e), fountain, spring.
fooi, (-e), n. tip, gratuity.
fooi, (ge-), tip.
fop, (ge-), cheat, fool, hoax.
foppertjie, fopspeen, (baby's) dummy.
forel, (-le), trout.
formaat, (-mate), size; shape.
formeel, (-ele), formal.
formule, (-s), formula.
formuleer, (ge-), formulate, word.
formulier, (-e), form; formulary.
fors, (-, -e), bold, robust, vigorous.
forseer, (ge-), force, compel.
fort, (-e), fort, fortress.
fortuin, fortune; wealth.
fortuinlik, (-e), fortunate, lucky.
fosfor, phosphorus.
fossiel, (-e), fossil.
foto, (-'s), photo(graph).
fotograaf, (-grawe), photographer.
fotografeer, (ge-), photograph.
fout, (-e), mistake; defect, fault.
fouteer, (ge-), make a mistake.
foutief, (-tiewe), faulty, wrong.
fraai, (-e), pretty, fine, handsome.
fragment, (-e), fragment, piece.
fraiing, (-s), edging, fringe; tassel.
framboos, (-bose), raspberry.
frank, (-e), n. franc.
frank, a. frank, free, bold.
frankeer, (ge-), frank, stamp, prepay.

Frankryk, France.
Fransman, (-ne, Franse), Frenchman.
frappant, (-e), striking.
frase, (-s), phrase.
frats, (-e), whim; buffoonery.
fratsemaker, buffoon, clown.
fregat, (-te), frigate.
fries, (-e), frieze, moulding.
Fries, (-e), Frisian.
frikkadel, (-le), rissole.
fris, (-, -se), fresh, cool; refreshing (drink), fit, hale, hearty.
frisseer, (ge-), crisp, curl, frizz(le).
frisgebou(d), (-de), strongly built.
frok, (-ke), frokkie, (-s), vest.
frommel, (ge-), crumple, crease.
frons, (-e), n. frown; scowl.
frons, (ge-), frown; scowl.
front, (-e), front; facade, frontage.
ftisis, phthisis.
fuchsia, vide foksia.
fuif, (fuiwe), celebration, spree.
fuif, (ge-), carouse, feast, revel.
fuik, (-e), fish-trap; hen-coop.
fundamenteel, (-tele), fundamental.
fungeer, (ge-), act (officiate) as.
funksie, (-s), function, capacity.
fusilleer, (ge-), shoot.
fut, go, push, spirit, mettle.
fyn, (-, -e), fine; delicate; choice, exquisite (wines); refined (people); subtle (distinction).
fynbesnaard, (-e), highly strung.
fyngevoelig, (-e), delicate; sensitive.
fynmeel, flour.
fyntuin, vegetable garden.
fyt, felon, whitlow.

ga!, faugh! phew!

gaaf, (gawe), fine, good, excellent.

gaan, (ge-), go; move, walk.

gaandeweg, by degrees, gradually, little by little.

gaap, (gape), n. yawn, yawning.

gaap, (ge), yawn; gape.

gaar, (well) cooked, done.

gaarne, gladly, readily, willingly.

gaas, gauze, netting.

gaat, vide gaan.

gaatjie, (-s), little hole; fingerhole.

gade, (-s), consort, spouse.

gadeslaan, (gadege-), observe, watch.

gading, taste, inclination, liking.

gaffel, (-s), prong; pitchfork.

gaip, (-e), uncouth person, boor.

gal, bile, gall.

galant, (-e), a. courteous, gallant.

galbitter, as bitter as gall.

galbult, heat-bump, urticaria.

galei, (-e), galley.

galery, (-e), gallery; drive (mining).

galg, (-e), gallow(-tree); gibbet.

Galileër, (-s), n., **Galilees**, (-lese), a. Galilean.

galjoen, (-e), galleon (ship and fish).

gallamsiekte, splenic fever.

galm, (-e), n. boom, peal.

galm, (ge-), bawl (of voice); (re)sound.

galmbord (klankbord), sound(ing)-board.

galop, n. gallop (of a horse).

galop, galoppeer, (ge-), gallop.

galsiekte, bilious complaint (of humans), gall-sickness (of animals).

galsterig, (-e), rancid, rank, strong.

gammat, (-s, -te), (young) Malay.

Gamsgeslag, Native(s).

gang, (-e), n. passage, corridor; gangway (railw.); tunnel (mining); gait (of a person); pace (of a horse); course (of a disease); trend (of conversation).

gangbaar, (-bare), current; valid; passable.

ganna(bos), (-s), ganna, lye-bush.

gans, (-e), n. goose.

gans, (-e), a. all, entire, whole.

gans, adv. absolutely, entirely.

gansegaar, altogether; – **nie**, by no means.

gapend, (-e), yawning, gaping.

gaping, (-e, -s), gap, hiatus.

gaps, steal, purloin.

gare, vide garing.

garing, gare, (cotton-)thread, yarn.

garingboom, American aloe.

garingklip, asbestos.

garnisoen, (-e), garrison.

gars, barley.

gas, (-te), n. guest, visitor.

gas, (-se), n. gas.

gasel, (-le), gazelle.

gaset, (-te), gazette.

gas(t)heer, host.

gasie, (-s), pay; wage(s), salary.

gasvry, hospitable.

gat, (-e), n. hole, gap, opening.

gawe, (-s), gift, talent; donation.

gawerig, (-e), excellent, fine.

geag, (-te), esteemed, respected; honourable.

gearm(d), (-de), arm-in-arm, armed.

gebaan, (-de), beaten (track).

gebaar, (-bare), gesture, gesticulation.

gebak, n. cake, pastry.

gebaken(d), gebaker(d): kort – wees, be hasty (peppery, touchy).

gebed, (-e), prayer; grace (at table).

gebeente, bones.

gebelg, (-de), angry, offended.

gebergte, (-s), mountain-range, mountains.

gebeur, (het –), happen, occur.

gebeurde: die –, the event (occurrence).

gebeurlik, (-e), contingent, possible.

gebeurtenis, (-se), event, occurrence.

gebied, (-e), n. dominion, territory (of a state); area; department, field, province, sphere.

gebied, (het –), command, direct, order.

gebiedend, (-e), commanding, compelling; urgent.

gebit, (-te), (set of) teeth; bit (of bridle).

geblus, (-te), slaked.

gebod, (-e, gebooie), command, order; decree.

geboë, arched, bent, bowed, curved.

gebonde, bound.

geboorte, (-s), birth.

gebore, born.

gebou, (-e), n. building, edifice, structure.

gebrek, (-e), lack, want, dearth, deficiency (of air); poverty; defect, fault, shortcoming.

gebrekkig, (-e), defective, faulty, broken.

gebreklik, (-e), crippled, deformed, lame.

gebroeders, brothers.

gebroedsel, (-s), brood.

gebroke, broken.

gebruik, (-e), n. use (of one's limbs); custom, habit, practice, usage; application, function; consumption (of foodstuffs).

gebruik, (-te), a. used, second-hand (car).

gebruik, (het –), use, employ; take (medicine), consume (coal).

gebruiklik, (-e), customary, usual.

gebukkend, (-e), crouching, stooping.

gebulk, bellowing, lowing.

gedaagde, (-s), defendant; respondent.

gedaan, (-dane), done, exhausted, finished.

gedaante, (-s), figure, shape; vision, apparition.

gedagte, (-s), idea, notion, thought; mind; memory; opinion.

gedagtenis, memory, remembrance; keepsake, souvenir.

gedagtestreep, dash.

gedagtig, mindful.

gedeelte, (-s), part, section; share.

gedeeltelik, (-e), a. & adv. partial (eclipse); partly, partially.

gedenk, (het –), bear in mind; commemorate.

gedenkboek, album, memorial volume.

gedenkwaardig, (-e), memorable.

gedien(d): nie van iets – wees nie, not be prepared to put up with something.

gediensTig, (-e), obliging; officious.

gedierte, (-s), creature; monster.

gedig, (-te), poem.

geding, (-e), action, law-suit; quarrel.

gedoe, bustle, concern, fuss.

gedoë, gedoog, (het –), suffer, tolerate.

gedoente, (-s), vide gedoe.

gedoriewaar, by gum!, really and truly!

gedra, (het –), behave, conduct oneself.

gedrag, behaviour, conduct.

gedrang, crowd, crush, throng.

gedrewe, chased, embossed.

gedrog, (-te), monster, monstrosity.

gedronge, compact, terse (style).

gedruis, (-e), noise, roar, rumbling, rush.

gedug, (-te), formidable; sound.

geduld, forbearance, patience.

geduldig, (-e), patient.

gedurende, for (a fortnight), during.

gedurig, (-e), a. constant, continual; continued (fraction, product).

gedurigdeur, vide gedurig(lik).

gedurig(lik), adv. constantly, continually.

gedwee, (gedweë), docile, meek.

gedwonge, compulsory, enforced; forced (smile); forcible (feeding).
gedy, (het –), flourish, prosper.
gee, (ge-), give; afford; yield; grant.
geel, n. yellow (colour); yolk (of an egg).
geel, a. yellow.
geelbaadjie: die – aanhê, be jealous.
geelbruin, tawny.
geelkapel, yellow cobra.
geelkoper, brass.
geelslang, cobra, "yellow snake".
geelsug, jaundice.
geelvink, yellow weaverbird.
geelwortel, carrot.
geen, g'n, a. & pron., no, not a, not any, not one, none.
geeneen, no-one, none.
geensins, by no means, not at all.
geër, (-s), giver.
gees, (-te), spirit; mind; wit; genius; ghost, spectre, apparition.
geesdodend, (-e), soul-deadening.
geesdrif, enthusiasm, zeal.
geesdriftig, (-e), enthusiastic, zealous.
geestelik, (-e), spiritual; mental (faculties); religious, sacred (songs).
geestelike, (-s), divine, minister.
geestig, (-e), bright, smart, witty.
gegewe, (-ns), n. datum, information; (pl.) data.
gegewe, a. given.
gegoed, (-e), well-off, well-to-do.
gegote, cast (iron).
gegroet!, hail!
gegrond, (-e), well-founded; legitimate (hope); sound (reasons); reasonable (doubt).
gehaastheid, hurry, hurriedness.
gehaat, (-hate), hated, hateful, odious.
gehalte, quality, grade, standard; proof (of alcohol).
gehard, (-e), tempered, hardened, hardy, seasoned (soldiers); inured.
geharwar, bickering(s), wrangling.
gehawen(d), (-de), battered; in rags.
geheel, (gehele), n. whole.
geheel, (gehele), a. complete, entire, whole.
geheel, adv. all, completely, entirely, quite, wholly.
geheelonthouer, teetotaller.
geheg, – aan, attached (devoted) to.
geheim, (-e), n. secret; mystery.
geheim, (-e), a. secret.
geheimenis, (-se), mystery.
geheimsinnig, (-e), dark, mysterious.
geheue, memory, remembrance.
geheuenis, memory.
gehoor, hearing; audience, hearers.
gehoorpyp, ear-trumpet; stethoscope.
gehoorsaam, (-same), a. dutiful, obedient.
gehoorsaam, (het –), obey; submit to.
gehug, (-te), hamlet.
gehumeur(d), (-de): goed (sleg) –, good (ill-)tempered.
gehuud, (-hude), married.
geil, fertile, rich (soil); lascivious.
geilsiekte, "geilsiekte" (stock disease).
geiser, (-s), geyser.
geit, (-e), goat; girl.
geitjie, (-s), lizard; shrew, vixen.
gejaag, (-de), a. flustered, hurried.
gejammer, lamentation(s), wailing(s).
gek, (-ke), n. fool; lunatic.
gek, (–, -ke), a. & adv. mad, crazy, foolish; queer, silly.
gek, (ge-), joke, jest.
gekant: – teen, antagonistic (hostile) to.

gekheid, folly, foolishness; joking, fun.
geklee(d), (geklede), dressed; dressy.
geklets, rubbish. twaddle.
geklik, (-e), foolish, silly, queer.
geknoei, bungling; scheming.
gekonfyt, (-e), – in, well-versed (skilled) in.
gekrenk, (-te), hurt, offended.
gekrui(d), (-de), seasoned, spiced; spicy.
gekrul, (-de), curly, wavy, frizzled.
gekskeer, (gekge-), banter, jest, joke.
gekunsteld, (-e), artificial, mannered.
gekyf, bickering, wrangling.
gelaat, (-late), countenance, face, mien.
gelag, n., die – betaal, pay the piper (fig.)
gelang: na – van, according (in proportion) to.
gelas, (het –), direct, instruct, order.
gelastigde, (-s), delegate, proxy.
gelate, resigned.
geld, (-e), n. money.
geld(e), (ge-), apply, be in force, be valid, hold (good), obtain, count; apply to, concern.
geldelik, (-e), monetary (reward), pecuniary (difficulties), financial (support).
geldgierig, (-e), avaricious, covetous.
geldig, (-e), valid (ticket, reason), binding (in law), legal, operative.
geldskieter, (-s), moneylender.
geldstuk, coin.
geldsugtig, (-e), vide geldgierig.
geldwissel, money-order.
gelede, a. suffered; vide ly, (ge-).
gelede, adv. ago, past; kort –, recently.
geledere, vide gelid.
geleë, lying, situated; convenient.
geleëner, vide gelegener.
geleentheid, occasion, opportunity.
geleerd, (-e), learned (man), scholarly (work); trained (horse).
geleerdheid, erudition, learning.
gelegener: ter – tyd, in due time.
gelei, n. jelly.
gelei, (het –), lead, escort, attend; convoy (ships); conduct (heat).
geleibrief, way-bill; permit; safe-conduct.
geleide, escort, guard, protection.
geleidelik, (-e), gradual(ly), by degrees.
gelei(d)er, (-s), conductor; guide; duct.
geleiding, conducting; conduction (of heat); (electric) wiring; conduit-pipes; main.
gelesene: die –, portion read; lesson.
gelid, (geledere), rank. file; generation.
geliefde, (-s), beloved, dearest, sweetheart.
geliefkoosde, favourite.
geliewe, please.
gelofte, (-s), solemn promise, vow.
Geloftedag, Day of the Covenant.
geloof, (-lowe), n. belief, faith; creed, religion; credit, credence, trust.
geloof, gelowe, (het –), believe, credit, vide glo.
geloofbaar, gelooflik, believable, credible.
geloofwaardig, (-e), credible, reliable.
gelowig, (-e), believing, faithful.
gelowige, (-s), believer; (pl.) the faithful.
geluid, (-e), sound, noise.
geluk, (-ke), n. happiness, joy; fortune, (good) luck; success.
geluk, (het –), succeed, have luck.
gelukbringer, -bringer, charm, mascot.
gelukkig, (-e), happy, fortunate, lucky.
geluksalig, (-e), blessed.
gelukslag, piece of good luck, godsend.
gelyksoeker, adventurer, fortune-hunter.
geluksvoël, lucky dog.

gelukwens, (gelukge-), congratulate, wish good luck (happiness, joy).

gelyk, (-e), n. iemand – gee, agree that a person is right; – hê, be right.

gelyk, (-e), a. alike, equal, indentical, same, flush, level; smooth.

gelyk, adv. equally, similarly, alike; simultaneously.

gelyk, (het –): – op, be (look) like, resemble.

gelyke, (-s), equal.

gelykenis, (-se), likeness, resemblance, similarity; parable (Bib.).

gelykheid, equality; similarity; evenness.

gelyklik, equally, in equal parts.

gelykmaak, (gelykge-), equalise, equate; level, smooth.

gelykmatig, (-e), equable; uniform; even; unruffled.

gelykmoedig, (-e), even-tempered.

gelykop, equally; deuce (in tennis); – speel, draw, play a draw.

gelyksoortig, (-e), similar, of the same kind.

gelykspel, draw, tie.

gelykstaan, (gelykge-), be equal.

gelykspel, (gelykge-), put on a par (with), place on the same level (as).

gelyktydig, (-e), simultaneous; contemporary.

gelykvloers, on the ground-floor; homely, plain.

gelykvormig, (-e), similar; uniform.

gelykwaardig, (-e), equivalent, of equal value.

gemaak, (-te), ready-made; affected, sham.

gemaal, (-male, -s), n. consort, spouse.

gemagtigde, (-s), proxy.

gemak, comfort, ease, facility; leisure.

gemaklik, (-e), easy, comfortable.

gemakshalwe, for convenience' sake.

gemak(s)huisie, closet, privy.

gemaksugtig, (-e), easy-going, easy-loving.

gemanier(d), (-de), well-bred, mannerly.

gematig, (-de), moderate, temperate.

gemeen, (gemene), a. & adv., common; general; public; ordinary, usual, base, mean, vulgar.

gemeenheid, meanness, shabbiness; vulgarity.

gemeensaam, (-same), familiar, intimate.

gemeenskap, community; intercourse; communication.

gemeenskaplik, (-e), common, joint; collective; community (singing).

gemeenslagtig, (-e), of common gender.

gemeente, (-s), community, congregation.

gemenebes, (-te), commonwealth.

gemene reg, Common Law.

gemeng, (-de), mixed, miscellaneous.

gemes, (-te), fatted (calf); stalled (ox).

gemiddeld, (-e), average, mean, medium.

gemis, lack, want.

gemmer, ginger.

gemoed, (-ere), mind, heart.

gemoedelik, (-e), genial, good-natured.

gemoei(d): mee –, at stake, involved.

gemors, mess(ing); filth.

gemsbok, vide **gensbok.**

gemunt, (-e), coined; – op, aimed at.

genaak, (het –), approach, come (draw) near.

genaakbaar, (-bare), accessible.

genaamd, called, named, by name.

genade, grace; mercy; pardon.

genadeslag, death-blow, knock-out blow.

genadig, (-e), gracious, merciful; lenient.

genant, (-e), namesake.

geneë, disposed, inclined, ready, willing.

geneentheid, inclination, affection, liking, love.

geneer, (het –), inconvenience, incommode.

genees, (het –), cure, heal; cover, get well again; be restored (to health).

geneesheer, doctor, physician.

geneesbaar, geneeslik, curable.

geneesmiddel, medicine, remedy, physic.

geneig, inclined, prone, apt (to).

gener: van nul en – waarde, null and void.

generaal, (-s), general.

geniaal, (-iale), brilliant, gifted.

genialiteit, brilliance, genius.

genie, (-ë), genius, man of genius.

geniekorps, corps of (military) engineers.

geniepsig, (-e), a. & adv. hurting, rough, malicious.

geniet, (het –), enjoy.

genitief, (-tiewe), genitive.

genoeë, genoege, (-ns), delight, joy, pleasure, liking; satisfaction.

genoeg, n. & adv. enough, sufficient; sufficiently.

genoege, vide **genoeë.**

genoeglik, (-e), agreeable; enjoyable.

genoegsaam, (-same), sufficient.

genoem(d), (-de), called, named.

genoop, obliged.

genoot, (-note), companion, partner.

genootskap, association, company, society.

genot, ((genietinge, genietings), delight, pleasure, enjoyment.

genote, enjoyed.

genotvol, (-le), vide **genotryk.**

gensbok, gemsbok, "gemsbok"; chamois.

Genuees, (-uese), Genoese.

genugtig, goeie: (my) –!, good gracious!

geografie, geography.

geologie, geology.

geoloog, (-loë), geologist.

geoorloof, (-de), allowed, lawful, permissible.

gepaar(d), (-de), coupled; in pairs.

gepantser, (-de), armoured, (train), armour-clad, iron-clad (ship); mailed (fist).

gepas, (-te), apt; becoming, fitting, proper.

gepastheid, aptness, fitness, propriety.

gepeupel, mob, populace, rabble.

geraak, (-te), offended, vexed.

geraamte, (-s), skeleton; framework.

geraas, (-ase), din, hubbub, noise.

gerade, advisable; **dit – ag,** think fit.

geredelik, (-e), a. & adv. promptly.

gereed, ready; finished; prepared.

gereedskap, implements, tools; utensils, tackle.

gereeld, (-e), fixed, orderly, regular.

gereformeerd, (-e), reformed.

gereg, (-te), n. course, dish.

gereg, n. justice; court (of justice), tribunal.

geregshof, court (of justice), law-court.

geregtelik, (-e), judicial (execution); legal (steps); forensic (medicine).

geregtig, entitled, justified, warranted.

gerek, (-te), lengthy, protracted.

gereserveer(d), (-de), reserved; reticent.

gerf, (gerwe), sheaf.

gerief, (geriewe), n. convenience; gadget.

gerieflik, (-e), comfortable, convenient.

geriewe: ten – van, for the convenience of.

geriffel, (-de), corrugated, ribbed.

gerig, judgment; **die jongste –,** doomsday.

gering, (-e), slight, small, trifling.

geringag, -skat, (geringge-), disparage, underestimate.

Germaan, (-mane), Teuton.

geroepe, called upon.

geroggel, rattling, death-rattle; gurgling.

gerug, (-te), report, rumour.

gerugmakend, (-e), sensational, epoch-making.

gerugsteun: – deur, supported (backed up) by.

geruime, considerable, ample, long (time).

geruis, rustle, rustling, rushing, swish.

geruit, (-e), a. checked, chequered.
gerus, (-te), a. calm, easy, quiet.
gerus, adv. safely; kom –, do come.
gerusstel, (gerusge-), reassure, relieve, set a person's mind at ease.
gerustheid, confidence, comfort, easiness, peace, security.
gesaaide, (-s), crop.
gesag, authority, power, prestige.
gesaghebbend, (-e), authoritative.
gesalfde, (-s), anointed.
gesame(nt)lik, (-e), a. complete (works), total (amount), joint (owners), united (forces), concerted (action).
gesame(nt)lik, adv. collectively, jointly.
gesang, (-e), song, hymn; warbling (of birds).
gesant, (-e), minister; ambassador.
gesantskap, (-pe), embassy, legation.
geseën, (-de), blessed; fortunate.
gesegde, (-s), expression, phrase, saying; predicate (gramm.).
gesel, (-le), n. companion, fellow, mate.
gesel, (-s), n. lash, scourge, whip.
gesel, (ge-), flog, lash, whip, scourge.
gesellig, (-e), sociable; cosy, snug; social (intercourse).
gesels, (het –), chat, converse, talk.
geselskap, (-pe), conversation; company, society.
geset, (-te), corpulent, stout, thickset; definite, fixed, regular, set (times).
gesete, seated; mounted.
gesien, (-e), seen; esteemed, respected.
gesig, (-te), face, countenance; view, prospect, sight; (eye-) sight; vision.
gesiggie, (-s), little face; pansy.
gesigseinder, horizon, skyline.
gesigspunt, aspect, point of view.
gesin, (-ne), family, household.
gesind, (-e), disposed, inclined, minded.
geskakeer(d), (-de), chequered, variegated.
geskape, created.
geskeie, divorced; separated.
geskenk, (-e), gift, present.
geskied, (het –), come to pass, happen.
geskiedenis, (-se), history; story, tale.
geskiedkundig, (-e), historical.
geskiedskrywer, -vorser, historian, historiographer.
geskik, (-te), able, appropriate, suitable.
geskil, (-le), difference, dispute, quarrel.
geskok, (-te), a. shocked.
geskool(d), (-de), practised, schooled, trained.
geskrif, (-te), document, writing; in –te, in writing, on paper.
geskut, n. artillery, guns, ordnance.
geslaag, (-de), successful.
geslag, (-te), n. family, race, lineage; gender, sex; generation; genus, tribe.
geslepe, cunning, sly; – glas, cut glass.
geslote, closed, locked, shut; reticent.
gesmoor(d), (-de), suppressed; strangled (voice); stewed (meat), fried (with onions).
gesnede, sliced (ham); graven (image).
gesneuwelde, (-s), person killed in action (pl.) casualties, dead.
gesog, (-te), in demand, sought after: affected, far-fetched, forced, studied.
gesond, (-e), healthy, sound, wholesome.
gesonde, a. sent; dispatched; vide send.
gesondheid, health; healthiness; soundness; sanity (of views).
gesondheidsleer, hygiene, hygienics.
gesout, (-e), salted; seasoned; immunised (med.).
gespanne, stretched; bent (bow); strained (relations); rapt (attention).

gespe(r), (-s), n. clasp, buckle.
gespe(r), (ge-), buckle, clasp; strap (on).
gespier(d), (-de), brawny, muscular.
gespikkel(d), (-de), speckled, spotted.
gesplete, cleft (palate), split.
gesprek, (-ke), conversation, discourse, talk.
gespuis, rabble, riff-raff, scum, vermin.
gestadig, (-e), constant; regular, steady.
gestalte, (-s), build, figure, stature.
gestaltenis, (-se), figure, shape.
gestamp, (-te), a.: –te mielies, samp.
gestand: sy belofte (woord) – doen, keep one's promise, redeem one's pledge.
gestel, (-le), n. constitution, system.
gestel(d): op iets – wees, stand on doing something.
gestel(d), conj. suppose, supposing.
gesteldheid, condition, nature, character, state.
gestem(d), (-de), disposed; tuned.
gesternte, (-s), constellation, star(s).
gesteur(d), gestoor(d), (-de), piqued, offended.
gestewel, (-de), booted.
gestig, (-te), n. institution, establishment, building, edifice; asylum, home.
gestoor(d), vide gesteur(d).
gestreep, (-te), striped, banded, streaked.
gesukkel, ailing; bungling; botheration; trouble.
geswa(w)el, (-de), sulphured (lit.); tipsy.
geswind, (-e), quick, rapid, swift, nimble.
geswolle, swollen (river); bombastic, stilted.
geswore, sworn.
getal, (-le), number.
getand, (-e), edged, jagged, toothed; cogged (wheel); serate(d).
getik, (-te), a. crack-brained; tipsy.
getoë, bred; gebore en –, born and bred.
getroos, (-te), a. comforted; ewe –, quite coolly.
getroos, (het –); jou baie moeite –, grudge (spare) no pains.
getrou, (-e), faithful, loyal, reliable, trusty; close (paraphrase); exact (copy).
getroud, (-e), married.
getuie, (-s), n. witness; deponent; second (at a duel).
getuie, getuig, (het –), testify, attest, depose.
getuienis, (-se), evidence, testimony; deposition.
getuigskrif, certificate; testimonial.
gety, (-e), tide.
geur, (-e), n. perfume, smell, aroma.
geurig, (-e), fragrant, sweet-smelling.
geut, (-e), gutter; drain, sewer; duct.
gevaar, (gevare), danger, peril, risk.
gevaarlik, (-e), dangerous, perilous.
gevaarte, (-s), colossus, monster; affair.
geval, (-le), n. case; event, instance, matter.
geval, (het –), please, suit.
gevange, captive, imprisoned.
gevangeneming, arrest, capture.
gevangenis, (-se), gaol (jail, prison).
gevange(n)skap, captivity, imprisonment.
gevat, (-te), clever, smart.
geveg, (-te), battle, engagement, fight.
geveins, (-de), feigned; pretended; hypocritical, assumed (indifference).
gevestig, (-de), fixed, established.
gevier(d), (-de), fêted, popular.
gevlek, (-te), speckled, spotted; stretched (hide).
gevleuel(d), (-de), winged.
gevoel, (-ens), feeling, sensation, sense, touch; emotion, sentiment.
gevoele, (-ns), feeling, opinion, sentiment, view.
gevoelig, (-e), sensitive, susceptible; sharp (lesson); heavy (defeat).
gevoelloos, (-lose), insensible; apathetic, callous, impassive, unfeeling; numb (of limb).

gevoelvol, (-le), full of feeling, tender.
gevoer, (-de), fed (animal); lined (coat).
gevolg, (-e), consequence, effect, result; following, retinue.
gevolglik, accordingly, consequently.
gevolgtrekking, (-e, -s), conclusion, inference.
gevolmagtigde, (-s), proxy, person holding power of attorney; (minister) plenipotentiary.
gevreet, (gevrete), mug, phiz.
gewaad, (gewade), attire, garb, raiment.
gewaag, (-de), a. risky; equivocal.
gewaand, (-e), supposed.
gewaar, geware, (het –), percieve, become aware of.
gewaarmerk, (-te), hall-marked.
gewaarword, (gewaarge-), become aware of, perceive; find out.
gewaarwording, (-e, -s), feeling, perception, sensation; experience.
gewag, mention.
gewapen(d), (-de), armed (soldier), reinforced (concrete).
gewas, (-se), growth; crop, harvest.
geweer, (-s, gewere), gun, rifle.
gewel, (-s), facade, front; gable.
geweld, force, violence.
gewelddadig, (-e), a. violent.
geweldenaar, (-s), oppressor, tyrant.
geweldig, (-e), a. enormous, powerful, mighty, violent.
geweldig, adv. awfully, dreadfully.
gewelf, (-welwe), arch, dome, vault.
gewen, (het –), accustom, habituate.
gewens, (-te), desired; desirable.
gewente, habit, custom.
gewer, (-s), donor, giver.
gewes, (-te), province, region, territory.
gewese, former, late, ex-.
gewestelik, (-e), regional; dialectal.
gewete, (-ns), conscience.
gewete(n)loos, (-lose), unprincipled, unscrupulous.
gewettig, (-de), justified, legitimate (hope).
gewig, (-te), weight; importance, moment.
gewigstoot, (gewigge-), put the shot.
gewigtig, (-e), momentous, weighty.
gewild, (-e), popular, studied.
gewillig, (-e), ready, willing; tractable.
gewin, n. advantage, gain, profit.
gewirwar, confusion.
gewis, (-se), a. certain, sure.
gewis, adv. certainly, to be sure.
gewislik, vide gewis, adv.
gewoel, bustle, stir; crowd, throng.
gewonde, (-s), wounded person.
gewoon, (-wone), accustomed; common, normal.
gewonne: dit – gee, yield the point.
gewoon, (– aan), accustomed, used (to).
    ordinary, regular, customary; plain (food); vulgar (fraction); average (citizen).
gewoonlik, (-e), a. & adv. common(ly), usual(ly).
gewoonte, (-s), habit, practice; custom, usage, use.
gewoonweg, downright, perfectly, simply.
gewrig, (-te), joint; wrist.
gewrog, (-te), creation, production, affair.
gewyd, (-e), consecrated; sacred.
geyk, (-te), legally stamped; stereotyped.
ghienie, (-s), guinea.
ghitaar, kitaar, (-s, -tare), guitar.
ghoen, (-e, -s), taw; (shooting-)marble; hopscotch stone.
gholf, golf.
ghong, (-e, -s), gong.
ghries, grease.

ghwano, guano, guano.
ghwar, (-re), lout, uncouth person.
gids, (-e), n. guide; directory.
giegel, giggel, (ge-), giggle, titter.
gier, (-e), n. vulture.
gier, (ge-), scream; whistle (of wind).
gierig, (-e), miserly, stingy.
gierigaard, (-s), miser.
giet, (ge-), pour (liquids); cast, mould.
gieter, (-s), watering-can; moulder.
gif, (-te), n. gift, donation, present.
gif, (-te, giwwe), poison, venom.
giftig, (-e), poisonous, venomous; virulent.
giggel, vide giegel.
gil, (-le), n. scream, shriek, yell.
gil, (ge-), scream, shriek, yell.
gilde, (-s), guild.
gimnastiek, gymnastics.
ginds, over there, yonder.
ginnega(a)p, (ge-), giggle, snigger, titter.
gips, gypsum; plaster of Paris.
giraf, (-fe, -s), giraffe.
gis, (-se), n. guess.
gis, n. yeast.
gis, (ge-), conjecture, guess.
gis, (ge-), ferment, rise, work.
gissing, (-e, -s), conjecture, supposition; estimate.
gister, yesterday.
gisteraand, yesterday evening, last night.
gistermôre, -oggend, yesterday morning.
gisting, ferment(ation); excitement.
git, jet.
gitswart, jet-black.
glaasogie, white-eye (bird).
glad, (-de), a. smooth, plain (ring); slippery (floor).
glad, adv. altogether, quite; smoothly; – nie, not at all, by no means.
glans, n. gloss, lustre; brilliancy, splendour, polish.
glans, (ge-), gleam, glisten; gloss, put a shine on (collars), polish.
glansryk, (-e), brilliant, radiant.
glas, (-e), glass; tumbler.
gla(a)sdeur, glass-door, French window.
glaserig, (-e), glassy; glazed (eyes).
glashelder, as clear as glass, crystal-clear.
glasmaker, glazier.
glasuur, n. enamel (of teeth); glaze, glazing (of pottery); icing (of cakes).
glasuur, (ge-), glaze.
glattendal (glad en al), altogether, quite.
gletser, (-s), glacier.
gleuf, (gleuwe), groove; slit.
glibberig, (-e), slippery, slithery, slimy.
glim, (ge-), glimmer, gleam, shine.
glimlag, n. smile.
glimlag, (ge-), smile, give a smile.
glinster, (ge-), glint, glitter, sparkle.
glip, (ge-), slide, slip.
glippe: die –, the slips (in cricket).
glips, (-e), mistake, slip.
gliserien, gliserine, glycerine.
glo, adv. evidently, presumably, seemingly.
glo, geloof, gelowe, (ge-, het geloof, – gelowe), believe; trust; think.
globaal, (-bale), a. general, rough.
gloed, blaze, glow, heat; ardour, fervour.
gloedvol, (-le), glowing (account).
gloei, (ge-), glow, be red-hot; be aglow.
gloeidraad, filament.
gloeiend, (-e), a. glowing; red-hot (iron); live (coals); ardent (love).
gloeilamp, electric bulb.
gloor, (glore), n. glow; lustre, splendour.

gloor, (ge-), glimmer; break (of day).
glorie, fame, glory, lustre.
glorieryk, (-e), glorious, famous.
gluur, (ge-), peep, peer, pry; leer.
gly, (ge-), slide; glide; slip.
glybaan, slide.
g'n, vide geen, a. & pron.
g'n, adv. not, never.
gô: sy – is uit, he is played out.
God, God; (pl. gode), god, idol.
goddank, thank God!, thank goodness!
Goddelik, (-e), divine, godlike, sublime.
goddeloos, (-lose), a. godless, impious, wicked, naughty.
godgeleerde, (-s), divine, theologian.
godgeleerdheid, theology.
godin, (-ne), goddess.
godsalig, (-e), godly, pious.
godsdiens, religion, faith; divine worship.
godsdienstig, (-e), devout, pious, religious.
godslastering, blasphemy.
godsonmoontlik, (-e), utterly impossible.
godsvrug, devotion, piety.
godvresend, (-e), God-fearing, devout, pious.
goed, n. 1. good.
goed, (-ere) n. 2. goods, property; estate; material, stuff, things; luggage; wares.
goed, (goeie), a. good; good-natured, kind, correct, proper.
goed, adv. well; correctly, right.
goedaardig, (-e), good-natured, kind-hearted.
goeddunke, pleasure; discretion.
goedertierenheid, loving-kindness, mercy.
goedgeefs, (-e), generous, liberal.
goedgesind, (-e), favourable; well-disposed.
goedgunstig, (-e), kind, obliging.
goedhartig, (-e), kind-hearted.
goedig, goeiig, (-e), good-natured.
goedhou, (goedge-), keep (of perishables).
goedjies, goods, things, knick-knacks.
goedkeur, (goedge-), approve (of), endorse, confirm; adopt (minutes); pass.
goedkeuring, approval, approbation; adoption (of minutes).
goedkoop, cheap, inexpensive.
goedmaak, (goedge-), make good, make up for, make restitution for, make amends for.
goedpraat, (goedge-), explain away.
goedskiks, willingly, with a good grace.
goedsmoeds, cheerfully; deliberately.
goedvind, (goedge-), think fit; approve of.
goeie, goodness!; – weet!, goodness knows.
goei(e)naand!, good evening!
goei(e)middag!, good afternoon!
goei(e)môre, -more!, good morning.
goei(e)nag!, good night!
Goeie Vrydag, Good Friday.
goël, gogel, (ge-), conjure, practise magic; dit –, a poltergeist manifests itself.
goëlaar, gogelaar, (-s), conjurer, magician.
goëlery, gogelary, conjuring, magic.
goeters, things.
goewerment, (-e), government.
goewernante, (-s), governess.
goewerneur, (-s), governor.
gogga, (-s), insect; bogey.
goiensak, goiingsak, gunny-bag; hessian.
golf, (golwe), n. wave; bay, gulf.
golf, golwe, (ge-), wave, undulate.
Golfstroom, Gulf-stream.
golwend, (-e), waving, wavy (hair); rolling; surging (crowd).
gom, (-me), n. gum.
gomlastiek, (India-)rubber.
gompou, kori-bustard.

gomtor, lout, uncouth person.
gondelier, (-s), gondolier.
gons, (ge-), buzz, drone, hum.
gooi, (-e), n. throw, cast.
gooi, (ge-), cast, fling, pitch, throw.
goor, (gore), dingy, dirty, putrid, rancid; sallow (face); threadbare (clothes).
Goot, (Gote), Goth.
gora, (-'s), gorra, gorê, (-s), waterhole (in riverbed).
gord, gort, (-e), n. band, belt, girdle.
gord, (ge-), gird, lace.
gordel, (-s), belt, circle, girdle; zone.
gordyn, (-e), curtain; blind.
gorilla, (-s), gorilla.
gorrel, (-s), n. throat, gullet, larynx.
gorrel, (ge-), gargle, gurgle.
gort, vide gord.
gort, groats, grits.
gortwater, barley-water.
Goties, (-e), n. & a. Gothic.
gou, a. & adv. rapid, quick(ly)), swift(ly); soon.
goud, gold.
goudbruin, auburn, chestnut.
goudgeel, gold-coloured, golden.
goudief, cutpurse, pickpocket.
goue, gold (coin); golden (hair, wedding).
gou-gou, quickly, in a jiffy (moment).
gouigheid, quickness; dexterity.
gousblom, calendula.
graad, (grade), degree, grade, rank.
graaf, (grawe), n. 1. earl; count.
graaf, (grawe), n. 2. spade.
graaf, grawe, (ge-), dig; burrow.
graag, gladly, readily, willingly.
graagte, eagerness.
graan, (grane), corn, grain; (pl.) cereals.
graansuier, (grain-)elevator.
graas, (ge-), feed, graze.
graat, (grate), fish-bone.
graatjie, (-s), n. small fish-bone, thin child.
graatjie(meerkat), thin-tailed meercat.
gradeer, (ge-), grade, gradate, graduate.
gradueer, (ge-), graduate.
graf, (-te), grave; sepulchre, tomb.
grafkelder, vault.
grafsteen, gravestone, tombstone.
grag, (-te), canal; ditch, moat.
gram, gram.
gramadoelas, rough country.
grammatika, (-s), grammar.
grammofoon, (-fone), gramophone.
gramradio, (-'s), gramradio.
gramskap, anger, ire, wrath.
granaat, (-nate), pomegranate; grenade, shrapnel; garnet.
granaatsteen, garnet.
graniet, granite.
grap, (-pe), fun, jest, joke.
grap(pe)maker, buffoon, joker, wag.
grapp(er)ig, (-e), amusing, funny.
gras, (-se), grass.
grasgroen, grass-green.
grasie, grace, pardon; gracefulness.
grasieus, (-e), elegant, graceful.
grasig, (-e), grassy.
graveer, (ge-), engrave; sink (dies).
gravin, (-ne), countess.
gravure, (-s), engraving, print, plate.
greep, (grepe), clutch, grasp, grip; hilt.
grein, (-e), grain.
greinhout, deal.
grenadella, granadilla, (-s), granadilla (grenadilla), passion-flower; passion-fruit.

grendel, (-s), n. bar, bolt.
grendel, (ge-), bolt.
grens, (-e), n. boundary, border; bound, limit.
grens, (ge-): – aan, adjoin, border on; verge upon.
grens, (ge-), cry, howl.
grensbalie, cry-baby.
grens(e)loos, (-lose), boundless, unlimited; infinite (misery).
gretig, (-e), desirous, eager; greedy.
grief, (griewe), n. grievance; offence, wrong.
grief, (ge-), gall, grieve, hurt.
Griek, (-e), Greek.
Griekwa, (-s), Griqua.
griep, influenza, flu(e).
grieselig, (-e), creepy, grisly, gruesome.
griffel, (-s), slate-pencil.
griffie, (-e), vide griffel.
gril, (-le), n. caprice, whim; shiver, shudder.
gril, (ge-), shiver, shudder.
grillerig, (-e), creepy, gruesome.
grillig, (-e), fanciful, whimsical, fickle; fitful (weather).
grimas, (-se), grimace.
grimeer, (ge-), make up.
grimlag, n. grin, sneer.
grimlag, (ge-), grin, sneer.
grimmig, (-e), angry, furious, grim.
grinnik, (ge-), grin, sneer, snigger.
grip(pie), furrow.
groef, (groewe), n. groove; furrow, wrinkle.
groef, groewe, (ge-), groove.
groei, n. growth; rising (of a river).
groei, (ge-), grow; rise.
groeikrag, vital force, vitality, vigour.
groen, n. green; greenery; verdure.
groen, a. green; fresh; immature.
groenigheid, greenness; green grass, greens.
groente, vegetables.
groentjie, (-s), greenhorn; fresher.
groenvoer, fresh fodder, green stuff.
groep, (-e), group, cluster, clump (of trees).
groepeer, (ge-), group, classify.
groepsgewys(e), in batches (groups).
groet, (-e), n. greeting.
groet, (ge-), greet, salute, take off one's hat, shake hands; say good-bye.
groete, groetnis, regards, greetings.
grof, (growwe), coarse, rude (remarks), rough (road), gross (carelessness), big (lie), bad (blunder), harsh (voice).
grofbrood, growwebrood, coarse (brown) bread.
grofgeskut, heavy ordnance (guns, artillery).
grofsmid, grofsmit, blacksmith.
grom, (ge-), growl, grumble, snarl.
grond, (-e), n. ground, earth; soil; land, bottom, foundation; reason.
grond, (ge-), base, found, ground.
grondboontjie, pea-nut, monkey-nut.
grondeloos, (-lose), bottomless, abysmal.
grondig, (-e), thorough, searching.
grondleêr, grondlegger, (-s), founder.
grondlegging, foundation.
grondslag, basis, foundation.
grondstof, element; raw material.

grondves, (ge-), found.
grondwet, constitution, fundamental law
groot, (grote), large, vast; big, tall; grown-up; great.
grootbek, braggart, swaggerer.
grootboek, ledger.
grootbring, (grootge-), bring up, rear.
groothandel, wholesale-trade.
groothartig, (-e), generous, magnanimous.
grootjie, (-s), granny, great grandmother; great grandfather.
grootliks, to a great extent, largely.
grootmaak, (grootge-), vide grootbring.
grootmens, adult, grown-up.
grootmoeder, grandmother.
grootmoedig, vide groothartig.
grootouers, grandparents.
grootpraat, (grootge-), brag, boast.
groots, (-e), grandiose, majestic: haughty; proud.
grootskeeps, (-e), on a large scale; princely.
grootspraak, boast(ing), bravado.
grootsteeds, (-e), grand, of a large town.
grootte, (-s), extent, greatness, size, tallness.
grootvader, grandfather.
grootwild, big game.
grootword, (grootge-), grow up.
gros, (-se), gross, mass.
groslys, list of prospective candidates.
grot, (-te), cave, grotto.
grotendeels, chiefly, largely, mainly.
grou, a. grey.
grou, (ge-), growl, snarl.
growwebrood, vide grofbrood.
growwerig, (-e), rather coarse (rough).
gruis, grit; gravel.
grusaam, (-same), gruesome, horrible.
gruwel, (-s), abomination, crime, horror.
gruwelik, (-e), atrocious; naughty.
gryns, (-e), n. grimace, grin, sneer.
gryns, (ge-), make a grimace, grin, sneer.
grynslag, n. sardonic smile; vide gryns, n.
grynslag, (ge-), vide gryns, ge-.
gryp, (ge-), catch, grab, grasp, grip, seize, lay hold of, snatch.
grys, (-e), grey (gray), grey-headed; hoary.
grysaard, (-s), grey-haired man, grey-beard.
guano, vide ghwano.
guerrilla-oorlog, guer(r)illa-warfare.
gul, (-le), cordial, frank, liberal.
gulden, (-s), n. guilder, Dutch florin.
gulde, a. golden.
gulhartig, (-e), vide gul.
gulp, (-e), n. fly, trousers-slit.
gulsig, (-e), gluttonous, greedy.
gummi, (India-)rubber.
gun, (ge-), allow, grant; ek – jou dit, you are welcome to it.
guns, (-te), favour; kindness, patronage, support.
gunsteling, (-e), favourite.
gunstig, (-e), favourable, propitious.
guur, bleak, inclement, raw, rough.
gyselaar, (-lare, -s), hostage; prisoner for debt.
gyseling, imprisonment for debt.

ha!, ah!, ha!, oh!.
haai, (-e), n. shark.
haai! interj. hullo!, hey!, I say!
haaihoei, hoeihaai, fuss.
haak, (hake), hook, hasp, clasp; clamp; square; T-square; bracket; peg; gaff; crook, stake.
haak, (ge-), hook; crochet; catch; delay, be delayed.
haak-en-steekbos, white-thorn.
haakplek, difficulty, hitch.
haaks, (-e), square(d), right-angle(d); **hulle is altyd –,** they are always at loggerheads.
haakspeld, safety-pin.
haal, (hale), n. pull; dash, stroke (of the pen); lash; stride.
haal, (ge-), fetch, go for, get, draw, pull; recover; catch.
haan, (hane), cock, rooster; cock, hammer (of gun); **hy is 'n ou –,** he is a topper.
haar, (hare), n. hair.
haar, a. right; – **om,** to the right, clockwise.
haar, (hare), pro. poss. her.
haar-af: die perd gaan –, the horse's hair is coming off.
haaragter, right-hind.
haarbuis(ie), capillary tube.
haard, (-e), fireplace, fireside, hearth; grate.
haarfyn, as fine as a hair; in detail.
haarkant, right side, off-side.
haarklowery, hair-splitting, quibbling.
haarknipper, hareknipper, hairclipper.
haarlaat, (ge-): **hy moes –,** he had to pay (the piper).
haarnaald, hair-pin.
haarnaasagter, second right-hind.
haarnaasvoor, second right-fore (-front).
haarsnyer, haresnyer, hairdresser.
haarvoor, right-fore (-front).
haarwurm, wire-worm; threadworm.
haas, (hase), n. hare.
haas, n. hasty, hurry, speed.
haas, adv. almost, nearly; practically.
haas, (ge-), hurry, make haste.
haasbek, having a tooth (teeth) missing.
haastig, (-e), hasty, hurried, in a hurry, speedy.
haat, n. hatred.
haat, (ge-), hate, detest.
haatdraend, (-e), vindictive, resentful.
haatlik, (-e), detestable, odious; spiteful.
had, vide **hê.**
hael, n. hail; shot.
hael, (ge-), hail.
haelbui, hailstorm, shower of hail.
haelgeweer, shotgun.
haelkorrel, hailstone; grain (pellet) of shot.
haelpatroon, shot-cartridge.
haglik, (-e), critical, desperate, precarious.
haikôna, aikôna, no, not at all.
hak, (-ke), n. heel.
hak, (ge-), chop. cut, bash, mince (meat).
hakhou, cut.
hakie, (-s), bracket; (little) hook.
hakkel, (ge-), stammer, stutter; stumble.
hakkelrig, (-e), stammering, stuttering.
hakskeen, heel.
hal, (-le), hall.
half, (halwe), half; semi-.
halfaam, alfaam, half-aum.
halfag(t), half past seven.
halfbakke, half-baked, slackbaked.
halfklaar, half-done.
halfmaan, half-moon; crescent, semicircle.
halfpad, half-way.
halfrond, (-e), n. hemisphere.

halfrond, (-e), a. half-round, hemispherical.
halfslyt, second-hand, half-worn.
halfuur, half an hour.
halfwas, (-se), half-grown.
halfweg, half-way; mid-off (cricket).
halfwys, half-wit.
halm(pie), (-s), blade, stalk.
hals, (-e), neck.
halsband, collar, neck-band; necklace.
halskettinkie, necklet.
halsoorkop, head over heels, precipitately.
halssnoer, necklace; gorget.
halsstarrig, (-e), headstrong, obstinate.
halt!, halt!, stop!
halte, (-s), halt; stopping-place, stop.
halter, (-s), halter.
halveer, (ge-), bisect, halve.
halwe, (-s), half.
ham, (-me), ham.
hamel, (-s), wether, hamel.
hamer, (-s), n. hammer; mallet (of wood).
hamer, (ge-), hammer.
hamerkop, head of a hammer; umber-bird.
hand, (-e), hand; handwriting.
handboeie, handcuffs, manacles, wristlets.
handbreed(te), hand's breadth.
handbyltjie, hatchet, chopper.
handdadig, vide **aandadig.**
handdoek, towel.
handdruk, handshake (-clasp, -grip).
handearbeid, manual labour; handicraft.
handel, n. commerce, business, trade.
handel, (ge-), act; deal, carry on business, trade.
handelaar, (-s), dealer, merchant, trader.
handelbaar, (-bare), docile, tractable.
handelend: – optree, take action.
handeling, (-e), action, act; transaction.
handelsaak, business; commercial matter.
handelskool, commercial school
handelsreisiger, commercial traveller.
handelsware, merchandise, commodities.
handelswyse, proceeding, procedure, behaviour.
hande-viervoet, on all fours.
handewerk, handiwork; handwork; needlework.
handgemeen: – raak, come to blows.
handgreep, grasp, grip; trick.
handhaaf, (ge-), maintain, vindicate; live up to.
handig, (-e), clever, handy, skilful.
handjievol, handful.
handkoffer, handbag, portmanteau.
handlanger, (-s), handyman; accomplice.
handleiding, guide, handbook, manual.
handperd, led-horse.
handrug, backhand.
handsak(kie), handbag; (lady's) vanity-bag.
handskêr, snips.
handskoen, glove; gauntlet.
handskrif, handwriting; manuscript.
handtastelik: – word, come to blows.
handtekening, signature.
handvat(sel), handle; ear, crutch.
handvol, (handevol), handful.
handwerk, vide **handewerk.**
handwyser, finger-post, signpost.
hanebalk, roof-beam, collar-beam, rafter.
hanekam, cockscomb (coxcomb).
hanepoot, (lit.) cock's foot (claw); (grapes) muscat of Alexandria, "honey-pots".
hanerig, (-e), cocky, quarrelsome.
hanetree(tjie), cock-stride.
hang, (-e), n. slope.
hang, (ge-), hang, be suspended; droop, suspend; be hanged.
hangbrug, suspension-bridge.
hangend(e), hanging, pending.

hanger, (-s), hanger; pendant.
hangkas, wardrobe.
hangklok, wall-clock.
hanglip, n. & a. sulky.
hangmat, hammock.
hanou, honou!, halt there! (to oxen).
hans, orphan; – grootmaak, hand-feed.
hanslam, hand-fed lamb, cosset.
hanswors, (-te), buffoon, clown.
hanteer, (ge-), handle, operate, work.
hap, (-pe), n. bite; morsel, mouthful.
hap, (ge-), bite, snap, snatch.
haper, (ge-), not function properly, miss, stick.
hard, (-e), a. & adv. hard, loud (voice); heavily; fast.
hard, (ge-), harden, steel (one's nerves).
hardebolkeil(tjie), bowler.
hardepad, hard labour.
harder, (-s), n. mullet, Cape herring.
hardhandig, (-e), hard-handed, harsh, rough.
hardhoofdig, (-e), headstrong, obstinate.
hardhorend, -horig, (-e), hard of hearing.
hardkoppig, (-e), headstrong, obstinate.
hardloop, (ge-), run; hurry; make haste.
hardlywig, (-e), constipated, costive.
hardnekkig, (-e), obstinate (person), stubborn (fight), persistent (cough).
hardop, aloud, loud.
hardvogtig, (-e), heartless, unfeeling.
ha(re)rig, (-e), hairy, hirsute.
haring, (-s), herring.
hark, (-e), n. rake.
hark, (ge-), rake.
harlekyn, (-e), buffoon, clown, harlequin.
harmonie, (-ë), harmony.
harmonies, (-e), hormonious, harmonic.
harmonieus, (-e), harmonious.
harmonika, (-s), accordion, concertina.
harnas, (-se), n. armour; cuirass.
harp, (-e), harp.
harpoen, (-e), harpoon.
harpoenier, (-s), harpooner.
harpuis, arpuis, n. resin, rosin.
harsings, brains.
harslag, (-te), pluck (of slaughtered animal).
harspan, head, skull.
hart, (-e), heart; mind; courage; core, centre.
hartbees, hartebeest.
hartbrekend, (-e), heart-breaking (-rending).
harte-aas, hartenaas, ace of hearts.
harte(n)boer, -(n)heer, -(n)tien, -(n)vrou, jack (knave), king, ten, queen of hearts.
hartedief, darling, love, pet.
hartelus: na –, to one's heart's content.
hartens, hearts (in cards).
hartkloppings, palpitation of the heart.
hartlam, darling, dearest.
hartlik, (-e), cordial, hearty.
hartroerend, (-e), pathetic, touching.
hartseer, n. grief, sorrow.
hartseer, a. sad, heart-sore, grieved (at heart).
hartstog, (-te), passion.
hartstogtelik, (-e), passionate, impassioned; ardent, keen.
hartsvanger, cutlass, hanger.
hartverlamming, heart-failure (-seizure).
hartverskeurend, (-e), heart-rending.
hartversterkinkie, (-s), cordial, drink, tot.
hartvormig, (-e), heart-shaped.
harwar, confusion; bickering, squabble.
hasepad: die – kies, take to one's heels.
haspel, (-s), reel.
haspel, (ge-), reel, bungle; wrangle.
hawe, n. goods, property, stock.
hawe, (-ns), n. harbour, port; dock; haven.

hawehoof, mole, pier, jetty.
hawer, oats.
hawerklap: om die –, every moment, for every trifle.
hawermeel, oatmeal.
hawermout, rolled oats; oatmeal-porridge.
hawersak, oat-bag; nose-bag.
hawik, (-e), hawk, goshawk.
hè! my! hey!
hê?, eh?, what?
hê, (had; gehad), have, possess.
Hebreeus, (-e), n. & a. Hebrew.
hebsug, covetousness, greed.
hede, n. this day, the present.
hede, adv. to-day, at present.
hede!, hene!, hete!, oh my!, good heavens!
hedendaags, (-e), a. modern, present-day.
hedendaags, adv. nowadays, at present.
heel, (hele), a. entire, whole; complete.
heel, adv. quite, very.
heel, (ge-), cure, heal.
heel, (ge-), fence, receive (stolen goods).
heelal, universe.
heeldag, the whole day; frequently.
heelhuids, with a whole skin, unscathed.
heelkragtig, (-e), curative.
heelkunde, healing art, surgery.
heeltemal, altogether, entirely, clean, quite, utterly.
heelwat, a. considerable number (of), a lot.
heen, away; êrens –, somewhere; nêrens – nie, nowhere.
heen-en-weertjie, 'n –, a moment; return-journey; return-ticket.
heengaan, n. death, departure.
heengaan, (heenge-), depart.
heenkome, refuge.
heenreis, n. outward voyage, forward journey.
heer, (here), army, host.
heer, (here), gentleman; lord; master; king (in cards).
Heer, Here, the Lord, God.
heerleër, host.
heerlik, (-e), delicious (food), glorious, lovely (weather), delightful (time).
heerlik(heid)!, Great Scott!
heers, (ge-), reign, govern; prevail.
heersend, (-e), ruling; prevailing.
heerser, (-s), heerseres, (-se), ruler.
heerskaar, heerskare, host.
heerskappy, (-e), dominion, mastery, rule, sovereignty.
heerssugtig, (-e), ambitious.
hees, (–, hese), hoarse, husky.
heet, (hete), a. hot; torrid.
heet, (ge-), call, name; be called (named); order, tell.
heethoof, hothead, hot-headed person.
heethoofdig, (-e), hot-headed.
hef, (-te, hewwe), n. handle, haft; hilt.
hef, (ge-), lift, raise; impose, levy.
hefboom, lever; fulcrum (zool.).
heffing, (-e, -s), levying (of taxes).
heftig, (-e), heated, vehement, violent.
heg, (-ge), n. hedge; vide haag.
heg, (-te), a. firm, solid, staunch.
heg, (ge-), affix, attach, heal.
hegpleister, adhesive (sticking) plaster.
hegtenis, custody, detention.
hei, heide, n. heath, heather; moor.
heiden, (-e, -s), heathen, pagan; gipsy.
heidens, (-e), heathen, pagan.
Heiland, Saviour.
heilig, (-e), a. holy, sacred.
heilig, (ge-), hallow, sanctify.

heiligdom, (-me), sanctuary, shrine; sanctum.
heilige, (-s), saint.
heiligskennis, desecration, sacrilege.
heilloos, (-lose), disastrous, fatal; impious.
heilsaam, (-same), beneficial, salutary.
heilsleër, salvation-army.
heimlik, (-e), secret; clandestine, private.
heimwee, homesickness.
heinde: – en ver, far and near (wide).
heining, (-s), enclosure, fence, hedge.
hek, (-ke), gate; boom.
hekel, n. dislike.
hekel, (ge-), crochet; censure, criticize, satirize.
hekkies, hurdles.
heks, (-e), n. witch; vixen.
hektaar, hectare.
hektogram, hectogram.
hektoliter, hectolitre.
hektometer, hectometre.
hel, n. hell.
hel, (ge-), dip, slant, slope.
helaas, alas, unfortunately.
held, (-e), hero.
heldedaad, heroic deed.
helder, (-e), clear, sonorous (sounds); vivid, bright; lucid (style).
heldhaftig, (-e), brave, heroic.
heler, (-s), healer; receiver, fence.
helfte, halfte, (-s), half.
Helleens, (-e), n. & a. Hellenic.
hellevaart, descent into hell.
helleveeg, shrew, vixen, hell-cat.
helling, (-e, -s), decline, slope; gradient.
helm, (-e, -s), helmet; helm; caul.
helmhoed, sun-helmet.
help, (ge-), aid, assist, help, succour; avail, be of use; attend to, serve.
hels, (-e), devilish, hellish, infernal.
helsteen, lunar caustic, silver nitrate.
hemel, (-e, -s), heaven; firmament, sky; tester (of bed); canopy (of throne).
hemelhoog, (-hoë), sky-high.
hemeling, (-e), celestial, inhabitant of Heaven.
hemels, (-e), celestial, heavenly.
hemelsbreed, (-breë), wide (difference).
hemelsnaam: in –, for Heaven's sake.
hemelswil: om –, for Heaven's sake.
Hemelvaart, Ascension.
hemp, (hemde), shirt; (lady's) chemise.
hempskakel, (skirt-)link; (cuff-) link.
hempsknoop, hemdeknoop, shirtbutton.
hempsknopie, shirt-stud.
hen, (-ne), hen.
hen(d)sop, (ge-), hands-up, surrender.
hengel, (ge-), angle.
hengelaar, (-s), angler.
hennep, hemp.
herberg, (-e), n. inn; accommodation.
herberg, (ge-), accommodate; shelter; harbour.
herbergsaam, (-same), hospitable.
herbore, born again, reborn, regenerate.
herbou, (het –), build again, rebuild.
Hercules, Herakles, Hercules.
herdenk, (het –), commemorate.
herdenking, (-e, -s), commemoration.
herder, (-s), n. (shep)herd; pastor.
herderlik, (-e), pastoral.
herderloos, (-lose), without a shepherd (pastor).
herdoop, (het –), rebaptize, rename.
herdruk, n. reprint, new edition.
herdruk, (het –), reprint.
Here, vide **Heer.**
herenig, (het –), reunite.
herereg(te), transfer-dues.
hergiet, (het –), recast.

herhaal, (het –), repeat, reiterate, say over again.
herhaaldelik, repeatedly, again and again.
herinner, (het –), jou –, call to mind, recall, recollect, remember.
herinnering, (-e, -s), recollection, reminiscence, memory; reminder; memento, souvenir.
herken, (het –), recognize; identify, know.
herkenbaar, (-bare), recognizable; identifiable.
herkies, (het –), re-elect.
herkiesbaar, (-bare), eligible for re-election.
herkoms, derivation, extraction, origin.
herkou, (ge-), ruminate, chew the cud; repeat.
herkry, (het –), recover, regain, get back.
herleef, -lewe, (het –), live again, return to life, revive.
herlees, (het –), read again, reread.
herlei, (het –), reduce; convert (money).
herleibaar, (-bare), reducible.
herlewing, rebirth, renascence, revival.
hermelyn, ermine.
hermiet, (-e), hermit.
herneem, (het –), take again; resume (one's seat); recapture (a fort).
hernieu, hernuwe, (het –), renew, renovate; resume (old friendship).
hernuwing, renewal, renovation; resumption.
heropen, (het –), reopen.
herower, (het –), reconquer, recover.
herroep, (het –), recall, revoke; repeal (laws), countermand (an order).
herrie, row, uproar; confusion.
herrys, (het –), rise again.
herrysenis, resurrection.
hersenskim, chimera, phantasm.
hersenskudding, vide **harsingskudding.**
hersien, (het –), revise, overhaul; reconsider (one's views).
herskep, (het –, het herskape), recreate, regenerate, transform, metamorphose.
herstel, n. restoration, reinstatement; rehabilitation; recovery; reparation.
herstel, (het –), mend, repair; restore (the monarchy), correct, rectify (a mistake), right (a wrong), make good (damage); reinstate; recover (from illness).
herstem, (het –), vote again.
hert, (-e), deer, hart, stag.
herstel, (het –), recount, count again.
hertog, (hertoë), duke.
hertogdom, duchy.
hertrou, (het –), remarry, marry again.
hervat, (het –), resume, restart.
hervorm, (het –), reform, remodel.
hervorming, reform, reformation (of church).
herwaarts, hither.
herwin, (het –), recover, regain; retrieve.
herwonne, regained, recovered.
heserig, (-e), slightly hoarse (husky).
het, vide **hê.**
hetsy: – . . . of (hetsy), either . . . or; whether . . . or.
hettetè, hittete: dit was so –, it was touch and go, it was a near thing.
heug, n.: teen – en meug, reluctantly.
heug, (ge-): dit – my nog, I still remember.
heugenis, memory, remembrance.
heuglik, (-e), memorable; joyful, glad.
heul, (ge-), – met, collude with.
heuning, honey.
heuningkwas: die – gebruik, coax, flatter.
heup, (-e), hip (man), haunch (animal).
heupjig, hip-gout, sciatica.
heuwel, (-s), hill.
hewel, (-s), n. siphon.
hewel, (ge-), siphon, draw off.

hewig, (-e), violent, sharp, fierce.
hiaat, (hiate), break, gap, hiatus.
hiasint, (-e), hyacinth.
hiel, (-e), heel; vide hak.
hiëna, (-s), hyena.
hier, here; close by.
hieraan, at (by, on, to) this.
hieragter, behind this; here(in) after.
hierbinne, in here, within.
hierbo, up here, overhead; in Heaven.
hierbuite, outside.
hierby, hereby, herewith; attached, enclosed (in letter).
hierdeur, -by (in consequence of, owing to, through) this; through here.
hierdie, this, (these).
hierheen, this way, hither.
hierin, in this, in here, herein.
hierjy, n. lout.
hierlang(e)s, this way, along here; hereabout(s).
hiermee, with this, herewith.
hierna, after this, hereafter; according to this.
hiernaas, next to this, alongside; next door.
hiernamaals, hereafter.
hiernatoe, this way, here.
hierom, for this reason.
hieromtrent, with regard to this; hereabout(s).
hieroor, about this, over this.
hierop, upon this, after this, hereupon.
hierso, here, at this place.
hierteen, against this.
hierteenoor, opposite, over the way; against this.
hiertoe, for this purpose; thus (so) far.
hieruit, from this, hence.
hiervan, of this, about this.
hiervoor, for this, in return for this.
hiet, (ge-), order.
hik, (-ke), n. hiccup.
hik, (ge-), hiccup.
hinder, (ge-), hamper, hinder, trouble; annoy, worry.
hinderlaag, ambush, ambuscade.
hinderlik, (-e), annoying, troublesome.
hindernis, (-se), hindrance, obstacle.
hinderpaal, bar, impediment, obstacle.
Hindoe, (-s), Hindu (Hindoo).
hings, (-te), stallion.
hingsel, (-s), handle; hinge; loop (of whip).
hink, (ge-), hobble, limp.
hinnik, (ge-), neigh, whinny.
hipnotiseer, (ge-), hypnotize.
hipokonders, ipekonders, hypochondria; caprices, whims.
historikus, (-se, historici), historian, historiographer.
histories, (-e), historical; historic.
hitsig, (-e), hot, lewd; in heat (animals).
hitte, heat.
hittete, vide hettetè.
ho!, ho!, stop!
hobbelagtig, (-e), bumpy, rough, uneven.
hobbelperd, rocking-horse.
hobbelrig, (-e), vide hobbelagtig.
hoe, how; what.
hoed, (-e), n. hat; bonnet.
hoed, (ge-), keep, tend, watch; guard, protect.
hoedanig, (-e), what, what kind (sort) of.
hoedanigheid, quality; capacity.
hoede, care, guard, protection.
hoedestander, hallstand.
hoef, (hoewe), n. hoof.
hoef, v. need.
hoefyster, horseshoe.
hoegenaamd: – nie, not at all.

hoek, (-e), corner; angle; (fish-) hook; narrow glen.
hoeka: van – (se tyd) af, (from) of old.
hoekig, (-e), angular; jagged (rocks).
hoekom, why, for what reason; wherefore.
hoeksteen, corner-stone; keystone.
hoender, (-s), fowl; chicken.
hoenderhok, poultry-house, fowl-run.
hoenderkop: hy is –, he is tipsy.
hoendervel: – kry, get gooseflesh.
hoepel, (-s), n. hoop.
hoepelbeen, bandy-leg, bow-leg.
hoëpriester, high priest, pontiff.
hoera!, hoerê!, hurrah!
hoërskool, hoër skool, high school.
hoes, (-te), n. cough.
hoes, (ge-), cough.
hoeseer, however much, much as.
hoes(t)erig, (-e), coughing.
hoeveel, how much, how many.
hoeveelheid, amount, quantity.
hoeveelste: die – van die maand is dit?, what day of the month is it?
hoever, how far; in –, (as to) how far.
hoewel, although, though; vide alhoewel.
hof, (howe), court; garden.
hoflik, (-e), courteous, obliging, polite.
hofmakery, love-making.
hok, (-ke), n. kennel (for dogs), pen (for sheep), sty (for pigs), run, house (for poultry), cage (for wild animals); den; quad.
hok, (ge-), bymekaar –, herd (huddle) together; hulle is ge–, they have been gated (given bounds).
hokaai!, hookhaai!, halt there! (to oxen).
hokkie, n. hockey.
hol, (-e), n. hole; cave, cavern; den, lair.
hol, n.: op –, running loose; op – gaan, bolt, stampede.
hol, (-le), a. hollow (tooth), empty (stomach), concave (lens); sunken (eyes).
hol, (ge-), run, rush, bolt, stampede.
holderdebolder, holderstebolder, head over heels, helter-skelter, pell-mell, topsy-turvy.
Hollander, (-s), Hollander, Dutchman.
Hollands, (-e), n. & a. Dutch.
holrug, hollow back, 'n teorie – ry, ride a theory to death.
holte, (-s), cavity, hollow, socket (of eye); pit (of stomach).
hom, him, it.
homoniem, (-e), n. homonym.
homp, (-e), chunk, hunk, lump.
hond, (-e), dog, hound; cur.
hondehok, (dog-) kennel.
honderd, (-e), hundred.
honderd-en-een: – moeilikheidjies hê, have a thousand and one troubles.
honderd-en-tien: al –, all the same.
honderdjarìg, (-e), of a hundred years, centennial; -e fees, centenary.
honderdjarige, (-s), centenarian.
honderdtal, a hundred; a century.
hondesiekte, distemper (in dogs).
hondmak, as tame as a dog.
honds, (-e), currish, churlish; brutal.
hondsdolheid, rabies; hydrophobia.
Hongaar, (-gare), Hungarian.
Hongaars, (-e), Hungarian.
honger, n. hunger.
honger, a. hungry.
honger, (ge-), hunger.
hongerig, (-e), (slightly, a bit) hungry.
hongersnood, famine.
honoreer, (ge-), honour, (a bill, a cheque).

honorêr, (-e), honorary.
honou!, vide **hanou.**
hoof, (-de), head; chief, leader; heading; principal.
hoof- . . ., chief, leading, main, principal.
hoofbestuurder, managing director; general manager.
hoofbrekens, brain-racking, worry.
hoofdelik, (-e), per head, per capita.
hoofgetal, cardinal (number).
hoofkussing, pillow.
hoofkwartier, headquarters.
hoofletter, capital (letter).
hooflyn, main line (railw.), trunk-line.
hoofpad, main road, high road.
hoofpyn, headache.
hoofreken(e), mental arithmetic.
hoofrol, leading (principal) part (rôle).
hoofs, (-e), ceremonious; courtly.
hoofsaak, main point (thing); (pl.). essentials.
hoofsaaklik, chiefly, mainly, principally.
hoofsin, principal clause (sentence).
hoofstad, capital, metropolis.
hoofstuk, chapter.
hooftrek, main feature, principal characteristic (trait); **in –ke,** in outline.
hoog, (hoë), high, tall, lofty (ideals), highpitched (voice); exalted (personage).
hoogag, (hoogge-), esteem highly, respect.
hoogagtend: – die uwe, respectfully yours.
hoogdrawend, (-e), high-flown, pompous.
hoogedele, right honourable.
hoogeerwaarde, right (most) reverend.
hooggeag, (-te), esteemed; **–te Heer,** Dear Sir.
hooggeregshof, supreme court.
hooggespan, (-ne), high(ly) strung.
hooghartig, (-e), haughty, high and mighty.
hooghou, (hoogge-), uphold, keep up.
hoogleraar, professor.
hoogmoed, pride, haughtiness.
hoogmoedig, (-e), proud, haughty.
hoognodig, (-e), urgently needed (necessary).
hoogpeil, high-water mark.
hoogs, extremely, highly.
hoogskat, (hoogge-), esteem (value) highly.
hoogspring, (hoogge-), do the high jump.
hoogstaande, eminent, of high standing.
hoogste, highest, sovereign, supreme; top, utmost.
hoogstens, at best, at most, at the outside, at the utmost, up to, not exceeding.
hoogte, (-s), height; altitude; pitch (of voice); rise, hill.
hoogtepunt, acme, culminating point, height, peak, pinnacle, zenith; high-water mark; crisis (of disease).
hoogty: – vier, be rampant, reign supreme.
hoogwater, high water, high tide.
hooi, hay.
hooimied, -miet, haystack.
hook!, hookhaai!, hokaai!, whoa!
hoon, n. scorn, jeer(s), taunt(s).
hoon, (ge-), deride, taunt, jeer (scoff) at.
hoop, (hope), n. 1. heap, pile; crowd, lot.
hoop, n. 2. hope.
hoop, (ge-), hope.
hoopvol, (-le), hopeful, sanguine; promising.
hoor, (ge-), hear.
hoorbaar, (-bare), audible.
hoorbuis, ear-trumpet, otophone.
hoorsê, hearsay.
hoort, v. so – dit, that's as it should be.
hop, n. hop; **– pluk,** pick hops.

hopeloos, (-lose), hopeless, desperate.
horing, (-s), horn; bugle; hooter (of motor); receiver (of teleph.)
horingdroog, (-droë), dry as dust (bone).
horingoud, (-oue), as old as the hills.
horison, (-ne, -te), horizon, skyline.
horisontaal, (-tale), horizontal, flat, level.
horlosie, oorlosie, (-s), watch; clock.
horrelpoot, crooked hoof, vide **horrelvoet.**
horrelpyp, hornpipe.
horrelvoet, club-foot, stump-foot, talipes.
horries, horrors, delirium tremens.
horte, jerks; met – en stote, by fits and starts.
hortensia, (-s), hydrangea.
hortjie, (-s), blind, shutter.
hospita, (-s), landlady.
hospitaal, (-tale), hospital; infirmary.
hot, left, near (side); **– om,** to the left, round the left.
hotagter, left-hind; **dit – kry (hê),** have a rough time.
hotagteros, left-hind ox.
hotelhouer, hotel-keeper, landlord.
hotnaasagter, second left-hind.
hotnaasvoor, second left-fore (-front).
hotvoor, left-fore (-front).
hou, (-e), n. blow, cut, lash, slash, stroke.
hou: a. – en trou, loyal and true.
hou, (ge-), contain, hold, keep; deliver, make (a speech), give (an address), observe (the Sabbath).
hou(d)baar, (-bare), tenable.
houding, (-e, -s), bearing, carriage; attitude; deportment; position, posture; poise; pose; conduct, demeanour.
houer, (-s), holder; bearer (of letter); licensee (of shop); container.
hout, (-e), wood; timber.
houterig, (-e), wooden; clumsy, stiff.
houtgerus, (-te), unsuspicious; unconcerned.
houthakker, wood-cutter; **–s en waterputters,** hewers of wood and drawers of water.
houtkapper, wood-cutter; woodpecker.
houtpop, wooden doll; **soos 'n – sit,** remain inactive.
houtskool, charcoal.
houvas, (hand)hold, support; mainstay.
houwitzer, (-s), houwitzer.
hovaardig, (-e), haughty, arrogant.
howeling, (-e), courtier.
howenier, (-s), gardener.
hu, (ge-), espouse, marry, wed; vide **trou, (ge-).**
hubaar, (-bare), marriageable.
Hugenoot, (-note), Huguenot.
huid, (-e), skin; hide (of animals).
huidarts, skin-specialist, dermatologist.
huidige, modern, present, of the present day.
huigel, (ge-), feign, pretend, sham.
huigelaar(ster), (-s), dissembler, hypocrite.
huigelagtig, (-e), canting, hypocritical.
huil, (ge-), cry, weep (of humans); howl, whine (of animals); bleed (of vines).
huilerig, (-e), tearful, whimpering.
huis, (-e), n. house, dwelling, home; household, family; firm; institution.
huisbesoek, pastoral visit; house-to-house call.
huisbraak, housebreaking, burglary.
huisdier, domestic animal.
huisgenoot, (-note), housemate, inmate; (pl.), household, family.
huisgesin, family, household.
huisgodsdiens, family-devotions (-prayers).
huisheer, master of the house; landlord.

huishen, house-bird, stay-at-home.
huishoue (-ns), n. household; housekeeping.
huishoudelik, (-e), household (expenses), domestic (affairs).
huishouding, vide **huishou(e),** n.
huishoudkunde, domestic science.
huishoudster, (-s), housekeeper.
huislik, (-e), domestic; home-loving, homy, homely.
huismoeder, mother of the family; matron.
huisraad, furniture; household effects.
huisvader, father of a family; housemaster (of hostel).
huisves, (ge-), house, lodge, take in.
huisvesting, accommodation; housing.
huisvlyt, home-industry.
huiswaarts, homeward(s).
huiswerk, homework; household work.
huiwer, (ge-), shudder, tremble, hesitate.
huiwerig, (-e), afraid, hesitating; shivery.
huiweringwekkend, (-e), horrible.
hul, (ge-), envelop, shroud, veil.
hulde, homage, tribute.
huldebetoon, mark of esteem (homage).
huldeblyk, tribute; testimonial.
huldig, (ge-), pay homage to, honour; recognise.
hul(le), pron. pers. they: them (acc.).
hul(le), pron. poss. their.
hulp, aid, assistance, help, support; succour, relief; rescue.
hulpbehoewend, (-e), destitute, needy helpless.
hulpmiddel, expedient, makeshift; aid, means.
hulpvaardig, (-e), helpful, ready to help.

hulpwerkwoord, auxiliary (verb).
hulsel, (-s), cover(ing), envelope, wrapper.
humeur, (-e), humour, mood, temper.
humeurig, (-e), moody; sulky.
humor, humour.
humoristies, (-e), humorous, humoristic.
hunker, (ge-), – na, crave for, hanker after.
huppel, (ge-), frisk, hop, skip.
hups, (-e), courteous, polite; lively, quick.
hurk, (ge-), squat.
hurke, (pl.) haunches.
hut, (-te), cottage, hut, hovel: cabin (on board ship); shack (of wood).
huur, n. hire, rent; rental; lease.
huur, (ge-), hire, rent (a house), engage (a servant), charter (a ship).
huurbaas, landlord.
huurgeld, rent, rental.
huurkontrak, lease.
huurling, (-e), hireling, mercenary.
huurmotor, hire-car, drive-yourself car.
huurrytuig, cab.
huwelik, (-e), marriage, wedding; wedlock.
huweliksboot(jie): in die – stap, get married.
huweliksvoorwaarde(s), marriage-contract (-settlement); antenuptial contract.
hy, he; it.
hyg, (ge-), gasp (for breath), pant.
hys, (ge-), hoist, pull (raise, haul) up.
hysbak, cage, skip.
hyser, (-s), hoister; crane; lift.
hyskraan, (lifting-)crane.

Iberies, (-e), Iberian.
ideaal, (-ale), ideal.
idealiseer, (geïdealiseer), idealize.
idee, (ideë, -s), idea, notion; opinion.
ideël, (ideële), ideal, imaginary.
identiek, (-e), identical.
identifiseer, (geïdentifiseer), identify.
idille, (-s), idyl(l).
idioom, (-iome), idiom.
idioot, (-iote), idiot; imbecile.
ieder, (-e), each, every.
iedereen, anyone, everybody, everyone.
iegelik, 'n –, everybody, everyone.
iemand, anybody, anyone, (some) one, somebody, a person.
Ier, (-e), Irishman; (pl.) the Irish.
Iers, (-e), n. & a. Irish.
iesegrimmig, (-e), bearish, surly.
ietermago, ietermagô (-'s), **ietermagog**, (-ge, -s), pangolin.
iets, pron. anything, something.
iets, adv. a. little, rather, somewhat, slightly.
ietwat, slightly, somewhat.
iewers, somewhere.
ignoreer, (geïgnoreer), ignore.
illumineer, (geïllumineer), illuminate.
illusie, (-s), illusion.
illustrasie, (-s), illustration.
illustreer, (geïllustreer), illustrate.
imiteer, (geïmiteer), imitate.
immer, ever, always.
immermeer, evermore.
immers, but, yet; indeed.
immigrasie, immigration.
immigreer, (geïmmigreer), immigrate.
imperfektum, (-ta), imperfect (tense).
imperialisme, imperialism.
implikasie, (-s), implication.
imponeer, (geïmponeer), impress (forcibly).
importeer, (geïmporteer), import.
imposant, (-e), imposing, impressive.
impressie, (-s), impression.
improviseer, (geïmproviseer), improvise, extemporize.
impulsief, (-iewe), impulsive.
imputeer, (geïmputeer), impute.
in, prep. in, into, within; during.
in, (gein), collect (debts), cash (cheque).
inagneming, observance.
inasem, (inge-), breathe, draw in, inhale.
inbaar, (-bare), collectable, leviable.
inbeeld, (inge-), jou –, fancy, imagine.
inbegrepe, vide **inbegrip**.
inbegrip: met – van, inclusive of.
inbegryp, included, including.
inbesitneming, occupation.
inbeslagneming, attachment, seizure; embargo (of ship); taking up (a person's time).
inbind, (inge-), bind (a book); take in.
inblaas, (inge-), blow into; suggest; breathe (infuse) into.
inblasing, instigation, suggestion.
inbly, (inge-), stay indoors; stay in (school).
inboek, (inge-), book, enter; indenture.
inboesem, (inge-), inspire into (with).
inboet, (inge-), plant in between, fill in, replace.
inboorling, (-e), native, (pl.) aborigines.
inbors, character, disposition, nature.
inbraak, burglary, housebreaking.
inbreker, (-s), burglar, housebreaker.
inbreuk, infraction, infringement; – **maak op**, encroach upon.
inbring, (inge-), bring in; put forward.
inburger, (inge-), become naturalized; become current.

indeel, (inge-), class(ify), group; graduate; incorporate in (with).
indeling, (-e, -s), classification, division.
indenk, (inge-): jou – in, realize, visualize.
inderdaad, indeed, in (point of) fact, really.
inderhaas, in haste, in a hurry, hurriedly.
indertyd, at the time; formerly.
indenk, (inge-): jou – in, realize, visualize.
Indiaan, (-ane), (Red) Indian.
indien, conj. if, in case.
indien, (inge-), bring in, introduce (a bill); lodge (a complaint), tender (one's resignation), move (a proposal); present (the budget); put in (a claim); present (a petition).
indienstreding, commencement of duties.
Indiër, (-s), Indian.
Indies, (-e), Indian.
indirek, (-te), indirect.
individu, indiwidu, (-e, -'s), individual.
individualis, indiwidualis, (-te), individualist.
individueel, indiwidueel, (-ele), a. & adv. individual(ly).
indommel, (inge-), drop off, doze off.
indompel, (inge-), dip (steep) in, immerse.
Indonesies, (-e), Indonesian.
indoop, (inge-), dip in(to).
indra(ag), indrae, (inge-), carry in(to).
indraai, (inge-), turn into (a road); screw in (a nut); wrap up (a parcel).
indring, (inge-), break into, penetrate into.
indringer, (-s), intruder, interloper.
indringerig, (-e), importunate, obtrusive.
indruis, (inge-), – **teen**, clash (conflict, be at variance, jar) with.
indruk, (-ke), n. impression.
indrukwekkend, (-e), imposing, impressive.
induik, (inge-), vide **indeuk**.
industrie, (-ë), industry.
industrieel, (-iële), a. industrial.
indut, (inge-), vide **indommel**.
ineen, close, together; vide **inmekaar**.
ineen- . . ., vide **inmekaar . . .**
ineens, at once, immediately, suddenly.
ineensluiting, fitting together, dovetailing.
ineenstorting, break-up, collapse, crash.
inent, (ingeënt), inoculate; vaccinate.
infaam, (-fame), downright (lie), infamous.
infeksie, infection, contagion.
infinitief, (-tiewe), infinitive (mood).
inflammasie, inflammation.
influensa, influenza, flu(e).
influister, (inge-), suggest, whisper to.
informasie, information; inquiry.
ingaan, (inge-), enter, go in(to); take effect.
ingaande – regte, import-duties; – **vanaf**, dating (with effect) from.
ingang, entrance, entry; way in.
ingebore, inborn, innate, native.
ingedagte, absent-minded, lost in thought.
ingee, (inge-), administer, give; suggest.
ingehoue, pent-up, restrained.
ingelê, ingeleg, (-de), inlaid; canned, pickled.
ingenieur, (-s), engineer.
ingenome: – met, charmed (taken up) with.
ingenomenheid, satisfaction.
ingesetene, (-s), inhabitant, resident.
ingeskape, vide **ingebore**.
ingeskrewe, enrolled; inscribed.
ingeslote, enclosed.
ingeslote, contributed, sent in.
ingetoë, modest, retired, reserved, sedate.
ingeval, in case; vide **geval**.
ingeval(le), hollow, sunken; emaciated.
ingevolge, in accordance with.
ingewande, bowels, intestines.

ingewikkel(d), **(-de)**, complex, complicated, involved, intricate.

ingewing, **(-e, -s)**, inspiration, suggestion; brainwave.

ingewortel(d), engrained, deep-seated.

ingewyde, **(-s)**, adept, initiated.

ingryp, **(inge-)**, intervene, take action; encroach upon.

ingrypend, **(-e)**, drastic, far-reaching.

inhaak, **(inge-)**, hook (hitch) in (to), take a person's arm.

inhaal, **(inge-)**, bring (fetch, gather, haul) in; catch (up with), overtake, make up (for).

inhalig, **(-e)**, covetous, grasping, greedy.

inham, **(-me)**, bay, creek, inlet.

inheems, **(-e)**, home, indigenous, native.

inhegtenisneming, arrest, apprehension.

inhou, **(inge-)**, contain, hold; check, restrain; retain, keep down (food); cancel, stop (payment), deduct (money); withdraw (from sale).

inhoud, contents; capacity; purport, tenor.

inja(ag), **injae**, **(inge-)**, drive in (to); rush in(to); overtake cause to take (medicine).

ink, **(-te)**, ink.

inkalf, **-kalwe(r)**, **(inge-)**, cave (calve) in.

inkamp, **(inge-)**, enclose, fence in.

inkeer, n. repentence; **tot – kom**, repent.

inkennig, **eenkennig**, **(-e)**, shy, timid.

inklaring, clearance.

inkleding, clothing, wording, phrasing.

inklee(d), **(inge-)**, clothe in words, phrase.

inklim, **(inge-)**, climb in(to); rebuke.

inkluis, included.

inkom, **(inge-)**, come in, enter, arrive.

inkomste, earnings, income, revenue.

inkoop, **(inge-)**, buy, purchase; buy in.

inkopies, small purchases; **– doen**, go shopping.

inkort, **(inge-)**, shorten; curtail.

inkpotlood, ink-pencil, indelible (pencil).

inkruip, **(inge-)**, creep (crawl) in(to); toady.

inkruiper, **(-s)**, toady; squatter; intruder.

inkuil, **(inge-)**, ensilage, ensile.

inlaat, **(-ate)**, n. intake; inlet.

inlaat, **(inge-)**, admit, let in; meddle (concern oneself) with.

inlading, load(ing), shipment; entraining.

inlands, **(-e)**, inland, indigenous, native.

inlas, **(inge-)**, insert, interpolate; mortise.

inlê, **(inge-)**, lay (put) in; can, preserve, pickle; inlay (with gold).

inleef, **-lewe**, **(inge-)**, adapt oneself (to); enter into.

inlei, **(inge-)**, introduce; preface.

inleiding, **(-e, -s)**, introduction; preface.

inlewer, **(inge-)**, give (hand, send) in; deliver up, surrender (arms).

inlig, **(inge-)**, enlighten, inform.

inloop, n. catchment(-area).

inloop, **(inge-)**, enter; call, drop in; overtake.

inluisteraar, **(angl.)** listener-in.

inlyf, **inlywe**, **(inge-)**, annex, incorporate.

inmaak, **(inge-)**, can, pickle, preserve, tin.

inmekaar, crumpled up, smashed; bent double, stooping.

inmekaar-. . ., vide **ineen . . .**

inmekaarsak, **(inmekaarge-)**, collapse, cave in.

inmekaarsit, **(inmekaarge-)**, assemble, build up, mount (machinery).

inmeng, **(inge-)**, mix up with; interfere with.

inmiddels, meanwhile, in the meantime.

inname, vide **inneming**.

inneem, **(inge-)**, bring in; take in (a dress); occupy, take up (room); capture, take (a fortress).

innemend, **(-e)**, attractive, fetching, taking, winning.

inneming, capture, taking.

innerlik, **(-e)**, inner (life), internal (forces); intrinsic (merit); inward (eye).

inpak, **(inge-)**, pack, do up (parcels).

inpalm, **(inge-)**, haul in (a rope); **alles –**, pocket everything.

inpas, **(inge-)**, fit in.

inpeper, **(inge-)**; **iemand –**, go for a person; give someone a hiding.

inprent, **(inge-)**, impress, inculcate, instil(l), drum (into the head . . .).

inrig, **(inge-)**, arrange, manage; fit (fix) up, furnish.

inrigting, **(-e, -s)**, arrangement, organization; structure; establishment, institution.

inruil, **(inge-)**, trade in, barter, exchange.

inruim, **(inge-)**: **plek –**, make room.

inry, **(inge-)**, ride in(to); break in (a horse), bring in.

inry(e), **inryg**, **(inge-)**, lace (tightly); tack (a dress), string (beads).

insage, inspection, perusal.

insak, **(inge-)**, sink in; collapse, sag.

insamel, **(inge-)**, collect, gather (in).

insê, **(inge-)**: **iemand –**, give a person a telling-off.

inseën, **(inge-)**, consecrate; ordain (clergyman).

inseep, **(inge-)**, soap; lather (for shaving).

insek, **(-te)**, insect.

insetting, **(-e, -s)**, decree (of Heaven).

insgelyks, likewise, similarly.

insien, **(inge-)**, look into; see, come to realise; understand.

insig, **(-te)**, insight; opinion, view.

insink, **(inge-)**, give way, sink down (in); subside; relapse.

insinking, subsidence; slump; relapse.

insinueer, **(geïn-)**, insinuate.

insit, **(inge-)**, put in; set in; insert; start (bidding); strike up (a song).

inskakel, **(inge-)**, switch on; engage; insert.

inskeep, **(inge-)**, embark; ship.

inskep, **(inge-)**, ladle in; dish up (food).

inskiet, **(inge-)**, throw (thrust) in(to); lose.

inskiklik, **(-e)**, complaisant, obliging.

inskryf, **-skrywe**, **(inge-)**, enrol(l), enter; register; subscribe (to a paper); tender.

inskrywing, **(-e, -s)**, enrol(l)ment, registration; entry; tender; application (for shares).

inslaan, **(inge-)**, drive in; batter (smash) in; take, turn down (a road); catch on, take; sink in.

insluimer, **(inge-)**, doze off.

insluit, **(inge-)**, enclose, lock in, shut in; include; contain.

insluk, **(inge-)**, swallow.

insonderheid, especially, particularly.

insout, **(inge-)**, salt; initiate (students).

inspan, **(inge-)**, inspan: harness (horses); yoke (oxen); set (a person) to do something; exert (one's strength).

inspanning, effort, exertion, strain.

inspekteer, **(geïn-)**, inspect.

inspekteur, **(-s)**, inspector, superintendent.

inspireer, **(geïn-)**, inspire.

inspraak, dictate(s) (of one's heart).

inspuit, **(inge-)**, inject, give an injection.

instaan, **(inge-)**,: **– vir**, answer for, vouch for; accept responsibility for, stand surety for.

installeer, **(geïn-)**, fix up, install; furnish, induct.

instamp, **(inge-)**, beat (ram) in.

instandhouding, conservation; maintenance; upkeep; preservation.

insteek, **(inge-)**, put in; thread (a needle).

instel, (inge-), establish, set up; institute, focus; adjust (instruments); propose (a toast).
instem, (inge-), agree; concur; chime in.
instinkmatig, (-e), instinktief, (-tiewe), a. & adv. instinctive(ly).
instoot, (inge-), force, push, (stave) in.
instop, (inge-), tuck (wrap) up; cram (stuff) in.
instort, (inge-), tumble down, fall in, collapse, relapse (of invalid).
instroom, (inge-), crowd (flock, flow, pour, stream) in(to).
instrukteur, (-s), instructor; drill-sergeant.
instrument, (-e), instrument, implement, tool.
instuur, (inge-), send in; vide **insend.**
insukkel, (inge-), get in (down) with difficulty.
insuur, (inge-), prepare yeast.
insyfer, (insypel), (inge-), infiltrate.
inteendeel, on the contrary.
inteken, (inge-), subscribe to; mark (on a map).
intekenaar, (-are, -s), subscriber.
intellektueel, (-uele), intellectual.
intelligent, (-e), intelligent; bright.
interes, interest.
interessant, (-e), interesting.
interesseer, (geïn-), interest; be interested in.
intern, (-e), internal.
internasionaal, (-ale), international.
interneer, (geïn-), intern.
internis, (-te), specialist in internal diseases.
interpunksie, punctuation.
intiem, (-e), intimate.
intog, entrance, entry.
intoom, (inge-), pull up, rein in; curb, restrain.
intrede, intree, n. entrance (upon office), entry (into); advent (of spring).
intree, (inge-), enter; set in.
intrek, n. **jou – neem by,** put up at (with).
intrek, (inge-), draw in, retract; march into; move into (a house); inhale (smoke); soak in; retract (a statement).

introduseer, (geïn-), introduce.
intuïsie, intuition.
intussen, meanwhile, in the meantime.
intyds, in time.
inval, n. incursion, invasion, raid; brain wave, idea.
inval, (inge-), drop (fall) in(to); collapse, tumble down; invade (a country), join (in singing); interrupt; start (work).
inventaris, (-se), inventory.
invlieg, (inge-), fly in(to); go for (a person).
invloed, (-e), influence.
invloedryk, (-e), influential.
invoeg, (inge-), insert, put in.
invoeging, (-e, -s), invoegsel, (-s), insertion.
invoer, (inge-), import (goods); introduce.
invorder, (inge-), collect; recover (debts).
inwag, (inge-), await, wait for.
inwen, inwin, (inge-), collect, gather.
inwendig, (-e), a. inner, interior, internal, inward.
inwendig, adv. inwardly, internally.
inwerk, (inge-): – op, act upon, affect, influence.
inwillig, (inge-), accede (agree) to, comply with, concede (demands), grant.
inwoner, (-s), inhabitant, resident (of city), inmate, occupant (of house), lodger.
inwoning, lodging.
inwoon, (inge-), live in; live (lodge) with.
inwortel, (inge-), strike (take) root.
inwy, (inge-), inaugurate, consecrate (a church).
ipekonders, hipokonders, hypochondria.
Iraans, (-e), Iranian.
ironie, irony.
irriteer, (geïr-), irritate.
Islam, Islam.
isolasie, isolation; insulation.
isoleer, (geïso-), isolate; insulate.
Israeliet, (-e), Israelite.
Italiaan, (-iane), Italian.
ivoor, ivory.

ja, yes, ay(e).

ja(ag), **jae**, (ge-), chase, pursue; hurry; race, rush, tear.

jaagsiekte, droning-sickness (in sheep).

jagspinnekop, vide **jagspinnekop**.

ja(a)psnoet, (-e), jackanapes; wise-acre.

jaar, (jare), year.

jaarblad, annual.

jaargang, volume (of a periodical).

jaargety, season.

jaarliks, (-e), a. & adv. annual(ly), yearly.

jaarring, annual ring, growth ring.

jaartal, date.

jaartelling, era.

jabroer, fellow without backbone, spunkless fellow.

jae, vide **ja(ag)**.

jag, (-te), n. hunt(ing); shooting; chase, yacht.

jag, (ge-), hunt, shoot, chase.

jagspinnekop, hunting-spider.

jagter, (-s), hunter, huntsman, sportsman.

jakkals, (-e), jackal.

jakkalsdraai, sharp turn; excuse.

jakkalsstreek, artifice, cunning, shrewdness.

jakker, (ge-), career along; gad about.

jakkie, (-s), coatee.

jakobregop, (-pe, -s), zinnia.

jakopeweroë, protruding eyes.

jaloers, (-e), jealous, envious.

jambe, (-s), iamb(us).

jammer, a. sorry.

jammer, (ge-), lament, wail.

jammerhartig, (-e), compassionate, soft-hearted.

jammerlik, (-e), miserable, pitiable, pitiful.

jammerte, pity; sorrow.

ja-nee, sure!, that's a fact!.

janfiskaal, (-ale, -s), butcher-bird, fiscal-shrike.

janfrederik, (-e, -s), Cape redbreast.

jangroentjie, (-s), sugar-bird.

janpiedewiet, (-e, -s), **janpierewiet**, bokmakirishrike.

jansalie, (-e), stick-in-the-mud.

jantjie: − **wees**, be jealous.

Jan tuisbly: **met − se kar ry**, stay at home.

Januarie(maand), (month of) January.

Japannees, (-ese), Japanese.

Japanner, (-s), Japanese, Jap.

japie, (-s), simpleton.

japon, (-ne), dress, frock.

japsnoet, vide **jaapsnoet**.

japtrap: **in 'n −**, in no time.

jarelang, (-e), for years together (on end).

jas, (-se), great-coat, overcoat.

jasmyn, jasmin(e), jessamin(e).

jaspis, jasper.

Javaan, (-ane), Javanese.

jawel, indeed, yes.

jawoord, acquiescence, consent; promise (of marriage).

jeens, to, towards, by; with.

jellie, (-s), jelly.

jenewer, gin.

jersie, (-s), jersey.

jeug, youth.

jeuk, n. itch(ing).

jeuk, (ge-), itch.

Jiddisj, Yiddish.

jig, gout.

Jobsgeduld, Job's patience.

Jobstyding, Job's news, message of ill-luck.

jodium, **jood**, iodine.

Joego-Slawië, (-e), Yugo-Slavia.

joernaal, (-ale), journal; logbook (mar.)

joernalis, (-te), journalist, pressman.

joggie, boy, sonny; caddy.

jok, (ge-), fib, tell fibs, tell stories.

jokkie, (-s), jockey.

jol, (ge-), make merry.

jolig, (-e), jolly, merry.

jolyt, merry-making, feasting.

jong, (-ens), n. boy.

jong, (attrib.), **jonk**, (predic.), young.

jongedogter, (young) girl.

jongeheer, young gentleman; Master (in address).

jongejuffrou, young lady; Miss (in address).

jongeling, (-e), young man, youth.

jongetjie, (-s), boy, youth.

jongetjieskind, boy.

jongkêrel, young man; lover.

jongman, young man, lad, stripling.

jongmeisie, young girl, lass.

jongos, young ox; tolly; −**se inspan**, vomit.

jongs: **van − af**, from childhood.

jongspan, children, kiddies, young folk.

jonker, (-s), (young) nobleman.

jonkman, young man; lover.

jonkvrou, young lady, maiden.

jood, vide **jodium**.

Jood, (Jode), Jew, Hebrew.

jool, fun, jollification, (students') rag.

joos: **dit mag − weet**, deuce (goodness) knows.

josie: **die − in wees**: have one's monkey up.

jota: **g'n − nie**, not an iota (jot).

jou, pron. pers. you.

jou, **jou(n)e**, pron. poss. your.

jou, (ge-), boo, hoot, barrack.

jubel, (ge-), exult, jubilate, shout for joy.

juffer, (-s), miss, mistress, missis.

juffrou, lady; teacher; Miss, Madam.

juig, (ge-), exult, rejoice.

juis, (-te), a. correct; exact, accurate, proper, right, precise.

juis, adv. exactly, precisely.

juistement, exactly, precisely, quite so.

juistheid, correctness, exactitude, precision.

juk, (-ke), yoke; beam (of balance).

jukskei, (-e), yoke-pin.

Julie(maand), (month of) July.

jul(le), pron. pers. you.

jul(le), pron. poss. your.

Junie(maand), (month of) June.

jurie, (-s), jury.

jurk, (-e), (night-) dress.

juweel, (-ele), jewel, gem; treasure (fig.).

juwelier, (-s), jeweller.

jy, you; − **weet nooit nie**, you never know.

kaai, (-e), quay, wharf.

kaak, (kake), jaw; gill (of fish); mandible (of insect).

kaal, (kale), bald (head); callow, unfledged (bird); bare, leafless (tree); naked (person).

kaalkop, n. baldhead; tuskless elephant.

kaalkop, a. & adv. baldheaded; hatless.

kaalperske, bald peach, nectarine.

kaap, (kape), n. cape, headland, point.

Kaapprovinsie, Cape Province.

Kaapstad, Cape Town.

kaart, (-e), n. card; map; chart; ticket.

kaartmannetjie, jack-in-the-box.

kaas, (kase), cheese; cheese-eater, Hollander.

kaaskop, blockhead; cheese-eater, Hollander.

Kaatjie: – Kekkelbek, chatterbox; kaatjie van die baan, cock of the walk.

kabaal, clamour, row, noise.

kabbel, (ge-), babble, lap, purl, ripple.

kabel, (-s), n. cable; hawser.

kabeljou, (-e), cod(fish), Cape cod.

kabinet, (-te), cabinet, ministry.

kaboedel, caboodle, lot.

kaboemielies, boiled mealies.

kabouter, (-s), brownie; gnome.

kader, frame, scheme.

kadet, (-te), cadet.

kaduks, in poor health; decrepit, seedy.

kaf, n. chaff.

kafee, (-s), café, coffee-house.

kafloop, (kafge-), beat, give a hiding (thrashing); finish, polish off (food).

kafpraatjies, nonsense, trash, small talk.

kaggel, (-s), fire-place.

kaiing, (-s), pl. greaves, brow(n)sels.

Kaïro, Cairo.

kajuit, (-e), cabin; ward-room.

kajuit(s)raad, council (of war).

kakao, cocoa.

kakebeen, jaw(-bone), jowl.

kakie, (-s), khaki; tommy; Englishman.

kakiebos(sie), Mexican marigold.

kakkerlak, (-ke), cockroach.

kalander, (-s), (corn-) weevil; vine-calander.

kalant, (-e), (sly) fox, rogue, scamp.

kalbas, (-se), calabash, gourd.

kalender, (-s), almanac, calendar.

kalf, (kalwers), n. calf.

kalf, kalwe, (ge-), calve (animals); cave in (ground).

kalfsoog, calf's eye; poached (fried) egg.

kalfsvleis, veal.

kali, potassium, potash.

kalk, n. lime.

kalklig, limelight.

kalkoen, (-e), turkey.

kalm, (-e), calm; cool, quiet; collected, composed.

kalmeer, (ge-), calm (down), pacify, soothe.

kalmweg, calmly, coolly, quietly.

kalwerhok, -kraal, calves' kraal.

kam, (-me), n. comb; crest (of a hill), ridge; cam, cog (of a wheel).

kam, (ge-), comb; card (wool).

kamas, (-te), legging, gaiter, spat.

kameel, (-mele), camel; giraffe.

kameelperd, giraffe, camelopard.

kamer, (-s), chamber, room.

kamera, (-s), camera.

kameraad, (-rade), comrade; chum, pal.

kamerwag, orderly.

kamma, kammakastig, -lielies, quasi, as of, make believe, would be, pseudo.

kamp, n. 1. combat, fight.

kamp, (-e), n. 2. camp; paddock.

kamp, (ge-), camp, encamp; fight, combat, struggle; te –e hê met, have to contend with.

kampanje, (-s), campaign.

kampeer, (ge-), (en)camp, camp out.

kamperfoelie, kanferfoelie, honeysuckle.

kampioen, (-e), champion.

kampvegter, fighter; champion, advocate.

kamrat, cog(-wheel), mortice-wheel.

kamta(g), kamtig, vide kamma.

kan, (-ne), n. can, jar, jug, mug, tankard.

kan, (kon), v. be able, can, may.

kanaal, (-nale), channel; canal; passage.

Kanadees, (-dese), Canadian.

ka(r)nallie, (-s), rascal, scamp.

kanarie, (-s), canary.

kandelaar, (-s, kandelare), candle-stick; agapanthus.

kandidaat, (-date), candidate, nominee, applicant (for a post).

kaneel, cinnamon.

kanfer, camphor.

kanferfoelie, vide kamperfoelie.

kangaroe, (-s), kangaroo.

kanker, cancer; (fig.), canker, pest.

kankerroos, cocklebur(r).

kanna, (-s), canna.

kanniedood, airplant.

kano, (-'s), canoe.

kanon, (-ne), cannon, gun.

kanonnier, (-s), gunner.

kans, (-e), chance; risk; turn.

kansel, (-s), pulpit.

kanselier, (-e, -s), chancellor.

kant, (-e), n. lace.

kant, (-e), n. side, border, edge, margin; direction, way; bank (of river).

kant: – en klaar, quite ready, ship-shape.

kant, (ge-); sig – teen, oppose.

kantel, (ge-), topple over; tilt, tip.

kantien, (-e), canteen.

kantoor, (-tore), office.

kap, (-pe), n. hood (of cart); shade (of lamp); cut (of axe); pawing (of horse); cowl (of chimney).

kap, (ge-), fell, cut down, chop; mince (meat); chip (in golf); chop (a ball in tennis); paw, hit out.

kapabel, (-e), able (to), capable (of).

kaparrang, (-s), wooden sandal, sabot.

kapater, (-s), n. castrated goat, kapater.

kapel, (-le), chapel.

kapel, (-le), cobra; geel, bruin –, Cape cobra.

kapelaan, (-s, -lane), chaplain.

Kapenaar, (-s, -nare), Capetonian; inhabitant of Cape Province.

kaper, (-s), privateer, freebooter, raider.

kapitaal, (-tale), n. capital, principal.

kapitalis, (-te), capitalist.

kapittel, (-s), n. chapter.

kapittel, (ge-), read a lecture, take to task.

kapkar, hooded cart.

kapok, n. kapok, seed-cotton; snow.

kapok, (ge-), snow.

kapokhaantjie, bantam-cock; little spitfire.

kapokhoender, bantam(-fowl).

kapokvoëltjie, Cape (penduline) tit.

kapot, broken, (gone) to pieces; done for, knocked up; in rags; out of order, gone smash.

kappertjie, (-s), orchid; nasturtium.

kappie, (-s), (sun-)bonnet; circumflex.

kapriol, kaperjol, (-le), caper, –le maak, cut capers.
kapsel, (-s), coiffure, hair-dress, head-dress.
kapsie, (-s): –(s) maak, raise objections.
kapstewel, top-boot.
kapstok, hat-rack, hall-stand.
kaptein, (-s), captain; chief.
kar, (-re), cart; car (motor).
karakter, (-s), character; role (rôle).
karaktertrek, characteristic, trait.
karamel, (-le, -s), caramel, burnt sugar.
karavaan, (-vane), caravan.
karba, (-'s) carboy, demi-john, wicker-bottle.
karbonkel, (-s), carbuncle; garnet.
kardinaal, (-nale), n. cardinal.
kardoes, (-e), paper-bag, paper-cornet.
karet, (-te), tortoise-shell.
karig, (-e), scanty, meagre, slender, frugal.
karikatuur, (-ture), caricature.
karkas, (-se), carcase; skeleton.
karkatjie, (-s), sty(e), hordeolum.
karkis, cart-box, box-seat.
karkoer, (-e), bitter melon, wild coloquint.
karmenaadjie, (-s), chop, cutlet.
karmosyn, crimson.
karnallie, vide ka(r)nallie.
karnuffel, (ge-), cuddle, hug; bully.
Karoo, Kar(r)oo.
karos, (-se), kaross, skin-rug.
karper, (-s), carp.
karring, (-s), n. churn.
karring, (ge-), churn.
karringmelk, buttermilk.
kartel, (-le, -s), n. cartel, trust.
kartel, (-s), n. notch; wave, curl.
kartel, (ge-), notch; wave (hair).
kartets, (-e), grape-shot, canister-shot.
karton, cardboard, pasteboard.
karwats, (-e), n. riding-whip, hunting-crop.
karwei, (ge-), ride transport.
karweier, (-s), transport-rider.
kas, (-te), n. wardrobe; bookcase; cabinet, cup-board; case; cash; exchequer; box, chest.
kas, (-se), socket.
kas, (ge-), deposit (money).
kasarm, (-s), barracks; die hele –, the whole caboodle.
kaskenade, (-s), prank, trick; to-do, uproar.
Kaspies, (-e), die –e See, the Caspian (Sea).
kassier, (-s), cashier; banker.
kastaiing, (-s), chestnut.
kastaiingbruin, chestnut, auburn.
kaste, (-s), caste.
kasteel, (-tele), castle; citadel; rook (in chess).
kasterolie, castor-oil.
kastig, quasi, as if (it were); vide kamma.
kastrol, (-le), stew-pan, saucepan, casserole.
kasty, (ge-), chastise, punish; chasten.
kasuaris, (-se), cassowary.
kasueel, (-ele), casual, accidental.
kat, (-te), cat.
katalogus, (-se), catalogue.
katar, catarrh.
katastrofe, (-s), catastrophe.
katderm, cat-gut.
katedraal, (-drale), cathedral (-church).
kategismus, catechism.
kategorie, (-ë), category.
katel, (-s), bedstead.
kater, (-s), tom-cat.
katjiepiering, (-s), gardenia.
katkisasie, confirmation(-class).
katkiseer, (ge-), catechize, give confirmation-classes; lecture, rebuke.
katlagter, (-s), babbler (bird); maxim.

katoen, cotton.
katoliek, (-e), catholic; universal.
Katoliek, (-e), n. & a. (Roman) Catholic.
katrol, (-le), pulley.
kats, (-e), n. cat (o' nine tails).
kats, (ge-), cat, thrash with cat.
katswink, dazed, unconscious.
kattebak, dickey.
kattekwaad, mischief, mischievous tricks, pranks.
katterig, (-e), cattish; chippy, seedy.
Kaukasies, (-e), Caucasian.
keb, (-s), cab.
keel, (kele), n. throat, gullet; gorge.
keël, cone, icicle, skittle.
keelgat, gullet.
keep, (kepe), n. notch, nick; tally.
keep, (ge-), notch, nick, indent.
keer, (kere), n. change, turn; time.
keer, (ge-), turn, turn round; shrink back; pre-vent, stop; defend; oppose; turn back (the sheep); check (the enemy); stem (the flood).
keerdam, barrage, weir.
keerkring, tropic.
keersy, reverse; other side; back.
kees, (kese), monkey; baboon.
kef, (ge-), yap, yelp, bark; squabble.
keil, (-e), n. wedge; top-hat.
keil, (ge-), fling, pitch; drive in a wedge.
keiser, (-s), emperor; Duitse K–, German Kaiser.
ke(r)jakker, (ge-), romp, gad about.
kekkel, (ge-), cackle; chatter.
kekkelbek, chatter-box, gossip.
kelder, (-s), n. cellar.
kelder, (ge-), cellar; slump, sink.
kelderverdieping, basement.
kelk, (-e), cup, chalice; calyx (of flower).
kelkie, (-s), wineglass; moonflower.
kelkiewyn, (-e), (Namaqua) sandgrouse.
kelner, (-s), waiter, steward.
Kelties, (-e), Celtic, Gaelic.
ken, kin, (-ne), n. chin.
ken, (ge-), know, be acquainted with, recognise.
kenbaar, (-bare), recognisable.
kenketting, kinketting, curb(-chain).
kenlik, (-e), recognisable; visible, obvious.
kenmerk, (-e), n. distinguishing mark; characte-ristic (feature).
kenmerk, (ge-), mark, characterize.
kenmerkend, (-e), characteristic, distinctive; out-standing, salient.
kenner, (-s), connoisseur, judge; authority.
kennetjie, (1) little chin.
kennetjie, (2) tip-cat (game).
kennis, knowledge; acquaintance(ship); con-sciousness.
kennisgewing, (-e, -s), notice, announcement.
kennismaking, (-e, -s), (making) acquaintance, meeting.
kennisneming, (-e, -s), (taking) cognisance; in-spection.
kenskets, (ge-), mark, characterise.
kensketsend, (-e), characteristic.
kenta(g), kentang, afraid (to play), funky.
kenteken, n. distinctive mark, characteristic; token, badge; symptom.
kenteken, (ge-), characterize.
kentering, (-e, -s), change, turn; transition.
kenwysie, signature tune.
keper: op die – beskou, on close inspection.
kêrel, (-s), chap, fellow; boy, young man, lover; fiancé.
kerf, (kerwe), n. nick, notch, jag, incision.
kerf, kerwe, (ge-), carve, notch; cut (tobacco); slice.

kerfstok, tally(-stick), nickstick; **baie op sy – hê**, have much to answer for.
ke(r)jakker, vide **kejakker**.
kerk, (-e), n. church; service; congregation.
kerker, (-s), n. jail (gaol), prison, dungeon.
kerker, (ge-), imprison, incarcerate.
kerkhof, churchyard, cemetery, graveyard.
kerkraad, church-council, consistory.
kerm, (ge-), groan, moan, whine.
kermis, (-se), fair.
kermisbed, shake-down, made-up bed.
kern, (-s), kernel, pith, heart; nucleus (of a comet); gist, root (of a matter).
kernagtig, (-e), pithy, terse.
kernkrag, nuclear power.
kernreaktor, nuclear reactor.
kernsplyting, nuclear fission.
kerrie, curry.
kers, (-e), n. candle.
Kersaand, Christmas-Eve.
Kersboom, Christmas-tree.
Kersdag, Christmas(-Day).
Kersfees, Christmas.
kersie, (-s), little candle; cherry.
Kersmis, Krismis, Christmas.
kersogie, white-eye; bush-warbler.
Kersvakansie, Christmas-holidays.
kersvers, fresh, quite new, piping (red-)hot.
kês, boiled sour milk, lopperd (milk).
kêskuiken, (mere) chicken, child, youngster.
ketel, (-s), kettle; cauldron; boiler.
ketter, (-s), n. heretic.
kettery, (-e), heresy.
ketting, (-s), chain.
keu, (-e, -s), (billiard-)cue.
keur, (-e), n. choice, selection; pick, flower; hallmark.
keur, (ge-), try, test, inspect; assay (metals).
keurig, (-e), exquisite, trim, dainty, choice.
keuring, (-e, -s), examination, inspection, assaying, testing; tasting.
keus(e), choice, selection; option.
kewer, (-s), beetle.
kiaat(hout), teak(-wood); Cape teak.
kibbel, (ge-), bicker, squabble.
kiek, (-e), n. snap(shot).
kiek, (ge-), snap.
kiel, (-e), n. keel; valley (of roof); corner.
kielie, (ge-), tickle.
kieliebak, armpit.
kiem, (-e), n. germ, embryo; seed.
kiem, (ge-), germinate, sprout, shoot.
kiemdodend, (-e), germicidal, antiseptic.
kiep!, shoo! (to fowls).
kiepersol(boom), umbrella-tree.
kiep-kiep, chick-chick!, chuck-chuck!
kierang, kurang, n. cheat(ing), deception.
kierang, kurang, (ge-), cheat, play false.
kierie, (-s), kerrie, (knob-)stick.
kies, (-e, -te), grinder, molar; cheek.
kies, (-e), a. delicate, considerate; nice.
kies, (ge-), choose, select; single (pick) out; elect.
kiesafdeling, -distrik, -wyk, constituency.
kiesbaar, (-bare), eligible.
kieser, (-s), constituent, voter, elector.
kieskeurig, (-e), fastidious, dainty, nice.
kiestand, molar(-tooth).
kiet(s), quits, even, equal.
kieu, (-e, kuwe), gill, branchia (pl.).
kiewiet, (-e), lapwing, plover, peewit.
kik, (ge-), make a sound.
kikker, (-s), frog.
kikvors, (-e), frog.
kil, (-le), chilly; cold, shivery.
kiloliter, kilolitre.

kilometer, kilometre.
kim, (-me), horizon.
kim, (ge-), get (become) mouldy.
kin, ken, vide **ken**, n.
kina, quinine.
kind, (-ers), child; kid(dy); baby, babe, infant.
kinderlik, (-e), childlike, innocent.
kindersorg, baby-care; child-welfare.
kinderspel(etjies), children's game, child's play.
kinds, (-e), doting, senile.
kindsbeen: van – af, from childhood.
kink, (-e), n. kink, hitch, knot.
kink, (ge-), turn, twist.
kinkel, (-s), vide **kink**, n.
kin-, kenketting, curb(-chain).
kinkhoes, (w)hooping-cough.
kinnebak, jaw(-bone), mandible.
kir, (ge-), coo.
kis, (-te), n. box, case; chest; coffin (for corpse); coffer; kist.
kis, (ge-), (place in a) coffin.
kisklere, best clothes, Sunday-best.
kitaar, ghitaar, (-are, -s), guitar.
kits: in 'n –, in a moment (jiffy).
kla(e), klaag, (ge-), complain; grumble, lament, wail.
klaar, (**klare**), ready, finished; clear, limpid; evident.
klaarblyklik, (-e), evident, clear.
klaarheid, clearness, clarity.
klaarkom, (**klaarge-**), get (be) done; manage.
klaarkry, (**klaarge-**), get ready (done), finish.
klaarpraat, done, finished.
Klaas Vaak, Klaas Vakie, Willie Winkie, sandman.
klad, (-de), n. blot, stain; blotch.
klad, (ge-), blot, stain; daub; scrawl.
kladboek, waste-book; scribbling-book.
kladpapier, blotting-paper, scribbling-paper.
kla(e), klae, vide **klaag**.
klaer, (-s), complainant; plaintiff (law).
klag, (-te), **klagte**, (-s), complaint; lamentation; accusation, charge.
klakkeloos, (-lose), a. & adv., groundless; offhand, without more ado.
klam, (-me), clammy, damp, moist.
klamp, (-e), n. clamp, cleat, bracket.
klandisie, custom, customers; patronage.
klank, (-e), n. sound, ring, tone.
klank, (ge-), sound, articulate, phone.
klanknabootsend, (-e), onomatopoetic.
klankgrens, sound barrier.
klant, (-e), customer, client.
klap, (-pe), n. slap, blow, lash, stroke, crack (of whip).
klap, (ge-), smack, clap; click (with the tongue); crack (with a whip).
klaploop, (klapge-), sponge, cadge.
klapper, (-s), n. coco(a)nut.
klapper, (-s), n. tell-tale; index, register, cracker; stop, explosive (phonetics).
klapper, (ge-), rattle; flap; chatter (teeth).
klapperhaar, coir.
klappertand, (ge-): **hy het ge– van die kou**, his teeth chattered with cold.
klapwiek, (ge-), clap (flap the wings).
klarigheid, readiness; **– maak**, prepare.
klas, (-se), class; form; grade; category.
klassiek, (-e), classic(al).
klassifiseer, (ge-), classify, sort.
klassikaal, (-kale), class (teaching).
klater, (ge-), rattle; splash.
klavier, (-e), piano(forte); vide **piano**.
klawer, (-s), clover; **-s** (pl.), clubs (in cards).
kledingstuk, garment, article of dress.

klee(d), (ge-), dress, clothe.
kleedjie, (-s), (table-)cloth, table-centre; saddle-cloth; rug; mat.
kleedkamer, dressing-room; cloakroom.
kleef, klewe, (ge-), cleave, cling, stick.
kleermaker, vide **kleremaker.**
klei, clay.
klein, little, small; slight; petty.
kleindogter, grand-daughter.
Klein Duimpie, Tom Thumb.
kleineer, (ge-), belittle, disparage.
kleingeestig, (-e), narrow-minded, petty.
kleingeld, change; petty cash.
kleingelowig, (-e), lacking in faith.
kleinhandel, retail-trade.
kleinigheid, (-hede), trifle, small thing.
kleinkind, grand-child.
kleinkry, (kleinge-), master; understand.
kleinmaak, (kleinge-), change (money); break up.
kleinmoedig, (-e), faint-hearted.
kleinneef, second cousin.
kleinood, (-ode), jewel, gem, treasure.
kleinserig, (-e), easily hurt; touchy.
kleinseun, grandson.
kleinsielig, (-e), petty, small-minded.
kleinspan, kleingoed, youngsters.
kleinsteeds, (-e), provincial, parochial.
kleintongetjie, uvula.
kleinvee, small stock, sheep and goats.
klem, (-me), n. accent, emphasis, stress; lockjaw; clamp, vice.
klem, (ge-), pinch, jam (one's finger), clench (one's teeth), tighten, clamp.
klemmend, (-e), forcible, cogent.
klemtoon, accent, stress; emphasis.
klep, (-pe), n. valve; flap (of bag); peak (of cap).
klep, (ge-), clapper, clatter; toll (of bell).
klepel, (-s), clapper, tongue.
klepligter, tappet.
klepper, (-s), n. rattle; –s (pl.), clacks.
klepper, (ge-), rattle; chatter (teeth).
klerasie, clothing, apparel, raiment.
klere, clothes, garments; dresses; gowns.
klerekas, wardrobe, clothes-press (-cupboard).
kleremaker, kleermaker, tailor.
klerk, (-e), clerk; –e (pl.), clerical staff.
klets, (ge-), splash; talk rot.
kletskous, chatterer, chatter-box.
kletsnat, wet through, soaking, soaked.
kletspraatjie(s), small talk, (idle) gossip.
kletter, (ge-), clash; pelt, clatter (rain).
kleur, (-e), n. colour; hue; complexion (of face); suit (of cards).
kleur, (ge-), colour; dye; flush, blush.
kleurling, (-e), coloured person
kleurryk, (-e), richly coloured, colourful.
kleursel, (-s), colouring; distemper.
kleurstof, pigment, dye.
kleurvas, (-te), fadeless, fast-dyed.
kleuter, (-s), tot, toddler.
klewerig, (-e), adhesive, sticky, gluey.
klief, kliewe, (ge-), cleave, split; plough, breast.
kliek, (-e), n. clique, coterie, set, party.
kliek, (ge-), form a clique.
kliënt, (-e), client, customer.
klier, (-e), gland.
klik, (-ke), n. cleek (golf); click (with tongue).
klik, (ge-), tell tales, split; click (with tongue).
klim, (ge-), climb, ascend, mount.
klimaat, climate.
klimaks, (-e), climax.
klimboontjie, runner-bean.
klimop, creeper, ivy, traveller's joy.

klingel, (ge-), tinkle, jingle.
kliniek, (-e), clinic.
klink, (-e), n. latch, catch.
klink, (ge-), sound, ring, clang, clink (glasses); clinch; rivet (bolts); nail.
klinker, (-s), vowel; clinker, hard brick.
klinkklaar, (-klare), pure; sheer.
klinknael, rivet.
klip, (-pe, -pers), stone; pebble; rock.
kliphard, (-e), as hard as stone.
klipkapper, stone-breaker (-dresser).
klipperig, (-e), stony, rocky.
klipplaat, flat slabs (ledges) of rock.
klipspringer, klipspringer.
klipsteenhard, very hard, hard as stone.
klipvis, dried cod; klipfish.
klits, (-e), n. bur(r); burdock.
klits (ge-), beat (eggs); thrash, smack.
klitsgras, -kruid, burdock, bur(r)weed.
kloek, (-e), a. brave, manly, stout.
kloek, (ge-), cluck.
kloekmoedig, vide **kloek.**
klok, (-ke), clock; bell; bell-jar.
klomp, (-e), crowd, number, lot; lump.
klomp, (-e), clog, wooden shoe.
klompie, (-s), a. bit, a little; small heap, handful; a few, some.
klont, (-e), n. lump, clod, nugget (of gold).
klont, (ge-), clot, curdle, coagulate.
klontjie, small lump; (suur)-s, (acid-)drops.
kloof, (klowe), n. chasm, gap, rift; gulf; ravine, kloof.
kloof, klowe, (ge-), cleave, split; chop (wood).
kloofhals, plunging neckline.
kloofsaag, rip-saw.
klooster, (-s), cloister, abbey.
klop, (-pe), n. knock, tap, rap; throb, beat.
klop, (ge-), knock, rap (at the door); pat (on the back); beat (whip) up (eggs); beat, throb, (of the heart); beat, defeat (someone); agree (with); balance, tally.
klopjag, round-up; police-drive.
klos, (-se), n. bobbin, spool; coil; lock (of sheep).
klots, (ge-), lap, splash.
klou, (-e), n. claw; paw; talon; fluke (of anchor); (bench-)clamp.
klou, (ge-), cling, stick; paw, clutch.
klouseer, -siekte, foot-disease (cattle).
klousule, (-s), paragraph, clause.
klouter, (ge-), clamber, climb, scramble.
klub, (-s), club.
klug(spel), farce, low comedy; joke, scream.
klugtig, (-e), farcical, droll, comical.
kluis, (-e), cell, hermitage; safe, safe-deposit.
kluisenaar, (-s), anchorite, hermit.
kluister, (ge-), chain, fetter, shackle.
kluit, (-e), clod, lump.
kluitjie, (-s), small clod (lump); dumpling, fib, lie.
kluts: die – kwyt wees (raak), be at sea (all abroad), flurried.
knaag, knae, (ge-), gnaw; prey (up)on; nag.
knaagdier, gnawer, rodent.
knaap, (knape), boy, lad; fellow, page.
knabbel, (ge-), nibble, gnaw, peck at.
knae, vide **knaag.**
knaend, (-e), gnawing; dull; ceaseless(ly); poignant (grief); unending (rain).
knak, (-ke), n. crack, snap; blow, set-back.
knak, (ge-), crack, snap; impair.
knal, (-le), n. bang, crack, clap.
knal, (ge-), bang, crack, crash, pop.

knaldemper, knalpot, silencer, exhaust(-box).
knap, (-pe), a. clever, smart; goodlooking, neat, spruce; tight (fitting).
knapbroekie, briefs.
knaphandig, (-e), dexterous, handy, skilful.
knars, (ge-), vide **kners.**
knee, knie, knieë, (ge-), knead; fashion, mould.
kneg, (-te), n. servant; slave; foreman.
knel, (ge-), pinch, squeeze; oppress.
knellend, (-e), oppressive.
knelter, vide **kniehalter.**
kners, (ge-), creak, grate; grind (teeth).
knetter, (ge-), crackle, sputter; crash.
kneukel, (-s), knuckle.
kneus, (-e), n. bruise, contusion.
kneus, (ge-), bruise; contuse.
knewel, (-s), n. whopper, stunner.
knibbel, (ge-), haggle, higgle.
knie, (-ë), n. knee.
knie, (ge-), vide **knee, (ge-).**
kniehalter, knelter, (ge-), kneehalter; handicap (a person).
kniel, (ge-), kneel.
knieserig, (-e), fretful, moping.
knieval, prostration.
knik, (-ke), n. rod; rut (in a road).
knik, (ge-), nod.
knip, (-pe), n. cut, snip (with scissors); catch (of door, purse); pinch (of salt); wink (of the eye).
knip, (ge-), cut, trim; pare (nails); punch (tickets); blink; wink (the eye).
knipmes, clasp-knife, pocket-knife.
knipoog, (ge-), wink.
knipsel, (-s), cutting, clipping.
knoei, (ge-), mess, bungle; intrigue.
knoes, (-te), knot, gnarl, node.
knoffel, knoflok, garlic.
knol, (-le), (old) crock (horse); bulb, tuber.
knoop, (knope), n. button; stud (collar); knot (in rope); expletive, oath.
knoop, (ge-), knot, tie; swear.
knop, (-pe), n. knob, handle (of door); bump; lump (in the throat); (push-)button; switch (electric); bud (of a plant).
knop, (ge-), bud.
knopkierie, club, knobkerrie.
knor, n. growl, grunt; – **kry,** get a scolding.
knor, (ge-), growl, grunt; grumble; scold.
knorrig, (-e), peevish, testy, surly.
knou, (-e), n. gnaw, bite; set-back.
knou, (ge-), gnaw; maul; injure.
knuppel, (-s), n. club, cudgel; niblick (golf).
knuppeldik, quite satisfied, stuffed.
knyp, (-e), n. pinch.
knyp, (ge-), pinch, squeeze.
knyper, (-s), clasper; claw; clip.
knyptang, pincers (big), nippers (small).
koddig, (-e), droll, comic(al), funny, odd.
koedoe, (-s), koodoo (kudu).
koeël, (-s), n. bullet, ball.
koeël, (ge-), pelt, throw; fire upon.
koeëllaer, ball-bearing.
koeëlrond, globular, spherical.
koei, (-e), cow.
koejawel, (-s), guava.
koek, (-e), n. cake.
koek, (ge-), cake, clot; knot; mat (hair); swarm together (bees).
koekeloer, (ge-), peep, spy, pry.
koekepan, (-ne), cocopan.
koekoekhen, speckled hen.
koekoekhoender, Plymouth Rock.
koeksoda, bicarbonate of soda.
koe(k)sister, (-s), sugar-dumpling.
koel, (-e), a. cool, cold, fresh.

koelbloedig, (-e), cold-blooded, in cold blood.
koelkamer, cold-storage (chamber).
koelte, (-s), coolness; breeze; shade; shady spot.
koens-, poenskop, hornless (ox, cow), pollard.
koepel, (-s), dome, cupola.
koepon, (-s), coupon.
koer, (ge-), coo.
koerant, (-e), newspaper, journal.
koerasie, courage, pluck.
koers, (-e), n. course, direction, route; price; exchange, rate (money).
koe(t)s, (ge-), crouch, dodge, duck.
koe(k)sister, sugar dumpling.
koester, (ge-), cherish, entertain; coddle, pamper (children); bask (in the sun).
koets, (-e), n. coach, carriage; sedan (motor).
koets, (ge-), vide **koes.**
koetsier, (-s), driver; cabman; coachman.
koevert, (-e), envelope.
koevoet, (-e), crowbar, lever, jemmy.
koffer, (-s), box, trunk, suitcase.
kofferradio, portable radio.
koffie, coffee.
koffiehuis, coffee-house, cafe.
koggel, (ge-), mimic, mock, imitate, tease.
koggelmander, (-s), -mannetjie, (-s), S.A. rock-lizard, agama.
kok, (-ke, -s), cook; caterer.
kokarde, (-s), cockade, badge, rosette.
koker, (-s), boiler; case, socket; quiver.
kokkewiet, (-e), bush-shrike.
kokon, (-s), cocoon.
kol, (-le), n. spot; stain; star (on horse); bull's eye (on target).
kolf, (kolwe), n. bat (cricket), club; butt (-end) (of gun); (distilling) receiver, flask.
kolf, kolwe, (ge-), bat (cricket).
koliek, colic.
koljander, coriander.
kolk, (-e), n. eddy; abyss; (air-)pocket.
kolk, (ge-), yawn (abyss); eddy (water).
kollega, (-s), colleague, confrère.
kollege, (-s), college; lecture.
kollekte, (-s), collection.
kollekteer, (ge-), collect, take up the collection (in church).
kolom, (-me), column; pillar.
kolon, (-ne), (army-)column.
kolonie, (-s), colony; settlement.
kolonis, (-te), colonist; settler.
kolossaal, (-sale), colossal, gigantic.
kolperd, horse with a star.
kolskoot, bull's-eye.
kolwer, (-s), batsman (in cricket).
kom, (-me), n. basin, bowl; washbasin.
kom, (ge-), arrive, come.
kombers, (-e), blanket.
kombineer, (ge-), combine.
kombuis, (-e), kitchen.
komediant, (-e), comedian.
komeet, (komete), comet.
komiek(lik), (-e), comic(al), droll, queer.
komies, (-e), comic(al), funny.
komitee, (-s), committee.
komkommer, (-s), cucumber.
komma, (-s), comma.
kommandant, (-e), commandant; commander.
kommandeer, (ge-), command, give orders; commandeer, requisition.
kommapunt, semicolon.
kommentaar, (-tare), comment(ary).
kommer, sorrow; distress, anxiety.
kommerloos, (-lose), care-free, untroubled.
kommernis, (-se), vide **kommer.**
kommervol, (-volle), distressful, wretched.

kommetjie, (-s), small basin; cup, bowl, mug.
kommissaris, (-se), commissioner.
kommissie, (-s), commission; committee.
kommunis, (-te), communist.
kompanie (-ë, -s), company (mil.)
kompanjie, (-ë, -s), company.
kompartement (-e), compartment.
kompas, (-se), compass.
kompenseer, (ge-), compensate, counterbalance.
kompeteer, (ge-), compete.
kompetisie, (-s), competition; league.
kompleet, (-plete), a. complete; utter (failure).
kompleet, adv. completely, utterly; just like.
komplement, complement.
kompliment, (-e), compliment.
komplot, (-te), plot, intrigue, conspiracy.
komponeer, (ge-), compose.
komponis, (-te), composer.
kompromis, (-se), compromize.
kompromitteer, (ge-), compromize.
koms, arrival, coming; advent (of Christ).
kondenseer, (ge-), condense.
kondisie, (-s), condition; form.
kondukteur, (-s), conductor, guard.
konferensie, (-s), conference.
konfoor, (-fore), chafing-dish, brazier.
konfyt, (-e), n. jam, preserve, comfits.
konfyt, (ge-): ge– **wees in,** be versed in; be an expert at.
kongres, (-se), congress.
koning, (-e, -s), king.
koninklik, (-e), royal, regal.
koninkryk, kingdom.
konjak, cognac, brandy.
konka, (-s), drum, tin.
konkel, (ge-), plot (and scheme), wangle, intrigue.
konklusie, (-s), conclusion, inference.
konkreet, (-krete), a. concrete.
konkurreer, (ge-), compete.
konsekwent, (-e), consistent, logical.
konsensie, conscience.
konsentrasie, concentration.
konsentreer, (ge-), concentrate, focus, fix.
konsep, (-te), concept, draft.
konsert, (-e), concert.
konsertina, (-s), concertina.
konserwatief, (-tiewe), n. & a. conservative.
konsistorie(kamer), vestry.
konsonant, (-e), consonant.
konstabel, (-s), constable, policeman.
konstant (-e), a. constant, uniform, steady.
konstrateer, (ge-), state; declare.
konstitusie, (-s), constitution.
konsuis, kwansuis, quasi, professedly.
konsul, (-s), consul.
konsulent, (-e), relieving clergyman.
kontak, (-te), contact, touch.
kontant, (-e), n. (hard) cash, ready money.
kontant, (-e), a. cash.
kontrak, (-te), contract, agreement.
kontras, (-te), contrast.
kontrei, (-e), country, part, region.
kontrole, control, check; supervision.
kontroleer, (ge-), control, check; supervise.
konvensie, (-s), convention.
konvooi, (-e), convoy.
konyn, (-e), rabbit, cony.
kooi, (-e), bed; cage.
kook, (ge-), boil (water), cook (food); boil, fume, seethe (with rage).
kooksel, (-s), boiling; decoction; batch.
kool, (kole), n. (1) coal, carbon.
kool, n. (2) cabbage.
koop, n. purchase, bargain.
koop, (ge-), buy, purchase.

koopbrief, deed of sale, purchase-deed.
koophandel, commerce, trade.
koopman, (-ne, -s, -liede, -lui), merchant.
koopwaar, -ware, merchandise.
koor, (kore), choir, chorus.
koord, (-e), cord; chord (maths.).
koorddanser(es), rope-dancer (-walker).
koors, (-e), fever.
koorsagtig, (-e), feverish; frenzied, hectic.
koorsblaar, blister, cold sore.
koorsig, (-e), feverish, febrile, pyretic.
koorspennetjie, clinical thermometer.
kop, (-pe), n. head; hill; cob (of maize).
kop, (ge-), cob (maize); head (cabbage, etc.).
kopbeen, skull.
koper, (-s), n. buyer, purchaser.
koper, n. copper.
koperkapel, (banded) cobra.
kopie, (-ë), n. copy, duplicate; manuscript.
kopkool, cabbage.
koppel, (ge-), couple, join; engage (gear).
koppelaar, (-s), n. clutch.
koppelteken, hyphen.
koppelwerkwoord, copula, copulative verb.
koppenent, head (of a bed).
koppie, (-s), small head; cup; hill, kopje.
koppig, (-e), headstrong, obstinate.
kopseer, headache.
kopskoot, shot in the head; knockout.
kopsku, bridle-shy: shy, evasive, timid.
kopspeel, (ge-), prance.
koraalrif, coral-reef, atoll.
Korana, (-s), Korana.
kordaat, bold, firm, plucky.
kordaatstuk, feat, achievement, bold deed.
Koreaans, (-e), n. Korean (Corean).
korente, korinte, (pl.) currants.
korf, (korwe), basket, hamper; (bee-)hive.
korfbal, basket-ball.
korhaan, (-hane), bustard.
koring, corn, wheat.
korinte, korente, (pl.) currants.
korporaal, (-s), corporal.
korps, (-e), corps, body.
korrek, (-te), right, correct; proper.
korreksie, (-s), correction.
korrel, (-s), n. grain, pellet; bead, sight (of gun); grape.
korrel, (ge-), aim (at); pick (grapes).
korrelkop, touchy (peevish) fellow; tufted head (of native).
korrelvat, (korrelge-), aim (at).
korrespondensie, correspondence.
korrigeer, (ge-), correct; set right.
kors, (-te), n. crust; scab (on wound).
korsie, (-s), crust.
korswel, (ge-), banter, jest, joke.
kort, (–, -e), a. short; brief.
kort, (ge-), shorten, clip.
kortaf, abrupt, curt, blunt, short.
kortasem, short-winded, puffed.
kortgebonde, short-tempered, touchy.
kortheidshalwe, for short, for briefness' sake.
korting, (-e, -s), reduction, discount.
kortkom, (kortge-), lack, need.
kort-kort, every now and again.
kortliks, briefly, shortly.
kortom, in short, in brief, in a word.
kortpad, short cut.
kortsigtig, (-e), short-sighted.
kortsluiting, short-circuit(ing).
kortstondig, (-e), short, short-lived.
kortvat (kortge-), take in hand, discipline.
kortweg, briefly, shortly, in short; curtly.
kortwiek, (ge-), clip the wings, frustrate.

kos, n. food, fare, victuals.
kos, (ge-), cost.
Kosak, (-ke), Cossack.
kosbaar, (-bare), expensive, costly; valuable (time); precious (stones).
kosganger, (-s), boarder.
kos(t)huis, boarding-house.
kosskool, boarding-school.
koste, cost(s), expenditure.
kostelik, (e), precious, splendid, excellent.
kosteloos, (-lose), free, gratis.
koster, (-s), sexton, verger.
kostuum, (-s), costume; fancy-dress.
kosyn, (-e), sash, frame.
kotelet, (-te), cutlet, chop.
kou, (-e), n. cage.
kou(e), n. cold.
kou, (ge-), chew, munch, masticate.
koubeitel, cold-chisel.
koud, [kou(e)], cold, chilly; frigid.
koudlei, (koudge-), walk (a horse) up and down; gull (a person).
kouekoors, ague, shivering fit, the shivers.
koulik, (-e), sensitive to cold, chilly.
kous, (-e), stocking.
kousband, garter, suspender; garter-snake.
koutjie, (-s), 1. chew(ing), cud; mouthful.
koutjie, (-s), 2. cage.
kouvoël, tawny eagle; cage-bird.
kraag, (krae), collar.
kraagmannetjie, maned lion.
kraai, (-e), n. crow.
kraai, (ge-), crow.
kraaibek, parrot-fish; pipe-wrench.
kraak, (krake), n. crack; flaw; fissure.
kraak, (ge-), crack; creak; (s)crunch (gravel).
kraal, (krale), 1. n. bead.
kraal, (krale), 2. n. pen, fold, kraal.
kraam, (krame), booth, stall.
kraan, (krane), tap, stopcock; crane, derrick.
kraanvoël, crane.
krabbel, (-s), n. scratch; scribble; sketch.
krabbel, (ge-), scratch; scrawl, scribble.
krabbetjie, krawwetjie, (-s), earring.
kraffie, (-s), water-bottle; decanter (for wine).
krag, (-te), strength, force, vigour, power, energy.
kragdadig, (-e), energetic, vigorous; effective, efficacious; powerful; potent.
kragsentrale, (electric) power-station.
kragtens, by virtue of, on the strength of.
kragtig, (-e), a. strong, powerful; nourishing, vigorous, forcible (language).
krakeel, (ge-), quarrel, wrangle.
krakie, (-s), small crack, flaw; highness (of meat).
kram, (-me), n. staple; clamp, cramp.
kramp, (-e), cramp, spasm.
krampagtig, (-e), convulsive, spasmodic (jerks); desperate (attempts).
kranig, (-e), bold, dashing, crack.
krank, (-e), sick, ill.
kranksinnig, (-e), crazy, insane.
kranksinnige, (-s), lunatic; maniac.
krans, (-e), 1. n. wreath, garland.
krans, (-e), 2. rock, ledge, krans.
krap, (-pe), n. 1. crab (-fish).
krap, (-pe), n. 2. scratch.
krap, (ge-), scratch; claw; paw.
kras, (–, -se) a. strong, vigorous.
kras, (ge-), scrape; screech; croak.
krat, (-te), crate, frame.
krater, (-s), crater.
krawwetjie, krabbetjie, (-s), earring.
kreatuur, (-ture), creature.
krediet, credit.

krediteer, (ge-), credit.
krediteur, (-e, -s), creditor.
kreef, (-te, krewe), crayfish; lobster.
kreeftegang, backward-march.
kreet, (krete), cry, scream, shriek.
kremetart, cream of tartar.
krenk, (ge-), hurt, offend, wound.
Kreool, (-ole), Creole.
Kretenser, (-s), Cretan.
Kretie: die – en Pletie, ragtag and hobtail.
kreuk, (-e), n. kreukel, (-s), crease, pucker.
kreuk, kreukel, (ge-), crease, pucker.
kreun, (-e), n. groan, moan.
kreun, (ge-), groan, moan.
kreupel, kruppel, a. cripple, lame, limping.
kreupelbos, -hout, brush-wood, thicket.
kriebel-, vide kriewel.
kriek, (-e), (house-) cricket.
krieket, cricket.
kriesel(tjie), (-s), bit, particle, crumb.
kriewel, kriebel, (ge-), tickle, itch; fidget.
kriewelrig, kriebelrig, (-e), itchy; fidgety; nettled (at).
krimineel, (-ele), criminal; outrageous.
krimp, (ge-), shrink, diminish, contract.
krimpystervarkie, small hedgehog.
kring, (-e), n. 1. circle, ring, orbit; quarter, walk of life; set.
kring, (-e), n. 2. carrion; beast, rotter.
kring, (ge-), curl, circle; mark with circles.
kringloop, cycle, circuit, circular course.
krink, (ge-), swing (round).
krinkel, (-s), n. crinkle.
krioel, (ge-), abound (swarm, teem) with.
krip, (-pe), n. manger.
krisant, (-e), chrysanthemum: aster.
kristal, (-le), crystal.
kristalhelder, as clear as crystal (daylight).
kriterium, (-s, -ria), criterion.
kritiek, (-e), n. criticism; review.
kritiek, (-e), a. critical, crucial.
krities, (-e), critical.
kritikus, (-se, -tici), critic.
kritiseer, (ge-), criticize; review (a book); censure
kroeg, (kroeë), bar, pub; students' club.
kroep, croup.
kroes, crisp(ed), frizzled; – voel, feel seedy.
kroeskop, curly-head; (person with) tufted hair.
krokodil, (-le), crocodile.
krom, a. bent, crooked, curved; hooked (nose).
krom, (ge-), bend, bow, crook, curve.
krombek, pick; (crook)bill; pipe-wrench.
kromming, (-e, -s), bend, curve, turn.
krompraat, (kromge-), lisp; speak (a language) imperfectly.
kromtrek, (kromge-), buckle, warp.
kroniek, (-e), chronicle.
kronkel, (-s), n. coil, twist(ing), kink.
kronkel, (ge-), coil, twist, wind.
kroon, (krone), n. crown; coronet; top; chandelier, electrolier, lustre (light).
kroon, (ge-), crown.
kroontjie, (-s), coronet; cowlick, crown (in hair).
kroonvervolger, public prosecutor.
kroos, issue, offspring, progeny.
krop, (-pe), n. crop, gizzard; head (of lettuce).
kropduif, cropper, pouter(-pigeon).
kropgans, pelican.
krot, (-te), den, hovel, shanty, kennel.
krui(e), (ge-), 1. season, spice, flavour.
krui(e), (ge-), 2. wheel, trundle (a barrow).
kruid, (kruie), herb; (pl.) spice.
kruidenier, (-s), grocer.
kruidjie-roer-my-nie(t), (-s), touchy person.

kruie, vide **krui, kruid.**
kruier, (-s), (luggage-)porter.
kruik, (-e), jar, jug, pitcher; urn.
kruin, (-e), crown, top; summit; crest (of wave).
kruinael(tjie), (-s), clove.
kruip, (ge-), creep, crawl; cringe, grovel.
kruis, (-e), n. cross; croup (of horse), crupper; small of the back (of man); loin; affliction, trial.
kruis, (ge-), cross; intersect; crucify; cruise.
kruisbande, (pair of) braces.
kruisbeeld, crucifix.
kruisement, mint.
kruiser, (-s), cruiser.
kruisig, (ge-), crucify.
kruising, cross(-breeding); crossing.
kruisvaarder, Crusader.
kruisverhoor, cross-examination.
kruisvra(ag), (ge-), cross-examine.
kruit, powder, gunpowder.
kruiwa, (wheel-)barrow.
kruk, (-ke), n. crutch; perch; crank; crock; stool.
kruk, (ge-), go on crutches; be ailing (crocked).
krukas, crankshaft.
krukkas, crankcase.
krukker, (-s), crock.
krul, (-le), n. curl; shaving (of wood); flourish (of pen).
krul, (ge-), curl; frizz, wave (hair).
krulhou, curly ball (in cricket); screw.
krullebol, curly-head.
krummel, (-s), n. crumb.
krummel, (ge-), crumble.
kruppel, vide **kreupel.**
kry, (ge-), get, receive, obtain, catch (a cold).
kryg, n. fight, war.
kryger, (-s), warrior.
krygshaftig, (-e), bellicose, martial, warlike.
krygsman, (-ne, krygsliede), soldier, warrior.
krygsraad, court martial, council of war.
krygsugtig, (-e), bellicose, warlike.
krygs, (ge-), scream, screech; cry; croak.
kryt, (1) chalk; crayon.
kryt, (2) arena.
kubiek, (-e), a. cube, cubic; **–e inhoud**, cubic content; **–e maat**, cubic measure.
kudde, (-s), flock.
kug, (-ge), n. (dry) cough.
kug, (ge-), cough.
kuier, n. visit, call, outing.
kuier, (ge-), call, visit; stroll.
kuiergas, guest.
kuif, (kuiwe), n. tuft, topknot; crest, hood.
kuiken, (-s), chicken; youngster.
kuikendief, Cape kite, harrier.
kuil, (-e), n. hole, pit; pool.
kuil, (ge-), put in pits, ensile.
kuiltjie, (-s), hole; dimple.
kuilvoer, (en)silage, silo(-fodder).
kuip, (-e), n. tub; vat.
kuip, (ge-), cooper; scheme, intrigue.
kuis, (-e), chaste, virtuous, virginal.
kuit, (-e), n. calf (of leg).
kuit, n. roe, spawn (of dish).
kul, (ge-), cheat, deceive.
kultuur, (-ture), culture; cultivation.
kundig, (-e), able, experienced, skilful.
kundigheid, learning, skill; **–hede** (pl.), accomplishments.
kuns, (-te), n. art; knack, trick, feat.
kunsleer, imitation-leather, leatherette.
kunsmatig, (-e), artificial.
kunsmis, artificial manure, fertilizer.
kunsrubber, synthetic rubber.
kunssinnig, (-e), artistic, art-loving.

kunsskilder, artist, painter.
kunstenaar, (-nare, -s), artist.
kunstig, (-e), artful, skilful, clever; artistic.
kurang, vide **kierang.**
kurator, (-e, -s), curator, custodian.
kurk, (-e), n. cork.
kurk, (ge-), cork, close (a bottle).
kurkdroog, (-droë), bone-dry.
kurk(e)trekker, cork-screw.
kurper, karper, (-s), carp.
kursief, (-iewe), in italics, italicized.
kursus, (-se), course, curriculum.
kurwe, (-s), curve, graph.
kus, (-se), n. (1) kiss.
kus, (-te), n. (2) coast, shore.
kus, n. (3): **te – en te keur**, in plenty, of a wide choice.
kus, (ge-), kiss.
kussing, (-s), cushion; pillow (of bed).
kussingband, balloon-tyre.
kussingsloop, pillow-case, pillow-slip.
kuur, (kure), cure; caprice, whim.
kwaad, n. evil, wrong, harm, mischief; injury, damage.
kwaad, a. & adv. angry, cross, vexed.
kwaadaardig, (-e), malicious, vicious; malignant, virulent (disease).
kwaaddoener, (-s), evil-doer; rascal, imp.
kwaadgeld: vir – rondloop, loaf about.
kwaadskiks, unwillingly.
kwaadspreker, -spreekster, scandalmonger, back-biter.
kwaadstoker, -stookster, mischief-maker.
kwaadwillig, (-e), malevolent, ill-disposed.
kwaai, bad-tempered, ill-natured, vicious; harsh, strict.
kwaaivri(e)nde, bad friends.
kwaak, (ge-), croak; quack.
kwaal, (kwale), ailment, disease.
kwadraatwortel, square root.
kwagga, (-s), quagga.
kwajong, (-ens), rascal, mischievous boy.
kwaksalwer, (-s), quack, charlatan.
kwal, (-le), jelly-fish.
kwalik, hardly, scarcely; **– neem**, take amiss (ill), resent.
kwaliteit, (-e), quality; capacity.
kwansel, (ge-), haggle, barter.
kwansuis, vide **konsuis.**
kwantiteit, (-e), quantity, amount.
kwarantyn, quarantine.
kwart, (-e), quarter; quart; crotchet.
kwartaal, (-tale), quarter; (school-)term.
kwartel, (-s), quail.
kwartier, (-e), quarter of an hour, quarter (of moon); (military) quarters, billet.
kwarts, quartz.
kwas, (-te), brush; tuft; tassel (ornament); knot (in wood), node.
kweek, n. couch-, quick-grass.
kweek, (ge-), cultivate (plants); foster (goodwill).
kweekgras, vide **kweek, n.**
kweekplaas, -plek, nursery; hotbed.
kweekskool, training-school (-college), (theological) seminary.
kweel, (ge-), carol, warble.
kweker, (-s), grower; breeder; nurseryman.
kwekery, (-e), nursery.
kwel, (ge-), torment, annoy, worry; tease.
kweper, (-s), quince.
kwes, (ge-), wound (an animal).
kwets, (ge-), grieve, offend; hurt (feelings).
kwesbaar, (-bare), vulnerable.
kwessie, (-s), matter, question; issue; quarrel.

kwetsend, (-e), offensive, outrageous.
kwetsuur, (-sure), hurt, injury, wound.
kwetter, (ge-), chirp, twitter.
kwik, mercury, quicksilver.
kwikstertjie, (-s), wagtail.
kwinkeleer, (ge-), twitter, warble.
kwinkslag, joke, quip, witticism.
kwispel, (ge-), wag the tail.
kwistig, (-e), lavish, liberal, prodigal.
kwitansie, (-s), receipt.
kwyl, n. drivel, slaver.
kwyl, (ge-), drivel, slaver.

kwyn, (ge-), languish; wither (plants); flag (interest); fall into decline.
kwyt, adv.: – **raak**, lose, get rid of.
kwyt, (ge-): **jou – van . . .,** acquit oneself of (a task).
kwytskel(d), (kwytge-), forgive (sins), let (someone) off; remit (taxes).
kyf, (ge-), dispute, quarrel, wrangle.
kyfagtig, (-e), quarrelsome.
kyk, n. aspect, look; view.
kyk, (ge-), look, see, view.
kyker, (-s), spectator; eye, pupil; telescope.

laaf, lawe, (ge-), refresh; try to restore consciousness.
laafnis, refreshment, relief.
laag, (lae), n. layer; bed, stratum (geology);
coat(ing) (of paint); course (of bricks).
laag, (lae), a. & adv. low, base, infamous, mean,
vile (creature), foul.
laaggety, ebb.
laaghartig, (-e), base, mean, vile.
laagte, leegte, (-s), valley, dip.
laagwater, low tide.
laai, n. (1) **in ligte –(e),** ablaze, in a blaze.
laai, (-e), n. (2) drawer; till; stock (of gun).
laai, (-e), n. (3) custom, habit, trick, dodge.
laai, (ge-), load, charge.
laaikas, chest of drawers; box (mining).
laaistok, ramrod.
laak, (ge-), blame, find fault with.
laakbaar, (-bare), reprehensible.
laan, (lane), avenue.
laars, (-e), boot.
laas, last.
laasgemelde, -genoemde, latter, last-named.
laaslede, last.
laaste, n. last one.
laaste, a. & adv. last; latest (reports).
laastelik, finally, lastly.
laat, (–, late), a. late.
laat, adv. late.
laat, (ge-), let; leave; allow, permit, let; stop;
refrain from (doing); make (person do a
thing); have (something) done.
laboratorium, (-s, -ria), laboratory, "lab."
lading, (-e, -s), load; cargo; charge.
laer, (-s), n. camp, lager.
laer, a. lower; primary (education).
laer, (ge-), lager, go into camp.
laerskool, laer skool, primary school.
laf, (lawwe), silly; insipid; cowardly.
lafaard, (-s), coward.
lafhartig, (-e), cowardly.
lag, n. laugh, laughter.
lag, (ge-), laugh.
lag-lag, laughingly; easily.
lagune, (-s), lagoon.
lagwekkend, (-e), laughable; ludicrous.
lak, n. sealing-wax; lac, lacquer (varnish).
lak, (ge-), 1. seal (letter); lacquer, japan.
lak, (ge-), 2. tackle, bring down hard.
lakei, (-e), lackey, footman.
laken, (-s), cloth; sheet (for bed).
lakense, cloth; **– pak,** cloth-suit.
lakleer, patent leather.
laks, (–, -e), lax, slack.
laksman, executioner; butcher-bird.
lakune, (-s), gap, blank.
lam, (-mers), n. lamb.
lam, a. paralysed; tired, weary, fatigued.
lam, (ge-), lamb.
lama, (-s), (1) lama (priest).
lama, (-s), (2) l(l)ama (animal).
lamlendig, (-e), miserable.
lammervanger, martial eagle.
lamp, (-e), lamp; valve (wireless).
lampetbeker, -kan, toilet-jug.
lamsak, (-ke), spunkless fellow, slacker.
lamsalig, (-e), miserable.
lamsiekte, "lamsiekte".
lamslaan, (lamge-), paralyse; render helpless.
lamvleis, lamb.
land, (-e), n. land; field; country; shore.
land, (ge-), land; disembark.
landbou, agriculture.
landboukunde, agriculture, agricultural science.
landdros, (-te), "landdros"; magistrate.

landelik, (-e), rural; country . . .; rustic.
landengte, isthmus.
landerye, cultivated fields (lands).
landgoed, (-ere), country-estate.
landkaart, map.
landman, farmer.
landmeter, (land-)surveyor.
landskap, (-pe), landscape.
landskas, (national) treasury.
landsman, (-ne, landsliede, -lui), country-man.
landstreek, region, district.
landverhuiser, emigrant.
lanfer, crêpe (crape).
lang (attrib.), **lank** (pred.), long; tall (person).
langasemsprinkaan, cricket.
langdradig, (-e), tedious, long-winded.
langdurig, (-e), long (illness); long-standing,
protracted.
lang(e)s, vide **langs.**
langgerek, (-te), long-drawn out.
langoog: **– wees,** be jealous (yellow-eyed).
langoor, long-ears; donkey.
langs, nest (to), beside; alongside of; along.
langsaam, (-same), a. slow, tardy, lingering.
langsaam, adv. slow(ly).
langsaam, next (door) to.
langsamerhand, gradually, by degrees.
langslewende, (-s), survivor.
langwa, long wag(g)on, perch-pole.
langwerpig, (-e), oblong.
laning, (-s), hedge.
lank, lang, long; a long time.
lankal, long, long ago.
lankmoedig, (-e), long-suffering, patient.
lank-uit, at full length.
lans, (-e), lance.
lanseer, (ge-), launch.
lanterfanter, (-s), idler, loiterer, loafer.
lantern, (-s), lantern.
lap, (-pe), n. rag; cloth (for wiping, rubbing);
patch; piece; remnant (of material); bandage
(round finger).
lap, (ge-), patch; mend; patch up.
lapel, (-le), lapel.
Lap(lander), Lapp, Laplander.
lappiesmous, ragman, pedlar.
larwe, (-s), larva, grub.
las, (-se), n. (1) weld, seam joint.
las, (-te), n. (2) burden, load; nuisance, trouble;
command, order.
las, (ge-), weld, join (together).
las, (ge-), instruct; vide **gelas.**
lasarus, leprosy.
lasbrief, warrant, order, writ.
lasdier, beast of burden.
laserstraal, laser beam.
laspos, (-te), nuisance, plague, bore.
laster, n. slander, calumny; libel.
laster, (ge-), slander; blaspheme.
lasterlik, (-e), slanderous, libellous; blasphemous
(against God).
lastig, (-e), difficult, awkward; trying, delicate
(question); troublesome; inconvenient.
lat, (-te), cane, stick; lath (support).
latei, (-e), lintel.
later, adv. later; later on, afterwards.
Latyn, Latin.
laventel, lavender.
lawa, lava.
lawaai, n. noise, din, uproar, row, tumult.
lawaai, (ge-), make a noise, kick up a row.
lawaaiwater, booze, spirits.
lawine, (-s), avalanche, snowslide.
lawwigheid, silliness, foolishness.
lê, leg, (ge-), put, place, lay; lie.

lede, a.: **met – oë,** regretful.
ledekant, bedstead.
ledemate, limbs.
ledig, (-e), a. idle.
ledig, (ge-), empty.
leed, harm; sorrow, grief, pain.
leedvermaak, malicious joy.
leedwese, regret.
leef, lewe, (ge-), live.
leeftog, subsistence; provisions.
leefwyse, way (manner) of living.
leeg, (leë), a. empty; vacant (seat, house).
leegdrink, (leegge-), drain, empty (one's glass).
leeghoofdig, (-e), empty-headed.
leegloop, (leegge-), run dry; become deflated (of tyre); idle, loaf.
leegloper, loafer, idler.
leegmaak, (leegge-), empty; clear (table).
leegsit, (leegge-), sit idle.
leek, (leke), layman.
leem, loam, clay.
leemte, (-s), gap, blank, lacuna; void.
leen, (ge-), borrow (from); lend (to).
leepoë, blear eyes.
leer, n. (1) leather.
leer, (lere), n. (2) ladder.
leer, n. (3) apprenticeship; doctrine; theory; teaching (of Christ).
leer, (ge-), teach (children); learn (language).
leër, (-s), n. army; host, multitude.
lêer, (-s), layer (hen); leaguer (for wine); sleeper (railway); file; register.
leergang, course of study.
leergierig, (-e), eager to learn, studious.
leerjonge, (-ns), apprentice.
leerling, (-e), pupil; disciple.
leerlooiery, tannery; tanning.
leermeester, teacher, tutor.
leerplan, syllabus, curriculum.
leersaam, (-same), instructive; docile.
leërskaar, host.
leerstelling, (-e, -s), dogma, doctrine, tenet.
lees, (-te), n. last, boot-tree; waist.
lees, (ge-), read.
leesbaar, (-bare), readable (book); legible (handwriting).
leesteken, punctuation-mark.
leeu, (-e, -s), lion.
leeubekkie, snap-dragon.
leeutemmer, lion-tamer.
leg, vide lê, (ge-).
legende, (-s), legend.
lei, (-e), n. slate.
lei, (ge-), lead, conduct, direct, guide.
leidak, slate-roof.
leidam, irrigation-dam.
leiding, lead; leadership, guidance, management; line; piping; (take the) lead.
leidraad, guiding line; guide, key, clue.
leidsman, leader, guide.
leier, (-s), leader; guide.
leiklip, slate.
leisel, (-s), rein.
lek, (-ke), n. leak(age); puncture (tyre).
lek, (ge-), (1) leak, be leaky.
lek, (ge-), (2) lick.
lekkasie, (-s), leak(age).
lekker, (-s), n. sweet.
lekker, a. & adv. nice, sweet, delicious; fine; tight, tipsy.
lekkerbekkig, (-e), sweet-toothed, fasticious.
lekkergoed, sweets, sweetmeats.
lekkerlyf, mellow, squiffy.
lekkerny, (-e), delicacy, dainty.
lektor, (-e, -s), lecturer.

lektuur, reading-matter; literature; reading.
lelie, (-s), lily.
lelieblank, (–, -e), lily-white.
lelik, n. ugly(-face).
lelik, (-e), a. ugly, nasty (fall); bad (language).
lelik, adv. nasty, badly.
lelikerd, (-s), ugly person, scarecrow, sight.
lem, (-me), blade.
lemmetjie, (-s), lime; vide **lem.**
lemoen, (-e), orange.
lende, (-s, -ne), loin.
lendedoek, loin-cloth.
lendelam, ramshackle; shaky, tottering.
lengte, (-s), length; longitude (geogr.): height (of person).
lengtegraad, degree of longitude.
lening, (-e), a. lithe, supple.
lenig, (ge-), alleviate (pain), relieve.
lening, (-e, -s), loan.
lens, (-e), lens.
lensie, (-s), lentil.
lente, (-s), spring.
lepel, (-s), spoon; ladle.
lêplek, place (room) to lie down; den.
leraar, (-s, lerare), minister; teacher.
lering, (-e), instruction.
les, (-se), n. lesson; lecture.
les, last; – bes, last but not least.
les, (ge-), quench (thirst), slake.
lesenswaard(ig), (-e), worth reading, readable.
lesing, (-e, -s), reading; lecture; version.
lessenaar, (-s), desk; writing-desk.
Let, (-te), Lett.
let, (ge-), mind.
Letlands, (-e), Latvian, Lettish.
letsel, (-s), injury; damage, harm.
letter, (-s), n. letter, character; type.
letter, (ge-), mark, letter.
letterdief, plagiarist.
lettergreep, syllable.
letterkunde, literature.
letterkundig, (-e), literary.
letterlik, (-e), a. literal (translation).
letterlik, adv. literally; to the letter.
Letties, Lets, (-e), Lettish, Latvian.
leuen, (-s), lie, untruth, falsehood.
leucnaar, (-s), liar.
leun, (ge-), lean.
leuning, (-s), back (of chair); rail(ing): support: banisters (stair-case); balustrade.
leuningstoel, easy chair, armchair.
leus, (-e), **leuse,** (-s), motto, device; slogan.
lewe, (-ns), n. life; quick.
lewendig, (-e), a. living, live (animals); lively (description); active; frisky (horse); bright (eyes); brisk (trade); keen (discussion).
lewendigdood, more dead than alive.
lewensbeskrywing, biography.
lewensgevaarlik, (-e), perilous.
lewenskets, biographical sketch.
lewenslang, (-e), -lank, lifelong, for life.
lewensloop, career.
lewensloos, leweloos, (-lose), lifeless; inanimate (nature).
lewenslustig, (-e), full of life, vivacious.
lewer, n. liver.
lewer, (ge-), furnish, supply; deliver; do (good work); furnish (proof).
leweransie, supply.
leweransier, (-s), furnisher, supplier; purveyor; caterer.
lewerik, leeurik, (-e), lark.
lewertraan, cod-liver oil.
liasseer, (ge-), file.
liberaal, (-ale), liberal, broadminded.

lid, (lede), limb (of body); member (of society); lid (of eye).
liddoring, corn.
lidmaat, (-mate), member (of church).
lidwoord, article.
lie(g), (ge-), lie, tell lies.
lied, (-ere), song, hymn.
liederlik, (-e), dirty, filthy; obscene.
lief, n. – en leed, the bitter and the sweet.
lief, (liewe), a. dear, sweet, kind, charming.
lief, adv. sweetly, nicely.
liefdadig, (-e), charitable, benevolent.
liefde, love.
liefdegawe, -gif, charity, alms.
liefderyk, (-e), loving, affectionate, kind.
liefdevol, (-le), full of love, loving.
liefhê, (liefgehad), love.
liefhebbend, (-e), loving, affectionate.
liefhebber, (-s), n. lover; enthusiast.
liefhebbery, (-e), hobby, fad.
liefie, (-s), darling, love; sweetheart; mistress.
liefkoos, (ge-), caress, fondle.
liefkry, (liefge-), grow fond of; fall in love with.
lieflik, (-e), lovely.
liefling, (-e), darling; favourite.
liefs, rather.
liefste, (-s), n. sweetheart, beloved; darling.
lieftallig, (-e), sweet, lovable, amiable.
lieg, vide **lie(g).**
liemaak, (liege-), fool, tease; sidestep, give (person) the dummy.
lier, (-e), lyre.
lies, (-e, -te), groin.
liewer(s), liewerste(r), rather; preferably.
liewerlee: van –, gradually.
lig, (-te), n. light.
lig, (-te), a. light; bright; blond, fair; slight, mild.
lig, adv. lightly; easily.
lig, (ge-), (1) lift, raise; weigh (anchor); clear (letter-box).
lig, (ge-), (2) give light; dawn; lighten.
liga, (-s), league.
ligdag, daylight.
liggaam, (-game), body; **vaste –,** solid.
liggaamlik, (-e), bodily; corporal (punishment); material; physical (training).
liggelowig, (-e), credulous; gullible.
liggeraak, (-te), touchy, over-sensitive.
liggewend, (-e), luminous, luminescent.
ligging, (-e, -s), situation; site; lie.
ligsinnig, (-e), frivolous, flippant.
ligtelaai(e): in –, in a blaze, ablaze.
ligter, (-s), lift.
likeur, (-e, -s), liqueur.
likkewaan, (-wane), iguana (leguan).
liksens, (-e), vide **lisensie.**
likwideer, (ge-), liquidate, wind up.
lila, lilac.
limf, lymph.
limonade, lemonade.
linde(boom), linden-tree, lime.
liniaal, (-iale), ruler.
linie, (-s), line; equator.
linieer, (ge-), rule.
linker, left; near (fore-leg, wheel).
linkerkant, left (side).
links, a. left-handed.
links, adv. to (on) the left.
linne, linen; cloth (binding of book).
linnekas, linen-press.
lint, (-e), ribbon; tape.
lintwurm, tape-worm.
lip, (-pe), lip.
lipstif, lipstick.

liriek, lyric, poetry, lyrics.
liries, (-e), lyric(al).
lis, (-te), (1) trick, ruse, device.
lis, lus, (-se), (2) noose; loop; tag.
lisensie, (-s), liksens, (-e), licence.
lisensieer, (ge-), license.
lispel, (ge-), lisp.
listig, (-e), cunny, wily, crafty, artful.
lit, (-te), joint; articulation.
Litauer, (-s), Lithuanian.
liter, (-s), litre.
literatuur, literature.
literêr, (-e), literary.
litteken, scar, cicatrice (cicatrix).
livrei, (-e), livery.
lob, (-be), lobe.
loef: die – afsteek, take the wind out of a person's sails.
loei, (-ge), low; roar.
loën, logen, (ge-), deny.
loënstraf, logenstraf, (ge-), belie, give the lie to.
loer, n.: op die – lê, lie in wait.
loer, (ge-), peep, peer; pry; lurk, watch.
loerie, (-s), lory (lourie).
loesing, (-s), hiding, thrashing, spanking.
lof, n. praise, commendation.
lof, (lowwe), n. leaves, foliage, leafage.
loflied, song (hymn, psalm of praise).
lofwaardig, (-e), laudable, praiseworthy.
log, (–, -ge), clumsy, unwieldy.
logen, vide **loën.**
logies, (-e), a. logical.
lojaal, (-jale), loyal.
lok, (-ke), n. lock, curl.
lok, (ge-), entice, lure, decoy.
lokaal, (-kale), n. room.
lokaas, bait, lure, decoy.
lokasie, (-s), location.
loket, (-te), pigeon-hole; box-office window, ticket-window; booking-office.
lokmiddel, bait, inducement, lure.
lokomotief, (-tiewe), locomotive, engine.
lokstem, lure, siren-voice, call.
lokvink, decoy, police-trap.
lokvoël, decoy(-bird).
lol, (ge-), be troublesome; nag.
lollery, nagging; nuisance, bother.
lolpot, nuisance, bore.
lomerig, (-e), drowsy, sleepy; languid.
lommer, foliage; shade.
lommerd, (-s), pawnbroker's shop.
lomp, (–, -e), a. clumsy, awkward.
lomperd, (-s), bumpkin, clodhopper, lout.
Londenaar, (-nare, -s), Londoner.
long, (-e), lung.
longontsteking, pneumonia.
lonk, (ge-), wink; give the glad eye.
lont, (-e), fuse; – **ruik,** smell a rat.
lood, n. lead; plumb-line; plummet.
loodgieter, plumber.
loodlyn, perpendicular, plumb-line.
loodreg, (-te), perpendicular, vertical.
loods, (-e), n. (1) pilot (of ship).
loods, (-e), n. (2) shed; hangar.
loods, (ge-), pilot (ship); direct, conduct.
loodsekering, lead-fuse, -plug.
loodswaar, leaden, like lead.
loof, n. foliage, leaves, leafage.
loof, lowe, (ge-), praise, glorify, extol.
loog, n. lye, lixivium, buck.
looi, n. tan.
looi, (ge-), tan; leather, thrash.
looiery, tanning; tannery; tanner's trade.
loom, (lome), drowsy; languid; heavy, dull.

loon, (lone), n. wages, salary, pay; reward.
loon, (ge-), reward, pay.
loontjie: boontjie kry sy –, it serves you right.
loontrekker, wage-earner.
loop, n. walking; walk, gait; running (of machine); course (of events); (pl.: lope), barrel (of gun); spruit, stream; course (of river).
loop, (ge-), walk; go; run.
loopbaan, career; orbit (of planet); track.
loopgraaf, trench.
loopplank, running-board; footboard; gangway.
loopplek, place for walking; pasturage; haunt, feeding-place.
loopprater, walkie-talkie.
loot, (lote), n. shoot, sucker; offspring.
loot, (ge-), draw lots, raffle (for); toss.
lootjie, (-s), (lottery-)ticket.
loper, (-s), walker; messenger; (carpet-) runner; master-key; bishop (chess); (pl.) buckshot, slugs.
lorrie, (-s), lorry.
los, (-, -se), a. loose; extra, spare (copy); undone, unfastened; detached, detachable; wanton; free (person).
los, adv. loosely.
los, (ge-), fire (shot); redeem (pledge); claim (goods); ransom (prisoner); release; let go.
losbandig, (-e), fast, dissipated, profligate.
losbars, (losge-), tear; burst out, explode, let fly; break (out); open fire.
losbrand, (losge-), open fire, let fly, launch out.
loseer, (ge-), board, put up, lodge.
losgoed, movable property; loose stuff.
loshand(e), with hands free.
losie, (-s), lodge; box (in theatre).
losies, board and lodging; accommodation.
losieshuis, -plek, boarding-house.
losknoop, (losge-), unbutton; untie, undo.
loskom, (losge-), get loose (away); get free (off); be released (discharged).
loskruit: met – skiet, fire with blanks.
loslippig, (-e), flippant, loose-tongued.
losloop, (losge-), be at large; run free (loose); idle; free-wheel.
loslopie, bye (cricket).
lospitperske, free-stone peach.
losprys, ransom.
losskakel, fly-half, stand-off half (rugby).
losslaan, (losge-), knock loose; earn (money).
losspeler, loose (wing) forward.
lossteek, (losge-), dig loose; let fly (at), lash out, go for, belabour.
lostrek, (losge-), pull (tear) loose; let out (fly).
lot, fate, destiny; lot.
lot, (-e), lottery-ticket; vide lootjie.
lotery, (-e), lottery; raffle; gamble.
lotgevalle, adventures.
lotjie: van – getik wees, have a screw loose.
lou, lukewarm (lit. & fig.), tepid.
louere, laurels.
louter, a. & adv. pure, sheer.
louter, (ge-), purify, refine, try, test.
lower, foliage.
lowergroen, bright (fresh, vivid) green.
lug, (-te), n. sky; air; atmosphere; scent, smell.
lug, (ge-), air, ventilate; vent.
lugband, pneumatic tyre.
lugdig, (-te), airtight.
lugdraad, aerial, antenna; overhead wire.
lughartig, (-e), light-hearted, happy-go-lucky.
lughawe, air-port.
lughou, lob (tennis); 'n – slaan, lob.
lugkasteel, castle in the air.
lugledig, n. vacuum.
lugmag, air-force.

lugpyp, windpipe, trachea.
lugreëling, air-conditioning.
lugruim, atmosphere, space.
lugspieëling, -spiegeling, mirage.
lugtig, (-e), a. airy; light-hearted; nervous; cautious; funky.
lugvaart, aviation, air-navigation.
lugwaardin, air hostess.
lui, a. lazy, indolent, slothful.
lui, (ge-), ring (bell), sound, peal; toll.
luiaard, (-s), lazy person; sloth (animal).
luid, (-e), loud.
luidens, according to.
luidkeels, at the top of one's voice.
luidrugtig, (-e), noisy, boisterous.
luidspreker, loudspeaker.
luier, (-s), n. (baby's) napkin; diaper.
luier, (ge-), loaf, laze, idle.
luik, (-e), n. shutter; hatch, trap-door.
luilak, (-ke), n. sluggard, lazybones, idler.
luim, (-e), mood, humour; whim.
luimig, (-e), humorous, witty.
luiperd, (-s), leopard, panther.
luis, (-e), louse.
luiskoors, typhus (fever).
luislang, python.
luister, n. splendour, lustre.
luister, (ge-), listen.
luisteraar, (-s), listener; eavesdropper.
luisterryk, (-e), splendid, brilliant.
luistervink, eavesdropper.
luitenant, (-e), lieutenant.
luiters, luters, leuters, innocent, unaware.
lukraak, (-rake), a. wild, random.
lukraak, adv. at random, haphazard.
lukwart, (-e), loquat.
lumier, n. break of day, dawn.
lumier, (ge-), break (of day), dawn.
lummel, (-s), n. gawk, simpleton, booby.
luns, (-e), lunspen, n. linch-pin, axle-pin.
lunsriem, axle-pin strap; dirty rascal.
lus, (-te), n. (1) desire, appetite; liking, inclination; lust, passion; delight, joy, pleasure, threat.
lus, (2) vide lis, (2).
lus, (ge-), like, feel like, feel inclined (for).
lusern, lucerne.
lus(t)hof, pleasure-garden.
lusteloos, (-lose), listless, languid, dull.
lustig, (-e), cheerful, merry, gay.
luters, leuters, vide luiters.
Luthers, (-e), Lutheran.
luttel, (-e), little.
luukse, luxury.
ly, (ge-), suffer; bear, endure.
lydelik, (-e), passive.
lydend, (-e), suffering; passive (voice).
lyding, (-e), suffering.
lydsaam, (-same), meek, patient.
lyf, (lywe), body; figure.
lyfband, belt, waist-band.
lyfie, (-s), little body; bodice.
lyfstraf, corporal punishment.
lyfwag, body-guard, life-guard.
lyk, (-e), n. corpse, dead body.
lyk, (ge-), look, seem, appear.
lykhuis, mortuary, morgue.
lykrede, funeral service (oration).
lykskouing, post-mortem (examination), autopsy; geregtelike –, inquest.
lykwa, hearse.
lym, n. glue; gum; bird-lime.
lym, (ge-), glue.
lyn, (-e), line; string, rope, cord.

lyn, (ge-), rule; line.
lynboot, liner.
lynolie, linseed-oil.
lynreg, perpendicular, straight.
lynsaad, linseed.
lynstaan, n. line-out (rugby).

lynstaan, (lynge-), line out; line up.
lys, (-te), n. list, register; cornice, moulding; skirting-board; frame (of picture); ledge; (picture-) rail.
lys, (ge-), frame.
lywig, (-e), corpulent; bulky, voluminous.

ma, (-'s), mother, mummy, mam(m)a.
maag, (mae, mage), stomach.
maag, (-de), vide maagd.
maag(d), (maagde), maid(en), virgin.
maagdelik, (-e), maidenly, virginal.
maagkoors, gastric fever.
maai, n. (loop na) jou –, go to blazes.
maai, (ge-), cut, mow, reap.
maaier, (-s), (1) mower, reaper.
maaier, (-s), (2) maggot.
maaifoedie, -foerie, (-s), scoundrel, blackguard.
maaimasjien, mowing-machine, harvester.
maak, (ge-), make; do.
maal, (male), n. (1) time.
maal, (male), n. (2) meal.
maal, (ge-), (1) grind, mill; pulverise.
maal, (ge-), (2) multiply.
maalklip, grinding-stone.
maalstroom, maelstrom, whirlpool.
maaltyd, meal, repast.
maan, (mane), n. moon.
maan, (ge-), warn, dun (for money).
maand, (-e), month.
Maandag, Monday.
maandblad, monthly (publication)
maandelang, (-e), a. 'n –e siekbed, an illness lasting months.
maandeliks, (-e), a. & adv. monthly, once a month, every month.
maanhaar, mane; central ridge (in farm-track).
maanhaarjakkals, maned jackal, aardwolf.
maar, but, yet, merely, only just.
maarskalk, (-e), n. marshal.
Maart, n. March.
maas, (mase), n. mesh, stitch.
maat, (mate), (1) measure, size, gauge; time, bar (music); measure, metre (poetry).
maat, (-s, maters), (2) mate, companion, partner.
maatband, tape-measure, measuring-tape.
maatloos, (-lose): maatlose verse, free verse.
maatreël, measure, precaution.
maatskaplik, (-e), social; joint (stock).
maatskappy, (-e), n. company; society.
maatstaf, measure, scale; standard, criterium.
maatstok, yard-stick; rule; (conductor's) baton.
Macedonies, (-e), Macedonian.
madam, (-s, -me), n. lady.
madeliefie, (-s), daisy.
maer, lean, thin; (fig.) meagre, poor.
maermerrie, shin.
mag, (-te), n. power, might, force, strength; control; authority.
mag, (praet.: mog), may, be allowed (permitted).
magasyn, (-e), n. store, warehouse; magazine.
magbrief, warrant, power of attorney.
magdom, lot(s), heap(s), crowd(s).
maghebber, (-s), authority, ruler.
magies, (-e), magic(al).
magistraat, (-ate), magistrate.
Magjaar, (-are), Magyar.
magnaat, (-ate), magnate, grandee.
magneet, (-ete), magnet, lodestone.
magneties, (-e), magnetic.
magteloos, (-lose), powerless, impotent.
magtig, (-e), powerful, mighty, potent.
magtig!, (interj.), Heavens!, Great Scott!.
magtig, (ge-), authorise, warrant, empower.
mahoniehout, mahogany.
majesteit, (-e), majesty.
majestueus, (-e), majestic.
majoor, (-s, -ore), major.
mak, (–, -ke), tame, docile, manageable, tractable.
makeer, (ge-), ail; lack, be wanting.

makelaar, (-lare, -s), broker.
maklik, (-e), easy, comfortable.
makou, (-e), muscovy duck.
makriel, (-e), Cape mackerel.
maksimum, (-s, -ima), maximum.
mal, (–, -le), mad, foolish, silly.
malariastreek, malarial region.
Maleier, (-s), Malay.
Maleis, (-e), Malay.
malkop, silly person, rattle-brain; tomboy.
mallemeule, merry-go-round.
malligheid, silliness; tomfoolery; nonsense.
malmokkie, marmotjie, (-s), guinea-pig.
mals, (-e), lush (grass), tender (meat).
maltrap, vide malkop.
malva, (-s), geranium, mallow.
mamba, (-s), mamba(-snake).
mammoet, (-e), mammoth.
man, (-ne, -s), man; husband.
mandaat, (-date), mandate.
mandaryn, (-e), mandarin.
mandjie, (-s), basket, hamper.
mandoor, (-dore, -s), foreman, mandoor.
manel, (-le), frock-coat.
maneskyn, moonlight, moonshine.
maneuvreer, (ge-), manoeuvre.
manewale(s), antics, capers.
mangaan, manganese.
mangat, man-hole
mangel, (-s), n. (1) tonsil.
mangel, (-s), (2) mangle, mangling-board.
mangelwortel, mangel(wurzel), mangold.
manhaftig, (-e), brave, manly; cheeky.
manie, (-ë, -s), craze, fad, mania, rage.
manier, (-e), fashion, manner, way.
manierlik, (-e), polite, well-mannered.
maniertjie, (-s), mannerism.
manifes, (-te), manfest(o).
manjifiek, (-e), magnificent.
mank, (-e), crippled, lame, limping.
mankoliek(ig), (-e), crocked, ill, seedy.
manlik, (-e), manly; masculine; male.
manmoedig, (-e), bold, brave, manly.
mannetjie, (-s), male; chappie, little fellow.
mans: hy is – genoeg om . . ., he is man enough to.
manskap, (-pe), crew; (pl.) men.
manslag, homicide, manslaughter.
mansmens, -persoon, male (person), man.
mantel, (-s), cloak, mantle; cape; casing, jacket, shell; fire-screen.
manteldraaier, turn-coat, weathercock.
manuskrip, (-te), manuscript.
mapstieks!, by Jove! my goodness!
maraboe, (-s), marabou.
margriet(jie), (-s), daisy, marguerite.
marine, navy.
marionet, (-te), marionette, puppet.
mark, (-e, -te), n. market.
markant, (-e), conspicuous, salient.
markeer, (ge-), mark; die pas –, mark time.
marmelade, marmalade.
marmer, n. marble.
marmot(jie), vide malmokkie.
Marokkaans, (-e), Moroccan.
Marokko, Morocco.
mars, (-e), march.
Mars, Mars.
Marseille, Marseilles.
marsjeer, (ge-), march.
marskramer, (-s), hawker, pedlar.
martel, (-e), rack, torture; torment.
martelaar, (-are, -s), martyr.
marteling, torture.
Marxisme, Marxism.
mas, (-te), mast; pole (gymnastics).

Masbieker, (-s), Mozambiquer.
masels, measles.
masjien, (-e), machine; engine.
masjinaal, (-ale), a. & adv. mechanical(ly); automatical(ly).
masjinerie, machinery.
masjinis, (-te), engineer (on ship), engine-driver (on train); scene-shifter.
masker, (-s), n. mask; disguise.
masker, (ge-), mask, veil.
massa, (-s), crowd, mass; lot, lump.
massaal, (-ale), wholesale.
masseer, (ge-), massage.
massief, (-iewe), massive, solid.
mastig!, gracious!
masurka, (-s), mazurka.
mat, (-te), n. mat, door-mat, floormat, bottom (of chair).
mat, (-te), a. languid, tired, weary; dead, dull (of gold); lustreless; dim; checkmate.
mate, degree, measure.
mateloos, (-lose), excessive, measureless.
materiaal, (-iale), material(s).
materie, matter.
materieel, (-iële), a. & adv. material(ly).
maters: sy – is dood, he has no equal.
matesis, mathematics.
matig, (-e), a. moderate; abstemious, sober, temperate.
matig, (ge-), moderate, modify, restrain (one's anger).
matinee, (-s), matinee.
matjiesgoed, n. bulrush.
matras, (-se), mattress.
matriek(eksamen), matric(ulation) (-examination).
matrikuleer, (ge-), matriculate.
matrone, (-s), matron.
matroos, (-ose), sailor.
matrys, (-e), matrix; mould.
Mattheüs, Matthew.
mauser, (-s), mauser.
mebos, mebos, dried and sugared apricots.
medalje, (-s), medal.
medaljon, (-s), medallion
Mede, Medes.
mede- . . ., co-, fellow- (in compounds).
mede-, meedeelsaam, (-same), communicative; expansive; liberal.
mede-, meedeling, (-e, -s), an announcement, communication, information.
mededinger, (-s), competitor, rival.
mede-, meedoë, compassion, pity, sympathy.
mededoënd, -dogend, (-e), compassionate, sympathetic.
mede-, meegevoel, fellow-feeling, sympathy.
medeklinker, consonant.
medely(d)e, compassion, pity, sympathy.
medelydend, (-e), compassionate.
medepligtig, (-e), accessary (accessory).
medepligtige, (-s), accomplice.
mede-, meewete, knowledge.
medies, (-e), medical.
medikus, (-se, -dici), medical man, medico, doctor, physician.
medisyne, (-s), medicine.
mediterreens, (-e), mediterranean.
medium, (-dia, -s), medium; means.
mede, partly, to some extent.
meebring, (meege-), bring along, bring with one; entail (delay); involve (danger).
meedeel, (meege-), communicate (news), inform (a person).
meeding, (meege-), compete.

meedoen, (meege-), join (in a game), take part, participate.
meedoënloos, (-lose), merciless.
meegee, (meege-), give, send along with; give way, yield.
meel, meal: **fyn –,** flour.
meelblom, flour.
meelpap, flour-paste; gruel.
meemaak, (meege-), go through, experience; take part in.
meen, (ge-), mean; intend; fancy, suppose, think.
meent, commonage.
meepraat, (meege-), join (take part) in (a conversation); put in a word.
meer, (mere), n. lake.
meer, a. & adv. more.
meerdere, (-s), superior.
meerderheid, majority; superiority.
meerderjarig, (-e), of age.
meerderman: as – kom, moet minderman wyk, honour comes first; the weakest goes to the wall.
meereken, (meege-), count (in), include.
meergegoed, (-e), better-off.
meerkat, mierkat, (-te), meercat.
meermaal, -male, frequently, more than once, often.
meerman, (-ne), merman.
meermin, (-ne), mermaid.
meerskuim, meerschaum.
meertou, mooring-cable.
meervoud, (-e), plural.
mees, adv. most(ly).
meesal, vide **meestal.**
meesleep, (meege-), carry along, drag along; carry (sweep) before it.
meesmuil, (ge-), simper, smirk, sneer.
meestal, meesal, mostly, usually.
meeste, greatest, most.
meestendeels, for the greater (the most) part; in the majority of cases.
meester, (-s), master; teacher.
meesteragtig, (-e), imperious; pedantic.
meesterlik, (-e), excellent, masterly.
meesterstuk, meesterwerk, masterpiece.
meet, n. starting-line, starting-point.
meet, (ge-), measure, gauge.
meetkunde, geometry.
meeu, (-e), (sea-)gull, sea-mew.
meewarig, (-e), compassionate.
meewerk, (meege-), co-operate, collaborate, assist; contribute towards.
meganies, (-e), mechanical.
Mei, May.
meiblom, May-flower.
meidoring, hawthorn, May-bush.
meineed, perjury.
meisie, (-s), girl.
mejuffrou, Madam (address without name), Miss (address with name).
mekaar, each other, one another.
Mekka, Mecca.
melaats, (-e), leprous.
melaatse, (-s), leper.
melaatsheid, leprosy.
melancholies, (-e), melancholy, depressed.
melasse, molasses.
meld(e), (ge-), announce, inform, mention, report, state.
meldenswaardig, (-e), worth mentioning.
melding, mention.
melerig, (-e), mealy, floury.
melk, n. milk.
melk, (ge-), milk.

melkbaard, down, soft beard.
melkery, (-e), milking; dairy-farming; dairy (-farm).
melkkos, milk-food, spoon-meat.
melkwit, milky white, as white as milk.
melodieus, (-e), melodious, tuneful.
melodrama, melodrama.
memorie, (-s), document; petition.
memoriseer, (ge-), memorize.
meneer, (-ere), gentleman; Mr (in address with name), Sir (in address without name); master; mister.
meng, (ge-), alloy (metals); blend (colours); mix (drinks); mingle (with people); adulterate, dilute.
mengelmoes, hodge-podge (hotch-potch), jumble, medley, mixture.
mengsel, (-s), blend; mixture.
menige, many, several.
menigeen, many a one.
menigmaal, frequently, often.
menigte, (-s), crowd, multitude.
menigvuldig, (-e), abundant, manifold.
mening, (-e, -s), idea, opinion, view; intention.
mens, (-e), n. human being, man, person; (pl.) men, people; visitors.
mens, pron. indef. one, you.
mensdom, mankind, humanity.
mensehater, misanthrope.
mensliewend, (-e), humane, philanthropic.
menslik, (-e), human.
menslikerwys(e), - gesproke, humanly speaking.
menslikheid, humanity; human nature.
mensvreter, man-eater, cannibal.
menuet, (-te), minuet.
merendeel, greater part, majority.
merendeels, for the greater (the most) part, mostly.
merg, murg, marrow.
meridiaan, (-iane), meridian.
meriete, merits.
merk, (-e), n. mark; brand (of articles), quality, sort; trademark; sign.
merk, (ge-) mark; notice, perceive, see.
merkbaar, (-bare), appreciable, noticeable, marked, perceptible.
merkteken, mark, scar, sign, token.
merkwaardig, (-e), noteworthy, remarkable.
merrie, (-s), mare.
mes, (-se), knife.
Mesopotamië, Mesopotamia.
messegoed, cutlery.
messel, (ge-), build, lay bricks.
messelaar, (-s), bricklayer, mason.
Messias, Messiah.
messtof, fertilizer, manure.
met, with.
metaal, (-ale), metal.
metaalkunde, metallurgy.
metafoor, (-fore), metaphor.
metamorfose, (-s), metamorphosis.
metdat, at the moment that.
meteen, at the same time.
meteens, (all) at once, suddenly, immediately.
meteoor, (-eore), meteor.
meteoriet, (-e), meteorite.
meteoroloog, (-loë), meteorologist.
meter, (-s), measurer, gauger; meter (of gas); metre (unit of length).
metgesel, (-le), companion, mate.
metode, (-s), method, plan, manner.
metodiek, method.
metodies, (-e), methodical.
Metodis, (-te), Methodist.

metonimie, metonymy.
metropolis, (-se), metropool, (-ole), capital (city), metropolis.
metropolitaans, (-e), metropolitan.
metrum, (-s, -tra), metre.
mette, matins; kort - maak met, make short work of.
mettertyd, in course of time, in due course, as time went on.
metterwoon: jou êrens - vestig, establish oneself (settle) somewhere.
meubel, (-s), article (piece) of furniture; (pl.) furniture.
meubelmaker, cabinet-maker, joiner.
meubelstuk, vide meubel.
meubileer, (ge-), fit up, furnish.
meublement, furniture.
meul, (-e), meule, (-ns), mill; (game of) noughts and crosses.
meulenaar, (-s), miller.
Midde(l)-Afrika, Central Africa.
middelbaar, (-bare), average, intermediate, mean, medium, middle; secondary (school).
middeldeur, across, asunder, in half, in two.
middeleeue, middle ages.
middelerwyl, meanwhile.
Middellandse: - See, Mediteranean (Sea).
middellyn, axis, centre-line, diameter.
middelmannetjie, ridge (in road).
middelmatig, (-e), middling, moderate, indifferent, mediocre, so-so.
middelpunt, centre, central point; hub, pivot.
middelrif, diaphragm, midriff.
middelslag, -soort, middling sort, medium, middlings.
midde(l)weg, middle course; mean; midway.
middernag, midnight.
mied, [-e(ns)], miet, (-e), heap, pile, (hay)stack.
mielie, (-s), maize, mealie.
mier, (-e), ant; -e hê, be fidgety, fidget.
mierhoop, vide miershoop.
mierkat, vide meerkat.
mier(s)hoop, ant-hill.
miet, n. vide mied.
miet, n. mite; tuberworm.
mik, (-ke), n. fork, forked post; forked stick (for catapult).
mik, (ge-), aim.
mika, mica.
mikpunt, aim; butt, target.
mikrofoon, (-fone), microphone.
mikroob, (-krobe), mikrobe, (-s), microbe.
mikroskoop, (-skope), microscope.
mikstok, forked stick.
mikstuur, (-ure), mixture.
Milaan, Milan.
mild, (-e), free-handed, generous, liberal; soft (rain).
milddadig, (-e), generous, liberal.
mildelik, (-e), a. & adv. lavish(ly).
milieu, (-'s), milieu, environment.
militêr, (-e), a. military.
miljoen, (-e), million.
miljoenêr, (-s), millionaire.
milligram, milligram.
millimeter, millimetre.
milt, (-e), milt, spleen.
mimiek, mimic art, mimicry.
min, minne, n. love.
min, a. & adv. few, little; less, minus.
minag, (ge-), disregard, disdain, despise.
minagting, contempt, disdain.
minder, a. & adv. fewer, less; inferior, lower.
mindere, (-s), inferior.
minderheid, minority; inferiority.

minderjarig, (-e), under age.
minderwaardig, (-e), inferior.
mineraal, (-ale), mineral.
miniatuur, (-ure), miniature.
minikopter, minicopter.
minimaal, (-ale), minimal.
minister, (-s), minister.
ministerie, (-s), cabinet, ministry.
minlik, (-e), amicable, friendly.
minnaar, (-s), lover.
minne: in der – skik, settle amicably.
minnebrief, love-letter.
minsaam, (-same), affable, gracious, kind.
minste, fewest, least, slightest, smallest.
minstens, at least, at the least.
mintig!, gracious!, goodness!
minuut, (-ute), minute.
mirakelspel, miracle-play.
mirre, myrrh.
mis, (-se), n. mass.
mis, (-te), n. fog, mist.
mis, n. dung, manure.
mis, a. & adv. amiss, wrong.
mis, (ge-), miss (the train); lose (the boat); spare,
do without (money).
misbruik, (-se), n. abuse, misuse; breach, betrayal (of trust).
misbruik, (het –), abuse, misuse.
misdaad, crime, offence.
misdadiger, (-s), criminal, evildoer.
misdeel(d), (-de), destitute, poor.
misdra, (het –), misbehave.
misdryf, (-drywe), n. offence, crime.
miserabel, (-e), miserable, rotten, wretched.
misgis, (het –), jou –, make a mistake.
misgun, (het –), (be)grudge, envy.
mishae, n. displeasure, annoyance.
mishandel, (het –), ill-treat, maltreat.
miskenning, want of appreciation.
miskien, perhaps.
miskruier, dung-roller, tumble-bug.
mislei (het –), deceive, mislead.
mislik, (-e), beastly, disgusting; bilious.
misluk, (het –), come to naught, fail, miscarry;
fall through; break down.
mismaak, (het –), deform, disfigure.
mismoedig, (-e), discouraged, dejected.
misnoeë, displeasure, dissatisfaction.
misnoeg, (-de), displeased, dissatisfied.
misoes, failure of crops; failure; wash-out.
mispel, (-s), medlar.
misreken, (het –), make a mistake.
misstap, false step, misstep.
mistig, (-e), foggy, misty.
mistroostig, (-e), dejected.
mistrouig, (-e), distrustful, suspicious.
misverstaan, (het –), misunderstand.
misvorm, (het –), vide mismaak.
miswurm, cutworm, caterpillar.
mite, (-s), myth.
mits, provided (that).
mobiel, (-e), mobile.
mobiliseer, (ge-), mobilize.
modaal, (-ale), modal.
modder, mud, ooze, sludge.
modderskerm, mud-guard.
moddervet, as plump as a partridge.
mode(s), fashion, style, vogue.
modegek, dandy, fop.
model, (-le), model, pattern; cut.
modemaakster, -maker, dressmaker.
modepop, doll, fine lady; vide modegek.
moderasie, moderation.
moderator, (-e, -s), moderator.
moderniseer, (ge-), modernize.

modieus, (-e), fashionable, stylish.
modiste, (-s), (up-to-date) dressmaker.
moed, courage, nerve, spirit.
moede: te –, at heart, in spirit.
moedeloos, (-lose), dejected, despondent.
moeder, (-s), mother; dam (of animals).
moederlik, (-e), maternal, motherly.
moedernaak, (-te), -nakend, (-e), stark naked.
moedersielalleen, quite alone.
moederskant: van –, on the mother's side.
moedig, (-e), brave, courageous, plucky.
moedswillig, (-e), n. & adv. petulant(ly), wan-
ton(ly), wilful(ly).
moedverloor, despondency.
moeg, (moeë), fatigued, tired, weary.
moeilik, (-e), a. & adv. difficult, hard.
moeilikheid, difficulty, scrape, trouble.
moeisaam, (-same), fatiguing, tiresome.
moeite, difficulty, trouble; labour, pains.
moeitevol, (-le), difficult, hard, toilsome, wearisome.
moenie!, don't!.
moer, (-e), mother, dam (of animals); dregs,
grounds, lees, sediment (of liquids); nut (on
bolt; seed-potato.
moeras, (-se), marsh, bog, swamp.
moerbei, (-e), mulberry.
moerhamer, (adjusting) spanner.
moersleutel, spanner, screw-wrench.
moesie, (-s), mole; beauty-spot.
moet, (-e), mark, dent, spoor.
moet, (pret.: moes), must, have to, be compelled
(forced, obliged) to; should, ought to.
mof, (mowwe), n. cross-breed.
moffie, (-s), mitten.
mofskaap, merino-sheep, wool-sheep.
Mohammed, Mohammed.
Mohammedaan, (-ane), Mohammedan.
moker, (ge-), hammer, strike, hit; give a thrashing; smash (tennis).
mol, (-le), n. mole.
moles(te), trouble.
molesteer, (ge-), annoy, molest.
mollig, (-e), chubby, plump, soft.
molwa(entjie), trolley, light waggon.
mombakkies, (-e), mask.
momenteel, (-ele), a. & adv. momentary.
mompel, (ge-), mumble, mutter.
monargaal, (-ale), monarchic(al).
monargie, (-ë), monarchy.
mond, (-e), mouth; estuary (of a river), muzzle
(of a gun).
mondelik(s), mondeling(s), (-e), a. & adv. oral(ly),
verbal(ly).
mondering, (-e, -s), equipment.
mondfluitjie, mouth-organ.
mondig, (-e), of (full) age, major.
monding, (-e, -s), mouth, estuary.
mondvol, (mondevol), mouthful.
Mongolië, Mongolia.
Mongool, (-ole), Mongol, Mongolian.
monnik, (-s), friar, monk.
monster, (-s), n. monster; freak.
monsters, (-s), n. sample, pattern.
monster, (ge-), muster (soldiers); (pass in)
review, inspect.
monstervergadering, mass-meeting.
monteer, (ge-), mount, set up, assemble, erect,
fit up, adjust; get up, stage (a play).
Montenegryn, (-e), Montenegrin.
monteur, (-s), assembler.
monteur-draaier, fitter and turner.
monument, (-e), monument.
mooi, a. & adv. beautiful, fine, handsome, nice,
pretty.

mooibroodjies: – bak, curry favour.
mooidoenery, airs and graces, put on.
mooie: jy is 'n –, you are a fine one.
mooipraat, (mooige-), coax; beg; try to persuade.
moois: iets –, something fine.
mooitjies, finely, prettily.
mooiweer: met iemand se goed – speel, play ducks and drakes with a person's things.
moondheid, power.
moontlik, (-e), a. & adv. possible; possibly, perhaps.
Moor, (More), Moor; blackamoor.
moor, (ge-), commit murder, kill, murder; maltreat, overwork.
moord, (-e), murder.
moorddadig, (-e), murderous, cruel.
moordenaar, (-s), murderer.
moordgierig, (-e), bloodthirsty.
moordkuil: van jou hart g'n – maak nie, speak one's mind freely.
moot, (mote), fillet, slice; valley, glen.
mopperig, (-e), disgrunted, grumbling.
mor, (ge-), grumble.
Morawië, Moravia.
môre, more, (-s), morning, morrow, to-morrow.
moreel, n. morale.
moreel, (-ele) a. moral.
môre-, morepraatjies: sy – en sy aandpraatjies kom nie ooreen nie, you cannot rely on his word.
môrestond: die – het goud in die mond, the early bird catches the worm.
mors, (ge-), mess, make a mess; spill (milk), waste (money).
morsaf, clean off, right through.
morsdood, stone-dead, stark-dead.
morsig, (-e), dirty, filthy, grimy.
mortier, (-e, -s), mortar.
mos, (-se), n. moss.
mos, n. must, grape-juice, new wine.
mos, adv. indeed.
mosbeskuit, must-bun (-rusk).
mosbolletjie, (-s), vide **mosbeskuit.**
moses, rival; master, superior.
mosie, (-s), motion, vote.
moskee, (moskeë, -s), mosque.
Moskou, Moscow.
mossel, (-s), mussel.
mossie, (-s), Cape sparrow.
moster(d), mustard.
mot, (-te), moth.
motel, motel.
motief, (-iewe), motive.
motiveer, (ge-), account for, give reasons for, motivate.

motor, (-e), motor; engine.
motor, (-s), motor-car, automobile.
motorkap, bonnet.
motreën, motreent, n. drizzle.
mou, (-e), sleeve.
mout, malt.
moveer, (ge-), attack, vex, bait.
mud, [-de(ns)], muid, bag.
muf, (muwwe), fusty, musty, stuffy.
muggie, (-s), gnat, midge.
muil, (-e), (1) mule; half-caste.
muil, (-e), (2) muzzle, mouth.
muilband, (ge-), gag, muzzle.
muis, (-e), mouse.
muishond, mongoose, weasel, polecat.
muisval, mouse-trap.
muisvoël, coly, mouse-bird.
muit, (ge-), mutiny, rebel, revolt.
mummie, (-s), mummy.
munisipaliteit, (-e), municipality.
munt, (-e), n. coin; money; mint, head.
munt, (ge-), coin, mint.
muntstuk, coin, piece of money.
murasie, (-s), dilapidated wall(s), ruins.
murg, marrow.
murg-van-groente, vegetable-marrow, squash.
murmel, (ge-), murmur; babble.
murmureer, (ge-), grumble, murmur.
mus, (-se), cap, night-cap; bonnet; tea-cosy.
musiek, music.
musikaal, (-ale), musical.
musikant, (-e), musician, player.
musikus, (-se), musician.
muskadel, muscat(el), muscadel.
muske(l)jaatkat, musk-cat, civet-cat.
muskiet, (-e), mosquito.
muur, (mure), wall.
muurkas, (built-in) cupboard.
muurtapyt, hangings, tapestry.
muwwerig, mufferig, (-e), rather musty.
my, pron. pers. me.
my, pron. poss. my, mine.
my, (ge-), avoid, fight shy of, shun.
mylpaal, mile-stone; landmark.
mymer, (ge-), brood, muse, ponder, meditate, be lost in reverie (thought).
mymering, (-e), day-dreaming, reverie.
myn, (-e), mine, pit.
mynbou, mining(-industry).
myne, mine.
mynersyds, on my part.
myngas, (fire-)damp, methane.
myntering, miner's phthisis.
mynveër, mine-sweeper.
mynwerker, miner; mine-worker.

'n, a, an.
na, adv. near.
na, prep. after; on.
na, prep. to: in, according to; after; at; of.
na-aap, (nage-), ape, mimic, imitate.
naaf, (nawe), hub, nave; boss.
naai, (ge-), sew, stitch.
naaimasjien. sewing-machine.
naaiwerk, sewing, needle-work.
naak, (-te), a. naked, nude, bare.
naak, (ge-), approach.
naald, (-e), needle (also of pine-tree, instrument, obelisk).
naaldekoker, needle-case; dragon-fly.
naald(e)werk, needle-work, sewing.
naam, (name), name.
naambord(jie), name-plate, door-plate.
naamgenoot, namesake.
naamlik, namely, to wit, viz.
naamloos, (-lose), (2) nameless, inexpressible.
naamval, case.
naamwoord, nomen; selfstandige –, noun.
naand, good evening!
naar, (nare), a. unpleasant; terrible; disagreeable; nasty; foul; miserable; giddy, faint.
naargeestig, (-e), dreary, gloomy.
naarheid, unpleasantness; giddiness.
naarstig, (-e), diligent, assiduous.
naas, next (to), beside; alongside of; next-door to.
naasaan, next to.
naasagter, the second from the rear.
naasbestaande, (-s), next of kin.
naaseergister, three days ago.
naasmekaar, alongside one another; abreast.
naasoormore, -môre, three days hence.
naaste, (-s), n. neighbour, fellow-man.
naaste, a. nearest; next.
naaste(n)by, roughly, more or less.
naasvoor, the second from the front.
naat, (nate), seam; suture; weld.
naberig, postscript; epilogue.
nabestaande, vide naasbestaande.
nabetragting, reflection, meditation.
nably, (nage-), stay behind, stay in.
naboots, (nage-), imitate, copy; mimic.
naburig, (-e), neighbouring.
naby, (-e), a. near.
naby, adv. near, close by (to), near by.
naby, prep. near, close to.
nabygeleë, near-by, neighbouring.
nabyheid, neighbourhood, vicinity.
nadat, vide na.
nadeel, (-dele), disadvantage; drawback; detriment.
nadelig, (-e), disadvantageous, detrimental; injurious.
nademaal, whereas.
nadenkend, (-e), meditative, pensive.
nader, (–, -e), nearer; further.
nader, (ge-), approach, draw near.
naderby, nearer.
naderhand, later on, afterwards.
nadink, (nage-), consider, reflect (upon).
nadoen, (nage-), imitate, mimic, copy.
nadors, after-thirst.
nadraai, sequel, after-effects, upshot.
nadruk, n. emphasis, stress.
nadruklik, emphatic(ally).
nael, (-s), n. nail; claw; rivet.
nael, (ge-), (1) nail.
nael, (ge-), (2) sprint, race, tear, fly.
na(w)el, navel.
naelloper, sprinter.
naelskraap: dit het – gegaan, it was a close shave (a near thing).

naeltjie, (-s), little nail; hyacinth; –s, cloves.
nag, (-te), night.
nagaan, (nage-), follow; trace; investigate; check.
nagaap, -apie, bush-baby, moholi lemur.
nagedagtenis, memory, commemoration.
nagemaak, (-te), imitation (-leather); counterfeit, artificial, spurious.
nagenoeg, nearly, almost, more or less.
nagereg, dessert.
nageslag, posterity.
Nagmaal, Holy Communion.
nagmerrie, nightmare; bugbear.
nagploeg, night-shift.
nagsê, (nagge-), say good-night.
nagtegaal, (-gale); nightingale.
nagtelik, (-e), nightly, nocturnal.
naguil, night-jar.
nagvoël, night-bird.
nahou, (nage-), keep in.
naïef, (naïewe), naïve (naïve), artless.
naja(ag), -jae, (nage-), run after, chase; seek (hunt) after.
najaar, autumn.
nakend, (-e), naked, bare.
nakom, (nage-), fulfil, keep; obey; do, perform; comply with.
nakomeling, (-e), descendant.
nakoming, fulfilment, performance.
nakyk, (nage-), look at, watch; check, look over; look up: overhaul.
nalaat, (nage-), leave behind; neglect; stop, leave off; leave; bequeath; omit.
nalatenskap, estate; heritage, inheritance.
nalatig, (-e), negligent, careless.
naleef, -lewe, (nage-), live up to; observe; comply with.
nalees, (nage-), read over; read up.
naloop, (nage-), run after, follow.
namaak, (nage-), copy, imitate; forge; counterfeit.
namaaksel, (-s), imitation, counterfeit.
Namakwa, (-s), Namaqua.
namate, as, in proportion to.
namens, on behalf of, for.
namiddag, afternoon.
nanag, after midnight.
naoes, after-crop.
Napels, Napels.
Napolitaans, (-e), Neapolitan.
napraat, (nage-), mimic; repeat words; echo, imitate the words (opinions) of.
nar, (-re), buffoon, jester, fool.
narig, (-e), a. wretched, miserable.
narkose, narcosis, anaesthesia.
narsing, (-s), narcissus.
nartjie, (-s), naartjie, mandarin (-orange).
nasaat, (-sate), descendant.
Nasarener, (-s) Nazarene.
Nasaret, Nazareth.
nasê, (nage-), say after, repeat.
nasie, (-s), nation.
nasien, (nage-), look over, read through, correct, audit, overhaul, inspect.
nasionaal, (-nale), national.
nasionalis, (-te), nationalist.
nasit, (nage-), chase, pursue, run after.
naskrif, (-te), postscript.
naslaan, (nage-), consult, look (turn) up.
nasleep, n. train, aftermath, sequel, after-effects.
nasmaak, after-taste.
naspeur, (nage-), trace, investigate.
naspoor, vide naspeur.
nastaar, (nage-), stare after.
nastreef, -strewe, (nage-), strive after, pursue; emulate.

nat, n. wet, damp.
nat, a. wet; moist, damp; tight, tipsy.
natmaak, (natge-), wet, water.
natreën, -reent, (natge-), be (get) caught in the rain.
natrium, sodium.
naturaliseer, (ge-), naturalize.
natuur, nature; disposition; (natural) scenery.
natuurkunde, physics.
natuurlik, (-e), a. natural; native.
natuurlik, adv. naturally.
natuurskoon, natural beauty, scenery.
navertel, (-), repeat.
naverwant, (-e), closely related.
navolg, (nage-), follow; pursue; imitate.
navolgenswaardig, (-e), worth following.
navorsing, investigation; research.
navra, (nage-), inquire.
navraag, inquiry; demand.
naweek, week-end.
naywer, jealousy, envy.
nè?, isn't it (he, she)?, not so?; yes?.
nederig, (-e), humble, modest, lowly.
nederlaag, vide neerlaag.
nedersetter, settler.
nedersetting, (-e, -s), settlement.
ne(d)erwaarts, downward(s).
nee, no.
neef, (-s), nephew; cousin.
neem, (ge-), take; book; engage; have.
neën-, vide negen-.
neer, down; op en –, up and down.
neerbuig, (neerge-), bend down.
neerdaal, (neerge-), come down, descend.
neerdrukkend, (-e), depressing.
neergeslaan, (-de), sad, heavy, doughy.
neerhaal, (neerge-), haul down; fetch down; pull down; lower.
neerhurk, (neerge-), squat (down).
neerkom, (neerge-), come down, descend, crash down; land.
neerkyk, (neerge-), look down.
neerlaag, nederlaag, (-lae), defeat, overthrow, reverse.
neerlaat, (neerge-), lower, let down.
neerlê, (neerge-), put (lay) down.
neersien, (neerge-), vide neerkyk.
neersit, (neerge-), put down.
neerslaan, (neerge-), strike (knock) down, fall down; cast down; beat down.
neerslag, down-beat; precipitate; downpour.
neerslagtig, (-e), depressed, dejected.
neersmyt, (neerge-), fling (chuck) down.
neerstort, (neerge-), fall down, collapse; crash; come down in torrents.
neerstryk, (neerge-), smooth down; come down, descend, alight.
neertrek, (neerge-), pull down; collar; tackle.
neervel, (neerge-), fell; strike down.
neet, (nete) nit.
neewoord, refusal.
neffens, vide naas.
negatief, (-tiewe), a. negative.
nege, nine.
negeer, (ge-), ignore; cut; disregard.
negende, neënde, (-s), ninth (part).
negentien, neëntien, nineteen.
negentig, neëntig, ninety.
negeoog, neën-, carbuncle.
Neger, (-s), negro.
negosie, wares, goods, trade.
negosieware, stock-in-trade, merchandise.
negosiewinkel, general store.
neig, (ge-), bend, bow, incline.

neiging, (-e, -s), inclination, disposition, tendency, bent.
nek, (-ke), neck: "neck" (between hills).
nekslag, blow in the neck; death-blow, finishing (knock-out) blow.
nêrens, nowhere.
nerf, (nerwe), n. vein, nervure (of leaf); grain (of wood, leather); skin.
nerf, nerwe, (ge-), grain (leather); (strip off) skin.
nering, (-e, -s), trade; occupation.
nes, (-te), n. nest; eyrie (of bird of prey); haunt; hole.
nes, adv. = net soos, just like; just as; as soon as; every time, whenever.
nesskop, (nesge-), make a nest.
net, (-te), n. net; netting; network.
net, (-, -te), a. neat; smart; clean, tidy; exact, accurate.
net, adv. (1), neatly.
net, adv. (2) just, exactly.
netelig, (-e), thorny, knotty; critical.
netjies, (-e), neat, tidy; clean; smart, dainty, trim, spruce, neat.
netjies, adv. neatly; nicely.
netnou, netnoumaar, just now; in a moment.
netto, net.
neuk, (ge-), hit, strike, flog.
neukery, (blinking) nuisance, mess-up.
neul, (ge-), be troublesome (a nuisance), nag.
neulkous, -pot, bore, plague, nuisance.
neurie, (ge-), hum.
neus, (-e), nose; prow (of ship); nozzle (of pipe, tube); toe-cap (of shoe), toe; point, shoulder of mountain).
neushoring, rhinoceros.
neut, (-e), nut; nutmeg.
neutraal, (trale), neutral.
neutraliseer, (ge-), neutralize.
newe(ns)gaand, (-e), enclosed, accompanying.
newel, (-s), mist, haze, fog.
newens, next to, beside; besides.
neweskikkend, (-e), co-ordinate.
neweproduk, by-product.
nie, not.
nie-blanke, non-European.
nie-lid, non-member.
niemand, no one, nobody, none.
nier, (-e), kidney; nodule (ore).
nies, (ge-), sneeze.
niet, nothing, nothingness.
nieteenstaande, notwithstanding, in spite of.
nietemin, nevertheless, none the less.
nietig, (-e), insignificant, trifling.
nietigheid, (-hede), insignificance; nullity (of marriage); trifle.
Nieu-Guinea, New Guinea.
nieumodies, (-e), fashionable, new-fashioned, stylish.
Nieu-Seeland, New Zealand.
niewers, vide nêrens.
nig, (-te), niggie, (-s), cousin; piece.
nikkel, nickel.
nikotien, nikotine, nicotine.
niks, nothing.
niksbeduidend, (-e), insignificant, trifling, worthless, good-for-nothing.
niksbetekenend, (-e), vide niksbeduidend.
niksnut, (-e), rotter, good-for-nothing, rogue, rascal.
nimf, (-e), nymph.
nimmer, never.
nimmermeer, never again, never more.
nippel, (-s), nipple.
nippertjie: op die –, in the nick of time.
nis, (-se), niche.

niveau, (-s), level, plane.
nivelleer, (ge-), level, take a level.
Noag, Noah.
nobel, (-e), noble.
nodeloos, (-lose), needless, unnecessary.
nodig, (-e), necessary; requisite.
nodige, n. what is necessary, essential; necessaries of life.
noem, (ge-), name, call, style; mention.
noemenswaard(ig), (-es), worth mentioning (speaking of).
noemer, (-s), denominator.
noen, noon.
nog, conj. (1) neither ... nor.
nog, a. & adv. (2) stil, yet further.
nogal, rather, quite, fairly.
nogmaals, once again, once more.
nogtans, yet, nevertheless, still.
nôi, nooi, (-ens), sweetheart, (best) girl.
nôientjie, nooientjie, (-s), girl, young lady; vide nôi.
nok, (-ke), ridge (of roof); cam (of wheel).
nokturne, (-s), nocturne.
nominasie, nomination.
nomineer, (ge-), nominate.
nommer, (-s), number, size (of shoe); event (sport); item (on programme); issue, number (of magazine).
nommer, (ge-), number.
non, (-ne), nun.
nood, need, distress; necessity; emergency.
noodgedronge, -gedwonge, from sheer necessity, compelled by necessity.
noodhulp, emergency-man; make-shift.
noodlot, fate, destiny.
noodlottig, (-e), fatal; ill-fated.
noodluik, escape hatch.
noodlydend, (-e), destitute; distressed.
noodsaak, n. necessity.
noodsaak, (ge-), force, compel, oblige.
noodsaaklik, (-e), a. necessary; essential.
noodsaaklikerwys(e), of necessity.
noodwa, breakdown truck.
noodwendig, (-e), a. necessary; inevitable.
noodwendig, adv. of necessity; inevitably.
nooi, n. vide nôi.
nooi, (ge-), invite.
nooit, never.
noop, (ge-), compel, induce.
Noor, (Nore), Norwegian.
noord, north.
Noord-Amerika, North America.
noorde, north.
noordelik, (-e), northern (hemisphere), northerly (direction).
noorderbreedte, north latitude.
noorderlig, northern lights, aurora borealis.
noordewind, north wind.
Noordpool, North Pole.
Noordsee, North Sea, German ocean.
noordster, polar star: load-star.
Noorman, (-ne), Northman, Norseman.
Noors, (-e), Norse, Norwegian.
noors, (-, -e), vicious (bull); heavy (soil).
Noorweë, Norway.
Noorweër, (-s), Norwegian.

noot, (note), note.
nopens, concerning.
noppies: in jou –, mighty pleased.
norm, (-e), norm, standard.
normaal, (-male), a. normal; standard.
Normandië, Normandy.
nors, noors, (-, -e), grumpy, morose, surly, sullen; vide noors.
nota, (-s), note; note (from the government).
notarieel, (-riële), notarial.
notaris, (-se), notary.
noteer, (ge-), note (down); quote (prices).
notisie, notice.
notule, minutes.
notuleer, (ge-), enter (record) in the minutes, minute.
nou, (-, -e), a. narrow; tight (clothes).
nou, adv. (1) narrowly; tightly.
nou, adv. (2) now, at present.
nou, interj. well.
noudat, conj. now that.
nougeset, (-te), narrow-minded; conscientious, scrupulous.
noukeurig, (-e), a. exact, accurate, precise; careful; close.
noukeurig, adv. exactly, accurately.
noulettend, (-e), precise, particular, strict, close; scrupulous.
nouliks, hardly, scarcely, barely.
nou-nou, in a moment (minute).
nousiende, particular, fastidious.
nousluitend, (-e), tight, close-fitting.
noustrop: – trek, work like a galley-slave, be hard pressed, struggle.
novelle, (-s), short story, novelette.
nu: – en dan, now and then; vide nou.
Nubiër, (-s), Nubian.
nugter, (-, -e), a. sober; sober-minded; level-headed; prosaic, matter-of-fact.
nugter, adv. soberly.
nuk, (-ke), whim, caprice, freak; mood.
nukkerig, (-e), sulky, moody, sullen.
nul, (-le), nought, cipher; zero (temperature); love (tennis): nil (rugby).
nut, use; benefit, profit.
nuttig, (-e), a. useful; profitable.
nuttig, adv. usefully; profitably.
nuttig, (ge-), partake of (meal).
nuus, news, tidings.
nuusblad, newspaper.
nuuskierig, (-e), inquisitive; curious.
nuut, (nuwe), new; modern; recent.
nuwe, vide nuut.
Nuwejaar, New Year.
Nuwejaarsdag, New Year's day.
nuweling, (-e), newcomer, beginner, novice; greenhorn; fresher, freshman.
nuwerig, (-e), newish, rather new.
nuwerwets, (-e), new-fashioned; modern.
nuwigheid, (-hede), novelty, innovation.
nyd, envy, bitter jealousy, enmity.
nydig, (-e), angry.
nyg, (ge-), bow, curts(e)y.
Nyl, Nile.
nyweraar, (-s), manufacturer.
nywerheid, (-hede), industry.

o, oh!; – so!, aha!.

oase, (-s), oasis.

objekteer, (ge-), object, raise objections.

observatorium, (-s, -toria), observatory.

odeur, (-s), scent, perfume.

oefen, (ge-), practise, exercise, train.

oefening, (-e, -s), practice, exercise, training.

oë(n)skou: in – neem, inspect; look at; review.

oënskynlik, (-e), a. apparent, ostensible.

oënskynlik, adv. apparently; ostensibly.

oeroud, (-oue), primeval, ancient.

oerwoud, primeval forest, virgin forest.

oes, (-te), n. crop, harvest; output.

oes, a. bad, feeble, miserable, shabby; off colour.

oes, (ge-), reap, harvest, gather; earn; beat, lick.

oester, (-s), oyster.

oestyd, harvesting-season, reaping-time.

oëverblindery, make-believe, pretence; deception.

oewer, (-s), bank (of a river), shore.

of, or; whether; (as) if; but.

offer, (-s), n. sacrifice, offering; victim.

offer, (ge-), sacrifice, offer, immolate.

offerande, (-s), offering, sacrifice.

offervaardig, (-e), willing to make sacrifices.

offisieel, (-siële), a. official.

offisieel, adv. officially.

offisier, (-e, -s), officer.

ofskoon, (al)though.

ofte: nooit – nimmer, never, on no account.

og, oh!

oggend, (-e), morning.

oggendstond, early morning.

ogiesdraad, wire-netting.

oker, ochre.

okkerneut, (-e), walnut.

okshoof, (-de), hogshead.

Oktober, October.

oktrooi, (-e), charter, patent, grant.

olie, (-s), n. oil.

olie, (ge-), oil, lubricate.

olieboom, castor-oil plant.

oliekoek, oil-cake; dough-nut; simpleton.

olienhout, oliewenhout, wild olive.

olifant, (-e), elephant.

olik, (-e), seedy, off colour, unwell.

olim: in die dae van –, in the days of yore.

olm, (-e), elm.

olyf, (olywe), olive.

Olyfberg, Mount of Olives.

om, adv. round; out; up, over.

om, prep. round, about, at; for.

om + te, to, in order to.

omarm, (–), embrace, fold in the arms.

omblaai, (omge-), turn over (a leaf).

omboor, (omge-), bind, hem, edge.

omboorsel, binding, edging, border.

ombring, (omge-), kill, put to death.

omdat, because, since, as, seeing that.

omdop, (omge-), turn inside out; curl (up); double up; fall down (over).

omdraai, (omge-), turn round (back, about); turn over; wrap in; twist.

omfloers, (–), cover, veil; muffle.

omgaan, (omge-), go round; take place, happen; associate (with).

omgang, association, (social) intercourse, dealings; circuit, rotation; round, lap.

omgee, (omge-), care, mind; hand round, pass round.

omgekeer(d), (-de), a. turned upside down (inside out); turned down, inverted; reversed.

omgekeer(d), adv. inversely; conversely.

omgekeerde, n. the reverse; converse.

omgekrap, (-te), untidy; confused; unruly; irritable, upset.

omgewe, omgeef, (–), surround, enclose.

omgewing, environment; vicinity.

omgrens, (–), bound; confine, restrict.

omhaal, n. bustle, commotion, fuss, to-do; – van woorde, verbosity.

omhaal, (omge-), persuade; pull down.

omhang, (omge-), put on, throw (overcoat, etc.) over one's shoulders.

omhê, (omgehad), have on.

omheen, about, round about.

omhein, (–), fence in (round), enclose.

omhels, (–), embrace.

omhoog, aloft, on high; up(wards).

omhulsel, (-s), wrapper, cover(ing); die stoflike –, the mortal remains.

omie, (-s), uncle.

omkantel, (omge-), fall over, topple over; tilt; upset, overturn, capsize.

om(me)keer, n. (complete) change, turn (of events); reversal.

omkeer, (omge-), turn (up, out, down, over), turn upside down; invert; reverse.

omkom, (omge-), come round; perish.

omkoop, (omge-), bribe; corrupt.

omkrap, (omge-), throw into disorder (confusion), disarrange; make a mess of, bungle.

omkry, (omge-), get down; get round, get on; while away (the time).

omlaag, (down) below; na –, down.

omliggende, neighbouring, surrounding.

omloop, n. (1) circulation; rotation.

omloop, (-lope), n. (2) ringworm.

omloop, (omge-), go (walk) round; revolve; knock down, run down.

omlyn, (–), outline, define.

omlys, (–), frame; set.

om(me)keer, vide omkeer, n.

om(me)sientjie: in 'n –, in the twinkling of an eye, in a jiffy.

ommesy, overleaf.

ommuur, (–), wall in.

ompad, roundabout way, detour.

omploeg, (omge-), plough.

ompraat, (omge-), persuade, talk over.

omrede, because.

omring, (–), surround, encircle.

omroep, (omge-), announce; broadcast.

omroeper, town crier; announcer.

omruil, (omge-), exchange; interchange.

omry, (omge-), knock down (over), run over; drive round.

omsendbrief, circular (letter).

omset, n. turnover; sale; returns.

omset, (omge-), turn over, convert into money; invert; transpose.

omsigtigheid, circumspection, caution.

omsingel, (–), surround, encircle.

omsit, (omge-), put round; sit round; turn round suddenly; transpose; transmute; invert; reverse; convert (into).

omskep, (omge-), transform, change.

omskryf, -skrywe, (–), paraphrase; define, describe; circumscribe (geom.).

omslaan, (omge-), strike (knock) down; fall down; capsize; turn over (page); turn down; turn up; fold (turn) back; change opinion.

omslag, (-slae), (1) cover, jacket; wrapper (of newspaper); cuff; turn-up.

omslag, (-slae), (2) brace.

omslagtig, (-e), roundabout, long-winded, tedious, detailed; prolix; wordy.

omsluier, (–), veil; conceal, cover.

omsluit, (–), surround; grip, clasp; fit (tightly).

omsmyt, (omge-), knock down (over), upset, overturn.

omsoom, (omge-), hem.

omsoom, (-), border, edge, fringe.

omspit, (omge-), dig (up).

omspring, (omge-), jump round; change one's opinion.

omstander, (-s), bystander, onlooker.

omstandig, adv. in detail.

omstandigheid, (-hede), circumstance, circumstantiality.

omstreeks, about, more or less.

omstreke, (pl.), vicinity, neighbourhood.

omswaai, (omge-), swing round; veer round.

omswerwing, (-e, -s), wandering.

omtrek, (-ke), n. outline; circumference (of a circle); perimeter (geom.); neighbourhood.

omtrent, adv. about, nearly; extremely.

omtrent, prep. about; with regard to.

omvang, girth, circumference; range, extent; size; magnitude.

omvangryk, (-e), bulky; comprehensive.

omvat, (-), include, comprise, embrace; take in; grip, clasp; span.

omvergooi, (omverge-), upset, knock, over; frustrate.

omverloop, (omverge-), knock down.

omvlie(g), (omge-), fly round; turn round suddenly.

omweg, (-weë), roundabout way, detour.

omwenteling, (-e, -s), revolution; rotation.

omwerk, (omge-), refashion, reconstruct; rewrite; dig, plough, cultivate.

omwoel, (omge-), dig up, turn up; throw into disorder; wriggle round.

onaangenaam, (-name), unpleasant, disagreeable; bad-tempered, unamiable.

onaansienlik, (-e), plain, unattractive; insignificant; inconsiderable.

onaardig, (-e), unpleasant, not nice; glad nie – nie, not at all bad.

onafgebroke, incessant, continuous.

onafhanklik, (-e), a. independent.

onafskeidelik, (-e), inseparable.

onbaatsugtig, (-e), unselfish, disinterested.

onbarmhartig, (-e), merciless, pitiless.

onbedagsaam, (-same), thoughtless, rash.

onbeduidend, (-e), insignificant, trifling, unimportant, trivial.

onbegaanbaar, (-bare), impassable.

onbegonne: dit is 'n – taak, that is attempting the impossible.

onbegryplik, (-e), inconceivable, incomprehensible.

onbeholpe, clumsy, awkward, crude.

onbekend, (-e), unknown.

onbekommerd, (-e), unconcerned, free from anxiety (care).

onbekook, (-te), rash, ill-considered.

onbekwaam, (-kwame), unable, incapable; unfit.

onbelangrik, (-e), unimportant, trifling.

onbeleef, (-de), impolite, rude, uncivil.

onbelemmerd, (-e), free, unimpeded, unhampered, unobstructed.

onbemin(d), (-de), not liked, unpopular.

onbenullig, (-e), stupid, dull, fatuous; trifling, paltry.

onbepaald, (-e), indefinite; uncertain.

onbeperk, (-te), unlimited, unrestricted.

onberedeneer(d), (-de), unreasoned; thoughtless, unreasoning.

onbereikbaar, (-bare), inaccessible, unattainable.

onberekenbaar, (-bare), incalculable.

onberispelik, (-e), irreproachable, faultless, immaculate.

onbesiens, unseen.

onbeskaaf, (-de), uncivilised, savage; unrefined.

onbeskaamd, (-e), impudent, insolent, unabashed.

onbeskof, (-te), rude, uncouth, ill-mannered.

onbeskrewe, blank, unrecorded; unwritten.

onbeskroom(d), (-de), undaunted, bold, fearless.

onbeskryflik, (-e), indescribable.

onbesonne, thoughtless, rash, wild.

onbesorg, (-de), light-hearted; unconcerned; undelivered (letter).

onbesproke, unreserved; irreproachable.

onbestaanbaar, (-bare), not existing; incompatible.

onbestendig, (-e), unsettled, changeable, unstable, inconstant.

onbestrede, unopposed, undisputed.

onbesuis, (-de), reckless, rash, ungovernable.

onbetaamlik, (-e), improper, indecent, unbecoming.

onbetroubaar, (-bare), unreliable.

onbetuig: hy het hom nie – gelaat nie, he gave a good account of himself.

onbevoeg, (-de), incompetent, unfit.

onbevooroordeeld, (-e), unprejudiced, impartial.

onbevredigend, (-e), unsatisfactory.

onbeweeglik, (-e), motionless; unyielding, immovable.

onbewimpeld, (-e), candid, open, frank.

onbewus, (-te), a. unconscious; unaware (of).

onbewus, adv. unconsciously; unknowingly.

onbillik, (-e), unfair, unreasonable.

onblusbaar, (-bare), unquenchable.

onbruik, disuse, desuetude.

onbruikbaar, (-bare), useless; naughty, disobedient.

onbuigbaar, (-bare), unbendable, inflexible; rigid; fixed (laws).

onbuigsaam, (-same), inflexible, rigid, firm.

ondank, ingratitude, thanklessness.

ondankbaar, (-bare), ungrateful, thankless; unprofitable.

ondanks, notwithstanding, in spite of.

ondenkbaar, (-bare), inconceivable.

onder, adv. below.

onder, prep. under, underneath, beneath; among; amid(st).

onderaan, at the foot of (the page); at the bottom of.

onderaards, (-e), underground.

onderbaadjie, waistcoat.

onderbewus, (-te), subconscious.

onderbewussyn, subconscious mind.

onderbreek, (-), interrupt; break.

onderdaan, (-dane), subject.

onderdak, shelter, home, accommodation.

onderdanig, (-e), submissive, obedient.

onderdeurspring, (onderdeurge-), pass under; iemand –, trick a person.

onderdruk, (onderge-), press down (under), hold down.

onderdruk, (-), oppress; suppress (a rebellion); quell; smother; repress.

onderduims, (-e), underhand, clandestine.

onderent, (-e), lower end, bottom end.

ondergaan, (onderge-), set (the sun); sink.

ondergaan, (-), undergo, endure, suffer.

ondergeskik, (-te), subordinate; inferior; subservient.

ondergronds, (-e), underground.

onderhandel, (-), negotiate (with), discuss terms, confer.

onderhawig, (-e), present; die –e saak, the case in question.

onderhewig, liable (to); subject (to).

onderhorig, (-e), dependent, subordinate; belonging to.

onderhou, (onderge-), hold down.

onderhou, (–), support, keep, provide for.
onderhoud, (1) support, maintenance.
onderhoud, (-e), (2) interview, conversation.
onderhoudend, (-e), amusing, entertaining.
onderkant, n. lower side, bottom.
onderkant, adv. below.
onderklere, underclothing, underwear.
onderkruip, (–), undersell, undercut; blackleg; swindle.
onderlangs, adv. lower down; along the lower parts.
onderleg: goed – wees in, have a good grounding in.
onderling, (-e), a. mutual.
onderling, adv. mutually; among (between) them.
ondermaans, (-e), sub-lunary, earthly.
ondermyn, (–), undermine, sap.
onderneem, (–), undertake, attempt.
ondernemend, (-e), enterprising.
ondernemingsgees, enterprise.
onderoffisier, non-commissioned officer.
onderonsie, family gathering, meeting of intimate friends.
onderrig, n. instruction, tuition.
onderrig, (–), teach, instruct; inform.
onderrok, underskirt, petticoat.
onderskat, (–), underestimate, underrate.
onderskei(e), (–), distinguish; discriminate.
onderskeid, different, distinction; discrimination.
onderskeidelik, respectively; severally.
onderskeiding, (-e, -s), distinction; honour, respect.
onderskeie, a. different; various.
onderskep, (–), intercept.
onderskikkend, (-e), subordinate.
onderskraag, (–), prop (up); support.
onderskryf, -skrywe, (–), endorse, sign, confirm.
ondersoek, n. investigation, examination, inquiry.
ondersoek, (–), investigate, examine; test; make researches; search.
onderspit: die – delf, be defeated.
onderstaande, under-mentioned.
onderstand, relief, aid, help.
onderstebo, upside-down, inverted; in confusion (disorder), upset; untidy.
onderstel, n. lower frame(-work), undercarriage, bogie, chassis.
ondersteun, (–), support, assist, aid.
onderstreep, (–), underline.
onderteken, (–), sign.
ondertoe, lower down, downward(s), to the bottom.
ondertrou, (–), intermarry.
ondertussen, meanwhile, in the meantime.
onderverdeel, (–), subdivide.
onderverhuur, (–), sublet.
ondervind, (–), experience, undergo.
ondervinding, (-e, -s), experience.
ondervoed, a. underfed, undernourished.
ondervra(ag), (–), (cross-)question, interrogate, (cross-)examine.
onderweg, on the way.
onderwerp, (-e), subject, topic, theme.
onderworpe, submissive; – **aan,** subject to.
onderwyl, (mean)while.
onderwys, n. education; teaching, instruction, tuition.
onderwys, (–), teach, instruct.
onderwyser, teacher, master.
ondeug, vice; mischievousness, roguery (roguishness); rascal, rogue.
ondeund, (-e), naughty, mischievous.
ondeurdag, (-te), thoughtless, rash; hare-brained.

ondeurdringbaar, (-bare), impenetrable; impervious.
ondeurgrondelik, (-e), unfathomable, inscrutable, impenetrable.
ondiens, disservice, bad (ill) turn.
ondier, monster, beast, brute.
ondig, (-te), leaky, not watertight.
onding, rubbish, monstrosity; absurdity.
ondoenlik, (-e), impossible; impracticable.
ondraagbaar, (-bare), too heavy to be carried; unwearable; unbearable.
ondraaglik, (-e), unbearable, intolerable, insufferable.
ondubbelsinnig, (-e), unequivocal, plain, unambiguous.
onduidelik, (-e), indistinct; faint, dim; obscure.
onedel, (-e), ignoble, base, mean.
oneens, at variance.
oneer, disgrace, dishonour.
oneerlik, (-e), dishonest, unfair.
oneffe, uneven; rough, bumpy.
oneg, (-te), illegitimate (child); false, artificial, counterfeit.
oneindig, (-e), a. endless, boundless.
oneindige, n. infinite, infinity.
onenigheid, (-hede), discord, strife, dispute, quarrel.
onervare, inexperienced.
oneweredig, (-e), disproportionate.
onfatsoenlik, (-e), rude; improper, indecent.
onfeilbaar, (-bare), infallible, unfailing.
ongeblus, (-te), unslaked (lime); unquenched (fire).
ongebruiklik, (-e), uncommon, unusual.
ongedaan, (-dane), undone.
ongedeer(de), (-de), unscathed, unharmed.
ongedierte(s), vermin; wild beasts.
ongeduld, impatience.
ongeduldig, (-e), impatient.
ongeërg, (-de), nonchalant, casual, cool.
ongeëwenaard, (-e), unequalled, unparalleled.
ongegrond, (-e), unfounded, ungrounded.
ongehoorsaam, (-same), disobedient.
ongekend, (-e), unknown; unparalleled.
ongekunsteld, (-e), simple, natural, artless.
ongeldig, (-e), invalid.
ongeleë, inconvenient, inopportune.
ongeleentheid, inconvenience.
ongeleer(d), (-de), unlearned (unlearnt); uneducated, illiterate; untrained.
ongelees, (-lese), unread.
ongeletter(d), (-de), not marked (unmarked); uneducated.
ongeloof, unbelief, disbelief.
ongeloofbaar, (-bare), **ongelooflik** (-e), incredible, unbelievable.
ongelowig, (-e), sceptical; incredulous.
ongeluk, (-ke), accident, mishap; misfortune, ill-luck; unhappiness.
ongelukkig, (-e), unhappy; unfortunate.
ongelukkig, adv. unfortunately.
ongelyk, n. wrong.
ongelyk, (-e), a. not level (smooth); uneven, unequal; not uniform; inconsistent.
ongemak, (-ke), discomfort, inconvenience.
ongemaklik, (-e), uncomfortable, troublesome.
ongemerk, (-te), unmarked; unnoticed.
ongenaakbaar, (-bare), inaccessible; unapproachable.
ongenade, displeasure; disgrace.
ongenadig, (-e), unmerciful, cruel; violent.
ongeneë, disinclined, unwilling.
ongeneesbaar, (-bare), incurable.
ongeneeslik, (-e), incurable.
ongenoeglik, (-e), unpleasant.

ongeoorloof, (-de), forbidden, unlawful.
ongepas, (-te), improper; unseemly.
ongepoets, (-te), rude, ill-mannered.
ongereeld, (-e), irregular; unregulated.
ongerief, inconvenience, discomfort; trouble.
ongerieflik, (-e), inconvenient; uncomfortable.
ongerus, (-te), anxious, uneasy.
ongerymd, (-e), absurd, ridiculous, silly.
ongesellig, (-e), unsociable (person); dull, dreary (place).
ongesiens, without having seen.
ongeskik, (-te), unfit, unsuitable, rude.
ongeskonde, undamaged, intact.
ongeskool, (-de), unskilled, untrained.
ongesond, (-e), unhealthy; unwholesome (food); sickly (complexion).
ongestadig, (-e), inconstant, fickle; unsettled.
ongesteld, (-e), indisposed, unwell.
ongesteur(d), -stoor(d), (-de), undisturbed.
ongetrou, (-e), unfaithful, disloyal.
ongetwyfeld, (-e), undoubted.
ongetwyfeld, adv. undoubtedly.
ongeval, (-le), accident, mishap.
ongeveer, about, nearly ; approximately.
ongevoelig, (-e), insensitive; insensible; impassive; cruel.
ongewens, (-te), unwished for, undesirable.
ongewettig, (-de), unauthorised; unwarranted.
ongewild, (-e), unintentional; unpopular.
ongewillig, (-e), unwilling; obstinate.
ongewoon, (-wone), uncommon; unfamiliar.
ongewoond, unaccustomed.
onguns, disfavour.
ongunstig, (-e), unfavourable; adverse.
onhandelbaar, (-bare), unmanageable.
onhandig, (-e), clumsy, awkward.
onhebbelik, (-e), ill-mannered, rude; huge.
onheil, calamity, disaster, evil.
onheispellend, (-e), ominous.
onherbergsaam, (-same), inhospitable.
onherkenbaar, (-bare), unrecognizable.
onherroepbaar, (-bare), onherroeplik, (-e), irrevocable, unalterable.
onherstelbaar, (-bare), irreparable, irretrievable.
onheuglik, (-e), immemorial.
onhoflik, (-e), discourteous, uncivil.
onhou(d)baar, (-bare), untenable.
onjuis, (-te), incorrect, inaccurate.
onkant, off-side.
onklaar, unfinished; out of order.
onkoste, expenses, charges.
onkreukbaar, (-bare), unimpeachable.
onkruid, weeds; good-for-nothing; rascal.
onkunde, ignorance.
onkundig, (-e), ignorant.
onlangs, (-e), a. recent.
onlangs, adv. recently, lately.
onledig: sig – hou met, busy oneself with.
onloënbaar, onlogenbaar, (-bare), undeniable, indisputable.
onlosbaar, (-bare), unredeemable.
onlus, (-te), aversion; listlessness; –te, riots, disturbances.
onmag, inability, impotence; swoon.
onmanierlik, (-e), unmannerly, rude.
onmeetlik, (-e), immense, immeasurable.
onmenslik, (-e), inhuman, brutal, cruel.
onmiddellik, (-e), a. immediate, direct.
onmiddellik, adv. immediately, directly.
onmin, variance, discord, strife.
onmisbaar, (-bare), indispensable, essential, necessary.
onmiskenbaar, (-bare), unmistakable.
onnatuurlik, (-e), unnatural; artificial, affected.
onnodig, (-e), unnecessary, needless.

onnosel, (-e), stupid, silly; innocent.
onnut, (-te), n. good-for-nothing, rogue.
onnutsig, (-e), naughty, mischievous.
onomstootlik, (-e), irrefutable.
onomwonde, a. plain (truth), frank.
onomwonde, adv. plainly, frankly.
onontbeerlik, (-e), indispensable.
onontwikkeld, (-e), undeveloped; uneducated.
onooglik, (-e), unsightly, unattractive.
onoordeelkundig, (-e), injudicious.
onoorganklik, (-e), intransitive.
onoorkoomlik, (-e), insuperable.
onoortrefbaar, (-bare), unsurpassable.
onoorwinlik, (-e), invincible, unconquerable.
onophoudelik, (-e), incessant, unceasing.
onpaar, not a pair, odd.
onpartydig, (-e), impartial, fair.
onpas: te –, out of season.
onpaslik, (-e), unsuitable, out of place.
onplesierig, (-e), unpleasant.
onraad, trouble, danger.
onraadsaam, (-same), unadvisable.
onredelik, (-e), unreasonable.
onreëlmatig, (-e), irregular.
onreg, injustice, wrong.
onregverdig, (-e), unfair, unjust; unrighteous; wrongful (action).
onrein, (-e), unclean, impure.
onroerend, (-e), immovable.
onrus, unrest, disturbance; anxiety.
onrusbarend, (-e), alarming, disquieting.
onrustig, (-e), restless; fidgety; uneasy, agitated.
onrusstoker, mischief-maker, agitator.
ons, pers. pron. we, us.
ons, poss. pron. our; die Onse Vader, the Lord's Prayer.
onsamehangend, (-e), disconnected, incoherent.
onsedelik, (-e), immoral.
onseker, (–, -e), a. uncertain, unsteady, problematical; unsettled.
onsigbaar, (-bare), invisible.
onsin, nonsense, rubbish.
onsindelik, (-e), dirty, uncleanly.
onsinnig, (-e), foolish, absurd, idiotic.
onskatbaar, (-bare), inestimable, invaluable.
onskeidbaar, (-bare), inseparable.
onskuld, innocence.
onskuldig, (-e), innocent.
onsmaaklik, (-e), unsavoury, unpleasant.
onstandvastig, (-e), inconstant, fickle.
onsterflik, (-e), immortal; undying.
onstigtelik, (-e), unedifying, offensive.
onstuimig, (-e), stormy, violent, impetuous (person); vehement.
onsuiwer, (–, -e), impure; unrefined; untrue; flat, false (note); faulty; inexact.
onsydig, (-e), neutral (state), impartial, neuter (gender).
ontaard, (–), degenerate, deteriorate.
ontasbaar, (-bare), intangible, impalpable.
ontbeer, (–), lack, miss, do without.
ontbering, (-e, -s), want, privation.
ontbied, (–), summon, send for.
ontbind, (–), undo; disband; dissolve, decompose.
ontbloot, (–), uncover (head), bare, unsheathe (sword); reveal.
ontboesem, (–), unbosom, unburden.
ontbrand, (–), take fire, burst into flame, ignite; break out (of war).
ontbreek, (–), be wanting, lack.
ontbyt, n. breakfast.
ontdek, (–), discover; find out, detect.
ontdekking, (-e, -s), discovery, revelation.
ontduik, (–), dodge; escape from, evade; elude.
onteenseglik, (-e), unquestionable.

onteer, (-), dishonour; violate, rape.
onteien, (-), expropriate; dispossess.
ontelbaar, (-bare), countless, innumerable, numberless.
ontembaar, (-bare), untamable, violent, ungovernable.
onterf, -erwe, (-), disinherit.
ontevrede, discontented, dissatisfied.
ontferm, (-): sig – oor, take pity on.
ontgaan, (-), escape, elude, evade.
ontgeld(e), (-): dit –, pay (suffer) for it.
ontgin, (-), bring under cultivation; exploit, work (mine).
ontglip, (-), slip from; escape.
ontgogel, -goël, (-), disillusion.
ontgroei, (-), outgrow; grow faster.
ontgroen, (-), initiate (a new student).
onthaal, (-hale), n. entertainment; reception (lit. & fig.).
onthaal, (-), entertain, treat.
onthef, (-): – van, exempt (free) from; relieve.
ontheilig, (-), desecrate, profane.
onthoof, (-), behead, decapitate.
onthou, (-), withhold from, keep from; remember, bear in mind.
onthul, (-), unveil; reveal, disclose.
onthuts, (-), disconcert, bewilder.
ontken, (-), deny.
ontkennend, (-), a. negative.
ontkiem, (-), germinate.
ontknoping, (-e, -s), unbuttoning; denouement.
ontkom, (-), escape.
ontlading, unloading; discharge.
ontleding, (-e, -s), analysis (of sentences); parsing (of words); dissection.
ontleed, (-), dissect; analyse; parse.
ontleen, (-): – aan, borrow from; derive from.
ontlening, (-e, -s), borrowing; derivation, adoption.
ontloop, (-), run away from, escape, elude; avoid.
ontluik, (-), open; expand; bud.
ontmoedig, (-), discourage, dishearten.
ontmoet, (-), meet (with); encounter; come across (a person).
ontneem, (-), deprive (of), take away.
ontnugter, (-), (make) sober; disillusion.
ontoeganklik, (-), inaccessible, unapproachable.
ontoegewend, (-e), unaccommodating, disobliging, unpliable.
ontoereikend, (-e), insufficient, inadequate.
ontoerekenbaar, (-bare), not imputable (to); irresponsible (for something).
ontplof, (-), explode, detonate.
ontplooi, (-), straighten; unfurl; unfold; reveal; develop, expand.
ontroer, (-), move, touch, affect.
ontroosbaar, (-bare), inconsolable, disconsolate.
ontrou, (-, -e), a. unfaithful, disloyal.
ontruim, (-), vacate; evacuate.
ontsag, awe, respect.
ontsaglik, (-e), a. awful; vast, huge.
ontsê, -seg, (-), deny; refuse.
ontset, (-), dismiss; relieve (town); appal. horrify.
ontsettend, (-e), a. terrible, awful.
ontsettend, adv. terribly, dreadfully.
ontsien, (-), stand in awe of; respect.
ontsier, (-), disfigure, deface, mar.
ontslaan, (-), dismiss, discharge.
ontslaap, (-), pass away.
ontslae: – van, rid of, free from.
ontslag, discharge, dismissal; release.
ontslape, passed away, deceased.
ontsluier, (-), unveil; disclose.

ontsluit, (-), unlock, open.
ontsmet, (-), disinfect, deodorize.
ontsnap, (-), escape.
ontsnap, (-), unfasten; unbend; relax.
ontspoor, (-), leave the rails, be derailed; laat –, derail.
ontspring, (-), jump away from; escape; rise (of river); be caused (by).
ontstaan, n. origin; development, rise.
ontstaan, (-), originate, begin; come into being; be formed.
ontsteek, (-), light, ignite; inflame.
ontstel, (-), upset, alarm, startle.
ontsteltenis, dismay, consternation.
ontstem, (-), disturb, ruffle.
ontstentenis: by – van, failing, in default of.
ontstoke, inflamed (wound).
ontsyfer, (-), decipher, make out.
onttrek, (-), withdraw.
ontvang, (-), receive; conceive; – my dank, accept my thanks.
ontvangs, (-te), receipt; reception; -te, returns, takings, revenue.
ontvanklik, (-e), receptive, susceptible.
ontvlam, (-), catch fire, flame up; inflame, stir up.
ontvlug, (-), escape, flee (from).
ontvoer, (-), kidnap (child), abduct.
ontvolk, (-), depopulate.
ontvou, (-), unfold.
ontwaak, (-), awake, wake up.
ontwapen, (-), disarm; pacify.
ontwerp, (-e), n. plan, design; scheme; draft, sketch; (parliamentary) bill.
ontwerp, (-), plan, design; project; draft; draw up; devise.
ontwikkel, (-), develop; generate.
ontwikkeld, (-e), developed; educated.
ontwil, sake; om my –, for my sake.
ontwortel, (-), uproot (lit. & fig.).
ontwrig, (-), dislocate, disrupt.
ontwyk, (-), avoid, shun, evade.
ontwykend, (-e), evasive (answer).
ontydig, (-e), untimely, unseasonable.
onuitputlik, (-e), inexhaustible.
onuitspreeklik, (-e), unspeakable, inexpressible.
onuitstaanbaar, (-bare), intolerable, unbearable.
onuitvoerbaar, (-bare), impracticable.
onuitwisbaar, (-bare), indelible, ineffaceable.
onvanpas, inconvenient; unsuitable, inappropriate.
onvas, (-te), soft (ground), faltering (steps, voice). shaking, unsteady (hand); light (sleep).
onveranderd, (-e), unchanged, unaltered.
onveranderlik, (-e), unchangeable, constant.
onverantwoordelik, (-e), not responsible, irresponsible (person); inexcusable.
onverbeterlik, (-e), incorrigible; first-rate.
onverbiddelik, (-e), inexorable, relentless.
onverbloem(d), (-de), a. undisguised, unvarnished (truth).
onverdeel(d), (-de), a. undivided.
overdeel(d), adv. entirely, wholly.
onverdien(d), (-de), unearned (wages); undeserved.
onverdraagsaam, (-same), intolerant.
onverganklik, (-e), imperishable, undying.
onvergeeflik, (-e), unpardonable.
onvergeetlik, (-e), unforgettable.
onvergenoeg, (-de), discontented, dissatisfied.
onverhoeds, adv. unexpectedly; suddenly.
onverklaarbaar, (-bare), inexplicable.
onverkry(g)baar, (-bare), unobtainable.
onverkwiklik, (-e), unpleasant, unsavoury.
onverminder(d), (-de), unabated.
onvermoë, inability, incapacity; impotence.

onvermoeid, (-e), untiring, tireless.
onvermurfbaar, (-bare), relentless, inexorable.
onvermydelik, (-e), inevitable, unavoidable.
onverpoos, (-de), uninterrupted, unceasing, unabating.
onverrig, (-te), undone; –ter sake, without having achieved one's object.
onversaag, (-de), undaunted, fearless.
onversadelik, (-e), insatiable.
onversadig, (-de), unsatiated, unsatisfied.
onversigtig, (-e), imprudent, rash.
onverskillig, (-e), indifferent; reckless (driver, etc.); careless.
onverskrokke, undaunted, intrepid.
onversoenlik, (-e), irreconcilable; implacable.
onverstaanbaar, (-bare), unintelligible; incomprehensible.
onverstandig, (-e), unwise, foolish.
onvervreem(d)baar, (-bare), inalienable (possessions); indefeasible (rights).
onverwags, unexpectedly, unawares.
onverwinlik, (-e), invincible.
onverwyld, immediately, at once.
onvoldaan, (-dane), unpaid; dissatisfied.
onvoltooi(d), (-de), unfinished, incomplete; imperfect (tense).
onvoorsien, (-e), unexpected, unforeseen.
onvoorsiens, unexpectedly.
onvoorwaardelik, (-e), unconditional, absolute.
onvri(e)ndelik, (-e), unkind, unfriendly.
onvrugbaar, (-bare), infertile (lit, & fig.); sterile (land, person, plant, discussion), unfruitful.
onwaar, (–, -ware), false, untrue.
onwaardig, (-e), unworthy.
onwaarskynlik, (-e), improbable, unlikely.
onwankelbaar, (-bare), unshakable, steadfast.
onweer, unsettled (bad) weather, storm.
onweerstaanbaar, (-bare), irresistible.
onwelvoeglik, (-e), indecent, improper.
onwelwillend, (-e), discourteous, disobliging.
onwenslik, (-e), undesirable.
onwetend, (-e), ignorant.
onwettig, (-e), illegal, illicit; naughty; illegitimate.
onwillekeurig, (-e), a. involuntary.
onwillekeurig, adv. involuntarily.
onwillig, (-e), unwilling, reluctant.
onwrikbaar, (-bare), unshakeable, steadfast.
oog, (oë), eye; fountain(-head); pub, bar.
ooggetuie, eyewitness.
oogklap, blinker; –pe, blinkers.
oogknip, wink; in 'n –, in the twinkling of an eye.
oogluikend: – toelaat, shut the eyes to.
oogmerk, aim, intention, object.
oogopslag, glance.
oogwenk, -wink, wink; in 'n –, in the twinkling of an eye.
ooi, (-e), ewe.
ooievaar, stork.
ooit, ever.
ook, also, as well, too, likewise, even.
oom, (-s), uncle.
oomblik, (-ke), moment.
oombliklik, (-e), a. instantaneous; momentary; immediate; fleeting.
oombliklik, adv. instantaneously, immediately, instantly.
oond, (-e), oven; furnace; (lime-) kiln.
oop, ope, open; empty (seat); vacant (post).
oopdraai, (oopge-), turn on, open.
oopgaan, (oopge-), open.
oopgooi, (oopge-), throw open, fling open (door); spread out (rug).
oophou, (oopge-), open (hand); keep unlocked; hold (keep) open; keep vacant.

ooplê, (oopge-), lie open; lie uncovered (exposed); lay open; expose.
oopmaak, (oopge-), open.
oopskuif, -skuiwe, (oopge-), slide up (open), shove (move) up (back).
oopsluit, (oopge-), unlock.
oopspalk, (oopge-), spread out, stretch out; open wide.
oopspring, (oopge-), burst open, fly open, crack.
oopstaan, (oopge-), be open.
oopsteek, (oopge-), prick, pierce.
oopstel, (oopge-), open; throw open.
ooptrek, (oopge-), open (drawer, etc.); give a thrashing.
oopval, (oopge-), fall open; become vacant.
oor, (ore), n. ear (of person, pitcher, etc.), handle.
oor, prep. over (head, shoulder, eyes, place); across (road, channel); more than, over (R3); beyond, above (a hundred); via, by way of (a place); (five minutes) past (the hour).
oor, adv. over.
oor, conj. because.
oorbekend, (-e), generally known; too well known.
oorbel(letjie), ear-ring, ear-drop.
oorbevolk, (-te), over-populated.
oorbieg, auricular confession.
oorbietjie, oribie, (-s), oribi.
oorbluf, (–), bluff, frighten, bully; fluster.
oorbly, (oorge-), remain, be left (over); stay.
oorblyfsel, (-s), remainder, remnant; remains; relic.
oorblywend, (-e), remaining.
oorbodig, (-e), superfluous, redundant.
oorboord, overboard.
oorbring, (oorge-), take over (across) bring, convey, transport, transfer (to another post); translate; take, deliver (message); tell (news, story).
oorbrug, (–), bridge.
oord, (-e), place, region, (holiday) resort.
oordaad, excess, superabundance.
oordadig, (-e), a. excessive, extravagant.
oordrag, by (during the) day.
oordeel, n. judgment, sentence (passed by the judge); verdict (of jury); opinion, view(s).
oordeel, (ge-), judge; be of opinion, consider, deem.
oordeelkundig, (-e), discerning; sensible.
oordink, (–), consider, ponder over.
oordra, (oorge-), carry over (across); assign; transfer (rights); cede; commit (authority to).
oordrag, (-te), transfer, conveyance; cession; assignment.
oordragtelik, (-e), metaphorical.
oordrewe, a. exaggerated; excessive; exorbitant (price); overdone.
oordryf, -drywe, (oorge-), drift across (the river); blow over (of weather).
oordryf, -drywe, (–), exaggerate, overdo.
ooreenkom, (ooreenge-), agree (with); correspond (to, with).
ooreenkoms, (-te), similarity, resemblance; agreement; treaty; contract.
ooreenkomstig, (-e), similar, corresponding, conformable.
ooreenstem, (ooreenge-), agree, concur.
ooreenstemming, agreement, harmony, concord.
oorerf, -erwe, (oorge-), inherit.
oorerflik, (-e), hereditary; inheritable.
oorgaan, (oorge-), go across, cross; go over (to another party); pass off (of sensations); stop; clear up (of weather), blow over; be promoted.

oorgang, (-e), going across; crossing; going over; adoption; transition, change; passage, transit.

oorganklik, (-e), transitive (verb).

oorgawe, handling over; surrender; transfer, cession (of rights).

oorgee, (oorge-), pass over, hand, reach; yield, surrender; give up, part with; hand over (to the police).

oorgehaal, (-de), cocked (gun); prepared, ready, on the point of.

oorgenoeg, more than enough.

oorgevoelig, (-e), over-sensitive; hypersensitive.

oorgroot, (-grote), vast, huge, immense.

oorhaal, (oorge-), fetch (over); cock (a gun), persuade, talk over.

oorhaastig, (-e), hurried, rash, reckless.

oorhand, upper hand, mastery, supremacy.

oorhandig, (-), hand (over), deliver.

oorhê (oorgehad), have left (over, to spare).

oorheen, over, across.

oorheers, (-), dominate (a person), predominate (over).

oorheersend, (-e), (pre)dominant; outstanding.

oorhel, (oorge-), lean, (hang) over, incline.

oorhoeks, (-e), a. diagonal; out of sorts.

oorhoeks, adv. diagonally.

oorhoop, in a heap; disarranged.

oorjaag, -jae (-), overdrive (horse, person), work (person) to exhaustion.

oorjaag, -jae, (oorge-), drive (chase) over (across); re-run (a race).

oorjas, overcoat.

oorkant, n. the other (opposite) side.

oorkant, prep. across, beyond.

oorkants(t)e, opposite (bank).

oorkom, (oorge-), come over (across), cross, get over; happen to, befall.

oorkom, (-), surmount.

oorkonkel, (-s), n. box on the ear.

oorkrabbetjie, -krawwetjie, (-s), ear-drop.

oorkruiper, earwig.

oorkruis, crosswise, diagonally.

oorkyk, (oorge-), look beyond; look over; go (look, read) over, go through; correct.

oorlaai, (-), overload; overstock (market); deluge (with); overwhelm (with praise).

oorlaai, (oorge-), transfer the load, tranship; load over again, reload.

oorlaat, (oorge-), leave; entrust (to).

oorlams, (-e), oorlam, (-se), clever, smart, handy; cunning; sly; sharp.

oorlas, nuisance, annoyance.

oorlede, oorlee, deceased, the late; – mnr. K., the late Mr K.

oorleef, -lewe, (-) survive, outlive.

oorleer, n. upper (leather), vamp.

oorleg, deliberation, consideration; consultation; judgment; care.

oorlewer, (oorge-), give (deliver) up (over); hand down.

oorlewering, (-e, -s), handing over; tradition.

oorlog, (-loë), war.

oorlogvoerend, (-e), belligerent.

oorloop, n. overflow(ing); landing; crossing.

oorloop, (oorge-), cross; run (flow) over, overflow.

oorloper, deserter.

oorlosie, vide horlosie.

oormaak, (oorge-), do over again; remake; stop (pain); transfer; remit; transmit.

oormaat, superabundance, excess.

oormag, superior power (numbers), odds.

oormatig, (-e), a. excessive; immoderate.

oormeester, (-), overpower, overcome.

oormoed, rashness; presumption.

oormoedig, (-e), rash, reckless.

oormôre, -more, the day after to-morrow.

oornag, (-), pass the night.

oorname, taking over.

oorneem, (oorge-), take from; take over; adopt, derive; copy.

oorpeinsing, (-e, -s), meditation, musing.

oorplaas, (oorge-), remove; transfer.

oorplant, (oorge-), transplant.

oorplasing, (-e, -s), removal, transfer.

oorreed, (-), persuade, induce.

oorrompel, (-), take by surprise, overwhelm, fall (swarm) upon, rush.

oorsaak, (-sake), cause, origin.

oorsaaklik, (-e), casual.

oorsê, (oorge-), say again, repeat.

oorsees, (-sese), oversea, transmarine.

oorsien, (oorge-), see on the other side; excuse, overlook.

oorsig, (-te), view; synopsis, summary.

oorsit, (oorge-), put over (across); take across; promote (at school); put into (another language).

oorskadu, (-), overshadow; eclipse, cloud, darken.

oorskat, (-), over-estimate, overrate.

oorskat, (oorge-), estimate (value) again, re-estimate.

oorskiet, n. remains; remainder, rest; surplus, remnant; leavings.

oorskot, (-te), vide oorskiet, n.; surplus; stoflike –, mortal remains.

oorskry, (-), cross; overstep, pass beyond; exceed; violate, infringe.

oorslaan, (oorge-), hit over; fold (turn) over; skip, omit, leave out, miss out; miss (a meeting); pass (over) by; misfire (of motor, gun).

oorslag, (-slae), overlapping part; hasp (and staple); flap.

oorspan, (-), span, extend across; overstrain.

oorsprong, (-e), origin, source.

oorspronklik, (-e), original; premeval.

oorstap, (oorge-), cross, step across (over); change; disregard.

oorsteek, (oorge-), cross (the street).

oorstelp, (-), overwhelm.

oorstroom, (oorge-), overflow; brim over.

oorstroom, (-), flood, inundate (lit. & fig.); deluge, swamp; overstock, glut.

oortap, (oorge-), pour (transfer) into another vessel.

oorteken, (-), over-subscribe (a loan).

oortel, (oorge-), (1) recount.

oortel, (oorge-), (2) lift over (across).

oortjie, (-s), farthing.

oortollig, (-e), a. superfluous, redundant.

oortollig, adv. superfluously.

oortreder, (-s), trespasser, transgressor, infringer (of law).

oortree, (-), transgress, infringe, break.

oortree, (oorge-), step over.

oortref, (-), surpass, excel, outclass.

oortreffend, (-e), superlative (degree).

oortrek, (oorge-), pull over; move (into another house); cross, trek over (across): upholster (furniture), cover.

oortrek, (-), overdraw.

oortreksel, (-s), cover, slip, case.

oortrokke: – rekening, overdraft.

oortuie, -tuig, (-), convince.

oorval, (-), (take by) surprise, overtake.

oorverdowend, (-e), deafening.

oorvertel, (-), tell over again, repeat.

oorvleuel, (-), outflank; surpass.

oorvloed, abundance, plenty.
oorvloei, (oorge-), overflow, flow (run) over, brim over; flood, inundate.
oorvloed, (-), overfeed.
oorvoer, (oorge-), lead across (over); convey, take across.
oorvoer, (-), overfeed; overstock.
oorvra, (oorge-), ask again.
oorvra, (-), overcharge.
oorwaks, (-e), box on the ear.
oorweë, -weeg, (oorge-), reweigh.
oorweë, -weeg, (-) consider, weigh (consequences, etc.).
oorweg, n. level-crossing.
oorweging, (-e, -s), consideration.
oorweldig, (-), overpower, overwhelm; overcome.
oorwelf, (-), overarch, span, vault.
oorwen, vide **oorwin.**
oorwig, preponderance.
oorwin, oorwen, (-), conquer, defeat.
oorwinnaar, (-d), conqueror, victor.
oorwinning, (-e, -s), victory.
oorwinter, (-), winter, hibernate.
oorwoë, considered.
oos, a. east.
Oos-Afrika, East Africa.
Oossee, die -, the Baltic.
ooste, (the east); **die O.,** the East.
oostelik, (-e), easterly, eastern.
Oostenryk, Austria.
Oosters, (-e), Oriental, Eastern.
ootmoed, humility, meekness.
ootmoedig, (-e), humble, meek.
op, prep. on, upon, in, at.
op, adv. up, on.
opaal, (opale), opal.
opbeur, (opge-), drag up; cheer up, comfort.
opblaas, (opge-), blow up, puff up, inflate; blast.
opbou, (opge-), build up; edify, benefit.
opbreek, (opge-), break up; strike (tents); break (pull) up (street); disperse.
opbrengs, -brings, (-te), yield, crop (of wheat), output; produce, proceeds.
opbring, (opge-), bring up; rear, (child), educate; vomit; yield (crop); bring in, realize.
opbrings, vide **opbrengs.**
opdaag, (opge-), arrive, turn up.
opdamp, (opge-), vaporize; evaporate.
opdat, (in order) that.
opdiep, (opge-), dig up (out), unearth.
opdis, (opge-), serve up, dish up.
opdoem, (opge-), loom (up).
opdoen, (opge-), do (up) (the hair); acquire (knowledge); catch (a cold), get, contract (disease).
opdok, (opge-), pay up; pay the piper.
opdons, (opge-), let (a person) have it, go for (a person); do (things) anyhow, bungle along.
opdra(ag), (opge-), carry up; wear out (clothes); instruct, charge; entrust (person) with (duty); dedicate (church, book).
opdraand, (-e), -draande, (-s), n. uphill path (road), rising ground.
opdraand, opdraans, a. and adv. uphill.
opdrag, (-te), instruction, order, commission, charge.
opdreun, (opge-), drone (on); make it hot for, drive (a person) on.
opdrifsel, (-s), drift, driftwood, debris.
opdring, (opge-), push on (forward); force (something) upon, intrude upon (a person).
opdringerig, (-e), intrusive, obtrusive.
opduik, (opge-), emerge, come to the surface; turn up, crop up.

opeen, one upon another, together.
opeenhoping, accumulation; crowd; congestion (traffic).
opeens, suddenly, all of a sudden.
opeenvolgend, (-e), successive.
opeet, (opgeëet), eat, eat (up), finish; devour, consume.
openbaar, n. public; **in die -,** in public.
openbaar, (-bare), a. public.
openbaar, (ge-), reveal, divulge, disclose.
openbaring, (-e, -s), revelation, manifestation, disclosure.
openhartig, (-e), frank, open (-hearted).
opening, (-e, -s), opening; aperture, gap, passage, chink.
openlik, adv. openly, publicly; frankly.
opera, (-s), opera.
operasie, (-s), operation.
operd, (opgeërd), earth up, bank up.
opereer, (ge-), operate.
operette, (-s), operetta.
opflikker, (opge-), flicker (flare) up, blaze up, cheer (brighten) up.
opgaaf, hut-tax.
opgaan, (opge-), go up, ascend.
opgaar, (opge-), collect, store up, rise; climb.
opgang, (-e), rise; ascent; growth; success, fame.
opgawe, (-s), statement (of facts), account; (official) return, report; exercise.
opgee, (opge-), pass (hand) up; give up, hand over; set (a problem); enumerate (items), state (reasons), specify (details); give up (patient, plan, hope), lose (courage); stop (smoking).
opgehewe, raised; swollen, inflamed.
opgekrop, (-te), pent-up (rage).
opgeruimd, (-e), cheerful, gay.
opgeskeep: - sit, be saddled (with something).
opgeskort, (-e), suspended (sentence).
opgeskote, grown up (boy), adolescent.
opgesmuk, (-te), showy, gaudy; bombastic (style).
opgetoë, elated, exultant, in high spirits.
opgewas(se): - wees teen, be a match for.
opgewek, (-te), cheerful, gay, cheery.
opgewonde, excited.
opgooi, (opge-), throw up, toss up; vomit.
opgraaf, -grawe, (opge-), unearth; exhume, (body); excavate.
ophaal, (opge-), draw up, pull up; hoist (flag); weigh (anchor); shrug (shoulders); turn up (the nose); collect (tickets); rake up, open up.
ophef, n. fuss.
ophef, (opge-), lift (up), raise (eyes, hand); abolish, repeal (law), revoke, annul; lift, raise (socially).
ophelder, (opge-), clear up; elucidate, illustrate; solve (mystery); brighten.
ophemel, (opge-), extol, write up.
ophoop, (opge-), heap up, pile up, heap together; accumulate; amass.
ophou, (opge-), hold up; support; keep on (hat); hold (breath); detain, keep (waiting); stop, leave off; keep up (one's position).
opinie, (-s), opinion.
opja(ag), (opge-), drive (chase) up; speed up (the road); flush (birds), put up (game), rouse, start; frighten away; force up.
opkeil, (opge-), wedge up; drive (urge) on, chastise, give it (a person) hot.
opklaar, (opge-), clear up (of weather); brighten (of face); elucidate, solve.
opknap, (opge-), tidy up (oneself, table, room); renovate, do up (house), retrim (dress); put (matter) right.

opknappertjie, (-s), tonic.

opkom, (opge-), come up; get up, stand up; rise (of sun); shoot forth, sprout, come up (of grass); spring up (of breeze), come on (of storm); attend (meeting), turn up; crop up, arise (of question); spring up.

opkoms, rising (of sun); rise (of a statesman); beginning; attendance.

opkoop, (opge-), buy up; forestall.

opkrop, (opge-), conceal, restrain, bottle up.

opkry, (opge-), get up; get on (a hat); use up, finish.

oplaag, impression, edition (of book).

oplaai, (opge-), load (up); give (person) a lift.

oplaas, finally, eventually, at last.

oplê, (opge-), put on, apply; impose (tax) upon, inflict (punishment) on; set (person at task).

oplei, (opge-), lead up; train (teacher), educate, bring up.

opleef, -lewe, (opge-), revive.

oplewer, (opge-), yield, bring in, produce, give; deliver.

oplet, (opge-), attend, watch.

oploop, (opge-), walk up, go up; slope upwards, rise; accumulate.

oplos, (opge-), dissolve; solve (problem); settle (dispute); work out.

oplossing, (-e, -s), solution.

opluister, (opge-), adorn add lustre to, illuminate; illustrate.

opmaak, (opge-), make (bed); do (up) (the hair); trim (hat); make up (in pages); make out (list); stir up, incite.

opmeet, (opge-), measure; survey.

opmerk, (opge-), notice; observe.

opmerking, (-e, -s), remark, observation.

opmerklik, (-e), remarkable, noteworthy.

opmerksaam, (-same), observant, attentive.

opnaaisel, (-s), tuck.

opname, (-s), taking; insertion; survey (of land); reception; record(ing).

opneem, (opge-), take up; pick up; count (votes); film, shoot; borrow (money); put in; include; absorb (heat), assimilate; look (person) up and down, take stock of.

opnoem, (opge-), name, mention, enumerate.

opnuut, again, afresh, anew.

opoffer, (opge-), sacrifice, offer up.

oponthoud, delay, stoppage; break down.

oppas, (opge-), try on (hat); look after, tend (flock), herd (sheep), nurse (patient); take care, look out, mind.

oppassend, (-e), well-behaved; steady.

oppasser, (-s), caretaker, attendant.

opper, (ge-), suggest, propose, raise (objection), broach (subject).

opperhoof, chief, head.

oppermag, supremacy, supreme power.

opperste, uppermost, highest, supreme.

oppervlak, (upper) surface.

oppervlakkig, (-e), superficial, shallow.

oppervlakte, surface; area; superficies.

Opperwese, Supreme Being, God.

opponent, (-e), opponent.

opposisie, opposition.

opraak, (opge-), run short, give out, be spent.

opraap, (opge-), pick (snatch, take) up.

opreg, (-te), upright, sincere, straight-forward, frank, open; genuine, pure.

oprig, (opge-), raise; erect (building); start (business), found (institution), float (company), form (society).

oproep, (-e), n. summons; appeal.

oproep, (opge-), summon, call up(on); summons; call out (up); call (together).

oproer, (-e), revolt, rebellion, mutiny.

oproerig, (-e), rebellious, riotous.

oproermaker, agitator, rioter.

opruim, (opge-), clear away, clear, tidy up; do away with.

opruiming, (-e, -s), clearing away, clearance; clearance-sale.

opruk, (opge-), jerk, (pull) up; advance.

opryg, -rye, (opge-), tack; lace.

opsê, (opge-), say (prayer); recite; terminate (agreement).

opsent, absent, absent; lost.

opset, (ground-)plan, framework; purpose, design.

opsetlik, (-e), a. intentional, deliberate.

opsie, (-s), option.

opsien, n.: – baar, cause a sensation.

opsien, (opge-), look up; shrink (from doing something).

opsienbarend, (-e), sensational.

opsiener, (-s), overseer, inspector; invigilator, commissioner.

opsig, (-te), respect.

opsigter, (-s), overseer; caretaker.

opsit, (opge-), (1) sit up; stay up; spoon; wait up.

opsit, (opge-), (2) put on (hat); swell (up); erect; raise (price); set up, start (business), establish; stake (money).

opskep, (opge-), scoop up; ladle out; serve up, dish up.

opskiet, (opge-), shoot up; sprout.

opskort, (opge-), reserve (judgment), postpone, (sentence); adjourn.

opskrif, (-te), inscription; heading (of chapter); caption; title.

opskud, (opge-), shake up; hurry up.

opskudding, (-s), commotion, stir, fuss, sensation.

opslaan, (opge-), hit (strike) up; bounce; turn up (collar); cock (hat), turn up; raise (eyes); pitch (tent).

opslag, (-slae), up-stroke; rise, increase; ricochet, bounce; self-sown oats, barley, etc.; young grass; storage.

opslagplek, store, shed.

opsluit, adv. absolutely.

opsluiting, (-e, -s), locking up (in); imprisonment, confinement.

opslurp, (opge-), lap up; absorb.

opsmuk, n. finery, trimmings, trappings.

opsmuk, (opge-), dress up, trick out (up), decorate; embellish (narrative).

opsoek, (opge-), look up (a word); call on, look up (a person) look for.

opsom, (opge-), sum up; summarize.

opspoor, (opge-), trace, track down, hunt down, find out.

opspraak, scandal; sensation.

opstaan, (opge-), stand up, rise, get up; revolt, rebel.

opstal, (-le), (farm-)buildings, premises.

opstand, (-e), rebellion, revolt, rising, insurrection.

opstanding, resurrection.

opstapel, -stawel, (opge-), build up; pile (heap) up, accumulate.

opsteek, (opge-), pin up; put up (the hair); hold up (hand); prick up (ears); light (lamp); incite, urge on.

opstel, (-le), n. composition, essay.

opstel, (opge-), place in position; mount (gun); frame (rule), draw up (report); draft.

opstook, (opge-), stir (fire); instigate, incite.

opstootjie, (-s), disturbance, riot, rising.

opstopper, (-s), taxidermist; blow.

opstry, (opge-), contradict; dispute.

opstyg, (opge-), ascend, rise; mount.
opsweep, (opge-), whip up; incite.
opsy, aside, aloof, away.
opteken, (opge-), note (down), set (write) down,
  record, enter.
optel, (opge-), (1) add (up), total up.
optel, (opge-), (2) pick up; lift; trouble.
optimis, (-te), optimist.
optog, (-te), procession; approach.
optooi, (opge-), adorn, decorate.
optrede, appearance; behaviour, conduct.
optree, (opge-), appear; play (act) a part; take
  action, act.
optrek, (opge-), draw (pull) up; raise; shrug
  (shoulders); erect; add up; lift, rise.
opvaar, (opge-), sail up; ascend.
opval, (opge-), strike.
opvang, (opge-), catch (snatch) up; catch (water);
  intercept.
opvarende, (-s), passenger.
opvatting, (-e, -s), view, opinion, idea.
opveil, (opge-), sell by auction.
opvlie(g), (opge-), fly up; jump up.
opvliegend, opvlieënd, (-e), quick-tempered.
opvoed, (opge-), educate, bring up, train.
opvoedkunde, education, pedagogy.
opvoer, (opge-), bring up; stage (lay), produce.
opvolg, (opge-), succeed; obey, follow.
opvoubaar, (-bare), collapsible, foldable.
opvreet, (opge-), devour.
opvulsel, (-s), stuffing, filling.
opwaarts, upward(s).
opwagting: sy – by iemand maak, wait (up)on
  somebody.
opwas, (opge-), (1) wash up.
opwas, (opge-), (2) grow up.
opwee(g), -weë, (opge-): – teen, counterbalance,
  make up for.
opwek, (opge-), rouse, wake up, raise from the
  dead; stir up; excite, provoke; generate.
opwel, (opge-), well up (out, forth), bubble up.
opwen, -win(d), (opge-), wind up; excite.
opwindend, (-e), exciting.
opwinding, excitement.
opwip, (opge-), rebound; jump up.
orakel, (-s), oracle.
oral(s), everywhere.
oranje, orange.
Oranjerivier, Orange River.
Oranje-Vrystaat, Orange Free State.
orde, (1) order.
orde, (-s), (2) order (Natural History); geestelike –, religious order.
ordelik, (-e), orderly, well-behaved.
orden, (ge-), put in order, arrange; ordain
  (minister of religion).
ordentlik, (-e), decent, respectable, fair, pretty,
  good.
ordentlikheidshalwe, for decency's sake.
order, (-s), order, command.
ordinansie, (-s), ordinance (of God).
ordonnans, (-e), orderly.
ordonnansie, (-s), ordinance.
orent, on end, upright, erect.
orgaan, (-gane), organ.
organisasie, (-s), organization.
organiseer, (ge-), organize.

orgelis, vide orrelis.
orgidee, (-deë), orchid.
oribie, vide oorbietjie.
Oriëntaal, (-tale), Oriental.
orig, (-e), (1) remaining.
orig, (-e), (2) meddlesome, intrusive.
origens, for the rest, otherwise.
orkaan, (-kane), hurricane.
orkes, (-te), orchestra.
ornament, (-e), ornament.
orrel, (-s), organ.
orrelis, (-te), organist.
ortodoks, (-e), orthodox.
os, (-se), ox.
oseaan, (-ane), ocean.
ossewa, ox-wag(g)on.
otjie, (-s), pig; grunter.
otter, (-s), otter.
Ottomaans, (-e), Ottoman.
ou, (-es), n. (old) fellow; one, a man, a chap.
ou, a. old, ancient.
oubaas, old gentleman (fellow, chap).
ouboet(a), ouboetie, eldest brother.
oud, old, aged.
oud-, former, ex-, old (student).
ouderdom, (-me), age; old age.
ouderling, (-e, -s), elder.
ouderwets, (-e), old-fashioned, out-of-date; precocious (child).
oudheid, oldness; antiquity.
oudheidkundige, (-s), archaeologist.
ouditeur, (-e, -s), auditor.
ouds: van –, formerly, of old.
oudsher: van –, from long ago.
oud-stryder, ex-soldier, veteran.
ouer, (-s), n. parent.
ouer, a. older; elder.
ouerig, (-e), oldish, not so young.
ouerlik, (-e), ouerlik, (-e), parental.
Oujaarsdag, last day of the year.
Oujaarsaand, New Year's eve.
oujongkêrel, bachelor.
oujongmeisie, old maid, spinster.
oujongnôi, -nooi, vide oujongmeisie.
oulaas: vir –, for the last time.
oulik, (-e), precocious (child); clever, tricky;
  neat.
oulap, (-pe), penny.
ouma, (-s), grandmother.
ouma-grootjie, great-grandmother.
oumannehuis, old men's home.
oupa, (-s), grandfather.
oupa-grootjie, great-grandfather.
outentiek, (-e), authentic.
outeur, (-s), author.
outjie, (-s), fellow, chap, boy.
outo, (-'s), motor-car.
outomaties, (-e), automatic.
outoriteit, (-e), authority.
outyds, (-e), old-fashioned; ancient.
ouvolk, (kind of) lizard.
ouvrou-onder-die-kombers, toad-in-the-hole.
owerheid, authorities, government.
owerigens, origens, for the rest, otherwise.
owerste, (-s), chief; prior.

pa, (-'s), pa, dad.
paadjie, (-s), (foot-)path, track, trail; parting (of hair).
paai, (ge-), coax, soothe; pat, stroke.
paaiboelie, (-s), bugbear, ogre, bogey.
paaiement, (-e), instalment.
paal, (pale), pole, post, stake.
paalspring, (paalge-), do polevaulting, -jumping.
paaltjie, (-s), stake; (fencing-) standard; (cricket) stump.
paap, (pape), pope; priest, parson.
paar, (pare), n. pair (of socks, eyes); couple (of people).
paar, adv. – **of onpaar**, odd or even.
Paasfees, Easter; (Jewish) Passover.
Paasvakansie, Easter-holidays.
pad, (paaie), road, way, path.
padda, (-s), frog, toad.
paddastoel, (poisonous) toadstool.
paddavis, tadpole.
padgee, (padge-), give way; make room.
padlang(e)s, along the orad; – **loop**, be straightforward; – **praat**, be outspoken (frank, candid).
padloper, tramp, vagabond; steamroller.
padvinder, path-finder; boy scout.
pag, lease; (quit)rent.
pagina, (-s), page.
pagter, (-s), lessee; tenant (-farmer).
pak, (-ke), pack, package, packet (of biscuits, candles), parcel, bundle (of papers); load, burden; suit (of clothes); hiding, thrashing.
pak, (ge-), pack (up); wrap (up); seize, grip, clutch; hold the attention.
pakhuis, store, warehouse.
pakkend, (-e), arresting, gripping, catchy.
pakket, (-te), parcel.
pakos, pack-ox.
pal, adv. firm, fixed, immovable.
paleis, (-e), palace.
Palestina, Palestine.
palet, (-te), palette.
paling, (-s), eel.
paljas, charm, spell, magic potion.
palm, (-s), palm.
palmiet, (-e), "palmiet," (bul)rush.
pamflet, (-te), pamphlet; lampoon.
pampelmoes, (-e), shaddock, pomelo.
pamperlang, (ge-), cajole, wheedle, coax.
pampoen, (-e), pumpkin; bumpkin.
pampoenkoekie, (-s), pumpkin-fritter.
pampoentjies, (pl.) mumps.
pan, (-ne), (frying-) pan; tile.
pand, (-e), pledge, security; forfeit.
pand, (ge-), pawn; pledge.
pandak, tile-roof.
pandoer, (-e, -s), pandour.
pandspeel, (pandge-), play (at) forfeits.
paneel, (-nele), panel.
pangeweer, flint-gun.
paniekerig, (-e), panicky.
pannekoek, pan-cake.
pant, (-e), (coat-)tail, flap.
pantoffel, (-s), slipper.
pantser, armour, mail, armour(-plating).
pantser, (ge-), armour, plate (ships).
pap, n. porridge; poultice (on a sore); pulp, mash; paste.
pap, a. & adv., soft, weak; flabby; punctured.
papa, (-'s), **pappa** (-s), papa, daddy.
papaja, (-s), pa(w)paw.
papawer, (-s), poppy.
papbroek, softy, milksop, funk.
papegaai, (-e), parrot, polly.
papelellekoors, sham-fever; trembles.

papie, (-s), chrysalis; cocoon.
papier, (-e), paper; (pl.) papers; documents.
papierdrukker, paper-weight.
papkuil, bulrush (Typha sp.).
papnat, soaking (dripping) wet.
Papoea, (-s), Papuan.
pappa, vide **papa**.
papsaf, -**sag**, (-te), quite soft.
papsak, softy, milksop.
paraat, (-rate), ready, prepared.
parabool, (-bole), parabola.
parade, (-s), parade.
paradoks, (-e), paradox.
paradys, (-e), paradise.
parafeer, (ge-), initial; paraph.
paraffien, paraffin(e).
paragraaf, (-grawe), paragraph; section.
parallel, n. & a. (-e), parallel.
parasiet, (-e), parasite.
pardoems!, flop!, splash!.
parenteties, (-e), parenthetic(al).
parfuum, n. perfume, scent.
pari, par.
park, (-e), park.
parkeer, (ge-), park (motors).
parket, parquet(-floor); front stalls.
parkiet (-e), parakeet.
parlement, (-e), parliament.
parlementêr, (-e), parliamentary.
parmant, (-e), cocky (cheeky) person.
parmantig, (-e), cheeky, pert, impertinent, impudent.
parodie, (-ë), parody, travesty.
paroniem, (-e), n. paronym.
parool, parole, password; word of honour.
pars, (ge-), press.
part, (-e), part, portion, share.
part, (-e), trick.
partikel, (-s), particle.
partuur, vide **portuur**.
party, (-e), n. party.
party, a. some.
partydig, (-e), partial, prejudiced.
partykeer(s), sometimes, occasionally.
partymaal, sometimes, at times.
Parys, Paris.
Parysenaar, (-nare, -naars), Parisian.
pas, (-se), n. pace, step; gait; (mountain) pass, defile, passage; pass, passport.
pas, n.: **te – kom**, come in useful (handy).
pas, adv. (only) just; newly, just, only; scarcely, hardly.
pas, (ge-), fit; fit on, try on (a coat); become, behove; suit, be convenient.
Pase, Easter.
pasella, present.
pasiënt, (-e), patient.
paskwil, (-le), lampoon; farce, mockery.
paslik, (-e), fitting, becoming; fair; in good condition, fit.
pasoppens: in jou – bly, mind one's steps (p's and q's), look out.
paspoort, (-e), pass, passport.
passaat, (-sate), trade(-wind); passage.
passasie, (-s), passage.
passasier, (-s), passenger.
passeer, (ge-), pass (also in card-games), go past, overtake; pass by.
passend, (-e), fitting, appropriate.
passer, (-s), (pair of) compasses.
passie, (-s), passion; craze.
passief, n. passive (voice).
pasta, paste.
pastei, (-e), pie, pastry, pasty.
pastoor, (-tore), pastor; priest, vicarage.

pastorie, (-ë), parsonage, rectory.
Patagonië, Patagonia.
patat, patatta, (-s), sweet potato; block-head.
patent, (-e), n. patent.
patent, (-e), a. patent; ingenious; excellent.
pateties, (-e), pathetic(al).
patos, pathos.
patriarg, (-e), patriarch.
patriot, (-te), patriot.
patrollie, (-s), patrol.
patroon, (-one), cartridge, pattern, model; patron, patron saint.
patrys, (-e), patridge, sandgrouse.
paviljoen, pawiljoen, (-e), pavilion, stand.
pê!, boo.
pedaal, (-dale), pedal.
pedagogie(k), pedagogy (pedagogics).
pedagoog, (-goë, -goge), pedagogue.
pedant, (-e), n. pedant.
peer, (pere), pear.
peer-, pereboom, pear-tree.
pees, (pese), tendon, sinew; string.
peesagtig, (-e), tendinous, sinewy.
peet, (pete), godfather, (-mother).
peetdogter, goddaughter.
peetjie, (-s), godfather; loop na jou –, go to the dickens.
peetoom, godfather.
peettante, godmother.
peil, n. level, gauge; standard.
peil, (ge-), gauge, fathom, sound, probe.
peillood, plummet, sounding-lead.
peins, (ge-), meditate, ponder, muse.
peits, (-e), whip.
pekel, n. pickle.
pekel, a. salt.
pekel, (ge-), pickle, salt, souse.
pelgrim, (-s), pilgrim.
pelikaan, (-kane), pelican.
peloton, (-ne, -s), platoon.
pels, (-e), fur; vide bont.
pen, (-ne), n. pen; nib; quill; spine; needle (for knitting).
pen, (-ne), n. pin, peg, spike.
pen, (ge-), pen, write.
pendoring, spike-thorn, long spine.
penisilline, (-ien), penicillin.
penkop, youth, youngster, cub.
pen(ne)lekker, quill-driver, pendriver.
pennemes, pen-knife.
pennie, (-s), penny.
penningmeester, treasurer.
penorent, straight up, erect, upright.
penregop, straight up, erect, vertical.
pens, (-e), paunch, belly.
penseel, (-sele), paint-brush; pencil.
pens en pootjies, adv. bodily.
pensioen, (-e), pension.
pensionaris, (-se) pensionary.
penwortel, tap-root, main root.
peper, pepper.
peper, (ge-), pepper.
peperduur, frightfully expensive.
peperkorrel, pepper-corn; –s (pl.), tufts of woolly hair.
peperwortel, horse-radish.
per, per, by.
perd, (-e), horse; knight (chess).
perdeby, wasp.
perdevlieg, horse-fly, botfly, cleg.
perdfris, healthy, hale and hearty.
perdgerus, calm, unconcerned.
perdry, (perdge-), ride (on horseback).
pêrel, (-s), pearl.
pêrel, (ge-), pearl, bead.

perfek, (-te), perfect.
periode, (-s), period.
perk, (-e), limit, bound; (grass-) lawn, plot; arena.
perkament, (-e), parchment, vellum.
perlemoen, perlemoer, mother-of-pearl.
permanent, (-e), permanent, lasting.
perron, (-s), platform.
pers, (-e), n. press.
pers, a. purple.
pers, (ge-), press, squeeze.
perseel, (-ele), lot, allotment, plot.
persent, per cent.
persentasie, (-s), percentage.
Persië, Persia.
perske, (-s), peach.
personeel, personnel, staff.
personifikasie, personification.
persoon, (-sone), person; actor, figure, appearance.
persoonlik, (-e), personal(ly).
perspektief, (-tiewe), perspective; view.
Peruaan, (-ane), Peruvian.
pes, (-te), pestilence, plague; pest.
pes, (ge-), pester, plague.
pessimis, (-te), pessimist.
pet, (-te), cap.
petalje, (-s), stir, fuss, commotion; pl. antics, escapades.
petieterig, (-e), small, tiny, weak.
petisie, (-s), petition, memorial.
petisionaris, (-se), petitioner.
petrol, petrol, motor-spirit.
peul, (-e), n. pod, husk.
peul, (-e), n. bolster, under-pillow.
peul, puil, (ge-), bulge, protrude.
peusel, (ge-), nibble, peck.
peuter, (ge-), fiddle, worry; tamper.
pianis, (-te), pianist.
piano, (-'s), piano.
piedewiet, vide pierewiet.
piek, (-e), pike; peak.
piekel, (ge-), lug, drag, carry.
piekfyn, grand, swell, spick and span.
piekniek, (-s), n. picnic.
piep, n. pip, roup.
piep, (ge-), chirp, squeak, peep.
pieperig, (-e), squeaky, piping (voice); weak(ly), sickly (person), soft.
piepjong, quite young, soft, tender.
piepkuiken, spring-chicken.
pier, (-e), n. pier, jetty.
pierewiet, (-e, -s), pilawit.
piering, (-s), saucer.
piesang, (-s), banana.
piet-my-vrou, (-e), red-chested cuckoo; whip-poor-will.
piets, (ge-), whip, flick.
pigmee, (-meë), pygmy.
pik, (-ke), n. peck; pick(-axe).
pik, n. pitch.
pik, (ge-), peck, bite; pick.
pikant, (-e), piquant, pungent, spicy.
pikdonker, pitch dark.
pikdraad, waxed end (thread).
pikkenien, (-s), picannin(ny).
pikkewyn, (-e), (jackass-)penguin.
pikswart, pitch black, jet black.
pil, (-le), pill.
pilaar, (-are), pillar, column; stalwart.
piloot, (-lote), pilot.
piment, allspice; pimento (-tree).
pimpel: – en pers, black and blue.
pinkie, (-s), little finger.
Pinkster, Whitsuntide, Pentecost.

Pinkstersondag, Whit Sunday.
pion, (-ne), pawn.
pionier, (-s, -e), pioneer.
piouter, pewter.
pipet, (-te), pipette.
piramide, (-s), pyramid.
Pireneë, Pyrenees.
pistool, (-tole), pistol (weapon).
pit, (-te), stone (of peach), pip (of orange), kernel; core, pith, marrow; wick (of a lamp).
pits(w)eer, boil, furuncle.
pittig, (-e), pithy (speech), terse (expression), racy, snappy (style).
pla(e), plaag, (ge-), vex, annoy, tease, bother, banter.
plaag, (plae), n. plague; nuisance.
plaas, (plase), farm; place.
plaas, (ge-), place, put, set (put) up, erect; locate, assign a place to, rank; insert.
plaas, vide pleks.
plaaslik, (-e), local.
plaasvervanger, deputy, substitute.
plaasvind, (plaasge-), take place, happen.
plaat, (plate), (door-, photographic, dental), plate; (marble) slab, engraving, print, picture; (gramophone-)record; sheet (of iron); patch, stretch (of bush).
plaatsing, plasing, placing.
plae, vide pla.
plafon, (-ne, -s), ceiling.
plagiaat, plagiarism.
plak, (-ke), n. ferule, strap, cane, stick.
plak, (ge-), paste, gum, stick, affix (stamp); paper (room).
plakkaat, (-kate), placard, poster; edict.
plakker, (-s), paperhanger; hanger-on; squatter (on a farm).
plakpapier, wall-paper.
plan, (-ne), plan, project, design; diagram.
planeet, (-ete), planet.
plank, (-e), plank, board; shelf.
plant, (-e), n. plant, herb.
plant, (ge-), plant; transplant; tackle (football).
plantasie, (-s), plantation.
plantegroei, vegetation.
plantkunde, botany.
plas, (-se), n. pool, puddle, plash.
plat, flat (roof), horizontal; level, even, smooth; coarse, broad.
platanna, (-s), clawed toad.
platdruk, (platge-), squeeze flat, crush.
platform, (-s), platform.
platina, platinum ore.
platinum, platinum.
platjie, (-s), wag, rogue, scamp.
platkopspykertjie, tack, drawing-pin.
platlê, (platge-), lie (down) flat; crush; run at full speed.
platloop, (platge-), run over, sweep away, finish off.
plato, (-'s), plateau.
platonies, (-e), platonic.
platriem, strap.
platsak, penniless.
platskiet, (platge-), shoot down (people); level (town) with the ground.
plattegrond, (ground-)plan (of building, town); (seating-) plan.
platteland, country(-districts); backveld.
plattrap, (platge-), trample under foot.
platweg, down-right, flatly; plainly.
plavei, (ge-), pave.
pleeg, (ge-), commit, perpetrate (crime).
pleegkind, foster-child.
plegtig, (-e), solemn, ceremonious, impressive.

plegtigheid, (-hede), ceremony, rite, function.
pleidooi, (-e), plea, argument, address.
plein, (-e), square.
pleister, (-s), n. plaster; stucco (on wall).
pleister, (ge-), plaster, stucco.
pleit, (ge-), plead.
pleitbesorger, counsel, advocate, lawyer; spokesman.
plek, (-ke), place, spot; room, space; seat; post, position.
pleks, plaas, instead of, in place of.
pleng, (ge-), shed (blood), pour out (wine); offer (a libation).
plesier, pleasure, enjoyment.
plesier, (ge-), please.
plesierig, (-e), pleasant, happy; cheerful.
plig, (-te), duty.
pligmatig, (-e), as in duty bound.
pligsbesef, pligsgevoel, sense of duty.
pligshalwe, as in duty bound, dutifully.
ploe(ë), ploeg, (ge-), plough.
ploeg, (ploeë), n. plough.
ploegbaas, gangboss, foreman; ganger.
ploeter, (ge-), plod, drudge.
plof, (plowwe), n. thud, flop.
plof, (ge-), thud, flop, thump.
plomp, a. awkward, clumsy, stout.
plons, (ge-), splash, plop.
plooi, (-e), n. fold, pleat, crease, wrinkle.
plooi, (ge-), fold, crease, pleat.
plotseling, (-e), a. sudden, abrupt.
plotseling, adv. suddenly, all at once.
pluiens, pluiings, (pl.), rags, tatters.
pluim, (-e), plume, feather, crest.
pluimbal, shuttle-cock.
pluimpie, little crest (plume); compliment.
pluimstryk, (ge-), flatter, fawn upon.
pluimvee, poultry.
pluis, a. in order.
pluis, (ge-), fluff, pick, make fluffy.
pluisie, (-s), (bit of) fluff, plug (of wadding), wad, piece of cotton-wool.
pluiskeil, top-hat.
pluk, (ge-), pick, pluck; cull; fleece.
plunder, (ge-), plunder, ransack (a town); rob (a man).
plus, plus.
plutokraat, (-krate), plutocrat.
poedelnaak, (-te), poedelnakend, (-e), stark naked.
poeding, (-s), pudding.
poeët, (poëte), poet.
poeier, (-s), powder.
poeier, (ge-), powder.
poel, (-e), pool, puddle.
poena(geweer), light rifle, small musket.
poenskop, koenskop, (-s), poll, pollard.
poësie, poetry.
poets, n. trick.
poets, n. polish.
poets, (ge-), polish, clean, shine.
pofadder, puff-adder.
poffertjie, fritter.
poging, (-e), -s), attempt, try, effort.
pohaai, bohaai, fuss, noise, to-do.
pok, (-ke), pock.
pokkel, (-s), lump of flesh, body.
pokkies, (pl.), smallpox.
pol, (-le), tuft, tussock, clump.
Pole, Poland.
poleer, (ge-), polish; smooth-bore.
polemiek, (-e), controversy, polemic.
polgras, tuftgrass.
poliets, smart, clever, knowing.
Polinesië, Polynesia.
polis, (-se), (insurance-)policy.

polisie, police.
polisieagent, policeman, constable.
politiek, n. politics; policy.
politikus, (-se, -tici), politician.
politoer, n. polish.
politoer, (ge-), polish.
pols, (-e), pulse.
pols, (ge-), sound.
polshorlosie, -oorlosie, wrist watch.
polvy, (-e), heel (of boot).
polys, (ge-), polish (lit. & fig.), burnish.
pomelo, (-'s), grape-fruit; pomelo.
Pommere, Pomerania.
pomp, (-e), pump.
pomp, (ge-), pump; hit, strike.
pompelmoes, vide **pampelmoes.**
pompstasie, pumping-station.
pondok, (-ke), hut, hovel.
ponie, (-s), pony.
pons, punch.
pont, (-e), pontoon; ferry(-boat).
ponton, (-s), pontoon.
poog, (ge-), attempt, endeavour.
Pool, (Pole), Pole.
pool, (pole), pole.
poolsee, polar (Arctic, Antarctic) sea.
poort, (-e), gate(way), entrance; pass.
poot, (pote), paw, hoof, foot (of animal), leg (of animal, table, etc.); paw.
pootjie, (ge-), trip (up).
poot-uit, exhausted, done up, dog-tired.
pop, (-pe), doll; puppet; figurehead.
populariseer, (ge-), popularize.
populasie, population.
populêr, (-e), popular.
populier, (-e), poplar.
por, (ge-), prod, poke; spur (egg) on.
porie, (-ë), pore.
pors(e)lein, porcelain, china (-ware).
porsie, (-e), part, share; helping.
portaal, (-tale), entrance hall, lobby; porch, landing.
portefeulje, (-s), portfolio: wallet.
portier, (-e, -s), porter; carriage-door.
port(o), postage.
portret, (-te), portrait, photo(graph).
Portugal, Portugal.
portuur, partuur, (-s), equal, match.
pos, post; post office; mail; postal delivery.
pos, (ge-), post (letters, pickets).
posbode, postman.
posduif, carrier-pigeon.
poseer, (ge-), pose; sit (to a painter).
posisie, (-s), position, situation, status.
positief, (-tiewe), a. & adv. positive; sure.
positiewe, n. pl. senses; consciousness.
poskantoor, post office.
posmeester, postmaster.
posseël, (postage) stamp.
postuur, (-ture), figure, shape.
posvat, (posge-), take post, take root; take up one's position.
poswissel, postal order, money order.
pot, (-te), pot, jar.
potas, potash, potassium carbonate.
potdig, (-te), tightly closed, air-tight.
potdoof, (-dowe), stone-deaf.
potensiaal, (-siale), n. potential.
potklei, potter's clay; sticky mud.
potlepel, ladle.
potlood, (-lode), **potloot** (-lote), lead pencil.
potsierlik, (-e), grotesque; ridiculous.
pottebakker, potter.
pou, (-e), peacock, peafowl, peahen.
pous, (-e), pope.

pousdom, papacy; papal state.
pouse, (-s), interval, pause.
pouseer, (ge-), pause, break off.
power, poor, meagre, thin.
Praag, Prague.
praal, splendour, pomp, glory.
praalbed, bed of state.
praat, n. talk.
praat, (ge-), talk, speak, converse.
praatjie, (-s), talk, rumour, story.
praatkous, talker, tattler.
praatlustig, (-e), talkative, garrulous.
praatsiek, garrulous, loquacious.
praatsugtig, (-e), garrulous, loquacious.
prag, beauty, splendour.
pragmaties, (-e), pragmatic.
pragstuk, beauty, masterpiece.
pragtig, (-e), beautiful, splendid.
praktiseer, (ge-), devise, contrive; cogitate, puzzle.
prakties, (-e), a. practical, workable.
praktiseer, (ge-), practise.
praktisyn, (-s), (legal, medical) practitioner.
praktyk, (-e), practice.
praterig, (-e), talkative, garrulous.
predestinasie, predestination.
predik, (ge-), preach.
predikaat, (-kate), predicate; title; mark.
predikant, (-e), minister, clergyman, parson.
predikasie, (-s), sermon; lecture.
predikatief, (-tiewe), predicative.
prediker, (-s), preacher.
predomineer, (ge-), predominate.
preek, (preke), sermon, homily.
preek, (ge-), preach; sermonize, reprove.
preekstoel, pulpit.
prefek, (-te), prefect.
prefereer, (ge-), prefer; – bo, prefer to.
prefiks, (-e), prefix.
prei, leek.
preliminêr, (-e), a. preliminary.
premie, (-s), premium; bounty, bonus.
premier, (-s), premier, prime minister.
premis, (-se), premise (premiss).
prent, (-e), picture, illustration, print.
prent, (ge-), impress, imprint (on).
preparaat, (-rate), preparation; slide.
Presbiteriaans, (-e), Presbyterian.
presensie, presence.
present, (-e), n. present, gift.
present, a. present.
presentasie, (-s), presentation.
preserveer, (ge-), preserve.
president, (-e), president; chairman.
presies, (-e), a. precise, exact, regular; neat, tidy.
presies, adv. precisely, exactly.
presipiteer, (ge-), precipitate.
prestasie, (-s), achievement, feat.
presteer, (ge-), achieve, accomplish.
pret, fun, pleasure.
pretensie, (-s), pretence; pretension.
pretmaker, joker, jester.
prettig, (-e), pleasant, enjoyable, jolly.
preuts, (-e), prim and proper, prudish.
prewel, (ge-), mutter.
prieel, (**priële**), **prinjeel,** (-jele), pergola, covered walk.
priem, (-e), awl, pricker; dagger.
priem, (ge-), pierce, prick.
priester, (-s), priest.
prik, (-ke), prick.
prik, (ge-), prick; tingle.
prikkel, (-s), stimulus, incentive, goad.
prikkel, (ge-), excite, irritate, provoke; stimulate; goad; tickle (the palate); sting.

pril: –le jeug, early youth.
prima, prime, first-rate, tiptop.
primaat, (**-mate**), primate.
primêr, (**-e**), primary (school, colours).
primitief, (**-tiewe**), primitive.
prinjeel, vide **prieel**.
prins, (**-e**), prince.
prinsipaal, (**-pale**), principal
prinsipe, (**-s**), principle.
prisonier, (**-s**), prisoner; convict.
privaat, (**-ate**), n. latrine, water-closet.
privaat, (**-vate**), a. & adv. private(ly).
probeer, (**ge-**), try, attempt; test (a gun), try out (a machine), taste, sample.
probleem, (**-bleme**), problem, question.
produk, (**-te**), product; (a literary) production; result, outcome.
produseer, (**ge-**), produce, turn out.
produsent, (**-e**), producer.
proef, (**proewe**), proof, test, trial, experiment; sample, specimen; dissertation; copy.
proe(f), (**ge-**), taste; sample.
proef, (**ge-**), try, test, assay.
proefneming, experiment.
proefondervindelik, (**-e**), experimental.
proefplaas, experimental station (farm).
proes, (**ge-**), sneeze; burst out laughing; giggle; snort (of a horse).
profeet, (**-fete**), prophet.
profesie, (**-ë**), prophecy.
professioneel, (**-nele**), professional.
professor, (**-s, -e**), professor.
profeteer, (**ge-**), prophesy.
profiteer, (**ge-**), profit (by), take advantage (of), avail oneself (of).
profyt, (**-e**), profit, gain.
program, (**-me**), program(me).
progressief, (**-siewe**), progressive.
proklameer, (**ge-**), proclaim.
prokurasie, (**-s**), power of attorney, proxy, procuration.
prokureur, (**-s**), attorney, solicitor.
promesse, (**-s**), promissory note.
promosie, (**-s**), promotion, rise; graduation (at university).
promoveer, (**ge-**), graduate, take one's (doctor's) degree.
pronk, show, ostentation; finery; pride.
pronk, (**ge-**), show off, parade; spread, buck.
pronker, (**-s**), fop, dandy.
pronk-ertjie, sweet pea.
pront, fluently, punctual(ly), regular(ly).
pront-uit, straight (out), directly, flatly.
prooi, prey.
prop, (**-pe**), cork, stopper (of bottle); bung (of cask); gag; wad; plug (in hole); lump (in throat).
prop, (**ge-**), cram, plug, close up.
propaganda, propaganda.
propageer, (**ge-**), propagate, diffuse.
proponent, (**-e**), candidate for the ministry.
proporsioneel, (**-nele**), proportionate(ly).
propvol, (**-le**), chock-full, crammed (with), stuffed (with).
prosa, prose.
prosedeer, (**ge-**), go to law, litigate.
prosedure, (**-s**), procedure.

proses, (**-se**), process, course (of action), method; lawsuit.
prospekteer, (**ge-**), prospect.
protektoraat, (**-rate**), protectorate.
protes, (**-te**), protest, protestation.
protesteer, (**ge-**), protest.
proviand, provisions, victuals, stores.
provinsie, (**-s**), province.
pruik, (**-e**), wig, periwig.
pruim, (**-e**), plum; quid, chew, (tobacco).
pruim, (**ge-**), chew.
pruimedant, (**-e**), prune.
Pruise, Prussia.
prul, (**-le**), rubbish, trash.
pruttel, (**ge-**), grumble; simmer.
pryk, (**ge-**), look splendid, shine; parade, show off.
prys, (**-e**), price, value; prize, reward; praise.
prys, (**ge-**), praise, extol, laud, glorify.
prysenswaardig, (**-e**), praiseworthy.
prysgee, (**prysge-**), abandon, deliver up (over), give up, hand over.
psalm, (**-s**), psalm.
psigiater, (**-s**), psychiater, psychiatrist.
psigologie, psychology.
publiek, n. public; audience.
publiek, (**-e**), a. public.
publiek, adv. publicly.
publiseer, (**ge-**), publish, make public.
puik, n. pick, elite, flower, cream.
puik, a. first-rate, choice, excellent.
puil, **peul**, (**ge-**), bulge, protrude.
puimsteen, pumice(-stone).
puin, ruins, debris.
puis, (**-te**), **puisie**, (**-s**), pimple, pustule.
punktueer, (**ge-**), punctuate.
punt, (**-e**), point; tip (of tongue, finger); spot, dot, (full) stop; item; matter; question; score, mark.
puntdig, (**-te**), epigram.
puntene(u)rig, (**-e**), particular, fastidious; squeamish, touchy.
puntig, (**-e**), pointed.
puntsgewyse, point by point, seriatim.
purgasie, (**-s**), purgative; purgation.
purper, n. & a. purple.
put, (**-te**), well.
put, (**ge-**), draw (water, inspiration).
putjie, (**-s**), hole (golf).
puts, (**-e**), well; (tar-)pot, bucket.
puur, (**pure**), pure; sheer; all.
pyl, (**-e**), arrow, barb, bolt, dart, shaft.
pyl, (**ge-**), dart, shoot, go straight.
pyler, (**-s**), shaft, pillar, pier.
pylreguit, straight as an arrow.
pylsnel, swift as an arrow.
pyn, pain, ache.
pyn, (**ge-**), ache, hurt, smart.
pynappel, pineapple.
pynbank, rack.
pynig, (**ge-**), torture, rack, torment.
pynlik, (**-e**), painful, distressing.
pynstillend, (**-e**), analgesic, soothing.
pyp, (**-e**), pipe; tube; (chimney-)flue; (trouser-)-leg.
pypkan, (**ge-**), fool, cheat; (football) sell the dummy.
pypkaneel, (whole) cinnamon.

raad, (-gewinge, -gewings), (1) advice, counsel.
raad, (rade), (2) council, board.
raadgee, (raadge-), advise, give advice.
raad-op: – wees, be at one's wit's end.
raadsaam, (-same), advisable, expedient.
raadsheer, councillor; bishop (chess).
raaf, (rawe), raven.
raai, (ge-), advise; guess.
raaisel, (-s), riddle, puzzle, enigma.
raak, (ge-), hit (mark); touch (ground); concern (person).
raak, a. & adv. to the point, effective, telling (blow).
raaklings, vide rakelings.
raaklyn, tangent.
raam, (rame), n. window; frame.
raam, (ge-), estimate; frame (picture).
raap, (rape), n. turnip; rape.
raap, (ge-), gather, pick up.
raapkool, turnip-cabbage, khol-rabi.
raar, (rare), a. queer, strange, odd.
raas, (ge-), make a noise; rave, storm, rage.
raat, (rate), remedy.
rabarber, rhubarb.
rabat, (-te), rebate, discount, reduction.
rabbedoe, (-ë, -s), rabbedoes, (-e), vide robbedoe(s).
rabbi, (-'s), rabbyn (-e), rabbi.
radar, radar.
radbraak, (ge-), break on the wheel; murder (language).
radeloos, (-lose), desperate.
radikaal, (-kale), a. radical.
radio, (-'s), radio, wireless.
radja, (-s), rajah.
radys, (-e), radish.
rafel, (-s), n. ravel, thread.
rafel, (ge-), fray (out), ravel (out).
raffinadery, (-e), (sugar-) refinery.
raffineer, (ge-), refine.
ragfyn, (–, -e), cobwebby, thin, flimsy.
ragitis, rickets.
rak, (-ke), rack, shelf, bracket.
rakelings: – verbygaan, graze past.
raket, (-te), racket (racquet); rocket.
rakker, (-s), rascal, rogue, knave.
ram, (-me), ram, tup; rammer.
raming, (-e, -s), estimate, calculation.
ramkie, Hottentot-guitar, ramkie.
rammel, (ge-), rattle, clatter, clank.
rammelkas, rattletrap, rickety car; rattle-box.
ramp, (-e), disaster, catastrophe.
rampokker, (-s), gangster.
rampsalig, (-e), wretched, miserable; doomed; fatal.
rampsoedig, (-e), disastrous.
rand, (-e), brim (of hat, cup); edge; brink (of precipice); margin (of paper); rim; border, boundary; fringe.
randeier, outer egg; wall-flower.
randsteen, kerb-stone.
rang, (-e), rank, grade, degree, class, order.
rangeer, (ge-), arrange; shunt (train).
rangorde, order.
rangskik, (ge-), arrange; classify; marshal.
rangtelwoord, ordinal number.
rank, (-e), n. tendril, shoot; clasper.
rank, (–, -e), a. slender, thin, slim.
rank, (ge-), trail, shoot tendrils; twine.
ransel, (ge-), flog, thrash, lick.
rant(jie), ridge.
rantsoen, (-e), ration, allowance; ransom.
rapat, quick, agile, numble.
rapport, (-e), report.
raps, (-e), n. flick, cut, lash, hit.
raps, (ge-), flick, hit, strike.

rariteit, (-e), curiosity, rarity, curio.
ras, (-se), n. race; strain, breed.
ras, (-se), swift, quick.
rasend, (-e), raving, fuming, storming, mad, furious.
raserny, rage, fury, frenzy.
rasionaal, (-nale), rational.
rasper, (-s), n. rasp, grater, scraper.
raspe(r), (ge-), rasp, grate.
rat, (-te), (cog)wheel.
ratel, (-s), n. (1) honey-badger, Cape badger.
ratel, (-s), n. (2) rattle.
ratel, (ge-), rattle.
rats, (–, -e), quick, swift, agile.
ravot, (ge-), romp.
reageer, (ge-), react.
reaksie, (-s), reaction.
realisme, realism.
rebel, (-le), rebel.
rebels, (-e), rebellious; furious; sulky.
red, (ge-), save, rescue.
redaksie, (-s), editoral staff; editorship; wording.
redakteur, (-s), editor.
reddeloos, (-lose), a. beyond help, irrevocable.
redding, (-e, -s), rescue, saving; salvation.
rede, (-s), (1) reason, cause.
rede, (2) reason, understanding.
rede, (-s), (3) speech, address.
rede, (-s), (4) ratio.
rededeel, part of speech.
redegewend, (-e), causal.
redekawel, (ge-), argue, reason.
redelik, (-e), rational; reasonable, fair.
redelikerwys, in reason, reasonably.
redeloos, (-lose), irrational, not gifted with reason, brute.
redenaar, (-s), orator.
redeneer, (ge-), argue, reason.
redetwis, (ge-), dispute.
redevoerder, (-s), speaker, orator.
redigeer, (ge-), edit (newspaper); draw up (document).
reduseer, (ge-), reduce.
reeds, already.
reëel, (reële), real.
reeks, (-e), series, sequence; row; line; set; train (of events).
reël, (-s), n. line; rule.
reël, (ge-), arrange, settle; organize; adjust.
reëlaar, (-s), governor; regulator.
reëling, (-e, -s), arrangement; regulation(s), rule(s); adjustment; organization.
reëlmatig, (-e), regular.
reëlreg, (-te), a. straight.
reëlreg, adv. straight(away).
reën, reent, (reëns), n. rain.
reën, reent, (ge-), rain.
reënboog, reent-, rainbow.
reep, (repe), strip, string.
referaat, (-rate), lecture, paper; report.
refereer, (ge-), refer.
referent, (-e), speaker, lecturer; reporter.
referte, (-s), reference.
refleksie, (-s), reflection.
reformasie, reformation.
reg, (-te), n. right, justice; claim; law.
reg, (-te), a. right, correct.
reg, adv. rightly; straight.
regaf, straight down.
regbank, court of justice.
regeer, (ge-), rule, reign; manage.
regering, (-s), rule, reign; government.
reggeaard, (-e), right-minded.
reghoek, rectangle.

regie, state control (monopoly); stage-manage-
ment; **onder** – **van**, produced by.
regiment, (-e), regiment.
regisseur, (-s), producer, stage-manager.
register, (-s), register; index.
registrateur, (-s), registrar.
regkom, (regge-), come right; recover.
reglement, (-e), rules, regulations.
regmaak, (regge-), repair; correct; rectify;
settle; fix up.
regmatig, (-e), rightful, lawful, fair.
regop, erect, perpendicular, vertical; straight up.
reg-reg, rêrig, very, really, terribly.
regruk, (regge-), pull straight, put straight.
regs, to the right; right-handed.
regsaak, lawsuit, case.
regsgeldig, (-e), legal, valid.
regsgeleerde, (-s), lawyer, jurist.
regsinnig (-e), orthodox.
regskape, upright, just, honest.
regsomkeer, right about turn.
regstreeks, (-e), a. direct, straight.
regstreeks, adv. directly, straight.
regsweë: van –, according to law.
regte, n. right; law; duties.
regter, (-s), n. judge, justice.
regter-, a. right, off.
regtig, really, truly, indeed; – **waar?**, really?,
indeed?
reguit, straight (line, road); honest, frank,
candid, straight.
regulasie, (-s), regulation.
reguleer, (ge-), regulate, adjust, time.
regverdig, (-e), a. just, righteous.
regverdig, (ge-), justify; sanctify.
rehabiliteer, (ge-), rehabilitate.
rei, (-e), chorus.
reier, (-s), heron.
reik, (ge-), reach, stretch.
reikhals, (ge-): – **na**, yearn (long) for.
reiling, vide **reling**.
rein, (–, -e), pure, chaste.
reinig, (ge-), purify, cleanse, clean.
reïnkarneer, (ge-), reincarnate.
reis, (-e), n. journey, trip; voyage.
reis, (ge-), travel, journey, tour.
reisdeken, (travelling-) rug.
reisies, resies, races.
reisvaardig, (-e), on the point of leaving.
rek, (-ke), n. (1) elastic; catapult.
rek, n. (2) elasticity.
rek, (ge-), stretch; draw out; extend, prolong
(discussion); protract; spin out.
rekbaar, (-bare), elastic, ductile, extensible.
reken, (ge-), reckon, calculate, estimate, compute; count, consider, regard.
rekening, (-e, -s), calculation, computation,
reckoning; account, bill.
rekenkunde, arithmetic.
rekenmeester, accountant.
rekenskap, account.
rekker, (-s), elastic; garter; catapult.
reklame, (-s), advertisement, boosting, réclame;
claim.
rekommandeer, (ge-), recommend.
rekonsilieer, (ge-), reconcile.
rekonstruksie, (-s), reconstruction.
rekord, (-s), record.
rekreasie, (-s), recreation.
rekruut, (-krute), recruit.
rektor, (-s), rector, principal.
relaas, (-lase), account, story, report.
reliek, (-e), relic.
reling, reiling, (-s), railing, rail.
rem, (-me), n. brake.

rem, (ge-), brake, pull, strain; curb.
remskoen, brake-shoe, (wheel-)drag; stick-in-
the-mud.
Renaissance, Renaissance (Renascence).
renbaan, racecourse.
rendier, reindeer.
renegaat, (-gate), renegade.
renons, aversion, dislike.
renoster, (-s), rhinoceros.
rens, sour (milk).
rente, (-s), interest.
rentenier, (-e, -s), n. retired person.
rentenier, (ge-), live on the interest of one's
money.
rentmeester, steward, manager.
reorganiseer, (ge-), reorganize.
rep, n.: **in** – **en roer**, in confusion (commotion,
tumult).
rep, (ge-): – **van**, mention.
repareer, (ge-), repair, mend.
repeteer, (ge-), repeat; rehearse (play); recur (of
decimal).
repliek, (-e), rejoinder, reply, counterplea.
reproduksie, (-s), reproduction.
reptiel, (-e), reptile.
republiek, (-e), republic.
republikein (-e), republican.
reputasie, (-s), reputation.
res, (-te), n. rest, remainder.
resent, (-e), recent.
resep, (-te), recipe; prescription.
reserveer, (ge-), reserve.
reserwe, (-s), reserve; reserves.
reses, (-se), recess.
resident, (-e), resident.
resies-, vide **reisies-**.
resitasie, (-s), recitation.
resiteer, (ge-), recite.
respek, respect, regard.
respekteer, (ge-), respect.
ressorteer, (ge-): – **onder**, be classed among,
come (fall) under.
restant, (-e), remainder.
resteer, (ge-), remain.
resultaat, (-tate), result, outcome.
resumeer, (ge-), summarize, sum up.
retireer, (ge-), retreat, retire.
retoer, return.
reuk, ruik, (-e), smell; scent; odour.
reun, (-s), gelding.
reunhond, dog.
reus, (-e), giant; colossus.
revisie, (-s), revision.
revolusie, (-s), revolution.
rewolwer, (-s), revolver, pistol.
rib, (-be, -bes), rib; rib (of wood, iron).
ribbekas, thorax.
ribbok, rhebuck.
ridder, (-s), n. knight.
ridder, (ge-), knight.
ridderlik, (-e), knightly; chivalrous.
ridderspoor, larkspur, delphinium.
riel, (-e), reel (dance).
riem, (-e), (1) thong, strap, riem.
riem, (-e), (2) oar.
riem, (-e), (3) ream (of paper).
riemspring, (riemge-), skip.
riet, (-e), reed, rush; thatch (of roof).
rietbok, reedbuck, rietbok.
rietskraal, very thin, reedy.
rif, (riwwe), reef (rock-formation); ledge; ridge;
edge.
riffel, (-s), n. wrinkle, fold, ridge, crinkle, ruffle,
ripple; edge.
riffel, (ge-), wrinkle, ripple; corrugate.

rig, (ge-), aim, direct.

rigsnoer, guide, directing principle, rule, example.

rigter, (-s), judge.

rigting, (-e, -s), direction; tendency, inclination.

riksja, (-s), rickshaw.

ril, (ge-), shudder, shiver, tremble.

rilling, (-e, -s), shudder, shiver.

rimpel, (-s), n. wrinkle, fold, line; ripple (of water).

rimpel, (ge-), wrinkle, line; ripple; pucker (knit) (one's brow); pucker.

ring, (-e), ring; circle; band; halo; presbytery, ring.

rinkel, (ge-), jingle, chink.

rinkhals, ring-neck, ring-necked (animal).

rinkink, (ge-), jingle; romp; gallivant, gad about.

rinneweer, (ge-), ruin, spoil.

riool, (-e), riool, (-ole), drain, sewer.

rioleer, (ge-), drain.

riskant, (-e), risky, hazardous.

rissie, (-s), chilli; termagant, vixen.

rit, (-te), journey, ride, spin.

ritme, (-s), rhythm.

rits, (-e), n. series, string, row.

ritsel, (ge-), rustle.

ritssluiter, zip fastener, zipper.

ritssluiting, zip fastening.

rittel, (ge-), shiver, shake.

ritteltit(s): die – kry, get the shivers.

rituaal, (rituale), ritual.

ritueel, (rituele), ritual.

rivier, (-e), river.

rob, (-be), seal.

robbedoe, (-ë, -s), robbedoes, (-e), tomboy, hoyden, romp, boisterous person.

robot, (-s, -te), robot.

robyn, (-e), ruby.

roede, (-s), rod, birch; rood ($\frac{1}{4}$ of an acre).

roei, (ge-), row, pull.

roekeloos, (-lose), reckless, rash, foolhardy; wicket, sinful.

roem, n. renown, glory, fame.

roem, (ge-), boast; praise, laud, extol.

Roemenië, R(o)umania.

roemryk, (-e), famous, glorious; magnificent.

roemsugtig, (-e), thirsting for fame.

roep, n. call, cry.

roep, roep, (ge-), call, cry, shout.

roeping, (-e, -s), calling, vocation.

roer, (-e, -s), n. (1) rudder, helm.

roer, (-s), n. (2) gun, rifle.

roer, n.: (3) in rep en –, in a stir.

roer, (ge-), stir, move; touch.

roereiers, scrambled eggs.

roerend, (-e), a. touching; moveable.

roering, stirring, motion; emotion.

roerpen, tiller.

roersel, (-e, -s), motive.

roes, n. (1) intoxication; excitement.

roes, n. (2) rust; blight, rust.

roes, (ge-), rust; corrode.

roes(e)moes, confusion, tumult.

roet, soot.

roete, (-s), route, road.

roetine, routine.

rof, (rowwe), rough.

roffel, n. ruffle (of drum), roll.

rofkas, n. rough-cast.

rofkas, (ge-), rough-cast.

rog, rye.

roggel, (ge-), expectorate; rattle.

rojaal, (-jale), royal; generous, liberal.

rok, (-ke), skirt, dress, gown.

rol, (-le), n. roll (of paper); scroll; register, list, roll; part (of an actor), rôle; cylinder, roller.

rol, (ge-), roll, tumble.

rolprent, film.

rolprentkamera, cine-camera.

rolskaats, roller-skate.

roltrap, escalator.

rolvark(ie), South African hedgehog.

roman, (-s), (1) novel.

roman, (-s), (2) roman (fish).

romanse, (-s), romance.

romanties, (-e), romantic.

Romein, (-e), Roman.

rommel, n. lumber, rubbish, trash.

rommel, (ge-), rumble; rummage.

rommel(a)ry, lumber, rubbish, litter.

romp, (-e), trunk; hull.

rond, (-e), a. round; circular.

rondawel, (-s), "rondavel", round hut (cottage).

rondborstig, (-e), open, candid, frank.

ronddans, (rondge-), dance about.

ronddra, (rondge-), carry about.

ronddraai, (rondge-), turn (twist) round (about); loiter (round).

ronddrentel, (rondge-), saunter about.

ronddwaal, (rondge-), wander about.

ronde, (-s), round; lap (of race-track); beat (of policeman).

rondgaan, (rondge-), go about (round).

rondgaande, travelling; – hof, circuit court.

rondhol, (rondge-), run (rush) about.

ronding, (-e, -s), rounding; camber.

rondjie, (-s), round.

rondkuier, (rondge-), go about visiting; stroll about.

rondkyk, (rondge-), look about.

rondlei, (rondge-), lead about; conduct, show (person) round (a place).

rondloop, (rondge-), walk (go, loaf) about.

rondloper, tramp, vagrant, loafer.

rondom, on all sides (of), all round.

rondomtalie, round and round.

rondreis, (rondge-), travel about, tour.

rondskrywe, circular letter.

rondspring, (rondge-), jump about; beat about the bush.

rondstrooi, (rondge-), scatter; spread (news).

rondswerf, -swerwe, (rondge-), roam (wander) about.

rondtas, (rondge-), grope about.

rondte, (-s), roundness; round; circle.

rondtrek, (rondge-), pull about; trek (journey, go, wander) about.

ronduit, frankly, straight out.

rondweg, frankly.

rong, (-e), rung, upright, support.

ronk, (ge-), snore; drone, purr.

roof, (rowe), n. (1) scab, crust.

roof, n. (2) plunder, robbery; booty.

roof, rowe, (ge-), plunder, rob, steal.

roofbou, overcropping.

roofdier, beast of prey.

roofgierig, roofsugtig, (-e), rapacious.

rooi, red.

rooibekkie, waxbill, widow-bird.

rooibok, impala.

rooibont, red and white.

rooidag, dawn, day-break.

rooijakkals, red fox (jackal).

rooikat, caracal, lynx.

rooimeerkat, -mierkat, bushy-tailed meercat.

rooimier, red ant.

rooivink, red bishop-bird, red Kaffir-finch.

rooiwater, red-water, Texas fever.

rook, n. smoke.

rook, (ge-), smoke.
rookmis, smog.
room, cream.
Rooms, (-e), Roman Catholic; Roman.
roomys, ice-cream.
roos, (1) erysipelas, the rose.
roos, (rose), (2) rose.
rooskleurig, (-e), rose-coloured, rosy; bright.
roosmaryn, rosemary.
rooster, (-s), n. gridiron, grill (for roasting); grate (in fireplace); time-table.
rooster, (ge-), roast, grill, toast.
ros, (-se), n. steed.
ros, (-se), a. ruddy, reddish-brown.
roset, (-te), rosette.
roskam, n. curry-comb.
roskam, (ge-), curry; rebuke.
rosyn, (-e), rosyntjie, (-s), raisin.
rot, (-te), n. rat.
rot, adv.: iemand – en kaal steel, steal everything a person possesses.
rotasie, rotation, turn.
rots, (-e), rock, cliff.
rotstuin, rockery.
rotsvas, (-te), firm as a rock, adamant.
rottang, (-s), rat(t)an, cane.
rotting, putrefaction.
rou, n. mourning.
rou, a. raw, uncooked; hoarse (voice).
rou, (ge-), mourn.
roubeklag, condolence.
rouklaag, (ge-), lament.
roukoop, smart-money.
rowe, (ge-), vide roof, (ge-).
rower, (-s), robber, bandit, brigand.
ru, (-we), rough (surface); raw (materials); crude (oil); coarse, unrefined, rude.
rubber, rubber.
rubriek, (-e), category, class; column (of a newspaper); heading, rubric.
rudimentêr, (-e), rudimentary.
rug, rûe(ns), ridge, hill; back.
ru-gare, -garing, cotton-thread.
rugbaar, known.
rugby, rugby, rugger.
ruggraat, backbone, spine.
rugsak, rucksack.
rugsteun, (ge-), support, back.
rugstring, vertebral column; loin.
ruig, (-, ruige, ruie), shaggy; shrubby, bushy.
ruik, reuk, n. smell; scent; vide reuk.
ruik, (ge-), smell, scent.
ruiker, (-s), bunch of flowers, bouquet.
ruil, n. exchange, barter.
ruil, (ge-), exchange, barter.
ruilhandel, barter.
ruim, (-e), n. hold (of a ship); nave.
ruim, (-, -e), a. spacious, roomy; wide, loose; ample, abundant.
ruim, adv. amply, abundantly.
ruim, (ge-), empty; ream, widen (hole).
ruimskoots, amply, abundantly.

ruimte, (-s), space, room; gap; capacity; scope; breadth (of view).
ruim(te)skip, space ship.
ruim(te)vaarder, astronaut, cosmonaut.
ruimtevaart, space travel.
ruimtevaartuig, space-craft.
ruimtevlug, astronautics, space travel.
ruimtevrees, agoraphobia.
ruimtuig, space-craft, -ship, -vessel.
ruïnasie, rinnewasie, ruination.
ruïne, (-s), ruins.
ruïneer, (ge-), ruin.
ruis, (ge-), rustle, murmur.
ruit, (-e), pane (of windows); lozenge; check (material).
ruite(ns), diamonds (cards).
ruiter, (-s), rider, horseman.
ruiterlik, (-e), frank(ly), open(ly).
ruitery, cavalry.
ruitjiesgoed, check.
ruk, (-ke), n. jerk, pull, tug; gust (of wind); time, while.
ruk, (ge-), jerk, pull, tug.
rukwind, gust of wind, squall.
rumatiek, rheumatism.
rumoer, n. noise, row, hubbub, din.
rumoer, (ge-), make a noise.
runderpes, rinderpest.
runnik, (ge-), neigh, whinny.
Rus, (-se), Russian.
rus, n. rest, peace; safety-catch; pause.
rus, (ge-), rest, repose.
rusbank, couch, sofa, settee.
rusie, (-s), quarrel, dispute.
Rusland, Russia.
ruspe(r), (-s), caterpillar.
rusteloos, (-lose), restless.
rustend, (-e), resting; retired; emeritus.
rustig, (-e), restful, tranquil, calm, peaceful.
ry, (-e), n. row, line, string; series, suite; course (of bricks).
ry, (ge-), ride, drive.
ry(e), ryg, (ge-), tack, shir(r), gather, run, baste; string (beads); lace (shoes).
ryk, (-e), n. kingdom, empire, realm; sphere.
ryk, (-, -e), a. rich, wealthy; fertile.
rykdom, (-me), wealth; abundance.
ryloop, (ge-), hitch-hike.
rym, (-e), n. rhyme.
rym, (ge-), rhyme; agree, correspond, tally.
rymelary, doggerel.
Ryn, Rhine.
ryp, n. hoar-frost.
ryp, (-, -e), a. ripe, mature.
ryp, (ge-), frost.
rys, n. rice.
rys, (ge-), rise.
rysig, (-e), tall.
rysmier, white ant, termite.
rytuig, (-tuie), vehicle; cab (for hire); coach, carriage.
rywiel, bicycle, cycle.

sa!, catch him!

saad, (sade), saat, (sate), seed.

saadhuisie, seed-capsule, seed-vessel.

saadskiet, (saadge-), run (go) to seed.

saag, (sae), n. saw.

saag, sae, (ge-), saw, cut, rip; scrape.

saagsel, sawdust.

saai, a. & adv. dull, humdrum, tedious.

saai, (ge-), sow, scatter.

saak, (sake), matter, business, case; cause; (law-)suit, (court-)case.

saakgelastigde, (-s), agent, representative, deputy, commissioner.

saaklik, (-e), business-like, thorough; impersonal; concise; real.

saal, (sale), n. hall, room; ward (in hospital).

saal, (-s), n. saddle.

saalboom, pommel; saddle-tree.

saam, same, together.

saambly, (saamge-), stay (live), together.

saamdoen, (saamge-), join in, join hands.

saamgaan, (saamge-), accompany, go along; go together, agree, go hand in hand; join in with; match.

saam-, samegesteld, (-e), compound; complex, complicated.

saamhok, (saamge-), herd together.

saamhorigheid, samehorigheid, solidarity, unity.

saamkom, (saamge-), come together, assemble, meet, unite; go (come) with (a person), come too.

saamkoppel, (saamge-), couple.

saamloop, (saamge-), meet, come together; accompany, go (come) with (a person).

saamloop, n. vide **sameloop**.

saampraat, (saamge-), join in the conversation; have a say in the matter.

saamroep, (saamge-), call together, convene, convoke.

saamsmelt, (saamge-), melt together, amalgamate, fuse, merge.

saamspan, (saamge-), unite, co-operate; conspire, plot (against).

saamstel, (saamge-), compose, make up, compile (a dictionary).

saamstem, (saamge-), agree; harmonize.

saamsweer, (saamge-), conspire, plot.

saamtrek, (saamge-), draw (pull) together; contract (muscles); concentrate (forces).

saamval, (saamge-), fall together, coincide.

saamvat, (saamge-), summarize; take along with one.

saamvoeg, (saamge-), join, unite.

saamwerk, (saamge-), work (act, pull) together, co-operate, collaborate.

saans, in the evening, of an evening.

saat, vide **saad**.

Sabbat, (-te), Sabbath.

sabel, (-s), n. (1) sable(-fur, -buck).

sabel, (-s), n. (2) sword, sabre.

sabotasie, sabotage.

Sadduseër, (-s), Sadducee.

sadisties, (-e), sadistic.

sae, vide **saag, (ge-)**.

saf, sag, (-te), soft; vide **sag**.

saffier, (-e), sapphire.

saffraan, saffron.

sag, saf, (-te), a. soft; light; gentle, mild.

sag, saf, adv. softly, gently, lightly.

sagaardig, (-e), mild, meek, gentle.

sage, (-s), legend, story; saga.

sagkens, gently, softly.

sagmoedig, (-e), mold, gentle, benign.

sagsinnig, (-e), gentle, mild.

sak, (-ke), n. sack; bag; pocket; pouch.

sak, (ge-), sink, drop, subside, go down; give milk.

sakdoek, handkerchief.

sakeman, business-man.

sakkerloot!, by gad!, by Jove!

sakkeroller, pickpocket.

Sakse, Saxony.

sal, shall (should), will (would).

salaris, (-se), salary, pay.

saldo, (-'s), balance.

salf, salwe, (ge-), anoint; salve.

salf, n. ointment, salve.

salie, sage; Salvia sp.

salig, (-e), blessed (blest); blissful.

Saligmaker, Saviour.

salm, salmon.

Salomo, Solomon.

salon, (-s, -ne), reception-room.

salon, (-s, -ne), salon; saloon.

salpeter, saltpetre, nitre.

saluut, (-lute), n. salute.

salvo, (-'s), salvo, volley, round.

Samaritaan, (-tane), n. Samaritan.

sambok, (-ke), sjambok.

sambreel, (-brele), umbrella.

same, vide **saam**.

samegesteld, (-e), vide **saamgesteld**.

samehang, n. coherence, order; cohesion; connection; context.

samekoms, meeting, gathering.

samelewing, society; cohabitation.

sameloop, saamloop, n. confluence (of rivers); concourse (of people).

samespraak, dialogue, conversation.

samespreking, conversation, discussion, interview; meeting.

samestelling, (-e, -s), composition; construction, assembly; compilation; texture; compound.

sameswering, (-e, -s), conspiracy, plot.

sampioen, (-e), mushroom, champignon.

sand, sand; grit.

sandaal, (-dale), sandal.

sandsuiker, crystallised sugar.

sang, song, singing.

sanger, (-s), singer; songbird; poet.

sangerig, (-e), melodious, tuneful.

sangstuk, song.

sanik, (ge-), din, drone, bother, nag.

sap, (-pe), juice; sap.

saploos, (-lose), sapless.

sapperig, sappig, (-e), juicy; succulent, sappy.

sardien, (-s), sardine.

Sardinië, Sardinia.

sarkasme, sarcasm.

sarkasties, (-e), sarcastic(ally).

sarkofaag, (-fae), sarcophagus.

sarsie, (-d), charge, sally; volley.

sat, satiated, tired (of), sick (of).

Satan, Satan, the devil.

satelliet, (-e), satellite.

Saterdag, Saturday.

satire, (-s), satire.

Saturnus, Saturn.

satyn, satin.

sawwe, sawwerig, vide **sag**.

saxofoon, (-fone), saxophone.

se, of, belonging to.

sê, n. say.

sê, seg, (ge-), say, tell.

sebra, (-s), zebra.

sede, (-s), custom, habit; (pl.) customs, habits; morals.

sedeer, (ge-), cede, assign.

sedelik, (-e), moral, ethical.

seder, (-s), cedar.

sedert, since; for.
sedertdien, since then.
sedig, (-e), modest, retiring, demure, coy; decorous.
sedisie, sedition.
see, (seë), sea, ocean; flood, torrent.
seë, sege, victory, triumph.
see-engte, strait.
seehoof, pier, jetty.
seekat, octopus; squid, cuttlefish.
seekoei, hippo(potamus); seacow, manatee.
seel, (-s), (1) (birth-)certificate.
seël, (-s), (2) stamp; seal.
seël, (ge-), seal (up); stamp (a letter).
seeleeu, sea-lion, seal.
seëlring, signet-ring.
seeman, (-ne, seeliede, seelui), seaman, sailor.
seën, (-s), drag-net, seine.
seën, (seëninge, seënings), n. blessing, benediction; godsend, boon.
seën, (ge-), bless.
seep, n. soap.
seep, (ge-), soap (in); lather (the face).
seëpraal, segepraal, (ge-), triumph (over).
seepsoda, caustic soda.
seer, (sere), n. sore; boil.
seer, a. sore, painful.
seer, adv. painfully; very (much), highly.
seespieël, sea-level.
seestraat, strait(s).
seëtog, segetog, triumphal procession.
seevaarder, (-s), navigator.
seëvier, segevier, (ge-), triumph (over); prevail.
seewier, sea-weed.
sefier, (-s, -e), zephyr.
seg, vide **sê**.
seggenskap, say, voice.
segregasie, segregation.
segregeer, (ge-), segregate.
segsman, informant.
segswyse, expression, saying.
seidissel, suidissel, sow-, milk-thistle.
seil, (-e), n. sail; tarpaulin; canvas.
seil, (ge-), sail.
seilnaald, sail-needle, packing-needle.
sein, (-e), signal.
sein, (ge-), signal; wire, telegraph.
seisoen, (-e), season.
sekel, (-s), sickle.
seker, (-, -e), a. certain; sure.
seker, adv. sure(ly), certain(ly), for sure.
sekering, (-e, -s), fuse (elec.).
sekerlik, certainly, surely, for sure.
sekondant, (-e), seconder; second.
sekonde, (-s), second.
sekondeer, (ge-), second.
sekretaris, (-se), secretary.
seks, sexuality; sex.
sekse, (-s), sex.
seksie, (-s), section (also mil.).
sekstant, (-e), sextant.
seksueel, (-ele), sexual, sex- . . .
sektaries, (-e), sectarian.
sekte, (-s), sect.
sekulariseer, (ge-), secularize.
sekundes, (-se, -di), secundus; proxy.
sekuriteit, (-e), surety, security.
sekuur, (-, kure), a. accurate, precise.
sel, (-le), cell.
selde, seldom, rarely, infrequently.
seldery, selery, celery.
seldsaam, (-same), rare, scarce.
selei, sjelei, jam; jelly.
seleksie, (-s), selection.
selery, seldery, celery.

self, n. self, ego.
self, pron. self.
selfbehae, self-complacency.
selfbewus, (-te), self-conscious; self-confident, self-assured.
selfbewustheid, self-confidence.
selfgenoegsaam, self-sufficient.
selfmoord, suicide, self-murder.
selfs, even.
selfstandig, (-e), a. independent, autonomous, self-reliant; self-supporting; substantive, substantival.
selfsug, selfishness, egoism.
selfsugtig, (-e), selfish, egoistic.
selfvoldaan, (-dane), self-complacent.
selluloïed, selluloïde, celluloid.
selonspampoen, (common) field-pumpkin.
semels, bran.
sement, n. cement.
semester, (-s), semester, term, half-year.
Semiet, (-e), Semite.
seminarie, (-s), seminary.
senaat, (-nate), senate.
senator, (-e, -s), senator.
sendeling, (-e), missionary.
sending, mission; consignment.
sening, (-s), sinew, tendon.
senit, zenith.
sens, seis, (-e), scythe.
sensasie, (-s), sensation, thrill.
sensitief, (-tiewe), sensitive.
sensueel, (-suele), sensual.
sensus, census.
sensuur, censure; censorship.
sent, (-e), cent, *omgereken tot rande en −e*, converted to rands and cents.
senter, (-s), centre (football).
sentimenteel, (-tele), sentimental.
sentimeter, centimetre.
sentraal, (-trale), central.
sentrale, (-s), (telephone-)exchange; power-station.
sentraliseer, (ge-), centralize.
sentrum, (-tra), centre.
senuwee, senuwee, (-s), nerve.
senu(wee)agtig, (-e), nervous, nervy.
seperig, (-e), soapy.
septer, (-s), sceptre.
septies, (-e), septic.
seraf, (-im, -s), seraph.
serebraal, (-brale), cerebral.
seremonie, (-s), ceremony; (pl.) formalities, ceremonial.
serge, sersje, serge.
serie, (-ë, -s), series; break (billiards).
sering, (-e), lilac.
sermeinpeer, (Saint) Germain-pear.
sero, vide **zero**.
seroet, (-e), cheroot, cigar.
serp, (-e), scarf, muffler, sash.
sersant, (-e), sergeant.
sersje, serge, serge.
sertifikaat, (-kate), certificate.
sertifiseer, (ge-), certify.
servet, (-te), table-napkin, serviette.
servies, (-e), (tea-)set, (dinner-)service.
serwituut, (-tute), servitude, casement, claim, charge.
Serwië, Serbia.
ses, (-se), six.
sessie, (-s), session, cession.
sestien, sixteen.
sestig, sixty; **jy is −**, you are silly.
set, (-te), n. move, trick; set; putt (golf).
set, (ge-), set, mount; set up, compose (type).

setel, (-s), seat (in parliament); throne; see (of pope); headquarters.
setel, (ge-), reside, be resident; have its headquarters (seat); sit.
setfout, misprint, printer's error.
setlaar, (-s), settler, immigrant.
setsel, (-s), type, matter, composition.
setter, (-s), compositor.
seun, (-s), son; boy, chap.
seur, (-s), sir, master.
seur, (ge-), bother, nag; delay, dawdle.
seurkous, bore, bothersome person.
sewe, (-s), seven.
sewejaartjie, (-s), everlasting.
sewentien, seventeen.
sewentig, seventy.
sfeer, (sfere), sphere; (fig.) region, domain.
sfinks, (-e), sphinx.
siaan, cyanogen.
Siam, (Thailand), Siam.
Siamees, (-mese), Siamese.
sianied, sianide, cyanide.
Siberië, Siberia.
Siciliaans, (-e), Sicilian.
Sicilië, Sicily.
sidder, (ge-), shiver, tremble, shake.
sie!, vide sies!
siebie, (-s), puppy, doggy.
siedend, (-e), seething, boiling.
siejy!, seijy!, sejy!, go (get) away!
siek, ill, sick, diseased.
siekerig, (-e), ailing.
sieklik, (-e), ailing, suffering, sickly; morbid.
siekte, (-s), illness, sickness, disease, malady; ill health.
siek(t)everlof, sick-leave.
siel, (-e), soul; heart; spirit, mind.
sieling, sjieling, (-s), shilling.
sielkunde, psychology.
sielsiek, (-e), mentally diseased.
sien, (ge-), see; notice, perceive, distinguish.
siener, (-s), seer, prophet; visionary.
sienlik, (-e), visible, perceptible.
siens: tot –, so long, bye-bye, cheerio!
sienswyse, opinion, way of thinking.
sier, (ge-), decorate, adorn, embellish.
sieraad, ornament, trinket.
sierlik, (-e), graceful, elegant.
sies!, bah!, phew!, sis!
sif, (-te, siwwe), sieve, strainer.
sif, (ge-), sieve, strain, screen, sift.
sifdraad, (fine) gauze, wire netting.
sifting, (-e, -s), sifting.
sig, n. sight, view.
sig, pron. oneself (him-, her-, itself, themselves).
sigaar, (-gare), cigar.
sigaret, (-te), cigarette.
sigbaar, (-bare), a. & adv. visible; perceptible; clear, manifest.
Sigeuner, (-s), gipsy.
sigorei, chicory.
sigsag, zigzag.
sigself, oneself, itself (him-, herself, themselves).
siklus, (-se, sikli), cycle.
siks: by my –!, upon my soul.
sikspens, (-e), sixpence.
Silesië, Silesia.
silhoeët, (-te), silhouette.
silinder, (-s), cylinder.
sillabe, (-s), syllable.
sillabus, (-se), syllabus.
silt, (-e), briny, saltish.
silwer, silver; silver-plate; silver coin.
silwerskoon, spotlessly clean.
simbaal, (-bale), cymbal.

simbool, (-bole), symbol, emblem.
simfonie, (-ë), symphony.
simmetries, (-e), symmetric(al).
simpatie, (-ë), sympathy.
simpatiseer, (ge-), sympathize (with).
simpel, (-e), silly, foolish, dotty, simple, plain; mere.
simptoom, (-tome), symptom.
Simson, Samson.
sin, (-ne), n. sense; mind; wish, liking, taste, fancy; sentence; meaning.
sinagoge, (-s), synagogue.
sindelik, (-e), clean, tidy; proper.
sindikaat, (-kate), syndicate, ring.
sinds, since; for.
sinsdien, since.
sing, (ge-), sing.
Singalees, (-lese), Cingalese, Ceylonese.
sinies, (-e), cynic(al).
sinjaal, (-ale), signal, sign.
sink, n. zinc; galvanized iron.
sink, (ge-), sink.
sinkings, neuralgia, rheumatism.
sinklood, sinker, sink.
sinkopee, syncope, elision, syncopation.
sinkplaat, n. (sheet of) galvanized (corrugated) iron.
sinkplaat, a. corrugated.
sinlik, (-e), sensual, carnal.
sinloos, (-lose), meaningless, senseless.
sinloos, (-lose), meaningless, senseless.
sinnebeeld, emblem, symbol.
sinnelik, (-e), of the senses, sensory.
sinneloos, mad, insane, senseless.
sinnigheid, liking, inclination.
sinodaal, (-dale), synodal, synodic(al).
sinode, (-s), synod.
sinoniem, (-e), n. synonym.
sinryk, (-e), full of (pregnant with) meaning, terse, significant.
sinsnede, clause, phrase, expression.
sinspeel, (ge-), allude; – op, allude to.
sint, (-e), saint.
sintaksis, syntax.
Sinterklaas, Santa Claus.
sintese, synthesis.
sintuig, sense-organ.
sinverwant, (-e), synonymous.
Sion, Zion.
sipier, (-e, -s), gaoler, warder.
sipres(boom), cypress(-tree).
sirene, (-s), siren.
sirkel, (-s), circle, ring.
sirkulasie, circulation.
sirkuleer, (ge-), circulate.
sirkus, (-se), circus.
sis, n. chintz, print.
sis, (ge-), hiss; sizzle.
sisteem, (-teme), system, method.
sistematies, (-e), systematic(al).
sit, n. comfortable, sitting position.
sit, (ge-), sit; put, place, stand; set.
sitaat, (-tate), quotation, citation.
siteer, (ge-), quote; cite (law).
sitplaas, -plek, seat.
sitroen, (-e), citron.
sitrus, citrus.
sitting, (-e, -s), sitting, session; seat (of a chair).
situasie, (-s), situation, position.
siviel, (-e), civil.
sjaal, (-s), shawl, wrap.
sjabloon, (-lone), pattern, stencil.
sjampanje, champagne.
sjarmant, (-e), charming.
sjef, (-s), chef (cook); chief.

sjelei, selei, jelly; jam.
sjerrie, sherry.
sjieling, sieling, (-s), shilling.
sjimpansee, (-s), chimpanzee.
Sjina, China.
sjokolade, chocolate, cocoa; chocolates.
sj(uu)t!, hist!, hush!.
skaad, (ge-), harm, damage.
skaaf, (skawe), n. plane.
skaaf, skawe, (ge-), plane, smooth; rub, scrape, bark (one's skin).
skaafbank, carpenter's bench.
skaafsel, (-s), shaving.
skaai, (ge-), pinch, pilfer.
skaak, n. chess.
skaakmat, checkmate.
skaal, (skale), scale, pair of scales, balance.
skaam, a. shy, bashful; ashamed.
skaam, (ge-), feel (be) ashamed, feel shame.
skaamte, (sense of) shame; bashfulness, shyness; modesty.
skaap, (skape), sheep (also fig.).
skaapkop, sheep's head; blockhead.
skaapsteker, rhombic, "sheepsticker".
skaar, (skare), n. (1) (plough-)share.
skaar, (skare), n. (2) notch, chip.
skaar, (skare), skare, (-s), n. (3) crowd, host, multitude.
skaar, (ge-), range, draw up.
skaars, (-, -e), a scarce, rare; scanty.
skaars, adv. scarcely, hardly.
skaats, (ge-), skate, rink.
skaats, (-e), skate.
skade, damage, harm injury, loos.
skadelik, (-e), harmful, injurious, noxious.
skadevergoeding, indemnification, compensation, damages.
skadu, (-'s), shadow.
skaduryk, (-e), a. shady, shadowy.
skaduwee, (-s), shadow.
skag, (-te), shaft (of mine, arrow); quill (of feather).
skakel, (-s), n. link; half(back) (rugby).
skakel, (ge-), connect; dial (teleph.).
skakelaar, (-s), switch.
skakering, (-e, -s), shade, nuance.
skalks, (-e), arch, roguish.
skamel, (-s), n. footstool; bogie (of wag(g)on, truck); transom.
skamel, (-, -e), a. poor, scanty, humble.
skamerig, (-e), shy, bashful.
skamper, (-, -e), scornful, bitter.
skandaal, (-dale), scandal, disgrace.
skande, shame, disgrace.
skandeer, (ge-), scan.
skandelik, (-e), disgraceful, shameful, scandalous, outrageous.
Skandinawië, Scandinavia.
skandvlek, n. stigma, disgrace.
skans, (-e), rampart, bulwark, trench.
skaplik, (-e), reasonable, fair, tolerable.
skare, (-s), skaar, (skare), crowd, host.
skarlaken, scarlet.
skarnier, (-e), hinge.
skarrel, (ge-), search, rummage, ransack; philander, chase.
skat, (-te), treasure, wealth; darling.
skat, (ge-), estimate (number), value, assess (property); esteem, appreciate.
skatbaar, (-bare), ratable, taxable.
skater, (ge-), roar with laughter.
skaterlag, n. burst (peal) of laughter.
skaterlag, (ge-), roar with laughter.
skatlik, (-e), dear, darling.
skatryk, very wealthy (rich).

skattig, (-e), dear, sweet.
skatting, (-e, -s), estimate, valuation; esteem, estimation; tribute.
skavot, (-te), scaffold.
skawe, (ge-), vide skaaf, (ge-).
skede, (-s), sheath.
skedel, (-s), skull, cranium.
skeef, (skewe), a. crooked, skew; oblique (angle, axis); sloping; distorted.
skeef, adv. crooked, askew, awry, amiss, wrong.
skeel, a. & adv. squinting, squint-eyed.
skeel, (ge-), differ; matter.
skeen, (skene), shin.
skeepgaan, (skeepge-), embark.
skeepvaart, navigation; shipping; marine.
skeer, (ge-), shave (the beard), shear (wool), cut, trim (hair).
skei, (-e), yoke-pin, skey.
skei(e), (ge-), part, divide, separate, divorce.
skei(d)baar, (-bare), separable.
skeidsregter, n. referee, umpire; arbitrator.
skeikunde, chemistry.
skel, (-le), a. shrill (voice); glaring.
skel, (ge-), ring.
skel, (ge-), scold, abuse, call names.
skel(d)woord, abusive word.
skelet, (-te), skeleton.
skelm, (-s), rogue, rascal, thief.
skelm, a., sly, cunning; dishonest; furtive.
skelmstreek, -stuk, piece of dishonesty, underhand (sharp) dealing.
skelvis, haddock.
skema, (-s), scheme, outline, plan.
skemer, n., dusk, twilight.
skemering, dusk, twilight; dawn.
skemerkelkie, sundowner.
skend, (ge-), disfigure, mutilate; violate; profane, desecrate; transgress (the law); defile.
skenk, (ge-), give, grant, present (endow) with.
skennis, violation, desecration.
skep, (-pe), n. scoop, ladle, shovel; spoonful (ladleful, spadeful), helping.
skep, (ge-), 1. scoop, ladle, dish up.
skep, (ge-), 2. create; establish, set-up.
skepdoel, drop-goal.
skepel, (-s), bushel.
skephou, half-volley (tennis).
skeplepel, ladle.
skeppend, (-e), creative.
skepper, (-s), creator; scoop, dipper.
skepsel, (-e), creature.
skepsel, (-s), coloured man, native; creation, work.
skepskop, drop(-kick).
skepties, (-e), sceptical.
skêr, (-e), (pair of) scissors; (pair of) shears.
skerf, (skerwe), (pot)sherd, fragment, splinter.
skerm, (-e, -s), screen (against light); curtain (in theatre).
skerm, (ge-), fence, parry; parade.
skermutseling, (-e, -s), skirmish, brush.
skerp, (-, -e), a. sharp, cutting, keen, acute, severe; acrid.
skerp, adv. sharply, severely, keenly, acutely, closely.
skerpioen, (-e), scorpion.
skerpsinnig, (-e), sharp, sharpwitted, acute, discerning.
skerpskutter, sharp-shooter; sniper.
skerts, n. joke, joking, jest, fun.
skerts, (ge-). joke, jest, make fun.
skets, (-e), n. sketch, (rough) draft.
skets, (ge-), sketch, outline, picture.
sketter, (ge-), blare; bray; rant; brag.

skeur, (-e), n. tear, rent (in cloth); crack, fissure; split (in party).

skeur, (ge-), tear (up), rend, rip; split.

skeurbuik, scurvy.

skewebek: – trek, pull faces (a wry face).

skielik, skierlik, (-e), a. sudden, quick.

skielik, skierlik, adv. suddenly.

skiereiland, peninsula.

skierlik, vide **skielik**.

skiet, n.: – gee, veer, slack.

skiet, (ge-), shoot, fire (a shot); blast (with dynamite); dart, rush.

skietlood, plumb, plummet.

skif, (ge-), separate, sort out, sift; (milk) (begin to) run, curdle; (material) become threadbare.

skig, (-te), arrow, bolt, dart; flash, ray.

skigtig, (-e), skittish, (inclined to be) shy.

skik, n. pleasure, enjoyment.

skik, (ge-), arrange, manage, order; settle, make up; be convenient, suit.

skiklik, (-e), obliging, accommodating.

skil, (-le), n. peel, rind, skin, scale.

skil, (ge-), peel, pare, skin.

skilder, (-s), n. painter.

skilder, (ge-), paint; depict, delineate, picture.

skilderagtig, (-e), picturesque.

skildery, (-e), picture, painting.

skildwag, sentinel, sentry.

skilfer, (-s), dandruff (on the head); scale, flake, tuft.

skilfer, (ge-), scale, flake, give off scales.

skilpad, (-paaie), tortoise (on land), turtle (in water); slowcoach.

skim, (-me), shadow, spectre, ghost.

skimmel, (-s), mildew, mould; fungus; blight; grey (horse), roan (horse).

skimmel, a. mouldy, mildewy, musty, stale; bashful; roan, grey.

skimmel, (ge-), grow mouldy (mildewy).

skimp, (-e), n. gibe, jeer; allusion, innuendo.

skimp, (ge-), scoff, jeer; allude, make covert references.

skimpdig, (-te), satire.

skinder, (ge-), slander; backbite.

skinderbek, gossip, slanderer.

skink, (ge-), pour; serve.

skinkbord, tray, salver.

skip, (skepe), ship, boat.

skipbreuk, shipwreck.

skipper, (-s), n. (sea-)captain, master.

skitter, (ge-), sparkle, glitter, shine.

skitterend, (-e), sparking, brilliant, glorious.

skob, skub, (-be), scale; vide **skub.**

skobbejak, (-ke), scoundrel, rogue, bounder, scamp, rascal.

skoei, (ge-), shoe.

skoeisel, footwear.

skoe(n), boot, shoe.

skoenlapper, cobbler, butterfly.

skoenmaker, bootmaker, shoemaker.

skof, (skowwe, skofte), lap, stage, trek; shift; hump, withers (horse), shoulders (ox).

skoffel, (-s), hoe, weeding-hook.

skoffel, (ge-), hoe, weed; dance.

skoffelpik, hoe.

skoffelploeg, cultivator.

skok, (-ke), shock, impact, concussion; jolt, jerk, jar.

skok, (ge-), (give a) shock, shake, jolt.

skolier, (-e), scholar, pupil.

skollie, (-s), hooligan, "skollie".

skommel, (-s), swing.

skommel, (ge-), swing, rock, oscillate, roll, wobble; (prices) fluctuate.

skooier, (-s), beggar, "loafer", tramp.

skool, (skole), school; shoal (of fish).

skoolhou, (skoolge-), teach, give lessons.

skoon, n. the beautiful.

skoon, (–, skone), a. clean, pure; fine, beautiful, handsome.

skoon, adv., clean, quite, completely, absolutely.

skoondogter, daughter-in-law.

skoonmaak, (skoonge-), clean, cleanse, clean out, clean up, weed (a garden-bed).

skoonmoeder, mother-in-law.

skoonskip: – maak, make a clean sweep.

skoonsuster, sister-in-law.

skoonvader, father-in-law.

skoonveld, n. (golf) fairway.

skoonveld, adv. clean gone.

skoor, n.: – soek, ask (look) for trouble.

skoor, (ge-), joke, tease; quarrel.

skoorsteen, chimney; funnel (of ship).

skoorvoetend, reluctantly.

skoot, skot, (skote), shot; report, crack; time, turn.

skoot, (skote), lap, bosom; fold.

skop, (-pe), n. shovel; scoop; spade.

skop, (-pe), n. kick.

skop, (ge-), kick; recoil.

skopgraaf, shovel.

skoppe(ns), (pl.) spades (cards).

skoppel-, skoppermaai, (-e), **skoppel-, skopper-maaier**, (-s), swing; – ry, swing.

skor, (–, -re), hoarse, husky, rough.

skorriemorrie, riff-raff, rabble.

skors, n. bark, rind.

skors, (ge-), suspend; adjourn.

skort, (ge-), be wrong, be wanting.

Skot, (-te), Scot, Scotchman.

skotig, (-e), gradually sloping.

skotskar, scotch-cart.

skottel, (-s), dish, basin.

skottelgoed, dishes and plates.

skottelploeg, disc-plough.

skouburg, (-e), theatre.

skouer, (-s), shoulder.

skouspel, (-spele), spectacle, sight, scene.

skout, (-e), sherif, bailiff.

skout-by-nag, rear-admiral.

skraag, (ge-), support, prop (up).

skraal, (–, skrale), thin, lean (of a person); poor (soil); bleak, cutting (wind); scanty, meagre (returns, hopes).

skraap, (skrape), n. scratch.

skraap, (ge-), scrape; pursue, chase.

skraapsug, stinginess, niggardliness.

skram, (-me), n. scratch, mark.

skram, (ge-), scratch, graze.

skrams, grazingly.

skrander, smart, clever, bright, sharp, ingenious, shrewd.

skrap, (ge-), scratch, strike out, cross out, cancel.

skrap(s), a. & adv. scarce(ly); barely.

skrede, (–, -s), step, stride.

skree, (skreë) skreeu, (-e), n. shout, cry, scream; shriek.

skree, skreeu, (ge-), shout, cry, scream; shriek; bawl.

skree(u)balie, cry-baby.

skreeulelik, (-e), a. frightfully ugly.

skrefie, chink, slit.

skrei, (ge-), cry, weep.

skreiend, (-e), crying, flagrant, shameful.

skriba, (-s), scriba, scribe.

skrif, (-te), writing, handwriting; exercise book.

skrifgeleerd, (-e), educated; cunning.

skriftelik, (-e), in writing, written.

skriftuur, (-ture), scripture, document.

skrik, n. fright, terror, alarm.

skrik, (ge-), start, be frightened (startled); get a fright.
skrikaanja(g)end, (-e), alarming, terrifying.
skrikbarend, (-e), alarming, terrifying.
skrikkeljaar, leap-year.
skrikkerig, (-e), jumpy, nervous, frightened, afraid; shy, skittish.
skrikmaak, (skrikge-), startle, alarm, frighten.
skrikwekkend, (-e), alarming, appalling.
skril, (-, -le), shrill; glaring (colours).
skrobbeer, (ge-), rebuke, reprove, reprimand.
skroef, (skroewe), n. screw; propeller (of boat, aeroplane); (jaw-)vice.
skroef, skroewe, (ge-), screw.
skroefhamer, wrench, spanner.
skroefturbinemotor, prop-jet.
skroei, (ge-), singe (hair); scorch (grass); cauterise (a wound).
skroewe, vide skroef, (ge-).
skroewedraaier, skroefdraaier, (-s), screw-driver.
skromelik, vide skroomlik.
skrompel, (ge-), shrivel, wither.
skroom, n. diffidence, timidity, modesty.
skroom, (ge-), hesitate, dread, be afraid.
skroomlik, (-e), shameful(ly), disgraceful(ly), bad(ly).
skroomvallig, (-e), timorous, bashful.
skrop, (-pe), (dam-)scraper.
skrop, (ge-), scrub, scour; scratch; scrape.
skrum, (-s), scrum, scrummage.
skrum, (ge-), scrum.
skrumskakel, scrum-half.
skryf, skrywe, (ge-), write; correspond.
skryfblok, writing-pad (-block).
skryn, (ge-), smart, cause pain.
skrynend, (-e), smarting, painful.
skrynwerker, cabinet-maker, joiner; carpenter.
skrywe, n. letter.
skrywe, vide skryf, (ge-).
sku, (-, -we), shy, bashful; reserved, unsociable; skittish (of horse, etc.).
skub, skob, (-be), scale, scutum.
skud, (ge-), shake; tremble; jolt; shuffle (cards).
skugter, (-, -e), timied, shy, coy.
skuif, (skuiwe), bolt (of a door), sliding-bolt; slide; slide-valve; puff (of smoke).
skuif, skuiwe, (ge-), push; shove; move.
skuifdeur, sliding door.
skuifel, (ge-), shuffle.
skuifie, (-s), slide; draw (at cigar, cigarette).
skuifmeul(e), (game of) noughts and crosses (lit.); excuse, pretext (fig.).
skuil, (ge-), shelter, take cover (shelter); hide.
skuilgaan, (skuilge-), hide.
skuilhoek, hiding-place, cover.
skuilhou, (skuilge-), hide, keep hidden.
skuilnaam, pen-name, pseudonym.
skuim, n. foam (on liquids, horses, round the mouth); froth; lather (of soap); dross (of molten metal); scrum; dregs, refuse.
skuim, (ge-), foam, froth; lather; skim; sparkle, bead; fume (with rage).
skuimbek, (ge-), foam at the mouth.
skuins, a. slanting, sloping, oblique; bevel(led).
skuins, adv. slantingly, obliquely, aslant, awry; askance.
skuinste, (-s), slope.
skuit, (-e), boat.
skuiwe, vide skuif.
skuiwergat, scaffolding-hole, putlog-hole; scupper-hole.
skuld, (-e), n. debt; fault, guilt.
skuld, (ge-), owe.
skuldbewys, acknowledgment of debt, IOU.

skuldeiser, creditor.
skuldenaar, (-s, -nare), debtor.
skuldig, (-e), guilty; culpable.
skulp, (-e), shell.
skurf, (skurwe), mangy, scabby (in animals), chapped, rough (in human beings); scaly.
skurk, (-e), blackguard, villain, scoundrel, rogue.
skut, (-s), n. shot, marksman.
skut, (-te), n. protection; screen; fence; pound (for stray animals).
skut, (ge-), protect; pound, impound.
skutkraal, pound.
skutsengel, guardian-angel.
skutter, (-s), shot, marksman.
skutting, (-s), protection; fence, hoarding, impounding.
skuur, (skure), n. barn, shed.
skuur, (ge-), rub; scrub; scour (pots); graze, chafe.
skuurpapier, sand paper, abrasive paper.
skyf, (skywe), target; slice (of watermelon), quarter (of orange); disc.
skyn, n. appearance, semblance; show, pretence; glimmer, glow.
skyn, (ge-), shine; seem, look, appear.
skynbaar, (-bare), a. apparent, seeming.
skyngeveg, sham fight, mock fight.
skynheilig, (-e), hypocritical.
skynsel, glow, light, glimmer.
sla(e), (pl.) cuts, lashes, blows.
Slaaf, (Slawe), Slav, Slavonian.
slaaf, (slawe), n. slave.
slaaf, slawe, (ge-), slave, toil, drudge.
slaafs, (-e), slavish, servile.
slaag, (ge-), succeed; pass.
slaags: – raak, come to blows; join battle.
slaai, lettuce; salad.
slaak, (ge-), breathe, heave, utter.
slaan, slaat, (ge-), strike, beat, hit; thrash, flog; slap, flap.
slaanbeurt, innings.
slaanding, something to hit with, cane.
slaap, sleep; (pl. slape), temple.
slaap, (ge-), sleep, be asleep.
slaapdrank, sleeping-draught, soporific.
slaapkous, drowsy-head, sleepy-head.
slae, vide sla(e).
slag, (slae), blow (of hand, sword); stroke (of clock, rower, swimmer); beat (of heart, pulse); lash (of whip); clap (of thunder); thump, thud, crash (of falling object); slap, smack (in the face); knack, trick, sleight of hand; turn, time; kink, turn, twist (in a rope); battle.
slag, (ge-), slaughter, kill; skin.
slagboom, barrier, bar.
slaggat, pot-hole.
slaghuis, butcher's shop, butchery.
slagoffer, victim.
slagpale, abattoir, slaughterhouse.
slagskip, battle-ship.
slagtand, tusk; fang, canine (tooth).
slagter, (-s), butcher.
slagting, slaughter, butchery.
slagvaardig, (-e), ready for the fray (for battle), game.
slagyster, (spring-)trap.
slak, (-ke), snail, slug; (pl. also) slag, clinker (of metal).
slampamper, (ge-), revel, make merry.
slang, (-e), snake; (hose-)pipe.
slank, (-, -e), tall (and slim), willowy, of fine figure; slim, slender.

slap, a. & adv. slack; soft; weak; flabby; limp; dull (trade).

slavin, (-ne), (female) slave.

slawe, (ge-), vide **slaaf**, (ge-).

slawerny, slavery, bondage, servitude.

slee, (sleë), sledge; sleigh (for persons only); sled (for goods only); carriage.

sleep, n. drag, tow; train.

sleep, (ge-), drag, pull, draw, haul, lug; tow, tug.

sleepboot, tug.

sleepsel, (-s), trail.

sleeptong: – **praat**, lisp.

sleeptou, tow-rope.

sleepvoetend, (-e), shuffling, lagging.

Sleeswyk, Schleswig, Sleswick.

sleg, (-te), a. bad; evil; poor; rotten.

sleg, adv., badly, ill; poorly.

sleg, (ge-), level, raze, demolish.

slegs, only, merely, but.

slenter, (ge-), saunter, stroll; slouch.

slenterslag, trick, dodge, roguery.

slet, (-te), slut, strumpet.

sleur, groove, rut, routine.

sleur, (ge-), vide **sloer**, (ge-).

sleurwerk, routine-work, grind.

sleutel, (-s), key; spanner.

sleutelbeen, collar-bone.

slib, silt, ooze, slime, mire.

slik, vide **slib** & **slyk**.

slim, (–, -me), smart, clever; crafty, cunning.

slimmerd, (-s), cunning fox, sly dog.

slimpraatjies, clap-trap, glib talk.

slinger, (-s), pendulum; sling; (starting-)handle, crank.

slinger, (ge-), swing, oscillate; sway, reel, lurch, roll; wind; hurl, fling.

slingerplant, creeper, climbing plant.

slinks, (–, -e), underhand, surreptitious.

slip, (-pe), tail, flap (of a coat); slit; tip.

slipdraer, pall-bearer.

sloep, (-e), sloop, dinghy, longboat.

sloer, (ge-), drag (on), dawdle, keep postponing (putting off); linger.

sloerie, (-s), slut, drab.

slof, (ge-), shuffle, shamble.

slonserig, (-e), slovenly, slatternly.

sloof, slowe, (ge-), drudge, toil, slave.

sloop, (slope), n. pillow-case, pillow-slip.

sloop, (ge-), level, demolish (a building); dismantle (a fort); break up; undermine; drain, sap (one's strength).

sloot, (slote), furrow, trench, ditch.

slordig, (-e), untidy, slovenly, dowdy; careless; shoddy.

slot, end, conclusion; peroration; (pl. -te); lock (of door, gun); clasp (of book); castle.

slotsom, conclusion.

Slowakye, Slovakia.

slowe, vide **sloof**, (ge-).

slu, [-(w)e], cunning, crafty, wily.

sluier, (-s), n. veil; fog.

sluiks: ter –, on the sly, stealthily.

sluimer, n. slumber.

sluimer, (ge-), slumber, doze.

sluip, (ge-), slink, sneak, steal; prowl.

sluipmoord, assassination.

sluis, (-e), sluice; lock.

sluit, (ge-, geslote), close; lock; close down; conclude (treaty); effect (insurance); make, (peace); end, conclude (letter, speech).

sluitboom, boom, barrier.

sluk, (-ke), n. swallow, gulp, mouthful, pull, draught.

sluk, (ge-), swallow; put up with, endure.

slukderm, gullet, oesophagus.

slurp, (ge-), gulp, guzzle.

slyk, mire, slime, mud; silt.

slym, phlegm, mucus, slime.

slymerig, (-e), slimy, mucous.

slymvlies, mucous membrane.

slyp, (ge-), sharpen, whet, grind; cut, polish (diamonds).

slypplank, knife-board.

slypsteen, grindstone, whetstone.

slyt, (ge-), wear out; pass, spend (one's days).

slytasie, wear (and tear), wastage.

smaad, n. contumely, abuse, insult.

smaad, (ge-), malign, revile, deride.

smaak, n. taste, flavour, liking.

smaak, (ge-), taste; enjoy; appear, seem.

smaaklik, (-e), palatable, delicious, enjoyable.

smaakvol, (-le), tasteful, in good taste.

smaal, (ge-), sneer.

smadelik, (-e), derisive, scornful.

smag, (ge-), languish, pine; yearn (for).

smak, thud, crash; smack (of the lips).

smal, (–, -le), narrow.

smarag, (-de), emerald.

smart, (-e), n. grief, sorrow, affliction, pain.

smartlik, (-e), painful.

smee(d), (ge-), forge, hammer, weld; invent (a lie); plan (conspiracy); coin.

smeek, (ge-), implore, beseech, beg.

smeer, n. grease; smear, stain.

smeer, (ge-), grease, lubricate; butter; rub, massage.

smeerlap, grease-rag; ragamuffin, dirty fellow, blackguard, swine, cad, skunk.

smelt, (ge-), melt, liquefy; fuse (wire); melt down, render (fat); smelt (ore); merge, fuse.

smeltdraad, fuse(-wire).

smeltkroes, crucible, melting-pot.

smerig, (-e), dirty, filthy, messy.

smet, (-te), stain, blot, blemish, taint.

smeul, (ge-), smoulder, glow.

smeulstofie, slow combustion stove.

smid, (-s, smede), smit, (-te), (black-)smith.

smiddags, in the (of an) afternoon; at noon, midday.

smoel, (-e), mug, face.

smokkel, (ge-), smuggle.

smoor, (ge-), smother, choke, throttle; stifle (sound); hush up (scandal); braise, stew.

smoordronk, dead drunk.

smoorklep, choke, throttle-valve.

smoorverlief, deeply in love.

smôrens, smorens: in the (of a) morning.

smous, (-e), n. pedlar, hawker.

smous, (ge-), hawk.

smul, (ge-), feast, regale oneself.

smyt, (ge-), fling, hurl, cast, pitch.

s'n: pa –, father's.

snaaks, (-e), funny, comical, droll, queer, strange.

snaar, (snare), n. string; lover, beloved.

snaar, (ge-), string (a racket, etc.)

snags, in the (of a) night.

snak, (ge-), gasp (for breath); yearn.

snap, (ge-), catch; understand; babble.

snaps(ie), tot, spot, drop, drink.

snars, sners: geen –, not a rap, not a hang.

snater, (-s), n. mug, jaw.

snater, (ge-), chatter, jabber.

snawel, (-s), bill, beak.

snedig, (-e), quick, smart, witty.

snee, (sneë), edge; caesura (in verse).

sneespapier, India-paper, tissue-paper.

sneeu, n. snow.

sneeu, (ge-), snow.

snel, (–, -le), a. & adv. fast, swift(ly), quick(ly), rapid(ly), speedy (speedily).

snel, (ge-), hurry, hasten, rush.
sneller, (-s), (1) trigger.
sneller, (-s), (2) sprinter; three-quarter.
snelskrif, shorthand, stenography.
sneltrein, express (train), fast train.
snerpend, (-e), biting, piercing (wind, cold); burning (pain).
snert, pea-soup; rot, rubbish, trash.
sneuwel, (ge-), fall, be killed (in action).
snik, (-ke), n. sob, gasp.
snik, (ge-), sob.
snikheet, snikkendheet, swelteringly hot.
snip, (-pe), snipe; perky (saucy) thing.
snipper, (ge-), snip, cut up.
snipperig, (-e), perky, saucy.
snippermandjie, waste-paper basket.
snit, cut (of a garment); edge (of knife).
snoei, (ge-), prune (fruit-trees); trim, clip, lop; cut (expenses).
snoek, (-e), "snoek", pike (European).
snoep, a. greedy, grasping, having.
snoep, (ge-), sneak, pinch, eat furtively; refuse to give.
snoepkroeg, snack bar.
snoer, (-e), n. line, string, lace.
snoer, (ge-), tie, string (up).
snoesig, (-e), dainty, ducky, sweet.
snoet, (-e), snout (of pig), muzzle, nose (of cat); mug, jaw.
snood, (snode), evil (plans), base (ingratitude), heinous (crime).
snor, (-re), moustache.
snor, (ge-), drone; purr; whizz.
snorbaardjie, moustache; whiskers.
snork, (ge-), snore; snort (of horse).
snot, snot, mucus (of the nose).
snou, (-e), n. snarl.
snou, (ge-), snarl (out), snap (out).
snuf, smell.
snuffel, (ge-), sniff, nose; ferret, pry, rummage.
snuif, n. snuff.
snuif, snuiwe, (ge-), take snuff; sniff.
snuistery, (-e), knick-knack, gimcrack.
snuit, (-e), n. snout (of pig), proboscis (of insect).
snuit, (ge-), blow one's nose; snuff.
snuiter, (-s), snuffers; kid, milksop.
snuiwe, vide snuif, (ge-).
sny, (-e), n. cut, gash, notch, slice.
sny, (ge-), cut; geld; sprint.
snyer, (-s), tailor; cutter, carver.
snysel(tjie)s, dough-threads.
so, so, thus.
sober, frugal; sober.
sodanig, (-e), such, such like; in such a way.
sodat, so that.
sodoende, in this (that) way, thus; so.
sodra, as soon as.
soe! ugh!, brr!, phew!
soebat, (ge-), beg, implore, entreat.
Soedan, Sudan.
soek, (ge-), look for (a pen, trouble), look (out) for (a job, a wife), look up (a word), seek (help), hunt for (a house), search.
soeklig, search-light, spot-light.
soel, (1) mild, soft; close, sultry.
soel, (2) sallow (of human complexion).
soen, (-e), n. kiss.
soen, (ge-), kiss.
soep, sop, soup.
soepee, (-s), supper.
soepel, (-, -e), supple, pliant, lithe.
soet, sweet.
soetjies, suutjies, softly, gently, quietly.

soetsappig, (-e), namby-pamby, sloppy, goody-goody, mealy-mouthed.
soetvloeiend, (-e), fluent, melodious.
so-ewe, just now, a moment ago.
soewerein, (-e), a. sovereign.
sofa, (-s), sofa.
sog, (-ge, söe), sow.
sog, wake (of a ship).
sogenaamd, (-e), a. so-called.
sogenaamd, adv. ostensibly, professedly.
soggens, in the (of a) morning.
soheentoe, soontoe, thither, there.
sok, (-ke), socket, sleeve; vide sokkie.
sokker, association-football, soccer.
sokkie, (-s), sock.
Sokrates, Socrates.
solang(e)s, (along) this (that) way.
solank, for the time being, so long.
soldaat, (-date), soldier.
soldeer, (ge-), solder.
solder, (-s), loft; ceiling.
soldy, wage(s), pay.
solied, (-e), solid, substantial; respectable; solvent.
sollisiteer, (ge-), apply.
solo, (-'s), solo.
som, (-me), sum.
somaar(so), vide sommer(so).
somber, (-, -e), sombre, gloomy.
somer, (-s), summer.
somers, (-e), summer- . . .
sommer, somaar, for no particular reason; just, merely; without further ado, straight off; immediately.
sommerso, somaarso, simply, just (as it was); after a fashion, so-so, in an off-hand way.
sommige, some.
soms, sometimes, at times, now and then.
somtyds, somwyle, = soms.
son, (-ne), sun.
sonate, (-s), sonata.
sonbesie, cicada.
sondaar, (-s), sinner; offender.
Sondag, Sunday.
sonde, (-s), sin; trouble.
sondebok, scapegoat.
sonder, without.
sonderling, (-e), queer, odd, peculiar.
sondig, (-e), a. sinful.
sondig, (ge-), sin; offend.
sondvloed, deluge.
sone, (-s), zone.
sonneblom, sunflower, helianthus.
sonnet, (-te), sonnet.
sonnewyser, sun-dial; gnomon.
sonnig, (-e), sunny.
sononder, n., sunset; adv., at sunset.
sonop, n. sunrise.
sonsondergang, sunset.
sonsteek, sunstroke.
soog, (ge-), suckle, nurse, nourish.
soogdier, mammal.
sooi, (-e), sod.
sooibrand, heartburn.
sool, (sole), sole.
soölogie, zoology.
soöloog, (-loge, -loë), zoologist.
soom, (some), hem; edge, border, fringe.
soom, (ge-), hem; border.
soontoe, soheentoe, thither, there.
soort, (-e), kind, sort, species, variety.
soortgelyk, (-e), of the same (that) kind, similar.
soortlik, (-e), specific.
soos, as: like, such as; just as.
sop, sap, juice. Vide soep.

Sophocles, Sophokles, Sophocles.
sopie, (-s), drink, tot.
sopperig, sapperig, (-e), juicy; sloppy.
sopraan, (-prane), soprano, treble.
sôre, sorg(e), (ge-), mind, see.
sorg, (-e), n., care; trouble, worry; anxiety, concern, solicitude; charge.
sorg(e), (ge-), vide sôre.
sorgbarend, (-e), alarming.
sorgsaam, (-same), careful, attentive.
sorgvuldig, (-e), careful, thorough.
sorgwekkend, (-e), alarming, causing anxiety.
sorteer, (ge-), sort, assort; grade.
sosatie, sosatie (sassate).
soseer, so much, to such an extent.
sosiaal, (-siale), social.
sosialis, (-te), socialist.
sosioloog, (-loge, -loë), sociologist.
so-so, so-so, after a fashion.
sosys, (-e), sausage, polony.
sot, (-te), n. fool.
sot, (–, -te), a. mad, crazy.
sotterny, (-e), foolishness; tomfoolery.
sou, vide sal.
sous, n. gravy; sauce, relish.
sous, (ge-), sauce; rain, pour, drizzle.
sousboontjies, bean-salad, salad-beans.
souskom, gravy-boat, sauce-boat.
sout, (-), n. salt.
sout, a. salt, briny.
sout, (ge-), salt; initiate.
soutpotjie, salt-cellar.
Soutsee, Dead Sea.
soutsuur, hydrochloric acid.
soveel, (soveel), so much, so many.
soveelste, umpteenth.
sover, so far, thus far, as far as.
sowaar, actually, to be sure, as sure as fate.
sowat, about, more or less, roughly.
sowel: – as, as well as.
Sowjet, (-s), Soviet.
spaan, (spane), scoop, ladle, skimmer; (roof) shingle; (for rowing) oar.
spaander, (-s), n. chip, splinter.
spaander, (ge-), scoot, skedaddle.
spaar, (ge-), save, put by, reserve, husband; spare (one's life, costs trouble).
spaarsaam, (-same), thrifty, economical.
spalk, (-e), n. splint.
spalk, (ge-), set (fractured leg), splint, stretch (hides).
span, (-ne), n. team; gang; span (of oxen; of the hand).
span, (ge-), stretch (rope); strain (eyes, muscles, attention); draw, bend (a bow); hobble (a horse), strap (a cow).
spandabel, (-e), extravagant, wasteful.
spandeer, (ge-), spend.
Spanjaard, (-e), Spaniard.
Spanje, Spain.
spannend, (-e), tight, tense; exciting, thrilling.
spanning, tension, strain, pressure; voltage; span (of bridge); suspense, excitement.
spansaag, bow-, frame-saw.
spanspek, musk-melon.
spantou, milking-strap, kneestrap.
spar, (-re), rafter (of roof); spruce-fir.
Spartaan, (-tane), Spartan.
spartel, (ge-), flounder, sprawl; struggle.
spasie, (-s), space, room, opening.
spasieer, (ge-), space.
spat, (-te), n. splash, spatter, stain, spot.
spat, (ge-), splash, splutter, spatter; take to one's heels.
spataar, varicose vein.

spatsel, (-s), splash, spatter.
speek, (speke), spoke.
speeksel, spittle, saliva.
speel, (ge-), play; act; chime; gamble.
speelbal, playing ball; sport, plaything, puppet.
speels, (-e), playful.
speelsiek, (–, -e), playful, frolicsome.
speel-speel, playing; easily.
speen, (spene), n. nipple, teat.
speen, (ge-), wean.
speenvark(ie), sucking-pig.
speer, (spere), spear; javelin.
spek, bacon, "spek"; blubber (of whale).
spekboom, spekboom, elephant's food.
spekskiet, (spekge-), fib.
spektakel, (-s), scene, uproar, rumpus.
spekulant, (-e), speculator.
spekuleer, (ge-), speculate.
spekvet, as plumb as a partridge, fatted; in good health, looking well.
spel, (-e), n. game; play, performance; playing; recreation.
spel, spelle, (ge-), spell.
speld, (-e), pin.
speld(e), (ge-), pin, fasten.
spelenderwys(e), speelsgewyse, playing, playfully, in play; jocularly.
speler, (-s), player; gambler; musician; actor; performer.
spelerig, (-e), playful, frolicsome.
speletjie, (-s), game; fun.
speling, play, allowance, scope.
spelle, (ge-), vide spel.
spelletjie, (-s), game.
spelling, (-e, -s), spelling.
spelonk, (-e), cave, cavern.
spens, dispens, (-e), pantry.
sper, (ge-), bar, block; distend.
spervuur, barrage.
spesery, (-e), spice.
spesiaal, (-siale), special; (adv.) specially.
spesialiseer, (ge-), specialise.
spesialiteit, special(i)ty; specialist.
spesifiek, (-e), specific.
spesifiseer, (ge-), specify.
speur, (ge-), notice, discover, detect; trail, track.
speurder, (-s), detective.
spie, vide spy.
spieël, (-s), n. looking-glass, mirror; level (of the sea).
spieël, (ge-), mirror, reflect.
spieëlbeeld, image; illusion.
spieëlglad, (-de), as smooth as a mirror.
spieëlglas, plate-glass.
spieëltafel, dressing-table.
spier, (-e), muscle.
spierwit, snow-white, pure white.
spies, (-e), spear, javelin, pike, lance.
spiets, (-e), speech; joke.
spikkel, (-s), n. spot, speck, speckle.
spikkel, (ge-), speckle.
spil, (-le), pivot, axle; halfback.
spin, (ge-), spin; purr (of a cat).
spinasie, spinach.
spinnekop, (-pe), spider.
spinnerak, (-ke), cobweb; gossamer.
spioen, (-e), n. spy, scout.
spioen, (ge-), spy, scout.
spioenasie, espionage.
spioeneer, (ge-), spy; scout.
spiraal, spiral, coil, helix.
spiritisme, spiritism, spiritualism.
spiritualisme, spiritualism.
spiritus, spirit(s).
spit, (-te), n. spit; spadeful; crick, lumbago.

spit, (ge-), dig.
spits, n. point, head; peak, summit, spire, pinnacle; van, forefront.
spits, (-, -e), a. pointed, sharp.
spits, (ge-), point.
spitsroei: – loop, run the gauntlet.
spitsvondig, (-e), subtle, ingenious, far-fetched, quibbling.
spleet, (splete), crack, fissure, crevice.
splinter, (-s), n. splinter, shiver, sliver, chip.
splinter, (ge-), splinter, shiver.
splinternuut, (-nuwe), brand new.
splits, (ge-), split (up), cleave; splice.
splyt, (ge-, gesplete), split, cleave.
spoed, n. haste, speed.
spoed, (ge-), speed, hasten, hurry.
spoedeisend, (-e), urgent.
spoedig, (-e), a. quick, speedy, early.
spoedig, adv. soon, quickly, speedily.
spoe(g), spu(ug), n. spittle, spit, saliva.
spoe(g), spu(ug), (ge-), spit, expectorate.
spoel, (-e), n. shuttle, spool, bobbin.
spoel, (ge-), flow, wash, rinse.
spoetnik, sputnik.
spog, (ge-), boast, brag, swank, show off.
spoggerig, (-e), boastful, bragging; showy; swanky.
sponning, (-s), groove, rabbet, slot.
spons, (-e), n. sponge; bung.
spons, (ge-), sponge.
sponssiekte, black quarter, quarter evil.
spontaan, (-tane), spontaneous.
spook, (spoke), n., ghost, spectre; fright, freak.
spook, (ge-), haunt, be haunted; struggle, fight.
spoor, (spore), n. (1) trace, track, trail, footmark, footprint; railway (line), rails, track; mark, sign, trace, vestige, indication; rut, track (of wagon).
spoor, (spore), n. (2) spur.
spoorlyn, railway line.
spoorslag, incentive, spur, urge.
spoorweg, railway.
sporadies, (-e), sporadic(al).
sport, (-e), (1), rung.
sport, (2) sport.
sportbyeenkoms, sports(-meeting).
sportief, (-tiewe), sporting.
spot, n. scorn, ridicule, mockery, banter.
spot, (ge-), mock, scoff, jeer; jest, joke.
spotdig, (-te), satire, satirical poem.
spotgoedkoop, dirt-cheap.
spottenderwys(e), mockingly, jeeringly.
spotterny, mockery; derision.
spotvoël, mocker, teaser.
spraak, speech.
spraakkuns, grammar.
spraaksaam, (-same), talkative, loquacious, garrulous, chatty, chattering.
sprake, talk, mention.
sprank(ie), spark.
sprankel, (ge-), sparkle, scintillate.
spreek, [(sprak), ge-, gesproke], speak.
spreekbuis, speaking-tube; mouthpiece.
spreekkamer, consulting-room.
spreekwoord, proverb, adage.
spreekwyse, manner of speaking (speech); idiom, expression.
spreeu, (-s), starling.
sprei, (-e), n. quilt, counterpane, coverlet.
sprei, (ge-), spread.
sprekend, (-e), speaking; telling, striking.
spreuk, (-e), motto, maxim, adage, proverb.
spriet, (-e), blade (of grass); feeler, antenna.
spring, (-e), n. jump, leap, bound.

spring, (ge-), jump, leap, spring, bound; hop, skip, caper; snap, crack, burst.
springhaas, jumping-hare.
springlewendig, (-e), brisk, alive and kicking.
springmielies, pop-corn.
springstof, explosive.
sprinkaan, (sprinkane), locust, grasshopper.
sprinkel, (ge-), sprinkle; damp.
sproei, spru, n. thrush, sprue.
sproei, (ge-), sprinkle, water; spray.
sproet, (-e), freckle.
sprokie, (-s), fairy-tale; fable, fiction.
sprong, (-e), jump, leap, bound; caper, gambol, hop.
spruit, (-e), n. shoot, sprout; offshoot, off-spring; tributary, small stream.
spruit, (ge-), shoot, sprout; issue, descend (from).
spruitkool, (Brussels) sprouts.
spu(ug), vide spoeg.
spuigat, scupper hole.
spuit, (-e), n. syringe, squirt; (water-)hose.
spuit, (ge-), spout, squirt; spray.
spy, (-e), spie, (-ë), pin, wedge, cotter.
spyker, (-s), nail.
spys, n. food.
spyskaart, -lys, menu, bill of fare.
spyt, n. regret, sorrow.
spyt, (ge-), regret, be sorry.
spytig, (-e), regrettable.
st!, hist!, hush!
staaf, (stawe), n. bar, rod; ingot.
staaf, stawe, (ge-), confirm, prove.
staak, (ge-), stop, knock off.
staal, steel.
staal, (ge-), steel (the nerves).
staaltjie, (-s), sample; instance; yarn.
staan, (staat), (ge-), stand.
staande, standing; permanent.
staander, (-s), standard.
staanspoor: uit die –, from the (very) start (beginning).
staan-staan, standing (stopping) every now and then, while standing.
staat, (state), n. state; condition; rank, position; statement, record, list, form.
staat, (ge-), vide staan.
staatkunde, (ordinary) politics; (far-seeing) statesmanship.
staatmaker, (-s), man on whom one can depend, prop, mainstay.
staatsie, state, ceremony, pomp; procession.
staatskoerant, government gazette.
staatsman, statesman, politician.
staatsreg, constitutional law.
staatsweë: van –, by (on behalf of) the government; on authority (of the goverment).
stabiel, (-e), stable, steady, firm.
stabiliseer, (ge-), stabilize.
stad, (stede), city, town.
stade: te – kom, stand in good stead, be of good use, come in handy.
stadhuis, hall, city hall.
stadig, (-e), slow, lingering.
stadion, (-s), stadium.
stadium, (-s, stadia), stage, phase, period; stadium (length).
stadsraad, town council, city council.
staf, (stawe), staff (support, sign of office or authority; body (of officers, nurses, etc.); mace (in Parliament); (marshal's) baton; (bishop's) crozier.
staker, (-s), striker.
staking, (-e, -s), cessation, stoppage (of activities); strike (of workmen); tie (of votes); suspension (of payment).

stal, (-le), n. stable (for horses), cowshed (for cattle).

stalles, (pl.), stalls (in theatre).

stalletjie, (-s), stall, booth; small stable.

stam, (-me), n. stem (of tree, plant), trunk (of tree); tribe, clan (of people), stock, race; stem (of word).

stam, (ge-), form stems (a stem); – **van**, descend, from.

st(r)amboel, vide **snaar**, n.

stamboom, genealogical tree, pedigree.

stamel, (ge-), stammer (out), falter.

stamp, (-e), n. knock, blow; bruise; stamp (of foot); stamping.

stamp, (ge-), knock, pound, hit, give a blow; stamp; pound, crush; bruise; bump, jolt; thud.

stamper, (-s), pounder, stamper; jumper(-drill); stamp; pestle; rammer; pistil (of flower).

stampvoet, (ge-), stamp one's feet (in anger); (of horses) paw the ground.

stampvol, (-le), crammed, packed, crowded.

stamverwant, (-e), akin, cognate, related.

stamverwantskap, affinity, kinship, relationship, community of race.

stand, (-e), position, posture, (of the body); state, condition, situation, degree, rank, standing, station (in life); class, circle, caste, order; position, level, height (of barometer).

standaard, (-e), standard.

standbeeld, statue.

stander, (-s), stand (for hats, umbrellas); cruetstand; post, upright.

standerd, (-s), standard, class.

standhoudend, (-e), lasting, permanent.

standjie, (-s), tiff, quarrel, row.

standpunt, standpoint, point of view.

standvastig, (-e), steadfast, resolute, firm, constant.

stang, (-e), bit (of a bridle); rod, bar.

stank, (-e), stench, stink.

stansa, (-s), stanza.

stap, (-pe), n. step, pace, stride; footstep.

stap, (ge-), walk, go on foot; hike.

stapel, (-s), n. pile, stack, heap; stocks (shipbuilding); stock (of cattle).

stapel, stawel, (ge-), stack, pile up, heap up; build.

stapelgek, stawelgek, raving mad.

star, (-re), stiff, fixed.

staroog, (ge-), stare (gaze) fixedly.

stasie, (-s), station.

stasioneer, (ge-), station.

stat, (-te), Bantu village (kraal).

staties, (-e), static.

statig, (-e), stately, solemn, dignified.

statistiek, (science of) statistics; (pl. -e), statistics, returns, figures.

status, status, position.

statuut, (-tute), statute, ordinance, regulation, articles (of association).

stawe, vide **staaf**, (ge-).

stawe, vide **stapel**, (ge-).

stawing, confirmation, proof, support.

stede, stee, stead, place.

stedelik, (-e), municipal, urban, civic.

stedeling, (-e), townsman, town dweller.

stee, vide **stede**.

steeds, (-e), a. urban, town- . . .

steeds, adv., always, ever, constantly, still.

steeg, (stege, steë), alley, lane.

steek, (steke), n. stitch; sting (from bee); stab, thrust (with dagger); dig, poke, prod (with finger); dig, thrust (pointed remark).

steek, (ge-), prick, stab, jab (with a knife),

thrust (with a sword); (insect) sting; (wound) burn, smart; (sun) burn, scorch; (pain) shoot, twitch.

steekhoudend, (-e), valid, sound.

steeks, (–, -e), jibbing.

steekvlieg, gadfly.

steel, (stele), n. handle (of tool); stem, stalk of flower); stem (of pipe); shaft (of spear).

steel, (ge-), steal.

steelkant, blind side.

steels, (-e), stealthy, furtive.

steen, (stene), brick; stone, rock.

steenbok, steenbok (steenbuck).

Steenbokskeerkring, tropic of Capricorn.

steenkool, -kole, coal.

steg, (-ge), n. stile.

steg, (ge-), make slips (cuttings).

steggie, stiggie, (-s), cutting, slip.

steier, (-s), n. scaffolding, staging.

steier, (ge-), rear (of horse); stagger.

steierplank, scaffolding-board.

steil, steep, bluff; straight (hair).

steilte, (-s), steepness; incline, declivity.

stekelagtig, (-e), prickly; (fig.) stinging.

stekeling, (-e), sharp, stinging, acrimonious; prickly.

stekelvark, porcupine.

stel, (-le), n. set; lot, bunch; under-carriage; suite (of rooms).

stel, (ge-), put, place; adjust, regulate, direct; fix; draw up, compose.

stelkunde, algebra.

stellasie, (-s), scaffolding, stand, structure, frame-work; (fruit-) tray.

stellig, (-e), a. positive (assertion), definite (promise), firm, fixed, certain.

stellig, adv. positively, definitely.

stelling, (-e, -s), proposition, theorem (math.); premise, supposition, hypothesis; thesis; (milit.) position.

stelp, (ge-), sta(u)nch, stop.

stelsel, (-s), system.

stelselmatig, (-e), systematic.

stelt, (-e), stilt.

stem, (-me), n. voice; vote.

stem, (ge-), vote, go to the poll, record (cast) one's vote; tune (a musical instrument).

stembande, (pl.), vocal chords.

stembus, ballot-box, poll.

stemmig, (-e), sedate, quiet, staid, sober.

stemming, (-e, -s), ballot, voting, vote, poll; mood, state of mind, humour, disposition; tuning.

stempel, (-s), n. stamp; seal; impression, imprint, (post-) mark, stamp, seal; hall-mark; stigma (bot.).

stempel, (ge-), stamp; hall-mark; mark, brand.

stemreg, franchise, vote; right to vote.

stenig, (ge-), stone (to death), lapidate.

stenografie, shorthand, stenography.

ster, (-re), star, luminary.

stereoskoop, (-skope), stereoscope.

stereotiep, (-e), a. stereotype.

sterf, sterwe, (ge-), die.

sterflik, (-e), mortal.

sterfling, sterweling, (-e), mortal.

steriliseer, (ge-), sterilize.

sterk, (–, -e), a. strong; virile, robust, powerful.

sterk, (ge-), strengthen; invigorate, encourage.

sterkwater, spirits (of wine), aqua fortis.

sterrekunde, astronomy.

sterrewag, (astronomical) observatory.

stert, (-e), tail, brush (of fox), pigtail; train, rear, back portion.

stertriem, crupper (of harness); loin-skin (of natives); jock-belt.

sterwe, vide **sterf**.

sterweling, vide **sterfling**.

steun, n. support, aid, assistance, help; stay, prop.

steun, (ge-), (1) support, help; back (up), prop (up), support; speak in support of, support (a motion).

steun, (ge-), (2) groan, moan.

steunpilaar, pillar, support; buttress.

steur, stoor, (ge-), disturb; be in the way, intrude; derange, inconvenience.

steurnis, stoornis, (-se), disturbance, nuisance.

stewe, (-ns), prow.

stewel, (-s), boot.

stewig, (-e), a. solid, stout, sturdy, strong, substantial.

stewig, adv. firm(ly), tight(ly).

stiebeuel, (-s), stirrup; footstall.

stiefdogter, stepdaughter.

stiegriem, stirrup-leather.

stier, (-e), bull; Taurus.

stif, (-te), small rod, style, pencil; pin, peg.

stig, (ge-), found (a business, a college), establish, form (a society), plant (a colony), institute, start (a fund).

stigtelik, (-e), edifying.

stik, (ge-), (1) stitch (with a machine).

stik, (ge-), (2) choke, be choked, stifle, be stifled.

stikdonker, a., pitch-dark.

stiksel, stitching.

stikstof, nitrogen.

still, (–, -le), a., quiet, still, calm; silent.

still, (ge-), allay (fears, pain); quiet, hush (the conscience); alleviate, still (pain); satisfy, appease (hunger).

still, interj., hush! keep quiet!; shut up!.

stilbly, (stilge-), keep (remain) quiet.

stilet, (-te), stiletto.

stilhou, (stilge-), stop, halt, come to a stop (halt), pull (draw) up.

stilisties, (-e), stylistic.

stilletjies, quietly, softly; on the quiet, on the sly, stealthily, secretly.

stilstand, standstill, stop, stoppage; stagnation.

stilswy(g)e, silence.

stilte, silence, stillness, quiet.

stimuleer, (ge-), stimulate.

stingel, (-s), stem, stalk.

stink, a. stinking, evil-smelling, fetid.

stink, (ge-), stink, smell bad.

stinkerd, (-s), stinkard, stinker, skunk.

stinkhout, stinkwood.

stinkmuishond, Cape polecat.

stip, (-pe), n., point, spot, dot.

stip, (-te), a. & adv., punctual, precise, accurate; strict; prompt.

stippel, (-s), n., spot, speck, point, dot.

stippel, (ge-), dot, point; stipple.

stiptelik, promptly, precisely, strictly.

stipuleer, (ge-), stipulate, demand.

stoei, (ge-), wrestle, romp.

stoel, (-e), n. chair, seat.

stoep, (-e), stoep.

stoer, (-e), sturdy, hardy, stout.

stoet, (-e), procession, train.

stof, (stowwe), n. (1) dust, powder.

stof, (stowwe), n. (2) material, stuff; matter; subject-matter.

stof, (ge-), dust, remove the dust.

stofbesem, hair-broom.

stofbril, goggles.

stofdig, (-te), dust-proof.

stoffasie, (-s), material, stuff; calibre.

stoffeer, (ge-), upholster, furnish.

stofferig, stowwerig, (-e), dusty.

stoflik, (-e), material; tangible.

stofnaam, name of material; (gram.) material noun.

stofsuier, vacuum cleaner.

Stoïsyn, (-e), Stoic philosopher.

stok, (-ke), stick, staff; pole; handle (of broom); stick, club (golf).

stok, (ge-), stop (of breath).

stokalleen, solitary, quite alone.

stokblind, (-e), stone-blind.

stokdoof, (-dowe), stone-deaf.

stoker, (-s), stoker, fireman; distiller; firebrand.

stokou, (predicatively: **stokoud**), very old.

stokperdjie, hobby-horse; hobby, fad.

stoksielalleen, quite (all) alone.

stokstil, stock-still, motionless.

stokstyf, (-stywe), as stiff as a poker.

stokverf, stopverf, putty.

stol, (ge-), clot, coagulate, congeal; freeze.

stolp, (-e), cover, bell-jar.

stom, (-me), dumb, mute, speechless; foolish, stupid, dull; poor, wretched.

stommeling, (-e), blockhead, ass.

stommerik, (-e), fathead, blockhead.

stommiteit, (-e), blunder; stupidity.

stomp, (-e), n. stump, stub.

stomp, a. blunt, dull; snub, stumpy; obtuse (angle).

stomp hoek, obtuse angle.

stomphoekig, (-e), obtuse-angled.

stompsinnig, (-e), stupid, dense, dull.

stonde, (-s), hour, time.

stoof, (stowe), n. stove.

stoof, stowe, (ge-), stew, braise, cook (meat), broil, swelter (in the sun).

stook, (ge-), fire, stoke (furnace); burn (coal); make (light) a fire; distil (spirits).

stoom, n. steam.

stoom, (ge-), steam.

stoor, (ge-), vide **steur**.

stoornis, vide **steurnis**.

stoot, (stote), n. push, thrust, dig; shot, stroke (billiards).

stoot, (ge-), push, thrust, knock, bump; jostle (in a crowd); butt, toss (with the horns).

stootkant, false hem.

stootkussing, buffer.

stop, (ge-), (1) stop (up), fill (up), plug (up) (a hole); fill (a pipe, a tooth); darn (a sock); stuff (birds); slip (into one's pocket); bundle (into a vehicle).

stop, (ge-), (2) stop, pull up, halt, come (bring) to a stop.

stoppel, (-s), stubble.

stopsit, (stopge-), stop, close down; put an end (a stop) to.

stopverf, stokverf, putty.

storie, (-s), story, yarn; fib.

storm, (-e, -s), n. storm, gale.

storm, (ge-), storm.

stormenderhand, by storm.

stormloop, (stormge-), storm, attack, rush, charge.

stormram, battering ram.

stort, (ge-), pour; spil (milk); shed (blood, tears); deposit, pay in (money); plunge (into water, misery).

stortbad, shower(-bath).

stortreën, -reent, n. downpour, deluge.

stortreën, -reent, (ge-), come down in torrents.

stortvloed, flood, torrent; deluge, mass.

stotter, (ge-), stutter, stammer.

stout, a. naughty, bad; bold, daring.

stouterd, (-s), naughty boy (girl).
stoutmoedig, (-e), bold, daring.
stowe, vide stoof, (ge-).
stoww(er)ig, vide stoff(er)ig.
straal, (strale), n. beam, ray (of light, hope); flash (of lightning); stream, jet (of water); radius (of a circle); gleam, flicker, (of hope).
straal, (ge-), shine; beam, glow, flash, radiate.
straalvliegtuig, jet aircraft.
straalvormig, (-e), radial.
straat, (strate), n. street; strait (of the sea).
straat, (ge-), face with stones, pave.
straatweg, highroad.
straf, (strawwe), n. punishment, penalty.
straf, (strawwe), a. ; adv. severe(winter); severe, stern (tone); rigid.
straf, (ge-), punish, chastise.
strafdoel, penalty goal.
strafsaak, criminal case.
strafskop, penalty kick, free kick.
strak, (–, -ke), tight, taut, tense; severe, hard, fixed.
strakkies, presently, in a minute; perhaps.
straks, perhaps; presently.
stram, (–, -me), stiff, rigid.
strand, (-e), n., beach, seaside; "strand", seaside resort.
strand, (ge-), strand, run ashore.
strandloper(tjie), sand-plover, -piper.
strandmeer, lagoon, coastal lake.
strategies, (-e), strategic(al).
strawasie, (-s), difficulty.
streef, strewe, (ge-), strive, endeavour.
streek, (streke), region, track, area, part; point (of compass); trick, wile, artifice, dodge, joke.
streel, (ge-), fondle, caress, stroke; gratify; flatter (one's vanity).
streep, (strepe), n. stroke, line; stripe; streak (of light); dash.
streep, (ge-), mark with a stripe; cane.
streepsak, grain-bag.
streepsuiker, cane-juice, a hiding.
strek, (ge-), stretch, reach, extend; last.
strekking, (-e, -s), tendency, drift, inclination; purport, tenor, sense, meaning.
strem, (ge-), curdle, coagulate; hinder, obstruct, hold up.
streng, (–, -e), strict, severe (winter, judge, sentence), stern, austere.
strengel, (ge-), plait, twine, twist.
streukel, vide struikel.
strewe, vide streef.
striem, (ge-), castigate, lash, cut.
strik, (-ke), n., knot, bow; snare, noose, trap (for catching); snag.
strik, (-te), a., strict, severe; precise.
strik, (ge-), tie (in a bow); snare.
strikvraag, poser, puzzling, question.
string, (-e), n., string; thread; skein (of yarn); strand (of rope); trace (of harness).
stroef, (stroewe), stiff; rough; gruff, surly, rough-mannered.
strofe, (-s), stanza, strophe.
stroming, (-e, -s), stream, current; tendency, drift, trend.
strompel, (ge-), stumble, hobble, limp.
stronk, (-e), n., stalk; stump.
strooi, n., straw.
strooi, (ge-), scatter (money, seeds); strew (flowers); sprinkle, dredge (meal, sugar).
strooibiljet, hand-bill.
strooihuis, stroois, struis, (-e), straw hut, Bantu-hut.
strooijonker, best man.
strooimeisie, bridesmaid.

stroois, vide strooihuis.
strooisuiker, castor-sugar.
strook, (stroke), n. strip, band; frill, flounce (needlework).
strook, (ge-), agree, tally, fit in.
stroom, (strome), n. stream; current (in ocean, of electricity); flood (of light, tears); flow, spate (of words).
stroom, (ge-), stream, flow, rush, pour.
stroom-op: altyd – wees, be contrary (perverse).
stroop, n., syrup, treacle; love (tennis).
stroop, (ge-), pillage, plunder; strip.
stroopkwas: met die – werk, butter up, flatter.
stroopsoet, as sweet as honey, honey-sweet; very sweet (good) (of child).
strooptog, raid, marauding expedition.
strop, (-pe), strap, brace, rope, halter; "strop" (for oxen).
strottehoof, larynx.
struik, (-e), bush, shrub.
struikel, streukel, (ge-), stumble, trip.
struikrower, robber, highwayman.
struis, vide strooihuis.
struktuur, (-ture), structure, texture.
struweling, stribbeling, (-e), trouble, row, ruction.
stry, (ge-), fight, combat, contend, struggle; argue; quarrel; contradict, deny.
stryd, fight, battle, struggle, conflict, war.
strydig, (-e), conflicting, contrary.
strydlustig, (-e), bellicose, pugnacious.
strydperk, arena, lists.
strydvaardig, (-e), ready (prepared) for war (battle).
stryk, n. stroke.
stryk, (ge-), 1. go, walk, stride, march.
stryk, (ge-), 2. smooth (one's hair); stroke (one's beard); iron (linen); draw the bow over (the strings); strike (the flag).
strykstok, bow, fiddlestick.
strykyster, flat-iron, (solid) sad-iron.
stu, (ge-), push, press; stow (cargo).
studeer, (ge-), study; prepare, read (for an examination).
studeerlamp, study-lamp, reading-lamp.
student, (-e), student.
studie, (-s), study.
stug, (–, -ge), reserved, stiff, difficult to deal with, unfriendly, curt.
stuif, stuiwe, (ge-), be dusty; fly, rush.
stuifmeel, pollen.
stuifswam, puff-ball.
stuip, (generally pl. –e), convulsion(s), seizure, fit(s).
stuiptrekking, (-e, -s), convulsion.
stuit, (ge-), check, arrest, stop.
stuitend, (-e), objectionable, offensive.
stuitig, stuitlik, (-e), objectionable.
stuitjie, (-s), stuitjiebeen, tail-bone.
stuiwe, vide stuif.
stuiwer, (-s), halfpenny.
stuk, (-ke), piece; article (of clothing, furniture), fragment, splinter; paper, document, piece; man (at chess).
stukkend, (-e), broken; tipsy; ugly; torn.
stukrag, driving-force, -power.
stuksgewys(e), singly, one by one.
stumper(d), (-s), bungler; poor blighter.
stustraal, ram-jet.
stut, (-te), n. prop, support, stay; buttress, stanchion; strut; truss.
stut, (ge-), prop (up), support, shore (up), truss (up).
stuur, (sture), n. (steering-)wheel; handles; tiller, rudder, helm (of ship).

stuur, (ge-), dispatch; drive (horses, motor); steer (ship); guide.
stuurboord, starboard.
stuurman, (-ne, -lui), steersman, man at the helm; (chief) mate; cox(swain).
stuurs, (-e), curt, cool, stiff, reserved, gruff, surly.
styf, (stywe), a. stiff, rigid; starched; firm.
styf, stywe, (ge-), starch; (fig.) stiffen.
styfhoofdig, (-e), obstinate, headstrong.
styg, (ge-), rise, ascend; climb.
styl, (1) style.
styl, (-e), (2) post (of door, bed), jamb; strut; stanchion, support.
stysel, starch.
stywe, vide **stuif, (ge-).**
subiet, suddenly; at once, straightaway.
sublimeer, (ge-), sublimate.
subsidie, (-s), subsidy, grant (in-aid).
subtiel, (-e), subtle.
suf, (suwwe), a. dull, stupid, thickheaded.
sug, (-te), n. (1) sigh; desire, thirst, love, passion.
sug, n. (2) pus, matter; (illness) dropsy.
sug, (ge-), sigh; sough (of wind).
suid, south.
suidelik, (-e), south, southerly; southern.
suiderbreedte, south latitude.
suidissel, seidissel, (-s), sowmilk-thistle.
Suidpoolsee, Antarctic Ocean.
suie, vide **suig.**
suier, (-s), sucker; piston, plunger (of pump); sucker (of plant).
suierstang, piston-rod.
suig, suie, (ge-), suck.
suig(e)ling, (-e), infant, baby.
suiker, sugar.
suikerbekkie, sugar-bird, sun-bird.
suikerbrood, sponge-cake; sugar-loaf.
suikersiekte, diabetes.
suikersoet, as sweet as sugar.
suil, (-e), pillar, column, obelisk, pile.
suinig, (-e), stingy, niggardly; parsimonious, frugal, thrifty.
suip, (ge-), guzzle, booze; drink (of animals).
suiplap, toper, boozer, soaker, tippler.
suis, (ge-), buzz, sing, tingle (in the ears); sough, rustle, sigh, moan (of wind); whiz(z).
suiwel, butter and cheese, dairy products.
suiwer, (-, -e), a., pure, clean, plain (truth), clear; sheer, pure (nonsense), correct (pronunciation).
suiwer, (ge-), purify (blood, air, language), clean, cleanse, purge; refine (sugar).
sukkel, (ge-), plod (on), trudge (on), drudge, toil.
sukkelrig, (-e), ailing, in indifferent health; ploddingly, slowly.
sukses, (-se), success.
sulfa, sulfa (sulpha).
sulke, a. & pron., (pl. pron.: -s), such; (pl.) such ones.
sult, brawn.
suring, (-s), sorrel, sheep-sorrel, dock.
sus, adv., thus.
sus, (ge-), hush, quiet; pacify, calm.
suspisie, (-s), suspicion.
suster, (-s), sister, (also) nurse.
suur, (sure), n. acid (chem.): acidity (of the stomach).
suur, (-, sure), a., sour, acid, acrid, peevish.
suurdeeg, yeast, leaven.
suurkanol, crabby fellow.
suurklontjies, acid-drops.
suurlemoen, lemon.
suurstof, oxygen.
suutjies, vide **soetjies.**

swaai, (-e), n. swing; sweep.
swaai, (ge-), swing, wield (a sceptre), wave, flourish; swing, sway (to and fro) reel; wheel (rugby).
swaan, (swane), swan; **jong** –, cygnet.
swaap, (swape), block head, simpleton.
swaar, (-, sware), heavy; massive; difficult, hard, stiff (examination); severe (illness, punishment).
swaard, (-e), sword.
swaardblom, -lelie, sword-lily, gladiolus.
swaarlywig, (-e), corpulent, stout.
swaarmoedig, (-e), melancholy, depressed.
swaartekrag, gravitation, force of gravity.
swaarweer, thundery weather, thunderstorm, -clap.
swaarwigtig, (-e), weighty, ponderous.
swa(w)el, (-s), n. 1. swallow.
swa(w)el, n. 2. sulphur.
swa(w)elstert, dovetail; swallowtail; V-shaped earmark; swallowtail(ed) (coat).
swaer, (-s), brother-in-law.
swagtel, (-s), n. bandage, swathe.
swagtel, (ge-), bandage, swathe.
swak, n. weakness, failing.
swak, (-, -ke), weak; feeble (voice); delicate (health, child); poor, bad (chance, show, memory); gentle, soft(er), weaker (sex).
swakkeling, (-e), weakling.
swaksinnig, (-e), mentally deficient.
swam, (-me), fungus; spavin.
swang: in –, in vogue.
swarigheid, (-hede), difficulty, obstacle.
swart, n. black.
swart (-, -e), a. black.
swartgallig, (-e), pessimistic, melancholy.
swartsmeer, (swartge-), blacken; vilify.
swartspan, team of black oxen, church-council.
swawel, vide **swa(w)el.**
Swede, Sweden.
sweef, swewe, (ge-), float, hover; glide, flit (by, past); soar (aloft).
sweefbrug, suspension bridge.
sweefspoor, aerial railway.
sweefstok, trapeze.
sweem, semblance, trace, shred.
sweep, (swepe), whip.
sweer, (swere), n. ulcer, tumour, abscess.
sweer, (ge-), 1. fester, ulcerate.
sweer, (ge-), 2. swear, vow.
sweerlik, surely, certainly, without a doubt.
sweet, n. sweat, perspiration.
sweet, (ge-), sweat, perspire; cure.
sweetvos, chestnut, sorrel.
sweis, (ge-), weld, forge.
swel, (ge-), swell, expand, dilate.
swelg, (ge-), swill (drink), guzzle (food).
swem, (ge-), swim.
swendel, (-s), n. swindle, fraud.
swendel, (ge-), swindle.
swenk, (-e), n. turn, swerve, side-step.
swenk, (ge-), swerve; swing round, wheel (about); change about.
swerf, swerwe, (ge-), rove, wander, roam, stray.
swerfling, swerweling, (-e), wanderer; tramp, vagabond; stray (child, dog).
swerm, (-s), n. swarm; (bees in) hive.
swerm, (ge-), swarm, cluster, crowd.
swernoot, (-note), **swernoter,** (-s), scoundrel, skunk.
swerwe, vide **swerf.**
swetrioel, swetterjoel, (-e), swarm, multitude.
swiep, (ge-), swish.
swier, n. flourish, swagger; gracefulness, elegance.

swier, (ge-), glide, carry oneself gracefully; be (go) on the spree.

swig, (ge-), give way, yield.

swik, (ge-), make a false step, stumble.

swingel, (-s), swingle(tree).

Switser, (-s), Swiss.

swoeë, swoeg, (ge-), toil, drudge; swot.

swoel, (-, -e), sultry, close.

swye, n. silence.

swye, swyg, (ge-), be (remain) silent.

swygsaam, (-same), silent, taciturn.

swymel, (ge-), be (become, feel) dizzy.

swyn, (-e), swine, pig.

sy, n. (1) silk.

sy, (-e), n. (2) side; flank (of army).

sy, pers, pron. she.

sy, poss. pron. his, its.

sy, v. dit – so, so be it.

sybok, angora-goat.

syde: ter –, aside, on one side.

sydelings, (-e), sidelong; lateral.

syfer, (-s), n. figure; bogey (golf).

syfer, (ge-), (1) figure, reckon, calculate.

syfer, (ge-), (2) ooze, filter.

syg, (ge-), ooze, filter; sink down.

syne, s'n: dit is Pa –, it is Father's.

synersyds, on his part, from his side.

sypaadjie, -pad, by-path; pavement.

sypel, (ge-), vide syfer, (ge-), (2).

sysie, (-s), (bird) seed-eater; siskin.

sywurm, silk worm.

ta, (-'s), father.
taai, (–, -e), tough; sticky; wiry, hardy, touch; dogged, tenacious.
taak, (take), task.
taal, (tale), language, tongue, speech.
taalkunde, philology, linguistics.
taamlik, (-e), a. fair, passable.
taamlik, adv. fairly, passably, tolerably.
taan, (ge-), dim, pale, fade; wane.
taankleurig, (-e), tawny, tan-coloured.
tabak, tobacco.
tabberd, tawwerd, (-s), dress, skirt.
tabel, (-le), table, list, index.
tabernakel, (-s), tabernacle.
tablet, (-te), tablet; lozenge.
taboe, taboo.
tafel, (-s), table; index.
taf(e)reel, [taf(e)rele], picture, description; scene.
tag(gen)tig, eighty.
tak, (-ke), branch, bough; antlers (of stag).
tak(t), tact.
takbok, deer, stag.
takel, (-s), n. tackle.
takel, (ge-), rig, tackle; knock about, dress down, maul, handle roughly.
takelblok, tackle, block.
takhaar, (-hare), Backvelder.
taks, n. portion, share.
taks, (ge-), estimate, reckon.
takseer, (ge-), appraise, estimate, value.
takt, vide **tak(t).**
taktiek, tactics.
tal, (-le), number.
talent, (-e), talent.
talm, (ge-), delay, linger, loiter, dawdle.
talryk, (-e), numerous, multitudinous.
tam, (–, -me), weary, tired, fatigued.
tamaai, huge, colossal, gigantic.
tamaryn, tamarind.
tamatie, (-s), tomato.
tamatiepruim, persimmon.
tamatiestraat: hy is in –, he is up the pole.
tamboer, (-e), drum; drummer.
tameletjie, (-s), butter-scotch, tameletjie.
tand, (-e), tooth; prong (of fork); cog.
tandarts, dentist, dental surgeon.
tandheelkunde, dentistry.
tand(e)pasta, dental cream, tooth-paste.
tang, (-e), (pair of) pincers; tongs (for sugar, coal, hair); pliers; forceps.
tangens, (tangente), tangent.
tans, nowadays, now.
tant(e), (-s), aunt(ie); missus, madam.
tap, (-pe), n. tap; spigot, plug, bung; tennon; trunnion.
tap, (ge-), tap, draw.
tapbeitel, socket-chisel.
tapisserie, (-ë), tapestry.
tapyt, (-e), carpet.
tarentaal, (-tale), guinea-fowl.
tarief, (-riewe), tariff; list (scale) of charges; rate, terms; fare.
tarra, tare.
tart, (ge-), defy, dare, provoke.
Tartaar, (-tare), Tartar.
tarwe, wheat.
tas, (-se), n. (1) bag, pouch, satchel, wallet.
tas, (ge-), grope, feel; touch.
tasbaar, (-bare), palpable, tangible.
Tasmanië, Tasmania.
tatoeëer, (ge-), tattoo.
tawwerd, vide **tabberd.**
te, prep, at, in; to.
te, adv. too.

teater, (-s), theatre.
tee, tea.
teë, adv. against.
teëblad, teenblad, counterfoil.
teëet, (teëgeëet): **sig – aan,** have a surfeit of.
teef, (tewe), bitch.
teëgaan, (teëge-), oppose, counteract, check, thwart.
teëgesteld, teengesteld, (-e), contrary, opposite.
teëgif, antidote.
teegoed, tea-things, cups and saucers.
teëhou, (teëge-), check, obstruct, prevent, retard, impede; press against, support.
teëkom, teenkom, (teëge-, teenge-), come across, meet.
teël, (-s), tile.
teel, (ge-), breed, raise (cattle); cultivate, grow (crop).
teelaarde, humus, vegetable earth.
teem, (ge-), whine, drawl.
teëmiddel, antidote.
teen, n.: **voor en –,** pro and con.
teen, prep. against; at; by.
teen-, vide **teë-.**
teenaan, against.
teendeel, contrary, opposite.
teenoor, opposite; over against, in contrast with.
teenoorgestel(d), (-de), opposite, contrary.
teenpraat, teëpraat, (teenge-, teëge-), contradict.
teensin, teësin, dislike, distaste, antipathy, aversion.
teensit, teësit, (teenge-): **sig –,** resist, offer resistance; bear up.
teenslag, teëslag, set-back, reverse.
teenspoed, teëspoed, adversity, ill-luck.
teenspreek, teëspreek, (teenge-, teëge-), contradict, deny.
teenstand, teëstand, resistance, opposition.
teenstander, teëstander, (-s), opponent, adversary.
teenstelling, teëstelling, (-e, -s), contrast.
teenstrydig, (-e), conflicting (opinions), contradictory, clashing.
teenswoordig, (-e), a. present, present-day.
teenswoordig, adv. nowadays, at present.
teenvoeter, teëvoeter, (-s), antipode.
teenvoorstel, teëvoorstel, counter-proposal.
teenwerp, teëwerp, (teenge-, teëge-), object.
teenwig, teëwig, counterpoise, counterbalance.
teenwoordig, (-e), present.
teer, n. tar.
teer, (–, tere), a. tender; frail, delicate.
teer, (ge-), (1) tar.
teer, (ge-), (2): **– op,** live on.
teergevoelig, (-e), sensitive, touchy, tender, delicate, susceptible.
teerhartig, (-e), tender-hearted.
teerling, die.
teerputs, tar-bucket.
teëval, (teëge-), be disappointing.
tegelyk, at once, at the same time; in one batch.
tegelykertyd, simultaneously, at the same time.
tegemoetgaan, (tegemoetge-), go to meet.
tegemoetkomend, (-e), obliging, compliant.
tegnies, (-e), technical.
tehuis, (-e), home, hostel.
teiken, (-s), target, mark.
teikenskiet, (teikenge-), shoot at a mark (target), have rifle-practice.
teister, (ge-), ravage, devastate, afflict.
teken, (-s), n. sign; signal; mark, trace, symptom (of disease); token.
teken, (ge-), sign (one's name); draw, sketch; portray, delineate, describe.

tekenaar, (-s), drawer, designer, caricaturist, cartoonist.
tekenend, (-e), characteristic; descriptive, telling.
tekort, (-e), deficit, deficiency, shortage.
tekortdoening, wronging, cheating (a person) out of something.
tekortkoming, (-e, -s), shortcoming, fault.
teks, (-te), text (of book, manuscript); words (of a song).
tekstiel, (-e), textile.
tekswoord, text.
tel, n. count.
tel, (ge-), count; number.
telefoneer, (ge-), telephone (phone).
telefoon, (-fone), telephone.
telefoonhokkie, telephone booth.
telegraaf, (-grawe), telegraph.
telegrafeer, (ge-), telegraph, wire.
telegram, (-me), telegram, wire.
teleskoop, (-skope), telescope.
teleurstel, (teleurge-), disappoint.
televisie, television.
telg, (-e), shoot; descendant, scion.
telkemaal, -male, time and again, again and again, every now and then; every time.
telkens: – as, whenever.
telling, (-e, -s), counting, count; numeration; addition; census; score.
telraam, abacus, calculating-frame.
telwoord, numeral.
tem, (ge-), tame, master, curb.
tema, (-s), subject, theme.
Temboeland, Tembuland.
temerig, (-e), drawling.
temmer, (-s), tamer.
tempel, (-s), temple.
temper, (ge-), temper, restrain; modify; mitigate; tone down, soften.
temperament, (-e), temperament; temper.
temperatuur, (-ture), temperature.
tempteer, (ge-), vex, irritate, tease.
ten, to, at, in.
tendens, (-e), tendency, purpose.
tender, (-s), tender.
tenger(ig), (-e), slender, fragile.
tenk, (-e, -s), tank.
tennis, tennis.
tenoor, (-nore), tenor.
tensy, unless.
tent, (-e), tent; booth (at fair); hood (of vehicle), tilt.
ten toon stel, (ten toon ge-), show, exhibit.
tenue, uniform, dress.
teoloog, (-loë, -loge), theologian.
teorie, (ë), theory.
tepel, (-s), teat, nipple.
ter, in (at, to) the.
teraardebestelling, internment, burial.
terdeë, thoroughly, soundly.
têre, vide **terg(e).**
tereg, rightly, justly.
teregkom, (teregge-), land, arrive; come right.
teregstel, (teregge-), put on trial; execute.
teregwys, (teregge-), reprove, reprimand; direct, show the way.
terg(e), têre, (ge-), tease, provoke, torment.
terggees, tease.
tering, consumption, phthisis.
terloops, (-e), a. casual, incidental.
terloops, adv. casually, incidentally.
term, (-e), term; expression.
terminus, (-se, termini), terminus.
termometer, thermometer.
termyn, (-e), term, period, time; instalment.
terneergedruk, (-te), dejected, depressed.

terneergeslae, vide **terneergedruk.**
ternouernood, hardly, scarcely, barely.
terpentyn, turpentine.
terras, (-se), terrace.
terrein, (-e), ground, (building-) site, plot; terrain; field, province (of thought, action) sphere, domain.
terriër, (-s), terrier.
terselfdertyd, at the same time.
tersluiks, stealthily, on the sly.
terstond, at once, directly.
tersy(de), aside.
tert, (-e), tart.
terug, back, backward(s).
terugbesorg, (–), return, send back.
terugbetaal, (–), repay, refund.
terugblik, (terugge-), look back (on).
terugdeins, (terugge-), shrink back.
teruggetrokke, self-contained, reserved.
terughoudend, (-e), reserved.
terugkeer, (terugge-), return, go back.
terugslaan, (terugge-), hit (strike) back; return (a ball); repulse; revert.
terugslag, recoil(ing), repercussion; backswing; return-stroke; back-fire; set-back.
terugwerkend, (-e), retrospective, retroactive.
terwyl, while, whilst, whereas.
tes, (-se), fire-pan, chafing-dish.
tesaam, tesame, together.
tesis, (-se), thesis.
tesourier, (-e, -s), treasurer.
tessie, (-s), vide **tes.**
testament, (-e), testament, (last) will (and testament).
teuel, (-s), bridle, rein.
teug, (teue), draught.
tevergeefs, in vain, vainly.
tevore, before, previously.
tevrede, satisfied, contented, content.
teweegbring, (teweegge-), bring about (to pass), cause.
tewens, at the same time, also.
tiekie, (-s), tickey.
tiekiedraai, (tiekiege-), ,,tiekiedraai'', dance.
tiemie, thyme.
tien, ten.
tien(d)er, (-s), teen-ager.
tienderjarige, teen-ager.
tiep, (-e), vide **tipe.**
tier, (-e, -s), n. tiger; South African leopard.
tier, (ge-), (1) thrive, prosper, flourish.
tier, (ge-), (2) rage, bluster, storm.
tierboskat, serval.
tierelier, (ge-), sing, warble.
tierlantyntjie, (-s), flourish; bauble, fallal, gewgaw, showy trifle.
tiermelk, tiger's milk; booze.
tifus, typhus (fever).
tik, (-ke), n. pat, tap, touch; rap; tick (of watch).
tik, (ge-), tick, click; pat, tap (on shoulder), touch.
tikmasjien, typewriter.
tikster, (-s), (lady-)typist.
timmer, (ge-), carpenter, do carpenter's work; build, construct.
timmerasie, (-s), framework (of roof), structure, scaffolding.
timmerman, (-s, -ne), carpenter.
tin, n. tin, pewter.
tingel, (ge-), jingle, tinkle.
tingerig, (-e), vide **tengerig.**
tingieter, tinsmith, tinman.
tinkel, (ge-), tinkle.
tintinkie, (-s), grass-warbler.
tint, (-e), n. tinge, tint, hue.

tintel, (ge-), tint, tinge.
tintel, (ge-), twinkle; sparkle; tingle.
tintel, n. tingling.
tip, (-pe), n. tip, point.
tipe, (-s), tiep, (-e), type.
tipies, (-e), typical.
tiran, (-ne), tyrant.
titel, (-s), title; heading (of chapter).
titel, (-s), dot (on i, j); tittle.
tjalie, (-s), shawl.
tjank, (ge-), whine, yelp, howl, whimper.
tjankbalie, cry-baby, squealer.
tjap, (-pe), n. stamp; postmark.
tjap, (ge-), stamp.
tjek, (-s), cheque.
tjello, (-'s), 'cello (violoncello).
tjienkerientjee, (-s), chinkerinchee.
tjilp, (ge-), chirp, twitter.
tjoekie, quod, prison.
tjoepstil, quite still (quiet).
tjou-tjou, hotchpotch (hodge-podge), chow-chow, pickles.
tob, (ge-), toil, drudge, slave.
toe, a. closed, shut.
toe, adv. then, at that time, in those days; to(wards).
toe, conj. when; as, while.
toebehoor(t), (–), belong to.
toebehoorsels, belongings, accessories.
toebehore, (-ns), (-s), parts; vide toebehoorsels.
toeberei, (–), prepare; season, mature.
toebind(e), (toege-), tie up, fasten.
toebring, (toege-), give (strike) (a blow); inflict (defeat, loss).
toebroodjie, (-s), sandwich.
toedien, (toege-), give (blow, beating), administer (medicine), mete out.
toedoen, n. instrumentality, aid.
toedrag: die juiste – van die saak, the ins and outs (all the particulars) of the case.
toeëien, (toegeëien): sig –, appropriate, usurp.
toef, toewe, (ge-), linger, tarry.
toegang, entrance; admission; approach.
toeganklik, (-e), accessible, approachable.
toegedaan: 'n mening – wees, hold an opinion (a view).
toegee, (toege-), give extra (into the bargain); admit, grant, concede; yield, give way (in).
toegeeflik, (-e), indulgent, lenient.
toegeneë, affectionate.
toegewend, (-e), indulgent, lenient; concessive (clause).
toehoorder, listener, hearer.
toejuig, (toege-), cheer; welcome.
toeka: van – se dae (tyd), af, from time immemorial.
toeken, (toege-), award (marks, prize), give, grant, allocate, allot; credit.
toekom, (toege-): dit kom my toe, it is my share, I have a right to it.
toekomend, (-e), future, next.
toekoms, future: in die –, in future.
toelaag, (-lae), toelae, (-s), grant, subsidy, allowance.
toelaat, (toege-), leave shut; allow, permit; admit (to place, class).
toelê, (toege-): sig – op, apply oneself to, go in for.
toelig, (toege-), explain, elucidate, illustrate.
toeloop, n. concourse, throng, crowd.
toenader, (toege-), approach.
toename, increase.
toeneem, (toege-), grow, increase; become (grow) worse.
toenmalig, (-e), then, contemporary.

toentertyd, at that (the) time.
toepas, (toege-), apply (rules); put into practice; enforce (law).
toepaslik, (-e), appropriate, apposite, applicable.
toer, (-e), n. tour, trip; spin, ride, trick, feat; stunt.
toer, (ge-), tour, make a trip.
toereikend, (-e), adequate, enough.
toereken, (toege-), impute, charge.
toerekenbaar, accountable, responsible.
toernooi, (-e), tournament, tourney.
toerus, (toege-), equip, fit out.
toesê, (toege-), promise.
toesig, supervision, care; invigilation.
toeskouer, (-s), spectator, onlooker.
toespeling, (-e, -s), allusion, insinuation.
toespraak, (-sprake), speech, address.
toespreek, (toege-), address, accost.
toestaan, (toege-), accede, grant (request), concede; allow.
toestand, state (of affairs), position, condition; situation.
toestel, (-le), apparatus; appliance, machine.
toestem, (toege-), consent; assent, grant.
toestroom, (toege-), flow (stream) towards; rush (flock) towards, come flocking in(to), pour in.
toet, n.: hy is 'n man van – (was hy beter, dan was hy goed), he is a real nincompoop (ninny, dud).
toet, (ge-), hoot, toot.
toets, (-e), n. test; assay; key (of piano); touch.
toets, (ge-), test, try; assay.
toetssteen, touchstone.
toeval, n. chance, accident; fit.
toevallig, (-e), a. accidental, casual, chance.
toevallig, adv. by chance, accidentally.
toevertrou, (–): iemand iets –, entrust a person with something.
toevlug, refuge, shelter; recourse.
toevoeg, (toege-), join; add.
toevoegsel, (-s), supplement, appendix.
toevoer, n. supply.
toewyding, dedication; devotion.
toewys, (toege-), award, grant, allot.
tog, (-te), n. journey, voyage, expedition; draught.
tog, adv. yet, nevertheless, still.
togryer, transport-rider, trekker.
toiens, toiings, rags, tatters.
tokkel, (ge-), pluck (the strings), strum.
tokkelok, (-ke), theological student.
toktokkie, (-s), tapping-beetle; tick-tock.
tol, (-le), n. (1) top.
tol, n. (2) toll, duty (duties), customs.
tol, (ge-), spin.
tolk, (-e), n. interpreter; mouthpiece.
tolk, (ge-), interpret.
tollie, (-s), tollie, young ox.
tombe, (-s), tomb.
ton, (-ne), ton; barrel, cask.
toneel, (-nele), stage; scene; theatre.
toneelskrywer, dramatist, playwright.
toneelspeler, actor, player.
toneelstuk, play.
tong, (-e), tongue.
tongval, dialect.
tongvis, sole.
tonnel, (-s), n. tunnel; subway.
tonnel, (ge-), tunnel.
tonnemaat, tonnage.
tontelbos, tinder-bush.
tooi, (ge-), decorate, adorn, deck, dress.
toom, (-s, tome), n. bridle.
toomloos, (-lose), unbridled, unchecked.
toon, (tone), n. (1) toe.
toon, n (2) tone; pitch (of voice); sound.

toon, (ge-), show.
toonaangewend, (-e), leading (lights).
toonbank, counter.
toonbeeld, example, model; paragon.
toor, (ge-), practise witchcraft, conjure, juggle; bewitch, put a spell on.
toordokter, witch-doctor, medicine-man.
toorn, wrath, anger.
toornaar, towe(r)naar, (-s), magician.
toornig, (-e), wrathful, angry.
toorts, (-e), torch.
top, (-pe), n. top; peak, summit; apex, vertex.
top, (ge-), top, lop; clip, trim.
top, interj. all right!, right oh!, agreed!
topaas, (-pase), topaz.
toppunt, top, peak, summit; apex; zenith, acme, height, pinnacle.
tor, (-re), beetle; country-bumpkin, boor, clodhopper.
toring, (-s), tower, steeple (of church).
torpedeer, (ge-), torpedo.
torring, (ge-), unpick, unstitch, rip open; worry, pester, bother.
tors, (ge-), carry.
tortelduif, turtle-dove.
tot, prep. till, until, to, as far as; – nog toe, hitherto.
tot, conj. until, till.
totaal, (-tale), n. total, total sum.
totaal, (-tale), a. total.
totaal, adv. totally, utterly, quite.
totstandkoming, coming into being, realization, declaration.
tou, (-e), n. string, twine, cord.
tou, (ge-), walk one after another.
toulei, (touge-), lead the oxen (team).
toustaan, (touge-), form a queue.
toutrek, (touge-), tug at the rope.
touwys, broken in, tamed; more or less at home in (used to) work.
tower, (ge-), vide toor.
tower-, vide toor-.
towerslag: soos met 'n –, as if by magic.
traag, (trae), slow, indolent, lazy, sluggish, dull, apathetic, torpid.
traak, (ge-), concern.
traan, (trane), n. (1) tear.
traan, n. (2) train-oil, fish-oil.
traan, (ge-), water (of eyes).
tradisie, (-s), tradition.
trag, (ge-), endeavour, try, attempt.
tragies, (-e), tragic.
traktaat, (-tate), treaty.
trakteer, (ge-), treat; entertain; regale.
tralie, (-s), bar, spike.
trans, (-e), pinnacle; firmament.
transitief, (-tiewe), transitive.
transito, transit.
transport, (1) transport, carriage.
transport, (-e), (2) transfer.
transporteer, (ge-), convey, transport; carry forward (book-keeping); transfer.
trant, manner, style, strain.
trap, (-pe), n. (1) stamp, trample, kick.
trap, (-pe), n. (2) step; staircase; degree, step.
trap, (ge-), tread, trample, kick; pedal; thresh; scoot.
trappel, (ge-), trample, stamp.
trapper, (-s), pedal (of bicycle); treadle.
trapsgewys(e), adv. by degrees, step by step, gradually.
trapsoetjies, -suutjies, (-e), chameleon; slow-coach.
trawant, (-e), satellite; henchman.
tred, pace, tread.

tree, (treë), n. pace, step.
tree, (ge-), step, walk, tread.
tref, (ge-), strike, hit; find, meet, come across; come upon, attack.
treffend, (-e), striking; touching.
tregter, (-s), funnel; hopper (in mill).
trein, (-e), train; retinue, following.
treiter, (ge-), plague, tease, annoy.
trek, (-ke), n. (1) pull; haul; draught (of air); migration, journey; stage; moving; feature (of face); trait, characteristic.
trek, n. (2) appetite; inclination, desire.
trek, (ge-), pull, draw, tug, haul, drag; journey, travel, go, march, trek; migrate; move; be draughty, warp, become warped; twitch (of muscles).
trekdier, draught-animal.
trekker, (-s), puller; trigger; corkscrew; forceps; drawer (of bill); tractor; trekker.
trekkings, convulsions, twitchings.
trekpleister, blister-plaster; attraction.
treksaag, cross-cut saw, whipsaw.
treksel, (-s), brew (of tea); enough coffee (tea) for a brew.
trem, (-me, -s), tram(-car).
trens, (-e), snaffle; loop.
treur, (ge-), grieve, mourn, pine.
treurig, (-e), sad, mournful.
treurspel, tragedy.
treurwilgerboom, treurwilkerboom, weeping-willow.
triestig, (-e), gloomy, miserable, dreary.
tril (ge-), tremble, vibrate, quiver, quake.
triomf, (-e), triumph.
triomfeer, (ge-), triumph (over).
trippel, n. tripple, amble.
trippel, (ge-), trip; amble, tripple.
troebel, troewel, (–, -e), a. turbid, muddy, cloudy.
troef, (troewe), n. trump(-card).
troef, (ge-), trump (lit. & fig.).
troei, vide tru.
troep, (-e), troop, company; troupe.
troetel, (ge-), caress, fondle, pet, pamper.
troewel, vide troebel.
trofee, (-feë), trophy.
troffel, (-s), trowel.
trog, (-ge, trôe), trough.
Troje, Troy.
trok, (-ke), truck.
trollie, (-s), trolley.
trom, (-me), drum.
trommel, (-s), n. drum; trunk; (ear-)drum.
trommel, (ge-), drum, beat the drum.
trommeldik, sated, full, filled.
tromp, (-e), muzzle (of fire-arm); trunk (of elephant); trumpet.
trompet, (-te), n. trumpet.
trompie, (-s), Jew's harp.
tromp-op, directly, immediately.
tronie, (-s), face; phiz, mug.
tronk, (-e), gaol (jail), prison.
troon, (trone), n. throne.
troon, (ge-), reign; be enthroned.
troop, (trope), trope.
troos, n. comfort, consolation.
troos, (ge-), comfort, console.
troosteloos, (-lose), disconsolate, inconsolable; dreary, dismal, forlorn.
trop, (-pe), flock, herd; crowd, multitude, lot; covey (of partridges); pack.
trope, (pl.) tropics.
tros, (-se), n. bunch, cluster, batch.
trots, n. pride.
trots, a. (–, -e), proud, haughty.
trots, prep. in spite of, notwithstanding.

trotseer, (ge-), defy, dare, brave.
trou, n. fidelity, loyalty, faith.
trou, a. (-, -e), faithful; loyal; true, trusty; regular (visitor); accurate.
trou, (ge-), marry, be (get) married.
troueloos, (e), faithless, false, disloyal.
trouens, indeed, as a matter of fact.
tru, troei!, back!, wait!,
tru, troei, (ge-), reverse (car), back.
trui, (-e), sweater, jersey.
tsaar, (tsare), Czar (tsar).
Tsjeg, (-ge), Czech.
Tsjeggo-Slowakye, Czecho-Slovakia.
tug, n. discipline; punishment.
tug, (ge-), punish, chastise, discipline.
tugteloos, (-lose), undisciplined; licentious.
tugtig, (ge-), punish, chastise.
tuig, (tuie), harness.
tuimel, (ge-), tumble, topple (over).
tuin, (-e), garden.
tuinbou, horticulture.
tuinier, (-e, -s), gardener.
tuinslang, garden-hose.
tuis, at home.
tuiste, (-s), home.
tuit, (-e), n. spout, nozzle; pout.
tuit, (ge-), tingle.
tulband, turban.
tulp, (-e), tulip; poisonous tulip.
turbine, turbine.
turbineskroef, turbo-prop.
turf, peat; turf; clayey soil.
turksvy(g), prickly pear.
Turkye, Turkey.
tussen, between; among.
tussenbei(de), so-so, passable, fair; – **kom (tree),** interfere, intervene.
tussendeur, adv. in between.
tussenkoms, intervention, mediation.
tussenpoos, interval.
tussentyd, interval, interim.
tussenverkiesing, by-election.
tussenvoeg, (tussenge-), insert.
tussenwerpsel, (-s), interjection.
tuur, (ge-), peer (at); pore (over a book).

twaalf, twelve.
twak, nonsense; **sy – is nat,** he is nowhere (no good).
twee, two.
tweederangs, (-e), second-rate.
tweedrag, discord, dissension.
tweegeveg, duel, single combat.
tweeklank, diphtong.
tweeledig, (-e), biarticulate; binary, binomial, double, dual.
tweeling, (-e), twins.
tweërlei, of two kinds.
tweeslag-, two-stroke.
tweesnydend, (-e), double-edged.
tweespalk, -spalt, discord, dissension.
tweestryd, duel; inward conflict; indecision.
tweetalig, (-e), bilingual.
twintig, twenty.
twis, (-te), n. quarrel, dispute, strife.
twis, (ge-), quarrel, dispute.
twisappel, bone of contention.
twisgierig, (-e), quarrelsome.
twissiek, (-e), quarrelsome, contentious.
twyfel, n. doubt.
twyfel, (ge-), doubt.
twyfelmoedig, (-e), wavering, vacillating, half-hearted.
twyg, [twy(g)e], twig; scion.
ty, (-e), tide.
tyd, (tye), time; season; tense (gram.).
tydelik, (-e), temporary, temporal.
tydelik, adv. temporarily, pro tem.
tydens, during.
tydgenoot, contemporary.
tydig, (-e), timely, seasonable.
tydig, adv. in good time.
tyding, (-e, -s), news, tidings.
tydkorting, pastime.
tydperk, period.
tydrowend, (-e), taking up much time.
tydsaam, (-same), slow, leisurely.
tydskrif, periodical, magazine.
tydstip, point of time; moment.
tydverdryf, pastime.
tydverspilling, waste of time.

u, pers. pron. you.

u, poss. pron., your.

ui, (-e), onion; jest, joke.

uier, (-s), udder.

uil, (-e), owl.

uilskuiken, blockhead, nincompoop, simpleton.

Uilspieël, buffoon, joker.

uintjie, (-s), edible bulbous plant.

uit, prep., out of, in, of, through, by, from, among.

uit, adv. & a., off, out, over, up, on.

uit, (ge-), utter, express, voice.

uit-asem, adv. & a. out of breath.

uitbak, (uitge-), bake (fry) well; fall into disfavour, lose one's popularity.

uitbars, (uitge-), burst (break) out, explode.

uitbeeld, (uitge-), depict, delineate.

uitblaker, (uitge-), blurt out.

uitboender, (uitge-), bundle out, expel.

uitboer, (uitge-), become bankrupt, lose favour.

uitbou, (uitge-), enlarge, extend.

uitbraak, n. escape; outbreak.

uitbraak, (uitge-), vomit, belch forth, disgorge.

uitbrei, (uitge-), spread, enlarge, extend.

uitbroei, (uitge-), hatch; concoct.

uitbuit, (uitge-), exploit.

uitbundig, (-e), exceeding, excessive; enthusiastic, exuberant; boisterous.

uitdaag, (uitge-), challenge; dare, defy.

uitdelg, (uitge-), destroy, exterminate; wipe out.

uitdien, (uitge-), last (its time); serve (its purpose, one's time).

uitdoof, -dowe, (uitge-), extinguish, quench.

uitdor, (uitge-), dry up (out), wither, shrivel (up).

uitdos, (uitge-), array, dress up.

uitdrukking, (-e, -s), expression, phrase, term, wording.

uitdruklik, (-e), a. definite, explicit, express.

uitdruklik, adv. definitely, emphatically.

uitdy, (uitge-), swell; expand.

uiteen, apart, asunder.

uiteenlopend, (-e), divergent, different.

uiteensit, (uiteenge-), explain, expound, state; space.

uiteenspat, (uiteenge-), break up, burst (asunder), explode, disrupt.

uiteinde, end, extremity; finality.

uiteindelik, at last, finally, ultimately.

uiter, (ge-), Vide uit, (ge-).

uiteraard, naturally, from the nature of the case.

uiterlik, n. appearance, exterior.

uiterlik, (-e), a. & adv. apparent(ly), outward(ly), at the latest, at the utmost.

uitermate, exceedingly, uncommonly.

uiters, utterly, extremely, supremely, very; to the last degree; at the latest.

uiterste, (-s), n. extreme, extremity, limit.

uiterste, a. extreme, farthest, last, outside, utmost, utter, very.

uitgaande, outward (mail); outward-bound (ship); pleasure-seeking.

uitgang, exit, outlet; issue; ending, termination (of a word).

uitgawe, (-s), costs, expense; edition, publication.

uitgebak, (-te), found out, in disfavour.

uitgebrei(d), (-breide), broad, extensive, vast, wide.

uitgee, (uitge-), distribute (food), issue (tickets); spend (money); edit, publish (book); pass out (ball).

uitgelate, exuberant, joyful, wanton.

uitgeleef, (-de), decrepit, worn out.

uitgemaak, (-te), established, settled.

uitgenome, barring, except, save.

uitgeslape, knowing, sly, shrewd.

uitgesonderd, barring, except, save.

uitgestorwe, deserted (town); extict (animal); deceased.

uitgestrek, (-te), extensive, large, vast.

uitgeteer, (-de), emaciated, wasted.

uitgevreet, (-vrete), big and strong, well-fed.

uitgewekene, (-s), emigrant refugee.

uitgewer, (-s), editor, publisher.

uitgifte, (-s), issue; output.

uitgraaf, -grawe, (uitge-), dig out, dig up, excavate; exhume (corpse).

uithaal, (uitge-), draw (pull, take) out; play (tricks); exert oneself.

uithaler, flashy, showy, smart.

uithoek, out-of-the-way place, remote corner, outlying district.

uithol, (uitge-), (1) cut (dig, hollow, scoop) out, excavate.

uithol, (uitge-), (2) run out; outrun.

uithonger, (uitge-), famish, starve.

uithou, (uitge-), (1) bear, suffer, stand, stick, endure; hold back (out).

uithou(dings)vermoë, endurance, stamina, staying-power.

uithuisig, (-e), never at home.

uiting, (-e, -s), expression, utterance.

uitkalf, -kalwe, (uitge-), cave in, hollow (wash) out (banks of a river), erode.

uitkeer, (uitge-), pay out, pay back; turn aside; head off (cattle).

uitklophou, knock-out blow.

uitknikker, (uitge-), bowl out, oust.

uitknipsel, clipping, cutting, scrap.

uitkoggel, (uitge-), deride, mock, mimic.

uitkom, (uitge-), appear, come out; (flowers) bud; (eggs) hatch; (facts) become known; (predictions) come true; turn out; work out; make ends meet.

uitkoms(te), issue, result; godsend, help, relief.

uitkryt, (uitge-), cry out; denounce.

uitkyk, n., prospect, view; outlook, attitude.

uitlaat, n. outlet; exhaust.

uitlaat, (uitge-), leave out; let out; let off, release; express; let drop (a hint).

uitlê, lay out; extend; explain, expound, interpret.

uitleef, -lewe, (uitge-), spend; live one's own life.

uitlewer, (uitge-), deliver, hand over, surrender; exchange; extradite.

uitlok, (uitge-), lure, tempt; elicit (an answer); call forth, evoke; ask for (trouble), provoke (a quarrel).

uitloof, -lowe, (uitge-), offer, promise.

uitlooi, (uitge-), tan, beat, thrash.

uitloop, n. overflow, outlet, spillway.

uitloop, (uitge-), go out, walk out; run out (liquids); bud, shoot, sprout.

uitloot, (uitge-), release (bonds); raffle (a prize).

uitmaak, (uitge-), break off (an engagement); constitute, form; decide, settle; decry, denounce, call.

uitmekaar, apart, asunder.

uitmond, (uitge-), debouch into; discharge, empty (itself) into.

uitmondig, mouth, outlet.

uitmoor, (uitge-), butcher, massacre.

uitmunt, (uitge-), excel, surpass.

uitnemend, (-e), excellent, eminent.

uitnodiging, invitation.

uitnooi, (uitge-), invite.

uitoefen, (uitge-), carry on, practise; exercise (influence); follow, pursue (a trade) hold, occupy (a post); discharge (duties); wield (power).

uitoorlê, (-), outmanoeuvre, outwit.

uitpak, (uitge-), unpack; pour out, unburden (one's heart).

uitpeul, (uitge-), 1. peel, shell (peas).

uitpeul, 2. vide **uitpuil**.

uitpluis, (uitge-), sift (evidence), investigate (matter), scrutinize, thresh out (a subject); pick (coir).

uitpuil, -peul, (uitge-), bulge; (eyes) goggle, protrude.

uitput, (uitge-), exhaust, wear out.

uitraak, (uitge-), get out; be broken off (engagement); go bankrupt.

uitreik, (uitge-), present, confer (a prize), distribute, hand out; issue.

uitreken, (uitge-), calculate, figure (reckon, work) out.

uitrig, (uitge-), accomplish, do, perform.

uitroei, (uitge-), root out, uproot, eradicate, exterminate, stamp out, annihilate.

uitroep, (uitge-), call, cry, exclaim, shout; declare (a strike); proclaim.

uitroepteken, exclamation mark.

uitrus, (uitge-), rest, have (take) a rest, repose; equip, fit out, rig (out).

uitrusting, equipment, outfit, kit.

uitsaai, (uitge-), scatter; disseminate; broadcast.

uitsak, (uitge-), bag (bulge) out, sag; drop out; begin to rain.

uitset, n. trousseau, outfit.

uitsetting, enlargement, dilation, inflation; expansion, extension; deportation; expulsion.

uitsien, (uitge-), look (out); look like; – **na,** look forward to.

uitsig, prospect, view; outlook.

uitsit, (uitge-), sit out; serve one's time; expand, extend, distend, dilate; cut out (a rival); post (a sentry); invest (money); put out, banish.

uitskakel, (uitge-), cut out, disconnect, switch off; declutch; rule out.

uitskei(e), (uitge-), leave off, stop, knock off, chuck (drop) it; excrete.

uitskel, (uitge-), abuse, scold, revile.

uitskep, (uitge-), bail out (water), ladle out (soup); scoop out.

uitskryf, -skrywe, (uitge-), write out, copy out; make out (invoice); issue (loan); call (election).

uitskud, (uitge-), shake (out); strip to the skin; rob, win (someone's money).

uitslaan, (uitge-), beat (strike) out; knock out; spread (stretch) out (wings); break out (rash, flames); sweat, exude (of wall).

uitslag, 1. rash, eruption; efflorescence.

uitslag, 2. result, issue, outcome.

uitsluit, (uitge-), lock out; bar, debar, exclude; preclude (doubt): rule out (possibility).

uitsluitend, (-e), a. & adv. exclusive(-ly).

uitsnuffel, (uitge-), ferret out, spy out.

uitsnuit, (uitge-), blow (one's nose).

uitsonder, (uitge-), except, exclude.

uitsondering, exception; exemption.

uitsonderlik, (-e), exceptional.

uitspansel, firmament, heavens, sky.

uitspattend, (-e), dissipated; excessive; loud.

uitspatting, (-e, s), debauchery, dissipation, excess.

uitspook, (uitge-), fight out, fight to the finish; settle by fighting.

uitspraak, pronunciation; pronouncement, utterance, finding, award, judgement, sentence, verdict.

uitspreek, (uitge-), pronounce; express, say.

uitspruit, (uitge-), bud, shoot (up), sprout (out); result from.

uitstaan, (uitge-), stand out; bulge out; bear, endure, stand, suffer.

uitstal, (uitge-), display, put out (for sale); parade, show off.

uitstek: by –, par excellence. tour, trip.

uitstedig, (-e), out of town.

uitstek, by –, par excellence.

uitstekend, (-e), excellent, first-rate.

uitstel, (uitge-), defer, delay, postpone.

uitstof, (uitge-), dust out; beat, lick.

uitstraal, (uitge-), emanate; emit, radiate.

uitstraat, (uitge-), pave.

uitstrek, (uitge-), expand; stretch out (hands); extend.

uitsuie, -suig, (uitge-), suck (out); bleed (labourers); drain, squeeze dry, impoverish (a country), extort (money).

uittap, (uitge-), draw (off).

uittart, (uitge-), challenge, defy, provoke.

uitteer, (uitge-), pine (waste) away.

uittog, departure, exodus; flight.

uittree, (uitge-), retire, resign, withdraw; step out.

uittrek, (uitge-), pull out; pull off; take off (coat); draw, extract (tooth); undress.

uittreksel, extract; abridgment, digest, excerpt, epitome.

uitvaar, (uitge-), sail (out), put to sea; bluster, rant, storm.

uitvaardig, (uitge-), issue, enact, decree.

uitval, n., sally, sortie; thrust; attack; outburst, quarrel.

uitvee(g), (uitge-), erase, sweep out (a room): wipe out (eyes).

uitverkoop, (–), sell off, clear, sell out.

uitverkore, chosen, elect, predestined.

uitvind, (uitge-), find out, discover; invent; ascertain.

uitvindsel, (-s), contrivance, device.

uitvloeisel, (-s), outcome, result.

uitvlug, (-te), n. excuse, evasion, loop-hole, pretext, subterfuge.

uitvoer, (uitge-), export (goods); execute (an order), carry out (a plan), fulfil (a promise), perform (a task), administer, enforce (the law); line (a hat).

uitvoerig, (-e), ample, detailed, minute, lengthy.

uitvra(ag), (uitge-), invite; examine, interrogate, question.

uitwaarts, outward(s).

uitwas, (-se), n., excrescence, outgrowth.

uitweg, way-out, outlet; escape, expedient, loop-hole.

uitwei(e), (uitge-), digress; – **oor,** dilate (enlarge) on.

uitwendig, (-e), external, outward.

uitwerk, (uitge-), work out (sum); elaborate (scheme), develop (idea); squeeze out, oust; bring about, effect.

uitwerpsel, (-s), excrement.

uitwis, (uitge-), blot (wash, wipe) out, efface, erase, expunge, obliterate.

uitwissel, (uitge-), exchange, cash (cheque).

uitwoed, (uitge-), subside, abate.

uitwoel, (uitge-), cease tumbling about; chase out; rouse.

uitwyk, (uitge-), step aside; give way; swerve; dodge; emigrate, go into exile.

uitwys, (uitge-), point out, show; prove; decide, pass judgement.

unaniem, (-e), unanimous, of one accord.

unie, union.

uniek, (-e), unique, unparalleled.

universeel, (-sele), universal, general, sole.

universiteit, (-e), university.

usurpeer, (ge-), usurp.

uur, (ure), hour.

uwe, yours; **die –,** yours truly.

uwentwil: om –, for your sake.

vaag, (vae, vage), vague, hazy, faint.

vaak, n. sleepiness.

vaak, a. sleepy, drowsy.

vaak, adv. often.

vaal, ashen, pale, tawny, grey; faded; dull, drab.

vaalstreep: die – vat, take the road.

vaalwater: in iemand se – kom, thwart a person.

vaam, (vame), vide **vadem**.

vaandel, (-s), colours, flag, standard, banner.

vaandrig, (-s), standard-bearer.

vaar, (ge-), sail, navigate, voyage.

vaardig, (-e), clever, skilful, deft.

vaart, navigation; speed; haste; course.

vaartjie: 'n aardjie na sy –, a chip of the old block.

vaartuig, (-tuie), vessel.

vaarwater, fairway; vide **vaalwater**.

vaarwel, n. farewell.

vaas, (vase), vase.

vaatdoek, vide **vadoek**.

vaatjie, (-s), keg, little tub (barrel), firkin; corporation; fatty.

vabond, vagebond, (-e), rogue, rascal, scamp, knave; vagabond, tramp.

vadem, (-s), **vaam (vame)**, fathom.

vader, (-s), father.

vaderland, fatherland, native country.

vadoek, vaatdoek, (-e), dish cloth, wash-cloth, face cloth.

vadsig, (-e), lazy, slothful, indolent.

va(g)evuur, purgatory.

vag, (-te), fleece, pelt.

vagebond, vide **vabond.**

vak, (-ke), pigeon hole, compartment; square; panel; subject; profession; trade.

vakansie, (-s), holiday(s), vacation.

vakarbeider, skilled labourer.

vakature, (-s), vacancy.

vakleerling, apprentice.

vakuum, (-s), vacuum.

val, (-le), fall; downfall; trap; slope; frill, valance.

val, (ge-), fall; drop.

valbrug, draw-bridge.

valbyl, guillotine.

valdeur, valluik, trap-door.

valies, (-e), travelling-bag, portmanteau.

valk, (-e), hawk, falcon, peregrine.

vallei, (-e), valley; dale, vale.

vals, (–, -e), a. false; counterfeit, base, spurious (coin); forged (signature); treacherous.

vals, adv. false.

valsaard, (-e, -s), perfidious (false) person.

valskerm, parachute.

valstrik, trap, snare, pitfall; snag.

van, (-ne), n. surname.

van, prep., of; from, with, for; by.

vanaand, to-night, this evening.

vanaf, from.

Vandaal, (-dale), Vandal.

vandaan, from.

vandaar, hence.

vandag, to-day (today).

vandat, since.

vandeesjaar, vandesejaar, (-week, -maand), this year (this week, this month).

vandisie, vendusie, (-s), auction (sale), public sale.

vaneen, asunder.

vaneffe, a minute ago, just now.

vang, (ge-), catch; capture, arrest.

vangstok, noose-handle; noose.

vangwa, pick-up (van), squad car.

vanhier, from here; hence.

vanielje, vanilla.

vanjaar, this year.

vanmekaar, asunder, to pieces.

vanmelewe, vans(e)lewe, in the old days, formerly.

vanself, of one's (its, his) own accord, of oneself, by itself (oneself).

vanselfsprekend, (-e), obvious, self-evident.

vanwaar, whence, from which.

vanweë, on account of, owing to.

varia, miscellanies.

varieer, (ge-), vary; range.

varing, (-s), fern, bracken.

vark, (-e), pig, swine, hog.

vars, fresh; new-laid (eggs).

vas, (-te), a. fast; firm, fixed, permanent.

vas, adv. firmly, fast.

vasberade, determined, resolute, firm.

vasbeslote, determined.

vasbind(e), (vasge-), tie (up), fasten.

vasbrand, (vasge-), burn (of food); seize (of engine); get stuck; be unable to pay (manage).

vasel, (-s), fibre, thread.

vashou, (vasge-), hold; hold fast (tight); hang on to.

vaskeer, (vasge-), corner, trap.

vaslê, (vasge-), be fastened; be chained (up); be moored; lie firm; pin (hold) cown; determine; purloin.

vasloop, (vasge-), run aground; collide with; **sig –**, find one's way blocked, get stuck; be cornered, get into trouble.

vasmaak, (vasge-), fasten, button up.

vaspraat, (vasge-): talk oneself into a tangle.

vasslaan, (vasge-), hammer in, nail down.

vassteek, (vasge-), fasten, pin (on); halt, stop (dead, short); stick, get stuck.

vasstel, (vasge-), fix, determine, settle (day); ascertain; appoint (place, time); establish (fact); stipulate; lay down (rule).

vasteland, continent.

vastrap, n. hop-dance, "vastrap".

vastrap, (vasge-), tread (stamp) down; stand firm; be unwavering, stand firm.

vastrek, (vasge-), pull tight; (drive into a) corner; swindle, take in.

vasval, (vasge-), stick (in the mud).

vat, n. (1) grip, hold.

vat, n. (2) barrel, cask, vat.

vat, (ge-), take; seize, catch; grasp; understand, see.

vatbaar: – vir, capable of; open to (conviction); susceptible to (cold, pain, kindness); susceptible of (impressions); amenable to; liable to.

vee, stock, cattle.

vee(g), (ge-), sweep.

veearts, veterinary surgeon.

veeg, (veë), n. wipe; swish (of tail), whisk; box, cuff (on the ear), slap; swipe.

veel, (–, vele), many; much.

veel, adv. much; often, frequently.

veel, (ge-), stand, bear, endure.

veelal, often, mostly.

veelbetekenend, (-e), significant, meaning.

veelbewoë, eventful; troublous.

veeleer, rather, sooner.

veeleisend, (-e), exacting.

veelmeer, rather.

veels: – geluk!, hearty congratulations!; **– te**, far too.

veelseggend, (-e), significant.

veelsydig, (-e), multilateral; many-sided, versatile; wide (knowledge).

veelvoud, (-e), multiple.

veelvoudig, (-e), manifold.

veelvuldig, (-e), frequent; manifold.

veer, (vere), n. (1) feather (of bird); spring (of car, watch).

veer, (vere), n. (2) ferry.
veer, (ge-), be springy (resilient); feather.
veerkombers, (eiderdown) quilt.
veerkrag, springiness; elasticity.
veertien, fourteen.
veertig, forty.
veestapel, stock, livestock.
veeteelt, stock-breeding, cattle-breeding.
veewagter, shepherd.
veg, (ge-), fight.
veglustig, (-e), pugnacious.
veil, a. jou lewe – hê, be ready to sacrifice one's
 life.
veil, (ge-), sell by auction, put up for sale.
veilig, (-e), safe, secure.
veiligheidshalwe, for safety's sake.
veiling, (-e, -s), public sale, auction.
veins, (ge-), simulate, feign, sham.
veinsaard, (-s), hypocrite, dissembler.
vel, (-le), n. skin (of person & animal), hide (of
 animal); sheet (of paper).
vel, (ge-), cut down, fell (tree); flog; pass (sentence).
veld, (-e), veld; field; grazing, pasture, vegetation.
veldbed, camp-stretcher.
veldheer, general.
veldslag, battle.
veldtog, campaign.
veldwerker, field(er), fieldsman.
velerlei, all kinds of, various.
velling, (-s), rim, fellow (felly).
vendusie, vide **vandisie**.
Venisië, Venice.
vennoot, (-note), partner.
venster, (-s), window; shelf (in wheat-stack).
vent, (-e), n. fellow, chap.
venter, (-s), hawker, street-vendor.
ventileer, (ge-), ventilate.
venyn, venom (lit. & fig.).
ver, (–, -re), a. far; distant.
veraangenaam, (–), make pleasant.
veraf, far (distant, away).
verafgo(o)d, (–), idolize.
verafsku, (–), detest, abhor, loathe.
verag, (–), despise, scorn.
veragtelik, (-e), despicable, vile; scornful (look).
veragter, (–), decline, deteriorate.
veral, especially, chiefly.
veralgemeen, (–), generalize.
verander, (–), change, alter.
veranderlik, (-e), changeable, fickle, inconstant;
 variable; unsettled.
verantwoord, (–), account for, answer for.
verantwoordelik, (-e), responsible, answerable.
verarm, (–), impoverish; become poor.
veras, (–), incinerate, cremate.
verassureer, (–), insure.
verbaas, (–), surprise, astonish.
verban, (–), banish, exile; expel.
verband, (-e), bond (of bricks), overlapping;
 bandage, dressing (of wound); bond (on property), mortgage; connection; context.
verbanneling, (-e), exile.
verbaster, (–), interbreed; degenerate.
verbeel, (–): sig –, imagine, fancy.
verbeelding, imagination, fancy.
verbeelding, (-e, -s), conceit; caprice, whims;
 hypochondriac(al).
verbelentheid, fancy, caprice, capriciousness;
 imagination.
verberg, (–), hide, conceal.
verbete, pent up, fierce, intense.
verbeter, (–), improve; correct; rectify (error);
 emend (text); reform (person); better.
verbeur, (–), forfeit; confiscate.

verbeusel, (–), waste (time, money), fritter (idle)
 away (time).
verbied, (–), forbid, prohibit; ban.
verbind, (–), join, connect; link (up); put through
 (to number 63); bandage, tie up; retie, re-
 fasten.
verbinding, (-e, -s), joining; linking (up); connection; junction (railway); dressing (of
 wound); compound, combination (chem.);
 union.
verbintenis, (-se); union; alliance, agreement;
 engagement.
verbitter, (–), embitter; exasperate.
verbleek, (–), turn (grow) pale; fade.
verbleik, (–), fade, pale.
verblind, (–), blind, dazzle.
verbloem, (–), disguise, gloss over.
verbluf, (–), dumbfound, non-pluss.
verbly, (–), gladden, delight.
verblyf, n. residence, abode; stay.
verbond, prohibition; embargo; suppression;
 ban.
verbode, prohibited, forbidden.
verboë, inflected, declined.
verbolge, wrathful, angry.
verbond, (-e), alliance, union, pact, league, coalition; covenant, treaty.
verborge, concealed, hidden.
verbou, (–), rebuild; cultivate, grow.
verbouereerd, (-e), flustered, embarrassed.
verbrand, (–), burn; burn (be burnt) to death;
 cremate (corpse).
verbrei, (–), spread (rumour); disseminate
 (doctrine), propagate.
verbroeder, (–), fraternize.
verbrokkel, (–), crumble (to pieces) (lit. & fig.);
 disintegrate, break (up).
verbrou, (–), make a mess (hash) of, spoil,
 bungle.
verbruik, (–), consume, use up.
verbrysel, (–), smash, crush, shatter, break.
verbuie, -buig, (–), twist, bend; decline, inflect
 (gram.).
verby, prep. past, beyond.
verby, adv. past; over; at an end.
verbypraat, (verbyge-): sy mond –, put one's foot
 in (to) it, drop a brick.
verbyster, (–), perplex, bewilder.
verdaag, (–), adjourn, prorogue, postpone.
verdag, (-te), suspicious; suspected (person,
 place); suspect (of statement), questionable
 (actions).
verdamp, (–), evaporate.
verdedig, (–), defend; stand up for.
verdeel, (–), divide; distribute.
verdelg, (–), destroy, exterminate.
verder, (–, -e), a. further, farther.
verder, adv. further, farther.
verderf, n. destruction, ruin.
verderf, -derwe, (–), ruin; corrupt.
verdien, (–), earn (salary), deserve (honour);
 merit (reward).
verdienste, (-s), wages; profit; merit.
verdienstelik, (-e), meritorious, deserving.
verdiep, (–), deepen; – raak in, become engrossed
 in.
verdieping, (-e, -s), deepening; floor.
verdiepinghuis, double-storey.
verdig, (-te), a. fictitious.
verdig, (–), invent (story).
verdigsel, (-s), fiction; fabrication; fable.
verdink, (–), suspect; vide **verdag**.
verdoem, (–), damn.
verdoesel, (–), blur; gloss over.

verdof, (-dowwe), (–), tarnish; dim (light); deaden (sound).

verdonker, (–), darken, cloud, dim.

verdoof, -dowe, (–), dull, deaden (sound); tarnish; anaesthetise (surgery), stupefy, stun.

verdor, (-de), a. withered, parched, shrivelled up.

verdor, (–), wither, parch, shrivel up.

verdorwe, perverted, depraved, corrupt.

verdowe, vide verdoof.

verdowend, (-e), stupefactive; narcotic.

verdra(ag), (–), endure, bear, stand.

verdraagsaam, (-same), tolerant, forbearing.

verdraai, (–), twist (arm); distort (words).

verdrag, (-drae), treaty, agreement.

verdring, (–), push aside (away), jostle, crowd out; oust, supplant.

verdrink, (–), drown, be drowned.

verdroog, -droë, (–), dry up, parch.

verdruk, (–), oppress; vide verdring.

verdryf, -drywe, drive away (out) chase away (out); expel, eject, oust, turn out; pass (while away) (time).

verduidelik, (–), explain, elucidate, illustrate.

verduister, (–), darken, obscure; grow dark; embezzle (money); darken, cloud.

verduistering, darkening; eclipse (of sun); embezzlement.

verdun, (–), thin, make thin; dilute.

verduur, (–), endure, bear, suffer.

verdwaal, (–), lose one's way, get lost.

verdwaas, (–), infatuate, knock silly.

verdwyn, (–), disappear, vanish.

veredel, (–), improve (stock); refine; elevate, ennoble.

vereelt, (-e), a. horny, callous, hard.

vereenselwig, (–), identify.

vereenvoudig, (–), simplify; reduce (fraction).

vereer, (–), honour, reverence, worship.

vereers, vide vir.

vereffen, (–), settle, pay (account), square.

vereis, (–), demand, require.

vereiste, (-s), requirement, requisite.

verenig, (–), unite, merge, amalgamate, combine; incorporate (in one body); join; V–de Volke, United Nations.

vererg, (–), annoy, irritate, vex.

vererger, (–), make worse, aggravate.

verewig, (–), immortalise, perpetuate.

verf, (verwe), n. paint, colour; dye.

verf, verwe, (ge-), paint; rouge; dye.

verflenter, (–), tear; become tattered.

verflou, (–), grow (become) faint; fade; weaken (of energy); flag (of interest); slacken; cool down; diminish.

verfoei, (–), detest, loathe, abominate.

verfoes, (–), spoil, bungle, muddle.

verfraai, (–), embellish, adorn.

verfris, (–), refresh.

verfrommel, (–), crumple, crush.

verg(e), (ge-), demand, require.

vergaan, (–), perish, decay, decompose; pass away; be wrecked (of ship), be lost.

vergaar, (–), collect, gather; amass, hoard.

vergader, (–), collect, gather; meet, assemble.

vergal, (–), gall; embitter; spoil.

vergange, adv. lately; the other day.

verganklik, (-e), perishable (goods); transient, transitory.

vergas, (–), (1) treat; – op, treat to.

vergas, (–), (2) gasify; vaporize.

vergasser, (-s), carburettor; vaporiser.

vergeef, (-gewe), (–), forgive, pardon.

vergeefs, (–), fruitless, futile.

vergeestelik, (–), spiritualize, sublimate.

vergeet, (–), forget.

vergeld(e), (–), repay, requite.

vergelding, reward, recompense, requital; retribution; reprisal.

vergeleke: – met, in comparison with.

vergelyk, (-e), n. compromise, agreement, settlement.

vergelyk, (–), compare.

vergelyking, (-e, -s), comparison; simile, equation (alg.).

vergemaklik, (–), facilitate.

vergenoeg, (–), content.

vergesel, (–), accompany, attend.

vergesig, (-te), prospect; vista; view.

vergesog, (-te), far fetched.

vergetelheid, oblivion.

vergewe, (1) vide vergeef.

vergewe, (–), (2) poison.

vergewis, (–): sig – van, make sure of.

vergiet, (–), shed.

vergif, (-giwwe, -te), poison; venom.

vergifnis, forgiveness, pardon.

vergiftig, (–), poison; envenom.

Vergilius, Virgil.

vergis, (–): sig –, make a mistake.

verglaas, (–), glaze; vitrify.

vergoddelik, (–), deify.

vergoed, (–), make good, compensate, indemnify; make it up to, repay.

vergoelik, (–), excuse, gloss (smooth) over, extenuate.

vergote, spilt (spilled) (blood).

vergroei, (–), grow out of shape; outgrow.

vergroot, (–), enlarge (portrait); increase; augment; magnify; exaggerate.

vergruis, (–), crush, pulverize; shatter, smash.

vergryp, (–): sig – aan, transgress, infringe (law), violate; commit an offence against.

vergun, (–), permit, allow; grant.

verhaal, (-hale), n. story, narrative, account; redress, remedy.

verhaal, (–), tell, narrate, relate.

verhaar, (–), lose the hair.

verhaas, (–), hasten, expedite.

verhandel, (–), negotiate (bill); barter (away), dispose of.

verhandeling, (-e, -s), treatise, essay, discourse, dissertation; lecture.

verhang, (–), rehang, hang otherwise.

verhard, (–), harden; become (make) callous.

verheerlik, (–), glorify, extol.

verhef, (–), lift; elevate; extol.

verheffend, (-e), elevating, ennobling.

verhelp, (–), remedy, rectify.

verhemelte, (-s), palate.

verheug, (–), gladden, delight.

verhewe, elevated; embossed; swollen; lofty, exalted, elevated, fine, sublime.

verhinder, (–), prevent, hinder.

verhit (–), heat, inflame.

verhoed, (–), prevent, avert.

verhonger, (–), famish, starve.

verhoog, (-hoë), n. platform, dais.

verhoog, (–), heighten; raise (salary), increase; promote; enhance (qualities); intensify.

verhoor, (-hore), n. hearing, trial, examination.

verhoor, (–), answer, hear (prayer); try (prisoner); examine.

verhouding, (-e, -s), (relation); proportion, ratio.

verhuis, (–), move (into house), remove; emigrate; pass away.

verhuur, (–), let (rooms), rent, let out; hire out, lease (farm).

verhuurder, (-s), lessor; landlord.

verinnerlik, (–), deepen, spiritualize.

verja(ag), -jae, (–), drive (frighten, chase, scare) away; drive out (enemy); dispel.
verjaar, (–), celebrate one's birthday.
verjaar(s)dag, birthday; anniversary.
verjaring, birthday; prescription (of debt).
verjong, (–), rejuvenate.
verkalk, (–), calcify, calcine.
verkas, (–), shift, decamp.
verkeer, n. intercourse; traffic.
verkeer, (–), be (in a certain position).
verkeerd, (-e), a. wrong; unreasonable, impossible.
verkeersknoop, traffic jam.
verken, (–), scout, reconnoitre.
verkies, (–), elect, choose; return (as M.P.), prefer.
verkiesbaar, (-bare), eligible; sig – stel, stand for, seek election.
verkiesing, (-e, -s), election (by vote); wish, choice.
verkieslik, (-e), preferable.
verkla(ag), -klae, (–), bring a change (an action) against, lodge a complaint against; accuse.
verklaar, (–), explain (meaning), elucidate; state, declare; testify, certify.
verklap, (–), let out, blab.
verklee(d), (–), disguise; change one's clothes.
verkleineer, (–), belittle, disparage.
verkleinwoord, diminutive.
verkleur, (–), fade, discolour, change (its) colour.
verkleurmannetjie, chameleon.
verklik, (–), let out, split on.
verkluim, (–), grow numb with cold; die of the cold.
verknies, (–), sig –, mope.
verknoei, (–), spoil, make a mess of.
verknog: – aan, attached (devoted) to.
verknorsing, sorry plight, fix.
verkoeler, (-s), radiator.
verkondig, (–), preach, proclaim; expound, advocate (policy).
verkoop, (–), sell.
verkoopbrief, deed of sale.
verkort, (–), make shorter; abbreviate (word); abridge (book); condense; while away (the time).
verkoue, n. cold, chill.
verkouentheid, cold.
verkrag, (–), violate (law, conscience); ravish, force.
verkrop, (–), swallow, pocket (insults); restrain (feelings).
verkrummel, (–), crumble.
verkry, (–), obtain; gain, win.
verkul, (–), cheat, take in, trick.
verkwansel, (–), barter away; throw away.
verkwik, (–), refresh.
verkwis, (–), waste, squander, dissipate.
verkyk, (–): sig – aan, stare (gaze, gape) at.
verkyker, (-s), telescope, field-glasses.
verlaag, (–), lower; reduce; debase, degrade.
verlaat, (–), leave; desert, abandon, forsake.
verlak, (–), lacquer, japan, varnish.
verlam, (–), paralyse; cripple.
verlang, (–), want, desire; long.
verlangste, (-s), longing, yearning.
verlê, -leg, (–), shift, remove; lie (down) in a different position; divert (road); mislay.
verlede, n. past.
verlede, a. past, last.
verleë, bashful, perplexed, embarrassed.
verleen, (–), give, grant, render.
verleentheid, bashfulness, embarrassment, confusion; trouble.

verleer, (–), unlearn (habit); forget.
verlei, (–), lead astray; tempt, entice.
verleidelik, (-e), tempting, enticing.
verlekker, (–): sig – in, take (a) pleasure (a delight) in.
verleng, (–), lengthen; protract (visit); extend; produce (line); renew (bill).
verlep, (–), fade, wilt, wither.
verlief, (-de), a. amorous, in love.
verlief, adv.: – neem, put up with.
verlies, (-e), loss, bereavement.
verlig, (–), (1) light (up), illuminate; enlighten.
verlig, (–), (2) lighten (burden); alleviate (distress), ease (pain), relieve.
verloën, -logen, (–), deny, repudiate, renounce.
verlof, permission, leave.
verlok, (–), tempt, allure, entice.
verloof, -lowe, (–), affiance, betroth.
verloop, n. course (of time, disease), progress (of disease).
verloop, (–), pass, elapse, expire.
verloopte, runaway, vagabond; dissipated.
verloor, (–), lose.
verlos, (–), save, deliver; redeem.
verlug, (–), (1) ventilate, air.
verlug, (–), (2) illuminate; illustrate.
verlustig, (–), amuse; revel in.
vermaak, (-make), n. pleasure, delight; pastime.
vermaak, (–), alter (clothes); amuse, entertain, divert; bequeath, leave (by will); make (person) jealous.
vermaaklik, (-e), amusing, entertaining.
vermaan, (–), admonish, warn.
vermaard, (-e), renowned, famous.
vermag, (–), have the power to.
vermeende, supposed (brother, heir), reputed, fancied.
vermeer, vide vomeer.
vermeerder, (–), increase, multiply.
vermeld, (–), mention, state, record.
vermeldenswaard(ig), (-e), worth mentioning.
vermeng, (–), mix; blend.
vermenigvuldig, (–), multiply.
vermetel, (–, -e), audacious, bold.
verminder, (–), diminish, decrease, lessen, reduce, lower, cut down.
vermink, (–), mutilate, maim, cripple; garble (statement).
vermis, (–), miss.
vermoë, (-ns), power; capacity; ability; wealth.
vermoed, (–), suspect; presume, suppose, surmise.
vermoedelik, adv. probably, presumably.
vermoei, (–), tire, fatigue, weary.
vermoënd, (-e), rich, wealthy.
vermom, (–), disguise, mask.
vermoor, (–), murder, kill.
vermors, (–), waste.
vermorsel, (–), crush, pulverize, smash.
vermuf, (–), become (get) musty (mouldy).
vermy, (–), avoid, shun; steer clear of.
vernaam, (-name), a. important; prominent; distinguished.
vernaam, adv. especially, particularly.
vernag, (–), pass (spend) the night.
verneder, (–), humble, degrade.
verneem, (–), hear, understand, learn; inquire.
verneuk, (–), cheat, swindle, defraud.
verniel, (–), destroy, ruin, wreck; ill-treat, overwork.
verniet, free, gratis; in vain.
vernietig, (–), destroy; annihilate; annual, reverse.
vernieu, vide vernuwe.
vernikkel, (–), nickel-plate.

vernis, (-), varnish; veneer (fig.).
vernoem, (-): 'n persoon -, name a child after
  somebody.
vernou, (-), narrow; take in (dress).
vernuf, ingenuity, genius; wit.
vernuwe, vernieu, (-), renew; renovate.
veronagsaam, verontagsaam, (-), neglect (duty);
  slight (person), ignore, disregard.
veronderstel, (-), suppose; assume.
verongeluk, (-), be killed in an accident; meet
  with disaster; perish; fail; miscarry (of plan).
veronreg, (-), vide verongelyk.
verontrus, (-), disturb, alarm, perturb.
verontskuldig, (-), excuse.
verontwaardig, (-), made indignant.
veroordeel, (-), condemn; sentence.
veroorloof, (-), permit, allow.
veroorsaak, (-), cause, give rise to.
verootmoedig, (-), humiliate, humble.
verorber, (-), eat up, consume.
verorden, (-), ordain, decree, order.
verordineer, (-), ordain, order.
verouder, (-), age, grow old; become obsolete.
verower, (-), conquer, capture.
verpag, (-), lease, put out to lease.
verpak, (-), pack; repack.
verpand, (-), pawn, mortgage, pledge.
verpersoonlik, (-), personify.
verpes, (-), infect; contaminate, corrupt, poison.
verplaas, (-), shift, remove, transfer.
verplant, (-), plant out, transplant.
verpleeg, verpleë, (-), nurse; care for.
verpletter, (-), crush, shatter, smash.
verplig, (-), force, compel, oblige.
verpot, (-te), a. feeble, stunted, poor.
verraad, treason, treachery, betrayal.
verraai, (-), betray; reveal.
verraderlik, (-e), treacherous, traitorous.
verras, (-), surprise.
verre, far.
verregaand, (-e), extreme, outrageous.
verrek, (-), strain, wrench, sprain.
verreweg, far and away, by far.
verrig, (-), do, perform, execute.
verrigting, (-e, -s), execution, performance;
  transaction; -e, proceedings, transactions;
  meeting, function.
verroer, (-), stir, move.
verroes, (-), rust, grow rusty.
verrot, (-), decay, putrefy.
verruil, (-), exchange, barter.
verruk, (-), enrapture, enchant, ravish.
verryk, (-), enrich.
verrys, (-), rise: spring up.
vers, (-e), (1) verse; stanza; poem.
vers, (-e), (2) heifer.
versaak, (-), forsake, desert, renounce; neglect.
versadig, (-), satisfy (appetite).
verslag, (-), make soft(er), soften (heart); ease,
  relieve (pain), alleviate, modify.
versamel, (-), gather; collect; assemble; amass,
  (riches); compile; store up.
versamelnaam, collective noun.
versand, (-), silt up.
verseël, (-), seal (up).
verseg, (-), refuse point-blank.
verseil: - raak onder, get mixed up with.
verseker, (-), assure, ensure, make certain; insure
  (life, etc.).
versend, (-), dispatch, consign, forward.
versene: die - teen die prikkels slaan, kick against
  the pricks.
verseng, (-), singe, scorch.
verset, (-): sig -, resist, offer resistance.
versie, (-s), heifer.

versier, (-), adorn; beautify; embellish, trim.
versiersuiker, icing-sugar.
versigtig, (-e), careful, cautious.
versilwer, (-), silver.
versin, (-), fabricate, invent, concoct.
versink, (-), (1) sink.
versit, (-), move, shift.
verskaf, (-), provide; furnish, supply.
verskans, (-), entrench.
verskeep, (-), ship; tranship.
verskeidenheid, variety, diversity.
verskeie, several; different, various.
verskerp, (-), sharpen; accentuate.
verskeur, (-), tear, devour; rent.
verskiet, n. distance; perspective; view; prospect.
verskiet, (-), spend (cartridges); change colour,
  fade; shoot (of star); shift (of pain).
verskil, (-), differ, vary.
verskimmel, (-), become mouldy.
verskoon, (-), change clothes (linen); excuse.
verskrik, (-), frighten, startle, terrify.
verskriklik, (-e), terrible, dreadful, horrible.
verskroei, (-), scorch, singe.
verskrompel, (-), shrivel (up), wither, shrink.
verskuif, -skuiwe, (-), shift, (re)move.
verskuil, (-), conceal, hide.
verskuldig, (-de), due, indebted.
verskyn, (-), appear; be published.
verskynsel, (-s), phenomenon.
verslaaf, -slawe, (-), enslave.
verslaan, (-), beat, defeat; go (turn) flat (stale).
verslaap, (-), sleep away; sig -, oversleep oneself.
verslae, dismayed, dumbfounded.
verslag, (-slae), report, account.
verslaggewer, reporter.
verslap, (-), relax; slacken; flag.
versleg, (-), make (grow) worse; degenerate.
verslind(e), (-), devour, consume.
verslons, (-), ruin; spoil.
verslyt, (-), wear out (away, off); become threadbare; while away.
versmaad, -smaai, (-), scorn, despise.
versmag, (-), languish; waste (pine) away.
versmoor, (-), smother, suffocate.
versnapering, (-e, -s), titbit, delicacy.
versnel, (-), accelerate, quicken.
versnelling, (-e, -s), acceleration; gear; rapids.
versnipper, (-), cut into pieces (bits).
versoek, (-), request; invite; tempt.
versoekskrif, petition.
versoen, (-), reconcile, conciliate; placate.
versondig, (-), irritate, annoy, bother.
versool, (-), new-sole; retread.
versôre, -sorg, (-), care for, attend to, provide
  for, look after.
versot: - op, keen on, fond of.
versper, (-), obstruct, bar, block.
verspil, (-), waste, squander, dissipate.
verspoel, (-), wash away.
verspot, (-te), silly, foolish.
verspreek, (-): sig -, make a slip of the tongue;
  drop a brick.
versprei, (-), spread (rumour, news), diffuse
  (light, heat); scatter: propagate; disseminate.
verspring, (verge-), jump far; do the long jump.
verspring, (-), jump, shift, move.
verstaan, (-), understand.
verstand, understanding, intelligence, intellect,
  mind, sense.
verstandig, (-e), a. sensible, wise.
verstar, (-), make rigid, stiffen.
versteek, (-), conceal, hide.
versteen, (-), petrify; harden.
verstek, default.
verstekeling, (-e), stowaway.

verstel, (–), (re)adjust; change gears; mend, repair (clothes).
versterk, (–), strengthen; fortify; reinforce; intensify.
versteur, vide verstoor.
verstik, (–), stifle, suffocate, choke.
verstok, (-te), hardened, confirmed.
verstoke: – van, deprived of.
verstom, (–), render speechless; become speechless.
verstomp, (–), blunt, dull, deaden.
verstoor, -steur, (–), disturb; annoy, vex.
verstoot, (–), cast off; repudiate.
verstop, (–), stop (up); clog; plug.
verstoteling, (-e), outcast, pariah.
verstout, (–), embolden.
verstrek, (–), furnish, supply.
verstreke, expired, elapsed.
verstrik, (–), trap, ensnare, entangle.
verstrooi, (–), scatter, disperse.
verstrooi(d), (-de), dispersed, scattered; absent-minded.
verstryk, (–), elapse, expire.
verstuit, (–), sprain (wrist, ankle).
verstyf, -stywe, (–), stiffen; grow numb.
versugting, (-e, -s), sigh.
versuiker, (–), saccharify; sugar (fig.).
versuim, n. omission; neglect.
versuim, (–), neglect; fail (to do); stay, delay.
versuip, (–), drown; be drowned.
versuur, (–), sour (lit. & fig.); turn (become) sour.
verswak, (–), weaken, grow (become) weaker; grow dim (faint).
versweer, (–), fester, ulcerate.
verswelg, (–), swallow up.
verswik, (–), sprain.
verswye, -swyg, (–), keep a secret, keep back, suppress (news).
vertaal, (–), translate.
vertak, (–), branch out, ramify.
verte, distance.
verteenwoordig, (–), represent.
verteer, (–), consume, use up; spend; digest.
vertel, (–), tell, relate.
vertoef, -toewe, (–), stay, wait, linger.
vertolk, (–), interpret.
vertoog, (-toë), representation, protest.
vertoon, (–), show; exhibit, display; screen, present; produce (play), perform.
vertraag, (–), delay; retard.
vertrap, (–), trample upon.
vertrek, (-ke), n. (1) room, apartment.
vertrek, n. (2) departure.
vertrek, (–), depart, leave; distort, twist (face).
vertroebel, (–), make turbid (muddy).
vertroetel, (–), spoil, pamper.
vertroos, (–), comfort, solace, console.
vertrou, (–), trust.
vertroud, (-e), reliable, trustworthy.
vertroue, confidence, faith, trust.
vertroulik, adv. confidentially.
vertwyfeling, desperation, despair.
vervaag, (–), grow faint (dim).
vervaard, (-e), alarmed, frightened.
vervaardig, (–), manufacture, make.
vervaarlik, (-e), awful, frightful.
verval, (–), decline, decay; become dilapidated, fall into disrepair; mature, become due (of bill); lapse (of life-policy); expire (of lease); fall away.
vervals, (–), falsify; forge; counterfeit (coin).
vervang, (–), take the place of; replace; be substituted for; relieve.
vervat, (–), change one's grip; resume, begin (start) again (anew); continue.

verveel, (–), bore; tire.
verveer, (–), moult (of birds).
vervel, (–), change (cast) its skin.
vervelend, (-e), boring, wearisome.
vervelens: tot – (toe), ad nauseam.
verversing, (-e, -s), refreshment.
vervlakste, confounded, blinking.
vervloë, gone by.
vervloek, (–), curse, damn.
vervlugtig, (–), evaporate, volatilize.
vervoeg, (–), conjugate (verb).
vervoer, (–), convey, transport, carry.
vervoering, rapture, ecstasy.
vervoermiddel, conveyance, vehicle.
vervolg, (–), continue; persecute; prosecute, institute legal proceedings against; plague, pester.
vervolgens, further, then, thereupon.
vervolgstorie, -verhaal, serial (story).
vervorm, (–), transform, remodel.
vervreem, (–), estrange, alienate.
vervroeg, (–), accelerate, fix at an earlier date.
vervrolik, (–), cheer up.
vervuil, (–), render (become, grow) filthy; grow rank (of plants, weeds); become abundant.
vervul, (–), fill (position, a part); fulfil (promise, desire); do, discharge (duty); perform (task, duty); grant (wish).
vervyf, (–), convert (a try), goal.
verwaand, (-e), arrogant, conceited.
verwaardig, (–): sig – om, condescend to.
verwaarloos, (–), neglect.
verwag, (–), expect.
verwant, (-e), a. related; kindred, allied.
verwar, (–), tangle, intertwine; confuse.
verwarm, (–), warm, heat.
verwater, (–), dilute; water down.
verweer, (–), (1) defend.
verweer, (–), (2) weather (of rocks).
verwek, (–), generate; cause, raise (storm, laugh); stir up, provoke, excite, rouse; produce (sensation).
verwelk, (–), fade, wither, wilt.
verwelkom, (–), welcome, bid welcome.
verwen, (–), spoil (child); pamper.
verwens, (–), curse.
verwerf, -werwe, (–), gain, win.
verwerk, (–), work up, elaborate, digest.
verwerp, (–), reject, repudiate.
verwerplik, (-e), objectionable, unacceptable.
verwenslik, (–), realize, actualize.
verwikkeling, (-e, -s), complication.
verwilder, (–), chase (drive) away, frighten (scare) away.
verwissel, (–), change; interchange, exchange.
verwittig, (–), inform, notify.
verwoed, (-e), fierce, furious, wild.
verwoes, (–), destroy; devastate, ravage.
verwonder, (–), astonish, surprise.
verworpeling, (-e), outcast, reprobate.
verwring, (–), twist, distort.
verwurg, (–), strangle, throttle.
verwyder, (–), remove; get rid of.
verwydering, removal; estrangement.
verwyf, (-de), a. effeminate.
verwyl, (–), stay; linger.
verwys, (–), refer; relegate.
verwyt, (–), reproach, blame, upbraid.
verydel, (–), frustrate, upset, foil.
vesel, (-s), fibre, filament, thread.
vestig, (ge-), establish, found; settle.
vesting, (-e, -s), fortress, stronghold.
vet, (-te), n. fat; grease.
vet, a. fat; fatty, greasy.
vete, (-s), feud, quarrel, enmity.

veter, (-s), boot-lace; stay-lace.
vetkoek, damper, dough-nut, "vetkoek".
vetsak, fatty, roly-poly.
vier, four.
vier, (ge-), celebrate, observe.
vierderangs, (-e) fourth-rate.
vierhoek, quadrangle, quadrilateral.
vierkant, (-e), n. square.
vies, a. & adv. annoyed, disgusted; offensive, foul.
vies, (ge-): sig –, be fed up.
vieslik, (-e), filthy, dirty, loathsome.
viets, smart, spruce, dapper.
vilet, (-te), stock.
vilt, felt.
vin, (-ne), fin.
vind(e), (ge-), find; think, deem.
vindingryk, (-e), ingenious; resourceful.
vinger, (-s), finger.
vingeralleen, all by oneself, all alone.
vingerhoed, thimble.
vingerwysing, (-e, -s), indication, warning.
vink, (-e), finch.
vinnig, (-e), fast, quick; sharp; cross, angry.
viool, (viole), violin.
viooltjie, (-s), violet; pansy.
vir, for, to; – eers (vereers), for the present, for the time being; to begin with; – lief neem, put up with; – seker, for sure.
virtuoos, (-tuose), virtuoso.
vis, (-se), n. fish.
vis, (ge-), fish.
visenteer, (ge-), search, inspect.
vise-voorsitter, vice-chairman.
visie, (-s), vision.
visier, (-e, -s), visor (of helmet); (back-)sight of gun).
visioen, (-e), vision.
visvang, (visge-), fish; nod.
vit, (ge-), find fault, cavil.
vitrioel, vitriol.
vla, custard.
vlaag, (vlae), gust (of wind); shower (of rain); fit (of rage).
Vlaams, (-e), Flemish.
Vlaandere, Flanders.
vlag, (vlae), flag; colours.
vlagdoek, bunting.
vlak, (-ke), n. level (of sea); plane (geom.); surface, plain; flat (of the hand).
vlak, (–, -ke), a. shallow (water); flat.
vlak, adv. – by, close (near) by.
vlakhaas, Cape hare.
vlakte, (-s), plain; stretch.
vlakvark, wart-hog.
vlam, (-me), n. flame; blaze.
vlam, (ge-), flame, blaze.
Vlaming, (-e), Fleming; die –e, the Flemish.
vlas, flax.
vlees, flesh; meat (food).
vleeslik, (-e), fleshy, carnal.
vleg, (ge-), plait (hair, straw); twist (rope); weave (mats).
vlegel, vleël, (-s), flail; churl, gawk.
vlegsel, (-s), plait, tress, braid; pigtail.
vlei, (-e), n. hollow, marsh, swamp, "vlei".
vlei, (ge-), flatter, wheedle, cajole.
vleis, vlees, meat.
vlek, (-ke), n. stain, smudge, blot, blemish.
vlek, (ge-), stain, soil, smudge.
vlerk, (-e), wing.
vlerksleep, (vlerkge-), make love (to).
vlermuis, bat.
vleuel, (-s), wing, vane, wing-three-quarter.
vleuelpiano, grand piano.

vlie(g), (ge-), fly.
vlied, (ge-), fly, flee.
vlieëkas, meat-safe.
vlieënier, vliegenier, vide vlieër (2).
vlieër, (-s), (1) kite.
vlieër, (-s), (2) aviator, flyer.
vlieg, (ge-), fly.
vlieg, (vlieë), n. fly.
vliegbaan, aerodrome.
vliegmasjien, vliegtuig, aeroplane.
vlies, (-e), fleece (of sheep); film (over eyes); membrane (in body).
vliet, (ge-), flow, run.
vlinder, (-s), butterfly.
vloed, (-e), flood, flood-tide; torrent, flow (of words).
vloei, (ge-), flow, run, stream.
vloeiend, (-e), flowing; fluent (style).
vloeipapier, blotting-paper.
vloeistof, liquid.
vloek, (-e), n. curse; oath.
vloek, (ge-), swear, curse, damn.
vloer, (-e), floor, flooring; threshing-floor.
vlok, (-ke), flake (of snow); tuft.
vlooi, (-e), flea.
vloot, (vlote), fleet, navy.
vlot, (-te), n. raft, float.
vlot, (–, -te), a. afloat; fluent, smooth.
vlot, adv. fluently.
vlot, (ge-), float; go smoothly.
vlug, n. flight, escape.
vlug, (-ge), a. fast, quick, swift.
vlug, (ge-), flee, fly.
vlughou, volley.
vlugsand, quicksand.
vlugsout, smelling-salts.
vlugteling, (-e), fugitive; refugee.
vlugtig, (-e), cursory (glance); flying (visit); transitory; rough (sketch); superficial; slight.
vly, (ge-), lay down, arrange.
vlym, (-e), n. lancet; fleam.
vlymend, (-e), acute, sharp; poignant (grief); scathing (sarcasm); stinging.
vlyt, diligence, assiduity, industry.
vod, (-de, -dens), rag, tatter.
voed, (ge-), feed; nourish.
voeding, feeding; food.
voedsaam, (-same), nutritious, nourishing.
voedsel, food, nourishment.
voeg, (voeë), n. joint, seam.
voeg, voeë, (ge-), add; join, weld, seam.
voegwoord, conjunction.
voel, (ge-), feel.
voël, (-s), bird.
voëlent, bird-lime; mistletoe.
voelhoring, feeler, tentacle, antenna.
voëlverskrikker, scarecrow.
voëlvry, outlawed.
voer, n. fodder; (chicken-)food.
voer, (ge-), (1) feed.
voer, (ge-), (2) lead, take, transport; bear (arms, name); wage (war); carry on (conversation).
voering, (-s), lining.
voerkuil, silo.
voersak, nose-bag; forage-bag.
voert!, away with you!, get (go) away!
voertsek, -sik, vide voert.
voertuig, carriage, vehicle (lit. & fig.).
voet, (-e), foot; base; footing.
voetbal, football.
voete-ent, voetenent, foot(-end).
voetganger, (-s), pedestrian; hopper.
voetlys, skirting-board.
voetslaan, (voetge-), walk, foot it, slog.
voetspoor, foot-print, track.

voetstap, footstep.
voetstuk, pedestal, base.
vog, (-te), liquid; moisture, damp.
vokaal, (-kale), n. vowel.
vol, (–, -le), full.
volbloed, thoroughbred (animal).
volbring, (–), fulfil, accomplish, achieve.
voldaan, (-dane), n. receipt.
voldaan, a. content, satisfied; paid.
voldoen, (–), satisfy, please.
voldoende, sufficient, adequate, enough.
voldonge: – feit, accomplished fact.
volg(e), (ge-), follow; pursue.
volgende, following, next.
volgens, according to.
volgorde, order, sequence.
volgsaam, (-same), docile, obedient.
volhard, (–), persevere, persist.
volhou, (volge-), maintain, keep up, sustain; persevere, persist.
volk, (-e, -ere), nation.
volkekunde, ethnology.
volkome, a. perfect; complete; absolute.
volksdrag, national dress.
volksetimologie, popular etymology.
volkslied, national anthem; popular song.
volk(s)planting, settlement, colony.
Volksraad, House of Assembly.
volledig, (-e), full (account), complete (set).
volledigheidshalwe, for the sake of completeness.
volleerd, (-e), accomplished, finished.
volmaak, (-te), a. perfect, consummate.
volmag, (-te), power of attorney; full powers.
volmagtig, (ge-), authorize.
volmondig, (-e), frank, candid.
volop, in plenty (abundance).
volprese: nooit –, surpassing.
volprop, (volge-), stuff, cram.
volsin, sentence, period.
volslae, complete, absolute.
volstaan, (–), suffice.
volstop, (volge-), stuff, cram.
volstrek, (-te), a. absolute.
volstrek, adv. absolutely, quite.
volstruis, (-e), ostrich.
voltallig, (-e), full, complete, fully attended.
voltooi, (–), finish, complete.
volstrek, (–), carry out; perform.
voluit, in full; at full length.
volvoer, (–), fulfil, accomplish.
volwasse, adult, grown-up, full-grown.
vomeer, vermeer, (ge-), vomit.
vomitief, (-tiewe), emetic.
vondeling, (-e), foundling.
vonds, (-te), find, discovery.
vonk, (-e), n. spark.
vonk, (ge-), spark.
vonkel, (ge-), sparkle.
vonkprop, sparking-plug.
vonnis, (-se), n. sentence, judg(e)ment.
vonnis, (ge-), sentence, condemn.
voog, (-de), guardian.
voogdy, guardianship.
voor, (vore), n. furrow; ditch.
voor, n.: die – en teë (teen), the pros and cons.
voor, prep. in front of, before.
voor, adv. in front.
voor, conj. before.
vooraan, in front; in the forefront.
vooraand, eve.
vooraanstaande, leading, prominent.
vooraf, beforehand, previously.
voorafgaan, (voorafge-), precede; lead.
voorasnog, as yet.
voorbaat: by –, in anticipation.

voorbarig, (-e), premature; hasty; presumptuous, arrogant.
voorbedag, (-te), premeditated.
voorbeeld, (-e), example; illustration, instance; specimen; copy.
voorbeeldig, (-e), exemplary.
voorbehoedmiddel, preservative; prevent(at)ive.
voorbehou, (–), reserve.
voorberei, (–), prepare.
voorberig, preface, foreword.
voorbeskik, voorbestem, (–), predestine.
voorbidding, intercession.
voorbly, (voorge-), maintain (keep) the lead.
voorbode, precursor; omen, portent.
voorbok, bell-goat, ringleader.
voorbrand, fire-break.
voorbring, (voorge-), bring up (in court); put forward.
voordat, before.
voordeel, (-dele), advantage, benefit, profit.
voordelig, (-e), profitable, advantageous.
voordoen, (voorge-), sig – as, pose (give oneself out) as.
voordra, (voorge-), recite (poem), declaim; render (musical composition); do a turn, put (present) (the case of).
voordrag, (-te), (good, bad) delivery, diction; recitation; lecture, address, recital.
vooreergister, three days ago.
voorent, fore-part, forefront.
voorgaan, (voorge-), walk (go) in front of, precede; lead the way; take precedence.
voorgaande, preceding.
voorgee, (voorge-), give a start; give odds; pretend.
voorgeewedstryd, handicap (-race).
voorgemeld, (-e), before-mentioned.
voorgenoem(d), (-de), vide voorgemeld.
voorgenome, proposed, intended.
voorgeskrewe, prescribed, set (book).
voorgeslag, ancestors, forefathers.
voorgestoelte, front seat.
voorgevoel, presentiment, foreboding.
voorgrond, foreground; forefront.
voorhamer, sledge-hammer.
voorhande, in stock (store).
voorheen, formerly, in the past.
voorhoede, van, vanguard; forwards.
voorhoof, forehead.
vooringenome, prejudiced, bias(s)ed.
voorjaar, spring.
voorkeer, (voorge-), stop, bar (block) the way; turn back (sheep).
voorkeur, preference.
voorkom, (voorge-), (1) gain the lead; appear in court; be found, occur; appear, seem.
voorkom, (–) (2) prevent; avert.
voorkome, -koms(te), appearance, air.
voorkry, (voorge-), get (20 yards) start, receive odds (points); reprimand.
voorlaaier(geweer), muzzle-loader.
voorlaaste, last but one.
voorlê, (voorge-), (1) lie in front; lie in wait.
voorlê, (voorge-), (2) put before, submit, state.
voorletter, initial; –s, initials.
voorliefde, predilection, liking.
voorlig, (voorge-), light; enlighten.
voorloper, leader; forerunner.
voorlopig, (-e), a. preliminary.
voorlopig, adv. for the time being.
voormalig, (-e), former, late.
voormeld, (-e), above-mentioned.
voornaam, Christian name.
voornaamwoord, pronoun.
voorneem, (voorge-): sig –, resolve.

voorneme, (-ns), intention, resolve.
vernoem(d), (-de), above-mentioned.
vooroor, forward, leaning forward.
vooroordeel, prejudice, bias.
vooroorloop, (vooroorge-), stoop.
voorop, in front.
vooropgeset, (-te), preconceived.
vooropstel, (vooropge-), postulate, premise.
voorouers, ancestors, forefathers.
voorperd, front horse, ringleader.
voorpoot, forepaw, foreleg.
voorportaal, porch, hall, vestibule.
voorpos, outpost.
voorpraat, (voorge-), stick up for, prompt.
voorpunt, front; forefront.
voorpunt, front; forefront.
voorraad, supply, stock.
voorradig, in stock (store).
voorrang, precedence; preference.
voorreg, privilege; prerogative.
voorsaat, (-sate), ancestor, forefather.
voorsê, (voorge-), prompt.
voorsê, (–), prophesy, predict.
voorsetsel, (-s), preposition.
voorsien, (–), foresee; provide, supply.
Voorsienigheid, Providence.
voorsit, (voorge-), place in front of, preside.
voorsitter, chairman, president.
voorskiet, (voorge-), advance, lend.
voorskieter, money-lender.
voorskoot, (-skote), apron.
voorskot, (-te), loan, advance.
voorskrif, (-te), prescription, instruction.
voorskrif, -skrywe, (voorge-), prescribe.
voorskyn: te – bring, produce.
voorslag, whip-lash; live-wire.
voorsorg, provision, precaution.
voorspel, n. prelude (mus.); prologue; forward-
play (rugby).
voorspel, (voorge-), (1) spell (word) to.
voorspel, (–), (2) foretell, prophesy.
voorspeler, forward (rugby).
voorspoed, prosperity.
voorspoedig, (-e), prosperous.
voorspooksel, (-s), (ill, good) omen.
voorspraak, intercession; mediator.
voorspring, (voorge-), forestall.
voorsprong, start; advantage.
voorstaan, (voorge-), stand in front; advocate,
champion.
voorstad, suburb.
voorstel, (-le), fore-carriage, proposal, motion.
voorstel, (voorge-), introduce; present (at court);
represent (scene); suggest; propose; move.
voorstelling, (-e, -s), representation; performance;
confirmation, conception, idea.
voorsten, voorstewe, stem, prow.
voortgaan, (voortge-), continue, go on, proceed.
voortgang, progress.
voortgeset, (-te), continued.
voortou, lead.
voortplant, (voortge-), propagate, transmit.
voortreflik, (-e), excellent, first-rate.
voortrek, (voorge-), favour; prefer.
voorts, further, besides.
voortsetting, continuation.
voortsit, (voortge-), continue; pursue.
voortskry, (voortge-), advance.
voortspruit, (voortge-): – uit, result (arise) from.
voortvarend, (-e), impetuous, impulsive.
voortvloei, (voortge-), flow along (on); – uit,
flow (result, arise, spring) from.
voortvlugtig, (-e), fugitive.
voortyds, formerly.
vooruit, in front of, in advance.

—T. Sakwb.

vooruitbetaal, (–), pay in advance.
vooruitdink, (vooruitge-), think ahead.
vooruitgaan, (vooruitge-), go first; get on, make
progress; improve.
vooruitkom, (vooruitge-), get on.
vooruitloop, (vooruitge-), walk on ahead of;
anticipate.
vooruitsien, (vooruitge-), look ahead; foresee.
vooruitsig, prospect, outlook.
vooruitstreef, -strewe, (vooruitge-), strive (to get
on), forge ahead.
voorvader, forefather, ancestor.
voorval, (-le), n. incident, event.
voorval, (voorge-), happen, occur, take place.
voorvegter, champion, advocate.
voorvoegsel, (-s), prefix.
voorwaar, indeed, truly.
voorwaarde, (-s), condition.
voorwaarts, (-e), forward.
voorwend, (voorge-), pretend, feign.
voorwerp, (-e), object, thing.
voos, (–, vose), spongy, woolly.
vorder, (ge-), get on, (make) progress.
vorder, (ge-), demand, ask.
vore: na –, to the front.
vorentoe, a. forward (pass); progressive (farmer);
smart, fine; first-class.
vorentoe, adv. forward; to the fore.
vorige, former, previous; last.
vorm, (-e, -s), n. form; shape; figure; mould
(for cake); voice (active & passive); formality,
form.
vorm, (ge-), form; shape, fashion.
vormleer, accidence (gram.).
vormlik, (-e), formal, conventional.
vors, (-te), n. (1) ridge, capping.
vors, (-te), n. (2) monarch, prince.
vors, (ge-), investigate, search.
vorstelik, (-e), princely, royal.
vort, gone, away.
vos, (-se), fox; bay, sorrel.
vou, (-e), n. fold; pleat; crease.
vou, (ge-), fold.
vra, vraag, (ge-), ask; question; charge.
vraag, (vrae), question; query.
vraagstuk, question, problem; rider.
vraagteken, question mark; query.
vraat, (vrate), glutton.
vraatsug, gluttony, voracity.
vraestel, examination paper.
vrag, (-te), load; cargo.
vragbrief, consignment-note, bill of lading.
vragmotor, motor lorry.
vragvry, carriage paid, post-free.
vrank, acid, tart, astringent.
vrat, (-te), wart.
vrede, peace.
vrederegter, justice of the peace.
vreedsaam, (-same), peaceful; peaceable.
vreemd, (-e), strange; foreign; queer.
vreemde, strange part (thing); foreign lands.
vreemdeling, (-e), stranger; foreigner.
vreemdsoortig, (-e), strange, motley.
vrees, vrese, n. fear, dread.
vrees, (ge-), fear, dread.
vreesaanja(g)end, (-e), terrifying.
vreesagtig, (-e), afraid; timid.
vreeslik, (-e), terrible, awful, dreadful.
vreeswekkend, (-e), awe-inspiring.
vreet, (ge-), feed on; gorge.
vrek, (-ke), n. miser, skinflint.
vrek, (ge-), die (of animals).
vrekte, mortality (of animals).
vreug(de), joy, gladness.
vriend, vrind, (-e), friend.

vriendelik, (-e), friendly, kind, amicable.
vriendskap, friendship; favour.
vriendskaplik, (-e), friendly.
vries, (ge-), freeze.
vrind, vide **vriend.**
vroed, (-e), wise.
vroedvrou, midwife
vroeër, (–, -e), a. earlier; former, previous.
vroeër, adv. earlier; formerly.
vroeg, (vroeë), a. and adv. early.
vroegtydig, adv. early, in good time.
vroe(g)-vroe(g), very early.
vroegpampoen, vegetable marrow, squash.
vroetel, (ge-), root (of pigs); burrow; wriggle, fidget.
vrolik, (-e), merry, cheerful; tipsy.
vroom, (–, vrome), pious, devout.
vrot, a. rotten, putrid, decayed.
vrot, (ge-), rot, decay, putrefy.
vrotpootjie(s), root-rot; eel-worm.
vrotsig, (-e), rotten, beastly.
vrou, (-e, -ens), woman; wife; queen (cards).
vroulik, (-e), womanly, feminine.
vrug, (-te), fruit (lit. & fig.)
vrugbaar, (-bare), fertile; prolific.
vruggebruik, usufruct.
vrugteboord, orchard.
vry, (–, -e), a. free; vacant.
vry, adv. freely; fairly.
vry, (ge-), court, flirt.
Vrydag, Friday; **Goeie V.,** Good Friday.
vryf, vrywe, (ge-), rub.
vrygesel, bachelor.
vrygewig, (-e), generous, liberal.
vryheid, (-hede), freedom, liberty.
vrykamer, spare (bed)room.
vrylaat, (vryge-), let off (free); release; leave (person) a free hand.
vryloop, (vryge-), free wheel.
Vrymesselaar, Freemason.
vrymoedig, (-e), frank, bold, unbashful.
vrypleit, (vryge-), get (person) off.
vrypostig, (-e), pert, forward, presumptuous.
vrysinnig, (-e), liberal.
vryskel(d), (vryge-), exempt; let off.

vryspreek, (vryge-), acquit; absolve.
vryspring, (vryge-), get off, escape.
vrystaan, (vryge-), be permitted.
Vrystaat, Free State.
vrystel, (vryge-), exempt.
vrywaar, (ge-): – teen (vir), (safe)guard against.
vrywel, well-nigh, practically.
vrywillig, (-e), free, voluntary.
vuil, (–, -e), a. dirty; filthy.
vuilgoed, dirt, rubbish; pus.
vuilis, vullis, dirt, refuse; pus; dirty swine (skunk).
vuis, (-te), fist.
vul, (-le, -lens), n. foal.
vul, (ge-), (1) foal.
vul, (ge-), (2) fill.
vulkaan, (-kane), volcano.
vullis, vide **vuilis.**
vulpen, fountain-pen.
vurig, (-e), fiery; ardent; fervent.
vurk, (-e), fork; pitchfork.
vuur, (vure), n. fire; fervour.
vuur, (ge-), fire.
vuur(h)erd, fireplace, hearth.
vuurhoutjie, (-s), oatch.
vuurmaakplek, fireplace, hearth.
vuurpyl, rocket; red-hot poker.
vuurspu(w)end, (-e), fire-spitting.
vuurtoring, lighthouse.
vuurvas, (-te), fire-proof.
vuurvreter, fire-eater; hothcad.
vuurwapen, firearm.
vuurwarm, boiling, hot; red-hot.
vy(g), (vye), fig.
vyand, (-e), enemy, foe.
vyandig, (-e), a. hostile, inimical.
vyeboom, fig-tree.
vyf, num. five.
vyftien, fifteen.
vyftig, fifty.
vyl, (-e), n. file.
vyl, (ge-), file.
vysel, (-s), mortar; screw-jack.
vywer, (-s), pond.

wa, (-ens), wag(g)on, van, truck; (railway-) carriage, coach; chariot.
waad, (ge-), wade, ford.
waag, wae, (ge-), risk, venture.
waaghals, dare-devil.
waagskaal, weegskaal: hy het sy lewe in die – gestel, he risked his life.
waagstuk, risk, daring deed.
waai, (-e), n.: **die – van die been,** the bend (hollow) of the knee.
waai, (-e), n. slap, smack.
waai, (ge-), blow; flutter; fan.
waaier, (-s), fan.
waak, (ge-), watch.
waaksaam, (-same), watchful, vigilant.
Waal, (Wale), Walloon.
waan, n. delusion.
waan, (ge-), imagine, fancy, think.
waansin, madness, insanity, lunacy.
waanwys, (–, -e), opinionated, bumptious.
waar, (ware), n. goods, ware(s).
waar, (–, ware), a. true.
waar, adv. where.
waar, conj. since, whereas.
waaraan, inter. pron. of (by, in, etc.) what?
waaraan, rel. pron. of (by, in, on, etc.) which.
waaragter, behind what?, behind which.
waaragtig, adv. truly, really.
waarbo, above (over) what?; above; (over) which.
waarborg, (-e), n. guarantee, security.
waarborg, (ge-), guarantee, safeguard.
waarby, near (by, etc.) what?; near (by, etc.) which.
waarde, (-s), value, worth.
waarde, a. dear.
waardeer, (ge-), appreciate, value.
waardeur, through what?; through (by) which.
waardevol, (-le), valuable.
waardig, (-e), worthy, dignified.
waarheen, where?; where . . . to?; where . . . to.
waarheid, (-hede), truth.
waarin, wherein?; in which.
waarlang(e)s, along (past, next to) what?; along (past, next to) which.
waarlik, truly, really, actually.
waarmee, with what?; with which.
waarmerk, (ge-), stamp, certify, hall-mark.
waarna, after which, at (to, etc.) what?; at (to, etc.) which.
waarnatoe, where . . . to?, to which.
waarneem, (waargeneem), observe; watch; make use of (an opportunity); attend to (one's duty); hold a temporary appointment.
waarnewens, beside which.
waarom, round what?; why, what for?; round which.
waaronder, under (beneath, among) what?; under (beneath, among) which.
waaroor, over (across, about, etc.) what?; over (across, about, etc.) which.
waarop, on (upon) what?; on (upon) which.
waarsê, (waargesê), tell fortunes.
waarsêer, (-s), fortune-teller.
waarsku, (ge-), warn, caution.
waarskynlik, (-e), a. probable, likely.
waarskynlik, adv. probably.
waarso, where.
waarsonder, without what?; without which.
waarteen, against what?; against which.
waartoe, to (for) what?; to which.
waartussen, between (among) what?; between (among) which.
waaruit, out of (from) what?; out of (from) which.

waarvan, of (about, from, etc.) what?; of (about, from, etc.) which.
waarvandaan, from where?; from which.
waarvoor, for what?; for (before, etc.) which.
waas, haze (in the air).
wa-as, axle-tree of a wag(g)on.
waatlemoen, vide **waterlemoen.**
wae, (ge-), vide **waag,** (ge-).
waenhuis, cart-shed, wag(g)onhouse.
wafel, (-s), waffle; wafer.
wag, (-te), n. watchman; sentry, guard.
wag, (ge-), wait.
waggel, (ge-), totter, reel, waddle; toddle.
wagter, (-s), watchman; shepherd.
wagwoord, password, watchword.
wakend, (-e), wakeful, vigilant.
wakker, awake; vigilant, active, brisk, smart.
waks, n. boot-polish, blacking.
waks, (ge-), polish, black.
wal, (-le), bank, shore, embankment.
walg, (ge-), nauseate, disgust.
Wallis, Wales.
Wallis(s)er, (-s), Welshman.
walm, (-e, -s), n. dense smoke; reek.
walm, (ge-), smoke.
wals, (-e), n. waltz; roller.
wals, (ge-), waltz; roll.
walvis, whale.
wanbegrip, false notion.
wand, (-e), wall.
wandaad, misdeed, outrage.
wandel, n.: **handel en –,** conduct of life.
wandel, (ge-), walk, take a walk; promenade.
wandluis, bug.
wang, (-e), cheek.
wangedrag, misbehaviour, misconduct.
wanhoop, n. despair, desperation.
wanhoop, (ge-), despair.
wanhopig, (-e), desperate, despairing.
wankel, (ge-), stagger; waver, vacillate.
wankelmoedig, (-e), irresolute, wavering.
wanklank, discord, jarring (discordant) note.
wanneer, adv. & conj. when.
wanorde, disorder, confusion.
wanskape, misshapen, deformed.
want, conj. because, as for.
wantrou, (ge-), distrust, mistrust.
wapen, (-s), n. weapon; badge.
wapen, (ge-), arm; reinforce (concrete).
wapper, (ge-), flutter, float, fly, wave.
war: in die –, in confusion.
warboel, confusion, muddle, tangle.
ware, goods, wares.
warhoofdig, (-e), scatter-brained.
warm, a. & adv. warm, hot.
warrel, (ge-), whirl, swirl.
warrelwind, whirlwind.
was, n. wax.
was, (ge-), (1) wax (of moon).
was, (ge-), (2) wash.
wasbak, wash-basin; washing-trough; sink.
wasem, n. vapour, steam; breath.
wasgoed, wash(ing), laundry.
wasig, (-e), hazy, vapoury; blurred.
wasser, waster (-s), washer.
wassery, (-e), hazy, vapoury, blurred.
wasser, waster, (-s), washer.
wassery, (-e), laundry-(works).
wat, inter. pron. what?
wat, rel. pron. who, that, which, what.
wat, indef. pron. something; whatever.
water, (-s), n. water; dropsy.
water, (ge-), water; make water.
waterdig, (-te), waterproof, watertight.
waterdraer, water-carrier; drone.

waterlei, (waterge-), irrigate, water.
waternat, soaked (to the skin).
waterpas, n. (water-)level.
waterskilpad, turtle.
waterstof, hydrogen.
watertand, (ge-): dit laat my –, it makes my mouth water.
watte, wadding; (med.) cotton-wool.
watter, what, which.
wawyd: – oop, wide open.
web, (-be), web.
wed, (ge-), bet, (lay a) wager.
weddenskap, (-pe), bet, wager.
Wederdoper, Anababtist.
wederhelf, better half.
wederkerig, (-e), mutual, reciprocal.
wederom, weersiens: (tot) –!, see you again!
we(d)erspannig, we(d)erstrewig, (-e), recalcitrant, rebellious.
we(d)ersyds, (-e), mutual.
wedervaar, (het –), befall, happen to.
wedloop, wedren, race.
wedstryd, match, competition, contest.
weduvrou, weduwee, widow.
wedywer, n. competition, rivalry.
wedywer, (ge-), compete, vie.
wee, (weë), n. woe, grief, pain.
wee!, interj. – my!, woe is me!
weë, weeg, (ge-), weigh.
weef, (ge-), weave.
weegskaal, (pair of) scales, balance.
week, (weke), n. week.
week, (–, weke), a. soft, tender.
week, (ge-), soak, soften, steep.
weeklaag, (ge-), lament, wail.
weekliks, (-e), weekly.
weelde, luxury; profusion, wealth.
weeluis, bug.
weemoed, melancholy, sadness.
ween, (ge-), weep, shed tears.
Weenen, Weenen.
weens, on account of, because of; for.
weer, n. weather.
weer, adv. again.
weer, (ge-), avert; exclude; defend.
weerbarstig, (-e), unruly, rebellious.
weerga, equal, match, peer.
weergalm, (ge-), v. resound, re-echo.
weergee, (weerge-), reproduce; render.
weerglas, barometer.
weerhaan, (lit. & fig.) weathercock.
weerhou, (–), restrain.
weerkaats, (–), reflect.
weerklink, (–), re-echo, resound.
weerlê, -leg, (–), refute, disprove.
weerlig, n. lightning.
weerlig, (ge-), lighten.
weerloos, (-lose), defenceless.
weersin, aversion, repugnance.
weerskante: aan –, on both sides.
we(d)erspannig, (-e), vide wederspannig.
weerspieël, (–), reflect, mirror.
weerspreek, (–), contradict, deny.
weerstaan, (–), resist, withstand.
weerstreef, -strewe, (–), oppose, resist.
weersye: (aan), –, on either side.
weerwil: in – van, in spite of.
weerwolf, wer(e)wolf; scarecrow.
weerwraak, revenge, retaliation.
wees, (wese), n. orphan.
wees, (is; was; ge–), be.
weesheer, Master of the Supreme Court.
weeshuis, orphanage.
weeskind, orphan.
weet, (wis, ge-), know.

weetgierig, (-e), eager to learn.
weg, (weë), n. way, road, route.
weg, adv. away; gone; lost.
wegbêre, (wegge-), put away; tuck in.
wegbring, (wegge-), take away.
wegdros, (wegge-), run away, desert.
weghelp, (wegge-), help to get away.
wegkruipertjie, hide and seek.
weglê, (wegge-), put aside.
wegmaak, (wegge-), do away with.
wegraak, (wegge-), get lost.
wegruim, (wegge-), clear away.
wegslaan, (wegge-), strike (beat, knock) away (off); swallow.
wegsteek, (wegge-), hide.
wegtoor, -tower, (wegge-), spirit away.
wegvoer, (wegge-), carry away, carry off, abduct.
wegwyser, guide; sign-post.
wei, (-e); weide, (-s), meadow; pasturage.
wei, n. whey.
wei(e), (ge-), graze, feed.
weids, (-e), grand, stately.
weier, (ge-), refuse, decline, deny.
weifel, (ge-), waver, hesitate.
weifelmoedig, (-e), irresolute, wavering.
weinig, (-e), little, few.
weiveld, pasture-land; pasturage.
wek, (ge-), (a)wake, call, rouse; create (curiosity), raise (hopes), rouse (indignation), stir.
wek, (ge-), (a)wake, call, rouse; create (curiosity), raise (hopes), rouse (indignation), stir.
wekker, (-s), alarm(-clock).
wel, n.: – en wee, weal and woe.
wel, adv. well.
welbehaaglik, (-e), comfortable; pleasant.
welbehae, pleasure.
welbespraak, (-te), well-spoken, fluent.
weldaad, boon, kind action.
weldadig, (-e), benevolent, charitable.
welbekend, (-e), right-thinking.
weldoener, (-s), benefactor.
weldra, soon, presently.
weledele: die – heer W. Smith, W. Smith, Esq.; Weledele Heer, Dear Sir.
weleer, formerly.
welf, welwe, (ge-), vault, arch.
welgaan, (welge-), fare well.
welgedaan, (-gedane), well-fed, plump.
welgeluksalig, (-e), blessed.
welgemoed, (-e), cheerful.
welgesteld, (-e), well-to-do, well-off.
welgevalle, pleasure.
welhaas, well-nigh, soon, shortly.
welig, (-e), luxuriant, rampant, rank.
weliswaar, indeed, it is true, to be sure.
welk, (ge-), fade, wither.
welke, inter. pron. what, which.
welkom, (-e), welcome.
wellig, perhaps, may be.
welluidend, (-e), melodious.
wellus, (-te), sensuality; delight.
welp, (-e), cub.
welriekend, (-e), fragrant, sweetsmelling.
welsand, wilsand, quicksand.
welslae, success.
welsprekend, (-e), eloquent.
welstand, health; well-being, welfare.
welsyn, well-being, welfare; health.
welvaart, prosperity; welfare.
welvarend, (-e), prosperous, thriving.
welvoeglik, (-e), becoming, seemly, decorous.
welwillend, (-e), benevolent, obliging.
wemel, (ge-), swarm, teem.
wen, (-ne), windlass.
wen, (ge-), accustom to.

wen, win, (ge-), win, again; reap.
wend(e), (ge-), turn.
wendam, catch-dam.
wending, (-s, -e), turn.
Wenen, Vienna.
wenk, (-e), hint.
wenkbrou, vide winkbrou.
wens, (-e), wish, desire.
wens, (ge-), wish, desire.
wentel, (ge-), revolve, rotate, wallow.
wentelbaan, orbit.
wenteltrap, (winding-)staircase.
werd, a. worth.
werda!, who goes there?
wêreld, (-e), world, region.
wêreldberoemd, (-e), world-famous.
wêrelds, (-e), worldly.
werf, (werwe), n. farmyard; shipyard.
werf, werwe, (ge-), recruit, enlist.
werk, (-e), n. work, labour.
werk, (ge-), work.
werkbaas, foreman.
werkesel, drudge, plodder.
werkgewer, employer.
werklik, (-e), a. real, actual, true.
werklik, adv. really, actually, truly.
werknemer, employee.
werksaam, (-same), industrious; – wees, work,
  (be employed).
werktuig, tool, implement, instrument.
werktuigkundige, (-s), mechanic(ian).
werktuiglik, (-e), mechanical, automatic.
werkwoord, verb.
werp, (ge-), throw, cast, hurl.
werplood, sounding-lead.
werpskyf, discus.
werskaf, (ge-), be busily engaged.
werwel, (-s), vertebra, button.
wes, n. vide weste.
wese, (-ns), creature, appearance; character;
  substance; existence.
wesel, (-s), weasel.
wesen(t)lik, (-e), real; essential, fundamental,
  material.
Wesleyaan, (-ane), Wesleyan.
wesp, (-e), wasp.
wes(te), west.
weste: buite –, unconscious.
Westers, (-e), Western, Occidental.
wet, (-te), n. law, act.
wete, knowledge.
wetens, knowingly.
wetenskap, science; knowledge.
wetenswaardig, (-e), worth knowing.
wetgeleerde, (-e), jurist, lawyer.
wetgewing, legislation.
wetlik, (-e), legal.
wetsontwerp, bill.
wetties, (-e), strict, rigid.
wettig, (-e), lawful, a. legal.
wettig, (ge-), legalize; justify, warrant.
wewenaar, (-s), widower.
wie, pron. who, whom.
wieë, wieg, (ge-), rock.
wieg, (wieë), n. cradle.
wiegel, (ge-), wobble, rock.
wiegelied, cradle-song, lullaby.
wiek, (-e), wing.
wiel, (-e), wheel.
wier, seaweed.
wierook, incense, frankincense.
wig, (-te), baby, babe, child, bairn.
wig, (-ge, wie), wedge.
wik, (ge-), weigh.
Wiking, (-e), Viking.

wikkel, (ge-), wrap, enfold, swaddle; involve;
  shake; hurry.
wiks, (ge-), slap, beat, flog.
wil, n. will, wish, desire.
wil, (wou, ge-), wish, intend, will.
wild, n. game.
wild, (-e), a. wild, savage, unruly.
wildebees, gnu, wildebeest.
wildernis, (-se), wilderness, waste.
wildtuin, game-reserve.
wildvreemd, (-e), quite strange.
wilg, (-e), willow.
wilge(r), wilkerboom, willow-tree.
willekeur, arbitrariness.
willekeurig, arbitrary.
willens: – en wetens, deliberately.
wilsand, welsand, quicksand.
wimpel, (-s), pendant, pennon.
wimper, (-e), (eye)lash.
win, vide wen.
wind, (-e), wind.
windbuks, air-gun; gas-bag, braggart.
winderig, (-e), windy; flatulent.
windhond, greyhound.
windmaak, (windge-), brag, boast, swank.
windmaker, a. smart, posh.
windmeul(e), windmill.
windorrel, (fig.) gas-bag, windbag.
windsel, (-s), bandage, swathe.
windskeef, (-skewe), skew, crooked, awry.
windskerm, windscreen.
windstilte, calm.
windstreek, point of the compass.
windswa(w)el, cliff-swallow.
wingerd, vineyard.
wink, (-e), n. swink, nod.
wink, (ge-), beckon; wink.
winkbrou, (-e), eyebrow.
winkel, (-s), n. shop, store; (work)shop.
winkelhaak, (carpenter's) square; (L-shaped tear
  in cloth).
winkelier, (-s), shopkeeper, shopman.
wins, (-te), profit, return; winnings.
winsgewend, (-e), profitable, paying.
winter, (-s), winter.
winter(s)hande, chilblained hands.
wip, (-pe), n. seesaw; trap; skip.
wip, (ge-),go up and down; wobble; tilt; whisk,
  skip, hop.
wipneus, turned-up (tip-tilted) nose.
wis, (ge-), wipe.
wis, (-se), a. certain, sure.
wiskunde, mathematics.
wispelturig, (-e), fickle, inconstant.
wissel, (-s), n. bill (of exchange), draft; points,
  switch (railway).
wissel, (ge-), exchange; interchange; change;
  cash (cheque), vary.
wisselbeker, floating trophy.
wisselbou, rotation of crops.
wisselstroom, alternating current.
wisseltand, milk-tooth.
wisselvallig, (-e), uncertain, precarious.
wit, n. white.
wit, a. white.
wit, (ge-), whitewash.
witborskraai, parson crow.
witseerkeel, diphtheria.
wittebroodsdae, honeymoon.
witvoetjie: – soek, curry favour.
woed, (ge-), rage.
woede, rage, fury.
woedend, (-e), furious.
woef!, bow-wow!
woeker, (g),e- practise usury; exert oneself.

woekeraar, (-s), usurer.
woel, (ge-), bustle, work hard, toss (about), fidget (about); (round).
woelig, (-e), restless, fidgety, busy.
woelwater, fidget, restless person.
Woensdag, Wednesday.
woeps!, flop!
woerts!, whiz(z).
woer-woer, whirr-whirr, whirligig.
woes, (-te), desolate, wild, fierce.
woestaard, (-s), brute, rough.
woesteny, (-e), wilderness.
woestyn, (-e), desert.
wol, wool.
wolf, (wolwe-), wolf.
wolfram, tungsten.
Wolga, Volga.
wolhaarpraatjies: wilde –, wild talk.
wolk, (-e), cloud.
wolkagtig, (-e), cloudy, cloud-like.
wolkbank, bank of clouds.
wolkekrabber, skyscraper.
wolwegif, strychnine.
wond, (-e), n. wound, injury.
wond, (ge-), wound, injure, hurt.
wonder, (-s), n. wonder, miracle, prodigy.
wonder, (ge-), wonder.
wonderbaarlik, (-e), miraculous, marvellous.
wonderlik, (-e), wonderful, strange.
wonderskoon, (–, -skone), exquisite.
wonderwerk, miracle.
woning, (-s), residence, dwelling.
woon, (ge-), live, reside, dwell.
woonagtig, resident, living.
woonstel, flat.
woord, (-e), word, term.
woordeboek, dictionary.
woordelik, (-e), verbal; verbatim.
woordeskat, vocabulary.
woordestryd, argument, dispute.
woordetwis, verbal difference, argument.
woordevloed, torrent (flow) of words.
woordewisseling, altercation, dispute.
woordhou, (woordge-), keep one's promise.
woordontleding, parsing.
woordryk, (-e), verbose, voluble.
woordvoerder, spokesman, mouthpiece.
word(e), (ge-), become, grow.
wording, genesis, birth, origin.
wors, (-e, -te), sausage.
worsbroodjie, hot dog.
worstel, (ge-), struggle, wrestle.
worstelstryd, struggle (for existence), contest.
wortel, (-s), n. root; carrot.
woud, (-e), forest, wood.
wraak, n. revenge, vengeance.

wraak, (ge-), disapprove of, object to.
wraakgierig, wraaklustig, (-e), revengeful, vindictive.
wraaksug, thirst for revenge.
wrak, (-ke), n. wreck, derelict.
wrang, (-e), bitter (fig.).
wreed, (wrede), cruel, inhuman.
wreedaard, (-s), brute, cruel person.
wreedaardig, (-e), cruel, inhuman.
wreek, (ge-), avenge.
wrewel, resentment, annoyance.
wring, (ge-), wring.
wroeging, (-e, -s), remorse.
wroet, (ge-), (fig.) burrow, grub.
wrok, n. grudge, rancour.
wrywing, (-e, -s), friction (also fig.).
wuf, (-te), frivolous.
wuif, wuiwe, (ge-), wave.
wurg, (ge-), strangle, throttle.
wurm, (-s), n. worm, maggot, grub.
wy(e), (ge-), ordain, devote; consecrate.
wyd, (wye), wide, broad, roomy.
wydlopig, (-e), verbose, long-winded.
wydsbeen, astride, astraddle.
wydte, (-s), width, breadth.
wyf, (wywe), vixen, shrew.
wyfie, (-s), female (animal).
wyk, (-e), n. quarter, ward.
wyk, (ge-), give way (ground), fall back, withdraw.
wyl, (-e), n. while, (short) time.
wyle, late, deceased.
wyn, (-e), wine.
wynbou, viticulture, wine-growing.
wynruit, rue.
wynstok, vine.
wynvlieg, wine-bibber, tippler.
wys(e), (wyse, wyses), n. manner, fashion; mood (grammar).
wys, (-e), a. wise, sensible; ill-tempered, vicious.
wys, (ge-), show, point out.
wysbegeerte, philosophy.
wyser, vide wyster.
wysgeer, (-gere), philosopher.
wysheid, wisdom; maak asof jy die – in pag het, pretend to all knowledge.
wysie, (-s), tune, melody.
wysig, (ge-), modify, amend.
wysmaak, (wysge-): iemand iets –, make a person believe something.
wysneus, wiseacre, prig, pedant.
wys(t)er, (-s), hand (of watch), pointer (of balance, etc.).
wyt, (ge-): iets aan iemand –, blame a person for something.

xilofoon, (-fone), xylophone.

Xhosa, Kôsa, (-s), X(h)osa.

ydel, (-e), vain (person, hope); idle (word), empty (talk).
yk, (ge-), gauge, stamp and verify.
yl, a. thin (air, beard), rare, rarified.
yl, (ge-), (1) be delirious, rave.
yl, (ge-), (2) hasten, hurry, rush.
ylhoofdig, (-e), light-headed, delirious.
ylings, hurriedly, hastily.
ys, n. ice.
ys, (ge-), shudder, shiver.
ysig, (-e), icy.
ysingwekkend, (-e), appalling, ghastly.
yskas, refrigerator, ice-safe.
yskoud, (-koue), icy-cold.

Ysland, Iceland.
yslik, (-e), horrible, ghastly, gruesome; enormous.
Yssee, Arctic Ocean.
yster, (-s), iron.
ysterklou: — in die grond slaan, take to one's heels; stand firm.
ysterlees, last, boot-tree.
ystervark, porcupine.
ywer, n. diligence, zeal, fervour.
ywer, (ge-), be zealous.
ywerig, (-e), diligent, zealous.
ywersugtig, (-e), jealous, envious.

Z

zeppelin, (-s), zeppelin.
zero, sero, (-'s), zero.
zits, (ge-), whiz(z).

Zoeloe, (-s), Zulu.
zoem, (-s), buzz, hum, drone.

Afkortings en Simbole

a annum, jaar.
aanw. aanwysend.
a.asb. of a.a.u.b. Antwoord as u blief.
Afr. CSV Afrikaanse Christen-Studentevereniging.
ACVV Afrikaanse Christelike Vrouevereniging.
A.D. Anno Domini (*in die jaar van ons Here*)
a.d. a dato (*vanaf datum*); ante diem (*voor die dag*).
adj. adjektief; adjudant.
ad lib. ad libitum (*na wens*)
adv. adverbium; advokaat.
akk. akkusatief.
al. alias (anders); alinea (reël).
alg. algemeen.
amp. ampère.
antw. antwoord.
appl. applous, applikant.
Apr. April.
art. artikel.
a.s. aanstaande.
ASB Afrikaanse Studentebond.
asb. asseblief.
asst. assistent.
ATKV Afrikaanse Taal- en Kultuurvereniging.
ATV Afrikaanse Taalvereniging.
a.u.b. as u blief.
Aug. Augustus.
a.w. aangehaalde werk.

B.A. Baccalaureus Artium.
bb. of brs. broeders.
B.Com. Baccalaureus Commercii.
B.D. Baccalaureus Divinitatis.
bep. bepaling.
bes. vnw. besitlike voornaamwoord.
bet. betaal; beteken; betekenis.
betr. betreklik.
bg. bogenoemde.
bl. bladsy; bladsye.
b.nw. byvoeglike naamwoord.
BO Bevelvoerende Offisier.
b.o. blaai om.
B.Sc. Baccalaureus Scientiae.
bv. byvoorbeeld.
b.v.p. been voor paaltjie.
bw. bywoord; bywoordelik.
byl. bylae.
byv. byvoeglik(e).

C Celsius.
c sent
ca. circa (*ongeveer*)
cf. confer(atur) (*vergelyk*).
Ch.B. Chirurgiae Baccalaureus.
Chr. Christus.
CJV Christelike Jongeliedevereniging.
cm sentimeter.
cresc. crescendo (*toenemend in sterkte*)

d. denarius (*pennie*)
dat. datief; datum.
D.D. Doctor Divinitatis.
d.d. de dato (*vanaf datum*).
def. definisie.
dept. departement.
Des. Desember.
dgl. dergelike.
Di. Dinsdag.
di. domini (*dominees*)
d.i. dit is.
dial. dialek; dialekties.
disk. diskonto.
dist. distrik.

D.Lit(t). Doctor Lit(t)erarum.
dnr. dienaar.
Do. Donderdag.
do. dito.
dos. dosyn.
DPW Departement van Publieke Werke.
D.Phil. Doctor Philosophiae.
dr. debiteur; dokter; doktor.
ds. dominus (*dominee*).
D.V. Deo Volente (*as God wil*).
dw. (dnr.), dienswillige (dienaar).
d.w.s. dit wil sê.

e.a. en ander(e).
Ed. Edele.
ed. edisie.
Ed.Agb. Edelagbare.
e.d.m. en dergelike (dies) meer.
eerw. eerwaarde.
e.g. eersgenoemde.
e.k. eerskomende.
Eks. Eksellensie.
ekv. enkelvoud.
ens. ensovoort(s).
e.s.m. en so meer.

FAK Federasie van Afrikaanse Kultuurvereninge.
fig. figuur; figuurlik.
FM frekwensiemodulasie.
fol. folio.
fr. frank.
fut. futurum (*toekomende tyd*).

g gram.
geb. gebore; gebou; geboul.
Gebr. gebroeders.
gen. genitief.
genl. generaal.
Geref. Gereformeerd.
Ges. Gesang.
get. geteken; getuie.
GGD grootste gemene deler.

h uur.
ha hektaar.
h.c. honoris causa (*eregraad*).
H. d. L. Heil die Leser.
H.Ed. Hoogedele.
H.Eerw. Hoogeerwaarde.
H.Eks. Haar Eksellensie.
Herv. Hervormd(e).
hfst. hoofstuk.
H.Gel. Hooggeleerde.
HJS Hoër Jongenskool.
hl hektoliter.
H.M. Haar Majesteit.
HMS Hoër Meisieskool.
HOD Hoër Onderwysdiploma.
HPK Hoofposkantoor.
hs. handskrif.
hss. handskrifte.
hulpww. hulpwerkwoord.
h/v hoek van.

ib(id). ibidem (*op dieselfde plek*).
id. idem (*dieselfde*).
i.e. id est (*dit is*).
i.e.w. in een woord.
ind. indikatief.
inf. infinitief.
ins. insonderheid.
i.p.v. in plaas van.
i.s. insake.

i.v.m. in verband met.

Jan. Januarie.
jg. jaargang.
jhr. jonkheer; jongeheer.
jl. jongslede.
jr. junior.

kap. kapitaal; kapittel.
kapt. kaptein.
k.a.v. koste, assuransie, vrag.
k.b.a. kontant by aflewering.
kg kilogram.
KGV kleinste gemene veelvoud.
Kie. Kompanjie.
kl kiloliter.
km kilometer.
k.m.b. kontant met bestelling.
km/h kilometer per uur.
kol. kolonel.
KP Kaapprovinsie.
kPa kilopascal.
kr. krediteer; krediteur.
k.s.b. kombuis, spens, badkamer.
kW kilowatt.
kw. kwartaal; kwadraat.

ℓ liter.
lg. laasgenoemde.
Lit(t).D. Lit(t)erarum Doctor.
l.l. laaslede.
L.L.B. Legum Baccalaureus.
LPR Lid van die Provinsiale Raad.
L.S. Lectori Salutem (*Heil die leser*).
luit. luitenant.
LUK Lid van die Uitvoerende Komitee.
LV Lid van die Volksraad.
LW Let Wel.

m meter.
M.A. Magister Artium.
Ma. Maandag.
maj. majoor.
maks. maksimum.
m.a.w. met ander woorde.
M.B. Medicinae Baccalaureus.
m.b.t. met betrekking tot.
M.D. Medicinae Doctor.
mej. mejuffrou.
mejj. mejuffroue.
mev. mevrou.
mevv. mevroue.
mg milligram.
m.i. myns insiens.
min. minimum; minister.
min minuut.
ml milliliter.
Ml megaliter.
mm millimeter.
Mnl. Middelnederlands(e).
mnr. meneer.
Mrt. Maart.
ms. manuskrip.
mss. manuskripte.
mv. meervoud.
My. Maatskappy.

N. noord.
n.a.v. na aanleiding van.
N.B. Nota Bene (*Let Wel*).
n.C. na Christus.
Ndl. Nederland /s(e).
Ned. Geref. Nederduits Gereformeerd.
Ned. Herv. Nederduits Hervormd.

nl. naamlik.
nm. namiddag.
NOIK Nederlandse Oos-Indiese Kompanjie.
nom. nominatief.
Nov. November.
nr. (no.) nommer.
Ns. Naskrif.
NUSAS Nasionale Unie van Suid-Afrikaanse Studente.
nv. naamval.
nw. naamwoord.

O oos.
o.a. onder andere.
ob. obiit (*is oorlede*).
oef. oefening.
o.i. onses insiens.
Okt. Oktober
o.m. onder meer.
onderw. onderwerp.
ong. ongeveer.
onvolt. onvoltooid.
oorg. oorganklik.
oorl. oorlede.
OP Oostelike Provinsie.
op. opus (*werk*).
opm. opmerking.
ord. ordonnansie.
oudl. ouderling.
OVS Oranje-Vrystaat.
OVSOV Oranje-Vrystaatse Onderwysersvereniging.
o.w. onder wie.

p. pagina; per; piano; pro.
p.a. per adres; per annum (per jaar).
par. paragraaf.
penm. penningmeester.
perf. perfectum.
pers. persoonlik.
Ph.D. Philosophiae Doctor.
Pk. Poskantoor.
p.m. per maand; per mensem; plus minus.
PMG posmeester-generaal.
pp. paginas.
p.p. per precurationem (*by volmag*).
P.R. Poste Restante; Provinsiale Raad.
pres. president.
prof. professor.
proff. professore.
prok. prokureur.
prop. proponent.
prov. provinsiaal; provinsie.
prox. proximo (*aanstaande*).
P.S. Post Scriptum.
Ps. Psalm.

qq. qualitate qua (*in die hoedanigheid van*).

r. radius; reël.
RAK Raad vir Atoomkrag.
RAU Randse Afrikaanse Universiteit.
resp. respektiewelik.
R.I.P. requiescat in pace (*rus in vrede*).
R.K. Rooms-Katoliek(e).
RSA Republiek van Suid-Afrika.
R.S.V.P. Répondez s'il vous plaît (*antwoord a.u.b.*).
RVK Rugbyvoetbalklub.

s sekonde; sub; sekundus.
SA Suid-Afrika; Senior Advokaat.
SAOU Suid-Afrikaanse Onderwysersunie.
SAP Suid-Afrikaanse Polisie.
SAS&H Suid-Afrikaanse Spoorweë en Hawens.

SAP Suid-Afrikaanse Polisie.
SAS & H Suid-Afrikaanse Spoorweë en Hawens.
S.Ed. Sy Edele.
S.Ed.Agb. Sy Edelagbare.
S.Eerw. Sy Eerwaarde.
sek. sekundus.
sekr. sekretaris.
sekre. sekretaresse.
S.Eks. Sy Ekselensie.
sen. senator.
sers. sersant.
sert. sertifikaat.
sg. sogenaamd.
S.H. Sy Heiligheid; Sy Hoogheid.
S.H.Ed. Sy Hoogedele.
s.i. syns insiens.
s.j. sonder jaartal.
S.M. Sy Majesteit.
s.nw. selfstandige naamwoord.
spr. spreker.
sr. senior.
ss. stoomskip.
St. Sint.
st. standerd; sterk.
str. straat.
sts. standerds.
subj. subjek; subjektief.
SWA Suidwes-Afrika.

t metrieke ton.
t.a.p. ter aangehaalde plaatse.
t.a.v. ten aansien van.
t.a.v. tout a vous (geheel die uwe).
teenw. teenwoordig.
telw. telwoord.
temp. temperatuur.
tes. tesourier.
Th(eol). D. Theologiae Doctor.
t.o.v. ten opsigte van.
t.t. totus tuus (geheel die uwe).
tw. tussenwerpsel.
t.w. te wete.

U Ed. U Edele.
UK Uitvoerende Komitee; Universiteit Kaapstad.
US Universiteit Stellenbosch.
univ. universiteit.

v. vers; vide (kyk).
v.a.b. vry aan boord.
vb. voorbeeld.
v.C. voor Christus.
V.D.M. Verbi Divini (Del) Minister.
ver. verbuiging; verbum.
verklw. verkleinwoord.
verl. verlede.
vgl. vergelyk.
v/h voorheen.
vk. vierkant(e).
vlg. volgende.
vm. voormiddag.
vnw. voornaamwoord.
voegw. voegwoord.
vol. volume.
volt. voltooid.
voors. voorsetsel; voorsitter.
voorv. voorvoegsel.
voorw. voorwerp.
v.o.s. vry op spoor.
vs. versus (teen).
VSA Verenigde State van Amerika.
VSB Vroue-Sendingbond.
VVO Verenigde Volke(-Organisasie).

W watt; Wes.
W. wissel.
WAT Woordeboek van die Afrikaanse Taal.
wed. weduwee.
WelEd. Weledele.
wnd. waarnemend.
wo. waaronder.
WP Westelike Provinsie.
ww. werkwoord.

ENGELS – AFRIKAANS

a (an), 'n.
aback, agteruit; **taken –,** verbluf.
abandon, v. opgee, verlaat.
abandon, n. oorgawe; onverskilligheid.
abashed, verleë, beskaamd; verbluf.
abate, verminder, afneem; bedaar.
abattoir, slagpaal.
abbey, abdy, klooster; kloosterkerk.
abbot, ab.
abbreviate, afkort, verkort; verklein.
abdicate, afstand doen van, neerlê.
abdomen, buik, maag.
abduct, ontvoer, skaak; wegvoer.
aberration, afwyking; misstap.
abet, aanhits, opstook; steun.
abeyance: in –, buite werking, agterweë.
abhor, verafsku, verag.
abhorrent, afskuwelik, afstootlik.
abide, bly; volhard; wag op; verdra.
ability, bekwaamheid; gawe, talent.
abject, a. kruipend; volslae.
abjure, afsweer, versaak.
ablative, ablatief.
ablaze, aan (die) brand; glansend.
able, bekwaam, knap; in staat.
able-bodied, sterk (geboud), weerbaar.
ablution, afwassing, reiniging.
abnormal, abnormaal; misvorm(d).
aboard, aan boord.
abode, verblyf, woning, tuiste.
abolish, afskaf; ophef; herroep.
A-bomb, atoombom.
abominable, afskuwelik, verfoeilik, gruwelik.
abomination, verafskuwing, gruwel.
aborigines, oorspronklike bewoners.
abound, oorvloei, volop wees.
about, prep. om, rondom; omtrent, ongeveer; met betrekking tot, oor; aan, by, in.
about, adv. om, rond.
above, prep. bo, bo-oor, bo-op; bokant; meer as.
above, adv. omhoog, bo(we).
above, a. bo(we)staande.
aboveboard, eerlik, reguit, rondborstig.
above-mentioned, bo(we)genoemd.
abrade, afskawe, afskuur; afvrywe.
abreast, naasmekaar.
abridge, verkort, afkort, inkort, beperk.
abroad, van huis, buitenshuis.
abrogate, herroep, ophef, afskaf.
abscess, geswel, verswering, abses.
absence, afwesigheid; gebrek.
absent, a. afwesig; verstrooid.
absolute, volstrek; totaal; absoluut.
absolutely, totaal, heeltemal, absoluut.
absolve, kwytskeld, vryspreek, ontslaan.
absorb, opsuig, intrek, absorbeer; in beslag neem.
abstain, (sig) onthou; wegbly, (sig) onttrek.
abstainer, afskaffer.
abstemious, onthoudend, matig.
abstract, a. afgetrokke, teoreties, abstrak.
abstract, v. afskei; af-, ont- uittrek; abstraheer; uittreksel maak.
abstruse, verborge, diepsinnig, duister.
absurd, onsinnig, dwaas, ongerymd.
abundance, oorvloed, rykdom, menigte.
abuse, v. misbruik, mishandel; uitskel.
abut, grens (aan).
abyss, afgrond.
Abyssinia, Abessinië.
acacia, akasia.
academy, akademie; hoërskool.
accede, toetree; instem, toestem.
accelerate, versnel; bespoed; vervroeg.
accelerator, versneller.

accent, n. aksent, nadruk, klem (-toon); uitspraak.
accentuate, beklemtoon, beklem, nadruk lê op.
accept, aanneem, ontvang, aanvaar.
acceptance, ontvangs; aanvaarding.
accepted, aangenome; gangbaar.
access, toegang; vermeerdering.
accessary, n. medepligtige; bybehoorsel.
accession, toetreding; aanvaarding; (troons)-bestyging; toestemming.
accessory, n. bykomstigheid, toebehoorsel, onderdeel.
accident, ongeluk; toeval.
acclaim, v. toejuig, verwelkom.
accommodate, aanpas; versoen; voeg, skik; van diens wees; inneem, herberg, bevat.
accommodating, inskiklik, tegemoetkomend.
accompany, begelei, vergesel.
accomplice, medepligtige, handlanger.
accomplish, uitvoer, tot stand bring.
accomplished, verfyn; begaaf; volmaak.
accord, v. ooreenstem; toestaan, versoen.
accordingly, gevolglik, bygevolg, aldus.
accost, aanspreek; aanklamp.
account, v. beskou; verklaar; verantwoord.
account, n. rekening; rekenskap; verklaring; verslag.
accountancy, boekhoukunde.
accountant, boekhouer; rekenmeester.
accrue, toeneem, oploop; voortspruit.
accumulate, ophoop; vermenigvuldig, opgaar.
accumulator, versamelaar; opgaarbattery.
accurate, noukeurig, nougeset.
accusative, akkusatief.
accuse, beskuldig, aankla.
accused, aangeklaagde, beskuldigde.
accustom, wen, gewoond maak.
ace, aas, een.
acetylene, asetileen.
ache, v. seer wees, pyn ly.
ache, n. pyn.
achieve, uitvoer, verrig; presteer.
acid, a. suur, wrang; skerp, bits(ig).
acid, n. suur.
acknowledge, erken, toegee.
acme, hoogtepunt, keerpunt.
acorn, akker, eikel.
acquaint, bekend maak, in kennis stel.
acquaintance, kennis; bekendheid; kennismaking.
acquiesce, berus, (sig) skik; instem.
acquire, verwerf, aanskaf.
acquisition, aanskaffing, aanlering; aanwins.
acquit, vryspreek, ontslaan; (sig) kwyt.
acre, acre.
acrid, bitter; wrang, skerp.
acrobat, kunstemaker, toudanser, akrobaat.
across, prep. oor; anderkant; deur.
across, adv. oormekaar, oorkruis.
act, v. handel, tewerk gaan; waarneem.
act, n. handeling, daad; bedryf; wet.
acting, a. agerend, waarnemend; werkend.
action, handeling, daad, werking; (reg)saak; geveg; aksie.
active, bedrywig, aktief, werksaam; werkend; **– voice,** bedrywende vorm.
actor, toneelspeler, akteur; dader; bewerker.
actual, werklik, wesenlik; teenswoordig.
actually, werklik, regtig, waarlik.
actuate, (aan)dryf, aansit, beweeg, moveer.
acumen, skerpsinnigheid, insig.
acute, skerp; fyn, skerpsinnig, gevat; akuut.
adage, spreekwoord, spreuk.
adamant, onversetlik, kliphard, staalhard.
adapt, geskik maak; aanwend; aanpas (by).

add, byvoeg, optel.
adder, adder; slang; –'s tongue, slangtong.
addict, oorgee aan; verslaaf aan.
addition, toevoeging, vermeerdering; optelsomme, optelling; byvoegsel.
addle, verwar; vrot (verrot).
address, v. aanspreek; adresseer; toespreek.
address, n. adres; toespraak, rede.
adduce, aanvoer, aanhaal, bybring.
adept, a. ervare, oulik, bedrewe.
adept, n. ingewyde, meester.
adequate, doeltreffend; genoegsaam, eweredig (aan).
adhere, vaskleef; aanhang; bly by.
adherent, kleefstof; aanhanger, voorstander.
adhesive, klewerig; vasklewend.
adieu, vaarwel, goeiendag.
adjacent, aangrensend, belendend; naby.
adjective, byvoeglike naamwoord.
adjoin, grens aan; aanheg.
adjourn, verdaag, skors, uitstel.
adjudicate, beoordeel, bereg; verklaar.
adjunct, a. toegevoeg, adjunk . . . ; hulp- . . .
adjunct, n. byvoegsel, aanhangsel.
adjure, besweer; smeek.
adjust, skik, reël; (ver)stel, regstel.
adjutant, adjudant.
administer, bestuur, waarneem, administreer; uitoefen; toedien.
admirable, bewonderenswaardig, uitstekend.
admire, bewonder, vereer, admireer.
admit, toelaat; aanneem; erken, toegee; toestaan.
admonish, vermaan, raai, waarsku, teregwys.
ado, gedoente, ophef.
adolescent, n. jeugdige persoon.
adopt, aanneem; oorneem; kies.
adore, aanbid, vereer, verafgod.
adorn, versier, tooi, opskik.
adrift, drywend; turn –, aan sy lot oorlaat.
adroit, behendig; tak(t)vol, handig.
adulation, vleiery, inkruipery.
adult, a. volwasse, uitgegroei.
adult, n. volwassene, grootmens.
adulterate, vervals; verdun; besmet.
advance, v. vooruitkom, vorder; nader; styg; vooruitbring; uitsteek; verhaas; bevorder, verhoog; voorbring, opper; voorskiet.
advantage, n. voordeel; voorsprong.
advent, koms, nadering; advent (R. Kerk).
adventure, n. onderneming, waagstuk, avontuur; voorval.
adventurer, geluksoeker, avonturier.
adventurous, avontuurlik, waaghalsig; ondernemend.
adverb, bywoord.
adversary, teenstander, opponent, vyand.
adversity, teenspoed, ongeluk.
advertise, aankondig, adverteer.
advertisement, aankondiging, bekendmaking; advertensie, reklame.
advice, raad; berig; advies.
advisable, raadsaam, gerade.
advise, (aan)raai; laat weet; meedeel, adviseer.
adviser, raadgewer, raadsman, adviseur.
advocate, n. advokaat; voorstander.
advocate, v. bepleit, voorstaan, aanbeveel.
aerate, lug; –d water, spuitwater.
aerial, n. lugdrade.
aerodrome, vliegveld.
aeroplane, vliegmasjien, vliegtuig.
aesthetic, esteties, skoonheids- . . .
afar, ver, in die verte.
affable, vriendelik, minsaam, inskiklik.
affair, saak, besigheid, affêre.

affect, voorgee, voorwend; hou van; raak, beïnvloed, werk op.
affectation, aanstellings, gemaaktheid.
affection, aandoening; liefde; siekte.
affectionate, toegeneë, liefhebbend; aandoenlik; minsaam.
affidavit, beëdigde verklaring.
affiliate, aansluit; aanneem.
affinity, verwantskap; ooreenkoms.
affirm, bevestig; verseker, bekragtig.
affix, v. aanheg, opplak; byvoeg; verbind.
afflict, bedroef, kwel, teister, besoek.
affluence, oorvloed, weelde, rykdom.
afford, verskaf, gee; oplewer.
afforest, bebos, bosse aanplant.
affray, oploop, vegparty, bakleiery.
affront, v. beledig, affronteer, trotseer.
afield, in die veld; op die slagveld.
aflame, in vlam, aan brand; gloeiend.
afoot, te voet; op die been; aan die gang.
aforementioned, voornoemd, voormeld.
afore-said, voornoemd.
afraid, bang, bevrees.
African, n. Afrikaan; South –, Suid-Afrikaner.
after, prep, na; agter.
after, adv. agterna, later.
after, conj. na(dat).
after, a. later, agter-, na . . .
aftermath, na-oes, nasleep, nadraai.
afternoon, agtermiddag, namiddag.
afterthought, later oorweging; uitvlug.
afterwards, naderhand, daarna, later.
again, weer, nog eens, opnuut; verder; aan die ander kant.
against, teen.
agape, met ope mond, verstom.
age, n. ouderdom, leeftyd, eeu.
age, v. oud word, verouder, oud maak.
agency, agentskap; werking, bemiddeling.
agent, agent; bewerker; werktuig, agens; middel.
agglomeration, opeenhoping, versameling.
aggrandizement, verryking, verheerliking.
aggravate, vererger.
aggregate, n. versameling; totaal; geheel.
aggression, aanval, aanranding; aggressie.
aghast, ontset, versteld.
agile, rats, vlug, lenig.
agitate, beweeg, skud; opwek, verontrus; agiteer.
agitator, oproermaker, onrusstoker.
aglow, gloeiend, verhit, warm; blosend.
ago, gelede.
agog, opgewonde, verlangend, belus.
agony, pyn, angs; foltering, kwelling.
agree, ooreenstem, instem, akkordeer, eens wees; stryk.
agreeable, aangenaam; gewillig.
agreement, ooreenstemming, ooreenkoms.
agriculture, landbou, landboukunde.
aground, aan die grond, gestrand.
ahead, vóór, vooruit, voorop, vooraan.
aid, v. help, bystaan.
ail, skeel, skort; siek wees.
ailment, siekte, ongesteldheid.
aim, v. mik, korrel.
aim, n. doel, oogmerk.
air, n. lug, windjie; houding; wysie.
air, v. lug; droogmaak; lug gee aan.
air-gun, windbuks, windgeweertjie.
airmail, lugpos.
airtight, lugdig.
aisle, vleuel; sygang; paadjie.
ajar, op 'n skrefie, op 'n kier.
akin, verwant.
alabaster, albas.
alacrity, lewendigheid; graagte, gretigheid.

alarm, n. alarm; skrik, angs; wekker.
alarm, v. skrikmaak.
alarm-clock, wekker.
alas, helaas.
albatross, albatros, stormvoël.
albumen, wit van eier, eiwit.
alcohol, alkohol; sterk drank.
alcove, alkoof; somerhuisie, prieel.
alert, waaksaam, wakker, vlug.
algebra, stelkunde, algebra.
alien, n. vreemde, uitlander.
alienate, vervreem; ontvreem; afkonkel.
alight, v. afstyg; uitstyg; land, neerstryk.
alight, a. aan die brand.
align, in gelid stel, opstel, rig.
alike, a. gelyk, eenders.
alike, adv. eenders; gelykop; eweseer.
alive, lewendig; in lewe.
all, a. alle, al die, algar; heel, die hele.
all, pron. algar, alles.
all, adv. heeltemal, totaal.
allay, verlig, versag, matig, verminder; bedaar.
allege, beweer, aanvoer.
allegiance, trou, getrouheid.
alleviate, verlig, versag, lenig.
alley, steeg, gang.
alliance, verbond, verwantskap; huwelik.
alligator, kaaiman, alligator.
allocate, aanwys, toeken; plek aanwys.
allot, toewys, toeken, toedeel.
allow, toestaan, toelaat, toegee.
allowance, vergunning; (aan)deel; toelae; afslag.
alloy, n. mengsel; allooi; kwaliteit.
all-round, a. alsydig, veelsydig.
allude: - to, sinspeel (doel) op, bedoel.
allure, aantrek, aanlok, verlei.
alluring, aanloklik, verleidelik.
allusion, sinspeling, toespeling.
alluvial, aangeslibte; rivier- . . .
ally, v. verbind, verenig.
ally, n. bondgenoot.
almanac, almanak, kalender.
almighty, a. almagtig; tamaai, yslik.
almond, amandel.
almost, amper, byna.
alms, aalmoes, liefdegawe.
aloe, aalwee (aalwyn), garingboom.
aloft, bo, omhoog, hoog; na bo.
alone, alleen, eensaam; net, enkel.
along, prep. lang(e)s, langsaan.
along, adv. aan, vooruit, deur.
alongside, naas(aan), langsaan.
aloof, apart, op 'n afstand, opsy.
aloud, hard(op), luid.
alphabet, alfabet, abc.
Alps, Alpe.
already, al, (al)reeds.
Alsation, Elsasser; wolf(s)hond.
also, ook, eweneens; verder.
altar, altaar.
alter, verander, wysig.
altercate, twis, kibbel, krakeel.
alternative, n. alternatief, keus.
although, al, (al)hoewel, ofskoon.
altitude, hoogte, diepte; hoë rang.
alto, alt (stem).
altogether, altesame; glad, heeltemal.
alum, aluin.
always, altyd, altoos, gedurig, aljimmer.
am, is.
amalgamate, meng, amalgameer, saamsmelt.
amass, ophoop, versamel.
amateur, amateur, dilettant, liefhebber.
amaze, verbaas, dronkslaan, verstom.
ambassador, gesant, ambassadeur.

amber, barnsteen, amber.
ambiguous, dubbelsinnig; onduidelik, duister.
ambition, eersug, ambisie; doel, strewe.
ambitious, eersugtig, ambisieus.
amble, v. pasgang (telgang) loop, trippel.
amble, n. telgang, pasgang, trippelgang.
ambulance, ambulans, veldhospitaal.
ambush, n. hinderlaag, val.
ambush, v. in 'n hinderlaag lok.
amend, wysig; verbeter; amendeer.
amends, make -, vergoed.
amenity, aangenaamheid, innemendheid; gerief.
American, Amerikaner.
amiable, vriendelik, beminlik, minsaam.
amicable, vriendelik, vriendskaplik.
amid, amidst, tussen, onder, te midde van.
amiss, verkeerd; kwalik.
ammonia, ammoniak, vlugsout.
ammunition, ammunisie, skietgoed.
amnesty, amnestie, vergifnis.
among, amongst, onder, tussen.
amount, v. bedra, beloop.
amount, n. bedrag, som; opbrengs; hoeveelheid.
amphiteatre, amfiteater; strydperk.
ample, ruim, wyd; oorvloedig.
amplify, uitbrei, vergroot; uitwei.
amply, ruim, ruimskoots, volop.
amputate, afsit, afsny, amputeer.
amuck, amok.
amuse, vermaak, amuseer.
amusing, vermaaklik, amusant, snaaks.
an, 'n.
anaemia, bloedarmoede.
anaesthetic, n. verdowingsmiddel.
anaesthetize, verdoof, onder narkose bring.
analogy, analogie, ooreenkomstigheid.
analyse, ontleed, analiseer; ondersoek.
analysis, ontleding, analise, opsomming.
anarchy, regeringloosheid, anargie; wanorde.
anatomy, ontleedkunde, anatomie.
ancestor, voorouer, voorvader.
ancestry, voorouers; afkoms, geboorte.
anchor, n. anker.
anchor, v. anker; vasmaak.
anchovy, ansjovis.
ancient, a. oud, outyds; ouderwets.
and, en.
anecdote, verhaaltjie, anekdote.
anew, weer, opnuut.
angel, engel(tjie); -'s food, vrugteslaai.
anger, n. boosheid, gramskap, toorn.
anger, v. vertoorn, kwaad maak.
angle, n. hoek; (hoekige) punt.
angler, hengelaar, visvanger.
Anglican, Anglikaans.
angry, kwaad, boos.
anguish, angs, benoudheid, pyn, foltering.
animal, n. dier.
animal, a. dierlik.
animate, v. besiel, aanspoor, opwek.
animate, a. lewend, lewendig.
animosity, vyandigheid; verbittering.
aniseed, anys(saad).
ankle, enkel.
annals, kronieke, jaarboeke, annale.
annex, v. aanheg, toevoeg; annekseer.
annex, annexe, n. aanhangsel, bylae; bygebou.
annihilate, vernietig, wegveeg, uitwis.
anniversary, n. verjaar(s)dag, gedenkdag.
announce, aankondig, (aan)meld.
annoy, lastig val, pla, kwaadmaak.
annoyance, las, ergernis, hindernis.
annual, a. jaarliks, jaar- . . .
annual, n. jaarboek, -blad; eenjarige plant.
annul, vernietig; nietig verklaar; ophef.

anoint, salf, smeer.
anomaly, onreëlmatigheid, anomalie.
anon, aanstons.
anonymous, naamloos, anoniem.
another, 'n ander, 'n ander een; nog een.
answer, n. antwoord; verdediging; oplossing.
answer, v. antwoord, beantwoord.
ant, mier.
antagonize, teenwerk; in die harnas ja.
antagonism, vyandskap; teenstrydigheid.
antagonist, teenparty, teenstander.
Antarctic, Antarktika.
antbear, -eater, erdvark, miervreter.
antecedent, n. antesedent; –s, verlede.
antelope, antiloop, wildsbok.
antemeridian, voormiddags.
antenna, voelhoring; lugdraad.
antenuptial: – contract, huweliksvoorwaarde(s).
anthem: national –, volkslied.
ant-hill, mier(s)hoop.
anthology, bloemlesing.
anthrax, miltsiekte.
anthropology, antropologie.
antibiotic, antibiotikum
anticipate, voor wees, voorkom; vooruit oor-
    weeg; voorsien, verwag; verhaas.
antics, bokkespronge, kronkelinge; malstreke.
antidote, teengif.
antipathy, antipatie, teensin, afkeer.
antiquated, verouderd, ouderwets, antiek.
antique, n. ou kunswerk.
antiseptic, n. ontsmettingsmiddel, -stof.
anvil, aambeeld.
anxiety, angs, onrus; begeerte.
anxious, besorg; begerig.
any, enige; iedere; elke; soveel (-ver, -lank, ens.).
anybody, iedereen, elkeen; iemand.
anyhow, adv. sommerso, in elk geval.
anyhow, conj. hoe dit ook al sy, in elk geval.
anyone, iedereen (enigeen), wie ook; iemand.
anything, alles, enigiets; iets.
anyway, hoe dit ook mag wees, in elk geval.
anywhere, orals; êrens.
apace, snel, hard; by elke tree.
apart, afsonderlik, apart; alleen; opsy.
apartment, vertrek, kamer.
apathy, ongevoeligheid, onverskilligheid, apatie.
ape, n. aap; naäper.
ape, v. naäap.
aperient, purgeermiddel, purgasie.
aperture, opening.
apex, punt, top, toppunt.
aphis, bladluis.
apiary, byehok, byehuis; byekamp.
apiece, (per) stuk, elk.
apologize, (sig) verontskuldig, ekskuus (versko-
    ning) vra (maak).
apoplexy, beroerte.
apostle, apostel, geloofsprediker.
apostrophe, toespraak; afkappingsteken.
appal, ontstel, verskrik, ontset.
apparatus, toestel(le), gereedskap, apparaat.
apparel, n. kleding, drag, gewaad.
apparently, blykbaar; klaarblyklik; skynbaar.
apparition, verskyning; spook, gedaante.
appeal, v. appelleer; 'n beroep doen (op).
appeal, n. beroep; appèl; (smeek)bede.
appear, verskyn; blyk, skyn; lyk; optree.
appease, bevredig; tot bedaring bring; stil, les.
append, aanhang, toevoeg, byvoeg.
appendicitis, blindedermontsteking.
appendix, aanhangsel; bylae; blindederm.
appetizer, aptytsnapsie.
appetite, eetlus, aptyt, sin, lus.
applaud, toejuig; prys.

apple, appel.
appliance, aanwending, toepassing; toestel.
applicant, sollisitant, applikant.
application, aanwending; aansoek; vlyt, ywer.
apply, aanwend, toepas; aansoek doen; aanvra;
    wend (tot).
appoint, bepaal; aanstel, benoem; uitrus.
appointment, bepaling; afspraak; aanstelling,
    benoeming; uitrusting.
appraise, takseer, waardeer, skat.
appreciable, merkbaar, aanmerklik.
appreciate, waardeer, op prys stel; vermeerder in
    waarde; appresieer.
apprehend, vang, arresteer; begryp; vrees.
apprentice, n. (vak)leerling; nuweling.
apprentice, v. 'n ambag laat leer; inboek.
approach, v. nader, nader kom.
approbation, goedkeuring, byval; aanbeveling.
appropriate, a. geskik, passend.
appropriate, v. (sig) toeëien, beslag lê op.
approval, goedkeuring; on –, op sig.
approve, goedkeur; bevestig; – of, goedkeur.
approximately, by benadering, naastenby.
apricot, appelkoos.
April, April.
apron, voorskoot, skort.
apt, geneig (tot); geskik; bekwaam, vlug.
aptitude, geneigdheid; geskiktheid; aanleg.
aqualung, duiklong.
aquaplane, ski-plank.
aquarium, akwarium.
Arab, Arabier; Arabiese perd.
arable, ploegbaar, beboubaar, bewerkbaar.
arbitrary, willekeurig, eiemagtig, arbitrêr.
arbitrate, as skeidsregter optree, beslis.
arc, boog.
arcade, booggang, winkelgang.
arch, a. skalks, skelm, ondeund.
arch, a. aarts- . . .
arch, n. boog, gewelf.
arch, v. buig, welf.
archaeology, oudheidkunde, argeologie.
archaic, verouderd, oud, argaïsties.
archer, boogskutter.
archipelago, argipel, eilandsee; eilandgroep.
architect, boumeester, argitek.
archives, argief (argiewe); argiefgebou.
archivist, argivaris, argiefbewaarder.
Arctic, noordelik, Noordpool.
ardent, vurig, gloeiend, blakend.
ardour, warmte, hitte; gloed, ywer, vuur.
arduous, steil; moeilik; swaar, inspannend.
are, v. is.
area, oppervlakte; gebied, wyk, ruimte.
arena, perk, strydperk, arena.
Argentine, Argentinië.
argue, redeneer, betoog; aandui; argumenteer.
argument, redenering, argument, bewys(grond);
    diskussie; inhoud.
arid, droog, dor, onvrugbaar.
aright, reg, tereg.
arise, opstaan, opkom; voortspruit, volg.
aristocrat, aristokraat; edelman.
arithmetic, n. rekenkunde, rekenkundeboek.
ark, ark.
arm, n. arm; tak; mou.
arm, n. wapen.
arm, v. wapen.
armament, bewapening, oorlogtoerusting.
armchair, leun(ing)stoel, armstoel.
armistice, wapenstilstand.
armour, n. harnas, wapenrusting, pantser.
armour, v. pantser, harnas.
armoury, wapenkamer, wapenhuis, arsenaal.
army, leër; menigte.

around, prep. rondom, om, om ... heen.
around, adv. rond; in die rondte.
arouse, wakker maak; in die lewe roep.
arrange, skik, rangskik, in orde bring, reël, inrig; ooreenkom, afspreek.
array, v. opstel, skik; uitdos, opskik; kleed.
arrear(s), agterstand, agterstallige; in -(s), agter.
arrest, v. teenhou, stut; in hegtenis neem, arresteer.
arrive, aankom, (aan)land.
arrogant, verwaand, aanmatigend, waanwys.
arrow, pyl.
arsenal, arsenaal, wapenhuis.
arsenic, n. arseen, arsenik.
arson, (opsetlike) brandstigting.
art, n. kuns; slag, streek, lis.
artery, slagaar.
article, n. onderdeel, lid, stuk, artikel; lidwoord.
article, v. verdeel; inskryf; aankla.
articulate, v. duidelik uitspreek; artikuleer.
artifice, lis, slimstreek, slenterslag.
artificial, kunsmatig, gekunsteld.
artillery, artillerie; geskut.
artisan, handwerksman, ambagsman.
artist, kunstenaar; arties.
arum-lily, varkblom, aronskelk.
as, adv. & conj. as, net as, soos, net soos; terwyl; aangesien.
as, pron. (as) wat.
asbestos, asbes, garingklip.
ascend, opstyg, bestyg, (op)klim, opvaar, opgaan, oploop, rys.
ascension: A- Day, Hemelvaartsdag.
ascent, bestyging; opgang; steilte.
ascertain, uitmaak, vasstel, vergewis.
ascribe, toeskryf, toeken.
ash, as.
ashamed, beskaamd; skaam, skamerig.
ashore, aan wal, aan land; gestrand.
Asia, Asië.
Asiatic, n. Asiaat.
aside, adv. opsy, apart.
aside, n. tersyspraak.
ask, vra; versoek; uitnooi; eis.
askance, skeef, skuins, van tersy.
askew, skeef, skuins.
aslant, skuins, dwars.
asleep, aan die slaap, in slaap.
asparagus, aspersie(s).
aspect, aanblik, voorkoms; uitsig; gesigspunt, oogpunt; aspek.
asperity, ruheid, skerpheid, strengheid.
aspersion, belastering; laster.
asphalt, n. asfalt, pad, teer.
aspirant, aspirant, kandidaat.
aspire, streef, begeer, aspireer.
ass, esel; domkop.
assagai, as(se)gaai.
assail, aanval, aanrand, bestorm.
assassinate, vermoor, sluipmoord pleeg (op).
assault, v. aanval, aanrand.
assault, n. aanval, bestorming, aanranding.
assay, v. toets, keur; beproef; probeer.
assemble, versamel, vergader, byeenkom.
assembly, vergadering.
assent, v. toestem, inwillig; instem.
assent, n. toestemming, instemming.
assert, laat geld; handhaaf; staan op; beweer, verklaar.
assess, skat; raam; aanslaan, belas.
asset, bate, besit.
assign, toewys; vermaak; aangee, bepaal; toeskryf.
assimilate, gelykmaak; verteer; assimileer.
assist, bystaan, help, ondersteun.

assistance, bystand, hulp, ondersteuning.
assistant, n. helper, handlanger, assistent.
associate, v. verenig, assosieer; omgaan met.
associate, n. metgesel; deelgenoot, medewerker; vennoot; medepligtige; medelid.
association, vereniging; verbinding; bond; omgang; assosiasie.
assortment, sortering, verskeidenheid.
assume, aanneem, aanvaar; (sig) aanmatig.
assuming, gestel(d); aanmatigend.
assumption, veronderstelling, vermoede; aanmatiging.
assurance, versekering; selfvertroue; (lewens)-versekering.
assure, verseker; verassureer.
astern, agter; agteruit; op die agterskip.
asthma, asma, benoudebors.
astir, op, in beweging, opgewonde.
astonish, verbaas, bevreem, dronkslaan.
astound, verbaas.
astray, verdwaal.
astride, wydsbeen (wydsbene).
astronaut, ruimtevlieër, ruimtereisiger.
astronomer, sterrekundige, astronoom.
astronomy, sterrekunde, astronomie.
astute, slim, slu, geslepe, oulik.
asunder, uitmekaar, aan stukke.
asylum, skuilplaas, toevlug(soord); mental -, gestig vir sielsiekes.
at, op, in, te, by; na; met; teen.
athlete, atleet, sportman.
Atlantic, Atlantiese Oseaan.
atlas, atlas.
atmosphere, atmosfeer, dampkring; lug.
atom, atoom, stofdeeltjie; greintjie.
atomic, atoom-; - pile, atoomstapel.
atone, boet, goedmaak.
atop, bo-op.
atrocious, wreedaardig, afskuwelik.
atrocity, wreedaardigheid, flater.
attach, vasmaak, aanheg; heg.
attack, v. aanval, bestorm; aantas.
attack, n. aanval; aantasting.
attain, bereik, verkry.
attempt, v. probeer, trag.
attempt, n. poging, onderneming; aanslag.
attend, ag gee, let op; bedien, verpleeg; begelei; bywoon.
attention, aandag, oplettendheid.
attentive, oplettend, aandagtig; beleef.
attest, v. getuig, verklaar.
attire, v. aanklee; optooi.
attire, n. kleding; tooisel, opskik.
attitude, houding, postuur.
attorney, prokureur.
attract, aantrek; boei.
attraction, aantrekking(skrag); bekoring.
attractive, aantreklik, bekoorlik.
attribute, n. eienskap, kenmerk, hoedanigheid.
auburn, goudbruin.
auction, verkoping, vandisie (vendusie); veiling.
auctioneer, vendu-afslaer.
auction-mart, verkooplokaal.
audacious, vermetel; brutaal; astrant.
audible, hoorbaar.
audience, gehoor; toehoorders; oudiënsie.
auditor, ouditeur.
auger, handboor.
aught, iets.
augment, v. vermeerder, vergroot, toeneem.
August, n. Augustus(maand).
aunt, auntie, tant(e), tannie.
auspicious, veelbelowend, gunstig, gelukkig.
austere, streng; onkreukbaar; eenvoudig.
Australia, Australië.

Austria, Oostenryk.
authentic, outentiek, oorspronklik; betroubaar.
author, dader; oorsaak; outeur.
authorize, magtig, outoriseer, reg gee.
authority, gesag; volmag; segsman; outoriteit.
authorities, owerheid, gesaghebbendes.
auto(mobile), outo(mobiel), motor(rytuig).
autocrat, alleenheerser, outokraat.
automatic, werktuiglik; outomaties.
autopsy, lykskouing.
autumn, herfs.
auxiliary, a. hulp- . . .
auxiliary, n. helper, bondgenoot.
avail, v. baat, help.
avail, n. baat, nut, voordeel.
available, beskikbaar, voorhande; dienstig.
avalanche, sneeuval, lawine.
avaricious, gierig, inhalig.
avenge, wreek, straf, wraak neem.
avenue, toegang; laan.
average, n. gemiddelde, deursnee.
average, a. gemiddelde, deursnee- . . .
averse, afkerig, onwillig.
aversion, afkeer, teensin (teësin); afsku.
avert, keer, afwend; afkerig maak, afkonkel.
aviary, voëlhuis, voëlhok.

aviator, vliegenier, vlieër.
avid, begerig, gretig; gierig.
avoid, vermy, ontwyk; ontduik.
avow, erken, bely.
await, opwag, wag op; te wagte wees.
awake, v. wakker word, ontwaak; wek.
awake, a. wakker; lewendig.
awaken, wakker maak; wakker word.
award, v. toeken, toewys.
award, n. toekenning; beloning; prys.
aware, bewus.
away, weg; voort.
awe, n. vrees, ontsag, eerbied.
awe, v. ontsag inboesem; bang maak.
awful, skrikwekkend, verskriklik, ontsettend.
awhile, 'n rukkie, 'n tydjie.
awkward, onhandig; vervelend; moeilik.
awl, els.
awning, seil, skerm, skutting.
awry, skeef, skuins; verkeerd.
ax(e), byl.
axis, as, spil.
axle, as.
ay(e), ja.
azalea, asalea.
azure, asuur, hemelsblou.

baa, blêr.
babble, v. brabbel; babbel; klets; verklap; kabbel (van water).
babe, babetjie, suigeling.
baboon, bobbejaan.
baby, babatjie, kindjie; kleintjie.
bachelor, vrygesel, oujongkêrel.
back, n. rug; agterkant; agterspeler.
back, adv. terug, agteruit; gelede.
back, v. (onder)steun; wed op; agteruit trap; agteruit laat gaan.
back, a. agterste; agterstallige.
backbite, (be)skinder, (be)laster.
backbone, ruggraat; beginselvastheid, pit.
backfire, terugslaan.
background, agtergrond.
backhand, n. handrug.
backveld, agterveld, platteland.
backward, a. agterwaarts; agterlik, traag.
backward, adv. agteruit; agteroor; na agter; na die verlede.
backwash, terugspoeling, trek.
backyard, agterplaas.
bacon, ontbytspek, (gerookte) spek.
bad, sleg, erg; stout; nadelig; naar, siek, ernstig (siek); ongunstig; vrot.
badge, ordeteken, onderskeidingsteken, kenteken; wapen.
badger, n. ratel.
badger, v. pla, treiter, kwel; agtervolg.
badly, sleg, erg; hard; baie, gevaarlik.
baffle, uitoorlê; verydel.
bag, n. sak, tas.
bag, v. in die sak stop; skiet; vang; inpalm; slap hang; knieë maak; sakkies maak.
bagatelle, bakatel; kleinigheid.
baggage, bagasie, reisgoed; parmant.
bagpipe, doedelsak.
bail, n. borg, borgtog.
bail, v. borgstaan; onder borgtog uitlaat.
bail, n. –s, balkies.
bailiff, balju; geregsbode.
bait, n. (lok)aas; verversing.
bait, v. aanhits; tretter; lok; aas aansit.
bake, bak.
baker, bakker.
balance, n. (weeg)skaal; vliegwiel; ewewig; (batige) saldo, oorskot; balans.
balance, v. weeg; balanseer; teen mekaar opweeg; slinger; vereffen, afsluit.
balcony, balkon.
bald, kaal, kaalkop.
bale, n. baal.
bale, v. in bale verpak, baal.
bale, v. uitskep, uithoos.
baleful, nadelig, heilloos, verderflik.
balk, baulk, v. versuim; wegvlieg, vassteek; in die weg staan; teenwerk; verydel.
ball, n. bal; bol; koeël; kluit.
ball, n. bal, dansparty.
ballad, ballade, lied.
ballast, n. ballas.
ball-bearing, koeëllaer.
ballet, ballet, toneeldans.
balloon, (lug)ballon.
balloon-tyre, ballonband.
ballot, n. stembriefie; stemming; loting.
ballot, v. (met (stem)briefies) stem; loot.
ballot-box, stembus.
ball-point: – pen, koeëlstif, bolpen, rolpen.
balm, balsem, salf; troos.
bamboo, bamboes, bamboesriet.
ban, v. verbied; ban, in die ban doen.
ban, n. ban, banvloek.
banal, banaal, alledaags, peuterig.

banana, piesang, banana.
band, n. band; dryfriem; bende; vereniging; korps; orkes.
bandage, n. verband; blinddoek.
bandage, v. verbind, blinddoek.
bandit, (struik)rower, voëlvryverklaarde.
bandmaster, orkesleier.
bandoleer, –ier, bandelier.
bandy-legged, hoepelbeen, met hoepelbene.
bane, vergif; verderf, vloek.
bang, v. slaan, bons, toeklap; klop.
bang, n. slag; bons, knal.
bang, interj. bom!, boems!
bangle, armband; voetring.
banish, verban, verdryf, uitsit.
banjo, banjo.
bank, n. bank; wal; oewer.
bank, v. in die bank sit, deponeer.
bankrupt, a. bankrot, insolvent.
banner, banier, vlag, vaandel.
banns, (huweliks)gebooie.
banquet, n. feesmaaltyd, banket.
bantam, kapokhoendertjie.
banter, n. gekskeerdery, skerts.
baobab, kremetartboom, baobab.
baptize, doop; naam gee; onderdompel.
bar, n. staaf, stang, tralie; slagboom; maatstreep (musiek); regbank, balie; buffet; kroeg, kantien; sandbank; hinderpaal; skoenbalkies.
bar, v. afsluit, uitsluit; verhinder, versper, belet.
barb, n. baard (van 'n vis); weerhaak.
barbarian, n. barbaar, onbeskaafde.
barbaric, barbaars.
barbel, baber.
barber, haarsnyer, barbier, (haar)kapper.
barber's shop, barbierswinkel, haarkapperswinkel, haarkapsalon.
bare, a. naak, kaal, bloot; leeg; skraal.
bare, v. ontbloot, kaal maak.
barebacked, bloots, sonder saal; kaalrug.
bare-headed, kaalkop, blootshoofs.
barely, ope(n)lik; enkel, alleen, maar, skaars, ternouernood.
bargain, n. ooreenkoms; slag, kopie.
bark, n. bas, skors, skil; vel, huid.
bark, n. blaf, geblaf.
bark, v. blaf; hoes; knal.
barley, gars.
barley-wheat, kaalgars, barlewiet.
barn, skuur.
barometer, weerglas, barometer.
baron, vryheer; baron.
barrack, n. barak; –s, barakke; kaserne.
barrack, v. uitjou.
barrage, dam(wal); gordynvuur.
barrel, vat, vaatjie; (geweer)loop.
barren, onvrugbaar; kaal.
barricade, v. verskans, barrikadeer.
barrier, slagboom; grenspaal; tolhek; hinderpaal; hindernis, versperring.
barring, uitgeslote, behalwe.
barrister, advokaat.
barrow, kruiwa; stootkar.
barter, v. ruil; kwansel; verruil.
base, a. gemeen, laag; minderwaardig; onedel.
base, n. grondslag, basis, fondament, voetstuk.
base, v. (grond)ves, baseer, grond.
base-line, agterlyn.
basement, fondament; ondergrondse verdieping, kelder.
bashful, skaam, skamerig, verleë.
basin, kom; skottel; bekken; stroomgebied.
basis, grondslag, fondament, basis.
bask, (sig) koester, bak.

basket, mandjie, korf.
basket-ball, korfbal.
bass, baars (soort vis).
bass, bas(stem).
bastard, n. baster, halfnaatjie.
bat, n. vlermuis.
bat, n. (krieket)kolf; kolwer.
bat, v. slaan (krieket), kolf.
batch, baksel; klomp, bondel, stel, trop.
bath, n. bad.
bath, v. bad.
bathe, v. baai, swem; afwas.
bathe, n. bad, (die) baai.
batsman, kolwer, slaner.
battalion, bataljon.
batter, v. rammel, beuk, deuk.
batter, n. deeg.
battery, battery; aanranding.
battle, n. (veld)slag, geveg, stryd.
battle, v. veg, stry, slag lewer.
bawl, hard skreeu, brul.
bay, n. baai, inham, golf.
bay, a. rooibruin, vos.
bay, v. aanblaf.
bayonet, n. bajonet.
bazaar, basaar.
bazooka, pantservuis.
be, wees, bestaan.
beach, n. strand, kus, wal.
beacon, n. baken; sein(vuur); vuurtoring.
bead, n. kraletjie, knoppie; druppel; korrel.
beak, bek, snawel; kromneus; tuit.
beaker, beker.
beam, n. balk; ploegbalk; disselboom; straal.
beam, n. straal.
bean, boontjie.
bear, beer; brombeer.
bear, v. dra; gedra; verdra; voortbring.
beard, n. baard.
bearer, draer, bringer, houer, toonder; lykdraer.
bearing, houding, gedrag; rigting; strekking; verhouding.
beast, bees, dier.
beat, v. slaan, uitstof; wen, klop; stamp.
beat: dead –, pootuit.
beat, n. slag, klap; klop; tik; rondte; wyk.
beating, pak, loesing; getrommel.
beautiful, pragtig, skitterend.
beautify, mooimaak, verfraai.
beauty, mooiheid, skoonheid, prag.
beaver, bewer; kastoorhoed.
because, omdat, oor.
beckon, wink, knik, wuif, sein.
become, word; pas; betaam.
bed, n. bed, kooi; lêplek; bedding.
bed-clothes, beddegoed.
bedding, beddegoed.
bedlam, gekkehuis, lawaaiboel.
Bedouin, Bedoeïen.
bedridden, bedlêend.
bedrock, rotsbed; grond.
bedroom, slaapkamer.
bee, by.
beef, beesvleis.
beefsteak, biefstuk.
beehive, by(e)nes, byekorf.
beer, bier.
beest, beestings, bies.
beetle, n. kewer, tor.
beetroot, beet, beetwortel.
befall, gebeur; oorkom, wedervaar.
befit, pas, voeg, betaam.
before, prep. voor.
before, adv. voor, voorop, vooruit; tevore.
before, conj. voor, voordat, eer.

beforehand, vantevore, vooraf, vooruit.
befriend, vriendskap betoon, guns bewys.
beg, bedel; smeek; vra; versoek.
beget, verwek, verkry.
beggar, bedelaar; vent.
begin, begin, aan die gang sit.
beginning, begin, aanvang.
begone, maak dat jy weg kom!, trap!
begrudge, beny, misgun.
beguile, bedrieg, fop.
behalf, belang; ontwil.
behave, (sig) gedra.
behaviour, gedrag, houding.
behead, onthoof, kop afkap.
behind, prep. agter; anderkant.
behind, adv. agter, agteraan, agterna, van agter, agterom.
behindhand, agter, agterstallig; agterlik.
behold, aanskou, beskou, sien.
beho(o)ve, betaam.
being, part, synde.
being, n. bestaan; wese; skepsel.
belated, vertraag.
belch, v. wind opbreek, oprisp; uitbraak.
beleaguer, beleër, omsingel, insluit.
Belgian, n. Belg.
belie, belieg; loënstraf, weerspreek.
belief, geloof, oortuiging, mening.
believe, geloof (glo), vertrou; meen.
belittle, verklein; kleineer, afkam.
bell, klok, bel; blomkelk.
bellow, v. brul, bulk, loei; bulder.
bellows, blaasbalk.
belly, n. buik, pens; holte.
belly, v. opswel, uitstaan, bolstaan.
belong, behoor(t), aan.
belongings, toebehorens, besittinge.
beloved, bemin(de).
below, prep. onder, benede, onderkant.
below, adv. onder, onderaan, aan die onderkant, benede, omlaag, laer as.
belt, n. gord(el), lyfband; stook; riem, dryfriem.
bemoan, beklaag, bejammer.
bench, bank, sitbank, draaibank, skaafbank; regbank.
bend, v. buig; span; buk; draai; knoop.
bend, n. buiging, draai, kromming.
beneath, prep. onder, benede.
beneath, adv. (na) onder, benede, ondertoe.
benefactor, weldoener..
beneficial, voordelig, heilsaam.
benefit, n. voordeel, nut.
benefit, v. tot voordeel wees, baat, goeddoen; voordeel trek, profiteer.
benign, minsaam; sagaardig; heilsaam.
bent, draai; neiging.
benumb, verkluim, verlam, verdoof.
benzine, bensien.
bequeath, vermaak, nalaat.
bequest, erfenis, legaat, vermaking.
bereave, beroof; ontneem.
bereavement, verlies.
berry, bessie.
berth, n. (aan)lêplek; kajuit; slaapbank; oortog; baantjie; give a wide –, uit die weg gaan.
berth, v. vasmaak, aanlê; lêplek gee.
beseech, smeek.
beseem, pas, voeg, betaam.
beset, omring; aanval.
beside, naas, langs, digby; buite(n), behalwe.
besides, buitendien; buite(n), behalwe.
besiege, beleër, omsingel.
besmirch, bevuil, besmeer.
best, a. beste.
best, n. bes(te).

best, adv. liefs.
bestial, beesagtig, dierlik.
bestir, roer.
best man, strooijonker, bruidsjonker.
best seller, treffer, suksesboek.
bestow, (op)bêre; skenk, verleen.
bet, v. wed.
bet, n. weddenskap.
betray, verraai; aandui, dui op.
betroth, verloof.
better, a. beter.
better, adv. beter; liewer.
better, n. meerdere; oorhand.
better, v. verbeter.
between, tussen, onder.
bevel, n. skuinste, hoek; winkelhaak.
bevel, v. skuins maak.
beverage, drank.
bevy, klompie, aantal, paar.
bewail, bejammer, beklaag, beween.
beware, oppas, op jou hoede wees.
bewilder, in die war bring, verbyster.
bewitch, beheks; bekoor, betower.
beyond, prep. anderkant, oorkant, buite(kant), oor, bo(kant), verby.
beyond, adv. verder.
bias, n. skuinste; oorhelling; vooroordeel.
bias, v. beïnvloed, bevooroordeel.
bib, n. borslap(pie).
Bible, Bybel.
bibliography, boekbeskrywing, bibliografie.
bicker, kibbel; klater, kletter.
bicycle, n. fiets, rywiel.
bid, v. gebied, beveel; bie(d).
bid, n. bod.
bide, afwag.
bier, baar.
big, groot, dik.
bigamist, bigamis.
bigoted, dweepsiek, bekrompe.
bile, gal; brommigheid.
bilingual, tweetalig.
bilious, galagtig, mislik; brommig.
bill, n. snawel, bek.
bill, n. briefie; rekening; wissel; plakkaat, aan-plakbiljet; wetsontwerp, saak.
billet, n. briefie; baantjie, betrekking.
billiards, biljart.
billion, biljoen.
billow, n. golf, brander.
billy-goat, bokram.
biltong, biltong.
bin, kas, kis, mandjie, bus, blik.
bind, bind, vasmaak, heg, verbind, inbind; ver-plig.
binder, (boek)binder; verband, nawelband; bindmasjien.
binding, a. verpligtend, bindend.
binocular, verkyker, toneelkyker.
biography, biografie, lewensbeskrywing.
biology, biologie.
bioscope, bioskoop.
birch, v. onder die lat kry, klop, slaan.
bird, voël; kêrel, vent.
bird-lime, voëllym.
birth, geboorte; stand, afkoms.
birthday, verjaar(s)dag, geboortedag.
birth-mark, moedervlek.
birth-rate, geboortesyfer.
biscuit, beskuit; koekie.
bisect, halveer, in twee deel.
bishop, biskop; raadsheer (skaakspel).
bison, bison, buffel.
bit, n. hap, byt; bietjie, stukkie; brokkie, boor; stang.

bitch, teef.
bite, v. byt; invreet; (skroef) vat.
bite, n. byt; hap; stukkie ete.
bitter, a. bitter, skerp, griewend.
bitter, n. bitter; –s, bitter.
bitumen, asfalt, aardharpuis, bitumen.
bizarre, bisar, grillig, vreemd.
blab, verklap, verklik.
black, a. swart, donker, somber, duister.
blackball, afstem, lidmaatskap weier.
blackboard, (skool)bord.
blacken, swart maak, swart smeer.
blackguard, n. skobbejak, smeerlap.
blackhead, swartkoppie; vetwurmpie.
blackmail, n. afpersing; brandskatting.
blackmail, v. afpers.
Black Maria, tronkwa; nagwa.
blacksmith, smid.
bladder, blaas; blaar; windsak.
blade, sprietjie; blad; halm; lem.
blame, v. beskuldig, blameer; laak, afkeur.
blame, n. skuld, blaam.
blameless, onberispelik; onskuldig.
blanch, bleik, wit maak; wit word.
blancmange, blanc-mange.
bland, innemend, beleef; vleierig.
blank, a. blank, blanko; onbeskrewe, oninge-vul(d); leeg; wesenloos.
blank, n. leegte, leemte; ruimte; weggelate woord.
blanket, n. kombers, deken.
blanket, v. toemaak, bedek.
blare, v. sketter, lawaai maak, brul.
blaspheme, laster, spot, vloek.
blast, n. rukwind; windstroom; gesketter; ont-ploffing.
blast, v. in die lug blaas, laat spring; verskroei, verwoes.
blatant, skreeuerig, lawaaierig; volslae.
blaze, n. vlam, bloed; uitbarsting.
blaze, v. vlam, oplaai; skitter; opvlam, uitbars; losbrand, skiet.
blaze, n. bles.
blazer, kleurbaadjie.
bleach, bleik, verbleik.
bleak, a. kaal, guur, onherbergsaam.
blear, dof, glasig.
bleat, v. blêr, bulk; tjank.
bleed, bloei, bloedsoort; bloedlaat.
blemish, vlek, klad, smet.
blend, v. vermeng, meng, berei; (wyn) versny.
blend, n. mengsel, soort; vermenging.
bless, seën; loof.
blessed, **blest**, geseën, geloof, geluksalig; ver-vlakste.
blight, n. roes; verderf, plaag, pes.
blight, v. verskroei, verderf, verwoes.
blighter, rakker; skobbejak.
blind, v. blind maak, verblind, bedrieg.
blind, n. blinding, rolgordyn, luik, hortjie; skerm; blinddoek; oogklap; voorwendsel, oëverblindery.
blindfold, v. blinddoek.
blindly, blindelings, roekeloos.
blindman: –'s buff, blindemol.
blink, v. knipoog; flits.
blinkers, oogklappe.
bliss, saligheid, geluk, heil, vreugde.
blister, n. blaar; trekpleister.
blithe, bly, opgewek, lustig.
blitz, blitsaanval, blitsoorlog.
blizzard, sneeustorm, sneeujag.
bloated, opblaas; opgeblase.
bloater, gerookte haring, bokkem.
blob, bobbel, blaas.

block, n. blok; vorm; katrol; drukplaat; hindernis.
block, v. versper, (ver)hinder, dwarsboom; blok
(krieket).
blockade, n. blokkade, insluiting.
blockhead, domoor, klipkop, swaap.
blond, blond, lig.
blonde, blondine, blonde meisie.
blood, n. bloed; sap; temperament, familie, verwantskap.
blood, v. bloedlaat; bloed laat ruik.
bloodhound, speurhond, bloedhond.
bloodshed, bloedstorting, bloedvergieting.
bloodshot, bloedbelope, rooi.
bloodthirsty, bloeddorstig, moordlustig.
blood-vessel, bloedvat, aar.
bloody, bloedig; bloederig.
bloom, n. bloei, bloeisel; fleur, krag; blos, waas.
bloom, v. bloei, blom.
blossom, n. bloei(sel), blom, bloesem.
blossom, v. bloei, blom.
blot, n. klad, vlek; smet, skandvlek.
blot, v. klad; beklad.
blotch, puis(ie); vlek, klad; vloeipapier.
blotting-paper, kladpapier, vloeipapier.
blouse, bloes, hempbaadjie.
blow, v. waai; blaas; hyg; snuit.
blow, n. slag, klap, hou; amp, skok.
blow-fly, brommer.
blown, uit-asem; opgeswel; bederf.
blub, huil, tjank, grens.
blubber, n. walvisspek; gegrens, getjank.
blubber, v. grens, tjank; huil-huil praat.
bludgeon, n. knuppel.
blue, a. blou.
blue, n. blou; blousel; die lug; die see.
blue, v. blou maak; in die blousel sit.
blue-bottle, koringblom; brommer.
blue gum, bloekomboom (blougom-).
bluff, a. stomp; kortaf, plomp; openhartig,
hartlik.
bluff, v. oorbluf; uitoorlê, grootpraat; bangmaak; wysmaak.
blunder, v. struikel; (sig) vergis, flater begaan,
knoei.
blunder, n. flater, fout, bok.
blunt, a. stomp, bot; kortaf, reguit.
blunt, v. stomp maak, bot maak, ongevoelig
maak.
blur, klad, (be)vlek; onduidelik maak, verwar;
uitwis, verdof.
blurt, – out, uitflap, verklap.
blush, v. bloos, rooi word.
blush, n. blos; bloed.
bluster, v. storm, lawaai, raas; swets.
boa, – constrictor, luislang.
boar, beer; wildevark.
board, v. met planke bespyker; bordpapier;
tafel; maaltyd, ete, losies; bestuur, raad;
boord.
board, v. met planke bespyker; loseer, maaltyd
neem; losies gee, maaltye verskaf; aan boord
gaan.
boarder, kosganger, kosleerling.
boarding-house, koshuis, losieshuis.
boarding-school, kosskool.
boast, v. spog, grootpraat; spog met.
boat, n. skuit, boot, skip; souspotjie.
bob, v. dobber, duik; buig; hap.
bode, voorspel.
bodice, lyfie.
body, n. liggaam, lyf; lyk; romp; inhoud, hoof-
deel; bak; mens, persoon; vereniging, mag,
trop, bende, massa.
body-guard, lyfwag.

bog, n. moeras.
bogus, vals, voorgewend, sogenaamd.
bogy, (bogey), duiwel, gees; gogga, skrikbeeld.
boil, n. puis, sweer, bloedvint, pitsweer.
boil, v. kook.
boiler, (stoom)ketel; warmwatertenk.
boisterous, onstuimig; luidrugtig.
bold, dapper, moedig; skerp, duidelik.
bolster, v. – up, steun; stut, oplap.
bolt, n. bout; knip, grendel; pyl; bliksemstraal.
bolt, v. grendel, die knip opsit; vasskroef, vas-
bout; op loop gaan; weghardloop.
bomb, n. bom.
bomb, v. bombardeer.
bombard, bombardeer.
bombastic, bombasties, hoogdrawend.
bond, n. band; verbond; verband, skuldbrief;
verpligting, verbintenis; pakhuis.
bond, v. verbind, verband lê; verband neem op;
in entrepôt opslaan.
bondage, knegskap; gevange(n)skap.
bone, n. been; graat.
bonfire, vreugdevuur.
bonnet, n. mus, kappie; kap.
bonny, hups, aardig, lief, aanvallig.
bonus, bonus, premie, ekstra.
boo, v. boe, uitjou; bulk, loei.
booby prize, poedelprys.
book, n. boek; geskrif, werk.
book, v. inskryf, boek; bespreek.
bookcase, boekrak, boekkas.
booking-office, kaartjieskantoor.
book-keeping, boekhou.
bookmaker, beroepswedder.
bookseller, boekhandelaar.
boom, n. (versperrings)boom; spriet.
boom, v. dreun; opleef; aanprys.
boom, n. oplewing; ophemeling.
boomerang, boemerang.
boon, n. seën, voordeel; guns.
boor, lomperd, onbeskofte vent.
boot, n. skoen, stewel.
booth, tent, kraam.
bootlace, skoenveter.
bootlegger, dranksmokkelaar.
booty, buit, roof.
booze, v. drink, fuif, suip.
borax, boraks.
border, n. rand, kant; grens; soom.
border, v. grens, begrens; omrand, omsoom.
bore, v. boor, hol maak.
bore, n. las, vervelende persoon.
bore, v. verveel.
born, gebore.
borough, stad; kiesafdeling.
borrow, leen (van), ontleen (aan).
bosh, bog, kaf, onsin.
bosom, boesem, bors; skoot; hart; siel.
botany, plantkunde, botanie.
botch, v. konkel, (ver)knoei.
both, albei, altwee, beide.
bother, v. hinder, pla, lol, neul.
bother, n. beslommering, geneul, geseur.
bottle, n. bottel, fles.
bottle-store, drankwinkel.
bottom, n. boom, bodem; grond; agterste; onderste; onderent.
bottom, a. onderste; laaste.
bough, tak.
boulder, klip, rots(blok).
bounce, v. opspring, terugstuit; huppel.
bounce, n. terugslag, opslag.
bound, v. begrens, beperk.
bound, v. opslag maak, huppel.
bound, n. sprong, opslag.

bound, a. klaar (om te vertrek), bestem(d); – **for**, met bestemming (na).
bound, p.p. gebonde, verplig.
boundary, grens, grenslyn; grenshou.
bounder, hierjy, skobbejak, rakker.
bountiful, mild, ryk, oorvloedig.
bounty, mild(dadig)heid; gawe, weldaad; handgeld; premie.
bouquet, ruiker, bos; geur; boeket.
bout, pot(jie), beurt, rondjie.
bovine, osagtig, beeste- . . .; vadsig, bot.
bow, v. buig; laat buig; (sig) onderwerp.
bow, n. buiging.
bow, n. boog; strykstok; strik, strikdas.
bow, n. boeg.
bowels, ingewande; binneste, hart.
bowl, n. kom, bak; beker; blad (van lepel); pypkop.
bowl, n. rolbal, –s, rolbalspel.
bowl, v. rol, boul, balgooi; rol.
bow-legged, hoepelbeen.
bowler, bouler; rolbalspeler.
bow-saw, spansaag.
box, n. doos, dosie, kis(sie), koffer, (teater)losie; bok, voorkis; afskorting; huisie.
box, v. klap, opstopper gee; boks.
boxer, vuisvegter, bokser.
Boxing Day, Tweede-Kersdag.
box-office, kaartjieskantoor.
boy, jongetjie, knaap, seun; kêrel.
boycott, boikot.
bra, buustelyfie, brassière.
brace, n. koppeling, klamp; stut; omslag; –s, kruisbande.
brace, v. vasmaak; versterk.
bracelet, armband; handboei.
bracket, n. rak(kie); klamp, arm, skraag; hakie.
bracket, v. saamvoeg; tussen hakies sit.
brackish, brak, brakkerig.
brad, kleinkop-spykertjie; skoenspykertjie.
bradawl, els.
brag, v. grootpraat, bluf, windmaak.
braid, v. vleg; omboor.
brain, n. brein, harsings; verstand.
brain wave, ingewing, blink gedagte.
braise, smoor.
brake, rem, briek.
bran, semels.
branch, n. tak, vertakking; vak, afdeling.
branch, v. vertak.
brand, n. brandmerk; merk, soort, klas, kwaliteit; roes.
brand, v. brandmerk.
brand-new, splinternuut.
brandy, brandewyn.
brass, (geel)koper; geld; onbeskaamdheid.
brass band, blaaskorps, benning.
brat, snuiter, bengel, skreeuerd.
brave, a. dapper, moedig, onverskrokke.
brave, v. trotseer, uitdaag.
brawl, v. rusie maak, twis.
brawl, n. rusie, twis, relletjie.
brawn, spier; sult.
brawny, gespier(d).
bray, v. & n. runnik, balk; skree.
braze, (hard) soldeer; kopersweis.
brazen, koper- . . ., brons . . .; onbeskaamd, brutaal.
breach, breking; deurbraak, verbreking, oortreding; verwydering, rusie; bres, gat.
bread, brood.
break, v. breek, aanbreek, afbreek, stukkend breek.

break, n. breuk; onderbreking, pouse; serie (in biljart).
break-down, instorting; vertraging, oponthoud, ongeluk.
breaker, brander.
breakfast, ontbyt, agtuur.
breast, n. bors; skoot; gemoed, hart.
breath, asem (adem); woord.
breathe, asemhaal.
breech, n. agterste; agterstuk (van 'n kanon); –es, broek.
breed, v. verwek, teel, kweek; uitbroei; voortbring, veroorsaak; oplei, opvoed.
breed, n. ras, soort, aanteel.
breeding, opvoeding, beskawing.
breeze, bries; rusietjie, standjie.
brevity, kortheid; beknoptheid.
brew, v. brou, meng.
brew, n. brousel, mengsel.
brewery, brouery.
bribe, n. omkoopgeld, omkoopprys.
bribe, v. omkoop.
brick, n. baksteen; blok; gawe kêrel, doring.
brick, v. messel; – **up**, toemessel.
bricklayer, messelaar.
bride, bruid.
bridegroom, bruidegom.
bridesmaid, strooimeisie, bruidsmeisie.
bridge, n. brug; vioolkam; rug (van die neus).
bridge, v. oorbrug; 'n brug lê (oor).
bridle, n. toom, teuel; beteueling.
bridle, v. toom aansit; beteuel.
brief, a. kort; beknop.
brief, n. uittreksel; dossier, stukke; saakbrief, opdrag; instruksie; akte.
brief, v. saamvat; as advokaat aanstel.
briefs, knapbroekie.
brigade, brigade; afdeling.
brigadier, brigadier.
brigand, (struik)rower.
bright, helder, duidelik; lewendig; knap; opgeruimd.
brighten, verhelder, opklaar; opvrolik.
brilliant, a. skitterend; briljant.
brim, n. rand, boord, kant.
brine, n. soutwater, pekel(water).
bring, bring, saambring, veroorsaak.
brink, rand, kantjie.
brisk, a. lewendig, wakker.
brisket, bors(vleis), borsstuk.
bristle, n. steekhaar, (borsel)haar.
Britain, Brittanje.
Britisher, Briton, Brit.
brittle, bros.
broach, v. aanbreek, (vat) oopslaan; aanroer.
broad, breed, wyd, ruim.
broadcast, v. uitsaai; uitbasuin.
broaden, verwyd, verbreed; rek.
brochure, brosjure.
broil, v. braai, rooster; bak, blaker, brand.
broke, p.p. gebreek; platsak, bankrot.
broken, stukkend, gebroke.
broker, makelaar; tussenhandelaar, agent.
bronchitis, brongitis.
bronze, a. brons- . . ., bronskleurig.
brooch, borsspeld.
brood, n. broeisel; gebroed, gespuis.
brood, v. broei, uitbroei, peins.
broody, broeis.
brook, n. spruit, beek.
brook, v. verdra, veel, gedoog.
broom, brem; besembos; besem.
broth, sop.
brother, broer, boet(ie); broeder.

brother-in-law, swaer, skoonbroer.
brow, winkbrou; voorkop; rand, kruin.
brown, a. bruin; donker.
browse, v. knabbel; graas, wei; grasduin.
bruise, n. kneus(plek), stampplek.
bruise, v. kneus, indeuk; fyn maak.
brunette, brunet, swartjie.
brunt: bear the –, die spit afbyt.
brush, n. borsel, kwas; besem; skermutseling.
brush, v. langes skuur; (af)borsel, afvee(g).
brushwood, bossies, kreupelhout, ruigte.
brusque, kortaf, bruusk.
brutal, dierlik; onmenslik.
brute, a. bruut, dierlik, onmenslik.
brute, n. (on)dier, wreedaard, onmens.
bubble, n. (water)blaas, lugbel, seepbel.
bubble, v. borrel, kook.
buck, n. (wilde) bokram, mannetjie; wild; modegek.
bucks, v. bokspring; vassteek, steeks wees.
bucket, emmer; bak.
buckle, n. gespe(r).
buckle, v. vasgespe(r); aangord; krom buig; omkrul.
buckshot, bokhael, lopers.
buck-waggon, bokwa.
buck wheat, bokwiet.
bud, n. bot, knop, kiem.
bud, v. bot, uitloop; ontluik; ent.
Buddhism, Boeddhisme.
budge, verroer, beweeg.
budget, n. sak; begroting.
budget, v. voorsiening maak, begroot.
buff, a. dofgeel, seemkleurig.
buff, v. poleer, fynskuur.
buffalo, buffel.
buffer, stootkussing, stampveer; buffer.
buffet, v. slaan, stamp, worstel met.
buffet, n. slag, stamp, stoot, hou.
buffet, n. buffet, (skink)toonbank.
bug, weelluis; wandluis; kewer.
bugbear, paaiboelie; gogga.
buggy, bokkie.
bugle, beuel, trompet(ter).
bugler, trompetblaser.
build, v. bou, oprig, maak.
build, n. bou; liggaamsbou, vorm.
builder, bouer, boumeester, kontrakteur.
building, gebou; bouery.
bulb, bol; **electric –**, gloeilamp.
bulge, v. uitstaan, opswel, uitpeul, uitsit.
bulk, n. vrag, lading; omvang, grootte; massa; meerderheid.
bulk, v. vertoon, lyk.
bulky, groot, omvangryk, lywig, dik.
bull, n. bul, mannetjie.
bull, n. (pouslike) bul.
bullet, koeël.
bulletin, bulletin, rapport.
bullet-proof, koeëlvry.
bullfight, stiergeveg.
bullfinch, bloedvink, rooivink.
bullfrog, brulpadda.
bullion, staafgoud, staafsilwer.
bullock, os.
bull's-eye, handlantern; kol; kolskoot.
bully, n. baasspeler, bullebak.
bully, v. baasspeel oor.
bully beef, blikkiesvleis.
bulrush, biesie, matjiesgoed, papkuil.
bulwark, bolwerk, verskansing, skans.
bump, v. stamp, stoot.
bump, n. stamp, slag; knop, kneusplek; bult, knobbel.

bumper, n. stamper, stoter.
bumptious, verwaand, aanstellerig.
bun, bolletjie.
bunch, n. bos(sie), tros; bondel.
bunch, v. (in) bossies maak; tros, koek.
bundle, n. bondel, pak, hoop, gerf, rol.
bundle, v. saambind, saampak.
bung, n. sponning, prop, tap; leuen.
bungle, knoei, konkel, verknoei.
bunion, eeltswelsel, eeltsweer.
bunk, n. kooi, slaapbank.
bunk, v. klas versuim, dros, stokkies draai.
bunker, n. bunker.
bunny, konyntjie.
buoy, n. seeboei; **life–**, reddingsboei.
buoy, v. **– up**, ophou, drywende hou; opbeur.
bur, burr, klits(gras); saadjie.
burden, n. las, vrag.
burden, v. belas, belaai, bevrag.
bureau, skryftafel; kantoor; buro.
bureaucratic, burokraties.
burgess, (stemgeregtigde) burger.
burglar, inbreker.
burglary, inbraak, huisbraak.
burgle, inbreek.
burial, begrafnis.
burly, vors, groot, swaarlywig.
burn, v. brand, verbrand; aanbrand.
burn, n. brandplek, brandwond.
burnish, polys, poets, vryf, skuur.
burr, v. bry; onduidelik praat.
burrow, n. gat, hol, lêplek.
burrow, v. grawe, gat grawe.
bursary, (studie)beurs.
burst, n. bars; skeur; uitbarsting, losbarsting; kragtige inspanning.
bury, begrawe; bedek; vergeet.
bus, n. bus.
bush, n. bos(sie), struik(e); bosveld.
bush, n. (naaf)bus.
bushbuck, bosbok.
bushel, skepel, boesel.
Bushman, Boesman.
business, besigheid; plig; saak, bedryf, handel.
business man, sakeman.
bust, borsbeeld: bors.
bustard, (wilde) pou.
bustle, v. woel, werskaf; haastig maak.
busy, a. besig, bedrywig.
busybody, bemoeial; kwaadstoker.
but, conj. maar, egter, dog.
but, prep. behalwe, buite(n).
butcher, slagter; wreedaard.
butcher, v. slag; 'n slagting aanrig.
butcher-bird, laksman.
butt, n. skryf; mikpunt.
butt, n. kolf, agterent; stomp(ie).
butt, v. stamp, stoot.
butter, n. botter; vleiery, stroop.
butter, v. (botter op) smeer.
butterfly, skoe(n)lapper, vlinder.
buttermilk, karringmelk.
buttock, boud, agterste.
button, n. knoop; knop; dop(pie).
button, v. (vas)knoop, toeknoop.
buttress, n. stut(muur); steunpilaar.
buy, koop; omkoop.
buzz, v. gons; **– off!**, trap!
buzz-bike, kragfiets, bromfiets.
by, prep. by; met; deur; op; na, volgens; per.
by, adv. verby; opsy.
by(e), ondergeskik, onder . . ., sydelings.

bye, n. loslopie.
bygone, a. uitgesterf; verby, vervloë.
by-law, regulasie, verordening.
by-product, afvalproduk.

byre, koeistal.
bystander, toeskouer.
byway, dowwe paadjie; kort paadjie; onbekende terrein.

cab, huurrytuig.
cabbage, kool, kopkool.
cabin, n. kajuit, hut; hok.
cabin-boy, kajuitjonge.
cabinet, kabinet; kas; ministerie.
cabinetmaker, skrynwerker.
cable, n. kabel.
cable, v. kabel, telegrafeer.
caboodle, boel, spul, sous, rommel.
cackle, v. kekkel; babbel, snater.
caddie, (gholf)joggie.
cadet, kadet.
cadge, bedel, klaploop; smous.
café, kafee.
cage, n. kooi, koutjie; hok; hysbak.
cajole, vlei, flikflooi; omkonkel.
cake, n. koek, gebak.
calabash, kalbas.
calamity, onheil, ramp; rampspoed.
calculate, (be)reken, uitreken.
calendar, kalender, almanak.
calf, n. kalf; kuit; snuiter.
calibre, kaliber, deursnee; gehalte.
calico, kaliko, katoen.
call, v. roep, be-, byeen-, in-, op-, toeroep; uit-
lees; noem, heet; besoek aflê, aangaan; opbel.
call, n. roep, geroep; (voël)gefluit; (roep)stem;
besoek.
calling, geroep; beroep; roeping.
callous, gevoelloos, verhard.
callow, kaal, sonder vere; baar, groen.
calm, n. kalmte, stilte.
calm, a. kalm, stil, bedaard.
calm, v. kalmeer, stilmaak, tot bedaring bring.
calumny, laster(ing), skindertaal.
calve, kalwe.
calyx, (blom)kelk.
cam, kam (aan 'n rat), nok.
camber, welwing, helling.
camel, kameel.
camellia, japonika.
camera, kamera, **in –,** met geslote deure.
camouflage, n. maskering, camouflage.
camouflage, v. maskeer, kamoefleer.
camp, n. kamp, laer.
camp, v. kamp(eer), laertrek.
campaign, n. kampanje, veldtog.
camp-bed, veldbed, voubed.
camphor, kanfer.
can, v. kan, in staat wees; mag.
can, n. kan(netjie), blik, kantien.
can, v. inlê, inmaak.
Canadian, Kanadees.
canal, kanaal; buis; groef.
canalize, kanaliseer.
canary, kanarie; sysie.
cancel, v. kanselleer; deurhaal; afsê, afskrywe;
herroep, intrek.
cancer, kanker; **Tropic of C.,** Kreefskeerkring.
candid, openhartig, eerlik.
candidate, kandidaat; applikant, sollisitant.
candle, kers.
candour, openhartigheid, eerlikheid.
cane, n. riet; bamboes; rottang; matwerk; lat,
(wændel)stok, kierie.
cane, v. onder die lat kry; ('n stoel) mat.
canister, trommel, blik; **-shot,** skroot.
canker, n. (mond)sweer; kanker, pes, verpestende
invloed.
canna, kanna, blomriet.
cannibal, kannibaal, mensvreter.
cannon, n. kanon.
canny, oulik, slim; versigtig.
canoe, kano.

canon, kanon, wet, (kerk)reël; domheer, kanun-
nik.
canopy, (troon)hemel, gewelf, dak.
cant, n. sektetaal, jargon; huigeltaal.
cant, v. mooipraatjies verkoop, huigel.
cantata, kantate.
canteen, kantien; veldkombuis; veldfles.
canter, v. in (op) 'n handgalop loop (ry).
canvas, seil; (skilder)doek; skildery.
canvass, bespreek, uitpluis; (stemme) werf; pols.
canvasser, (stemme)werwer.
cap, n. pet; mus; doppie.
cap, v. graad toeken; kies vir die eerste (internasionale) span; kroon opsit, troef, oortref.
capable, bekwaam; geskik, in staat, kapabel.
capacity, bekwaamheid, vermoë; hoedanigheid,
kapasiteit; inhoud, volume.
cape, n. kaap; **The C.,** die Kaap, Kaapland.
Cape, a. Kaaps; **– cart,** kapkar.
cape, mantel, kraag.
Cape Colony, Kaapkolonie.
caper, bokspring.
capillary, haarvormig; haarfyn; kapillêr; **– tube,**
haarbuisie.
capital, a. hoof-...; uitstekend, eersteklas.
capital, n. kapitaal, hoofsom; hoofstad; hoofletter.
capitalist, kapitalis.
capitulate, kapituleer.
capricious, grillig, wispelturig, vol nukke.
Capricorn: Tropic of C., Steenbokskeerkring.
capsize, omslaan, omkantel.
capsule, doppie; skaaltjie; kapsule.
captain, n. kaptein.
captivate, bekoor, boei, inneem, vang.
captivity, gevange(n)skap, ballingskap.
capture, n. vangs; gevangeneming.
capture, v. vang; buitmaak, inneem.
car, rytuig, wa, motor.
caramel, karamel; gebrande suiker.
carat, karaat.
caravan, karavaan.
carbide, karbied.
carbon, koolstof.
carbon copy, deurslag.
carbuncle, karbonkel.
carburetter, -or, vergasser.
carcass, karkas, geraamte.
card, n. kaart; re(i)siesprogram.
cardboard, bordpapier, karton.
cardigan, wolonderbaadjie, knooptrui.
cardinal, a. kardinaal, vernaamste, hoof-...
cardinal, n. kardinaal.
care, n. sorgvuldigheid.
care, n. sorg, hoede; besorgdheid; sorgvuldigheid.
care, v. omgee, (sig) bekommer.
career, n. loopbaan; vaart.
career, v. snel, vlieg, ja.
carefree, sorgvry, onbesorg.
careful, oppassend, sorgvuldig, versigtig.
careless, sorgeloos, onoplettend, slordig, onverskillig, roekeloos, agterlosig.
caress, v. liefkoos, streel, paai, verwen.
caretaker, oppasser, opsigter.
cargo, lading, vrag.
caricature, karikatuur, spotprent.
carnation, ligrooi; angelier.
carnival, karnaval; feesviering.
carnivorous, vleisetend.
carol, n. vreugdelied; Kerslied.
carp, n. karper.
carp, v. vit, bedil, brom.
Carpathian: – Mountains, die Karpate.
carpenter, timmerman.

carpet, n. tapyt.
carriage, rytuig, (trein)wa; onderstel; vervoer; vrag; vervoerkoste; houding.
carrion, aas.
carrot, (geel)wortel.
carry, dra, vervoer, oordra; bevat.
cart, n. kar, voertuig, rytuig.
cart, v. (met 'n kar) vervoer, ry.
cartage, vervoer; vrag, karweiloon.
cartoon, ontwerptekening; spotprent.
cartridge, patroon; **blank –,** loskruit.
carve, (voor)sny; uitsny.
case, n. geval, saak; omstandigheid; hofsaak; naamval.
case, n. koffer, trommel, kis, doos; koker, huisie, sak, oortreksel, band.
cash, n. kontant(geld); kas, kasgeld; **hard –,** klinkende munt.
cash, v. (in)wissel, trek, honoreer, uitbetaal.
cash book, kasboek.
cashier, n. kassier.
cashier, v. afdank, afsit, ontslaan.
cask, vat.
casket, dosie, kissie.
Caspian, Kaspies.
cast, v. gooi, werp, strooi; afwerp; vorm, rang-skik, optel; rolle verdeel.
cast, n. gooi; optelling; opwerpsel; rolverdeling; afgietsel; soort, slag.
castaway, skipbreukeling; verworpeling.
caste, kaste, stand.
castigate, straf, tugtig; suiwer.
cast iron, n. gietyster; gegote yster.
castle, n. kasteel, slot.
castor-oil, kasterolie, wonderolie.
casual, toevallig, terloops; onverskillig.
casually, terloops, in die verbygaan.
casualty, ongeval; sterfgeval, verlies.
cat, n. kat; kats (strafwerktuig).
catacomb, katakombe, grafkelder.
catalogue, n. katalogus, lys, pryskoerant.
catapult, rekker.
cataract, waterval; star.
catarrh, katar, slymvliesontsteking.
catastrophe, katastrofe, ramp, onheil; ontkno-ping.
catch, v. vang; gryp, vat, vaspak; betrap; háal, inhaal; vashaak.
catch, n. vangs, vang; vanger; strikvraag, strik; knip, haak.
catching, aansteeklik; aantreklik; pakkend.
catchy, pakkend, aantreklik.
catechize, katkiseer, ondervra.
catechism, kategismus.
category, kategorie, klas, soort.
cater, voedsel (verversinge) verskaf.
caterer, leweransier.
caterpillar, ruspe(r).
caterwaul, miaau, kattegekerm.
catgut, dermsnaar; snaar.
cathedral, n. katedraal, domkerk.
Catholic, Katoliek.
cat-o'-nine-tails, kats.
cattle, vee, beeste; stomme vee.
caucus, koukus, partyvergadering.
cauliflower, blomkool.
cause, n. oorsaak, rede, beweegrede, grond, aan-leiding; (reg)saak.
cause, v. veroorsaak, teweegbring, bewerk, maak dat, laat.
causeway, straatweg; spoelbrug.
caustic, a. bytend, brandend, skerp.
caution, n. versigtigheid, omsigtigheid; verma-ning, waarskuwing.
caution, v. vermaan, waarsku; skrobbeer.

cautious, versigtig, omsigtig, behoedsaam.
cavalry, ruitery, perderuiters.
cave, n. spelonk, grot, gat; fraksie.
cavern, spelonk, grot, gat.
caviar(e), kaviaar, sout viskuit.
cavil, v. vit, bedil, haarklowe.
cavity, holte.
caw, kras, krys.
cease, v. ophou, stop, staak.
ceaseless, onophoudelik.
cedar, seder(boom); sederhout.
cede, op-, afgee, afstand doen van; sedeer, oor-dra.
ceiling, plafon.
celebrate, vier; herdenk; verheerlik.
cell, sel; hokkie; vakkie; kluis; graf.
cellar, n. kelder; wynvoorraad.
cellarage, kelderruimte; kelderhuur.
cello, violonsel, tjello.
celluloid, selluloïed.
Celsius: 100 degrees–, 100 grade Celsius.
cement, n. sement; band.
cement, v. segment; lym, vind, heg.
cemetery, begraafplaas,kerkhof.
cenotaph, gedenksteen; graf.
censor, sensor, keur-, sedemeester.
censure, v. afkeur; berispe; sensureer.
census, sensus, volkstelling.
cent, sent; **per–,** per honderd, persent.
centenary, eeufees.
centigram, sentigram.
centilitre, sentiliter.
centimetre, sentimeter.
centipede, duisendpoot.
central, sentraal, middel- . . .; midde- . . .; hoof- . . .
centralize, sentraliseer.
centre, n. middel, middelpunt, sentrum; spil; hoof; **– of gravity,** swaartepunt.
centre, a. midde, middelste.
century, honderd jaar, eeu; honderdtal.
cereal, n. graansoort; -s, graan, grane.
ceremonial, a. seremonieel, vormlik.
ceremony, seremonie, plegtigheid; vormlikheid.
certain, seker, gewis, stellig.
certificate, n. sertifikaat, getuigskrif, diploma.
certify, verseker, verklaar, getuig; waarmerk; sertifiseer.
cession, afstand, sessie.
chafe, v. vryf, skuur, skaaf; irriteer; wrewelig (ongeduldig) wees.
chaff, n. kaf; bog, waardelose ding.
chaff, v. terg, pla, vir die gek hou.
chaffinch, Europese vink, boekvink.
chagrin, n. ergernis, teleurstelling.
chain, n. ketting; reeks; -s, boeie, kettings; ge-vange(n)skap.
chain, v. boei, aan die ketting lê.
chair, n. stoel; voorsitter(stoel); professoraat.
chairman, voorsitter.
chalk, n. kalk, kryt.
challenge, v. uitdaag; uittart; aanroep, halt roep; protes aanteken, wraak.
chamber, kamer; slot, rewolwerloop; pot, uil.
chameleon, trapsoetjie, verkleurmannetjie.
chamfer, v. groef; skuinsmaak.
chamois: – leather, seemsleer.
champ, kou, byt, knaag.
champagne, sjampanje.
champion, n. kampioen, baas- . . .
champion, v. verdedig, veg vir, bepleit.
chance, n. kans, geleentheid; toeval, geluk.
chance, a. toevallig.
chance, v. gebeur; riskeer, waag.
chancellor, kanselier.

chandelier, kroonkandelaar.
change, v. verander (van); verruil, omruil, verwissel; kleinmaak; ver-, omklee; oorstap.
change, n. verandering; ruil, verwisseling; kleingeld; skoon klere; omkleding; oorstap(ping).
changeable, veranderlik.
channel, n. kanaal, sloot, bed(ding); groef.
chant, v. sing; singende resiteer.
chaos, chaos, warboel.
chap, n. kêrel, vent.
chap, v. bars, spring, skeur.
chaplain, kapelaan.
chapter, hoofstuk, kapittel.
char, (ver)brand, verkool.
character, n. karakter, kenmerk, stempel; hoedanigheid, soort; kenteken; letter(teken); rol.
characterize, kenskets.
characteristic, n. karaktertrek, kenmerk, eienaardigheid.
charcoal, houtskool.
charge, n. las; lading, skoot; sarsie, aanval; prys,
koste; taak, opdrag; sorg.
charge, v. laai; oplaai, belas; opdra; vra, in
rekening bring; aanval, beskuldig.
charitable, vrygewig; liefdadig; vriendelik.
charity, liefde, menseliefde; vrygewigheid, lief-
dadigheid.
charm, n. bekoring, betowering; gelukbringer;
toormiddel, -spreuk.
charm, v. bekoor, betower; toor.
charming, bekoorlik, betowerend.
chart, n. tabel; (see)kaart.
charter, n. grondwet; oktrooi.
charter, v. huur; bevrag.
chary, versigtig; suinig, karig.
chase, v. jag, jaag, najaag, agtervolg; agternaloop.
chasm, kloof, afgrond.
chassis, onderstel, geraamte, raam.
chaste, kuis, rein; suiwer, gekuis.
chastise, kasty, straf, tugtig.
chat, v. babbel, gesels.
chatter, v. babbel; snater; klap(pertand).
chatterbox, babbelbek, -kous, kekkelbek.
cheap, goedkoop; waardeloos.
cheat, v. bedrieg, fop, kul, flous.
check, v. skaaksit; stuit, stop; rem, weerhou,
beteuel; kontroleer; toets, nareken.
check, n. ruit; geruit, geruite stof.
checkmate, n. skaakmat.
checkmate, v. skaakmat sit, uitoorlê.
cheek, wang; astrantheid, koelbloedigheid.
cheeky, astrant, parmantig, brutaal.
cheep, piep.
cheer, n. stemming; toejuiging.
cheer, v. bemoedig, opvrolik; (toe)juig.
cheerful, opgewek, blymoedig, opgeruimd.
cheese, kaas.
cheetah, jagluiperd.
chemical, n. skeikundige stof; chemikalie.
chemist, apteker; skeikundige.
chemistry, skeikunde, chemie.
cheque, tjek, wissel.
cherish, koester, versorg; liefhê.
cheroot, seroet.
cherry, n. kers(ie), -boom.
chess, skaak(spel); **play –,** skaak speel.
chessmen, skaakstukke.
chest, kis, kas; bors(kas); **– of drawers,** laaikas,
klerekas.
chestnut, n. kastaiing; sweetvos(perd); ou grap.
chew, kou; pruim; peins, oordink; **– the cud,**
herkou.
chicken, kuiken; hoender-, kuikenvleis; jong
snuiter.

chicken-pox, waterpokkies.
chicory, sigorei.
chide, berispe, knor, uitskel.
chief, a. vernaamste, hoof- . . .
chief, n. leier, aanvoerder, hoofman, hoof.
chiefly, hoofsaaklik, vernaamlik, veral.
chieftain, hoof, opperhoof, kaptein.
chilblain(s), winterhande, -voete.
child, kind.
childhood, kindsheid, kindsdae.
childish, kinderagtig; kinderlik.
childlike, kinderlik.
chili, rissie.
chill, n. kilheid; koudheid; kou(e); verkoue-
(ntheid); onvriendelikheid.
chill, a. koud, kil, fris; koel.
chilly, kouerig; koulik, verkluimerig; koel.
chime, n. klokke; klok(ke)spel; kloklied.
chime, v. lui, slaan, speel; klokke lui.
chimney, skoorsteen, lamppyp; opening.
chimpanzee, sjimpansee, mensaap.
chin, ken.
China, China (Sjina).
Chinaman, Chiness (Sjinees).
chinaware, porseleingoed, -waar.
chink, n. spleet, bars.
chink, v. (laat) klink, rinkel.
chintz, sis.
chip, n. spaander, splinter, snipper.
chip, v. afsny, afsplinter; (laat) spring.
chirp, piep, tjilp.
chisel, n. beitel; **cold- –,** koubeitel.
celebrate, vier; herdenk; verheerlik.
chlorine, chloor.
chloroform, n. chloroform.
chloroform, v. onder chloroform sit.
chock-full, propvol.
chocolate, sjokolade.
choice, n. keus, voorkeur, beste, keur.
choice, a. uitgelese, uitgesogte, keurig.
choir, koor.
choke, v. (ver)stik, verwurg; smoor, demp; opstop, verstop.
choke, n. smoorklep, demper.
choose, kies, uit-, verkies.
chop, v. kap, hou, kloof.
chop, n. kap, hou; stuk; karmenaadjie, kotelet;
golfslag.
chopper, kapper, houer; byl, vleisbyl.
chord, snaar, koord.
chord, akkoord.
chorus, koor; refrein.
Christ, Christus.
christen, doop.
Christian, n. Christen; Christin.
Christian, a. Christelik; **– name,** voornaam.
Christmas, Kersfees, Kersmis.
Christmas-box, Kersgeskenk.
chromium, chroom.
chronic, chronies, langdurig, slepend.
chronological, chronologies.
chrysalis, papie.
chrysanthemum, krisant; aster; gousblom.
chubby, mollig, rondwangig.
chuckle, stilletjies lag, grinnik; klok.
chum, n. maat, vriend.
chunk, stuk, klomp, brok.
church, kerk.
churchyard, kerkhof.
churlish, lomp, onbeskof, honds; inhalig.
churn, v. karring, omroer; bruis, kook.
churn, n. karring.
chute, stroomversnelling; glybaan.
chutney, blatjang.
cigar, sigaar.

cigarette-case, sigaretkoker.
cinch, buikgord; voordeel; seker ding.
cinder, sintel, uitgebrande steenkool, as.
cinder-track, asbaan, sintelbaan.
cine-camera, rolprentkamera.
cinema, bioskoop, kinema.
cinnamon, kaneel.
circle, n. sirkel, kring, omtrek; sirkelloop; geselskap; galery, balkon.
circle, v. omsluit; omtrek; kringe maak, ronddraai; rondgaan; omsingel.
circuit, omtrek; rondreis; sirkelgang; stroomkring; **short –**, kortsluiting.
circuit-court, rondgaande hof.
circular, a. sirkelvormig, kringvormig; rondgaande; **– staircase**, wenteltrap.
circular, n. sirkulêre, omsendbrief.
circulate, rondgaan, in omloop wees, sirkuleer; laat rondgaan, in omloop bring.
circumference, omtrek.
circumflex, kappie.
circumspect, omsigtig, behoedsaam.
circumstance, omstandigheid; feit; besonderheid.
circumstantial, bykomstig; omstandig; **– evidence**, bykomende getuienis.
circus, sirkus; arena, strydperk, plein.
cistern, tenk, bak; dam; spoelbak.
citadel, sitadel, burg, vesting.
cite, dagvaar; aanhaal, siteer.
citizen, burger; stadsbewoner, inwoner.
citrus, sitrus.
city, stad.
city hall, stadhuis, stadsaal.
civet-cat, muskeljaatkat.
civic, burgerlik.
civics, burgerleer.
civil, burgerlik, burger- . . . ; siviel; beleef.
civilization, beskawing.
civilize, beskaaf.
claim, v. eis, aanspraak maak op; beweer.
claim, n. eis, vordering, aanspraak; bewering; kleim.
clamber, klouter.
clammy, klam, vogtig, taai, klewerig.
clamour, n. lawaai, geroep, geskreeu.
clam(p), n. kram; klem, skroef.
clamp, v. klem, (vas)klamp; las.
clan, stam; kliek; klas, soort.
clandestine, skelm, agterbaks, heimlik.
clang, v. skal, bons, kletter, lui.
clank, v. rammel, raas, klink.
clank, n. gerammel, geklank.
clap, n. klap, slag, knal.
clap, klap; toejuig.
clapperclaw, baklei, byt en krap, uitskel.
claptrap, effekbejag, mooipraatjies.
clarify, ophelder, opklaar, suiwer; helder word.
clash, v. bots, stoot; klink; indruis (teen), in stryd wees met.
clash, n. bons, stamp; gerammel; botsing.
clasp, n. klamp, haak, gespe(r), kram; handdruk; omhelsing.
clasp, v. vashaak, toegespe(r), omhels.
class, n. klas, rang, stand; orde.
class, v. klassifiseer, indeel.
classic, klassiek; **–s**, klassieke.
classical, klassiek.
classify, klassifiseer, indeel, rangskik.
clatter, v. kletter, rammel; trappel.
clause, klousule; artikel; bysin, sinsdeel.
claw, n. klou, poot; knyper, haak.
claw, v. klou, krap.
clay, klei; stoflike oorskot.
clean, a. skoon, suiwer, rein; netjies.

clean, v. skoonmaak, suiwer, opruim, aan die kant maak, poets.
clean, adv. skoon; totaal, heeltemal, glad.
cleanliness, sindelikheid, reinheid.
clear, a. helder, klaar; duidelik; skerp; deurdringend; skoon; oop, vry.
clear, v. skoonmaak, ophelder; op-, wegruim; leegmaak; trap; oorspring; uitklaar; afbetaal, vereffen; (tafel) afneem; ooptrek, opklaar (van die weer); vryspreek, suiwer; uitverkoop.
clearing, oop plek, skoon plek; opruiming; klaring.
cleave, kloof, splits, skei; klief, deursny.
cleave, kleef, vaskleef; getrou bly.
clemency, genadigheid; sagtheid.
clench, **clinch**, (om)klink, ombuig; (tande) vasbyt; (vuiste) bal; beklink, beseël.
clergyman, predikant, dominee.
clerk, klerk.
clever, slim, skrander, oulik, knap.
cliché, drukplaat, cliché; gemeenplaas.
click, v. tik, klik.
client, klant, kliënt.
cliff, krans, rots, klip.
climate, klimaat; (lug)streek.
climax, klimaks, hoogtepunt, toppunt.
climb, v. klim, klouter; beklim, bestyg.
climber, klimmer; klimplant.
cling, vassit, (aan)kleef, (vas)klem.
clingstone, taaipit.
clink, n. klink.
clinker, klinker, harde baksteen.
clip, v. (af)knip, skeer, snoei.
clip, n. skeersel.
clipper, knipper; skeermasjien, skêr; klipper (seilskip).
clipping, (uit)knipsel, skeersel.
clique, kliek.
cloak, n. mantel; dekmantel.
cloakroom, kleedkamer; bagasiekantoor.
clock, klok, horlosie.
clod, klont, kluit; blok, knul.
clog, n. blok (aan die been); klomp.
clog, v. belemmer; verstop; teenhou.
cloggy, kluiterig, klonterig; klewerig.
cloister, n. klooster, kruisgang, suilegang.
close, a. toe, gesluit, dig; nou, bekrompe; bedompig; geheimsinnig, agterhoudend; suinig; naby, digby; dig op mekaar; getrou.
close, v. toemaak, sluit; besluit, afsluit, eindig.
close, n. sluiting, slot, einde.
closet, n. privaatkamer; gemak(s)huisie.
clot, n. klont, klodder, (bloed)stolsel.
clot, v. klont, saampak; stol.
cloth, laken, tafellaken.
clothe, klee(d), beklee; inklee; bedek.
clothes, klere; beddegoed; linnegoed.
clothes-basket, wasgoedmandjie.
cloud, n. wolk.
cloud, v. (be)wolk; oorskadu, benewel.
cloud-burst, wolkbreuk.
cloudy, bewolk, newelagtig; wolkerig, troebel; duister, onduidelik.
clout, n. hou, slag; doek, lap.
clout, v. 'n hou gee.
clove, (krui)naeltjie.
clown, nar, hanswors, harlekyn; lomperd.
club, n. kierie, knots; gholfstok; klawer (kaart); klub.
club, v. (dood)slaan.
clubfoot, horrelvoet.
cluck, klok (van 'n hen).
clucking, broeis.
clue, leidraad; aanduiding; wenk; sleutel.
clump, bos, klomp; blok.

clumsy, onhandig, lomp.
cluster, n. bos(sie), trop, klompie.
cluster, v. 'n tros vorm, swerm, koek.
clutch, v. gryp, vat, ruk.
clutch, n. greep, gryp; klou; koppeling, koppelaar (van 'n motor).
coach, n. koets, rytuig, (spoor)wa, poskar; breier, afrigter.
coach, v. voorberei, oplei; brei, afrig.
coagulate, stol, strem, dik word, klont.
coal, n. (steen)kool.
coalition, samesmelting; koalisie.
coal-scuttle, kolebak, -emmer.
coal-tar, koolteer.
coarse, grof, ru, lomp, onbehoorlik.
coast, n. kus.
coat, n. baadjie; manel; (oor)jas; bekleding; verflaag.
coat, v. beklee, bedek, oortrek; verf.
coax, flikflooi, soebat, pamperlang.
cob, mannetjieswaan; poon; (mielie)kop.
cobbler, (skoen)lapper; knoeier; ysdrank.
cobra, kobra; **banded –**, koperkapel; **Cape –**, geelslang.
cobweb, spinnerak; net, web.
cocaine, kokaïen.
cock, n. (hoender)haan; weerhaan; haan (van 'n geweer); haantjie, doring; kraan.
cock, v. optrek; oorhaal.
cock-eyed, skeel; skuins, krom.
cockle-burr, kankerroos.
cockpit, stuurstoel (op 'n vliegtuig).
cockroach, kakkerlak.
cockscomb, hanekam.
cocksure, positief, seker; aanmatigend.
cocky, parmantig, verwaand.
cocoa, kakao.
coconut, klapper; klapperdop.
coconut-oil, klapperolie.
cocoon, papie.
cod, kabeljou.
coddle, vertroetel, verwen.
code, kode; wetboek, regulasies.
codlin(g)-moth, appelmot.
codliver-oil, visolie, lewertraan.
coerce, (af)dwing, beteuel, forseer.
coffee, koffie.
coffee-grounds, koffiemoer.
coffee-pot, koffiekan.
coffer, koffer, (geld)kas; –s, skatkis; fondse.
coffin, n. (dood)kis.
cog, n. kam, tand; kamrat, tandrat.
cogent, klemmend, oortuigend; dringend.
cogitate, peins, oorweeg, oordink.
cognac, konjak, fransbrandewyn.
conere, saamkleef, saamhang.
cohesion, samehang, verband; kohesie.
coil, v. opdraai, oprol, slinger, kronkel.
coil, n. bog, kronkeling; rol; (haar)lok; (induksie)klos, -spoel.
coin, n. munt(stuk), geld(stuk).
coin, v. munt, geld slaan; versin, uitdink.
coincide, saamval; ooreenstem.
coincidence, sameval, sameloop; ooreenstemming; toeval.
coir, klapperhaar.
cold, a. koud.
cold, n. kou(e); verkoue.
cold-chisel, koubeitel.
colic, koliek.
collaborate, saam-, meewerk.
collaborator, medewerker.
collapse, v. inmekaarsak, in duie stort; opvou, inmekaarvou; misluk.

collar, n. boordjie, kraag; halsband; borsriem; ring, band.
collar-bone, sleutelbeen.
colleague, kollega, ampgenoot.
collect, v. versamel, bymekaarmaak, vergader; bymekaarkom; insamel, kollekteer.
collective, gesame(nt)lik, gemeenskaplik, kollektief, verenigde, versamel- . . .
college, raad, genootskap; kollege.
collide, bots, in botsing kom, aanvaar, aanry.
collie, colly, Skotse herdershond, kollie.
colliery, steenkoolmyn, kolemyn.
collision, botsing, aanvaring, aanryding.
collusion, onderhandse samewerking (verstandhouding).
colon, dubbele punt.
colon, dikderm.
colonel, kolonel.
colonize, koloniseer, neerset.
colonist, kolonis, volksplanter, neersetter.
colony, kolonie, volksplanting, nedersetting.
colossal, kolossaal, reusagtig.
colour, n. kleur, tint; skyn.
colour, v. kleur, verf; oordryf, vermom, verdraai; kleur verleen; bloos.
colour-bar, kleurslagboom.
colt, jong perd; nuweling; slaanding.
column, kolom; pilaar; (leër)afdeling.
coma, bedwelming, swym; koma.
comb, n. kam; (heuning)koek.
comb, v. kam; kaard; skei, sif.
combat, n. geveg, stryd, kamp; **single –**, tweegeveg.
combat, v. (be)stry, (be)veg, worstel.
combination, verbinding, vereniging, kombinasie; samespanning; hempbroek.
combine, v. verbind, verenig, saamvat; saamsmelt; kombineer.
combine, n. sindikaat, trust, kartel; stroper (by koringoes).
combustible, brandbaar, ontvlambaar.
combustion, verbranding; brand.
come, kom.
comedian, komediant; toneelspeler.
comedy, komedie, blyspel.
comely, bevallig, aantreklik; gepas.
comet, komeet, stertster, roeister.
comfort, n. troos, vertroosting; verligting; gemak, gerief; voldoening.
comfort, v. troos, vertroos, opbeur.
comfortable, gemaklik, gerieflik, behaaglik.
comforter, trooster, fopspeentjie; serp.
comic(al), komiek(lik), komies, grappig, snaaks, koddig.
comma, komma; **inverted –s**, aanhalingstekens.
command, v. beveel, gebied; aanvoer, die bevel voer oor; beheers; beskik oor; uitsig gee op, uitsien op; afdwing.
command, n. bevel, gebod, las, opdrag; aanvoering; meesterskap, beheersing.
commander, bevelvoerder, -hebber; kommandeur; eerste offisier; kommandant.
commander-in-chief, opperbevelhebber.
commanding, bevelend; bevelvoerend; beheersend; indrukwekkend.
commandment, gebod.
commando, kommando.
commemorate, gedenk, herdenk, vier.
commence, begin, aanvang.
commend, aanbeveel, prys; toevertrou.
commendable, aanbevelenswaardig, loflik.
comment, n. uitleg(ging); opmerking; aanmerking, kommentaar.
comment, v. aanmerk; **– on**, op-, aanmerkinge maak op, kritiseer.

commentary, verklaring, uitleg, kommentaar.
commerce, handel; verkeer; omgang.
commercial, kommersieel, handeldrywend, handels- . . . , verkeers- . . . ; – traveller, handelsreisiger.
commission, n. las, opdrag; volmag; kommissie; (die) begaan, pleging.
commissioner, kommissaris; kommissielid, opsiener; High C., Hoëkommissaris.
commit, toevertrou; begaan, pleeg; verwys; verbind.
committee, komitee, kommissie.
commodity, gerief; handelsartikel.
common, a. gewoon, algemeen; publiek; gemeenslagtig; ordinêr; laag, sleg.
commonage, weireg; dorpsgrond, meent.
commonly, gewoonlik, meestal, deurgaans; gewoon; gemeen, sleg.
commonplace, a. gewoon, alledaags.
commonplace, n. gemeenplaas.
common-room, personeelkamer.
commonwealth, gemenebes.
commotion, beweging; opskudding; opstand.
communicate, meedeel; oorbring; Nagmaal bedien (gebruik); gemeenskap hou; in verbinding wees, oorlê; ineenloop (van vertrekke).
communication, meedeling; gemeenskap; verbinding; verkeersmiddel(e), verkeersweë; kommunikasie.
communion, omgang; gemeenskap; Nagmaal.
communism, kommunisme, gemeenskapsleer.
communist, kommunis; a. kommunisties.
community, gemeenskap.
commutator, (stroom)wisselaar.
compact, n. ooreenkoms, verdrag.
compact, a. dig, beknop, kompak.
companion, n. metgesel, maat, kameraad.
company, n. geselskap; gaste; maatskappy, genootskap.
comparative, vergelykend; betreklik; – degree, vergrotende trap.
compare, v. vergelyk; wedywer; trappe van vergelyking noem.
comparison, vergelyking.
compartment, afdeling, vak; kompartement.
compass, n. omtrek; omvang, bestek; grens; bereik; kompas.
compasses, (pair of) –, passer.
compassion, medelye, erbarming.
compatible, bestaanbaar, verenigbaar.
compatriot, landgenoot.
compel, noodsaak, verplig; afdwing.
compère, aankondiger, seremoniemeester.
compensate, skadeloos stel, vergoed, vergeld.
compete, wedywer, konkurreer, meeding.
competent, bevoeg, bekwaam.
competition, mededinging, wedywer; wedstryd; kompetisie.
competitor, mededinger, deelnemer.
compile, versamel, saamstel, kompileer.
complain, kla(e) (klaag).
complainant, klaer; eiser.
complaint, klag(te), aanklag; kwaal.
complaisance, tegemoetkomendheid; inskiklikheid.
complement, n. aanvulling; voltooiing; volle getal, taks; komplement (wiskunde).
complete, a. volledig, voltallig, kompleet; totaal, volkome, volmaak.
complete, v. voltooi; voltallig maak.
complex, a. ingewikkeld, samegestel(d).
complexion, (gelaats)kleur.
compliance, inskiklikheid; instemming; in – with, ingevolge, ooreenkomstig.
complicate, v. ingewikkeld maak.

compliment, n. pluimpie.
compliment, v. gelukwens; kompliment maak.
comply, inwillig; – with, voldoen aan; toestem in.
component, n. bestanddeel.
compose, saamstel, (uit)maak; rangskik; besleg; kalmeer; set (van drukwerk).
composedly, bedaard, rustig, kalm.
composition, samestelling, verbinding; opstel; toonsetting; geaardheid.
compost, mengsel; gemengde bemesting, kompos.
compound, a. samegestel(d).
compound, n. mynkamp; kampong.
comprehend, begryp, verstaan; insluit.
compress, v. saamdruk; saampers; saamvat.
compress, n. kompres, nat verband.
comprise, v. omvat, insluit; bestaan uit
compromise, n. skikking, vergelyk ooreenkoms.
compromise, v. skik, vergelyk tref; kompromitteer.
compulsion, dwang, geweld.
compulsory, gedwonge, verpligtend.
compute, bereken, uitreken; skat.
comrade, maat, kameraad.
concave, hol, holrond, konkaaf.
conceal, verberg, verstop, wegsteek; bedek, verswyg, geheim hou.
conceit, verwaandheid, verbeelding.
conceited, verwaand, eiewys.
conceive, opvat; (sig) voorstel; glo, begryp; uitdink.
concentrate, saamtrek, konsentreer
conception, begrip, voorstelling, opvatting, konsepsie.
concern, v. betref, aangaan, raak.
concern, n. saak; aangeleentheid.
concerned, betrokke; besorg.
concerning, aangaande, met betrekking tot.
concert, n. samewerking; konsert.
concertina, konsertina.
concession, bewilliging; begunstiging; vergunning; konsessie.
concise, beknop, bondig.
conclude, besluit, eindig; aflei.
conclusion, slot, einde; gevolgtrekking, konklusie.
conclusive, afdoende, oortui(g)end.
concoct, saamflans; brou; smee(d) beraam.
concoction, brousel; versinsel.
concord, ooreenstemming, harmonie.
concrete, a. konkreet, tasbaar.
concrete, beton.
concur, instem; saamstem; saamval.
concurrent, ewewydig; gelyktydig, samevallend; instemmend.
concussion, (hersen)skudding, skok; botsing.
condemn, veroordeel; afkeur.
condense, kondenseer, verdig; saampers.
condescend, neerbuig, (sig) verwaardig.
condition, n. toestand, staat; voorwaarde, stipulasie; kondisie; rang, stand.
conditional, a. voorwaardelik, kondisioneel.
condole, kondoleer, simpatie betuig.
condone, vergewe; goedmaak.
conducive, bevorderlik (vir).
conduct, n. gedrag; bestuur, beheer.
conduct, v. gedra; lei; bestuur; dirigeer.
conduction, geleiding.
conductor, geleier; bestuurder; kondukteur; dirigent, orkesleier; bliksemafleier; geleidraad.
cone, keël, keil, dennebol.
confectioner, koekbakker, lekkergoedmaker.
confederate, n. bondgenoot; saamgesworene.
confederation, bondgenootskap, konfederasie.
confer, toeken, verleen; beraadslaag.

conference, byeenkoms, konferensie; onderhoud, bespreking, beraadslaging.
confess, erken, beken, bely, bieg.
confide, vertrou, toevertrou, meedeel, opbieg.
confidence, (self)vertroue; vrymoedigheid.
confident, seker, oortuig; vrymoedig.
confidential, vertroulik, in vertroue; konfidensieel.
confine, v. beperk, bepaal, begrens, insluit; opsluit.
confirm, bevestig; goedkeur; versterk.
confiscate, beslag lê op, konfiskeer.
conflict, n. stryd, botsing, worsteling.
conflict, v. bots, in stryd wees (met).
confluence, samevloeiing.
confluent, n. bystroom.
conform, vorm (na); skik (na), aanpas (by), voeg (na).
conformity, ooreenkoms, gelykvormigheid; in – with, ooreenkomstig.
confound, in die war stuur; dronkslaan.
confront, teenoor mekaar stel, bymekaar bring.
confuse, verwar, deurmekaar maak.
confusion, verwarring; wanorde; verleentheid.
confute, weerlê.
congeal, bevries, stol, dik (hard) word.
congenial, geesverwant, simpatiek, geskik.
congestion, ophoping, stremming; kongestie.
congratulate, gelukwens, felisiteer.
congregate, versamel, vergader, byeenkom.
congregation, vergadering; gemeente.
congress, kongres, byeenkoms.
conjoin, aansluit; saamsluit, verbind.
conjugate, v. vervoeg; een word.
conjunction, voegwoord; verbinding, vereniging.
conjure, besweer; oproep; toor, goël, oë verblind.
conjurer, -or, toornaar, goëlaar.
connect, verbind; aansluit.
connected, verbonde; samehangend.
connection, -nexion, verbinding; verband; aansluiting; gemeenskap; samehang; betrekking; konneksie.
connive: – at, oogluikend toelaat.
connoisseur, kenner, fynproewer.
connote, beteken; bybetekenis hê; insluit.
conquer, verower, oorwin, verslaan; seëvier.
conqueror, oorwinnaar, veroweraar.
conscience, gewete, konsensie.
conscientious, nougeset, pliggetrou.
conscious, bewus.
consciousness, bewustheid; bewussyn; lose –, bewussyn verloor, flou word.
consecrate, v. heilig, wy; toewy; inseën.
consecutive, opeenvolgend; – number, volgnommer.
consent, v. in-, toestem, inwillig.
consequence, gevolg, uitwerking; gevolgtrekking; belang, betekenis.
consequently, gevolglik, dientengevolge.
consequent, gevolglik; logies, konsekwent.
conservative, behoudend, konserwatief.
conservatory, broeikas; konserwatorium.
conserve, v. bewaar, in stand hou; inlê.
consider, beskou; oorweeg.
considerable, aansienlik, aanmerklik.
considerate, bedagsaam, voorkomend, hoflik.
consideration, beskouing, oorweging; vergoeding; bedagsaamheid; betekenis.
considering, aangesien.
consign, toevertrou; oorlewer, oordra; afstuur.
consignee, geadresseerde.
consignment, oordrag, oorlewering; afsending; (be)sending; – note, vragbrief.
consignor, afsender.
consist: – of, bestaan uit.

consistence, -cy, dikte, digtheid, vastheid; konsekwensie.
consistent, konsekwent, beginselgetrou; – with, in ooreenstemming (verenigbaar) met.
consolation, troos, vertroosting.
console, v. (ver)troos, opbeur.
consolidate, vas word, hard word; versterk; bevestig; verenig, konsolideer.
consonant, medeklinker, konsonant.
consort, n. gemaal (gemalin); metgesel.
conspicuous, opvallend; uitblinkend.
conspire, saamsweer, saamspan; beraam.
constable, konstabel, polisieagent.
constant, a. standvastig; bestendig; trou; voortdurend, aanhoudend.
consternation, ontsteltenis, verslaentheid.
constipation, hardlywigheid, konstipasie.
constituency, kiesers; kiesafdeling.
constitution, samestelling; gesteldheid, gestel; staatsvorm; grondwet; konstitusie.
constrain, dwing; bedwing; verplig, noodsaak; vashou; opsluit.
constrict, toedruk, saamtrek, beperk.
construct, saamstel; maak, bou, oprig.
constructive, opbouend; konstruktief.
construe, uitlê, verklaar; opvat; verbind.
consul, konsul.
consult, v. raadpleeg, beraadslaag.
consume, verteer; verbruik; uitteer.
consumer, verbruiker; deurbringer.
consumption, vertering, verbruik; tering.
contract, aanraking; kontak.
contagious, aansteeklik, besmetlik.
contain, inhou, bevat, insluit; bedwing.
contaminate, besoedel, bevlek, besmet.
contemplate, beskou; (be)peins; beoog.
contemporary, n. tydgenoot; kollega (nuusblad).
contempt, veragting, minagting.
contend, stry, worstel; wedywer; beweer.
content(s), n. inhoud; omvang.
content, a. tevrede, vergenoeg.
contention, twis; bewering; kontensie.
contest, v. bestry, beveg, betwis; stry.
context, verband, samehang.
continent, a. matig, onthoudend; kuis.
continent, n. vasteland, kontinent.
contingency, toeval(ligheid); gebeurlikheid.
continual, aanhoudend, voortdurend.
continue, aanhou, volhou; vervolg, voortsit; volhard; bly; verleng.
continuous, onafgebroke, aanhoudend.
contortionist, (woord)verdraaier; slangmens.
contour, omtrek, lyn, hoogtelyn.
contraband, n. smokkelwaar; sluikhandel.
contract, n. ooreenkoms, verdrag, kontrak.
contract, v. ooreenkoms; inkrimp, saamtrek.
contradict, weerspreek, teëpraat.
contrary, a. teenoorgesteld; teengesteld; dwars; koppig, eiewys.
contrary, n. teenoorgestelde, teendeel; on the –, inteendeel.
contrast, n. teenstelling, kontras.
contravene, oortree; teenstaan, teenwerk.
contribute, bydra; meewerk.
contrive, bedink, versin; regkry; bestuur.
control, n. beheer, toesig; bedwang; kontrole.
control, v. beheers; bedwing, beteuel; toesig hou; kontroleer.
controller, opsigter; kontroleur.
controversy, stryd(vraag), twispunt, geskil, polemiek.
convalesce, aansterk, beter word.
convene, saamroep, belê; vergader.
convenience, gerief, gemak; geskiktheid.
convenient, gerieflik; geskik.

convent, klooster.
convention, byeenkoms; ooreenkoms; gebruik, tradisie; konvensie.
conventional, konvensioneel, gebruiklik; vormlik.
converge, (in een punt) saamloop.
conversant, bekend (met), bedrewe (in).
conversation, konversasie, gesprek.
converse, v. praat, gesels, konverseer.
converse, n. (die) omgekeerde, teenoorgestelde.
conversion, omkering; bekering; omsetting.
convert, v. omsit, verander (in, tot), omwissel; bekeer.
convex, bol(rond).
convey, vervoer, (oor)dra, oorbring; meedeel, gee; sê, beteken.
conveyance, vervoer, vervoermiddel; oordrag; transport.
convict, n. bandiet, dwangarbeider.
convict, v. skuld bewys; skuldig vind; oortuig.
convince, oortuig.
convocation, byeenroeping; vergadering, konvokasie.
convoy, n. konvooi; geleide.
convulsive, krampagtig, stuipagtig.
coo, koer; liefkoos.
cook, n. kok.
cook, v. kook; bewerk, vervals.
cookery, kookkuns.
cool, a. koel; bedaard, kalm.
cool, v. afkoel, verkoel.
coop, n. fuik, hoenderhok.
co-operate, saamwerk, meewerk, koöpereer.
co-opt, koöpteer.
co-ordinate, a. gelyk, newegeskik.
co-ordinate, v. gelykstel; neweskik; koördineer.
cope, v. – with, opgewasse wees teen; voldoen aan, raad weet met.
copious, oorvloedig; uitvoerig; ryk.
copper, koper; kopergeld; pennie.
copy, n. koppie; afskrif; nabootsing, reproduksie; eksemplaar; kopie.
copy, v. kopieer; afskrywe; oorskrywe; naboots, namaak.
coral, koraal.
cord, n. tou, lyn, koord, string, band; rib; vocal –s, stembande.
cordial, a. hartlik; hartsterkend.
corduroy, ferweel; ferweelbroek.
core, kern, pit, hart, binneste.
cork, n. prop; kurk; dobber.
cork, v. toekurk, prop opsit; 'n kol gee.
corkscrew, n. kurktrekker.
cork-tipped, met kurk(mondstuk).
corn, n. korrel; graan; koring.
corn, n. liddoring.
cornea, horingvlies.
corner, n. hoek.
corner, v. vaskeer.
corner-stone, hoeksteen.
cornet, kornet; kornetblaser; kardoes.
cornice, kroon(lys).
coroner, lykskouer; –'s inquest, (geregtelike) lykskouing.
corporal, corporeal, a. liggaamlik, stoflik; – punishment, lyfstraf.
corporal, n. korporaal.
corporation, korporasie, vereniging, liggaam, bestuur; buik.
corps, korps, afdeling.
corpse, lyk, dooie liggaam.
corpulent, swaarlywig, geset, korpulent.
corpuscle, liggaampie, stoffie, atoom.
correct, v. verbeter, nasien, korrigeer; berispe.
correct, a. reg, korrek, noukeurig, presies.

correlate, v. korreleer.
correspond, ooreenkom, ooreenstem; korrespondeer.
correspondence, ooreenkoms; briefwisseling.
corridor, gang, korridor.
corroborate, bevestig, bekragtig.
corrode, wegvreet; verroes; vergaan.
corrugate, rimpel; golf; –d iron, sink(plaat); –d iron roof, sinkdak; –d road, sinkplaatpad, riffelpad.
corrupt, a. bedorwe; omkoopbaar.
corrupt, v. bederf; verlei; omkoop.
corset, bors(t)rok, korset.
cosmetic, kosmetiek, skoonheidsmiddel.
cosmonaut, ruimreisiger.
cosmopolitan, a. kosmopolities.
cost, n. prys, koste.
cost, v. kos.
cost price, inkoopsprys.
costume, (klere)drag; kostuum; pak; rok.
cosy, a. behaaglik, gesellig.
cosy, n. teemus.
cot, n. katel; (kinder)bedjie; wieg.
cottage, hutjie; huisie.
cotton, n. katoen; garing.
cotton-wool, watte.
couch, n. rusbank, sofa; bed, siekbed.
cough, hoes.
council, raad; – of war, krygsraad.
councillor, raadslid.
counsel, n. raad, plan; beraadslaging; raadgewer, advokaat.
counsel, v. aanraai.
counsellor, raadgewer, raadsman.
count, n. graaf.
count, v. tel, optel, meetel; reken, ag.
countenance, n. gesig, voorkoms.
countenance, v. toelaat; begunstig, steun.
counter, n. blokkie, skyfie; toonbank.
counter-, teen-.
counteract, teenwerk; ophef; verydel.
counterfeit, a. nagemaak, oneg, vals.
counterfoil, teenblad; kontrabiljet.
country, land; landstreek; vaderland; platteland.
countryman, landgenoot.
coupé, koepee.
couple, n. paar, span.
couple, v. verbind, in verband bring; koppel.
coupon, koepon; rentebewys; kaartjie.
courage, moed, dapperheid, koerasie.
course, n. loop, gang; vaart; loopbaan, koers, rigting; (ren)baan; kursus, leergang; ry, reeks; laag.
court, n. hof; kantoor, geregshof, regbank; hofhouding; baan.
court, v. die hof maak; vry (na); soek.
courteous, beleef, hoflik, hoofs.
court martial, krygsraad.
cousin, neef (niggie).
cover, v. (be)dek, oordek; beskerm; beheers; bestryk; aanlê op; betaal; dek.
cover, n. (be)deksel; deksel; band, omslag; skuilplaas; dekmantel; dekkingsfonds.
cover-girl, fotomeisie.
covert, a. bedek, geheim, onderlangs.
covet, begeer.
covetous, begerig; gierig, inhalig.
cow, n. koei; wyfie.
coward, lafaard, bangbroek.
cowardly, lafhartig.
cowherd, beeswagter.
coy, sedig, skaam, bedees.
crab, n. krap; kreef; wen(as).
crack, n. (ge)klap; kraak, knak, bars; baasspeler, -skieter.

crack, v. kraak, klap, bars, knap, skeur.
crack, a. uithaler- . . . , baas- . . .
cracker, neutkraker; klapper; klinker.
crackle, kraak; knapper, knetter.
cradle, n. wieg; bakermat; raamwerk.
craft, ambag, handwerk; vaartuig; behendigheid, geslepenheid.
crafty, handig, slim, slu, listig.
crag, krans, rots.
cram, v. volstop, instop; inswelg.
cramp, n. kramp; klamp, anker.
cramp, v. kram, klamp.
crane, n. kraanvoël; kraan; hewel.
crane, v. (nek) uitrek.
crank, v. draai, (aan)slinger.
crank-case, krukkas.
crank-shaft, krukas.
crate, krat, mandjie, kis, hok.
crater, krater.
crash, v. raas; neerstort; verpletter; bots.
crave, bid, smeek, uitroep (om), verlang (na).
craving, verlange, behoefte, begeerte, lus.
crawl, v. kruip; aansukkel.
crayfish, (rivier)kreef.
crayon, n. (teken)kryt.
craze, n. gekheid, gier, manie; mode.
crazy, gek, waansinnig; lendelam.
creak, v. kraak, knars.
cream, n. room.
cream, a. roomkleurig.
creamery, botterfabriek.
crease, n. vou, plooi, rimpel; streep (krieket).
crease, v. vou, plooi, rimpel, kreukel.
create, skep; voortbring; veroorsaak; benoem.
creature, skepsel; mens; huurling; dier.
credible, aanneemlik; geloofwaardig.
credit, n. vertroue, geloof; aansien; eer; krediet.
credit, v. geloof, krediteer.
creditor, skuldeiser, krediteur.
credulous, lig-, goedgelowig.
creed, geloof, geloofsbelydenis.
creep, v. kruip, sluip.
cremate, verbrand, veras.
crematorium, krematorium.
creole, n. kreool.
cress, bronkors, waterkers.
crest, n. kuif; kam; pluim; maanhare; (skuim)top, kop, kruin; wapen.
crevasse, ysskeur.
crevice, skeur, spleet.
crew, bemanning.
cricket, kriek(ie).
cricket, krieket.
crime, misdaad; wandaad.
Crimea, The, Die Krim.
criminal, misdadig; krimineel.
crimson, a. karmosyn(rooi).
cringe, ineenkrimp; kruip; witvoetjie soek.
crinkle, v. krinkel, frommel, kreukel.
cripple, a. kreupel, mank.
cripple, n. 'n kreupele, 'n manke.
crisis, keerpunt, krisis.
crisp, a. kroes; krullerig; bros; fris, opwekkend; lewendig, beslis.
criterion, maatstaf, toets, kriterium.
critic, kritikus, resensent, beoordelaar.
critical, kritiek, haglik; krities; vitterig.
criticize, kritiseer, resenseer, beoordeel; vit.
croak, kwaak; vrek.
crochet, v. hekel.
crochet-hook, hekelpennetjie.
crock, v. breek, seermaak.
crock, n. erdepot; knol, kruk.
crockery, erdegoed, breekgoed.
crocodile, krokodil.

crony, boesemvriend, boetie.
crook, n. haak; staf; boef.
crook, v. buig; bedrieg, fop.
crooked, krom, verdraai; mismaak; slinks, oneerlik.
croon, v. neurie, brom.
crop, n. krop; handvatsel, steel; rysweep; gewas, gesaaide, oes.
cross, n. kruis; (ras)kruising; kruisproduk, baster.
cross, v. kruis; deurkruis; oorgaan, oorsteek; dwarsboom, teenwerk; verbygaan by mekaar.
cross, a. dwars, oorkruis; verkeerd; kwaad, kwaai.
cross-bar, dwarshout; swingel; draaghoutjie.
cross-examine, kruisvra(ag).
cross-eyed, skeel.
crossing, kruising, kruispunt, oorgang.
cross-road, dwarspad.
crouch, hurk, buk; kruip.
croup, kroep.
crow, n. kraai.
crow, v. kraai; brabbel; spog.
crowbar, koevoet, breekyster.
crowd, n. menigte, klomp, hoop; gedrang.
crown, n. kroon; krans; kruin; bol (van hoed).
crown, v. (be)kroon.
crown prosecutor, publieke vervolger, staatsaanklaer.
crown-wheel, kroonrat, dryfrat.
crucial, kruisvormig; kritiek, beslissend.
crucify, kruisig, kruis.
crude, ru; onbeholpe; onafgewerk; onryp; ongesuiwer(d).
cruel, wreed, wreedaardig, onmenslik.
cruet-stand, standertjie; asynstelletjie.
cruise, v. kruis, vaar.
cruise, n. tog, vaart.
cruiser, kruiser.
crumb, n. krummel.
crumble, krummel; (af)brokkel.
crumpet, plaatkoek.
crumple, kreukel, verfrommel.
crunch, v. kraak, hard kou, knars.
crupper, stertriem; kruis (van 'n perd).
crusade, kruistog, -vaart.
crusader, kruisvaarder.
crush, v. plat druk; onderdruk; verpletter, vermorsel; verkreukel.
crusher, stamper.
crust, n. kors; roof; aanbrandsel; aansetsel.
crust, v. kors (vorm); aanbrand.
crutch, kruk; steun.
crux, knoop, moeilikheid.
cry, n. skreeu, (ge)roep, kreet, gil; klag, bede, roepstem.
cry, v. roep, uitroep, skreeu; ween.
crystal, n. kristal.
cub, n. welp.
cube, n. kubus; derdemag; – root, kubiekwortel.
cubby-hole, paneelvak, -kassie, -kissie.
cubicle, slaap-, baaihokkie.
cucumber, komkommer.
cud, herkoutjie.
cuddle, liefkoos, omhels.
cudgel, n. kierie, stok.
cue, wenk, aanwysing; wagwoord.
cue, keu; biljartstok; haar-, pruikstert.
cuff, n. omslag, mansjet, (hemps)mou.
cuff, v. klap, oorveeg gee.
cuff-link, mansjetknoop, mouskakel.
cuisine, kookkuns, keuken; tafel, ete.
cul-de-sac, doodloopstraat, blinde steeg, sakstraat.
cull, pluk; uitsoek, uitvang.

culminate, die hoogtepunt bereik, kulmineer.
culpable, skuldig, strafbaar.
culprit, skuldige, boosdoener.
cultivate, bewerk; (aan)kweek, verbou; beskaaf; beoefen.
cultivator, kweker, verbouer; skoffelploeg, -eg.
culture, n. verbouding, kweking; beskawing; ontwikkeling, kultuur.
culvert, riool; spoelgat, duiksloot.
cumbersome, cumbrous, lastig, hinderlik.
cumulative, ophopend; kumulatief.
cunning, a. slim; geslepe; bedrewe.
cup, n. koppie; beker; kelkie.
cupboard, kas, muurkas, koskas.
Cupid, Kupido.
cupidity, begerigheid, hebsug.
cur, brak(kie); skobbejak, skurk.
curable, geneeslik, geneesbaar.
curate, (hulp)predikant.
curator, opsigter; voog: kurator.
curb, n. kenketting; rem, beteueling.
curb, v. inhou, beteuel; bedwing.
curd, dikmelk, stremsel.
curdle, dik word; stol (van bloed).
cure, n. (genees)middel; genesing.
cure, v. genees; verhelp, regmaak; inlê, sout, rook, droogmaak.
curfew, aand-, nagklok.
curio, kuriositeit, kunsvoorwerp.
curious, weetgierig; nuuskierig; merkwaardig, seldsaam.
curl, n. krul; (haar)lok.
curl, v. krul, kronkel, draai.
curler, krulpen.
curly, gekrul, krullerig, krul- . . .
currant, korent.

currency, omloop; gangbaarheid; munt.
current, a. lopende; in omloop, gangbaar; aangenome, algemeen.
current, n. stroom; stroming; loop, koers.
curriculum, kursus, leerplan.
curry, n. kerrie.
curry, v. roskam; brei; vel, klop.
curry-comb, roskam.
curse, v. vloek, vervloek, laster.
cursory, oppervlakkig, vlugtig; kursories.
curt, kortaf, bits(ig).
curtail, verkort, inkort, besnoei.
curtain, n. gordyn; skerm.
curve, v. buig, draai, 'n bog maak.
curve, n. boog; kromme; bog, draai.
cushion, n. kussing.
custard, vla.
custody, bewaring; hegtenis; voogdyskap.
custom, gewoonte, gebruik; klandisie.
customer, klant.
custom-house, doeanekantoor, tolhuis.
cut, n. sny; kap; hou; raps; keep; snit, fatsoen, vorm.
cut, v. sny; kerf; kap; raps, 'n hou gee; snoei; knip; klief; aanslaan; grief.
cute, oulik, slim, geslepe.
cutlery, messeware, messegoed, tafelgereedskap.
cutlet, kotelet, karmenaadjie.
cutting, uitknipsel; uitgrawing; steggie.
cycle, n. kringloop; fiets.
cyclone, sikloon, warrelwind, windhoos.
cylinder, silinder.
cynic, a. sinies; bytend, skerp.
cypress, sipres.
Czech, n. Tsjeg, Bohemer.
Czecho-Slovakia, Tsjeggo-Slowakye.

dab, n. tikkie, kloppie; spatsel.
dad, daddy, pa, pappie.
daddy-longlegs, langbeenspinnekop.
daffodil, affodil, geel narsing.
daft, dwaas, gek, mal.
dagger, dolk.
dahlia, dahlia.
daily, a. & adv. daagliks, dag- . . .
daily, n. dagblad.
dainty, a. fyn, sierlik, delikaat; kieskeurig.
dairy, melkery; melkkamer.
dairy farm, melkboerdery.
dairyman, melkboer.
dairy produce, suiwelproduk(te).
dais, verhoog; troonhemel.
daisy, madeliefie; margriet.
dally, dartel, speel; drentel, treusel.
dam, n. damwal; dam.
dam, v. opdam; stuit, keer.
dam, n. moe(de)r.
damage, n. skade; onkoste, skadevergoeding.
damage, v. beskadig, bederf; benadeel.
dame, dame; vrou; huisvrou; adellike dame.
damn, v. verdoem, veroordeel; benadeel, skend; afkeur; vloek.
damp, a. vogtig, klam.
dance, v. dans.
dance, n. dans; bal, dansparty.
Dane, Deen; Deense hond.
danger, gevaar, bedreiging.
dangerous, gevaarlik.
dangle, swaai, bengel, slinger.
Danube, Donau.
dapple-grey, appelskimmel.
Dardanelles, Dardanelle.
dare, durf; waag; trotseer.
daredevil, waaghals.
daring, n. durf, vermetelheid.
daring, a. koen, vermetel, astrant.
dark, a. donker; duister, geheim(sinnig).
dark, n. donker; duister(nis); duisterheid.
darken, donker word; donker maak, verduister.
darling, n. liefling, liefste, skat, hartlam.
darling, a. skatlik, liefste.
darn, v. stop, heelmaak.
dart, n. werppyl.
dart, v. gooi; skiet; straal; wegspring, pyl.
dash, v. klets; klots; gooi, smyt; slaan; bespat; stuif, vlieg; neerslaan.
data, gegewens.
date, n. dadel.
date, n. datum; dagtekening; jaartal.
date, v. dateer, dagteken.
dative, datief.
daub, v. besmeer, bepleister, beklad.
daughter, dogter.
daughter-in-law, skoondogter.
dawdle, draai, seur, drentel.
dawn, n. dagbreek, môreskemering.
day, dag; daglig; dagbreek.
daybreak, dagbreek.
day-dream, lugkasteel, mymering.
daze, v. verbyster, bedwelm; verblind.
dazzle, verblind; verbyster.
deacon, diaken; geestelike.
dead, a. dood; styf, dom; dooierig.
dead-alive, lewendig-dood.
dead-beat, poot-uit.
deaden, verdoof, temper; verstomp.
deadlock, dooie punt.
deadly, dodelik.
dead march, treurmars, dodemars.
deaf, doof.
deafen, doof maak; verdoof.
deaf-mute, doofstom.

deal, n. deel, gedeelte, hoeveelheid, klomp, boel; beurt (om kaarte te gee); (handel)-saak, slag.
deal, v. deel, ver-, uitdeel, toedeel, gee; handel.
deal, greinhout.
dealer, handelaar.
dean, fakulteitsvoorsitter, dekaan.
dear, a. lief, dierbaar; duur, kosbaar; **D. Sir,** geagte heer.
dearly, baie, erg, teer; duur.
death, dood; sterfgeval, (die) afsterwe.
death-bed, sterfbed.
death-duty, sterfreg, suksessiereg.
debacle, hopelose mislukking, fiasko.
debar, uitsluit, verhinder, belet.
debase, verlaag, verneder; vervals.
debate, n. debat, bespreking.
debate, v. debatteer, bespreek.
debility, swakheid, kragteloosheid.
debit, n. skuld, debet.
debit, v. debiteer, boek teen; belas.
debit balance, nadelige saldo.
debris, puin; opdrifsels.
debt, skuld.
debtor, skuldenaar, debiteur.
decade, tiental; dekade.
decadent, verwordend, dekadent.
decagram(me), dekagram.
decalitre, dekaliter.
decametre, dekameter.
decamp, verkas.
decapitate, onthoof.
decarbonize, ontkool.
decathlon, tienkamp, dekatlon.
decay, v. vergaan, verval; bederf.
decay, n. verval, agteruitgang; verrotting, bederf.
deceased, oorledene, afgestorwene.
deceit, bedrog, misleiding.
deceive, bedrieg, mislei, fop; verlei.
December, Desember.
decent, fatsoenlik, betaamlik; ordentlik.
decentralize, desentraliseer.
deceptive, bedrieglik, misleidend.
decide, besluit, uitmaak, beslis; oordeel.
decided, beslis, bepaald; nadruklik.
deciduous, bladwisselend; afvallend.
decimal, a. tientallig; desimaal – **system,** tientallige stelsel.
decimal, n. tiendelige (desimale) breuk.
decipher, ontsyfer; uitmaak.
decision, beslissing, uitspraak, besluit; uitslag; beslistheid.
deck, n. dek.
declare, verklaar; aankondig, bekend maak, aangee (by doeane).
decline, v. afhel, afhang, afdraand loop; buig; agteruitgaan, afneem; weier.
decline, n. verval, agteruitgang; afdraand.
declutch, loskoppel, uittrap.
decompose, oplos, ontleed; ontbind.
decompression, drukverligting.
decorate, versier, tooi; dekoreer.
decorum, fatsoen, welvoeglikheid.
decoy, v. verlok, lok.
decoy, n. lokmiddel; lokvoël.
decrease, v. verminder, afneem.
decree, v. verorden, bepaal.
decrepit, lendelam, gebreklik; afgeleef.
dedicate, (toe)wy, opdra.
deduce, aflei; gevolgtrekking maak; herlei.
deduct, aftrek.
deduction, aftrek(king), korting; gevolgtrekking; herleiding.
deed, daad, handeling; akte, dokument.
deeds office, registrasie-, aktekantoor.
deem, oordeel, dink, ag, meen.

deep, a. diep; diepsinnig; grondig; geheimsinnig, donker; innig.
deface, skend, vermink; uitwis.
defalcation, tekort; verduistering.
defame, belaster, beskinder.
default, n. gebrek, versuim, ontstentenis.
defeat, v. (oor)win; verydel; vernietig.
defeat, n. neerlaag; verydeling; vernietiging.
defect, gebrek, fout; tekort, defek.
defence, verdediging, teenstand; beskerming; verweer; verdedigingswerk, bolwerk.
defend, verdedig; verweer; beskerm.
defendant, verweerder; verdediger.
defer, uitstel, verskuiwe; draal, draai.
deference, eerbied, ontsag, respek.
defiance, uittarting, trotsering.
deficient, gebrekkig, ontoereikend; mentally –, swaksinnig.
deficit, tekort, nadelige saldo.
defile, v. bevuil, besmet; besoedel.
define, bepaal, omskrywe; omlyn; definieer.
definite, bepaald; presies, noukeurig.
deform, vervorm, mismaak, skend.
defraud, bedrieg.
defray, bekostig, (die koste) bestry, betaal.
deft, (knap)handig, knap, vaardig, netjies.
defunct, a. oorlede.
defy, trotseer, tart, uitdaag, spot met.
degenerate, v. ontaard, verbaster, versleg, degenereer.
degrade, verlaag, verneder; ontaard.
degree, graad, trap; klas, rang.
deign, (sig) verwaardig.
dejected, neerslagtig, bedruk, bek-af.
delay, v. vertraag, uitstel, verhinder, teenwerk; versuim, draai.
delay, n. vertraging, uitstel, versuim.
delectable, genoeglik, heerlik.
delegate, n. afgevaardigde, gemagtigde.
delete, uitkrap, deurstreep, uitwis.
deliberate, v. beraadslaag; oorweeg.
deliberate, a. weloorwoë; opsetlik; tydsaam; vasberade.
delicate, fyn, teer; tenger; fyngevoelig; lekker; delikaat.
delicious, heerlik, verruklik.
delight, n. genoeë, genot, behae, lus.
delimit, afbaken, delimiteer.
delineate, afbeeld, teken, skets.
delinquent, oortreder, skuldige.
delirious, ylhoofdig, waansinnig; verruk.
deliver, bevry, verlos; afgee; uitlewer; oorgee.
delivery, verlossing; (af)lewering.
delude, mislei, fop.
deluge, n. vloed, oorstroming; sondvloed.
deluge, v. oorstroom; oorstelp.
delusion, misleiding; oogverblinding; waan.
delve, grawe, delwe (dolwe).
demand, v. eis, vorder, verlang, vra.
demeanour, gedrag, houding, handelwyse.
demented, gek, kranksinnig.
demobilize, demobiliseer, (leër) ontbind.
democracy, volksregering, demokrasie.
democratic, demokraties.
demolish, vernietig; sloop; verslind.
demon, bose gees, duiwel.
demonstrate, uitlê, verklaar; aantoon; demonstreer.
demoralize, demoraliseer; bederf, verknoei.
demur, v. beswaar maak; pruttel.
demure, sedig, stemmig; preuts.
den, hol, lêplek; hok, bof.
denationalize, denasionaliseer.
denizen, n. bewoner; inheemse plant (ens.).
denominator, aanduier; noemer (van 'n breuk).

denote, aandui, aanwys, bepaal; beteken.
denounce, aankla, veroordeel.
dense, dig; dom, stom.
density, digtheid; stomheid.
dent, n. deuk (duik).
dentist, tandedokter, tandarts.
dentistry, tandheelkunde.
denude, ontbloot, blootlê.
deny, ontken, verloën; ontsê; weier.
depart, vertrek; heengaan.
department, departement, afdeling; gebied.
departure, vertrek; heengaan; afwyking.
depend, afhang; reken (op).
dependable, be-, vertroubaar.
depict, afteken, skilder, beskrywe.
deplete, leeg maak, uitput; uitdun.
deplorable, betreurenswaardig, jammerlik.
deplore, betreur; bekla.
depopulate, ontvolk.
deport, (sig) gedra; uitsit, deporteer.
depose, afsit; getuig.
deposit, n. belegging; storting, deposito; neerslag.
deposit, v. neersit, neerlê; stort, deponeer.
depot, opslagplaas, bêreplek.
depraved, ontaard.
deprecate, afkeur, opkom teen; afbid.
depreciate, agteruitgaan, depresieer.
depreciation, waardevermindering, depresiasie.
depress, af- in-, neerdruk; neerslagtig maak.
depression, daling, druk; laagte, kom; neerslagtigheid; depressie.
deprive, beroof, ontneem; afsit.
depth, diepte; diepsinnigheid.
deputation, afvaardiging, deputasie.
deputy, plaasvervanger, gemagtigde, plaasvervangende, vise-.
derail, laat ontspoor; ontspoor.
deranged, van die verstand af.
derelict, verlate, onbeheer(d).
deride, bespot, uitlag.
derivation, afleiding, herleiding; herkoms, afkoms.
derogatory, benadelend; kleinerend.
derrick, kraan, hyspaal, boortoring.
descend, af-, neerdaal, afklim, afstyg, land, afkom; sink; afstam.
descendant, afstammeling, nakomeling.
descent, af-, neerdaling, afstyging; afkoms; helling, afdraand; pad na onder; landing.
describe, beskrywe; omskrywe.
desecrate, ontheilig, ontwy.
desert, n. verdienste.
desert, n. woestyn, woesteny wildernis.
desert, v. verlaat; in die steek laat; dros.
deserve, verdien.
design, v. ontwerp; bestem; bedoel.
design, n. plan, ontwerp; opset; oogmerk; versoek.
desire, n. begeerte, wens, verlange.
desire, v. begeer, verlang, wens.
desirable, begeerlik, wenslik.
desist, ophou (met).
desk, lessenaar; skoolbank; kateder.
desolate, a. eensaam, verlate; troosteloos.
despair, n. wanhoop, vertwyfeling.
despair, v. wanhoop, in vertwyfeling raak.
despatch (dispatch), n. afsending, versending; (die) af-, doodmaak; haas, spoed.
desperate, wanhopig, radeloos; roekeloos.
despise, verag, verfoei; versmaad.
despoil, plunder, beroof.
despondent, moedeloos, neerslagtig.
despotism, dwingelandy, despotisme.
dessert, nagereg.

dessert-spoon, dessertlepel.
destination, (plek van) bestemming.
destined, (voor)bestem(d); voorbeskik.
destitute, behoeftig; brandarm; verlate.
destroy, verniel, vernietig, verwoes.
destroyer, vernieler; torpedojaer.
detach, losmaak, afsonder.
detail, n. besonderheid, kleinigheid.
detain, ophou, (ver)hinder, vashou; weerhou, agterhou; gevange hou; op skool hou.
detect, ontdek, gewaar word, agterkom.
detective, speurder.
detective story, speurverhaal.
deter, terughou, weerhou, afskrik, keer.
deteriorate, versleg, ontaard; bederf.
determination, beslissing; vasberadenheid.
determine, bepaal, vasstel; besluit, beslis.
detest, verfoei, verafsku.
dethrone, onttroon, afsit.
detonator, (slag)doppie; knalpatroon.
detour, omweg, ompad; uitweiding.
detrimental, nadelig, skadelik.
deuce, gelyk (tennis).
devastate, verwoes, verwoesting aanrig.
develop, ontwikkel; onthul, ontvou.
development, ontwikkeling; ontvouing.
deviate, afwyk, afdwaal.
device, leus; oogmerk; lis; uitvinding; middel.
devil, n. duiwel.
devilment, kwajongstreek, ondeundheid.
devise, versin, smee(d).
devoid, ontbloot.
devolve, afskuiwe; neerkom (op).
devote, (toe)wy, oorgee, offer.
devour, verslind, verteer, opvreet.
devout, vroom, plegtig; opreg.
dew, dou.
dext(e)rous, regs; handig, behendig, rats.
diabetes, suikersiekte, diabetes.
diagnosis, diagnose, (siekte)bepaling.
diagonal, n. oorhoekse lyn.
diagram, figuur, tekening, diagram.
dial, n. sonwys(t)er; wys(t)erplaat; (telefoon)-skyf.
dial, v. oplui, aanskakel, draai.
dialect, dialek, tongval.
dialogue, dialoog, samespraak, tweespraak.
diameter, middellyn, deursnee.
diamond, diamant; ruit.
diarrhoea, diarree.
diary, dagboek.
dice, n. dobbelstene.
dictate, v. dikteer, voorlees; voorskrywe.
dictation, diktee; bevel.
dictator, diktator.
dictionary, woordeboek.
diddle, flous, fop, uitoorlê.
die, v. sterf, doodgaan; vrek (van diere).
diesel: – engine, dieselmasjien.
diet, n. dieet; leefreël.
diet, v. op dieet stel, dieet hou.
differ, verskil.
difference, verskil, onderskeid; geskil.
different, verskillend, anders.
differential, n. ewenaar, differensiaal.
differentiate, onderskei; verskil maak.
difficult, moeilik, swaar, lastig.
difficulty, moeilikheid; beswaar.
diffident, bedees, beskeie.
diffuse, v. versprei, uitsprei, uitgiet.
dig, v. grawe, spit; snuffel.
digest, v. verteer; verwerk; verkrop.
digestion, spysvertering; verwerking.
digger, delwer.
digit, vinger, toon; syfer (onder 10).

dignified, waardig, deftig; verhewe.
digress, afdwaal, uitwei, afwyk.
dilapidated, verval(le), bouvallig.
dilate, uitsit, swel; rek.
dilemma, moeilikheid, verleentheid.
diligent, ywerig, naarstig, vlytig.
dilute, verdun, verswak.
dim, a. dof, skemerig, gedemp.
dim, v. dof word, verduister; dof maak, benewel.
dimension, afmeting, grootte, omvang.
diminish, verminder, afneem, inkrimp.
diminutive, n. verkleinwoord(jie).
dimple, n. kuiltjie.
din, n. geraas, gedreun, lawaai.
dine, eet, dineer; ete verskaf; – out, uit eet.
dingy, donker; naar; vuil.
dining-car, eetsalon, restourasiewa.
dining-room, eetkamer.
dinner, n. middagete, eetmaal, dinee.
dip, v. insteek, indompel; (vee) dip; (laat) sak; afhel, skuins loop.
diphtheria, witseerkeel.
diphthong, tweeklank, diftong.
diploma, getuigskrif, diploma.
diplomat, diplomaat.
dire, verskriklik, ontsettend, aaklig.
direct, a. direk, reguit, onmiddellik; lynreg(te); uitdruklik, ronduit.
direct, v. bestuur, reël, rig; aanwys, verwys; beveel; (brief) adresseer.
direction, bestuur; rigting; aanwysing; bevel, las; voorskrif.
director, direkteur, bestuurder, leier.
directory, voorskrifboek; adresboek.
dirt, vullis (vuilis), vuilgoed, vuiligheid; modder, slyk.
dirt-cheap, spotgoedkoop.
dirt-heap, vullishoop, ashoop.
dirty, a. vuil, smerig, morsig; gemeen, vieslik.
dirty, v. vuil maak, besmeer; besoedel.
disadvantage, nadeel; skade, verlies.
disagree, verskil (van mening), nie akkordeer (strook) nie; rusie maak.
disagreeable, onaangenaam; onplesierig; nors.
disappear, verdwyn, wegraak.
disappoint, teleurstel; verydel.
disapprove, nie saamstem nie.
disarmament, ontwapening.
disarrange, deurmekaar maak.
disaster, ramp, ongeluk.
disastrous, noodlottig, rampspoedig.
disband, ontbind, afdank; uiteengaan.
disbelieve, nie glo nie; betwyfel.
disc, sien **disk.**
discard, wegwerp, afdank; weggooi.
discern, onderskei, uitmaak, gewaar.
discerning, met deursig, oordeelkundig.
discharge, v. los, aflaai; losbrand, aftrek; ontlaai; ontslaan; vryspreek; nakom.
discharge, n. lossing; ontploffing; ontlading; ontslag; vryspraak; nakoming.
disciple, dissipel.
discipline, n. dissipline, oefening; tug(tiging).
disclaim, afstand doen van; loën, teenspreek.
disclose, blootlê, openbaar.
discolour, vlek; (laat) verkleur (verbleik).
discomfort, n. ongemak, ongerief; kommer.
disconnect, losmaak, loskoppel; ontbind.
discontented, ontevrede, misnoeg, brommerig.
discord, wanklank; tweedrag, twis.
discount, n. korting, diskonto.
discount, v. (ver)diskonteer, inwissel; korting gee; buite rekening laat.
discourage, ontmoedig; afraai.
discourteous, onbeleef, onwellewend, lomp.

discover, ontdek, uitvind; openbaar, verraai, onthul.
discredit, n. diskrediet, oneer, skande.
discredit, v. oneer aandoen; betwyfel.
discreet, versigtig, tak(t)vol; swygsaam.
discrepancy, teenstrydigheid, verskil.
discretion, oordeel, oorleg; versigtigheid; willekeur, goeddunke; diskresie.
discriminate, onderskei.
discuss, bespreek, beredeneer.
disdain, v. verag, versmaad, minag.
disease, siekte, kwaal.
disembark, aan land sit; land.
disengaged, vry, los; onbeset; ontslaan.
disfavour, n. ongenade, onguns.
disfigure, vermink, skend, ontsier.
disgrace, n. skande; ongenade.
disgrace, v. in die skande steek, skande (oneer) aandoen.
disgraceful, skandelik, skandalig.
disgruntled, brommerig, misnoeg.
disguise, v. vermom, verklee; verbloem.
disguise, n. vermomming; voorwendsel.
disgust, n. teensin, afkeer, walging.
disgust, v. stuit, walg.
dish, n. skottel; gereg.
dish, v. opskep; – up, opdien, opdis.
dish-cloth, vaatdoek (vadoek).
dishearten, ontmoedig; afskrik.
dishonest, oneerlik, onopreg.
dishonour, n. skande, oneer.
dishonour, v. onteer; ('n wissel) dishonoreer, weier.
dishonourable, eerloos; onterend.
disillusion, ontnugter, ontgoël.
disinclined, ongeneig, afkerig, teensinnig.
disinfect, ontsmet.
disinfectant, ontsmettingsmiddel.
disintegrate, uitmekaar val; ontbind, oplos.
disinter, opgrawe; opdiep.
disinterested, belangeloos; onpartydig; onbaatsugtig.
disjointed, ontwrig; onsamehangend.
disk, disc, skyf; diskus.
disk-plough, skottelploeg.
dislike, v. nie hou van nie.
dislike, n. afkeer, teensin, hekel.
dislocate, verplaas; ontwrig, verswik.
disloyal, ontrou, dislojaal.
dismal, naar, aaklig, somber.
dismay, n. ontsteltenis, verslaentheid.
dismay, v. (laat) ontstel, onthuts.
dismiss, wegstuur, laat gaan; afdank, ontslaan; bedank; ('n plan) laat vaar; terugstuur (krieket).
disobedient, ongehoorsaam.
disobey, ongehoorsaam wees aan.
disorder, n. wanorde, verwarring; oproer; kwaal.
disorderly, wanordelik, rumoerig.
disorganize, in wanorde bring, in die war stuur.
disown, verloën, verwerp.
disparage, kleineer, neersien op.
disparity, ongelykheid, verskil.
dispassionate, bedaard, besadig.
dispel, verdryf, wegja; wegruim.
disperse, verstrooi, uitmekaar jaag; versprei.
displace, verplaas; vervang.
display, v. vertoon, uitstal, ten toon stel, openbaar.
displease, mishaag, vererg.
displeasure, misnoeë, mishae.
dispose, skik, rangskik; reël, inrig; stem; beskik; – of, van die hand sit; kafloop, afreken mee; (argumente) weerlê.
disposition, rangskikking; inrigting; geaardheid.

disprove, weerlê.
dispute, v. redetwis, argumenteer; betwis.
dispute, n. redetwis, dispuut; geskil & twis.
disqualify, ongeskik maak; diskwalifiseer.
disregard, v. veronagsaam.
disrespectful, oneerbiedig.
disrupt, uiteenskeur.
dissatisfied, ontevrede, misnoeg, teleurgestel.
dissect, ontleed.
dissemble, veins, voorwend; ontveins.
disseminate, uitsaai, versprei, rondstrooi.
dissension, tweedrag, verdeeldheid.
dissent, n. meningsverskil; afskeiding.
dissipate, verstrooi, verdryf; verkwis.
dissolute, losbandig, bandeloos, liederlik.
dissolve, oplos, ontbind, smelt.
dissuade, afraai.
distance, n. afstand, distansie; verte.
distant, ver, verwyder(d), weg; koel.
distaste, afkeer, teensin.
distasteful, onsmaaklik.
distemper, n. hondesiekte.
distemper, n. muurkalk, kalkverf.
distemper, v. verf, wit, kalk.
distend, uitsit, swel, rek.
distil, distilleer, stook; afdruppel.
distinct, afsonderlik; duidelik, helder; bepaald.
distinction, onderskeiding; onderskeid, verskil; vernaamheid.
distinctive, kenmerkend; apart; vernaam.
distinguish, onderskei; kenmerk.
distort, verdraai, verwring, skeef trek.
distortion, verdraaiing, distorsie (radio).
distract, aftrek; aflei; verwar.
distress, n. nood, ellende.
distribute, uitdeel, (ver)deel, versprei.
district, distrik; wyk, streek, gebied.
distrust, v. wantrou, verdink.
distrust, n. wantroue; agterdog.
disturb, steur (stoor), pla, hinder.
disuse, n. onbruik.
ditch, n. sloot, voor.
ditto, ditto (dito), dieselfde.
ditty, liedjie.
dive, v. (in)duik, (in)dompel; insteek.
divergent, uiteenlopend.
diversion, afleiding; ontspanning.
divert, aflei; wegkeer; onttrek; afwend; vermaak.
diverting, vermaaklik, amusant.
divide, v. (ver)deel; skei.
divide, n. waterskeiding.
dividend, dividend; deeltal.
divine, a. goddelik, godsdienstig.
divisible, deelbaar.
division, (ver)deling; deelsomme; afdeling; skeiding, grens; verdeeldheid.
divisor, deler, divisor.
divorce, n. egskeiding; skeiding.
divorce, v. laat skei; skei.
divulge, openbaar, uitlaat, verklap.
dizzy, duiselig, duiselingwekkend.
do, v. doen, maak, verrig.
docile, leersaam, geseglik; mak.
dock, n. (skeeps)dok.
doctor, n. dokter, doktor.
doctrine, leer(stelling), dogma; leerstelsel.
document, n. dokument, stuk, akte.
dodder, n. dodder.
dodder, v. beef, tril; strompel, waggel.
dodge, v. draai, jakkalsdraaie maak; rondspring; vryspring; ontduik.
dodge, n. draai, slenterslag, uitvlug.
doe, hinde; haas-, konynwyfie.
dog, n. hond; reun; kram, haak.
dog, v. agtervolg; opspoor.

dogmatic, dogmaties, leerstellig.
dog-tired, doodmoeg, so moeg as 'n hond.
doing, n. werk, bedryf, doen en late.
doldrums, windstilte; neerslagtigheid.
doleful, droewig, treurig.
doll, pop.
dollar, daalder; (Amerikaanse) dollar.
dolomite, dolomiet.
domain, domein; gebied.
dome, dom, koepel.
domestic, a. huis- . . . , huislik, huishoudelike;
binnelands; – science, huisvlyt, huishoudkunde.
dominant, (oor)heersend, dominerend.
dominate, oorheers; uitsteek bo.
domineering, heerssugtig, baasspelerig.
dominion, heerskappy; gebied; gewes.
donation, skenking, gif, geskenk, donasie.
donkey, esel, donkie; domkop.
donor, skenker, gewer.
doom, n. vonnis, oordeel; ondergang.
door, deur.
doorkeeper, portier, deurwagter.
dope, v. bedwelm maak.
dope-addict, dwelmsugtige.
dormant, slapend, rustend, stil.
dormitory, slaapsaal.
dose, n. dosis, dop.
dose, v. medisyne gee.
dot, n. punt, stippel.
dote: – on, versot wees op.
dotty, simpel, getik.
double, a. & adv. dubbel(d), tweevoudig, tweeledig; twee maal; vals.
double, v. dubbel, verdubbel; hardloop; dubbel
vou; omseil; omspring, terughardloop.
double, n. die dubbel(d)e; dubbelganger; dubbel-
spel (in tennis).
double-faced, huigelagtig, geveins, vals.
double-storey(ed), -storied house, (twee)verdie-
pinghuis.
doubt, n. twyfel, weifeling; argwaan.
doubt, v. twyfel; weifel; betwyfel; nie vertrou nie.
doubtful, twyfelagtig, onseker; weifelend.
doubtless, ongetwyfeld, bepaald, stellig.
dough, deeg.
dour, hard, streng; stuurs.
dove, duif.
dovecot(e), duiwehok.
dovetail, n. swa(w)elstert.
dowdy, a. slordig, slonsig, smaakloos.
down, n. dons(ies), donshaartjies.
down, prep. af; van af; langes af.
down, adv. af, neer, (na) onder.
downfall, val; ondergang.
downhearted, mismoedig, neerslagtig.
downhill, berg af, bult af.
downpour, stortbui.
downright, regaf; volslae, pure.
downstairs, onder, benede; na benede.
downtrodden, verdruk, vertrap.
downward(s), na onder, ondertoe.
dowry, bruidskat.
dowse, water wys (met die stokkie).
doze, dut, dommel, sluimer, visvang.
dozen, dosyn.
drab, a. vaal; grou; eentonig, vervelig.
draft, (sien draught), n. afdeling; (bank)wissel;
skets, ontwerp.
draft, v. opstel; ontwerp.
drag, v. sleep; eg; rem.
drag, n. remskoen; blok aan die been; eg;
sleepsel; vertraging.
dragon, draak.
dragon-fly, naaldekoker.

drain, v. afwater, aftap; leegdrink; drooglê; uitput; dreineer.
drain, n. riool, afvoersloot; dreineerpyp.
drama, drama; toneelspel; dramatiese kuns.
dramatist, toneelskrywer.
drape, oortrek, omhang; drapeer.
drapery, kledingstowwe, klerasie; drapering.
drastic, drasties, deurtastend.
draught, sien draft, n. trek, tog; sluk; drank(ie);
ontwerp; diepgang (van 'n skip.)
draughts, dambord.
draughtsman, tekenaar, ontwerper.
draw, v. trek, aantrek, wegtrek; (rook) intrek;
uittrek; uitskep; uithaal, te voorskyn bring;
(uit)rek; teken.
draw, n. trek; skyfie (rook); pluk; aantreklikheid; uitloting; lotery; gelykspel.
drawback, beswaar, nadeel; skadusy.
drawer, trekker; tekenaar, laai.
drawing, trek(king): tekening.
drawing-board, tekenbord.
drawing-pin, drukspykertjie; duimspykertjie.
drawing-room, sitkamer, salon.
drawl, v. aanstellerig (temerig) praat.
dread, v. vrees.
dread, n. vrees, skrik, angs.
dreadful, verskriklik, ontsettend, vreeslik.
dream, n. droom; hersenskim.
dream, v. droom.
dreary, naar, aaklig; eentonig, vervelig.
dredge, v. dreg, bagger.
dregs, moer; oorskiet.
drench, v. drenk, papnat maak.
dress, v. aantrek, klee; versier, optooi; (wond)
verbind, behandel; afrig, dresseer; regmaak;
kam, roskam; skoonmaak, klaarmaak; (hare,
plante) knip, snoei; gelyk maak, glad maak;
bemes.
dress, n. kleed; klere; kleredrag; rok.
dressing-gown, kamerjas, huisjas.
dressing-room, kleedkamer.
dressing-table, spieëltafel.
dressmaker, modemaker (-maakster).
dribble, v. druppel; kwyl; dribbel (in voetbal).
drift, n. (die) drywe; trek; neiging; koers; bedoeling; drif.
drift, n. (die) drywe; trek; neiging; koers; bedoeling; drif.
drift, v. afdrywe, wegdrywe.
drill, v. boor; dril, oefen.
drill, n. boor; dril, oefening.
drink, v. drink; opdrink.
drink, n. drank.
drip, v. drup; laat drup.
dripping, gedrup, gelek; braaivet.
drive, v. drywe, aan-, voortdrywe, aanja; stuur,
bestuur, ry; ('n dryfhou) slaan.
drive, n. rit(jie), rytoertjie; pad; dryfjag; slag,
hou; dryfhou (in tennis, gholf); krag, ywer.
drivel, n. kwyl; geklets.
driver, bestuurder; koetsier; masjinis; dryfstok
(in gholf).
drizzle, mot-, stofreent.
droll, snaaks, koddig.
dromedary, dromedaris.
drone, n. waterdraer; gebrom, gegons.
drone, v. brom, gons.
droop, v. afhang; kwyn; sink; laat sak.
drop, n. druppel; sopie; oorbel; klontjie; val,
daling; skepskop; acid –s, suurklontjies.
drop, v. val; laat val; laat vaar, opgee; ophou.
dropper, afleier (paaltjie).
dropsy, water(sug).
drought, droogte.
drown, verdrink, versuip.

drowsy, slaperig, vaak, lomerig.
drub, slaan, pak gee.
drudge, v. sloof, slaaf, swoeg.
drug, n. medisyne; bedwelmende middel.
drug, v. 'n bedwelmende middel ingee.
drum, n. trom(mel), tamboer; silinder; bus.
drummer, tamboer(slaner).
drunk, a. dronk, beskonke.
drunkard, dronkaard, dronklap.
dry, a. & adv. droog, dor; dors(tig); ongeërg; droë (wyn).
dry, v. droë, uitdroog; droog word; droog maak; afdroë.
dry-clean, (uit)stoom; droogskoonmaak.
dry-dock, droogdok.
dual, a. tweeledig, tweevoudig, tweetallig.
dubious, twyfelagtig, onseker, weifelend.
duchess, hertogin.
duck, n. eend; nul, eier.
duck, v. (in)duik, wegduik; indompel; (weg)koes, (weg)buk.
duct, buis, pyp, kanaal.
dud, a. waardeloos, onbruikbaar, prullerig.
due, n. skuldig, betaalbaar; passend.
duel, n. tweegeveg.
dug, speen, tepel.
dug-out, kano; loopgraaf.
duke, hertog.
dull, bot, dom; dof; stomp; vervelend; betrokke (lug).
dull, v. bot (dof, stomp) maak, verstomp; verswak, verdoof, verflou.
duly, behoorlik, na behore, passend; op tyd.
dumb, stom, spraakloos; stilswyend.
dumbfound, dronkslaan, verstom, verbluf.

dummy, n. pop; blinde(man) (in kaartspel); fopspeentjie.
dump, n. plof, bons; mynhoop.
dump, v. neerplof, aflaai.
dumpling, kluitjie, bolletjie.
dun, a. vaalbruin, donkerbruin.
dunce, stommerik, domkop.
dune, duin.
dung, mis.
dung-beetle, miskruier.
dupe, v. bedrieg, fop, beetneem.
duplicate, v. verdubbel; kopieer.
duplicator, afrolmasjien, kopieermasjien.
durable, duursaam, sterk; bestendig.
duration, duur, voortduring.
during, gedurende, tydens.
dusk, skemer; halfdonker.
dust, n, stof.
dust, v. afstof, bestrooi; uitstof.
dustbin, vullisbak, vuilgoedbak.
duster, stoffer, stofdoek.
dusty, stowwig (stoffig), stowwerig (stofferig).
Dutch, a. Hollands, Nederlands.
duty, plig; diens; belasting, invoerreg.
dwarf, n. dwerg.
dwell, woon, bly.
dwindle, agteruitgaan, verminder.
dye, n. kleurstof, verf; kleur.
dye, v. verf, kleur.
dynamite, n. dinamiet, springstof.
dynamo, dinamo.
dynasty, dinastie, vorstehuis.
dysentry, buikloop.
dyspepsia, slegte spysvertering.

each, a. elke, iedere.
each, pro. elk, elkeen, iedereen; stuk.
eager, gretig, begerig; ywerig, vurig.
eagle, arend, adelaar.
ear, n. oor; gehoor.
ear, n. aar; saad (saat); kop.
ear-drum, oortrommel, trommelvlies.
ear-guard, oorskut.
earl, graaf.
early, vroeg (vroeë).
earn, verdien; verwerf.
earnest, n. erns.
earnest, a. ernstig; ywerig.
earnings, verdienste, loon.
earth, n. grond, aarde; gat, hol; grondsluiting.
earthenware, n. erdegoed, aardewerk.
earthenware, a. erde- . . .
earthly, aards.
earthquake, aardbewing.
earthworm, erdwurm.
earwig, oorkruiper, oorwurm; vleier.
ease, n. gemak, rus, verligting.
ease, v. verlig, stil; gerusstel; laat skiet ('n tou).
easel, (skilders)esel.
easily, (ge)maklik; fluit-fluit.
east, oos.
Easter, Pase; Paasvakansie.
eastern, a. oosters; oostelik.
East India, Oos-Indië.
eastward(s), ooswaarts.
easy, (ge)maklik.
easy-chair, gemaklike stoel, leun(ing)stoel.
easy-going, geskik, sorgloos, onbesorg.
eat, eet.
eaves, (onderste) dakrand, geut.
eavesdrop, afluister, luistervink speel.
ebb, v. eb, afneem, wegvloei; verval, agteruitgaan.
ebb-tide, eb. ebgety.
ebony, ebbehout.
eccentric, a. sonderling, eksentriek.
echo, n. weerkaatsing, weerklank, eggo.
echo, v. weerklink, weergalm; napraat.
eclipse, n. verduistering, eklips.
economic, ekonomies.
economize, besuinig, bespaar.
economy, staathuishoudkunde; spaarsaamheid.
ecstasy, vervoering, verrukking.
eczema, uitslag, ekseem.
eddy, v. maal, draai, warrel.
edge, n. snee, skerpkant; skerpte; kant, rand.
edgeways, -wise, op sy kant, skuins.
edible, eetbaar.
edict, edik, verordening.
edify, stig.
edit, redigeer.
edition, uitgaaf, druk, oplaag, edisie.
editor, redakteur.
educate, opvoed, oplei.
education, opvoeding, opleiding; opvoedkunde.
eel, paling, aal.
eerie, eery, huiweringwekkend.
effect, n. uitwerking, gevolg, uitslag, effek; indruk.
effect, v. uitwerk, bewerkstellig.
effective, doelmatig, doeltreffend; geskik.
efficient, doeltreffend; kragdadig; geskik.
effigy, beeld, beeltenis, afbeeldsel.
effluent, n. uitloop.
effort, (krags)inspanning, poging.
effusive, rojaal, hartlik; woordryk.
egg, n. eier.
egg, v. – on, aanhits, aanspoor.
egg-cup, eierkelkie.
egoist, egoïs, selfsugtige mens.

Egyptian, n. Egiptenaar.
eiderdown: – quilt, veerkombers, donskombers.
eight, ag; – o'clock, ag(t)uur.
eighteen, agt(t)ien.
eighty, tag(gen)tig.
eisteddfod, eisteddfod.
either, a. & pro. albei; een van beide.
either, adv. conj. of.
eject, uitwerp, uitskop; uitskiet.
elaborate, a. uitvoerig; fyn afgewerk.
eland, eland.
elapse, verstryk, verloop.
elastic, a. rekbaar, elasties; veerkragtig.
elastic, n. rek, gomlastiek.
elated, verheug, uitgelate; opgeblase.
elbow, n. elmboog; kromming.
elbow, v. stoot, dring, druk.
elder, a. ouer.
elder, n. ouderling; ouere.
elderly, bejaard.
eldest, oudste.
elect, v. kies, uitkies, verkies.
election, (ver)kiesing, eleksie; keuse.
election-day, stemdag.
electorate, kiesers, keurvorstedom.
electric, elektries.
electrician, elektrisiën.
electricity, elektrisiteit.
electron, elektron.
electronic, elektronies.
elegant, sierlik, bevallig, swierig.
elegy, treursang.
element, element, bestanddeel, grondstof; beginsel.
elementary, elementêr, aanvangs-.
elephant, olifant.
elevate, oplig, ophef; verhef, veredel.
elevator, (hys)kraan, hystoestel; ligter, hyser;
graansuier.
eleven, elf; elftal (in krieket).
elf, elf, (berg)gees, kaboutertjie.
elicit, uittrek, uitlok, ontlok.
eligible, verkiesbaar; verkieslik.
eliminate, verwyder, uitskakel; wegwerk; elimineer.
elk, elk, eland.
ell, el.
ellipse, ellips.
elocution, voordragsleer, spraakles, elokusie.
elope, wegloop, (sig) laat skaak; skaak.
eloquent, welsprekend; veelseggend.
else, anders.
elsewhere, êrens anders, elders.
elucidate, ophelder, verhelder, toelig.
elude, ontwyk; ontduik; ontvlug.
elusive, elusory, ontwykend; ontduikend, misleidend.
Elysian, geluksalig, hemels; Elisies
emaciation, vermaering, uittering.
emanate, uitstraal, uitvloei.
emancipate, vrystel, vrylaat; emansipeer.
embalm, balsem.
embankment, indyking; wal, dyk, kaai.
embark, inskeep.
embarrass, hinder, belemmer; verbouereerd (verleë) maak; bemoeilik.
embassy, gesantskap; gesantskapsgebou.
embellish, verfraai, opsier.
embers, (warm) as, (lewendige) kole.
embezzle, verduister, ontvreem.
embitter, verbitter, vergal.
emblem, sinnebeeld, embleem.
embodiment, beliggaming, verpersoonliking.
embrace, v. omhels; omvat, insluit.
embrace, n. omhelsing, omarming.

embrocation, smeergoed.
embroidery, borduurwerk; opsiersel.
embryo, vrugkiem.
emerald, n. smarag.
emerge, opkom, te voorskyn kom; voor die dag kom; blyk.
emergency, (geval van) nood.
emery-paper, skuurpapier, poleerpapier.
emetic, braakmiddel, vomitief.
emigrant, emigrant, landverhuiser.
emigrate, emigreer, verhuis, trek.
eminent, hoog, verhewe; uitstekend; eminent.
emotion, aandoening, ontroering, emosie.
emperor, keiser.
emphasis, klem, nadruk; klemtoon.
emphasize, nadruk lê op, beklem(toon).
empire, (keiser)ryk; (ryks)gebied.
employ, v. in diens neem (hê); gebruik, aanwend, besig.
employ, n. diens.
employee, werknemer, beampte, bediende.
employer, werkgewer, baas.
employment, diens, besigheid, vak, bedryf; aanwending, gebruik.
empty, a. leeg; ydel, betekenisloos, hol.
empty, v. leegmaak; uitloop.
emulate, nastreef, wedywer met; ewenaar.
enable, in staat stel, die geleentheid verskaf.
enamel, n. erd, emalje, enemmel.
encamp, kamp opslaan, laer trek, kampeer.
encase, toemaak, insluit, toespyker.
enchanting, betowerend, bekorend, verruklik.
enclose, in-, insluit; omring; omhein, inkamp.
enclosure, afsluiting; kamp; hok; skutting; bylae.
encounter, v. tref, teenkom, ontmoet.
encourage, aanmoedig; aanspoor; aankweek.
encroach, (– on), inbreuk maak (op), die grense oorskry, indring.
encumber, bemoeilik, belemmer, beswaar.
encyclop(a)edia, ensiklopedie.
end, n. end; einde; punt; doel; (sigaret)stompie.
end, v. ophou, eindig; stop; 'n einde maak aan.
endanger, in gevaar bring.
endear, bemind maak.
endeavour, v. streef, trag, (sig) beywer.
endeavour, n. strewe, poging.
ending, slot; afloop; uitgang; uiteinde.
endorse, endosseer; onderskrywe; oordra.
endorsement, endossement; onderskrywing.
endowment, skenking; aanleg.
endure, verdra, uitstaan; duur, aanhou.
enduring, blywend, durend.
enemy, n. vyand; duiwel.
enemy, a. vyandelik.
energy, energie, (gees)krag; werksaamheid; arbeidsvermoë.
enforce, afdwing (gehoorsaamheid); (die wet) uitvoer.
enfranchisement, vrystelling; verlening van stemreg.
engage, (ver)bind, verpand; verloof; in diens neem; in beslag neem; slaags raak, aanval.
engagement, verbintenis; afspraak; verlowing; besigheid; geveg.
engine, masjien; motor; lokomotief; werktuig.
engine-driver, masjinis.
engineer, n. boukundige, ingenieur.
England, Engeland.
English, a. Engels.
Englishman, Engelsman (pl. Engelse).
engross: –ed in, verdiep in.
engrossing, boeiend.
engulf, opsluk, verswelg; instort.
enhance, verhoog, vergroot, vermeerder.

enigma, raaisel.
enjoy, geniet, hou van.
enjoyment, genot, vermaak, plesier.
enlarge, uitbrei; uitsit; oordryf; – upon, uitwei oor.
enlighten, inlig, voorlig; verlig.
enmity, vyandigheid; vyandskap.
enormous, ontsaglik, tamaai; ontsettend.
enough, genoeg, voldoende.
enquire, sien inquire.
enrage, woedend maak, vertoorn, versondig.
enrich, verryk.
enrol, inskryf, registreer; te boek stel; diens neem, aansluit.
ensilage, n. inkuiling; kuilvoer.
ensuing, daaropvolgende; gevolglike.
ensure, verseker; bewerk; besorg.
enter, in- of binnegaan, -tree, -vaar, -kom; binnedring; inskryf, opskryf.
enteric, – fever, ingewandskoors, tifus(koors).
enterprise, onderneming; ondernemingsgees.
entertain, onderhoud; onthaal; koester.
entertainment, onthaal, ontvangs; vermaak.
entirely, heeltemal, totaal, volkome.
enity, wese, bestaan; geheel, entiteit.
entomology, insektekunde, entomologie.
entrails, ingewande, binnegoed.
entrance, n. ingang; binnekoms; toegang, toelating, intree; portaal; toegang.
entreat, smeek, bid, soebat; bejeën.
entry, binnekoms, intog; ingang, toegang; aanvaarding; inskrywing; boeking, pos.
enumerate, opsom, tel.
enunciate, uitdruk, uitspreek, formuleer.
envelop, inwikkel, omwikkel, hul (in).
envelope, koevert, omslag; omhulsel.
envious, jaloers, afgunstig.
environment, omgewing; omstandighede.
envoy, gesant, verteenwoordiger.
envy, n. jaloesie, naywer, afguns.
envy, v. beny, jaloers (afgunstig) wees op.
epic, n. epos, heldedig.
epidemic, n. epidemie, heersende siekte.
epilepsy, vallende siekte, epilepsie.
epilogue, narede, slotrede, epiloog.
episode, episode; voorval, geskiedenis.
epitaph, grafskrif.
epitome, uittreksel, samevatting.
epoch, tydstip, tydperk, tydvak.
equal, a. gelyk(waardig).
equal, n. gelyke, weerga.
equality, gelykheid; gelykwaardigheid.
equator, ewenaar, ewenagslyn.
equilibrium, ewewig, balans.
equinox, nagewening.
equip, toerus; uitrus; beman; uitdos.
equivalent, gelyk(waardig), ekwivalent.
era, tydperk; jaartelling.
eradicate, ontwortel, uitroei.
erase, uitwis, uitvee, uitkrap.
eraser, uitveër.
erect, a. (pen)regop, (pen)orent.
erect, v. oprig; stig, bou; opstel, opwerp.
erosion, verwering, wegspoeling; erosie.
err, sondig; dwaal, 'n fout begaan, (sig) vergis.
errand, boodskap; opdrag, las.
erratic, onseker, wisselvallig, ongelyk.
error, fout, vergissing; dwaling.
erudition, geleerdheid, belesenheid.
erupt, deurbreek, uitbreek; uitbars.
escalator, roltrap.
escapade, kwajongstreek, eskapade.
escape, v. ontvlug, ontsnap.

escape, n. ontkoming, ontsnapping.
escort, v. (be)gelei, vergesel, eskorteer.
espionage, spioenasie, bespieding.
essay, n. proef; poging; opstel; verhandeling.
essence, wese, kern; aftreksel; geur; reukwerk.
essential, a. wesenlik; noodsaaklik; essensieel.
essentially, hoofsaaklik, in wese.
establish, vestig; stig, oprig; instel; vasstel, bewys, staaf.
establishment, stigting; nedersetting; instelling; bevestiging; vasstelling; gestig; inrigting; huishouding; saak.
estate, rang, stand; boedel; eiendom; landgoed; staat.
esteem, v. skat, ag; hoogag, waardeer.
esteem, n. agting, skatting; hoogagting.
Esthonian, Estlander.
estimate, n. skatting; begroting.
estimate, v. skat, raam, waardeer.
estimation, mening; skatting, hoogagting.
estrange, vervreem.
estuary, mond, monding.
etching, ets; etswerk.
eternal, a. ewig, ewigdurend.
eternity, ewigheid.
ethics, sedeleer, etiek.
ethnic, volkekundig; etnologies.
ethnology, volkekunde, etnologie.
etiquette, etiket, wellewendheidsvorme.
etymology, (woord)afleiding, etimologie.
eucalyptus, gomboom; bloekomboom.
eulogy, lof, lofspraak, -rede; ophemeling.
euphemism, eufemisme, verbloeming.
Europe, Europa.
European, n. Europeaan, Europeër; Europese (vrou).
evacuate, ontruim; leegmaak.
evade, (vraag) ontwyk, (wet) ontduik.
evaluate, bereken, besyfer.
evangelist, evangelis.
evaporate, verdamp, vervlieg; uitwasem.
eve, aand; vooraand.
even, a. gelyk, gelykmatig; eenvormig; glad; plat.
even, adv. selfs.
evening, aand.
event, gebeurtenis, voorval; geval; uitslag; (sport)nommer, wedstryd.
eventful, bewoë.
eventually, uiteindelik, ten slotte.
ever, altoos, ewig; ooit.
evergreen, bladhoudend, groenblywend.
everlasting, a. ewigdurend; knaend.
everlasting, n. sewejaartjie; kanniedood.
evermore, ewig, altyd.
every, elke, iedere, al.
everybody, iedereen, elkeen.
everyday, a. daeliks, gewoon.
everyone, iedereen, algar.
everything, alles.
everywhere, oral(s), alom, allerweë.
evidence, getuienis; bewys; blyk(e).
evidently, klaarblyklik; blykbaar.
evil, a. sleg, kwaad, boos.
evil, adv. sleg.
evil, n. kwaad, euwel; onheil.
evil-doer, boosdoener.
evolution, ontwikkeling; evolusie.
evolve, ontvou, ontplooi, ontwikkel; aflei.
ewe, ooi.
exact, a. noukeurig, presies, stip.
exacting, veeleisend, streng.
exactly, adv. noukeurig, juis, presies.
exaggerate, vergroot, oordrywe.

examination, eksamen; ondersoek; ondersoeking; verhoor.
examination-paper, vraestel.
examine, ondersoek, toets; verhoor, ondervra.
example, voorbeeld; model.
exasperate, vertoorn, terg.
excavate, uitgrawe; uithol; opgrawe.
exceed, oortref; oorskry.
exceedingly, uitermate, uiters, bowemate.
excel, oortref, uitmunt; uitblink.
excellent, uitstekend, uitmuntend, voortreflik.
except, -ing, prep. behalwe, uitgesonderd.
exception, uitsondering; teenwerping.
exceptional, uitsonderlik, buitengewoon.
excerpt, n. uittreksel, ekserp.
excess, oormaat; oordaad; buitensporigheid, onmatigheid.
exchange, n. ruil(ing); uitwisseling; wisselkoers; sentrale (geld)beurs.
exchange, v. (om)ruil, verruil, wissel.
excise, n. – duties, aksyns(belasting).
excite, opwind; aanspoor; prikkel.
excited, opgewonde.
excitement, opgewondenheid, opwinding, spanning; aansporing.
exciting, opwindend, spannend.
exclaim, uitroep.
exclude, uitsluit.
excursion, uitstap(pie), ekskursie; uitweiding.
excuse, v. verontskuldig, verskoon.
excuse, n. verskoning; ekskuus.
execute, uitvoer, volbring, ten uitvoer bring; voltrek ('n vonnis); teregstel, ter dood bring.
executioner, beul, laksman, skerpregter.
executive, a. uitvoerend.
executive, n. uitvoerende mag, uitvoerende amptenaar.
executor, uitvoerder; eksekuteur, boedelbesorger.
exemplary, voorbeeldig.
exempt, v. vrystel, onthef, ontslaan.
exercise, n. oefening; uitoefening; opgawe.
exercise, v. oefen; uitoefen; oefening neem; dril.
exert, aanwend, te pas bring, uitoefen.
exertion, aanwending; inspanning.
exhale, uitwasem, uitasem, uitdamp.
exhaust, v. uitput; leegmaak.
exhaust, n. afvoer; uitlaatpyp; knalpot.
exhausted, uitgeput.
exhibit, v. ten toon stel, vertoon; uitstal.
exhibition, vertoning; uitstalling; tentoonstelling.
exhilarating, opwekkend, verfrissend.
exhort, waarsku; aanspoor.
exhume, opgrawe.
exile, n. verbanning, ballingskap; balling.
exile, v. verban, uitban.
exist, bestaan, wees, leef, voorkom.
existence, bestaan, aansyn.
exit, uitgang.
exodus, uittog, eksodus.
exonerate, suiwer, vrypleit; onthef.
exorbitant, buitensporig, verregaand.
exorcise, besweer, uitdryf, (uit)ban.
exotic, uitheems, vreemd.
expand, uitbrei; ontwikkel; swel; toeneem.
expanse, uitgestrektheid, oppervlakte.
expect, verwag; vermoed.
expectant, verwagtend; aanstaande.
expectation, verwagting; vooruitsig; hoop; afwagting.
expectorate, spu (spuug), spoe(g).
expendable, misbaar, afskryfbaar.
expedient, a. dienstig, gerieflik, raadsaam.
expedient, n. (red)middel, plan, uitweg.

expedite, bevorder, bespoedig, aanhelp.
expedition, bevordering; aansending; spoed; onderneming; tog, ekspedisie.
expel, uitsit, wegja, verdryf, verban.
expense, uitgawe, (on)koste.
expensive, duur, kosbaar, verkwistend.
experience, n. ondervinding, ervaring.
experience, v. ondervind, ervaar, belewe.
experiment, n. proef(neming), eksperiment.
experiment, v. proewe neem, eksperimenteer.
expert, a. bedrewe; deskundig.
expert, n. deskundige, vakman.
expiate, boet, boete doen, vergoeding doen.
expire, uitadem; doodgaan; verval; verstryk.
explain, duidelik maak, verklaar.
explanation, verklaring, uitleg.
explicit, uitdruklik, stellig, bepaald.
explode, ontplof, spring; uitbars; laat, ontplof.
exploit, n. prestasie, kordaatstuk.
exploit, v. eksploiteer, ontgin; uitbuit.
explore, ondersoek, navors, verken, eksploreer.
explosion, uitbarsting, ontplofffing.
explosive, n. ontploffingsmiddel.
exponent, vertolker; beliggaming; wortelgetal.
export, v. uitvoer, eksporteer.
export, n. uitvoer.
expose, openbaar, blootlê; blootstel; ontbloot; aan die kaak stel.
expositor, uitlêer, verklaarder, vertolker.
expostulate, 'n vertoog hou, vermaan; – with, vermaan, kapittel (oor).
expostulation, vertoog, teenwerping.
exposure, blootstelling; ontbloting; ontmaskering; beligting.
express, v. uitdruk; te kenne gee; vertolk; betuig.
expression, uitdrukking; gesegde.
expressly, uitdruklik; spesiaal, ekspres.
expropriate, onteien, eksproprieer.
expulsion, uitsetting, verdrywing; verbanning.
exquisite, uitgesog, voortreflik, keurig.
extemporize, uit die vuis praat; improviseer.

extend, uitsteek, uitbrei; (tydperk) verleng.
extensive, uitgebreid, omvattend.
extent, omvang; mate.
extentuating, versagtend.
exterior, a. buitenste; van buite; uitwendig.
exterior, n. buitekant; uiterlik.
exterminate, uitroei, verdelg.
external, buitekantse, buitenste; uitwendig; uiterlik; ekstern.
extinct, uitgedoof; uitgesterf; verouderd; afgeskaf.
extinguish, doodmaak, blus; doodblaas; vernietig.
extirpate, uitroei, uitdelg.
extol, loof, verheerlik, ophemel.
extort, afpers, afdwing; uitforseer.
extra, a. ekstra; buitengewoon; addisioneel.
extra, n. ekstra; toegif.
extract, n. ekstrak, aftreksel; uittreksel.
extract, v. uittrek; uittreksel maak; uithaal.
extradite, uitlewer; uitlewering bewerk.
extraordinary, buitengewoon; sonderling, snaaks.
extravagant, onmatig; buitensporig; verkwistend, oordadig; spandabel.
extreme, a. uiterste, verste, uiteindelike.
extreme, n. uiterste.
extremely, uiters, hoogs, uitermate.
extricate, ontwar, losmaak; verlos.
exuberant, weelderig, oorvloedig; uitgelate.
exude, uitsweet, vog afgee.
exult, juig, jubel.
exultant, jubelend, juigend, opgetoë, uitgelate.
eye, n. oog.
eye, v. aanskou, waarneem, sien.
eyebrow, winkbrou.
eyelashes, ooghare, wimpers.
eyelid, ooglid.
eye-opener, openbaring.
eyesight, gesig, oë.
eyesore, doring in die oog.
eyewitness, ooggetuie.

fable, n. fabel, sprokie; versinsel.
fabulous, fabelagtig; legendaries; ongelooflik.
face, n. gesig, voorkome; voorkant; sy(kant); wys(t)erplaat.
face, v. in die oë sien; in die gesig staar; staan teenoor; die hoof bied; uitsien op.
facetious, grappig, geestig; snaaks.
facilitate, vergemaklik; (aan)help.
facility, gemak; vaardigheid, vlotheid.
facing, a. teenoor.
fact, feit, daadsaak; daad.
faction, party; partygees.
factor, oorsaak; agent; deler; faktor.
factorize, in faktors ontbind.
factory, (handels)kantoor, fabriek.
faculty, aanleg; vermoë; bevoegdheid; fakulteit.
fad, idee, manie, gier, stokperdjie.
fade, verbleek, verkleur; verlep, verwelk; kwyn; verswak (radio).
fag, n. vuilwerk; moeite, las; groentjie.
fail, v. ontbreek, kortkom; verswak; faal; (motor) weier; misluk, misloop; in die steek laat; sak, druip.
failing, n. gebrek, swak(heid).
failure, mislukking; tekortkoming; gebrek, fout.
faint, a. flou, swak; dof, vaag.
faint, v. flou (bewusteloos) word.
fair, n. kermis.
fair, a. mooi, fraai; blond, lig; taamlik, goed; suiwer, skoon, rein; regverdig, billik; opreg, eerlik.
fair-play, skoon spel; that is not –, dit is kurang.
fairway, vaarwater; skoonveld (gholf).
fairy, n. (tower)fee.
fairy-tale, sprokie.
faith, geloof; vertroue; trou.
faithful, getrou; gelowig.
fake, n. bedrog; voorwendsel; vervalsing.
fake, v. voorwend, namaak, vervals.
fall, v. val, daal, sink, stort, sak.
fall, n. val; daling; instorting; afdraand, helling; waterval.
fallacy, bedrog; dwaalbegrip; onjuistheid.
fallow, a. braak.
false, vals; verkeerd; onwaar; oneg.
falsify, vervals.
falter, stamel, hakkel; weifel; strompel.
fame, roem, vermaardheid; faam.
familiar, a. (goed)bekend; gemeensaam, familiaar; vertroud; alledaags.
family, (huis)gesin, familie; afkoms.
family-tree, stamboom.
famine, hongersnood; gebrek, nood.
famish, verhonger.
famous, beroemd; vermaard; uitstekend.
fan, n. waaier; skroef.
fan, v. (koel) waai; aanblaas.
fanatic, n. dweper, dweepsugtige.
fan-belt, waaierband.
fancier, liefhebber, kweker.
fancy, n. verbeelding, fantasie; inval, gril; liefhebbery.
fancy, v. verbeel; voorstel; dink, glo; hou van.
fancy(-dress) ball, gekostumeerde bal.
fang, tand, slagtand; giftand; tandwortel.
fantastic, denkbeeldig, fantasties.
fantasy, fantasie; verbeeldingskrag; gril.
far, a. ver, afgeleë, verwyderd.
far, adv. ver, verreweg; veel; diep.
farce, n. klug(spel).
fare, n. reisgeld, vragprys; passasier; vrag; ete, gereg.
fare, v. gaan, vaar.
farewell, vaarwel.
far-fetched, vergesog.

farm, n. (boer)plaas, boerdery.
farm, v. boer; bebou.
farmer, boer; landbouer.
farmyard, werf.
farrier, hoefsmid; perdedokter.
farthing, oortjie.
fascinate, bekoor, betower, boei.
fashion, n. mode; manier; fatsoen.
fashion, v. vorm, fatsoeneer, vou, buig.
fashionable, modieus.
fast, v. vas.
fast, a. vas, stewig; blywend; kleurvas; vinnig, snel, vlug; los(bandig).
fast, adv. vas, ferm; diep; styf; dig.
fasten, vasmaak, toemaak; bevestig; vestig (op).
fastidious, kieskeurig, lastig, puntene(u)rig.
fat, a. vet; dik; ryk; vrugbaar.
fat, n. vet.
fatal, dodelik; noodlottig; fataal; beslissend.
fatalism, fatalisme.
fatality, noodlottigheid; noodlot; (dodelike) ongeluk; ramp.
fate, noodlot; bestemming, lot.
fateful, noodlottig; beslissend.
father, n. vader.
father-in-law, skoonvader.
fathom, n. vaam (vadem).
fathom, v. vadem; peil.
fatigue, n. vermoeienis; afmatting.
fatiguing, vermoeiend, afmattend.
fatten, vet maak; vet word.
fatty, a. vetterig, vet(agtig).
fatty, n. vetsak.
fatuous, laf, dwaas, onbenullig.
faucet, (tap)kraan.
fault, gebrek; fout; skuld.
fauna, fauna; diere(wêreld).
favour, n. guns; begunstiging; skrywe, brief.
favour, v. begunstig; bevoorreg; voortrek.
favourable, gunstig; goedgesind.
favourite, n. gunsteling, liefling.
fawn, n. jong hert.
fawn, a. vaalbruin.
fear, n. vrees; angs.
fear, v. vrees, bang wees (vir).
fearful, verskriklik, vreeslik; bang.
fearless, onbevrees, onverskrokke.
feasible, uitvoerbaar, doenlik, prakties.
feast, n. fees; (fees)maal, onthaal.
feast, v. feesvier; smul; fuif.
feat, kordaatstuk, prestasie.
feather, n. veer; pluim.
feature, n. kenmerk; trek; hoofpunt.
February, Februarie.
federation, (statebond), federasie.
fee, n. honorarium, vergoeding; salaris; (skool-, eksamen-, inskrywings-)geld.
feeble, swak; flou; sleg, pap.
feeble-minded, swaksinnig; besluiteloos.
feed, v. voed; voer; kos gee.
feed, n. voeding; voer, kos.
feel, voel; betas.
feeler, voeler; voelhoring.
feeling, n. gevoel; gesindheid.
feign, voorgee, voorwend; veins, huigel.
feint, v. liemaak, 'n skynbeweging maak.
felicitate, gelukwens, felisiteer (met).
fell, a. wreed, fel, woes.
fell, v. vel; om-, afkap; neerslaan.
fellow, maat; kêrel; vent; lid; weerga.
felon, fyt.
felt, n. velt (vilt).
female, a. vroulik; vroue- . . . ; wyfie- . . .
feminine, vroulik; verwyf.
fence, n. draad, heining; heler.

fencing, (die) skerm, skermkuns.
fend: – off, afweer.
ferment, v. gis; laat gis; ophits; broei.
fern, varing.
ferocious, wild, woes, wreed, kwaai.
ferry, n. pont.
fertile, vrugbaar.
fertilize, vrugbaar maak; bevrug; bemes.
fertilizer, messtof, kunsmis.
fervour, ywer, (gees)drif; vuur, gloed.
fester, v. etter, sweer, loop; kanker.
fester, n. sweer, verswering.
festival, n. feesdag; feesviering; fees.
fetch, v. haal, gaan haal; trek; behaal, opbring.
fête, n. fees(dag), fête.
fetish, fetisj, afgod.
feud, twis, vyandskap, vete.
fever, koors; opgewondenheid.
few, min, weinig.
fiasco, mislukking, fiasko.
fib, v. jok, kluitjies vertel.
fibre, vesel.
fickle, wispelteurig, veranderlik, vol grille.
fiction, verdigsel, versinsel; verdigting; fiksie; roman-literatuur.
fictious, nagemaak; denkbeeldig, versonne.
fiddle, n. viool.
fidelity, trou; getrouheid.
fidget, v. woel, vroetel; lastig wees.
field, n. veld; land; gebied; speler(s).
field, v. veldwerk doen (krieket); (bal) vat (vang).
fielder, veldwerker.
fieldglass, verkyker.
field-marshal, veldmaarskalk.
fiend, bose gees; besetene, woeste duiwel.
fierce, woes, onstuimig, woedend.
fiery, vurig; vlammend; opvliegend.
fifteen, vyftien; rugbyspan.
fifty, vyftig.
fig, n. vy(g); vyeboom.
fight, v. veg; baklei (met).
fight, n. geveg, stryd; twis.
fighter, vegter; bokser; jagvliegtuig.
figure, n. gedaante, vorm, figuur; postuur, gestalte; beeld; syfer.
figure, v. afbeeld, teken; verbeel.
file, n. vyl.
file, v. vyl; polys.
file, n. papierhaak; lias; lêer; rol; ry, gelid, tou.
file, v. inry(g), rangskik, liasseer; deponeer; in gelid marsjeer.
fill, v. vul, vol maak; vol word; ('n tand) stop; opvul; vervul; ('n pos) beklee.
fill, n. bekoms.
fillet, strook; lendestuk.
filling, vulsel, stopsel.
film, n. laag, vlies; film; rolprent.
film star, rolprentster.
filter, v. filtreer; suiwer; deursyg.
filth, vuilgoed, vullis; smerigheid.
filthy, vuil, smerig; – lucre, vuil gewin.
Fin(n), Fin.
fin, vin.
final, a. laaste, slot- . . . , einde . . . , beslissend; finaal.
final, n. eindeksamen; eindwedstryd.
finance, n. finansies.
financial, geldelik, finansieel.
finch, vink.
find, v. vind, ryk; bevind; verskaf.
find, n. vonds; ontdekking.
finding, uitspraak; bevinding.
fine, n. boete.
fine, v. beboet.

fine, a. fyn; dun, skerp; mooi, fraai, suiwer; edel; pragtig, heerlik, lekker.
finger, n. vinger.
fingerprint, vingerafdruk.
finish, v. voltooi, eindig; klaarkry, ophou; afwerk; doodmaak.
finish, n. einde, end, slot; afwerking.
finished, klaar; afgewerk; volmaak.
fir, den(neboom); dennehout.
fire, n. vuur; brand; skietery; koors; hartstog; ywer; vurigheid.
fire, v. aan die brand steek; skiet; opstook; aanspoor; afdank.
fire-brigade, brandweer.
fire-engine, brandspuit.
fire-escape, reddingstoestel; brandtrap.
firefly, vuurvlieg, glimwurm.
firm, n. firma; (handels)naam.
firm, a. vas, hard, massief; stewig, heg; vasberade, ferm; trou.
first, a. eerste; vroegste; voorste; vernaamste.
first, n. die eerste; begin.
first, adv. eers, eerste.
fish, n. vis.
fish, v. vis, visvang; hengel.
fish-bone, visgraat.
fisherman, visser.
fishing-rod, visstok, hengelstok.
fishing-tackle, visgereedskap.
fish-pond, visvywer, visdam.
fission, splitsing.
fissure, bars, skeur; kloof, spleet; naat.
fist, n. vuis; handskrif.
fit, n. toeval; bui, nuk.
fit, v. pas; geskik maak; aanpas.
fit, n. (die) pas, (die) sit; snit.
fit, a. passend, gepas; geskik; bekwaam; behoorlik; bruikbaar; gesond.
fitting, a. passend, gepas; aanpassend.
five, vyf.
fix, v. vasmaak, -sit, -spyker, -heg, (be-)vestig; vasstel; beslis, keuse doen; dik word; fikseer.
fix, n. knyp, moeilikheid.
fixed, vas; vasgestel(d); vasstaande; bepaald.
fixture, (spyker)vaste voorwerp; vastigheid; (vasgestelde) datum; afspraak; wedstryd.
fizz, v. bruis, borrel.
flabbergast, dronkslaan, verbluf.
flabby, pap, papperig, slap, slapperig.
flag, n. vlag.
flagrant, verregaande; flagrant.
flagstone, plaveisteen.
flair, flair, aanleg.
flake, n. vlok; skilfertjie, stukkie.
flake, v. vlok; afskilfer.
flame, n. vlam; hitte; vuur.
flame, v. vlam, brand; skitter, blink.
flamingo, flamink.
Flanders, Vlaandere.
flange, flens, rand.
flank, n. flank, sy; kant, vleuel.
flannel, n. flennie.
flap, v. flap, klap, slaan.
flap, n. flap, slag; klap; lelletjie; lappie.
flapper, vlieëplak; ratelaar; bakvissie.
flare, v. flikker, opvlam, gloei.
flash, v. flikker, vonkel, skitter; glinster; opvlam; flits.
flash, n. flikkering, flits, straal, skig.
flask, fles, veldfles.
flat, n. plat kant; woonstel, kamerwoning.
flat, a. plat; gelyk; glad; eentonig.
flat, adv. plat; sing –, vals sing.
flat-iron, strykyster.

flatten, plat maak; gelyk maak; plat word; gelyk word.
flatter, vlei, flikflooi; streel.
flavour, n. geur; smaak; aroma.
flavouring, n. geursel, smakie.
flaw, n. bars, skeur; fout, gebrek.
flax, vlas.
flea, vlooi.
fleck, v. vlek; stippel.
flee, vlug; ontvlug, ontwyk.
fleece, n. vlies; vag; skeersel.
fleece, v. skeer; pluk.
fleet, n. vloot.
fleet, a. vlug, rats, geswind, vinnig.
fleeting, vlugtig, verbygaand.
Fleming, Vlaming.
Flemish, a. Vlaams.
flesh, n. vlees (vleis).
flex, v. buig.
flex, n. (elektriese) koord.
flexible, buigbaar; buigsaam, inskiklik.
flick, tik; raps; klap.
flicker, v. flikker; fladder, wapper; tril.
flight, n. vlug; trek; swerm; – of stairs, trap.
flighty, lighoofdig, lossinnig; wispelturig.
flinch, terugdeins; krimp.
fling, v. gooi, werp, slinger; storm.
flippant, ligsinnig, onverskillig, onbesonne.
flirt, v. koketteer, flirt.
flit, v. sweef, fladder; swerf, trek.
float, n. sierwa; vlot; dobber; blaas; vryfplank (van 'n messelaar).
float, v. drywe, swem, vlot, dobber; laat drywe; (maatskappy) oprig; ('n lening) uitskryf.
fleck, n. trop, swerm, skaar, kudde.
flog, slaan, klop, uitstof.
flogging, pak (slae), loesing.
flood, n. vloed; stroom; oorstroming; sond-vloed; stortvloed.
flood, v. oorstroom; nat lei; laat oorloop; vloei.
floor, n. vloer, bodem; verdieping.
floor, v. vloer insit; plat slaan; dronkslaan.
florid, bloemryk; opsigtig; blosend.
florin, tweesjielingstuk, (20c).
florist, bloemis; (blo(e)mkweker.
flotilla, flottielje.
flotsam, wrakhout, opspoelsel; oesterkuit.
flounce, n. strook, opnaaisel.
flour, meelblom, fynmeel.
flourish, v. floreer, tier, welig groei.
flow, v. vloei; stroom.
flow, n. stroom; vloed; golwing.
flower, n. blom (bloem); bloei; fleur; bloeisel.
flower, v. bloei, blom.
flower-bed, blombedding, -akkertjie.
flower-girl, strooimeisie; blommeverkoopster.
flu, griep, influensa.
fluctuate, skommel; wissel.
fluent, vloeiend; vlot; vaardig.
fluff, dons, pluisie, vlokkie.
fluid, n. vloeistof; fluïdum.
fluke, n. gelukskoot.
flurry, v. aanjaag, verbouereerd maak.
flush, v. deurspoel; onder water sit; gloei, bloos; die bloed na die wange jaag.
fluster, v. deurmekaar maak, in die war bring.
flute, n. fluit; fluitspeler; groef(ie).
flutter, v. fladder; beef, tril; swaai.
fly, n. vlieg.
fly, v. vlie(g); vlug; waai, wapper.
fly, a. oulik, oorlams, geslepe.
fly-half, losskakel.
foal, n. vul(letjie).
foal, v. vul.
foam, skuim.

focus, v. instel; op een punt saamtrek.
fodder, voer.
foe, vyand.
fog, n. mis, newel; be in a –, benewel wees.
fog, v. mis; mistig maak; benewel.
fog-horn, mishoring.
foil, v. van die spoor lei; uitoorlê, verydel.
fold, v. vou.
fold, n. vou; plooi; hoek.
fold, n. kraal; hok; kudde.
foliage, blare, loof, gebladerte.
folio, folio.
folk, mense.
folk-song, volksliedjie.
follow, volg, na-, opvolg; aanhang.
following, a. volgende; onderstaande.
following, n. volgelinge, aanhang, gevolg.
folly, dwaasheid, gekheid, stommiteit.
foment, baai, pap, aankweek, aanstook.
fond, verlief; liefhebbend; be – of, lief wees vir; hou van.
fondle, v. troetel, liefkoos, streel.
food, voedsel, spys, ete, kos; stof.
fool, n. dwaas, gek, nar.
fool, v. vir die gek hou; bedrieg, fop.
foolish, dwaas, gek; dom.
foolscap, folio(papier).
foot, n. voet; onderent, voetenent.
football, voetbal.
footing, staanplek, vastrapplek; voet; voetstuk.
footprint, (voet)spoor.
for, prep, vir; om; in plaas van; gedurende.
for, conj. want, omdat, aangesien, omrede.
forage, n. voer.
forage, v. soek, wei, plunder.
forbid, belet, verbied.
forbidding, terugstotend, afskrikkend.
force, n. krag, mag; geweld; dwang.
force, v. dwing, noodsaak; afdwing.
forced, gedwonge; gesog, onnatuurlik.
forceful, kragtig, gespierd.
ford, n. drif.
ford, v. deurwaad, deurgaan,
fore, a. voor- . . .
fore, n. voorpunt; boeg; voorgrond.
foreboding, voorspelling; voorgevoel.
forecast, v. voorspel; beraam.
forefather, voorvader.
foregone: – conclusion, uitgemaakte saak.
foreground, voorgrond.
forehead, voorkop, voorhoof.
foreign, vreemd; buitelands, uitheems.
foreigner, vreemde(ling), buitelander.
foreman, voorman; voorsitter (van die jurie).
foremost, voorste; mees vooraanstaande.
forerunner, voorloper, voorbode, voorspel.
foresee, voorsien, vooruitsien.
foresight, vooruitsiendheid; oorleg; voorvisier.
forest, woud, bos.
forestall, voorspring; voorkom.
forestry, bosbou, bosboukunde; houtvestery.
foretell, voorspel, voorsê, profeteer.
foreword, voorwoord, inleiding.
forfeit, v. verbeur, inboet.
forge, v. smee(d); versin, bedink; namaak.
forget, vergeet.
forgetful, vergeetagtig; be – of, vergeet.
forgive, vergewe, kwytskeld.
forgiveness, vergifnis; kwytskelding.
forgo, afsien van, afstand doen van.
fork, n. vurk; gaffel; mik.
fork, v. splits, vertak.
forlorn, verlate, verlore; moedverlore.
form, n. vorm, gedaante, fatsoen; orde; formali-teit; bank; klas; kondisie; in –, op stryk.

form, v. vorm; maak; set; oprig, stig; rangskik.
formal, vormlik; formeel; uitdruklik.
formality, formaliteit, vormlikheid.
former, a. vroeër, vorige, gewese, voormalige.
former, pron. eerste, eersgenoemde.
formerly, vroeër, vanmelewe.
formidable, gedug; ontsagwekkend.
formula, formule; voorskrif, resep.
formulate, formuleer, onder woorde bring.
foresake, verlaat, in die steek laat; versaak.
fort, fort, skans, vesting.
forth, voort, vooruit; uit; voortaan; voorts.
forthcoming, nadurende, aanstaande.
forthright, reguit; meteens.
forthwith, onverwyld, meteens.
fortify, versterk; fortifiseer; aanmoedig.
fortitude, lewensmoed; vasberadenheid.
fortnight, veertien dae.
fortress, fort, vesting, bolwerk.
fortuitous, toevallig.
fortunate, gelukkig, voorspoedig; gunstig.
fortune, n. geluk, fortuin; kans; lot, voorspoed; rykdom.
fortune-teller, waarsêer (-segster).
forty, veertig; – winks, 'n dutjie.
forum, forum; markplaas; regbank.
forward, a. voorstel; voorwaartse; gevorderd; vroegryp; voorbarig; vrypostig.
forward, n. voorspeler.
forward(s), adv. vooruit, (na) vorentoe, voorwaarts.
forward, v. bevorder; bespoedig; aanstuur.
fossil, n. verstening, fossiel.
foster, voed, kweek, koester, bevorder.
foster-child, pleegkind, aangenome kind.
foul, a. vuil, smerig; troebel; gemeen, vals; skandelik, snood.
foul, n. vuil spel.
found, grondves, stig, oprig.
found, giet; smelt.
foundation, fondament, grondslag; stigting.
founder, n. stigter, oprigter, grondlêer.
founder, v. vergaan; misluk; val.
foundling, vondeling.
foundry, (metaal)gietery.
fount, bron(aar), fontein; oorsprong.
fountain, bron, (spring)fontein, oorsprong.
fountain-pen, vulpen.
four, vier.
fourteen, veertien.
fowl, n. voël, wildevoël; hoender.
fowl-run, hoenderhok; -kamp.
fox, n. vos, jakkals.
fox-terrier, foksterriër.
fraction, onderdeel, deeltjie; breuk.
fracture, n. breuk.
fracture, v. breek, bars.
fragile, teer, broos, swak, breekbaar.
fragment, stuk, deel, fragment.
fragrant, geurig, welriekend, lekkerruik- . . .
frail, a. teer, tenger; swak; verganklik.
frame, v. omlys, raam; ontwerp; vorm, skik.
frame, n. lys, raam(werk); kosyn; ontwerp; (gemoed)stemming.
frame-saw, spansaag.
franc, frank.
France, Frankryk.
franchise, stemreg, burgerreg.
frank, a. openhartig, eerlik, reguit.
frank, v. frankeer.
frantic, wild, woes, rasend, waansinnig.
fraud, bedrog; bedrieër.
fray, n. geveg, stryd.
fray, v. (uit)rafel, (ver)slyt.
freak, gier, gril; wispelturigheid.

freckle, n. sproet, vlek.
freckled, vol sproete, sproeterig; gespikkel.
free, a. vry; los, ongedwonge; vrypostig; verniet; vrygewig.
free, v. vrymaak, bevry; losmaak; verlos.
freedom, vryheid; gemak; vrypostigheid.
Freemason, Vrymesselaar.
freeze, v. vries; verkluim; (laat) bevries.
freight, n. vrag, lading; vraggeld.
French, a. Frans.
Frenchman, Fransman.
frenzy, waansin, dolheid, raserny.
frequent, v. dikwels besoek, (daar) boer.
frequently, dikwels, herhaaldelik.
fresh, a. fris; vars, nuut; parmantig.
freshen, op-, verfris; opsteek (van wind).
fresher, groentjie, nuweling.
fret, v. knies, (sig) bekommer.
friar, monnik.
friction, wrywing, friksie.
Friday, Vrydag; **Good** –, Goeie Vrydag.
friend, vriend(in).
friendly, vriendelik; vriendskaplik.
frieze, fries.
frigate, fregat.
fright, skrik; voëlverskrikker.
frighten, skrikmaak; bangmaak.
frightened, verskrik, bang.
frigid, koud; onvriendelik, vervelig.
frill, n. val(letjie).
frisky, lewendig, uitgelate, dartel.
fritter, n. snippertjie, skyfie; frituur; koekie.
frivolous, ligsinnig; beuselagtig; niksbeduidend.
fro: to and –, heen en weer.
frockcoat, manel.
frog, padda.
frolic, v. skerts, korswel, jakker.
from, van, vanaf, vandaan; volgens.
front, n. front; voorkant; bors (van hemp).
front, a. voorste, voor- . . .
frontier, grens.
frost, n. ryp; mislukking.
frost, v. ryp; doodryp; dof maak.
frostbitten, bevries, verkluim.
froth, skuim.
frown, n. frons.
frown, v. frons.
frugal, spaarsaam, matig; voordelig.
fruit, vrug, vrugte.
fruitful, vrugbaar.
frustrate, dwarsboom, verydel, uitoorlê.
fry, v. braai, bak.
fuddle, v. besuip; dronk maak; verwar.
fuel, n. brandstof, vuurmaakgoed.
fugitive, n. vlugteling, wegloper, droster.
fulfil, vervul; verwesenlik, uitvoer; voldoen (aan), volbring.
full, a. vol; volledig; voltallig.
full, adv. vol, ruim, heeltemal, ten volle, baie.
full-back, heelagter.
full-blooded, volbloed- . . . ; volbloedig.
full-grown, uitgegroei, volwasse.
full stop, punt.
fully, ten volle, volkome; ruim.
fulminate, bliksem; ontplof; uitvaar (teen).
fumble, v. knoei, onhandig wees.
fume, n. damp, (uit)wasem(ing).
fume, v. berook; damp; kook (van woede).
fumigate, uitrook, ontsmet.
fun, pret, plesier, vermaak; grap.
function, n. werk; amp, waardigheid; funksie.
function, v. werk; fungeer; funksioneer.
fund, n. voorraad; fonds, kapitaal.
fundamental, fundamenteel, grond- . . . ; prinsipieel.

funeral, n. begrafnis; lykstasie.
fungus, paddastoel, swam, fungus.
funk, n. vrees; bangbroek.
funk, v. bang word (wees); weghardloop van.
funnel, tregter; (lug-, skoorsteen-)pyp.
funny, snaaks, koddig, grappig.
fur, n. pels, bont; kim (op wyn); beslag (op die
tong).
furious, woedend, woes, rasend.
furl, opvou, oprol, inslaan.
furlong, furlong.
furlough, n. verlof.
furnace, oond; smeltkroes.
furnish, meubileer; uitrus; verskaf.
furniture, meubels, huisraad; toebehorens.
furrow, n. voor, sloot, grip; rimpel; riffel.

further, a. & adv. verder, meer, nader.
further, v. bevorder, aanhelp.
furthermore, verder; boonop, bowendien.
furtive, heimlik, steelsgewyse.
fury, woede, raserny, drif; furie.
fuse, v. smelt, saamsmelt; uitbrand.
fuse, n. lont; smeltdraadjie.
fuselage, geraamte, romp (van vliegmasjien).
fusion, smelting, fusie; samesmelting.
fuss, n. drukte, lawaai, rumoer; ophef.
fussy, omslagtig, seurderig, lollerig.
futile, vergeefs, vrugteloos; beuselagtig.
future, a. toekomstig; aanstaande; toekomende.
future, n. toekoms; vervolg; toekomende tyd.
fuzzy, gerafel; donserig.

gab, he has the gift of the –, sy mondwerk is goed.

gabble, v. babbel; (af)rammel; mompel.

gable, gewel(top).

gad, slenter; – about, rondslenter.

gadget, uitvindinkie; gerief.

Gaelic, Gaelies.

gaff, n. vishaak; gaffel (van 'n skip).

gag, v. muilband, die mond snoer; (woorde) inlas.

gaiety, vrolikheid; pret, vermaak; opskik.

gain, n. wins, profyt; baat.

gain, v. wen; voordeel trek.

gait, gang, stap, houding.

gaiter, slobkous, stofkamas; binnesool.

gala, gala, fees(telikheid).

gale, storm, sterk wind.

Galilee, Galilea; voorportaal, kapel.

gall, n. gal.

gallant, a. galant, hoflik; dapper; fier, trots; statig, swierig.

gallery, galery; gang.

gallivant, rondflenter, pierewaai, rondrits, rondjol, rondjakker, rinkink.

gallop, n. galop.

gallop, v. galop, galoppeer.

gallows, galg.

galore, volop, in oorvloed, soos bossies.

galosh, oorskoen.

galvanize, galvaniseer; –d iron, sink(plaat).

gamble, v. dobbel, speel.

gamble, n. dobbelary, dobbelspel; waagstuk.

gambol, v. bokspring, huppel.

game, n. spel, spel(l)etjie; pot(jie); wedstryd; wild.

game, a. klaar, gewillig, bereid, sportief.

game, a. lam, mank, kreupel.

gamma: – ray, gammastraal.

gander, gansmannetjie.

gang, trop, bende; ploeg.

ganger, voorman, opsigter, ploegbaas.

gangrene, kouevuur.

gangway, paadjie, deurloop; loopplank.

gaol (jail), n. tronk, gevangenis.

gaol, (jail), v. in die tronk sit, opsluit.

gaoler (jailer), tronkbewaarder, sipier.

gap, opening; leemte, gaping; verskil.

gape, v. gaap; – at, aangaap.

garage, n. garage, motor(waen) huis.

garbage, afval, uitskot.

garden, n. tuin.

gardener, tuinier; tuinman.

garden-hose, tuinslang, -spuit.

gardenia, katjiepiering.

gargle, v. gorrel.

garland, n. krans; segekrans; bloemlesing.

garlic, knoflok (knoffel).

garment, kledingstuk; kleding, gewaad.

garnet, granaat(steen).

garret, solderkamer.

garrison, n. garnisoen, besetting.

garrotte, v. wurg.

garrulous, babbelsiek, praatagtig, spraaksaam.

garter, kousband.

gas, n. gas; wind, bluf.

gas, v. gas, deur gas verstik; bluf, grootpraat.

gas-bag, windbuks, bluffer, grootprater.

gash, n. sny, hou, keep.

gash, v. sny, 'n hou gee, 'n keep gee.

gasket, seising, vulsel, pakking, voering.

gasp, v. snak (na asem), hyg.

gasp, n. snak; snik, hyging, ademtog.

gastric, maag-....

gate, hek; poort; sluis; toegang; ontvangste.

gather, vergader; versamel; pluk; oes; plooi; verstaan.

gathering, vergadering; insameling; sweer.

gaudy, a. opsigtig, spoggerig.

gauge, n. maat, standaard; spoorwydte; kaliber; meter.

gauge, v. meet; peil; toets; yk.

Gaul, Gallië; Galliër; Fransman.

gaunt, maer, skraal, uitgeteer, hol.

gauntlet, kaphandskoen.

gauze, gaas; wasigheid, dynserigheid.

gay, vrolik, plesierig; los(bandig); kleurig.

gaze, v. staar, strak, kyk, tuur.

gaze, n. (starende) blik.

gazelle, gasel, springbok.

gazette, n. gaset; (staats)koerant.

gear, n. uitrusting; gereedskap; rat(te).

gear-lever, versnellingsknop; stelarm.

gem, edelsteen; juweel, kleinood; briljant.

gender, geslag.

general, a. algemeen; gewoon.

general, n. generaal.

generalize, saamvat, generaliseer; veralgemeen.

generally, gewoonlik, in die reël, oor (in) die algemeen, oor die geheel.

generate, voortbring; veroorsaak; ontwikkel; opwek.

generation, voortbrenging; veroorsaking; ontwikkeling; opwekking; geslag, generasie.

generator, voortbrenger; generator, dinamo.

generous, edelmoedig, mild; rojaal; oorvloedig.

genesis, genesis; oorsprong.

genet, muskeljaatkat.

genial, vriendelik, hartlik, joviaal; aangenaam.

genitive, genitief.

genius, genie; (beskerm)gees; genius.

genteel, fatsoenlik, beskaaf; lieftallig.

gentle, a. sag; lief; deftig.

gentleman, heer; witman; meneer.

genuine, waar, opreg, eg, onvervals.

geography, geografie; aardrykskunde.

geology, aardkunde, geologie.

geometry, meetkunde; plane –, vlak(ke) meetkunde; solid –, stereometrie.

geranium, geranium; malva.

germ, n. kiem.

German, n. Duitser; Duits.

Germany, Duitsland.

germicide, n. kiemdoder.

germinate, (ont)kiem, uitloop; voortbring.

gesticulate, gebare maak, gestikuleer.

gesture, gevaar, (hand)beweging.

get, v. (ver)kry, verwerf, behaal, in die hande kry; ontvang, verdien; hê; word, raak; maak.

geyser, geiser; warmwatertoestel; spuitbron.

ghastly, aaklig, afgryslik; spookagtig; doodsbleek.

ghost, gees; spook; skaduwee.

ghostly, geestelik; spookagtig.

giant, n. reus.

gibber, v. brabbel, brabbeltaal, praat.

gibberish, koeterwaals, wartaal.

gibbet, n. galg.

gibe, jibe, v. spot, skimp, uitkoggel.

giddy, a. duiselig, dronk; duiselingwekkend; ligsinnig; wispelturig.

gift, n. gif, gawe, present.

gifted, begaaf, talentvol; begiftig.

gigantic, reusagtig, reuse-...

giggle, v. giggel, (giegel).

gill, n. kieu (mv. kuwe); belletjie; kaak.

gilt, a. vergul(d).

gimlet, handboor.

gimmick, foefie.

gin, n. jenewer.

ginger, n. gemmer; vuur, moed; rooikop.

ginger-beer, gemmerbier.

gingerly, versigtig, behoedsaam.
gipsy, sigeuner(in).
giraffe, kameel(perd).
gird, gord, opgord; aangord; wapen.
girder, dwarsbalk.
girdle, n. gordel, (broek)gord; buikriem.
girdle, v. omsluit.
girl, meisie; nôi.
girth, n. buikgord; gordel, buikriem; omvang.
gist, hoofsaak, kern.
give, v. gee, aangee; meegee; insak; skiet (van 'n tou).
given, gegewe.
gizzard, krop.
glacier, gletser.
glad, bly, verheug.
gladden, verbly, verheug; opvrolik.
gladness, blydskap, opgewektheid.
glamour, betowering, bekoring, aantreklikheid.
glamour-girl, prikkelpop.
glance, v. flikker, skitter; 'n blik werp; – off, afskram.
glance, n. blik, oogopslag; skramshou; flikkering, skynsel.
gland, klier; sel.
glare, v. flikker; woedend aankyk.
glare, n. skittering; woeste blik.
glaring, verblindend; skreeuend; woes; – injustice, skreiende onreg.
glass, glas; verkyker; weerglas; sopie; –es, bril.
glaze, v. glas (ruite) insit; verglaas; glans; glasig word; (oë) breek.
glaze, n. glans; glasuur; glasige blik.
gleam, n. straal, skyn, flikkering.
gleam, v. straal, skyn, flikker, blink.
glee, rondsang; blykskap, vrolikheid.
glen, dal, vlei.
glibly, glad, los; oppervlakkig.
glide, v. gly, skuiwe, sweef; sluip.
glimmer, v. lig, skyn, flikker, skemer.
glimmer(ing), n. skynsel, flikkering.
glimpse, n. glimp; vlugtige blik, kykie.
glimpse, v. skrams raak sien.
glint, v. glinster, blink.
glisten, glinster, blink.
glitter, v. skitter, glinster, vonkel.
gloat, lekkerkry; – over, (sig) verlustig in.
globe, bol, globe; glaaskap.
globule, bolletjie; druppeltjie, koeëltjie.
gloom, n. donkerte, skemer; somberheid.
glorify, verheerlik; prys, ophemel.
glorious, glorieryk; glansryk; salig (dronk).
glory, n. glorie; roem, eer; trots.
gloss, n. glans, skyn, mooi uiterlik.
gloss, v. laat glans, poets; – over, bemantel, doekies om draai.
glove, handskoen.
glow, v. gloei, blaak, brand.
glow, n. gloed, vuur.
glowing, gloeiend; vurig; lewendig.
glow-worm, vuurvliegie, glimwurm.
glue, n. lym.
glue, v. lym; vasplak; (oë) strak rig.
glut, v. volprop, oorlaai; versadig.
glut, n. versadiging, oorlading.
glutton, vraat, gulsigaard, gulsbek.
glycerine, gliserien.
gnarled, kwasterig, knoesterig.
gnash, kners.
gnat, muggie.
gnaw, knabbel, knaag; wegvreet, verteer.
go, v. gaan; loop, wandel, reis; weggaan, verdwyn, val; reik; geldig wees.
go, n. (die) gaan; wegspring; vaart; energie, fut.
goad, v. prikkel, aanspoor, drywe.

goal, n. doel, doelpunt; wen-, eindpaal.
goalkeeper, doelverdediger.
goal-line, doellyn.
goat, bok; he-, bokram; she-, bokooi.
goatherd, bokwagter.
goblin, kabouter.
god, (af)god.
God, God.
godfather, peetoom.
godmother, peettante.
godsend, godsgawe, uitredding.
goggles, stofbril, oogklappe; dronksiekte.
gold, n. goud; geld, rykdom.
golden, goue; gulde.
gold-fish, goudvis.
golf, n. gholf.
golfer, gholfspeler.
golf-links, gholfgrond, -baan.
gong, ghong.
good, a. goed; bekwaam, geskik; gaaf; eg; soet.
good, n. (die) goeie; nut, welsyn.
good-bye, vaarwel.
good-evening, (goeie)naand.
good-for-nothing, niksnuts.
good-natured, goedaardig; goedig.
goodness, goedheid; geskiktheid, bekwaamheid; deug.
goods, goed, goedere.
goods train, goederetrein, vragtrein.
goose, gans; uilskuiken, stommerik.
gooseberry, appelliefie.
gooseflesh, hoendervleis.
gore, v. deurboor; stoot.
gorge, n. keel, strot; kloof.
gorgeous, pragtig, skitterend, oordadig.
gorilla, gorilla.
gory, bloed(er)ig.
gospel, evangelie.
gossip, n. praatjiesmaker, -maakster; skinderpraatjies.
gossip, v. babbel, skinder.
Gothic, Goties; barbaars.
gouge, n. hol beitel, gutsbeitel.
gouge, v. uitbeitel, uithol; uitsteek.
gout, jig; druppel; vlek.
govern, regeer, bestuur; lei, beheer, beheers.
governess, goewernante.
government, n. goewerment, regering.
governor, goewerneur, bewindvoerder; reëlaar.
governor-general, goewerneur-generaal.
gown, n. rok, kleed; toga; (kamer)japon.
grab, v. gryp, skraap; vang, pak.
grace, n. guns, genade; grasie; swier; fatsoen; uitstel; tafelgebed.
grace, v. sier; vereer; begunstig.
graceful, bevallig, bekoorlik, grasieus.
gracious, genadig; innemend; grasieus.
grade, n. graad; gehalte; helling.
grade, v. gradeer, rangskik; meng.
gradient, helling; hellingshoek; gradiënt.
gradual, a. geleidelik; trapsgewyse.
graduate, v. gradeer; gradueer.
graduation, gradering, indeling; graadverdeling; graadverlening; – day, gradedag.
graft, n. ent; oorentsel.
graft, v. ent; oorent.
graft, n. omkopery.
grain, n. graan; korrel; grein(tjie); draad, nerf.
grain-elevator, graansuier.
gram, gramme, gram.
grammar, grammatika, spraakkuns.
grammatical, grammatikaal, grammaties.
gramophone, grammofoon.
gramradio, gramradio.
granadilla, grenadilla, granadilla, grenadella.

granary, graanskuur, -pakhuis.
grand, groot; groots; hoofs; pragtig, mooi, fraai.
grandchild, kleinkind.
grandeur, grootheid; grootsheid; prag.
grandfather, grootvader, oupa.
grandiose, groots; spoggerig.
grandmother, grootmoeder, ouma.
granite, graniet.
grant, v. toestaan; veroorloof; skenk, verleen; toegee, toestem, erken.
grant, n. vergunning; toelae; verlening; skenking.
grape, druif.
grape-fruit, jaar-, bitterlemoen, pomelo.
graph, n. grafiese voorstelling, grafiek.
graphite, grafiet, potlood.
grapple, n. haak; greep; worsteling.
grapple, v. aanklamp; aanpak, beetpak.
grasp, v. vasgryp, pak; begryp, vat.
grasp, n. greep; vashouplek; bereik; verstand.
grasping, inhalig, skraapsugtig.
grass, n. gras; weiveld, -land.
grasshopper, sprinkaan, sprinkaankriek.
grass-widow, grasweduwee.
grassy, grasryk; grasagtig; gras- . . .
grate, n. vuur(h)erd; rooster; tralie.
grate, v. rasper; knars; kras; kraak; skuur.
grateful, dankbaar; aangenaam.
grater, rasper.
grating, n. traliewerk, tralies.
gratis, gratis, verniet, kosteloos.
gratitude, dankbaarheid, erkentlikheid.
gratuity, gif, toelae, gratifikasie.
grave, n. graf, grafkuil.
grave, a. swaar, gewigtig, ernstig; somber.
gravel, n. gruis; graweel(steen).
gravestone, grafsteen.
graveyard, kerkhof, begraafplaas.
gravitate, graviteer; sak; oorhel, aangetrek word; (diamante) sif.
gravity, erns; gewigtigheid; swaartekrag; centre of –, swaartepunt; specific –, soortlike gewig.
gravy, sous.
gray, sien grey.
graze, v. wei, graas.
graze, v. skrams raak, skram; skaaf, skuur.
grease, n. vet, teer, ghries.
grease, v. smeer.
great, groot; lang; dik.
Great Britain, Groot-Brittanje.
Greece, Griekeland.
greed, hebsug, begerigheid; gulsigheid.
greedy, gulsig, snoep; hebsugtig.
Greek, n. Griek; Grieks.
green, a. groen; onervare; fris, jong.
green, n. groen; groenigheid; setperk (gholf).
greengrocer, groentehandelaar.
greet, v. groet, begroet, verwelkom.
greeting, groet; -s, groete.
gregarious: – instinct, kuddegevoel, -instink.
grenade, granaat.
grey, a. grys, grou, vaal.
greyhound, windhond.
grid, rooster; tralie; motorhek.
grief, leed, droefheid, verdriet.
grievance, grief, krenking; beswaar.
grieve, bedroef; grief, krenk; treur.
grievous, ernstig; drukkend; smartlik.
grill, n. rooster; braaivleis.
grill, v. (op die rooster) braai.
grim, nors, grommig, streng.
grimace, v. grimasse maak, gryns.
grin, v. gryns, meesmuil, grinnik.
grin, n. gryns(lag), spotlag.
grind, v. maal; slyp; swoeg, blok.

grindstone, slypsteen.
grip, n. (hand)greep, vat, houvas; hand(reiking); beheer; begrip; handvatsel.
grip, v. gryp, beetpak, vat; boei.
gripe, n. –s, koliek, krampe.
grisly, aaklig, afgryslik, grieselig.
grit, n. gruis; pit, fut, durf.
grit, v. knars, kraak.
grizzled, grys, peper-en-sout(kleurig).
grizzly, n. grysbeer.
groan, v. kreun, steun, kerm.
groan, n. kreun, gesteun, gekerm.
grocer, kruidenier.
grocery, kruideniersware.
groggy, aangeskote; slingerig: bewerig.
groin, lies, sy.
groom, n. staljong, perdekneg; oppasser; kamerheer; bruidegom.
groom, v. roskam, versorg; oppas.
groove, n. groef, gleuf; (sleur)gang.
groove, v. groef, keep, uitgroef, uitkeep.
grope, (rond)tas, (in die donker) voel.
gross, n. gros.
gross, a. groot; vet; grof; onbeskof; walglik; sinlik; – sum, bruto bedrag.
grotesque, a. grotesk, potsierlik, grillig.
ground, n. grond.
ground, v. grond, grondves; baseer; staaf; na die grond lei; grondvat; strand.
ground-floor, benede-verdieping; on the –, gelykvloers.
groundnut, grondboontjie.
ground-plan, plattegrond, grondplan.
group, n. groep; klomp(ie); party.
group, v. groepeer.
grouse, v. brom, kla, mopper.
grove, bome, bos.
grovel, kruip, in die stof wentel.
grow, groei; kweek, verbou; word.
growl, v. knor; brom, kla, mor; dreun.
growl, n. knor; gebrom, gemor; snou.
grub, n. wurm; maaier; sukkelaar; kos, eetgoed.
grudge, n. pik, wrok, hekel.
gruesome, aaklig, afskuwelik, afsigtelik.
gruff, nors, stuurs, bars, grof.
grumble, v. brom, pruttel, kla, mor; grom, knor; rommel, dreun.
grumpy, a. brommerig, nors, knorrig.
grunt, v. knor, gor-gor; brom, grom.
guano, ghwano.
guarantee, v. waarborg.
guard, n. wag; kondukteur; bewaker; beskerming, hoede.
guard, v. oppas, bewaak, behoed; op jou hoede wees; waak (teen).
guardian, bewaker; bewaarder, opsiener, oppasser; kurator; beskermer; voog.
guava, koejawel.
guess, v. raai, gis, skat; dink, glo.
guest, gas, kuiergas.
guffaw, v. brullend lag, brul, skaterlag.
guide, n. gids; leidsman; leidraad.
guide, v. lei, die weg (pad) wys, rondlei; raadgee; bestuur, stuur.
guile, lis, slimheid, bedrog.
guillotine, n. guillotine, valbyl; sluiting.
guilt, skuld.
guilty, skuldig.
guinea, ghienie.
guinea-fowl, tarentaal, poelpetaat.
guinea-pig, marmotjie.
guitar, ghitaar (kitaar).
gulf, golf; draaikolk; afgrond; kloof.
gull, n. seemeeu.
gullet, slukderm, keel(gat); sloot, kloof.

gullible, liggelowig, simpel, onnosel.
gully, kloof, sloep(ie); sloot(jie), voortjie.
gulp, v. wegsluk; inswelg.
gulp, n. sluk, mondvol, teug.
gum(s), n. tandvleis.
gum, n. gom.
gum, v. (vas)gom, lym.
gumboil, sweer(tjie), abses.
gum-tree, gomboom.
gun, geweer; kanon.
gunner, kanonnier, artilleris.
gunny, goiing.

gunpowder, (bus)kruit.
gurgle, v. borrel, klok.
gush, v. stroom, spuit, oorborrel; dweep.
gust, ruk, vlaag, bui.
gusty, winderig, vlaerig, onstuimig.
gut, n. derm; (derm)snaar; –s, ingewande.
gutter, n. geut, voortjie.
guy, n. gek, dwaas, voëlverskrikker.
guzzle, gulsig eet en drink.
gymnasium, gimnasium; gimnastiekkamer.
gymnastic, -s, gimnastiek.
gypsum, gips.

ha, ha!

haberdashery, garing en band, kramery.

habit, n. gewoonte, gebruik; kleed, kostuum.

habitable, bewoonbaar.

habitually, uit gewoonte, gereeld.

hack, v. kap, keep, hou, skop; kug.

hack, n. knol: ryperd; broodskrywer.

hackney, n. ryperd; sukkelaar, sloof.

hack-saw, ystersaag.

haddock, skelvis.

h(a)emorrhage, bloeding, bloedvloeiing.

h(a)emorrhoids, aambeie.

haft, hef, handvatsel.

hag, heks, ou wyf.

haggard, vervalle, ontdaan, verwilderd.

haggle, v. afding; twis, kibbel.

Hague: The –, Den Haag.

hail, v. & n. hael.

hail, v. begroet; (aan)roep, praai; – **from**, af-komstig wees van.

hair, haar (hare).

hairdresser, kapper.

hairpin, haarnaald.

hair-trigger, sneller.

hairy, harig, behaard.

hale: – **and hearty**, fris en gesond.

half, a. half.

half, n. helfte, halwe.

half, adv. half.

half-back, skakel, spil.

half-crown, halfkroon.

half-time, speeltyd; pouse, rustyd.

halfway, adv. halfpad, -weg.

hall, saal; voorportaal; huis; hal.

hallow, heilig, heilig verklaar.

hall-stand, (hoede)stander, hoederak, gangrak.

halt, v. tot staan (stilstand) bring; stop, tot staan (stilstand) kom.

halt, n. halt, stop; halte, stopplek.

halter, halter; strop.

halve, halveer, (gelyk) deel.

ham, dy; ham.

hamburger, frikkadelbroodjie.

hamlet, dorpie, gehug.

hammer, n. hamer; haan (van 'n geweer).

hammer, v. hamer, moker.

hammock, hangmat.

hamper, n. mandjie.

hamper, v. hinder, belemmer.

hand, n. hand, handbreedte; handvol; handteke-ning, handskrif; wyster; werksman.

hand, v. aangee, afgee.

hand-bill, strooibiljet.

hand-cart, stootkarretjie.

handcuff, n. (hand)boei.

handcuff, v. boei.

handicap, n. voorgif; agterstand; nadeel, belem-mering, las; hendikep.

handicap, v. voorgee; agter-, terugsit; kniehalter; hendikep.

handicapper, voorgeër.

handicap-race, voorgeewedstryd.

handiwork, hand(e)werk.

handkerchief, sakdoek.

handle, n. handvat(sel), steel, hingsel, kruk, oor, hef, stuur; vat.

handle, v. bevoel, betas; hanteer; baasraak; behandel; handel.

handlebar(s), stuur(stang).

handshake, handdruk.

handsome, knap, aansienlik; edelmoedig.

handwriting, handskrif.

handy, handig, behendig, vaardig; gerieflik, ge-skik; byderhand.

hang, v. hang, ophang; behang; plak.

hang, n. hang; slag.

hangar, vlieg(tuig)loods, hangar.

hangman, laksman, beul.

hanker, hunker; – **after**, snak na.

haphazard, a. toevallig; wild.

happen, gebeur, plaasvind, geskied.

happiness, geluk.

happy, gelukkig, bly.

happy-go-lucky, onbesorg, sorgloos; onverskil-lig.

hara-kiri, hara-kiri, selfmoord.

harangue, v. 'n gloeiende toespraak hou; op-sweep.

harass, lastig val, teister, bestook, kwel, pla, terg; vermoei.

harbour, n. hawe; toevlugsoord.

harbour, v. herberg; koester.

hard, a. hard, styf, dik; moeilik, swaar; hewig; streng, hardvogtig; skerp.

hard, adv. hard, swaar, moeilik; dig.

hard-board, kartonplank.

harden, hard; hardmaak; hard word; verhard.

hardened, gehard; verhard; verstok.

hard-hearted, hardvogtig.

hardly, skaars, nouliks, ternouernood.

hardship, teenspoed; ontbering.

hardware, ysterware.

hare, haas.

hare-brained, dwaas, roekeloos, onbesuis.

harlequin, harlekyn.

harm, n. skade, nadeel, kwaad.

harm, v. beskadig, skaad, benadeel.

harmful, nadelig, skadelik.

harmless, onskadelik; onskuldig.

harmonious, harmonieus, welluidend; harmo-nies; eensgesind.

harmonize, harmonieer, ooreenstem; in ooreen-stemming bring; harmoniseer.

harmony, harmonie; eensgesindheid.

harness, n. tuig; harnas, wapenrusting.

harness, v. optuig, inspan.

harp, n. harp.

harpoon, n. harpoen.

harpoon, v. harpoen(eer).

harrow, n. eg.

harrow, v. eg; pynig, folter, kwel.

harsh, grof; vrank; fel, skel, rou; bars, nors, streng; wreed, hard.

hartebeest, hartbees.

harvest, n. oes, (figuurlik ook oogs).

harvest, v. oes; (in)oogs, insamel.

hash, v. fynmaak, klein kap.

hash, n. fynvleis; opgewarmde kos; mengelmoes.

hashish, hasjisj, (mak) dagga.

hasp, n. knip, klink, neusie; string; oorslag; grendel.

haste, haas, spoed.

hasten, gou maak, (sig) haas; haastig maak, aanja; verhaas, bespoedig.

hasty, haastig, gehaas, gejaag; vinnig, snel, voortvliegend, driftig.

hat, hoed.

hatch, n. onderdeur; luik.

hatch, v. uitbroei.

hate, haat.

hateful, haatlik; gehaat.

hatred, haat, wrok, vyandskap.

haughty, hoog, trots, hoogmoedig.

haul, v. trek, hys, sleep; aanhaal; draai.

haul, n. (die) trek, sleep; vangs, wins.

haunch, heup; boud; dy; **sit on one's –es, op jou hurke sit.**

haunt, v. (êrens) boer; ronddwaal; agternaloop; **ghosts – the place, dit spook daar.**

haunt, n. lêplek, boerplek.
have, v. hê, besit; kry, ontvang, neem, gebruik; beetneem, flous.
haven, hawe; skuilplaas, toevlug.
haversack, rug-, knapsak; hawersak.
havoc, verwoesting.
hawk, n. hawik, valk.
hawk, v. smous.
hawker, smous, venter, marskramer.
hawser, kabel, tou, tros.
hawthorn, meidoring, haagdoring.
hay, hooi.
hay fever, hooikoors.
hayrick, -stack, hooimiet (-mied).
hazard, n. dobbelspel; gevaar, risiko; kans, toeval.
hazard, v. waag, riskeer; opper.
hazardous, gewaag, riskant, gevaarlik.
haze, waas, wasigheid, dynserigheid.
hazy, wasig, newelig, dynserig; vaal.
he, hy.
head, n. kop, hoof; verstand; lewe; oorsprong, bron; voorman, leier, bestuurder, prinsipaal; bo-ent, koppenent; punt, top.
head, v. eerste wees, lei; kop.
headache, hoofpyn, kopseer.
header, kopskoot.
head-hunter, koppesneller.
heading, opskrif, titel, hoof.
headlong, kop-vooruit; halsoorkop.
headman, (opper)hoof, hoofman.
headmaster, hoof(onderwyser).
headquarters, hoofkwartier.
headstrong, koppig, eiewys.
headway, vooruitgang; make –, vorder.
heal, genees, gesond word; gesond maak.
health, gesondheid, welstand.
heap, n. hoop; klomp, boel.
heap, v. stapel; – up, ophoop, opstapel.
hear, hoor, verneem; luister na; verhoor.
hearer, hoorder, toehoorder.
hearing, n. gehoor; verhoor; oor.
hearsay, hore-sê (hoorsê); by, from, on –, van hore-sê (hoorsê).
hearse, lykwa; (dood)baar.
heart, hart, boesem, siel; gemoed; liefde; moed; kern.
heart-ache, hartseer, harteleed, -pyn.
heart-broken: he was –, hy was ontroosbaar.
heartburn, sooibrand, suur.
hearten, opwek, moed inpraat.
heartfelt, innig, diepgevoelde.
hearth, (h)erd, haard.
heart-rending, hartverskeurend.
heartsore, hartseer; seer.
hearty, hartlik, opreg, innig; flink.
heat, n. hitte, warmte; uitdunwedloop; vuur, opwinding.
heat, v. verhit.
heated, verhit, warm; driftig, vurig.
heater, verwarmer, stofie.
heath, hei, vlakte; heide.
heathen, n. heiden; ongelowige.
heathen, a. heidens.
heat-wave, hittegolf.
heave, v. (op)hef, (op)hys; dein, swel; kokhals, brul; gooi; slaak, uitstoot.
heave, n. rysing, deining, swelling.
heaven, hemel; lug(ruim).
heavy, swaar; moeilik; drukkend; bedruk.
Hebrew, n. Hebreër; Hebreeus.
heckle, uitslaan; hekel; ondervra; roskam.
hectic, a. teringagtig; wild, woes.
hectogram(me), hektogram.
hectolitre, hektoliter.

hector, n. baasspeler, bullebak.
hedge, n. heg, heining, skutting.
hedgehog, krimpvarkie, rolvarkie.
heed, v. pas op, let op, ag gee op.
heed, n. ag, oplettendheid, hoede.
heedless, agteloos, onverskillig, onoplettend, sorgloos.
heel, n. hak, hiel; hoef; hakskeen, polvy; agterstuk, onderstuk.
heel, v. hak aansit; (uit)haak (voetbal).
heel, oorhel, hiel; ('n skip) krink.
hefty, swaar, gewigtig; hard.
he-goat, bokram.
heifer, vers.
height, hoogte; hoogtepunt, toppunt.
heighten, verhoog, vermeerder; verhef.
heinous, afskuwelik, verskriklik, snood.
heir, erfgenaam.
heirloom, erfstuk, familiestuk.
helicopter, helikopter.
heliograph, n. heliograaf.
helium, helium, songas.
hell, hel; dobbelhol.
helm, helmstok, roer(pen).
helm(et), helm(et), helmhoed.
help, v. help, bystaan; (be)dien.
help, n. hulp, bystand; helpster; middel, raad.
helpful, nuttig; behulpsaam.
helping, n. hulp; porsie, skep(pie).
helpless, hulpeloos; onbeholpe.
hem, n. soom, kant, boord.
hem, v. (om)soom; – in, insluit.
hemisphere, halfrond, hemisfeer.
hemp, hennep; tou, galgtou; hasjisj.
hemstitch, n. soomsteek.
hen, hen.
hence, hiervandaan af; van nou af; hieruit, daarom; five years –, oor vyf jaar.
henceforth, henceforward, van nou af, voortaan, hiervandaan af.
hen-coop, hoenderhok, fuik.
her, haar; that is –s, dit is hare.
herald, v. boodskap, aankondig; inlui.
herb, kruid, bossie.
herbalist, kruiekenner; kruiedokter.
herd, n. kudde, trop.
herd, n. herder, (vee)wagter.
herd, v. oppas, kyk na; saamhok.
here, hier; hierheen, hiernatoe.
hereabouts, hier rond, hier êrens.
hereafter, adv. hierna, voortaan; hiernamaals; verder op, agter in.
hereafter, n. the –, die hiernamaals.
hereby, hierby, hierdeur, hiermee.
heredity, erflikheid; oorerwing.
herein, hierin.
hereof, hiervan.
hereon, hierop.
heresy, kettery.
heretic, ketter.
hereto, hiertoe; tot hier.
hereupon, hierop.
herewith, hiermee.
heritage, erf(e)nis, erfdeel, erfgoed.
hermit, kluisenaar.
hero, held; halfgod, heros.
heroic, heldhaftig, dapper, helde-, heroïes, heroïek.
heroism, heldemoed, heldhaftigheid.
heron, reier.
herring, haring.
herself, haarself; sy self.
hesitate, aarsel, weifel.
hessian, goiingsak.
heterogeneous, ongelyksoortig, heterogeen.

hew, v. kap; slaan.
hibernate, oorwinter; luilak.
hiccup, hik.
hide, v. verberg, wegsteek; weg-, verstop; weg-
kruip, verskuil.
hide, n. vel, huid.
hide-and-seek, wegkruipertjie.
hideous, afskuwelik, afgryslik.
hiding, loesing, pak.
hiding-place, skuilplaas, wegkruipplek.
hierarchy, hiërargie; priesterheerskappy.
higgledy-piggledy, a. & adv. deurmekaar, onderstebo, hot en haar.
high, a. hoog; verhewe; adellik, sterk; hoog-
lopend, hewig.
High Church, Engelse Kerk.
highflown, high faluting, bombasties, hoogdrawend, aanstellerig.
high-handed, eiemagtig, outokraties.
Highlander, Hooglander.
highlands, hooglande.
highly, hoog, hoogs; hoëlik.
high-minded, edeldenkend, edelmoedig.
highness, hoogte; hoogheid.
high priest, hoëpriester.
high school, hoërskool.
high-spirited, fier; vurig, lewendig.
high-strung, hooggespanne; oorgevoelig.
high water, hoogwater.
highway, grootpad.
hike, v. stap, 'n wandeltog maak.
hilarious, vrolik, opgeruim, uitgelate.
hill, n. bult, heuwel, kop(pie), rant(jie).
hilt, handvatsel, greep, geves, hef.
him, hom.
Himalaya, Himalaja.
himself, hom, homself; self.
hind, a. agter- . . . , agterste; – leg, agterbeen.
hinder, v. hinder, belemmer; verhinder.
hindrance, hindernis, belemmering.
Hindu, Hindoo, Hindoe.
hinge, n. skarnier, hingsel; spil.
hinge, v. draai, hang; rus op, afhang van.
hinny, v. runnik.
hint, n. wenk, toespeling.
hint, v. 'n wenk gee, sinspeel op.
hip, n. heup; hoekspar (van dak).
hippopotamus, seekoei, hippopotamus.
hire, v. huur; verhuur; – put, verhuur.
hire-purchase, koop op afbetaling, huurkoop.
his, sy, syne; it is –, dit is syne.
hiss, v. sis, fluit, blas; uitfluit.
historic(al), geskiedkundig, histories.
history, geskiedenis; verhaal, storie.
hit, v. slaan, moker; 'n klap (slag, hou) gee;
raak, tref.
hit, n. hou, slag; raakskoot; steek, skimp.
hitch, v. vashaak; ruk.
hitch, n. ruk, plug; slag, knoop; haakplek, hape-
ring.
hitch-hike, ryloop, duimry.
hither, hierheen, hiernatoe.
hitherto, tot hier toe, tot nog toe.
hive, n. byekorf, by(e)nes; swerm.
hoard, n. hoop, stapel, voorraad, skat.
hoard, v. ophoop, opstapel, oppot.
hoarding, skutting.
hoarfrost, ryp.
hoarse, hees, skor.
hoary, grys, grou.
hoax, v. fop, om die tuin lei.
hoax, n. foppery, grap, gekskeerdery.
hobble, v. strompel, hobbel; (perde) span.
hobble, n. strompeling; spanriem.
hobby, stokperdjie, liefhebbery; ponie.

hock, hakskeensening; skenkel.
hockey, hokkie.
hoe, v. skoffel; (grond) losmaak.
hoe, n. skoffel.
hog, (burg)vark; smeerlap.
hoist, v. ophys; opblaas.
hoist, n. (die) oplig; ligter, hystoestel.
hold, v. hou, inhou, behou, vashou; besit, hê;
daarvoor hou, meen; volhou; (plek) inneem.
hold, n. vat, greep; vatplek, houvas.
hold, n. (skeeps)ruim.
hole, n. gat; pondok.
hole, v. gate maak; tonnel; inslaan, ingooi; – out,
'n putjie maak (gholf).
holiday, vakansie(dag).
Holland, Holland, hollandslinne.
Hollander, Hollander.
hollow, a. hol; leeg; laag; oneg, vals.
hollow, n. holte; leegte; laagte.
hollow, v. uithol; krom buig.
holster, holster, pistoolsak, saalsak.
holy, a. heilig, gewyd.
homage, hulde, eerbetoon.
home, n. tehuis, tuiste, huis, woonplek; bof,
doel.
home, adv. huis toe, na huis; tuis; raak.
Homer, Homerus.
homer, posduif.
homesick: be –, heimwee hê.
homestead, opstal, woonhuis.
homeward(s), huiswaarts, huis toe, na huis.
homicide, manslag, doodslag.
homogeneous, homogeen, gelyksoortig.
homonym, homoniem.
homophone, homofoon.
hone, n. oliesteen.
hone, v. slyp, aansit.
honest, eerlik, opreg; eerbaar.
honey, heuning; soetlief, skat.
honeycomb, heuningkoek.
honeymoon, wittebroodsdae.
honorary, ere- . . .
honour, n. eer; eerbewys; eergevoel; –s, eerbe-
wyse; honneurs.
honour, v. eer, respekteer; eer betoon; honoreer.
honourable, eervol; eerwaardig, agbaar; opreg,
eerlik.
hood, n. kap (van 'n mantel, kar, ens.).
hoodwink, blinddoek; flous, uitoorlê.
hoof, n. hoef, klou; poot.
hook, n. haak, hakie, kram(metjie); vishoek;
hoek, draai.
hook, v. (aan)haak, vasmaak; trek (in gholf,
krieket); (uit)haak (in voetbal).
hooligan, straatboef.
hoop, n. hoepel; band, ring.
hooping-cough, kinkhoes.
hoot, v. jou, uitjou, uitfluit; toet; hoehoe.
hooter, fluit, sirene, toeter.
hop, n. sprong (spring), huppelpas.
hop, v. spring, hup, huppel; eenbeentjie-spring,
hink; dans.
hope, n. hoop, verwagting; –s, verwagtinge.
hope, v. hoop, verwag.
Horace, Horatius.
horde, horde, swerm, bende.
horizon, gesigseinder, kim, horison.
horizontal, a. horisontaal; gelyk, waterpas.
horn, n. horing; voelhoring.
hornet, wesp.
horoscope, horoskoop.
horrible, verskriklik, afskuwelik, aaklig.
horrid, aaklig, naar.
horrify, met afgryse vervul.
horror, afsku, afgryse, gruwel.

horse, n. perd, perderuiters.
horseback: on –, te perd.
horse-fly, perdevlieg.
horseman, (perde)ruiter.
horse-power, perdekrag.
horse-radish, ramenas, peperwortel.
horseshoe, hoefyster.
horticulture, tuinbou.
hose, kous(e); broek; tuinslang.
hospital, hospitaal, siekehuis; gashuis.
hospitality, gasvryheid, herbergsaamheid.
host, leër, bende, skaar.
host, gasheer; waard.
hostage, gyselaar; pand.
hostel, herberg; losieshuis, koshuis.
hostile, vyandig, vyandelik.
hot, warm, heet; vurig, hewig, kwaai; – dog,
    worsbroodjie.
hotel, hotel.
hothead, heethoof, dwarskop.
hothouse, broeikas.
hound, n. (jag)hond.
hound, v. agtervolg.
hour, uur.
house, n. huis; parlement(shuis); saal; skouburg.
house, v. huisves, herberg, onder dak bring;
    opbêre.
household, n. huisgesin; huis.
housekeeper, huishou(d)ster.
housemaster, huisvader; inwonende onderwyser.
housewife, huisvrou.
hovel, pondok; afdak.
hover, fladder, sweef.
hovercraft, lugkussingvoertuig, skeervoertuig.
how, hoe.
however, egter, maar, ewewel, hoe dit sy.
howitzer, houwitser.
howl, v. tjank, huil, gier.
howler, tjanker, skreeuer; flater.
hub, naaf; spil, middelpunt.
huddle, v. opeenhoop; oprol, inkrimp; opeen-
    dring, koek.
hue, kleur (skakering), tint.
huff, brombui, kwaai nuk.
hug, v. omhels, vasdruk, vasklem.
huge, tamaai, enorm, groot.
Huguenot, Hugenoot.
hull, dop; buitenste, rand, skil; romp.
hum, v. gons, brom, zoem; neurie.
human, a, menslik, mens(e)- . . .
humane, mensliewend, humaan.
humanity, mensheid; menslikheid; mensliewend-
    heid; humaniteit.
humanity, menslik; menslikerwys.
humble, a. nederig; beskeie; onderdanig, diens-
    willig.
humble, v. verneder, verootmoedig.
humbug, v. kul, fop, bedrieg, swendel.
humdrum, a. eentonig, vervelig, saai.

humid, vogtig, klam.
humiliate, verneder, verkleineer.
humility, nederigheid.
humorous, humoristies, grappig.
humour, n. bui, humeur; humor.
humour, v. sy sin gee; paai.
hump, skof; boggel; bultjie.
humus, teelaarde, humus.
hunch, v. opbuig, krom trek.
hunch, n. bult; boggel; suspisie.
hunchback, boggel(rug).
hundred, honderd, honderdtal.
hundredfold, honderdvoud(ig).
Hungarian, Hongaar; Hongaars.
Hungary, Hongarye.
hunger, n. honger; lus, hunkering.
hunger, v. honger (na), hunker (na).
hungry, honger, hongerig; begerig.
hunt, v. jag; jaag.
hunter, jagter; skietperd.
hurdle, hek(kie).
hurl, smyt, gooi, slinger.
hurrah, hurray, hoera (hoerê)!
hurricane, orkaan.
hurry, n. haas, haastigheid, gejaagdheid.
hurry, v. haastig wees, gou maak, jaag, gejaag
    wees; aanjaag.
hurt, v. seermaak; benadeel.
hurtle, (aan)bons, smyt; vlieg; gons.
husband, n. man, eggenoot.
hush, n. stilte.
hush, v. stilmaak; stilbly.
husk, n. skil, dop, buitenste.
husk, v. afskil, uitdop.
husky, vol doppe; dor; skor; poolhond.
hussy, flerrie; snip.
hustle, v. stamp en stoot, dring, druk; woel, op-
    keil; jaag, gou maak.
hut, hut, huisie, pondok.
hybrid, n. baster, halfnaatjie.
hydrangea, hortensia.
hydrant, brandkraan.
hydraulic, hidroulies, water- . . .
hydrochloric: – acid, soutsuur.
hydrogen, waterstof.
hydrophobia, hidrofobie, hondsdolheid.
hyena, hiëna, (strand)wolf.
hygiene, gesondheidsleer, higiëne.
hymn, n. himne, (lof)sang, gesang.
hyperbole, hiperbool, oordrywing.
hyphen, n. koppelteken.
hypnotize, hipnotiseer.
hypnotism, hipnotisme.
hypochondria, hipokonders (ipekonders).
hypocrite, skynheilige, huigelaar, veinsaard.
hypodermic, hipodermies, onderhuids.
hypotenuse, hipotenusa.
hypothesis, hipotese, onderstelling.
hypothetic(al), hipoteties, veronderstellend.
hysteric(al), histeries.

I, ek.
Iberian, Iberies.
ice, n. ys.
ice, v. ys; bevries; (koek) glaseer.
iceberg, ysberg.
ice-cream, roomys.
ice-floe, ysblok, ysskots.
Iceland, Ysland.
icicle, yskegel, ysnaald.
icing, glasering; (koek)suiker.
idea, idee; denkbeeld, begrip.
ideal, a. ideaal, volmaak; denkbeeldig.
ideal, n. ideaal.
idealize, idealiseer.
identic(al), dieselfde, einste, identiek.
identify, vereenselwig; gelykstel; herken; aanwys; identifiseer.
identity, identiteit, eenselwigheid.
ideology, ideologie; ideëleer.
idiom, idioom; taaleie.
idiomatic, idiomaties.
idiot, idioot, dwaas.
idle, a. ledig, werkloos; vry; ongegrond; ydel, nutteloos.
idle, v. leegloop, luilak; – away, verbeusel.
idol, afgod; wanvoorstelling; dwaalbegrip.
idolise, verafgood, aanbid, vereer.
idyl(l), idille.
if, as, indien, ingeval; of.
ignite, aan die brand steek; aan die brand raak.
ignition, ontbranding, ontsteking.
ignition coil, ontstekingsklos, vonkspoel.
ignoble, onedel, laag; skandelik.
ignominious, skandelik, smadelik.
ignorant, onkundig, onwetend; onbekend (met).
ignore, ignoreer, oor die hoof sien.
iguana, likkewaan.
Iliad, Ilias.
ilk, klas; sleg.
ill, a. siek; sleg.
ill, adv. sleg; kwalik; moeilik.
ill, n. kwaad, euwel; –s, euwels.
illegal, onwettig.
illegible, onleesbaar, onduidelik.
illegitimate, onwettig; ongeoorloof; oneg.
ill-fated, ongelukkig, rampspoedig.
ill-feeling, kwaaivri(e)ndskap.
illicit, ongeoorloof, onwettig.
illiterate, ongeletterd, ongeleerd.
ill-mannered, ongemanierd, onmanierlik.
illness, siekte, ongesteldheid.
illogical, onlogies.
ill-treat, mishandel, sleg behandel.
illuminate, verlig; illumineer.
ill-use, mishandel, sleg behandel.
illusion, sinsbedrog, hersenskim, illusie.
illustrate, toelig, ophelder; kenskets; illustreer.
illustrious, beroemd, deurlugtig, roemryk.
ill-will, teensin; kwaadwilligheid.
image, n. beeld; ewebeeld; afbeelding.
imaginary, denkbeeldig.
imagination, verbeelding; verbeeldingskrag.
imagine, (sig) verbeel, (sig) voorstel, begryp.
imbecile, n. swaksinnige, idioot.
imbue, indrink, opneem; deurtrek.
imitate, navolg; na-aap, naboots, imiteer.
immaterial, onstoflik, van geen belang.
immature, onryp, onvolgroei.
immediately, onmiddellik, dadelik.
immense, ontsaglik, enorm; kolossaal.
immerge, immerse, indompel.
immigrant, n. immigrant, inkomeling.
immigrate, immigreer, intrek.
imminent, nakend, ophande; dreigend.
immobile, onbeweeglik, immobiel.

immoderate, onmatig, oordrewe, onredelik.
immodest, onbeskeie; onbetaamlik.
immoral, onsedelik, immoreel; sedeloos.
immortal, onsterflik; onverganklik.
immovable, onbeweeglik, onbeweegbaar, onwrikbaar.
immune, onvatbaar, immuun, vry.
imp, kwelgees, ondeug, vabond.
impact, botsing, skok, stamp, slag.
impair, benadeel; verswak.
impala, rooibok.
impale, deurboor.
impart, meedeel, deelagtig maak, oordra.
impartial, onpartydig.
impassable, ondeurganklik, ondeurwaadbaar, onbegaanbaar.
impasse, dooie steeg; dooie punt.
impassioned, hartstogtelik, vurig, opgewonde.
impassive, ongevoelig, onaandoenlik; lydelik.
impatient, ongeduldig; onverdraagsaam.
impeach, beskuldig, in twyfel trek.
impeccable, sonder sonde, onberispelik, volmaak.
impede, hinder, belemmer, teenhou.
imperative, a. gebiedend; dringend.
imperative, n. gebiedende wys, imperatief.
impel, aanspoor, aandryf, moveer; voortbeweeg.
impending, dreigend, ophande (synde).
impenetrable, ondeurdringbaar; ondeurgrondelik; ontoeganklik.
imperfect, a. onvolmaak, onvolkome.
imperial, kieserlik; vorstelik; ryks . . .
imperil, in gevaar bring (stel).
impersonate, voorstel, verpersoonlik; (sig) uitgee vir; vertolk.
impertinent, parmantig, onbeskaamd, astrant; nie ter sake nie.
imperturbable, onverstoorbaar.
impervious, ondeurdringbaar; ontoeganklik.
impetuous, onstuimig, voortvarend.
impetus, vaart, krag, beweegkrag; aandrang.
impi, impie.
implacable, onverbiddelik, onversoenlik.
implement, n. werktuig, (stuk) gereedskap.
implement, v. aanvul; vervul; uitvoer.
implication, verwikkeling; bedoeling; implikasie.
implicit(ly), stilswygend; inbegrepe; onvoorwaardelik, blind.
implore, smeek, bid.
imply, insluit, behels; bedui; sinspeel op.
impolite, onbeleef, ongemanierd.
import, v. invoer; beteken; te kenne gee.
import, n. invoer; betekenis; belang(rikheid).
important, belangrik, gewigtig, van betekenis.
impose, oplê; indruk maak op.
imposing, indrukwekkend.
impossible, onmoontlik; onuitstaanbaar.
imposter, bedrieër, opligter.
impotent, magteloos, hulpeloos; impotent.
impound, skut; beslag lê op.
impoverish, verarm; uitput.
impracticable, onuitvoerbaar, ondoenlik; onprakties; onhandelbaar, onbegaanbaar.
impregnable, onneembaar; onaantasbaar.
impress, v. indruk, inprent; stempel; indruk maak op, tref.
impression, indruk; stempel; druk, oplaag.
impressionable, gevoelig, vatbaar.
imprint, n. stempel.
imprint, v. (af)druk, inprent; stempel.
imprison, in die tronk sit, opsluit.
imprisonment, opsluiting, gevange(n)skap; tronkstraf.
improbable, onwaarskynlik.
impromptu, a. & adv. uit die vuis, impromptu.

improper, onbehoorlik, onfatsoenlik, ongepas; oneg, verkeerd.
improve, verbeter; bewerk.
improvise, improviseer, uit die vuis lewer.
imprudent, onversigtig, onverstandig, onbesonne.
impudent, onbeskaamd, skaamteloos, brutaal.
impulse, (aan)drang; prikkel, aansporing.
impunity, strafloosheid; with –, strafloos.
impure, onsuiwer, onrein; vervals; onkuis.
impute, toeskryf (aan), wyt (aan); aantyg, die skuld gee van.
in, prep. in, op, by.
in, adv. in, binne.
in, n.: –s and outs, besonderhede.
inability, onbekwaamheid; onvermoë.
inaccessible, onbereikbaar; onbeklimbaar, ontoeganklik; ongenaakbaar.
inaccurate, onnoukeurig, foutief, verkeerd.
inactive, werkloos, traag, flou, on-, inaktief.
inadequate, ontoereikend, onvoldoende.
inadvertent, onopsetlik; onoplettend; agtelosig; onbewus.
inalienable, onvervreembaar.
inane, a. leeg; betekenisloos, sinloos, dwaas.
inanimate, lewensloos; doods.
inapplicable, ontoepaslik, ongeskik.
inarticulate, onduidelik, onverstaanbaar; stom.
inattentive, onoplettend, agtelosig; onhoflik.
inaudible, onhoorbaar.
inaugurate, inwy, inhuldig; open.
inborn, aan-, ingebore, ingeskape.
incalculable, onberekenbaar; ontelbaar.
incapable, onbekwaam; onbevoeg.
incarnation, beliggaming, vleeswording.
incautious, onversigtig.
incense, n. reukwerk, wierook; bewieroking.
incense, v. kwaad maak, vertoorn.
incentive, n. aansporing, spoorslag; dryfveer.
incessant, onophoudelik, aanhoudend, knaend, voortdurend.
incident, n. voorval, gebeurtenis, insident.
incidentally, toevallig, terloops.
incinerate, (tot as) verbrand; veras.
incipient, beginnend, in die beginstadium.
incisor, snytand, voortand.
incite, aanspoor, opwek; aanhits, oprui.
inclement, guur; onbarmhartig.
inclination, neiging; geneentheid.
incline, v. (sig) buig, (sig) neig, oorhel.
incline, n. helling, skuinste; af-, opdraand.
include, insluit, omvat, meetel.
incoherent, onsamehangend.
income, inkomste.
incomparable, onvergelyklik, weergaloos.
incompatible, onverenigbaar; onbestaanbaar met.
incompetent, onbevoeg; onbekwaam, ongeskik.
incomplete, onvolledig; onvoltallig.
incomprehensible, onbegryplik.
inconceivable, ondenkbaar, onbegryplik.
inconsiderate, ondegsaam; onhoflik.
inconsistent, ongelyk, veranderlik; teenstrydig; inkonsekwent.
inconsolable, ontroosbaar.
inconstant, veranderlik, onbestendig, onstandvastig.
incontinent, onmatig; ontugtig; onbeheers.
inconvenient, ongerieflik, ongemaklik, ongeleë, lastig.
incorporate, v. inlyf, verenig, inkorporeer.
incorrect, onjuis, verkeerd, inkorrek.
incorruptible, onverganklik, onomkoopbaar.
increase, v. vermeerder, vergroot, verhoog, verbeter.
increase, n. vermeerdering, toename.
incredible, ongelooflik, ongeloofbaar.

incredulous, ongelowig, twyfelsugtig, skepties.
increment, vermeerdering; (loons)verhoging.
incriminate, beskuldig, inkrimineer.
incubate, uitbroei; broei; ontwikkel.
incubator, broeimasjien; kweektoestel.
inculcate, inprent.
incumbent: – (up)on, rustend op.
incur, (sig) blootstel aan.
incurable, ongeneeslik.
indebted, verskuldig, skuldig.
indecent, onbehoorlik, onbetaamlik, onfatsoenlik, onwelvoeglik, onsedelik.
indeed, werklik, regtig, inderdaad.
indefatigable, onvermoeibaar, onvermoeid.
indefinite, onbepaald, vaag, onduidelik.
indelible, onuitwisbaar; – pencil, inkpotlood.
indemnify, skadeloos stel; vrywaar.
indent, v. (uit)tand; (letters) inspring; bestel.
independence, onafhanklikheid.
independent, a. onafhanklik.
indescribable, onbeskryflik; vaag.
indeterminate, onbepaald; vaag.
index, n. wys(t)er; wys(t)er; inhoudsopgawe; klapper; indeks.
India, Indië.
Indian, a. Indies; Indiaans; **Red –,** Indiaan, Rooihuid.
indicate, aandui, aan die hand gee.
indicative, n. aantonende wys, indikatief.
indicator, wys(t)er; aanwys(t)er; aangeër.
indifferent, onverskillig; onpartydig; middelmatig.
indigenous, inheems, inlands.
indigent, behoeftig, nooddruftig, arm.
indigestion, slegte spysvertering, indigestie.
indignant, verontwaardig (oor).
indignity, belediging, onwaardige behandeling.
indirect, indirek, onregstreeks.
indiscreet, onbesonne; onbeskeie.
indiscriminately, blindelings, voor die voet.
indispensable, onmisbaar, onontbeerlik.
indisposed, ongeneë; ongesteld; afkerig.
indisputable, onbetwisbaar.
indistinct, onduidelik; dof, vaag; verward.
indistinctness, onduidelikheid.
indistinguishable, nie te onderskei nie; onsigbaar.
individual, a. individueel; alleenstaande.
individual, n. individu, enkeling.
indivisible, ondeelbaar.
indolent, lui, traag, vadsig.
indomitable, ontembaar; onbuigbaar.
indoors, binnenshuis, binne.
induce, oorhaal, beweeg, noop; veroorsaak, te voorskyn roep; aflei.
inducement, beweegrede, lokmiddel, verleiding.
induct, inlei; installeer; inwy; bevestig.
indulge, toegee aan, koester; verwen; die vrye loop gee.
indulgent, toegeeflik, inskiklik, meegaande.
industrial, a. industrieel, nywerheids- . . .
industrious, ywerig, vlytig, werksaam.
inebriety, dronkenskap; dranksug.
inedible, oneetbaar.
ineffective, ondoeltreffend, vrugteloos.
inefficient, onbekwaam; ondoeltreffend.
ineligible, onverkiesbaar; ongeskik, ongewens.
inept, onvanpas, misplaas; ongerymd, dwaas.
inequality, ongelykheid; veranderlikheid.
ineradicable, onuitroeibaar, onuitwisbaar.
inert, traag, bewegingloos, log.
inestimable, onskatbaar, onberekenbaar.
inevitable, onvermydelik, noodwendig.
inexcusable, onverskoonbaar, onvergeeflik.
inexhaustible, onuitputlik.
inexorable, onverbiddelik.

inexpedient, onraadsaam, ondienstig.
inexperienced, onervare, rou.
inexplicable, onverklaarbaar.
inexpressible, onuitspreeklik, onnoembaar.
infallible, onfeilbaar; onbedrieglik.
infamous, skandelik, skandalig; berug.
infancy, kindsheid, kinderjare; jeug.
infant, n. klein kindjie, babetjie, suigling.
infantry, infanterie, voetgangers, voetvolk.
infant-school, bewaarskool.
infatuation, versotheid; verliefdheid.
infect, aansteek, besmet, verpes.
infectious, aansteeklik, besmetlik.
infer, aflei, opmaak; bedoel.
inferior, a. laer; ondergeskik; minderwaardig.
inferior, n. ondergeskikte, mindere.
infernal, hels; ellendig, vervlaks(te).
inferno, inferno, hel.
infest, teister, vervuil, verpes.
infidel, n. ongelowige.
infinite, a. & adv. oneindig.
infinitive, (die) infinitief, onbepaalde wyse.
inflame, (laat) ontvlam, (laat) ontbrand; verhit, aanvuur, inflammasie kry.
inflammable, brandbaar, ontvlambaar; opvlieënd.
inflammation, ontsteking, inflammasie; ontbranding.
inflate, opblaas, oppomp.
inflected, verboë.
inflection, inflexion, verbuiging (gram.); buiging.
inflict, oplê, toebring, laat ondergaan.
influence, n. invloed, inwerking.
influence, v. beïnvloed, invloed (uit)oefen op.
influenza, griep, influensa.
influx, instroming, toevloed.
inform, meedeel, berig.
informal, informeel.
information, inligting, informasie; klagte, beskuldiging; kennis; kennisgewing.
infringe, oortree, breek, skend.
infuriate, woedend (rasend) maak, vertoorn.
infuse, ingiet; inboesem; laat trek (van tee).
ingenious, oulik, vernuftig, vindingryk.
ingenuous, ope(n)hartig; ongekunsteld.
ingestion, opneming, inbrenging.
ingot, staaf, baar.
ingratitude, ondankbaarheid.
ingredient, bestanddeel, ingrediënt.
inhabit, bewoon, woon in.
inhabitant, inwoner, bewoner.
inhale, inasem, intrek, insluk.
inherent, onafskeidelik verbonde (met), inherent.
inherit, erf, oorerf.
inheritance, erfnis, erfporsie; oorerwing.
inhibition, verbod; stuiting, inhibisie.
inhospitable, ongasvry; onherbergsaam.
inhuman, onmenslik.
iniquitous, onregverdig; verderflik.
initial, n. voorletter.
initial, v. parafeer.
initiate, v. aanvang, begin; inwy, inlei; ontgroen.
initiative, n. inisiatief; ondernemingsgees.
inject, inspuit.
injure, beseer; beskadig, verongeluk.
injury, besering, wond; nadeel, skade; onreg.
injustice, onregverdigheid; onreg.
ink, n. ink.
inland, adv. landwaarts, na die binneland.
inlet, opening, ingang; inham.
inmost, binneste; diepste, innigste.
innate, aan-, ingebore, ingeskape.
inner, binne-...., binneste, innerlik, inwendig.
innermost, binneste; diepste, innigste.
innings, beurt(e).

innocent, a. onskuldig; argeloos.
innocuous, onskadelik.
innovation, nuwigheid, verandering.
innoxious, onskadelik.
innumerable, ontelbaar, talloos.
inoculate, (in)ent.
inopportune, ontydig, ongeleë.
inordinate, buitensporig, oordrewe, ongereeld.
inquest, ondersoek, (lyk)skouing; **coroner's** –, geregtelike lykskouing.
inquire, enquire, verneem, navraag doen.
inquisitive, nuuskierig.
insane, kranksinnig, gek, mal.
insanitary, ongesond, onhigiënies.
insatiable, onversadelik, onversadigbaar.
inscription, inskrywing, opskrif.
inscrutable, onnaspeurlik, ondeurgrondelik.
insect, insek, gogga.
insecticide, insekpoeier, -gif.
insecure, onveilig, onseker, los.
insensible, onwaarneembaar; gevoelloos; bewusteloos; onbewus.
inseparable, onskeidbaar; onafskeidelik.
insert, insteek, invoeg, inlas; plaas.
inside, n. binnekant, binneste.
insidious, verraderlik; listig.
insight, insig.
insignificant, onbeduidend, niksbeduidend, onbetekenend, gering, nietig.
insincere, onopreg, onwaar.
insinuate, indring; insinueer.
insipid, laf, flou, smaakloos.
insist, aandring (op); aanhou, volhard (by).
insolent, parmantig, onbeskaamd, brutaal.
insoluble, onoplosbaar.
insolvent, a. bankrot, insolvent.
insomnia, slaaploosheid, insomnia.
inspan, inspan.
inspect, ondersoek, nasien; inspekteer.
inspector, inspekteur; opsiener.
inspiration, ingewing, inspirasie; besieling.
inspire, inboesem, besiel, aanvuur; inasem; inspireer.
instal(l), installeer; bevestig; inrig; aanlê.
instalment, gedeelte; paaiement.
instance, n. voorbeeld, geval, instansie.
instant, a. dringend; onmiddellik.
instant, n. oomblik.
instead: – **of**, in plaas van, pleks.
instep, wreef, voetrug.
instigate, opstook, aanspoor; op tou sit.
instil(l): – **into**, inprent.
instinct, n. natuurdrif, instink.
instinctive, instinkmatig, instinktief.
institute, v. stig, instel; vasstel.
institution, instelling, oprigting, stigting; institusie; aanstelling; instituut, inrigting, wet.
instruct, onderwys gee, onderrig; gelas.
instruction, onderwys, onderrig.
instructor, leermeester, instrukteur.
instrument, instrument; werktuig; middel.
insubordinate, ongehoorsaam, weerspannig.
insufficient, ontoereikend, onvoldoende.
insulin, insulien.
insult, v. beledig, affronteer.
insulate, afsonder; isoleer.
insulator, isolator.
insurance, versekering, assuransie.
insure, verassureer, verseker.
insurgent, a. opstandig, oproerig.
insurmountable, onoorkomelik.
intact, onaangeroer, ongeskonde, heel.
intangible, ontasbaar; onbevatlik.
integer, heel (integraal) getal; geheel.
integral, a. heel, volledig, integraal.

integrate, v. volledig maak; integreer.
integrity, onomkoopbaarheid; integriteit.
intellect, verstand, denkvermoë, intellek.
intellectual, intellektueel, verstandelik.
intelligence, verstand, intellek; oordeel, begrip; vernuf; tyding.
intelligent, skrander, intelligent.
intelligible, verstaanbaar, begryplik, bevatlik.
intend, van plan (voornemens) wees, meen.
intense, intens, groot, lewendig, sterk, hewig, kragtig, diep.
intensify, versterk, verdiep, vererger.
intent, n. bedoeling, voorneme, oogmerk.
intent, a. vasbeslote; ingespanne; gespanne.
intention, bedoeling, oogmerk, plan.
inter, v. begrawe, ter aarde bestel.
intercede, as bemiddelaar optree, tussenbeide kom; voorspraak wees.
intercept, onderskep; afsny; teenhou.
interchange, v. (uit)wissel, (om)ruil, vervang.
intercom, binnetelefoon.
intercourse, gemeenskap, omgang, verkeer.
interdict, n. verbod; skorsing; interdik.
interest, n. belang; aanspraak; deel; voordeel; belangstelling; rente.
interesting, belangwekkend, interessant.
interfere, (sig) bemoei (inlaat) met; tussenbeide kom.
interim, n. tussentyd.
interior, n. binneste-..., binneland: interieur.
interject, tussenvoeg; uitroep.
interjection, tussenwerpsel, uitroep.
interlude, tussenspel; pouse: tussenbedryf.
intermediary, n. tussenpersoon, bemiddelaar.
intermediate, a. tussen-..., tussentyds.
interminable, eindeloos.
intern, interneer.
intern(e), inwonende geneesheer (by hospitaal)
internal, inwendig; innerlik; binne-...
international, a. internasionaal.
interpret, (ver)tolk, verklaar, uitlê.
interpretation, uitleg, verklaring; vertolking.
interpreter, uitleêr, verklaarder; tolk.
interrogate, ondervra.
interrupt, onderbreek, steur, in die rede val.
intersect, sny, kruis.
interval, tussentyd; pouse, rustyd; tussenruimte.
intervene, tussenbeide kom; ingryp; tussenin kom; gebeur.
interview, n. onderhoud, persgesprek.
intestine, n. derm; –s, derms, ingewande.
intimate, a. vertroulik; innig, diep, nou; intiem.
intimate, v. te kenne gee, laat verstaan.
intimidate, bang maak, intimideer.
into, in, tot in.
intolerable, ondraaglik, onuitstaanbaar.
intoxicate, dronk maak, bedwelm.
intransitive, a. onoorganklik, intransitief.
intrepid, onverskrokke, onversaag, dapper.
intricate, ingewikkeld, verwikkeld, moeilik.
intrigue, v. konkel, knoei.
introduce, invoer; indien; voorstel.
introduction, invoering; inleiding; indiening; voorstelling.
introspection, selfwaarneming, introspeksie.
intrude, opdring; indring, lastig val.
intuition, intuïsie.
inundate, oorstroom; oorstelp.
invade, inval (in); inbreuk maak op.
invalid, a. ongeldig.
invalid, n. sieke, swakke, invalide.
invaluable, onskatbaar.

invasion, inval, strooptog; skending.
invent, uitvind; uitdink, bedink, versin.
invention, uitvinding; versinsel.
inventory, n. inventaris, lys.
inverse, a. omgekeer(d).
invert, v. omdraai, omkeer; –ed commas, aan-halingstekens.
invest, klee; omsingel, vaskeer; (geld) belê.
investigate, ondersoek, navors, uitpluis.
invidious, aanstootlik; onbenydenswaardig.
invigilate, toesig hou, oppas.
invigorating, versterkend; opwekkend.
invincible, onoorwinlik.
invisible, n. die onsienlike.
invisible, a. onsigbaar.
invite, v. (uit)nooi, vra; versoek; (aan)lok.
invoice, n. faktuur.
involuntarily, onwillekeurig, vanself.
involve, betrek in, verwikkel in; meebring.
involved, ingewikkeld; betrokke in.
inwardly, inwendig; innerlik.
inwards, adv. na binne, binnewaarts.
inyala, njala, basterkoedoe; boom.
iodine, jodium, jood.
I.O.U., skuldbewys.
Iran, Iran.
irascrible, sleggehumeurd, driftig, opvlieënd.
irate, kwaad, woedend.
Ireland, Ierland.
iris, swaardlelie; iris.
Irishman, Ier.
irksome, vermoeiend, vervelend, ergerlik.
iron, n. yster; brandyster; strykyster.
iron, v. stryk.
ironmonger, ysterhandelaar.
irony, ironie.
irrational, onredelik; redeloos.
irregular, a. onreëlmatig; ongereeld; ongelyk.
irrelevant, nie toepaslik nie, nie ter sake nie.
irreparable, onherstelbaar.
irreproachable, onberispelik.
irresistible, onweerstaanbaar; verleidelik.
irresolute, besluiteloos.
irrespective: – of, afgesien van.
irresponsible, onverantwoordelik.
irrevocable, onherroeplik.
irrigate, besproei, natlei, irrigeer.
irritable, prikkelbaar, liggeraak, knorrig.
irritate, prikkel, vererg, ontstem, irriteer.
Isaiah, Jesaja.
island, eiland.
isolate, afsonder, afskei; isoleer.
Israelite, Israeliet.
issue, v. uit-, voortkom, ont-, voortspruit, ont-staan; uitvaardig; uitgee; versprei.
issue, n. uitvloeisel; uitgang; uitweg; nakome-lingskap; uitslag; (geskil)punt, strydvraag, uitgawe; uitreiking.
isthmus, landengte; ismus.
it, dit; hy.
Italian, Italiaan, Italianer; Italiaans.
italic, n. –s, kursiefdruk.
Italy, Italië.
itch, v. jeuk.
item, n. nommer (op 'n program); pos (op 'n rekening); artikel (op 'n lys).
itinerary, n. reisplan; reisverhaal; reisgids.
its, sy, van hom, daarvan.
itself, self, homself; in –, op sigself.
ivory, n. ivoor.
ivy, klimop.

jab, v. steek, stoot, sny.
jabber, v. babbel, ratel, snater, kekkel.
jack, v. opdomkrag.
jackal, jakkals.
jacket, baadjie; omslag; skil.
jade, v. afjakker, uitput, flou ry.
jagged, ru, skerp, ongelyk; vol skare.
jail, sien gaol, n. tronk, gevangenis.
jailer, (gaoler), tronkbewaarder, sipier.
jalopy, rammelkas.
jam, n. (fyn)konfyt.
jam, v. vasdruk, vasknyp; haak; volprop.
jamb, sykosyn, deurstyl.
jangle, v. rammel; krys; twis.
January, Januarie.
Japan, Japan.
Japanese, n. Japannees, Japanner; Japannees, Japans (taal).
jar, v. knars, kras; twis; skok.
jar, n. fles, kruik, pot.
jargon, jargon, brabbeltaal.
jasper, jaspis.
jaundice, n. geelsug.
jaunt, n. uitstappie, plesierritjie.
jaunty, lugtig, swierig.
Javanese, Javaan; Javaans.
jaw, n. kaak, kakebeen; bek.
jawbone, kakebeen.
jaw-breaker, tongknoper.
jazz, jazz.
jealous, jaloers, naywerig, afgunstig.
jealousy, jaloesie, afguns, naywer.
jeans, kuitbroek.
jeep, utilileitswa.
jeer, v. spot, skimp (op), hoon.
Jehovah, Jehova.
jelly, jellie.
jemmy, breekyster; (gaar) skaapkop.
jeopardize, in gevaar stel, op die spel sit.
jerk, v. ruk, pluk; smyt, stamp, stoot.
jersey, jersie, trui.
jest, v. skerts, korswel.
jet, git.
jet, n. straal; bek, tuit, kraan, spuit; – aircraft, straalvliegtuig.
jet, v. spuit, straal, uitskiet.
jetblack, gitswart.
jetsam, wrakgoed, seedrif, opdrifsel.
jettison, oorboord gooi.
jetty, hawehoof, pier, kaai.
Jew, n. Jood; –'s harp, trompie.
jewel, n. juweel, kleinood, edelsteen; skat.
jeweller, juwelier.
jib, v. vassteek, steeks word; omdraai.
jiff(y), in a –, in 'n kits.
jig, n. horrelpyp; horrelpypdeuntjie.
jigsaw, figuursaag.
jigsaw puzzle, legkaart.
jilt, v. afsê, laat loop, fop.
jingle, v. klingel, rinkel; rymel.
jingo, jingo.
j(i)ujitsu, joejitsoe.
jive, v. wild dans.
job, n. (stuk) werk; baantjie; good –, 'n goeie ding.
jockey, n. jokkie, reisiesjaer.
jocular, grapp(er)ig, skertsend.
jocund, lustig, opgewek; aangenaam.
jog, v. stamp, ruk; stoot, aanstoot; (geheue) opfris; – along, on, aansukkel.
join, v. (ver)bind, vasmaak, saamvoeg, vasknoop;

aansluit (by), toetree (tot), (sig) verenig met; gepaard gaan met; aangrens.
join, n. voeg, lasplek; verbinding(spunt).
joiner, skrynwerker.
joint, n. voeg, las(plek); lit, gewrig; skarnier; verbinding; karmenaadjie.
joint, a. gesame(nt)lik, gemeenskaplik, mede-. . .
joint, v. las, voeg; deel, stukkend sny.
joist, n. dwarsbalk.
joke, n. grap, gekheid.
joke, v. 'n grap (grappe, grappies) maak, gekskeer, korswel, speel.
joker, grappemaker; vent, asjas; (swart) Piet, boer (in kaartspel).
jolly, jolig, vrolik, plesierig; aangeklam.
jolt, stamp, skok.
jostle, v. stamp, druk, dring, stoei.
jot, n. jota.
journal, dagboek; (dag)blad, tydskrif.
journalist, joernalis, koerantskrywer.
journey, n. reis, tog.
journey, v. reis, trek.
jovial, joviaal, lustig, gul.
joy, n. vreugde, blydskap, genoeë.
joyful, bly, vreugdevol, vrolik.
joystick, stuurstok.
jubilant, juigend, jubelend, triomfant.
jubilee, jubeljaar; jubileum.
Judah, Juda; Judas.
judge, n. regter; skeidsregter, beoordelaar.
judge, v. regspreek; uitspraak doen, oordeel; beoordeel; skat.
judg(e)ment, oordeel; vonnis; mening.
judicial, regterlik, geregtelik; oordeelkundig.
judicious, oordeelkundig, verstandig.
jug, n. beker, kruik.
juggle, v. goël, toor; knoei, verdraai.
juggler, goëlaar; bedrieër.
juice, sap (sop); gastric –, maagsap.
juke-box, blêrkas.
July, Julie.
jumble, n. warboel, rommel; gehobbel.
jumble-sale, rommelverkoping.
jump, v. spring, opspring; oorspring.
jump, n. sprong, spring.
jumper, springer; springboor.
jumper, kiel, jakkie.
junction, vereniging, verbinding; bindplek, las; saamloop; knoop(punt) (van spoorlyne).
juncture, vereniging; voeg, naat, las; sameloop (van omstandighede), tydstip.
June, Junie.
jungle, boswêreld, wildernis; warboel.
junior, a. junior, jonger, jongste.
junk, n. jonk (Chinese skip).
jurisdiction, regsgebied; regspraak; regsbevoegdheid; jurisdiksie.
jurisprudence, regsgeleerdheid.
jury, jurie, geswLorenes.
just, a. regverdig; billik, gegrond; geregtig; verdiend; juis, presies.
just, adv. net, presies, juistement; eenvoudig.
justice, geregtigheid, regverdigheid, reg; billikheid; justisie; regter.
justify, regverdig, wettig; verdedig; verantwoord, verskoon, goedpraat.
jut, v. vooruitsteek, uitspring, oorhang.
jute, goiing, jute.
juvenile, a. jeugdig, jeug-. . .
juvenile, n. jeugdige persoon.

kaiser, keiser.
klaeidoscope, kaleidoskoop.
kangaroo, kangaroe.
Karoo, Karoo.
kaross, karos.
keel, n. kiel; skip, vaartuig.
keen, a. skerp; bytend; vurig; heftig; ywerig; belangstellend; begerig.
keep, v. hou; behou; bewaar; oppas, beskerm; gehoorsaam, nakom, gestand doen, vervul; in ag neem; onderhou; in voorraad hou; goed bly.
keep, n. onderhou(d); bewaring; kasteel.
keeper, bewaarder, opsiener, oppasser.
keeping, bewaring; ooreenstemming.
keepsake, aandenking.
keg, vaatjie.
kennel, n. hondehok; hok, pondok.
kennel, n. geut, voor.
Kentish, Kenties.
kerb, rand van sypaadjie; sypaadjie.
kerb-stone, randsteen, trottoirsteen.
kernel, pit; kern.
ketchup, tamatiesous.
kettle, ketel.
kettle-drum, (ketel)tamboer, pouk.
key, sleutel; verklaring, vertaling, antwoordboek; toonaard; trant; klawer, toets, noot; wig, pen.
khaki, kakie.
kick, n. skop; skopper; krag, pit.
kick, v. skop; (sig) verset, (sig) teësit.
kick-off, afskop.
kid, n. boklammetjie; bokvel, snuiter.
kidnap, skaak, ontvoer.
kidney, nier.
kill, v. doodmaak, vermoor; uit die weg ruim.
kiln, oond.
kilogram(me), kilogram.
kilometre, kilometer.
kilowatt, kilowatt.
kilt, n. kilt, Skotse rokkie.
kin: next of –, bloedverwant(e).
kind, n. soort, klas, ras, slag; aard.
kind, a. vriendelik, goedhartig, lief.
kindergarten, kindertuin.

kindle, aan die brand steek, laat ontvlam.
kindly, goedhartig, welwillend.
kindred, a. verwant; gelyksoortig.
king, n. koning, vors; (by kaarte) heer; (by dambord en skaak) koning.
kingdom, koninkryk.
kiosk, kiosk; tuinhuis; stalletjie.
kipper, n. gerookte haring.
kiss, n. soen, kus; (kus)karambole.
kiss, v. soen, kus.
kit, vaatjie; uitrusting.
kitchen, kombuis.
kite, kuikendief; vlieër; skraper.
kleptomaniac, kleptomaan.
knack, slag, kuns, handigheid.
knapsack, knapsak, ransel.
knave, skelm, skobbejak, karnallie; boer (in kaartspel).
knead, knee (knie); brei; masseer.
knee, n. knie; hoek, bog.
kneecap, knieskyf; kniekap, knieskut.
knee-halter, kniehalter.
kneel, kniel.
knickerbocker, pofbroek, gesperbroek.
knife, n. mes; dolk; lem.
knight, n. ridder; perd (by skaakspel).
knit, brei; saamvleg, saambind.
knitting-needle, breinaald.
knob, n. knop; klont.
knobkerrie, knopkierie.
knock, n. klop; stamp, stoot; slag.
knock, v. klop; slaan, 'n hou gee, stamp.
knocker, klopper.
knock-on, v. aanslaan.
knock-out (blow), uitklophou.
knot, n. knoop, stik, lissie; band; bolla; groep, klompie.
knot, v. knoop, aanmekaarknoop, vasbind; (ver)bind.
know, v. weet, ken, herken.
knowingly, op veelseggende manier; bewus.
knowledge, kennis, verstand.
knuckle, n. kneukel; skinkel(been).
koodoo, kudu, koedoe.
kraal, n. kraal.

laager, n. laer; kamp.
label, n. etiket, kaartjie; seël.
laboratory, laboratorium, werkwinkel.
labour, n. werk, arbeid; taak.
labour, v. werk, arbei; swoeg; sukkel.
labourer, arbeider, dagloner, werksman.
labyrinth, doolhof, labirint.
lace, n. veter; (ryg)band; kant; boorsel.
lace, v. inryg, toeryg; vasryg; deurryg.
lack, n. gebrek, behoefte, tekort.
lack, v. ontbeer; ontbreek, kortkom.
lactic, melk- . . . ; – **acid,** melksuur.
lad, seun, knaap (knapie), kêreltjie.
ladder, n. leer.
ladder, v. lostrek, leer (van 'n kous).
ladle, n. potlepel, soplepel.
ladle, v. skep; – **out,** uitskep.
lady, dame, vrou (van die huis); lady.
ladybird, lieweheersbesie, boomskilpadjie.
lag, v. agterbly; – **behind,** agter raak.
lagoon, -une, strandmeer, lagune.
lair, lêplek; afdak, skuur.
lake, meer.
lamb, n. lam; skaapvleis, lamsvleis.
lamb, v. lam.
lame, adj. kreupel, mank, gebreklik; onbevredigend.
lame, v. verlam, kreupel maak.
lament, v. betreur, beklaag, beween; weeklaag.
lamp, lamp.
lance, n. lans; lansier.
land, n. land, grond; landgoed; landstreek.
land, v. land, aanland, aankom; aan wal sit; beland; grond vat, val; wen; uittrek, ophaal; besorg; bring.
landdrost, landdros.
landing, n. landing; landingsplek; trapportaal.
landscape, landskap.
landslide, grondverskuiwing; politieke omkeer.
lane, pad (paadjie), steeg, deurgang; gang.
language, taal, spraak; styl.
languid, loom, dooierig, lusteloos.
languish, verflou, wegkwyn, agteruitgang.
languor, loomheid, lusteloosheid; drukkendheid.
lank, dun, lang en skraal.
lantern, lantern.
lap, n. skoot; pand; klap.
lap, n. rondte (by wedrenne).
lap, v. (op)lek, opslurp; kabbel, spoel.
lapdog, skoothondjie.
lapel, lapel, kraagpunt.
Lapp, n. Laplander, Lap.
lapse, n. fout; misstap, afdwaling, afwyking, glips, afval, val; verloop.
lapse, v. afdwaal, val, verval, terugval; verloop, verbygaan; gly, glip.
larceny, diefstal.
lard, n. varkvet.
large, adj. groot, ruim, uitgestrek, breed, omvangryk.
large, n.: **at** –, vry, los, op vrye voet; breedvoerig.
largely, in groot mate, grotendeels, vernaamlik, hoofsaaklik; ruimskoots.
lark, n. lewerik.
lark, v. pret maak, gekskeer.
larkspur, ridderspoor.
larva, larwe.
larynx, strottehoof, larinks.
laser: – **beam,** laserstraal.
lash, n. hou, raps; plak; voorslag; ooghaartjie.
lash, v. raps, slaan; vasknoop.
last, n. lees.
last, adj. laaste, verlede, jongslede; uiterste.
last, n. laaste.

last, adv. die laaste; eindelik.
last, v. aanhou; voortduur; goed bly; uithou.
latch, n. knip, klink.
late, adj. laat; te laat; vorige, gewese; wyle.
late, adv. laat, te laat; onlangs, vroeër.
lately, onlangs; in die laaste tyd.
latent, verborge, onsigbaar, sluimerend, slapend, latent.
lathe, draaibank.
lather, n. seepskuim, skuim (van 'n perd).
lather, v. inseep, seep smeer; skuim, uitlooi.
Latin, n. Latyn.
latitude, breedte(graad); omvang; speling.
latrine, latrine.
latter, laasgenoemde, tweede, laaste van twee.
lattice, traliewerk, latwerk.
laud, v. prys, loof, verheerlik; ophemel.
laudable, lofwaardig, loflik; gesond.
laugh, n. lag; gelag.
laugh, v. lag.
laughable, belaglik; lagwekkend, grappig.
laughter, gelag, laggery.
launch, v. werp, slinger; van stapel laat loop; uitstuur; aan die gang sit.
launch, n. barkas; plesierbootjie.
laundry, washuis, wassery, wasinrigting.
laurel, n. lourier; louerkrans.
lava, lawa.
lavatory, waskamertjie, toiletkamer.
lavish, adj. kwistig; volop, oorvloedig.
lavish, v. met kwistige hand uitdeel; verkwis.
law, n. wet; reg; regspraak; balie.
law-court, geregshof, landdroshof, magistraatshof.
lawful, wettig; wetlik; geoorloof.
lawless, wetteloos, sonder wet; losbandig.
lawn, n. grasperk.
lawsuit, hofsaak, proses.
lawyer, advokaat, regsgeleerde, prokureur.
lax, los, slap, laks; nalatig.
laxative, n. purgeermiddel, lakseermiddel.
lay, adj. leke- . . . ; wêreldlik.
lay, v. lê; neerlê; neerslaan, platdruk; laat bedaar; rig, mik; wed; ('n strik) span; ('n komplot) smee; ('n gees) besweer.
layer, n. laag; lêer; inlêer (van plant).
lazy, adj. lui, traag.
lead, n. lood; potlood; peillood.
lead, v. lei; (aan)voer; dirigeer; voor wees.
lead, n. leiding; watervoor; (koppel)riem; hoofrol.
leader, leier, voorman, aanvoerder; voorperd; hoofartikel.
leading, adj. vernaamste, voorste.
leaf, n. blaar; blad; velletjie.
league, n. (ver)bond, verbintenis.
leak, n. lekplek; **spring a** –, 'n lek kry.
leak, v. lek.
lean, adj. maer, skraal, dun.
lean, v. leun, steun; laat leun (steun, rus); neig, geneig wees; oorhel.
lean-to, afdak.
leap, v. spring; oorspring.
leap, n. sprong.
leap-year, skrikkeljaar.
learn, leer; verneem, te hore (te wete) kom.
learned, geleerd.
learner, leerling, beginneling, groene.
learning, geleerdheid, kunde; (die) leer.
lease, n. huur; huurkontrak; huurtyd.
lease, v. huur; verhuur; pag; verpag.
leash, n. koppel(riem).
leash, v. vasbind, vaskoppel.
least, adj. minste, geringste, kleinste.
least, n. die minste.

leather, n. leer; leerwerk; riem.
leave, n. verlof.
leave, v. laat; nalaat; agterlaat; laat staan, laat lê, laat bly; verlaat; vertrek.
lecture, n. (voor)lesing; klas, kollege; vermaning.
lecture, v. 'n lesing hou; klas hê; vermaan.
lecturer, lektor, spreker.
ledge, rotslys, (rots)bank; rant; rif; lys.
ledger, grootboek; steierplank.
lee, lykant.
leech, bloedsuier; arts.
leek, prei.
leer, v. lonk; gluur; gryns.
left, adj. linker- . . . ; links.
left, adv. links, aan (na) die linkerkant.
leg, been; poot (van 'n tafel); (broeks)pyp; boud (vleis).
legacy, legaat, nalatenskap, skenking.
legal, wettig, wetlik; regs- . . .
legalize, wettig, legaliseer.
legend, legende; opskrif, randskrif.
legging, kamas; beenskut.
leg-guard, beenskut.
legible, leesbaar.
legion, legioen; legio.
legislate, wette maak.
legislation, wetgewing.
legitimate, adj. eg, wettig; wetlik.
leisure, vrye tyd, ledige uurtjies.
length, lengte; afstand; duur.
lemonade, limonade.
lend, leen, uitleen.
lemon, suurlemoen.
lengthen, verleng; rek.
lenient, sag, genadig, toegewend.
lens, lens.
lentil, lensie.
leopard, luiperd.
leprosy, melaatsheid.
Lesbian, Lesbiër; a. Lesbies.
less, prep. min; – three, min drie.
lessee, n. huurder, pagter.
lessen, verminder.
lesson, les; leesstuk.
lessor, verhuurder.
lest, uit vrees dat, (op)dat . . . nie.
let, v. laat; toelaat, toestaan; verhuur.
lethargy, slaapsug, dooierigheid.
letter, n. letter; brief.
letter-box, briewebus.
lettuce, (krop)slaai.
level, n. waterpas, paslood; peil, standaard; vlak.
level, adj. waterpas, gelyk; egalig; gelykmatig.
level, v. gelykmaak; nivelleer; mik, korrel vat.
level-crossing, oorgang.
lever, n. hefboom, stelarm; ligter.
levy, v. hef; invorder; oproep, aanwerf.
lewd, ontugtig, wellustig, onkuis.
liable, verantwoordelik.
liana, bobbejaantou, slingerplant.
liar, leuenaar.
libel, n. laster; smaadskrif.
libel, v. belaster, beklad.
libellous, lasterlik.
liberal, adj. vrygewig, goedhartig; vrysinnig.
liberate, bevry, vrylaat, vrymaak.
liberty, vryheid.
librarian, bibliotekaris.
library, biblioteek, boekery; uitgawe.
licence, verlof, vergunning; lisensie; losbandigheid; (digterlike) vryheid.
license, 'n lisensie verleen, lisensieer.
licensee, n. lisensiehouer, gelisensieerde.
lick, v. lek; klop.
lid, deksel; lid.

lie, n. leuen.
lie, v. lieg.
lie, v. lê; rus.
lie, n. ligging; die lê; rigting.
lieu: in – of, in plaas van.
lieutenant, luitenant.
life, lewe; lewenswyse.
life-belt, reddingsgordel.
life-assurance, lewensversekering.
lifeless, lewe(ns)loos.
lifetime, leeftyd.
lift, v. (op)lig, (op)hef, optel; verhef.
lift, n. (die) oplig, opheffing; ligter, hyser.
ligament, gewrigsband, ligament.
light, n. lig; lewenslig.
light, adj. lig, ligkleurig.
light, v. opsteek; aan die brand steek; verlig.
light, adj. lig; bros, los; vlug.
light, adv. lig, los.
lighten, ligter maak; ligter word; verlig.
lighter, aansteker; ligter.
lighthouse, vuurtoring.
lightning, weerlig, blits, bliksem.
like, adj. soos; gelyk; eenders, dieselfde.
like, prep. soos, so.
like, conj. soos.
like, n. gelyke, weerga.
like, v. hou van; aanstaan.
likely, waarskynlik; geskik; aanneemlik.
liking, sin, lus, smaak; geneentheid.
lilt, n. vrolike deuntjie (wysie); ritme.
lily, n. lelie.
limb, n. lit; tak; uitloper; –s, ledemate.
lime, n. kalk; (voël)lym.
lime, n. lemmetjie.
limelight, kalklig.
limestone, kalksteen, kalkklip.
limit, n. grens, grenslyn; toppunt.
limit, v. begrens; bepaal, beperk.
limited, beperk.
limp, v. mank (kreupel) loop, mank wees.
limp, adj. slap, buigsaam; pap.
limpid, helder, deurskynend.
line, n. tou, lyn; streep, ry; reël; reeks, koers; linie; spoor; vak; besigheid; reëltjie; skeepvaartlyn; soort; gelid.
linen, linne; linnegoed.
linen-press, linnekas.
liner, lynboot, linieboot.
linesman, grensregter.
linger, talm, toef; aarsel; sukkel.
linguist, taalkenner; taalkundige.
liniment, smeergoed, smeersel.
lining, voering, bekleding.
link, n. skakel.
link, v. aaneenskakel, aanmekaar skakel, verbind.
links, gholfbaan.
linoleum, linoleum.
linseed oil, lynolie.
lion, leeu.
lip, lip; astrantheid; rand.
liqueur, likeur, soetsopie.
liquid, n. vloeistof.
liquidate, likwideeer, vereffen; afwikkel.
liquor, vog; (sterk) drank.
lisp, v. lispel, sleeptong praat.
list, n. lys, rol; band.
list, v. 'n lys maak van.
list, v. oorhel, oorhang, skuins hang.
listen, luister.
listener, luisteraar.
literal, n. drukfout, skryffout.
literal, letterlik.
literacy, letterkundig, literêr; geletterd.

literature, letterkunde, literatuur, lettere.
Lithuanian, Litaus; Litauer.
litigate, prosedeer, 'n saak maak.
litre, liter.
litter, n. draagbaar; ruigte, kooigoed; afval; rommel; werpsel.
little, adj. klein; weinig; kleinsielig.
little, n. weinig, min.
little, adv. weinig.
live, adj. lewendig, lewend; gloeiend (van kole); onontplof; gelaai; onder stroom.
live, v. leef (lewe), bestaan, voortleef; woon.
livelihood, broodwinning, bestaan.
lively, lewendig, vrolik, opgewek.
liver, lewer.
livery, livrei; mondering.
livestock, lewende hawe, vee.
livid, blou, loodkleurig, doodsbleek.
living, adj. lewendig; lewend.
living, n. lewensonderhoud, broodwinning, bestaan; lewenswyse, lewe.
lizard, akkedis.
llama, lama.
load, n. vrag: las; gewig; pak.
load, v. laai, oplaai; bevrag.
loaf, n. brood.
loaf, v. leegloop, rondslenter; jou lyf wegsteek; bedel.
loam, leem, teelaarde, kleierige grond.
loan, n. lening.
loan, v. uitleen.
loathe, verafsku, verfoei, walg van.
loathsome, weersinwekkend, walglik.
lob, v. 'n lugskoot slaan; voortsukkel.
lobby, n. (voor)portaal, voorsaal: wandelgang (van parlementsgebou).
lobe, lob; (oor)lel.
lobster, kreef; rooibaadjie.
local, adj. plaaslik; lokaal.
localize, lokaliseer, tot een plek beperk.
locate, die plek aanwys; lokaliseer.
location, plekbepaling; lokasie.
lock, n. (haar)lok, krul.
lock, n. slot, klem (ook van 'n geweer); (kanaal)-sluis.
lock, v. sluit, toesluit; insluit.
lockjaw, klem (in die kake).
locksmith, slotmaker.
locomotive, n. lokomotief.
locust, sprinkaan.
lodge, n. huisie; tuinierswonig; (vrymesselaars)-losie.
lodge, v. huisves, losies verskaf, herberg; (klag) indien; vassit, bly steek.
lodger, loseerder, kosganger.
lodging, huisvesting; woonplek.
lodging, huisvesting; woonplek, losies; indiening.
loft, solder; galery; duiwehok.
log, n. blok; log (van skip); logboek; puntelys.
logarithm, logaritme.
log-book, logboek, skeepsjoernaal; dagboek; logaritmetafel.
logic, logika, redeneerkuns.
logical, logies.
loin, lendestuk; –s, lendene.
loin-cloth, lendekleed.
loiter, draal, draai, talm; slenter.
London, Londen.
lonely, eensaam; verlate.
long, adj. lang; langdurig; (lang) gerek.
long, adv. lang.
long, v. verlang.
long-distance: – call, hooflynoproep.
longing, n. verlange, hunkering, begeerte.
longitude, geografiese lengte.

long-winded, langasem- . . . ; omslagtig, langdradig.
look, v. kyk, sien; lyk; daar uitsien.
look, n. blik; gesig, gelaat; uitdrukking; voorkome.
look-out, uitkyk; wag; uitsig.
loom, v. opdoem, opskemer.
loop, n. oog, lissie; hingsel; bog.
loophole, kykgat, skietgat; uitweg.
loose, adj. los; slap; ruim, wyd.
loosen, losmaak; los word; laat skiet.
loot, n. roof, buit.
loot, v. plunder, roof, buitmaak.
lop, v. afkap; snoei.
lope, v. lang hale gee, draf.
loquacious, babbelsiek, praatlustig.
loquat, lukwart: lukwartboom.
lord, n. heer, meester; lord.
lore, leer, kennis.
lorry, vragmotor, lorrie.
lose, verloor; verlies(e) ly; kwyt raak; verbeur.
loss, verlies, skade.
lot, n. lot; (aan)deel; erf; klomp(ie), bossie, hoop (hopie) hoeveelheid.
lotion, wasmiddel, water.
lottery, lotery.
loud, adj. luid, hard; luidrugtig.
loud, adv. luid, hardop.
lounge, v. slenter, rondlê, drentel.
louse, luis.
lovable, lief, beminlik.
love, n. liefde; liefling, skat, beminde; nul (in tennis).
love, v. liefhê, bemin, baie hou van.
lovely, lieflik, heerlik; kostelik.
lover, kêrel, vryer; liefhebber; minnaar; bewonderaar.
loving, liefhebbend; liefdevol, liefderyk.
low, adj. laag; plat; sag; swak; nederig, gering; klein, min; gemeen.
low, adv. laag; sag.
low, v. bulk, loei.
lower, v. stryk, laat sak; verlaag, daal, sak (van prys); verswak; verneder, verlaag.
lowly, gering, eenvoudig, nederig, beskeie.
loyal, lojaal, getrou.
loyalty, lojaliteit, getrouheid.
lozenge, ruit; tablet(jie).
lubricate, olie, smeer, gladmaak.
lucern(e), lusern.
lucid, helder, duidelik; blink(end).
luck, geluk, toeval.
luckily, gelukkig.
lucrative, winsgewend, voordelig.
ludicrous, belaglik, lagwekkend, dwaas.
luggage, bagasie, passasiersgoed.
lull, v. sus; kalmeer, paai, bedaar.
lull, n. stilte, rus, verposing.
lullaby, wiegelied.
lumbago, lendepyn, spit (in die rug).
lumber, n. rommel, prulle; timmerhout.
lumber-jacket, bosbaadjie, windskerm.
lumberman, houtkapper.
luminous, liggewend, skitterend, stralend, lumineus.
lump, n. stuk, klont; klomp, hoop; knop, bult.
lunar, maan(s) . . .
lunatic, n. kransinnige, mal mens.
lunch, n. middagete, noenmaal.
lung, long.
lunge, v. stoot, steek; (weg)spring; slaan; skop.
lurch, n.: leave in the –, in die steek laat.
lurch, v. slinger, steier.
lure, v. (aan)lok, weglok.

lurid, somber, aaklig.
lurk, v. skuil, op die loer lê.
luscious, suikersoet, lekker; oorlaai.
lush, adj. sappig, mals.
lust, n. wellus, begeerte, sug.
lustre, glans, skittering; luister, roem; lugter, kroonkandelaar.
lute, n. luit.

Lutheran, Luthers; van Luther.
luxurious, weelderig.
luxury, weelde, weelderigheid, oorvloed; lekkerny; genot, weeldeartikel.
lye, loog.
lynch, lynch.
lynx, los; rooikat (S.A.)
lyric, n. liriese gedig.

ma, ma.
macabre, aaklig, grieselig.
macadamize, macadamiseer, gruis.
macaroni, macaroni.
Mach: (– number), Mach (– getal).
Machiavellian, Machiavellisties, gewetenloos.
machination, sameswering; konkelary.
machine, masjien, toestel.
machinery, masjinerie; meganiek; opset.
mackintosh, reënjas.
mad, a. gek, mal; kranksinnig.
madam(e), madam, mevrou; juffrou.
madden, mal (woedend) maak.
madness, kranksinnigheid; dwaasheid.
Madonna, Madonna.
maelstroom, maalstroom, draaikolk.
magazine, tydskrif; pakhuis, loods; kruithuis.
maggot, maaier; gier.
magic, n. towerkuns; heksery; toorkrag.
magic, toweragtig, betowerend.
magician, towe(r)naar.
magistrate, landdros, magistraat.
magnanimous, grootmoedig.
magnate, magnaat; geldman.
magnesium, magnesium.
magnet, magneet.
magnetic, magneties.
magnificent, pragtig, heerlik; groots.
magnify, vergroot; groter maak; ophemel.
Magyar, Magjaar; Magjaars.
mahogany, n. mahoniehout(boom).
maid, meisie(tjie); maagd; diensmeisie.
maiden, n. meisie; maagd; leë boulbeurt.
mail, n. pos; possak; poskar; postrein.
maim, v. vermink, skend; 'n knou gee.
main, n. krag; hoofleiding.
main, a. vernaamste, grootste; eerste.
mainland, vasteland.
mainly, vernaamlik, hoofsaaklik.
mainmast, groot mas.
main road, hoofweg, grootpad.
mainspring, slagveer; dryfveer.
main street, hoofstraat.
maintain, volhou; handhaaf; ophou; voer; ondersteun; volhou.
maize, mielies.
majestic, majestueus, groots, verhewe.
majesty: Your –, U Majesteit.
major, n. majoor; mondige; senior.
major, a. groter; hoof . . ., groot.
major-general, generaal-majoor; veggeneraal.
majority, meerderheid; mondigheid.
make, n. vorm; maaksel, fabrikaat; soort.
make, v. maak, vorm; vervaardig; doen; verhef; opmaak; voorberei; (toespraak) hou; trek; aflê; (geld) verdien; (oorlog) voer; forseer; begaan; voorgee.
make-believe, n. skyn.
make-up, versinsel; vermomming, grimering.
malaria, malaria.
male, n. mannetjie, manspersoon.
male, a. manlik, mans- . . . ; mannetjies- . . .
malevolent, kwaadwillig, boosaardig.
malice, kwaadwilligheid; hatigheid.
malicious, boos; kwaadwillig, boosaardig; voorbedag.
malign, v. beskinder, beklad.
malignant, boosaardig; skadelik; kwaadaardig; kwaadgesind.
malinger, siek aanstel, siekte voorwend.
mallet, (hout)hamer.
malt, n. mout.
Malta, Malta. – **fever**, Maltakoors, bokkoors.

Maltese, Maltees; Malteser.
mamba, mamba(slang).
mam(m)a, mama (mamma).
mammal, soogdier.
mammoth, mammoet.
man, n. man; mens; die mens, die mensdom.
man, v. beman, beset.
manacle, v. boei.
manage, v. bestuur, lei; sôre; regkry; baasraak, beheer; behandel.
management, bestuur, administrasie, beheer; oorleg.
manager, bestuurder, direkteur, baas.
managing, besturend; prakties.
managing director, (hoof)bestuurder.
mandate, n. mandaat; lasbrief; opdrag; volmag.
mandible, (onder)kakebeen.
mandolin(e), mandolien.
mane, maanhaar, mane.
man-eater, mensvreter, kannibaal.
manganese, mangaan, bruinsteen.
mange, skurfte, onsuiwer(heid).
manger, krip; trog.
mangle, v. verskeur, vermink; verknoei.
mango, mango; mangoboom.
manhole, mangat.
manhood, manlikheic ; manlike jare.
mania, manie; gier; waansin.
maniac, n. waansinnige, maniak.
manicure, v. manikuur.
manifest, v. duidelik maak; bewys; openbaar; verskyn.
manifesto, manifes.
manifold, a. menigvuldig, veelsoortig.
manipulate, hanteer, manipuleer; bewerk.
manly, manlik, manmoedig, manne- . . .
manner, manier, wyse; aanwensel; soort, gewoonte.
mannerism, aanwensel; gemanierdheid.
mannerly, goedgemanierd, manierlik.
manoeuvre, n. maneuver, krygsoefening; slim plan.
manoeuvre, v. maneuvreer; intrigeer, bewerkstellig.
manse, pastorie, predikantshuis.
manslaughter, manslag.
mantel(piece), skoorsteenmantel.
mantle, n. mantel; dekmantel; bedekking.
manual, n. handboek.
manual, a. hand- . . .
manufacture, n. vervaardiging; fabrikaat, maaksel.
manufacture, v. vervaardig, maak.
manufacturer, vervaardiger, fabrikant.
manure, n. mis, messtof.
manure, v. bemes, misgee.
manuscript, n. manuskrip, handskrif.
many, a. baie, veel.
map, n. kaart, landkaart.
mar, skend; bederwe.
marabou, maraboe.
marauder, plunderaar, buiter.
marble, n. marmer; albaster.
marble, a. marmer- . . .
March, Maart.
march, n. mars; stap, skof; beloop, verloop.
march, v. marsjeer; stap; laat marsjeer.
mare, merrie.
margarine, margarine, kunsbotter.
margin, n. kant; wins, oorskot; speling, (speel)-ruimte; skeiding, grens.
marigold, gousblom.
marine, a. marine- . . . , see- . . . , skeeps- . . .

mark, n. merk, merkteken; doelwit; kruisie; stempel; punt; spoor; blyk.
mark, v. merk, stempel, teken; noteer; aangee; laat merk; afmerk; opmerk; oplet.
market, n. mark; afsetgebied.
market, v. verkoop, bemark.
marking-ink, letterink, merkink.
marksman, skutter, skerpskutter.
marmalade, marmelade; lemoenkonfyt.
maroon, v. (op 'n verlate eiland) agterlaat.
maroon, a. rooibruin.
marquis, -quess, markies.
marriage, huwelik, bruilof, eg.
married, getroud, huwelik- . . .
marrow, n. murg (merg), pit.
marry, v. trou, in die huwelik tree.
marsh, moeras, vlei.
marshal, n. maarskalk; seremoniemeester.
marsupial, n. buideldier.
mart, mark; vendu(sie)lokaal; handelsentrum.
marten, marter; marterbont, marterpels.
martial, oorlogs- . . . , krygs- . . . ; – law, krygswet.
Martian, Marsbewoner.
martingale, springteuel; dubbele inset.
martyr, n. martelaar, lyer.
martyr, v. martel, pynig, folter.
marvel, n. wonder; verbasing.
marvel, v. wonder, verbaas wees (oor), (sig) verbaas (verwonder) (oor).
marvellous, wonderbaarlik, wonderlik.
mascot, gelukbringer, talisman.
masculine, manlik; mannetjiesagtig, managtig; sterk, fors, ru.
mash, v. meng; fynmaak.
mask, n. masker; vermomming; mombakkies; voorwendsel.
mask, v. vermom, verklee; verberg.
mason, n. messelaar; Vrymesselaar.
mass, n. mis.
mass, n. massa; hoop, klomp.
mass, v. vergader, ophoop, konsentreer.
massacre, n. slagting, bloedbad, moord.
massacre, v. vermoor, bloedbad aanrig.
massage, v. masseer, vrywe.
massive, swaar, massief.
mast, n. mas.
master, n. meester, baas; besitter; kaptein; weesheer; werkgewer; bobaas; onderwyser; jongeheer.
master, v. (oor)meester, meester maak van; onderwerp; baasspeel (oor); baasraak; ('n taal) aanleer.
master-key, loper.
masterpiece, meesterstuk.
mastiff, waghond; boerboel; kettinghond.
mat, n. mat.
mat, a. mat, dof.
match, n. vuurhoutjie.
match, n. gelyke, partuur; wedstryd.
match, v. verbind (in die huwelik); pas (by mekaar); teen mekaar opgewasse wees.
mate, n. maat; kameraad; man; mannetjie (wyfie); hulp; stuurman.
mate, v. (skaak)mat sit.
material, n. materiaal, stof, boustof.
material, a. stoflik, materieel, liggaamlik; wesenlik, belangrik.
materialize, verwesenlik (word); voordeel lewer; materialiseer.
maternal, moederlik, moeder(s)- . . .
maternity home (hospital), kraaminrigting.
mathematics, wiskunde, matesis.
matinée, matinee, middagvoorstelling.
matricide, moedermoord; moedermoordenaar.

matriculate, matrikuleer.
matriculation, matrikulasie.
matrimony, huwelik, eg.
matrix, gietvorm, matrys.
matron, dame, huisvrou; matrone, huismoeder.
matter, n. stof, materie; inhoud; ding, voorwerp, onderwerp, saak; etter; kwessie.
matter, v. van belang wees, op aankom.
matter-of-fact, droog, saaklik nugter.
mattress, matras.
mature, v. ryp word, uitgroei, ontwikkel; ryp maak; (wissel) verval.
mature, a. ryp, ontwikkel(d).
maul, mall, n. voorhamer. moker.
maul, v. slaan; moker; toetakel, kneus.
mauve, ligpers, dofpers, mauve.
maw, maag, pens; bek.
mawkish, sentimenteel; wee, naar, walglik.
maxim, prinsipe, grondbeginsel; leus.
maximum, maksimum, grootste hoeveelheid.
May, n. Mei(maand); bloeityd.
may, might, v. mag, kan.
mayor, burgemeester.
mayoress, burgemeestersvrou; burgemeesteres.
maze, n. doolhoof, labirint; warboel.
me, my; ek; **it's –,** dis ek.
meadow, weiland, grasland, weide.
meagre, maer, arm, skraal, onvrugbaar, dor, armsalig.
meal, meel.
meal, maal, maaltyd, kos.
mealie, mielie.
mealie-borer, mielierusper.
mean, n. middelweg, middelmaat; (die) gemiddelde; **–s,** middele; geld, rykdom; manier, wyse.
mean, a. gemiddeld, middel- . . . , middelmatig; gemeen, laag; armoedig; suinig.
mean, v. bedoel; beteken; voornemens wees; bestem.
meander, v. kronkel, slinger, ronddwaal.
meaning, n. betekenis; bedoeling; plan.
meaning, a. veelbetekend, betekenisvol.
meantime: in the –, intussen.
meanwhile, intussen.
measles, masels; **German –,** Duitse masels.
measure, n. maat; maatstaf; hoeveelheid; maatemmer, -glas; maatreël; metrum; grens.
measure, v. meet, maat neem; skat; af-, op-, toemeet; goed bekyk.
measurement, maat, inhoud; (op)meting.
meat, n. vlees (vleis); kos.
meat-pie, (vlees)pastei(tjie).
mechanic, n. ambagsman; werktuigkundige.
medal, gedenkpenning, medalje.
meddle, bemoei (met), lol (met), inlaat (met). inmeng, torring (aan).
meddler, lolpot, bemoeial.
Medes, Mede.
medi(a)eval, middeleeus.
median, mediaan; mediaanaar.
mediate, v. bemiddel, tussenbei kom.
medical, a. medies, geneeskundig, genees- . . .
medicine, n. geneesmiddel, medisyne; geneeskunde.
mediocre, middelmatig.
meditate, oordink, (be)peins; voornemens wees.
Mediterranean (Sea), Middellandse (See).
medium, n. middel; middelslag; hulp(middel); voertaal; medium.
medium, a. middelmatig, deursnee- . . .
medley, n. mengelmoes, mengeling, potpourri.
meek, gedwee, sag(moedig), ootmoedig.
meerkat, meerkat.

meet, v. ontmoet; raak loop; tegemoetkom; voldoen aan, bevredig; byeenkom.
meeting, samekoms, byeenkoms, ontmoeting; samevloeiing.
melancholy, a. swaarmoedig, droefgeestig, swartgallig, treurig.
mellow, a. ryp, sappig; sag, mals, beleë; vrolik, aangeskote.
mellow, v. ryp word (maak); temper, versag.
melodious, welluidend, sangerig, melodieus.
melodrama, melodrama.
melody, (sang)wysie, melodie; gesang.
melon, spanspek.
melt, v. smelt; oplos; ontdooi.
member, lid, lidmaat; deel, afdeling.
memorable, (ge)denkwaardig, heuglik.
memorial, n. gedenkteken; versoekskrif, adres.
memorize, van buite (uit die kop) leer.
memory, geheue; (na)gedagtenis; herinnering.
menace, n. bedreiging, dreigement.
menace, v. (be)dreig.
mend, v. regmaak, repareer; herstel; lap, las, stop.
menial, a. slaafs; diensbaar; laag.
meningitis, harsingvliesontsteking.
mental, geestelik, geestes- . . . , verstandelik, verstands- . . .
mentality, mentaliteit; denkwyse.
mention, n. gewag, melding.
mention, v. (ver)meld, noem.
menu, spyslys, spyskaart, menu.
mercenary, n. huurling, huursoldaat.
mercenary, a. gehuur; omkoopbaar; inhalig, geldsugtig.
merchandise, koopware, negosie (goed).
merchant, (groot)handelaar, koopman.
merciful, genadig, barmhartig.
merciless, ongenadig, meedoënloos.
mercury, kwik(silwer).
mercy, genade, barmhartigheid; seën.
mere, a. adv. net, louter, bloot.
merely, net, louter, slegs.
merge, indompel; oplos; (laat) saamsmelt.
meridian, n. middaglyn, meridiaan.
merit, n. verdienste, deug; verdienstelikheid, waarde.
merit, v. werd wees, verdien.
meritorious, verdienstelik.
mermaid, meermin.
merman, meerman.
merry, vrolik, prettig, opgeruimd.
merry-go-round, mallemeule.
mesh, n. netwerk; maas; strik, val.
mesmerize, hipnotiseer.
mess, n. gereg, gemeenskaplike ete; hondekos; deurmekaarspul, warboel, wanorde; vuilgoed; vuilheid.
mess, v. saameet; verknoei, deurmekaar maak; bemors.
message, boodskap, berig.
messenger, boodskapper, bode; voorbode; loopjong.
Messiah, Messias, Messias.
Messrs, Menere.
metal, n. metaal; klipgruis; glaspys.
metal, a. metaal- . . .
metallurgy, metaalkunde; metallurgie.
metamorphosis, metamorfose.
metaphor, beeldspraak, beeld, metafoor.
metaphysics, metafisika.
mete, v. meet, uitdeel.
meteor, meteoor; vallende ster.
meteorology, weerkunde, meteorologie.
meter, meter.
method, metode, manier; stelsel.

methodic(al), metodies, sistematies.
Methodist, n. Metodis.
meticulous, nougeset, angsvallig.
metre, digmaat, versmaat, metrum.
metre, meter (lengtemaat).
metropolis, hoofstad, metropool.
mettle, moed, energie, ywer, vuur.
mew, v. miaau.
Mexican, Mexikaans, Mexikaner.
mica, mika.
microbe, mikrobe.
microscope, mikroskoop.
midday, n. middag.
middle, n. middel, midde, middelpunt, middelweg.
middle, a. middelste, middel-, tussen-.
middle-aged, van middelbare leeftyd.
middling, a. adv. middelmatig, so-so.
midge, muggie; dwergie.
midget, dwergie.
midnight, n. middernag; pikdonkerte.
mid-off, halfweg (in krieket).
mid-on, halfby (in krieket).
midwife, vroedvrou, ouvrou.
might, n. mag, krag, geweld.
mighty, magtig, kragtig, geweldig, sterk; groot.
migraine, skeel hoofpyn, migraine.
migrant, a. rondtrekkend, trek- . . .
migrate, trek, verhuis, swerwe.
mild, sag, sagaardig; goedhartig; mild, lig; flou; versagtend; a – climate, 'n sagte klimaat.
mildew, n. skimmel, weer.
mile: nautical –, seemyl.
milestone, mylpaal.
militant, vegtend, strydend; strydlustig.
military, a. militêr, oorlogs- . . .
milk, n. melk; skimmed –, afgeroomde melk; fresh –, soetmelk; condensed –, gekondenseerde melk, blikkiesmelk.
milk, v. melk.
milk-shake, bruismelk.
milksop, papbroek, melkmuil.
milk-white, spierwit, melkwit.
mill, n. meul, fabriek; spinnery.
mill, v. stamp, maal; rondmaal; klits; (munt) kartel.
miller, meulenaar.
milliard, miljard.
milligram, milligram.
millilitre, milliliter.
millimetre, millimeter.
milliner, hoedemaker, hoedemaakster; modemaker, modemaakster.
million, miljoen.
millionaire, miljoenêr.
millstone, meulsteen.
mimic, v. namaak, na-aap, naboots; uitkoggel.
mimosa, doringboom.
mince, v. (fyn)maal, gemaak praat.
mince(d)-meat, gemaalde vleis.
mind, n. verstand, intellek, gees; gemoed; mening, opvatting; sin; neiging, gevoelens, doel, voornemens; gedagte, herinnering.
mind, v. herinner, onthou; oplet, oppas; sôre, na kyk; omgee.
mine, n. myn; bron (van rykdom, ens.).
mine, v. grawe, delwe; ontgin; uithol; myne lê.
mine, pron. myne, my, van my.
miner, delwer, mynwerker; mynîeer.
mineral, n. mineraal, delfstof, erts.
mingle, meng, vermeng, deurmekaarloop.
miniature, a. klein, miniatuur- . . .
mini-car, minimotor.
minicopter, minikopter.
minimum, n. minste, minimum.

minimum, a. minimaal, minimum- . . .
minister, n. minister; gesant; predikant.
ministry, ministerie; ministerskap; ampsverrigting; geestelikheid; sorg; hulp.
minor, a. minder, kleiner, onmondig, junior, ondergeskik; onbeduidend, gering; van laer rang.
minority, minderjarigheid; minderheid.
mint, n. munt; hoop.
mint, v. munt; uitvind, maak.
mint, n. kruisement.
minus, minus, min; sonder; waardeloos.
minute, n. minuut; oomblikkie; **the –s,** die notule.
minute, a. klein, gering; haarfyn.
miracle, n. wonder, wonderwerk.
miraculous, wonderbaarlik, wonder- . .
mirage, lugspieëling; waan, bedrog.
mire, n. modder; vuiligheid.
mirror, n. spieël.
mirror, v. weerspieël, weerkaats.
mirth, vrolikheid, joligheid.
misanthrope, mensehater, misantroop.
misapprehension, misverstand.
misbehave, sleg gedra.
misbehaviour, wangedrag.
misbelief, ongeloof; wangeloof, dwaalleer.
miscalculate, misreken; verkeerd (be)reken.
miscarry, misluk; verlore gaan (van 'n brief).
miscellaneous, gemengd, deurmekaar; veelsydig; verskillend, veelsoortig.
mischief, kwaad, onheil, skade; kattekwaad.
mischief-maker, kwaadstoker, onheilstigter.
mischievous, nadelig, verderflik, ondeund.
misconception, wanbegrip.
misconduct, n. wangedrag; wanbestuur.
misconduct, v. sleg gedra; sleg bestuur.
miscount, v. verkeerd (op)tel; vertel.
misdeed, oortreding, misdaad.
miser, vrek, gierigaard; ellendeling.
miserable, ellendig, ongelukkig; miserabel.
misery, ellende, armoede, nood.
misfire, v. weier, kets.
misfortune, ongeluk, ramp.
misgiving, argwaan; vrees, besorgdheid.
mishap, ongeluk, ongeval.
misjudge, verkeerd beoordeel; verkeerd oordeel.
mislead, verlei, mislei; bedrieg, kul.
misplace, verkeerd plaas, misplaas.
misprint, n. drukfrout.
misprint, v. verkeerd (af)druk.
misquotation, verkeerde aanhaling.
misquote, verkeerd aanhaal.
misrepent, verkeerd voorstel; verdraai.
misrule, v. sleg regeer; sleg bestuur.
miss, n. juffrou, mejuffrou; nôi(entjie); meisie.
miss, n. misskoot; gemis, verlies.
miss, v. mis; verpas, versuim; ontbeer; mis (skiet, skop, slaan), ens.
misshapen, mismaak, misvorm, lelik.
missile, werptuig, gooiding, projektiel.
missing, verlore, ontbrekend, weg.
mission, sending, opdrag; roeping, bestemming, sendingpos.
missionary, n. sendeling; gesant; bode.
mist, n. mis, newel; motreën; waas.
mistake, n. fout, vergissing, abuis.
mistake, v. verkeerd verstaan; verwar, verwissel.
mistaken, verkeerd; onjuis.
mister, meneer, heer, die heer.
mistletoe, mistel(tak), voëlent.
mistress, mevrou, vrou; onderwyseres; eienares.
mistrust, n. wantroue, verdenking.
mistrust, v. wantrou, twyfel aan, verdink.
misty, newelagtig, mistig; onduidelik.

misunderstand, verkeerd begryp.
misunderstanding, misverstand, geskil.
misuse, n. misbruik; mishandeling.
misuse, v. misbruik; mishandel.
mitigation, versagting, verligting.
mitre, lysboek, verstek; – **box,** verstekblok; biskopsmus; myter.
mix, aanmaak, meng, deurmekaar maak; berei; omgaan.
mixture, mengsel; mikstuur; drankie.
mix-up, deurmekaarspul; mengelmoes.
moan, n. gekerm, geklaag, gesteun.
moan, v. kerm, steun; weeklaag; betreur.
moat, grag, sloot.
mob, n. gepeupel, gespuis; bende, menigte.
mobile, beweeglik; los; vlottend; mobiel.
mobilize, mobiliseer, mobiel maak.
mock, v. (be)spot, hoon; uitkoggel, naboots; verydel.
mock fight, skyngeveg.
mock trial, skynverhoor; skynhof.
mode, manier, wyse, vorm; mode.
model, n. model; voorbeeld; toonbeeld.
model, v. modelleer, vorm, boetseer.
moderate, a. gematig, matig, middelmatig; taamlik; redelik; billik.
moderate, v. matig, temper; in toom hou; afkoel; modereer.
modern, modern, nuwerwets.
modernize, moderniseer.
modest, beskeie, sedig, ingetoë; fatsoenlik; matig.
modesty, beskeidenheid; eerbaarheid.
modify, wysig, verander; matig.
modulate, reguleer, stel; moduleer.
mohair, sybokhaar.
Mohammedan, n. Mohammedaan.
moist, a. nat, vogtig, klam(merig).
moisten, natmaak, bevogtig.
moisture, vog, vogtigheid, klamheid.
molar, kiestand, maaltand.
molasses, stroop, suikerstroop, melasse.
mole, n. moesie, moedervlek.
mole, n. mol.
molecule, molekule, stofdeeltjie.
mole-hill, molshoop.
molest, moveer, hinder, molesteer.
mollycoddle, v. (ver)troebel, verwen.
moment, oomblik; oogwenk; belang.
momentous, gewigtig, belangrik.
momentum, dryfkrag, vaart.
monarch, monarg, koning, (alleen)heerser.
monarchy, monargie; koninkryk, keiserryk.
monastery, klooster.
Monday, Maandag.
monetary, geldelik, geld- . . .
money, geld, munt.
money-box, spaarpot, gelddosie.
moneylender, geldskieter.
money-order, poswissel.
Mongolian, Mongools, Mongool.
mongrel, n. baster; basterhond.
monk, monnik; drukkersklad.
monkey, n. bobbejaan; stamper.
monkey-nut, grondboontjie, apeneutjie.
monocle, oogglas, monokel.
monologue, alleenspraak, monoloog.
monopolize, monopoliseer; in beslag neem.
monopoly, monopolie, alleenhandel; alleenreg.
monotonous, eentonig, vervelend, monotoon.
monsoon, moeson; reënseisoen.
monster, n. monster, gedrog.
monstrous, monsteragtig; afgryslik, onmenslik; reusagtig.
month, maand.
monthly, n. maandblad, maandskrif.

monthly, a. maandeliks, maand- . . .
monument, monument, gedenkteken.
mood, stemming, bui, luim; wyse.
moody, nukkerig, buierig; swaarmoedig.
moon, n. maan.
Moor, Moor.
moor, v. aanlê, vasmaak, anker.
moose, (Amerikaanse) eland.
moot, v. bespreek, opper.
mop, v. opvrywe, dweil; afvee.
mope, v. (sig) verknies, druil.
moped, kragfiets, bromfiets.
moral, n. moraal, les; ewebeeld; –s, sedes.
moral, a. moreel, sedelik.
morale, n. moreel, moed, selfvertroue.
morality, sedelikheid; sedekunde; sedelike ge-
    drag.
morbid, sieklik, ongesond, siekte- . . .
more, meer, ander, nog, groter.
moreover, origens; daarenbowe, bowendien,
    verder, buitendien, boonop.
morgue, lykhuis.
moribund, sterwend, doodsiek.
Mormon, Mormoon.
morning, n. môre, oggend.
Moroccan, Marokkaans; Marokaner.
morose, stuurs, nors, stug.
morphia, morfia.
morphology, morfologie, vormleer.
morsel, stukkie, happie, brokkie.
mortal, n. sterfling.
mortal, a. sterflik; dodelik; dood(s)- . . . , mens-
    lik, mense- . . .
mortality, sterflikheid; sterfte(syfer).
mortally, dodelik; sterflik; menslik.
mortar, n. vysel; klei; mortier.
mortgage, verband, hipoteek.
mortgage, v. verpand, verband neem (op).
mortified, gekrenk, beledig.
mortise, n. tapgat.
mortuary, n. lykhuis; begraafplaas.
mosque, moskee.
mosquito, muskiet.
moss, n. mos; moeras.
most, a. meeste, uiterste, grootste; die meeste.
most, adv. die meeste, mees, uiters.
mostly, meestal, grotendeels, hoofsaaklik.
motel, motel.
moth, mot, nagvlinder.
mother, n. moeder, ma; vroutjie.
mother country, vaderland.
mother-in-law, skoonmoeder.
mother-of-pearl, perlemoen (perlemoer).
mother-tongue, moedertaal; grondtaal.
motion, n. beweging; gang; gebaar; voorstel,
    mosie.
motion, v. (met 'n gebaar) wys, toewink.
motive, n. beweegrede, motief, dryfveer.
motive, a. bewegend, dryf- . . .
motor, n. motor, outo.
motor-cycle, motorfiets.
mottled, gevlek, bont, gestreep.
motto, motto, leus, sinspreuk.
mould, n. (los)grond, teelaarde.
mould, n. vorm; matrys; stempel; tipe.
mould, v. vorm, maak, giet, modelleer.
mould, n. skimmel, kim.
mould, v. skimmel (word); kim.
mould, n. roes, roesvlek.
moulder, verval, vergaan, vrot.
moulding, lyswerk, lys, fries.
moulding-plane, lysskaaf.
moult, verveer; verhaar; vervel; verloor.
mound, n. hopie, heuweltjie; wal, skans.

mount, v. opklim, styg, rys; opstel, regsit.
mountain, n. berg, kop.
mountainous, bergagtig, berg- . . .
mounted, berede, te perd.
mourn, treur, rou (oor), betreur, beween.
mourner, treurende, roudraer.
mournful, treurig, droewig, bedroef.
mouse, n. muis; blouoog.
mouse-trap, (muis)valletjie; slagystertjie.
moustache, snor(baard), knewel.
mouth, n. mond; bek; monding, uitloop; ope-
    ning.
mouthful, mondvol, hap, sluk.
mouth-organ, mondfluitjie.
mouthpiece, mondstuk; woordvoerder.
movable, a. beweeglik, los; roerend.
move, n. beweging; set, stoot; stap, maatreël.
move, v. beweeg, roer, gaan, loop; aandrywe;
    verplaas; trek, omtrek; werk; voorstel.
movement, beweging, gang; meganiek.
moving, beweeg- . . . ; aandoenlik; dryf- . . .
mow, v. maai, sny; – down, afmaai; wegmaai.
mower, maaier; snymasjien.
much, a. baie, veel, erg.
muck, n. vuilgoed; gemors.
muck, v. he –s about, hy slenter rond; – up,
    verknoei.
mucky, vuil, smerig; gemeen.
mucus, slym.
mud, modder, slyk; vuilgoed.
muddle, n. deurmekaarspul, verwarring; knoei-
    werk.
muddle, v. verwar; knoei; troebel maak; dronk
    maak.
muddy, n. modderig; troebel; morsig.
mudguard, modderskerm.
muffle, v. toedraai, toemaak; demp; toesnoer;
    blinddoek.
muffler, halsdoek; serp.
mug, n. beker.
mug, n. uilskuiken, esel.
muggy, bedompig, swoel, broeierig.
mulberry, moerbei.
mule, muil; dommerik.
multi-coloured, veelkleurig, bont.
multiple, n. veelvoud; least common –, kleinste
    gemene veelvoud.
multiple, veelvoudig, veelsoortig.
multiply, vermenigvuldig; vermeer(der); ver-
    groot.
multitude, menigte, hoop, skare.
mumble, v. mompel, prewel; kou.
mummy, mummie.
mumps, pampoentjies.
munch, vreet, hard kou, knabbel.
mundane, aards, wêrelds.
municipal, munisipaal; stads- . . .
municipality, stadsraad, munisipaliteit.
murder, n. moord.
murder, v. moor, vermoor; radbraak.
murderer, moordenaar.
murdurous, moorddadig, moord- . . .
murky, donker, duister; dik.
murmur, v. murmel, ruis; mompel, mor, fluister.
muscle, spier; spierkrag.
Muscovy, Rusland; – duck, makou.
muscular, gespierd; spier- . . .
museum, museum.
mushroom, n. paddastoel; sampioen.
music, musiek.
musical, musikaal, musiek- . . .
musician, musikus; musikant.
musk melon, spanspek.
must, v. moet; verplig wees.
mustard, moster(d).

muster, versamel; toeloop.
musty, muf, (be)skimmel; verander.
mute, n. stomme; figurant.
mute, a. stom, stil, sprakeloos.
mutilate, vermink, skend.
mutiny, n. opstand, oproer, muitery.
mutiny, v. opstaan, muit, oproerig word.
mutter, v. pruttel; prewel; mompel.
mutton, skaap; skaapvleis.
mutual, wederkerig, wedersyds, onderling, gemeenskaplik.
muzzle, n. snoet, bek; loop, mond (van geweer); muilband.

muzzle, v. muilband; besnuffel; stil maak.
muzzle-loader, voorlaaier.
muzzy, suf; hoenderkop.
my, my.
myopic, bysiende.
myriad, a. ontelbaar, talloos.
myself, ekself, myself.
mysterious, geheimsinnig, raaiselagtig.
mystery, geheim, raaisel; misteriespel.
mystic(al), a. verborge, geheimsinnig.
myth, mite, fabel, storie, sage.
mythology, mitologie, gode- en heldeleer.

nag, v. lol, sanik, pruttel, seur.
nail, n. nael; spyker.
nail, v. vasspyker; beslaan; vang.
naïve, naïef, eenvoudig, ongekunsteld.
naked, naak (nakend), bloot.
name, n. naam, benaming.
name, v. noem, opnoem, benoem, vernoem.
nameless, naamloos; nameloos; onbekend.
namely, naamlik.
nanny(-goat), bokooi.
nap, n. dutjie, slapie.
Napoleonic, Napoleonties, van Napoleon.
narcotic, slaapmiddel, verdowingsmiddel.
narrate, vertel, verhaal, beskrywe.
narrative, n. verhaal, vertelling, relaas.
narrow, a. nou, smal, knap, eng; bekrompe.
narrow, v. vereng, beperk, vernou.
narrow-minded, kleingeestig, bekrompe.
nasty, vuil, vieslik, morsig, smerig; onaangenaam, slegs; naar, onaardig, gemeen, lelik.
nation, nasie, volk.
national, nasionaal, volks- . . . , staats- . . .
nationalist, nasionalis.
native, a. aangebore; inheems; geboorte- . . .
natty, netjies, keurig, fyn; handig.
natural, a. natuurlik; ongekunsteld, ongedwonge; ongesog; natuur- . . .
naturalize, naturaliseer.
naturally, natuurlik(erwyse).
nature, natuur; geaardheid, aard, inbors, karakter; soort.
naught, nul, niks.
naughty, ondeund, stout, onwettig, gruwelik.
nausea, mislikheid, seesiekte.
nauseate, walg, mislik maak.
naval, see- . . . , skeeps- . . . , marine- . . .
nave, naaf (van 'n wiel).
nave, skip (van 'n kerk).
nave-ring, naafband.
navel, nawellemoen.
navigate, bevaar; stuur; vaar.
navigation, skeepvaart, seevaart.
navigator, seevaarder.
navy, vloot, seemag, marine.
Nazarene, Nasarener.
near, a. na, nabysynde, nabygeleë; nou verwant;
  dierbaar.
near, adv. naby, digteby; byna.
near, prep. by, naby, digteby; na aan.
near, v. nader, naby kom.
nearly, byna, amper(tjies), haas.
near-sighted, bysiende.
neat, a. netjies; ordelik, sindelik; suiwer; keurig.
nebulous, newelagtig; vaag.
necessary, a. nodig, noodsaaklik, noodwendig.
necessary, n. necessaries of life, lewensbehoeftes.
necessitate, noodsaak, dwing, verplig.
necessity, noodsaaklikheid, behoefte.
neck, nek, hals; pas, engte.
necklace, halsketting, halssnoer.
necktie, das.
nectar, nektar, godedrank.
nectarine, kaalperske, nektarien.
need, n. nood, behoefte, gebrek.
need, v. nodig hê, (be)hoef, makeer.
needful, a. nodig, noodsaaklik, onmisbaar.
needle, naald; breipen, breinaald; kompasnaald,
  magneetnaald.
needless, onnodig, nodeloos.
needlework, naaldewerk; handwerk.
needs, n. behoeftes, benodigdhede.
needy, behoeftig, hulpbehoewend.
nefarious, goddeloos, gruwelik.
negation, ontkenning, negasie.

negative, a. negatief, ontkennend.
negative, v. ontken; weerspreek; afstem.
neglect, v. verwaarloos, versuim, veronagsaam,
  nalaat.
neglectful, nalatig, agtelosig.
negligible, onbeduidend, nietig.
negotiate, verhandel, handel dryf; onderhandel.
Negro, Neger.
neigh, v. runnik, hinnik.
neighbour, n. buurman, buurvrou.
neighbourhood, buurte, nabyheid; omgewing,
  omtrek.
neither, pron. geen (van twee), geeneen (van
  beide).
neither, adv. ook nie, ewemin.
neither, conj.: . . . nor, nòg . . . nòg.
nephew, neef, broerskind, susterskind.
nepotism, nepotisme, voortrekkery.
nerve, n. senuwee, lewe; moed, durf.
nerve, v. sterk (maak), krag gee.
nervous, senuweeagtig, skrikkerig.
nest, n. nes.
nest, v. nes maak; nes hê.
nestle, nestel; nes skop; tuis maak.
net, n. net; strik.
net(t), n. netto, suiwer.
nether, onder(ste), laer, benede.
Netherlands, Nederland, die Nederlande.
netting, netwerk, gaas, sifdraad.
nettle, n. (brand)nekel, netel.
nettle, v. vererg, irriteer.
neuralgia, sinkings, senuweepyne.
neuritis, neuritis, senuwee-ontsteking.
neurotic, a. senusiek, neuroties.
neuter, a. onsydig; geslagloos.
neutral, a. neutraal, onsydig, onpartydig.
neutralize, neutraliseer, ophef; neutraal verklaar.
never, nooit, nimmer.
nevermore, nimmermeer, nooit weer nie.
nevertheless, nietemin, almaskie.
new, nuut; vars; groen.
newcomer, nuweling.
new-fashioned, nuwerwets, nieumodies.
new-laid, vars(gelê).
newly, onlangs, pas.
news, nuus, tyding, berig.
newspaper, koerant, nuusblad.
New Year's Day, Nuwejaarsdag.
next, a. naaste, volgende, aanstaande, aan-
  kom(m)ende; langsaan.
next, adv. vervolgens, (daar)na.
next, prep. lang(e)s, langsaan, neffens, naasaan.
next, n. volgende.
nib, pen (punt), punt.
nibble, v. knabbel, peusel; vit.
nice, lekker, aangenaam; mooi, gaaf, vriendelik,
  liefies; fyn.
nick, n. kerf, keep.
nick, v. kerf (keep) insny; fop; vang.
nickel, v. vernikkel.
nickelplated, versilwer(d).
nickname, n. bynaam.
nicotine, nikotien; pypolie.
niece, niggie, susterskind, broerskind.
niggardly, inhalig, suinig, gierig.
nigh, naby, byna.
night, nag, aand.
nightdress, slaapklere, naghemp.
nightingale, nagtegaal.
nightmare, nagmerrie.
nil, nul, niks.
nimble, rats, vinnig, vlug.
nincompoop, bog, uilskuiken, niksnuts.
nine, nege.
nineteen, negentien.

ninety, negentig.
nip, v. byt, knyp.
nipper, knyper; seuntjie; (pl.) knyptang.
nitrate, n. nitraat.
nitric, salpeter- . . . ; – acid, salpetersuur.
nitrogen, stikstof.
no, a. geen (g'n).
no, adv. nee; niks.
nobility, adel; edelheid.
noble, n. edelman.
noble, a. adellik; edel, grootmoedig; groots.
nobody, niemand.
nocturnal, nagtelik.
nod, v. knik; insluimer.
nod, n. (hoof)knik, wenk.
nodule, knoesie; kwassie; knoppie.
nohow, glad nie; look –, oes lyk.
noise, n. geraas, lawaai, rumoer.
noiseless, stil, geluidloos, geruisloos.
noisy, luidrugtig, lawaaierig, raserig.
nomadic, nomadies, swerwend.
nom de plume, skuilnaam, pennaam.
nominal, nominaal.
nominate, nomineer, benoem; vasstel.
nomination, nominasie, benoeming.
nominative, nominatief.
nominator, voorsteller; noemer (van 'n breuk).
non-commissioned, onder(offisier).
non-committal, vaag, niksseggend, ontwykend.
non-conductor, nie-gelei(d)er.
nondescript, a. sonderling, vreemdsoortig.
none, pron. geeneen, niemand; niks.
none, a. geen, niks.
none, adv. niks.
nonentity, onding; nul, nulliteit.
non-member, nie-lid.
nonplus, v. verwar, verleë maak.
nonsense, onsin, dwaasheid.
noon, middag, twaalfuur.
noose, n. strik, lis, strop.
nor, nog, ook nie; neither . . . –, nòg . . . nòg.
norm, norm, standaard.
normal, a. normaal.
Norman, Normandies, Normandiër.
Norse, Noors.
north, n. die noorde.
north, a. noord(e)- . . . ; noordelik.
north, adv. noord, noordwaarts.
northern, noordelik, noord(er)- . . .
northwards, noordwaarts, na die noorde.
north-wester, noordwestewind.
Norway, Noorweë.
Norwegian, Noor; Noors; Noorweegs.
nose, n. neus; reuk; tuit.
nostalgia, heimwee.
nostril, neusgat.
not, nie.
notable, a. vernaam; merkwaardig; merkbaar.
notary, notaris.
notch, n. keep, kerf, skaar (in 'n mes).
notch, v. keep, kerf; behaal.
note, n. noot (in musiek); toon; teken; nota,
  aantekening; briefie.
note, v. oplet; aanteken.

notebook, aantekeningboek.
noted, beroemd, bekend, vermaard.
noteworthy, opmerkenswaardig.
nothing, niks, nul; glad nie.
nothing, n. nietigheid, nul.
notice, n. kennis, aandag, notisie, opmerksaam-
  heid; kennisgewing, aankondiging, berig.
notice, v. opmerk, merk, ag slaan op.
noticeable, merkbaar; openlik.
notice-board, aanplakbord.
notify, bekend maak, kennis gee, aankondig,
  meedeel, rapporteer.
notion, begrip, idee, denkbeeld.
notorious, welbekend (van feite); berug (van
  persone).
notwithstanding, ondanks, nieteenstaande; nietemin, tog.
noun, selfstandige naamwoord.
nourish, voed; aankweek, koester.
nourishing, voedsaam.
novel, a. nuut; eienaardig, vreemd.
novel, n. roman.
novelty, nuwigheid.
November, November.
novice, nuweling, groene.
now, adv. nou.
now, n. (die) hede, (die) teenswoordige.
nowadays, teenswoordig; hedendaags.
nowhere, nêrens, niewers.
noxious, skadelik, verderflik.
nozzle, neus, snoet; tuit, bek; mondstuk.
nuclear, kern-; – reactor, kernreaktor.
nucleus, kern, pit.
nude, n. naakfiguur.
nude, a. kaal, naak, bloot.
nudge, v. aanstoot, stamp (in die ribbe).
nudge, n. steek, stamp, stoot, prik.
nugget, (goud) klont, klomp.
nuisance, (oor)las, stoornis, plaag; laspos.
null, nietig, ongeldig, kragteloos.
nullify, verydel, ophef.
numb, a. gevoelloos, dood.
number, n. nommer, getal, klomp, aantal, party.
number, v. nommer, tel.
numberless, ontelbaar, talloos.
numeral, telwoord; syfer.
numeric(al), numeriek, getal(s)- . . .
numerous, talryk, baie; groot.
numskull, swaap, esel, uilskuiken.
nun, non.
nurse, n. verpleegster, suster; kindermeid, kin-
  deroppasster, kinderjuffrou.
nurse, v. verpleeg, oppas; soog, versorg; bewaar,
  opspaar; koester (bv. 'n grief).
nursemaid, kindermeid, kindermeisie, -oppasster.
nursery, kinderkamer; kwekery; kweekdam;
  kweekplaas.
nursing-home, verpleeginrigting.
nurture, v. kweek, opvoed, grootmaak, troetel.
nut, neut; moer(tjie) (van 'n skroef); klont.
nutcracker(s), neutkraker.
nutmeg, neut.
nutritious, voedsaam.
nuzzle, snuffel, vroetel; aankruip teen.

o(h), o!
oak, akkerboom, eik(e)boom.
oar, n. roeispaan, (roei)riem.
oasis, oase.
oath, eed; vloek(woord).
oatmeal, hawermeel.
oats, hawer.
obdurate, verhard, koppig, verstok.
obedient, gehoorsaam.
obey, gehoorsaam (wees), luister na.
obituary, n. dood(s)berig.
object, n. voorwerp; oogmerk, doel; plan, bedoeling; objek.
object, v. beswaar maak.
objectionable, aanstootlik, laakbaar.
objective, a. objektief.
objective, n. mikpunt, doel.
objector, beswaarmaker.
obligation, verpligting; verbintenis.
oblige, verplig; diens bewys, van diens wees.
obliterate, uitvee, uitwis; vernietig.
oblivion, vergetelheid.
oblivious, vergeetagtig; ongevoelig; onbewus.
oblong, a. langwerpig.
obnoxious, aanstootlik, onaangenaam.
obscene, vuil, liederlik, onkies, obseen.
obscure, a. duister; onduidelik, onbekend; afgeleë.
obscure, v. verdof, verduister; verberg; in die uitsig belemmer.
obsequious, slaafs, onderdanig, kruiperig.
observant, oplettend, opmerksaam.
observation, waarneming; opmerking, aanmerking.
observatory, sterrewag, observatorium.
observe, waarneem, gadeslaan, dophou; opmerk, aanmerk; vier; nakom, naleef.
obsess, kwel, agtervolg.
obsession, kwelling, las, obsessie.
obsolete, verouder(d), uit die mode.
obstacle, hinderpaal, struikelblok.
obstacle-race, hindernis-wedloop.
obstinate, koppig, hardnekkig, halsstarrig, styfhoofdig.
obstruct, belemmer; versper.
obtain, (ver)kry, verwerf, behaal; geld.
obtrude, opdring, indring.
obtuse, stomp; dof; bot, dom.
obverse, voorkant.
obviate, uit die weg ruim, verwyder; voorkom.
obvious, duidelik, vanselfsprekend.
occasion, n. geleentheid; aanleiding.
occasionally, nou en dan, af en toe.
occidental, westers, westelik.
occult, a. verborge, geheim, okkult.
occupant, besitter, bewoner; insittende.
occupation, inbesitneming, besetting; beroep, ambag.
occupier, bewoner.
occupy, in besit neem, beset, ('n betrekking) beklee; bewoon; beslaan, inneem; in beslag neem.
occur, voorkom; opkom, byval; plaasvind, voorval.
occurrence, gebeurtenis, voorval.
ocean, oseaan.
octagon, aghoek, oktogoon.
octave, oktaaf; agtal.
October, Oktober.
octopus, seekat, oktopus.
oculist, oogdokter, -arts; oogkundige.
odd, ongelyk, onewe; orig; snaaks. sonderling, raar.
odds, verskil; geskil, onenigheid; kanse, voordeel; oormag.

ode, ode.
odious, haatlik, verfoeilik.
odour, ruik (reuk), geur.
of, van, aan, deur, op, uit, in.
off, adv. af, weg; ver.
off, prep. van . . . af (weg); van.
off, a. ander; regter, haar.
offal, afval; oorskiet, brokkies.
off-chance, moontlikheid, geluk.
offence, aanstoot, ergernis; oortreding, misstap.
offend, aanstoot gee, beledig; oortree.
offender, oortreder; belediger.
offensive, a. beledigend, aanstootlik; walglik; sleg, onaangenaam (van ruik); aanvallend.
offensive, n. aanval, offensief.
offer, v. aanbied; offer; opper, maak.
offer, n. aanbod; bod; voorstel.
office, taak, plig; amp, betrekking; kantoor, buro.
officer, n. amptenaar, beampte; bestuurslid; offisier; konstabel.
official, a. amptelik, amps- . . . ; offisieel.
official, n. beampte, amptenaar.
officiate, 'n amp waarneem; 'n diens lei, voorgaan, voorsit; – as, optree as.
officious, bemoeisiek, half-amptelik, offisieus.
offshoot, loot, spruit.
often, dikwels, baiemaal, herhaaldelik.
ogle, v. (toe)lonk, verliefderig aankyk.
oh, o; ag, og.
oil, n. olie.
oil, v. olie, smeer.
oilstone, oliesteen.
ointment, salf, smeersel, smeergoed.
old, a. oud, ou; ouderwets, bejaard.
old-fashioned, ouderwets.
oligarchy, oligargie, paarmansregering.
olive, n. olyf(boom); olyftak; olyfkleur.
Olympic: – games, Olimpiese spele.
omelet(te), omelet, eier(panne)koek, struif.
omen, voorteken.
ominous, onheilspellend, dreigend.
omit, weglaat, uitlaat, oorslaan; nalaat, versuim.
omnibus, (omni)bus.
omnipotent, almagtig, alvermoënd.
omniscient, alwetend.
on, prep, op, op, by, aan, teen, met, na, oor.
on, adv. aan; deur, verder.
once, adv. eenmaal, eenkeer.
once, conj. sodra, as.
once, n. eenmaal.
oncoming, a. naderende, aanstaande.
one, a. een; enigste.
one, pron. ('n) mens; een.
one, n. een.
onion, n. ui.
onlooker, toeskouer.
only, a. enigste.
only, adv. maar, slegs, net, pas, alleen.
only, conj. maar, alleen, as.
onto, op, tot by, na.
onus, las, verantwoordelikheid, onus.
onward(s), adv. voorwaarts, verder.
ooze, n. modder, slyk; looiwater.
ooze, v. syfer, lek; uitsweet.
opal, opaal.
opaque, ondeurskynend; duister, onduidelik.
open, a. oop; blootgestel; openbaar, ope(n)lik; openhartig, rondborstig; vatbaar.
open, v. oopmaak; oopgaan; begin; blootlê, openbaar maak; inlei.
opening, n. opening; aanvang, begin; inleiding; kans.
openly, ope(n)lik, rondborstig.

opera, opera.
operate, werk, uitwerking hê op; veroorsaak; werk met, bestuur; sny, opereer.
operation, werking; bewerking; werksaamheid; beweging; operasie.
operator, werker; telegrafis; operateur.
opinion, mening, sienswyse, opinie.
opium, opium.
opponent, teenstander, teenparty, opponent.
opportune, geleë, gunstig, geskik.
opportunist, opportunis.
opportunity, geleentheid, kans.
oppose, bestry, opponeer, teenwerk.
opposite, a. teenoorgestel, ander.
opposite, n. die teenoorgestelde, teendeel.
opposite, adv. (aan die) ander kant, (aan die) oorkant.
opposite, prep. regoor, teenoor, oorkant, anderkant.
opposition, teenstand, weerstand; teenstelling, teenparty, opposisie.
oppress, onderdruk, verdruk.
oppressive, onderdrukkend; benoud, drukkend.
optical, gesigs- . . . , opties.
optician, gesigkundige, optisiën.
optimism, optimisme.
option, keuse; opsie, voorkeur.
optional, na keuse, opsioneel.
or, of, anders; either . . . -, òf . . . òf.
oracle, orakel, godspraak.
oral, mondeling; mond- . . .
orange, n. lemoen; oranje(kleur).
Orange, n. Oranje.
orang-outang, orang-oetang.
orator, redenaar, spreker.
orb, bol, sfeer; oog(appel); kringloop.
orbit, oogholte; baan, kringloop; wentelbaan; v. wentel.
orchard, boomgaard, (vrugte)boord.
orchestra, orkes.
orchid, orgidee.
ordain, orden, inseën; bepaal, vasstel; bestem, beskik; beveel, verordineer.
ordeal, beproewing; vuurproef, toets.
order, n. orde; rang, stand; klas, soort; volgorde, skikking; bevel, las, gebod, order; bestelling.
order, v. gelas, beveel, gebied; voorskryf; kommandeer; bestel; inrig, reël, in orde bring; bepaal, beskik.
orderly, a. ordelik, ordeliewend; gereeld, reëlmatig.
ordinance, ordonnansie; reglement, ordinansie.
ordinary, a. gewoon, alledaags, gebruiklik, ordinêr.
ordnance, artillerie, grofgeskut.
ore, erts.
organ, orrel; orgaan; mondstuk.
organization, organisasie, reëling.
organize, organiseer, reël, inrig.
organism, organisme.
orgy, drinkparty, drinkgelag.
Orient, n. die Ooste, Oriënt.
orient, orientate, v. die ligging bepaal; oriënteer.
Oriental, n. Oosterling.
origin, oorsprong, afkoms; oorsaak.
original, a. oorsponklik, origineel.
originate, ontstaan, voortspruit.
ornament, n. sieraad, ornament.
ornate, ryk versier(d), bloemryk.
orphan, n. wees(kind).
orphanage, weeshuis.
orthodox, ortodoks, regsinnig.
oscillate, slinger, skommel; aarsel; ossilleer.
ostensibly, oënskynlik, kastig, konsuis.
ostracize, verban; uitsluit, uitdrywe.

ostrich, volstruis.
other, a. ander; anders.
other, n. ander.
otherwise, anders.
otter, otter.
ought, v. moet, behoort.
our, ons (onse).
ours, ons s'n, ons.
oust, uitdryf, verdryf, verdring, uitlig.
out, adv. uit, buite; dood; bekend.
out, prep. uit.
out-and-out, deur en deur, deeglik.
outboard, buiteboord-.
outbreak, uitbarsting; oproer; (die) uitbreek.
outbuilding, buitegebou.
outburst, los-, uitbarsting.
outcast, verworpeling, verstoteling.
outclass, oortref, oorskadu.
outcome, uitslag, gevolg, resultaat.
outdo, oortref, baasraak.
outdoor, buitelug- . . . , opelug . . . , buite- . . .
outfit, uitrusting, toerusting.
outflow, uitloop; uitstroming.
outgrow, uitgroei, verbygroei; vergroei.
outing, uitstappie, kuiertjie.
outlandish, uitheems, vreemd.
outlaw, n. voëlvryverklaarde.
outlaw, v. verban, voëlvry verklaar.
outlay, uitgawe, onkoste; ontwerp.
outlet, uitgang; uitweg; mond (van 'n rivier); afvoerpyp.
outline, n. omtrek, skets.
outline, v. skets, die hooftrekke gee.
outlive, oorleef, langer leef as.
outlook, vooruitsig; uitkyk; uitsig, gesig; kyk.
outpost, voorpos, buitepos.
output, produksie, opbrings.
outrage, n. vergryp, aanranding, gewelddaad.
outrage, v. aanrand, verkrag, geweld aandoen.
outright, adv. heeltemal, skoon; ope(n)lik, ronduit, rondborstig.
outside, n. buitekant; uiterlik; uiterste.
outside, a. buite- . . . , buitenste; uiterste.
outside, adv. buitekant, na buite.
outsider, oningewyde, buitestaander, buiteperd.
outspan, v. uitspan.
outstanding, uitstaande, onbetaal(d); prominent, buitengewoon.
outstay, langer bly as.
outstrip, verbyhardloop; verbystrewe.
outward, a. uiterlik, uitwendig; buite- . . .
outward, adv. na die buitekant.
outwardly, (na die) uiterlik.
outwards, buitekant toe, na buite.
outweigh, swaarder weeg as.
outwit, fop, uitoorlê, te slim wees vir.
oval, a. ovaal, eiervormig.
oven, oond.
over, adv. oor; omver, onderstebo, om; verby.
over, prep. oor, bo, by, oorkant.
over, n. (boul)beurt.
overalls, oorbrock, oorpak, oorrok.
overbearing, baasspelerig, heerssugtig.
overboard, oorboord.
overcast, bewolk, betrokke, toegetrek.
overcharge, v. oorbelas, oorlaai; te veel vra (laat betaal).
overcoat, jas.
overcome, v. oormeester, te bowe kom.
overcome, a. oorstelp, verslae.
overconfident, oormoedig.
overdo, oordryf; te gaar kook; ooreis.
overdraft, oortrokke bankrekening.
overflow, v. oorloop, oorstroom.
overhand, oorhands.

overhaul, nakyk, opknap; inhaal.
overhead, a. lug- . . . , bogrondse.
overhear, afluister, toevallig hoor.
overlap, gedeeltelik dek, oormekaar val, gedeeltelik saamval.
overload, oorlaai.
overlook, uitkyk op; oor die hoof sien.
overpower, oorweldig, oormeester; oorstelp.
overrun, oorstroom, platloop; vervuil, wemel.
oversea, a. oorsees.
oversight, vergissing, versuim; toesig.
overstep, oorskry, te buite gaan.
overt, ope(n)lik, openbaar.
overtake, inhaal; oorval.
overthrow, v. omvergooi; verslaan.

overtime, adv. na ure; **work –,** oorwerk doen.
overtime, n. oortyd, oorure.
overturn, v. omslaan; omgooi; verslaan.
overwhelm, oorweldig, oorstelp.
overwork, v. oorwerk.
owe, skuld; verskuldig wees.
owing to, prep. as gevolg van, weens.
owl, uil.
own, a. eie.
own, v. besit; erken, beken.
owner, eienaar, besitter, baas.
ox, os.
ox-waggon, ossewa.
oxygen, suurstof.
oyster, oester.

pa, pa.
pace, n. tree, stap; gang, vaart.
pace, v. stap; afstap; aftree; trippel, 'n pas loop; die pas aangee.
pacer, trippelaar, pasganger; gangmaker.
pacific, vreedsaam; **P. Ocean**, Stille Oseaan.
pacify, tot bedaring bring, kalmeer, paai.
pack, n. pak, bondel; bende, klomp, trop.
pack, v. pak, wegpak, inpak, verpak; volstop.
package, pak(kie), bondel.
packet, pakkie; pakket.
packhorse, pakperd.
packing-needle, seilnaald.
pact, ooreenkoms, verbond, verdrag.
pad, n. kussinkie; saaltjie; vulsel; beenskut; skryfblok; voetsool.
pad, v. (op)stop, opvul, beklee.
padding, stopsel, vulsel; bladvulling.
paddle, v. roei; in die water plas.
paddock, kamp; park; speelgrond.
padlock, n. hangslot.
page, n. bladsy, pagina.
pageant, vertoning, praal; historiese optog.
page-boy, page, livreikneg, (hotel)joggie, boodskappertjie; sleepdraertjie; edelknaap.
pain, n. pyn, leed, verdriet, smart.
pail, emmer.
pain, v. pyn, pynig, seermaak; kwel; leed of smart veroorsaak.
painful, pynlik, seer.
painstaking, ywerig, werksaam; presies, noulettend.
paint, n. verf; blanketsel.
paint, v. verf, skilder; beskrywe.
painter, skilder.
pair, n. paar.
pair, v. paar; twee-twee opstel.
palace, paleis.
palatable, smaaklik, lekker, aangenaam.
palate, verhemelte; smaak.
pale, a. bleek, vaal; dof, flou.
pale, v. bleek of dof word, verbleek, verdof; verskiet.
palette, palet.
paling, pale, paalheining, skutting.
pall, n. lykkleed; sluier.
pall, v. smaakloos word, walg.
pallbearer, slippedraer.
palliate, versag, verlig; verontskuldig, verbloem.
pallor, bleekheid.
palm, n. (hand)palm; palm(boom).
palpable, tasbaar, duidelik.
palpitate, klop, pols, tril.
paltry, niksbeduidend, nietig, klein.
pamper, vertroetel, verwen, bederwe.
pamphlet, pamflet, vlugskrif, brosjure.
pan, n. pan.
pancake, pannekoek.
pancreas, alvleesklier, pankreas.
pandemonium, pandemonium.
pane, (venster)ruit, glasruit.
panegyric, n. lofrede.
panel, n. paneel; naamlys, naamrol; baan; rol.
panel-beater, duikklopper.
pang, skerp pyn, steek; kwelling.
panic, n. paniek, plotselinge skrik.
panorama, vergesig, panorama.
pansy, gesiggie.
pant, v. hyg; snak (na).
panther, panter, luiperd.
pantomime, gebarespel, pantomime.
pantry, spens.
papa, pa(pa), pappie.
papaw, papaja.

paper, n. papier; koerant; vraestel; –s, dokumente.
paper, v. plak.
paper-fastener, papierklem(metjie).
parable, gelykenis.
parabola, parabool.
parachute, valskerm, daalskerm.
parade, n. optog; vertoning; parade(plein).
parade, v. parade hou, (laat) marsjeer; te koop loop met, spog met.
paradise, paradys; hemel.
paradox, paradoks.
paraffin, n. paraffien(olie), lampolie.
paragraph, n. paragraaf.
parallel, a. parallel, ewewydig; ooreenstemmend.
parallelogram, parallelogram.
paralyse, verlam; ontsenu, paraliseer.
paramount, vernaamste, hoogste, opperste, opper-....
paraphrase, v. omskrywe, parafraseer.
parasite, parasiet; klaploper.
paratroops, valskermtroepe.
parcel, n. pak(kie), pakket.
parch, (ver)skroei, verdroog.
parchment, perkament.
pardon, n. vergifnis, genade; ekskuus.
pardon, v. vergewe, vryspreek.
pare, (af)skil, afsny, (af)knip; snoei.
parent, ouer; bron, oorsaak; –s, ouers.
parental, ouderlik.
parenthesis, parentese; hakies.
par excellence, by uitnemendheid.
pariah, uitgeworpene, verstoteling.
parish, gemeente, parogie.
park, n. park; wildtuin.
park, v. omhein, toemaak; parkeer.
parley, v. onderhandel, bespreek, praat.
parliament, parlement.
parliamentary, parlementêr, parlements-....
parlour, voorkamer, sitkamer; salon.
parlous, gevaarlik; moeilik, lastig.
parochial, parogiaal; eng, bekrompe.
parody, n. parodie, spotdig; bespotting.
parquet, n. parketvloer.
parrot, n. papegaai; na-aper.
parry, v. afweer, keer, afwend, pareer.
parsimonious, spaarsaam, suinig, gierig.
parsley, pieters(i)elie.
parsnip, witwortel.
parson, predikant, dominee.
parsonage, pastorie.
part, n. deel, gedeelte, stuk, part; rol; aandeel, kant, party.
part, v. (ver)deel; skei, afskeid neem; breek.
partake, deelneem (aan); 'n deel hê in; geniet.
partial, partydig; gedeeltelik; **be – to**, 'n voorliefde hê vir.
participate, deelneem aan, 'n deel hê in.
participle, deelwoord, partisipium.
particle, deeltjie, stukkie, greintjie; partikel.
particular, a. besonder, buitengewoon; kieskeurig, punteneurig.
particular, n. –s, besonderhede.
parting, afskeid; skeiding; paadjie (in die hare).
partisan, **-zan**, partyman, volgeling.
partition, n. verdeling; afdeling; skeiding; afskorting.
partition, v. (ver)deel; 'n afskorting maak; afskei.
partly, gedeeltelik, vir 'n gedeelte, deels.
partner, n. vennoot; maat.
partridge, patrys.
party, party; geselskap; geselligheid.
pass, v. verbygaan, passeer; deurgaan; toelaat; aanneem; slaag; te bowe gaan; aangee; stryk,

trek; (vonnis) uitspreek; deurbring; pas (in kaartspel).
pass, n. (verlof)pas; handbeweging.
pass, n. (berg)pas, nek, deurgang.
passable, gangbaar, taamlik; begaanbaar.
passage, deurgang, -tog, -vaart, -reis; oorgang, -tog; passasie; reisgeld; gang.
passenger, passasier, reisiger.
passer-by, verbyganger.
passion, hartstog, passie; drif.
passive, lydend; lydelik; passief.
passport, pas(poort).
past, a. verby; verlede; afgelope; oud- . . .
past, n. verlede.
past, prep. oor, verby.
past, adv. verby.
paste, n. deeg; pap; pasta; lym.
paste, v. plak, aanplak, vasplak.
pastel, pastel.
pastime, tydverdryf; spel, speletjie.
pastor, predikant, pastoor, herder.
pastoral, a. pastoraal, herderlik.
pastry, pastei, gebak; koek.
pasture, n. wei(veld), weiplek, gras(veld).
pat, v. tik, klop; platstryk; streel.
patch, n. lap; pleister; ooglappie; stuk(kie), lap(pie).
patch, v. lap, heelmaak.
patent, a. gepatenteer(d), patent; duidelik; – leather, lakleer.
patent, n. patent, oktrooi.
patent, v. patenteer.
path, pad, weg.
pathetic, aandoenlik, patetles.
pathological, patologies.
patience, geduld, lankmoedigheid.
patient, n. pasiënt, lyer, sieke.
patient, a. geduldig, verdraagsaam.
patois, dialek; kombuistaal; patois.
patriarch, aartsvader, patriarg.
patriot, patriot, vaderlander.
patrol, n. patrollie, rondte.
patrol, v. patrolleer, die rondte doen.
patron, beskermheer; patroon; –s, klandisie.
patter, v. kletter, ratel, klater; trippel, trappel, klap.
pattern, patroon, model; voorbeeld.
paunch, buik, pens.
pauper, arme, behoeftige.
pause, n. verposing, pouse.
pause, v. wag, pouseer, afbreek, stilbly.
pave, plavei, (uit)straat, uitlê.
pavement, sypaadjie; plaveisel.
pavilion, pawiljoen, tent.
paw, n. poot, klou.
pawn, n. pion.
pawn, n. pand.
pawn, v. verpand, in pand gee.
pay, n. betaling, loon.
pay, v. betaal; beloon, vergeld; boet.
payable, betaalbaar; winsgewend.
payment, betaling, loon.
pea, ertjie.
peace, vrede; rus, kalmte, stilte.
peaceful, vreedsaam, rustig, stil.
peach, n. perske; perskeboom.
peacock, pou(mannetjie).
peak, n. punt, spits, (berg)top, piek.
peal, v. lui, (weer)galm, (weer)klink.
peanut, grondboontjie, apeneutjie.
pear, peer.
pearl, n. pêrel.
pearl-barley, pêrelgars, gort.
peasant, boer, landbouer.
pebble, kiesel(steen).

peck, v. pik.
peculiar, besonder, eienaardig; snaaks, raar, vreemd.
pedagogue, pedagoog, skoolmeester.
pedal, n. pedaal; trapper.
pedestal, voetstuk.
pedestrian, n. voetganger.
pedigree, n. stamboom, geslagsboom.
pedigree, a. stamboek- . . .
pedlar, smous, bondeldraer.
peel, v. (af)skil, afdop; afskilfer.
peel, n. skil, dop.
peep, v. loer, gluur, kyk.
peep, n. kykie, (die) loer.
peer, n. weerga, gelyke; edelman.
peg, n. pen; kapstok.
peg, v. vaspen, met penne vasslaan.
pelican, pelikaan.
pellet, proppie; pilletjie; koeëltjie.
pell-mell, adv. deurmekaar, holderstebolder, onderstebo; halsoorkop.
pellucid, helder, duidelik; deurskynend.
pelt, n. vel, huid.
pelt, v. gooi, koeël.
pen, n. hok, kraal.
pen, n. pen.
penal, straf- . . . ; strafbaar.
penalise, straf, beboet.
penalty, straf, boete; – (kick), strafskop.
pencil, potlood; griffel; stralebundel.
pending, a. hangende, onbeslis.
pendulum, slinger.
penetrate, binnedring, deurdring; deurgrond.
penetrating, deurdringend, skerp.
penguin, pikkewyn.
penicillin, penisilline (penisillien).
peninsula, skiereiland.
penitent, a. boetvaardig, berouvol.
penitentiary, n. strafgevangenis.
penknife, sakmes, knipmes, pennemes.
penny, pennie, oulap.
pension, n. pensioen; losieshuis.
pensionary, n. pensionaris.
pensive, peinsend, in gedagte versonke.
Pentecost, Pinksterfees, Pinkster.
people, n. mense; volk, nasie.
people, v. bevolk.
pepper, n. peper.
peppermint, peperment.
per, deur, per.
perambulator, kinderwaentjie.
perceive, bespeur, bemerk; begryp.
per cent, persent, per honderd.
perceptible, waarneembaar, merkbaar.
perch, n. (dwars)stok, (dwars) houtjie (in 'n voëlhok), sitplek.
percolate, deursyfer, filtreer.
peremptory, beslissend; gebiedend; dringend.
perennial, a. standhoudend; altyddurend.
perfect, a. volmaak, perfek.
perfect, v. voltooi; verbeter.
perfection, volmaaktheid.
perfidious, trouelODS, vals, verraderlik.
perforate, perforeer.
perform, maak, doen, verrig; vervul, nakom, uitvoer; opvoer, speel.
performance, vervulling; opvoering, vertoning; prestasie; voorstelling.
performer, speler, voordraer.
perfume, n. geur, reuk; odeur, reukwater.
pergola, prieel.
perhaps, miskien, altemit, dalk, straks.
peril, n. gevaar; risiko.
perimeter, omtrek, buitegrens.
period, tydperk, periode.

periodical, n. tydskrif.
periphrasis, omskrywing, perifrase.
periscope, periskoop.
perish, omkom, vergaan.
perishables, bederfbare ware.
perjury, meineed.
perm[anent) wave], vaste golwing.
permanent, blywend, permanent.
permeate, deurdring, deurtrek.
permission, toestemming, verlof.
permit, v. toelaat, toestaan, vergun.
permit, n. verlofbrief, pas.
pernicious, dodelik, verderflik, skadelik.
perpendicular, a. loodreg, vertikaal; regop, penorent.
perpetrate, pleeg, begaan, bedrywe.
perpetual, ewigdurend, lewenslang.
perpetuate, verewig, bestendig.
perplex, in die war bring, verbyster, verbouereer.
persecute, vervolg; lastig val, pla(e).
persevere, volhard, aanhou, volhou.
Persian, n. Pers; Persies.
persiflage, jillery, korswel.
persimmon, dadelpruim, tamatiepruim.
persist, volhard, volhou, aanhou.
person, persoon, mens.
personal, persoonlik; indiwidueel; eie.
personally, persoonlik.
personify, verpersoonlik, beliggaam.
perspective, n. perspektief; gesig.
perspicacity, skranderheid.
perspiration, sweet, perspirasie.
perspire, (uit)sweet, uitwasem, perspireer.
persuade, oorreed, ompraat, oorhaal.
pert, astrant, vrypostig, parmantig.
pertinacity, hardnekkigheid; volharding.
pertinent, gepas, saaklik, pertinent.
perturb, verontrus.
peruse, sorgvuldig (deur)lees.
pervade, deurtrek, deurdring.
perverse, verkeerd, eiewys; pervers.
pervert, n. afgedwaalde; verdorwene.
pessimism, swartgalligheid, pessimisme.
pest, pes, plaag; plaaggees, kwelgees.
pester, lastig val, pla(e).
pestilence, pes, pestilensie.
pestle, stamper.
pet, n. troeteldier; hanslam, ens.; liefling.
pet, v. (ver)troetel, verwen.
petal, blomblaartjie.
peter: – out, opraak, doodloop.
petition, n. versoek, versoekskrif, petisie.
petition, v. versoek; smeek; petisioneer.
petrify, versteen; laat lam skrik.
petrol, petrol.
petticoat, onderrok.
petty, nietig, beuselagtig, kleingeestig.
petulant, prikkelbaar, iesegrimmig.
pew, (kerk)bank.
pewter, piouter, tin.
phantom, spook(sel), gedaante; hersenskim.
Pharisee, Fariseër; skynheilige.
phase, stadium; gestalte; fase.
pheasant, fisant.
phenomenal, merkwaardig, verbasend.
philanthropist, mensevriend, filantroop.
Philistine, Filistyn; bekrompe kêrel.
philosopher, wysgeer, filosoof.
philosophy, filosofie, wysbegeerte.
phlegm, slym; traagheid, koelheid.
phlegmatic, flegmaties, onverskillig.
ph(o)enix, feniks.
phone, n. telefoon.
phone, v. opbel, oplui.
phonetic, foneties.

phonogram, fonogram.
phosphate, fosfaat.
phosphorus, fosfor.
photo-finish, fotobeslissing; – camera, wenpaal-
  kamera.
photo(graph), n. portret, foto.
photographer, afnemer, fotograaf.
phrase, n. segswyse; uitdrukking; sinsnede,
  sinsdeel; frase.
phthisis, (myn)tering.
physical, fisies; liggaamlik, liggaams- . . .
physician, dokter, geneesheer.
physics, natuurkunde, fisika.
physiology, fisiologie, natuurleer.
physique, liggaamsbou.
piano, klavier, piano.
piccalili, atjar.
piccaninny, klonkie, pikkenien.
pick, v. pik; steek, prik; skoonmaak; (af)pluk;
  (op)pik; peusel; kies, uitsoek; afeet.
pick, n. keuse.
pick, n. pik, kielhouer.
picket, n. paal, pen; (brand)wag; pos.
pickle, n. pekel; moeilikheid.
pickle, v. inlê, inmaak; insout.
pickpocket, sakkeroller.
picnic, n. piekniek, veldpartytjie.
picnic, v. piekniek maak.
picture, n. prent; skildery; toonbeeld.
picture, v. voorstel, skilder, beskrywe.
picture-gallery, skilderyemuseum.
picturesque, skilderagtig.
pie, pastei.
piebald, bont.
piece, n. stuk, deel, lap(pie).
piecemeal, stuksgewyse.
pier, seehoof, hawehoof; pilaar.
pierce, deursteek, oopsteek, deurboor.
pig, n. vark; varkvleis; morsige vent.
pigeon, n. duif; swaap, uilskuiken.
pigeon-hole, n. gaatjie; vakkie, hokkie.
pigheaded, koppig, eiewys; dom.
pig-iron, ru-yster.
pigment, kleurstof, pigment.
pigsty, varkhok.
pile, n. hoop, stapel, klomp; brandstapel.
pile, v. opstapel, ophoop.
piles, n. aambeie.
pilfer, ontfutsel, skaai, steel.
pilgrim, pelgrim.
pill, n. pil.
pillage, v. plunder, verwoes.
pillar, n. (steun)pilaar.
pillar-box, briewebus.
pillion, vrouesaal, agtersaaltjie.
pillow, n. kussing; peul.
pillow-case, kussingsloop.
pilot, n. loods.
pilot, v. lei, stuur, loods; die pad wys.
pimple, puisie.
pin, n. speld; pen, stif, spy, luns.
pin, v. vassteek, vasspelde; deursteek.
pinafore, voorskoot.
pincers, knyptang, tangetjie; knypers.
pinch, n. knyp; knypie, snuifie.
pinch, v. knyp, druk, knel; suinig (vrekkig) wees.
pine, n. denneboom.
pine, v. kwyn, vergaan, versmag.
pineapple, pynappel.
ping-pong, tafeltennis.
pinion, n. vlerkpunt, slagveer; vleuel.
pinion, n. tandrat.
pink, a. angelierrooi, ligroos.
pinnacle, n. torinkie, top; toppunt.
pioneer, n. baanbreker, pionier.

pious, vroom, godsdienstig.
pip, n. piep (hoendersiekte).
pip, n. pit.
pipe, n. pyp, buis; fluit.
pipe-wrench, pypsleutel, kraaibek.
piquant, skerp, prikkelend, pikant.
pique, n. wrok, hekel, pik.
pirate, n. seerower; rowerskip; letterdief.
pistil, stamper.
pistol, n. pistool, rewolwer.
piston, suier; klep.
piston-rod, suierstang.
pit, n. put, kuil; gaatjie; afgrond; bak, parterre
(in die skouburg).
piston-rod, suierstang.
pit, n. put, kuil; gaatjie; afgrond; bak, parterre
(in die skouburg).
pitch, n. pik.
pitch, v. (tent) opslaan; uitstal; gooi; stamp (van
'n skip).
pitch, n. (krieket)baan; hoogte; graad; toestand;
staanplek.
pitch-dark, pikdonker.
pitchfork, n. gaffel, hooivurk.
piteous, jammerlik, erbarmlik, ellendig.
pitfall, vanggat, strik, val; valstrik.
pitch, pit, kern; murg; krag.
pitiful, medelydend; ellendig, treurig.
pitiless, meedoënloos, wreed.
pity, n. medelyde, jammer(te).
pity, v. bejammer, jammer kry, beklaag.
placard, n. aanplakbiljet, plakkaat.
placate, paai, bevredig; versoen.
place, n. plek, plaas; huis; posisie.
place, v. (neer)sit, plaas, regsit, aanstel; (geld)
belê; tuis bring.
place-kick, stelskop.
placid, vreedsaam, stil; bedaard, kalm.
plague, n. plaag, pes; pestilensie; las.
plague, v. (met plae) besoek, teister; lastig val,
kwel, versondig.
plain, a. duidelik, helder; eenvoudig; alledaags,
eerlik; onopgesmuk.
plain, n. vlakte.
plainly, duidelik; openhartig; eenvoudig.
plaintiff, eiser, klaer.
plaintive, klaend, klaag- . . .
plait, n. (haar)vlegsel; vou, plooi.
plait, v. vleg; vou, plooi.
plan, n. plan, bedoeling, voorneme, oogmerk;
manier; skets, ontwerp.
plan, v. planne maak, prakseer, beoog; ontwerp.
plane, n. skaaf.
plane, v. skawe.
plane, n. vlak; gelykte; trap, peil, basis.
plane, n. vliegtuig.
planet, planeet.
plank, n. plank; verkiesingsleus.
plant, n. plant, gewas; masjinerie, uitrusting,
gereedskap.
plant, v. plant, beplant; vestig, stig.
plantation, plantasie; volk(s)planting.
plaque, plaatjie, medalje.
plasma, groenkwarts; plasma.
plaster, n. pleister; pleisterkalk.
plaster, v. (be)pleister; besmeer.
plastic, plastiek(stof).
plate, n. plaat; bord; naambord; vaatwerk,
goudwerk, silwerwerk, metaalwerk; beker;
bekerwedren.
plateau, tafelland, hoogvlakte, plato.
plateglass, spieëlglas.
platform, n. verhoog, tribune, platform.
platinum, platina (erts); platinum.
platitude, gemeenplaas.

Platonic, Platonies.
platoon, peleton, afdeling.
platter, vlak skottel.
plausible, aanneemlik, glad.
play, v. speel; bespeel.
play, n. spel; vermaak; toneelstuk.
player, speler.
playful, uitgelate, dartel, vrolik, speels.
playground, speelplek, speelterrein.
plaything, speeldingetjie; speelbal.
playtime, speeltyd.
plea, pleidooi, argument; pleit.
plead, pleit, smeek, soebat; bepleit.
pleasant, aangenaam, genoeglik.
please, beval, aanstaan, behaag.
pleasing, aangenaam, innemend.
pleasure, genot, genoeë, vermaak; begeerte.
pleat, plooi, vou.
plebiscite, volksbesluit, volkstemming.
pledge, n. pand; waarborg; belofte.
pledge, v. verpand; jou woord gee.
Pleiades, Sewester, Plejade.
plenary: – power, volmag.
plenipotentiary, gevolmagtigde.
plentiful, oorvloedig, volop.
plenty, n. oorvloed.
plenty, adv. oorvloedig, baie, volop.
pleurisy, borsvliesontsteking, pleuris.
pliant, buigsaam, slap; inskiklik.
pliers, knyptang, (draad)tang.
plight, n. toestand, posisie.
plod, v. swoeg, beur, sukkel, sloof.
plot, n. erf, bouperseel; intrige; sameswering.
plot, v. skets, (uit)teken, ontwerp; saamsweer.
plough, n. ploeg.
plough, v. ploeg (ploeë, ploe); klief.
plover, waterkiewietjie; strandloper.
pluck, n. ruk, pluk, trek; harslag; moed, durf.
pluck, v. (af)pluk; trek, ruk; kaalmaak.
plucky, moedig, dapper.
plug, n. prop, pen, tap, stop; pluisie.
plug, v. (toe)stop, 'n prop insteek.
plum, pruim; die beste.
plumage, vere.
plumb, n. skietlood.
plumb, v. peil, meet; waterpas maak.
plumber, loodgieter.
plume, n. pluim, veer; veerbos.
plump, a. dik, rond, vet, geset; mollig.
plunder, v. roof, plunder, steel.
plunder, n. roof, buit; wins.
plunge, v. (in)spring, duik.
plunge, n. sprong, indompeling; waagstuk.
plunger, suier; dobbelaar; duiker.
pluperfect, voltooid-verlede (tyd).
plural, meervoud.
plus, n. plus(teken).
plusfours, kardoesbroek.
plush, pluis, ferweel.
plutocrat, kapitalis, plutokraat.
ply, v. hanteer, gebruik; uitoefen, verrig.
pneumonia, longontsteking.
poach, v. eier sonder dop kook; posjeer.
poach, v. stroop; oortree; steel.
poacher, stroper; wilddief.
pocket, n. sak; holte.
pod, n. peul, dop.
poem, gedig.
poetry, poësie, digkuns; gedigte.
poignant, skerp, bytend, bitsig; pynlik.
point, n. stippeltjie; puntjie; punt; teken.
point-blank, botweg, reguit, rondborstig.
point-duty, verkeersdiens.
pointer, wys(t)er; stok; jaghond; patryshond;
naald.

poise, v. balanseer; (laat) hang; swewe.
poise, n. ewewig; houding.
poison, n. gif, vergif.
poison, v. vergiftig, vergewe; verbitter.
poisonous, giftig; verpes; verderflik.
poke, v. stoot, stamp, steek; roer.
poker, vuuryster.
Poland, Pole.
pole, n. pool.
Pole, Pool.
polecat, muishond.
police, polisie.
policeman, polisie-agent, konstabel.
policy, staatsmansbeleid; staatkunde; politiek, gedragslyn; beleid, oorleg.
policy, polis.
polish, blinkmaak, polys, poleer, poets, verfyn, beskaaf.
polish, n. glans, skyn; smeer(sel), (skoen)waks, politoer; verfyning.
polite, beleef, vriendelik, hoflik.
politician, staatsman, politikus.
politics, politiek; staatkunde, staatsleer.
poll, n. kop; stembus.
poll, v. top, afsny; (horings) afsae; stem.
poll, n. poenskopbees.
pollard, n. poenskopdier; semels.
pollen, stuifmeel.
pollinate, bestuif.
polling-booth, stemburo, -bus.
poll-tax, hoofbelasting.
pollute, besoedel, besmet; vuil maak.
polo, polo.
polony, polonie.
polyester, poliëster
polygamy, veelwywery, poligamie.
polyglot, a. veeltalig, poliglotties.
polygon, veelhoek, poligoon.
pomade, n. pommade, (haar)salf, haarolie.
pomegranate, granaat, granaatappel.
pommel, n. knop, swaardknop; saalknop.
pomp, prag, praal, vertoon.
pompous, skitterend; verwaand; hoogdrawend.
pond, dam, poel, vywer.
ponder, (be)peins, oordink; mymer.
ponderous, swaar, gewigtig; lomp; droog.
pontoon, pont(on).
pony, ponie, bossiekop; R50.
poodle, poedel(hond).
pooh, ag, bog!
pool, n. dam(metjie), poel, plas; kuil.
pool, n. pot, inset; ring, trust.
pool, v. in die pot gooi; saammaak.
poor, a. arm, behoeftig, armoedig; skraal, onvrugbaar; gering, klein; armsalig, treurig; beskeie, nederig.
poorhouse, armhuis.
poorly, ellendig, armoedig; siekerig; laag, gemeen.
popcorn, springmielies.
pope, pous; –'s nose, stuitjie.
popgun, propgeweertjie, knalgeweertjie.
poplar, populier(boom).
poppy, papawer.
popular, volks-...., gewild, populêr; gewoon.
population, bevolking, populasie.
porcelain, porselein.
porch, (voor)portaal.
porcupine, ystervark.
pore, n. sweetgaatjie, porie.
pore, v. kyk, tuur, staar.
pork, varkvleis.
pornography, pornografie.
porous, poreus.
porpoise, bruinvis, seevark.

porridge, pap.
port, n. hawe; hawestad; port (wyn).
portable, draagbaar, vervoerbaar, lig; – radio, draradio.
portend, voorspel, bedui, beteken.
portfolio, briewesak; portefeulje.
porthole, patryspoort, kajuitvenstertjie.
portion, n. (aan)deel, porsie, erfdeel.
portrait, portret; skildering, beeld.
portray, skilder, beskrywe; afbeeld.
Portuguese, Portugees.
pose, n. houding, pose; aanstellings.
pose, v. poseer; (vraag) stel; plaas.
position, posisie, stelling; ligging; houding; status, rang, stand; betrekking; toestand.
positive, a. positief, vas, bepaald, stellig; seker, oortuig, beslis.
possess, besit, hê.
possession, besitting, eiendom; besit.
possible, a. moontlik, gebeurlik; doenlik.
possible, n. uiterste; maksimum.
possibly, moontlik, dalk, miskien.
post, n. stut, paal, styl.
post, v. aanplak; bekend maak; – up, aanplak.
post, n. pos; poskantoor, poswese.
post, v. haas, jaag; pos.
post, n. pos, posisie, betrekking; fort.
postage, posgeld.
postage stamp, posseël.
postal order, posorder.
post box, briewebus.
postcard, poskaart.
poster, aanplakbiljet; aanplakker.
posterior, a. later; agter-...., agterste.
posterity, nageslag, nakomelingskap.
posthumous, nagelate; posthuum.
postman, posjong, briewebesteller.
postmaster, posmeester.
post-mortem, lykskouing.
post office, poskantoor.
post office box, posbus.
postpone, uitstel, verskuif.
postscript, naskrif.
posture, n. houding, postuur; toestand.
pot, n. pot, kan; (kamer)uil; blompot.
potash, potas.
potassium, kalium.
potato, aartappel (ertappel); sweet –, patat.
potent, magtig, sterk.
pot-hole, slaggat (pad).
potential, a. potensieel, latent, moontlik.
potion, drank, gifdrank.
pot-pourri, mengsel, allegaartjie.
potter, v. peuter, prutsel, sukkel.
pottery, pottebakkery; erdewerk.
pouch, n. sak(kie); patroonsak; tabaksak; beursie; buidel.
poultice, n. pap.
poultry, pluimvee.
pounce, v. neerskiet op, bevlie, gryp.
pound, n. skut, skutkraal, skuthok.
pound, v. skut, in die skut ja.
pound, v. (fyn)stamp; timmer, moker, papslaan.
pour, v. giet, gooi, (in)skink; stort, uitstort, stroom; stortreën.
pout, v. pruil, suur gesig trek.
poverty, armoede, gebrek; skaarste.
powder, n. poeier; stof; (bus)kruit.
powder, v. poeier; fynmaak, fynstamp.
power, mag, krag; vermoë, gesag, beheer, invloed.
powerful, sterk, magtig; invloedryk.
powerless, magteloos, kragteloos.
power station, sentrale.

pox: small –, kinderpokkies; **chicken** –, water-pokkies.
practical, prakties, doelmatig.
practically, prakties; feitlik, so te sê.
practice, praktyk; oefening; gewoonte, gebruik; uitvoering.
practise, toepas, beoefen, uitoefen; praktiseer; oefen.
practitioner, praktisyn.
Prague, Praag.
praise, n. lof, eer, roem.
praise, v. prys, ophemel, loof.
praiseworthy, prysenswaardig, loflik.
pram, kinderwaentjie; melkkarretjie.
prance, steier, bokspring; spog, pronk.
prank, n. grap, poets; kaskenade, streek.
prate, v. babbel, klets, snater, sanik.
prattle, v. babbel, snater.
pray, bid, smeek; versoek.
prayer, gebed, bede; versoek.
prayer-meeting, biduur.
preach, preek; verkondig.
preamble, inleiding, voorrede.
prearrange, vooraf skik (bepaal).
precarious, onseker, wisselvallig; gevaarvol.
precaution, voorsorg, voorsorg(s)maatreël.
precede, voorgaan, voorafgaan.
precedence, voorrang, superioriteit.
precedent, n. voorbeeld, presedent.
preceding, voorafgaande, vorige.
precept, bevel, voorskrif, bevelskrif.
precinct, gebied.
precious, a. kosbaar; kostelik; edel.
precipice, afgrond, krans, steilte.
precipitate, n. presipitaat, afsaksel, neerslag.
precipitate, a. (oor)haastig, onbesonne.
precipitate, v. (neer)stort, neergooi; verhaas, bespoedig; (laat) afsak.
precipitous, steil; oorhaastig.
précis, opsomming, kort inhoud, oorsig.
precise, presies, nougeset, sekuur; juis.
preclude, uitsluit; belet, voorkom.
precocious, vroeg (ryp); oulik, vrypostig, astrant.
predatory, roof- . . . , roofsugtig.
predecessor, voorganger; voorvader.
predestine, vooraf bepaal, voorbeskik.
predetermine, vooraf bepaal; predestineer.
predicament, toestand; moeilike posisie.
predicate, n. gesegde; predikaat.
predict, voorspel, voorsê.
predilection, voorliefde; partydigheid.
predominant, oorheersend.
predominate, die oorhand hê, oorheers; in die meerderheid wees.
preface, n. voorwoord, inleiding.
preface, v. inlei.
prefect, hoof, prefek.
prefer, verkies, voorkeur gee aan, prefereer; bevorder; inlewer.
preferable, verkieslik.
preferably, liewers, by voorkeur.
preference, voorkeur; voorrang.
prefix, n. voorvoegsel, prefiks.
pregnant, swanger, vrugbaar; betekenisvol, veelseggend.
prehistoric, voorhistories.
prejudice, n. vooroordeel; nadeel, skade.
prejudice, v. afbreuk doen aan, benadeel; bevooroordeeld maak.
preliminary, a. voorafgaande, inleidend(e), voorbereidend(e), preliminêr.
prelude, n. inleiding, voorspel.
premature, voorbarig, ontydig; te vroeg.
premeditate, vooraf bedink (beraam).

premier, n. eerste minister, premier.
premise, **premiss**, n. premis; –s, plek, gebou, werf.
premise, v. vooropstel.
premium, beloning, prys; premie; onderriggeld.
premonition, waarskuwing, voorteken.
preoccupied, afgetrokke, mymerend.
preparation, voorbereiding; klaarmakery; preparaat.
prepare, (voor)berei, gereed maak, klaarmaak, oplei; prepareer.
preposition, voorsetsel.
prepossessing, innemend.
preposterous, ongerymd, belaglik, gek.
prerequisite, n. noodsaaklike vereiste.
prerogative, prerogatief, voorreg.
Presbyterian, a. Presbiteriaans.
prescribe, voorskryf; voorskrifte neerlê.
prescription, resep, voorskrif; (die) voorskryf; verjaring.
presence, teenwoordigheid, aanwesigheid; voorkome.
present, a. teenwoordig, aanwesig; huidig; onderhawig.
present, n. die teenwoordige, die hede.
present, n. geskenk, present.
present, v. voorstel; (ver)toon; oplewer; indien, aanbied.
presentiment, voorgevoel.
presently, netnou, aanstons (aans).
preserve, n. konfyt, ingelegde vrugte; wildpark.
preserve, v. bewaar, beskerm, behoed, behou; inlê, inmaak.
preside, voorsit, presideer.
president, voorsitter; president.
press, n. gedrang; haas, gejaagdheid; menigte; pers; (druk)pers, drukkery.
press, v. druk, pers; pars; platdruk, saamdruk; aandring, dwing.
pressing, dringend; dreigend.
pressure, druk, drukking.
prestige, reputasie, prestige, gesag.
presume, veronderstel, vermoed, aanneem; waag, die vryheid neem.
presumption, veronderstelling; verwaandheid.
presumptuous, verwaand, vermetel.
presuppose, aanneem, veronderstel.
pretence, skyn, voorwendsel.
pretend, voorgee, maak asof, beweer.
pretentious, pretensieus, aanmatigend; verwaand.
pretext, voorwendsel, ekskuus.
pretty, a. mooi, lief, aanvallig.
pretty, adv. taamlik.
prevail, die oorhand kry; heers.
prevailing, heersend, algemeen.
prevaricate, rondspring, uitvlugte soek.
prevent, verhinder, belet, verhoed; teëhou; voorkom.
previous, a. vorige, voorafgaande.
previously, vantevore, vooraf, vooruit.
prey, n. prooi; buit, roof; slagoffer.
prey, v.: – **upon**, roof, plunder.
price, n. prys; waarde.
priceless, onbetaalbaar, kostelik.
prick, n. steek; prikkel; gaatjie; kwelling, wroeging.
prick, v. prik, steek; spits; kwel.
prickle, v. steek, prik.
pride, n. hoogmoed; trotsheid, trots.
pride, v.: – **oneself (up)on**, jou roem op, trots wees op.
priest, priester, geestelike.
prig, pedant, wysneus.

primary, vroegste, oorspronklike; eerste, primêr, elementêr; vernaamste.
prime, n. begin, eerste stadium; bloeityd.
prime, a. vernaamste, belangrikste, eerste, prima, eersteklas; primêr, fundamenteel, oorspronklik.
prime, v. laai; afrig; inpomp.
primer, voorloper.
primitive, oudste, oorspronklike, eerste, oer . . . ; outyds, primitief.
prince, prins; vors, heerser.
principal, a. belangrikste, hoof- . . .
principal, n. hoof; prinsipaal; hoofpersoon, baas, lasgewer; kapitaal.
principle, beginsel, grondslag; prinsipe.
print, n. druk, afdruk; spoor, merk; prent, plaat; sis.
print, v. afdruk, merk, stempel; druk; in drukletter skryf.
prior, adv. vroeër, voorafgaande, eerste.
priority, prioriteit, voorkeur.
prism, prisma.
prison, gevangenis, tronk.
prisoner, gevangene, prisonier; bandiet.
private, a. privaat, persoonlik, eie; konfidensieel; afgesonder.
private, n. gewone soldaat.
privation, ontbering, gebrek.
privilege, n. voorreg, privileg(i)e.
privilege, v. bevoorreg; vrystel.
privy, a. geheim, verborge.
prize, n. prys, beloning; buit.
prize, v. waardeer, op prys stel.
prize, v. oopmaak, oopbreek.
pro, voor; – **and con**, voor en teë.
probable, waarskynlik.
probationary, proef- . . .
probe, v. peil, ondersoek; sondeer.
probity, opregtheid, eerlikheid.
problem, probleem, vraag(stuk); raaisel.
procedure, handelwyse, prosedure.
proceed, voortgaan; te werk gaan.
proceeding, handelwyse; –s, verrigtinge, handelinge; stappe, maatreëls.
proceeds, opbrings, wins(te).
process, loop, gang, ontwikkeling; metode; hofsaak; proses.
procession, optog, stoet.
proclaim, aankondig, proklameer, verklaar; uitroep.
procrastinate, uitstel, sloer, talm.
procurable, verkrygbaar.
procure, (ver)kry, besorg, verskaf.
prod, v. steek; aanspoor, aanpor.
prodigal, a. verkwistend; oorvloedig, rojaal.
prodigious, verbasend; enorm, ontsaglik.
prodigy, wonder(mens), wonderkind.
produce, n. produkte; opbrings, produksie.
produce, v. opbring, oplewer; veroorsaak; lewer; wys; opvoer; uitgee; verleng; voortbring; produseer.
producer, produsent; regisseur.
product, produk, voortbrengsel.
production, produksie; voortbrengsel, produk; opvoering.
profane, a. ongetwyfeld; heidens; oneerbiedig, profaan.
profess, verklaar, erken; bely, betuig; voorgee; onderwys.
profession, verklaring, erkentenis; beroep, professie.
professional, a. professioneel, beroeps- . . . , vak- . . .
professor, belyer; professor, hoogleraar.
proffer, v. aanbied, aanpresenteer.

proficient, bekwaam, knap, bedrewe.
profile, n. profiel; vertikale deursnee.
profit, n. wins, voordeel, profyt.
profits, v. wins maak, wen, voordeel trek uit; baat, help.
profitable, voordelig, winsgewend.
profiteer, v. woekerwins maak, jou sak vul.
profligate, a. losbandig, ontugtig.
profound, diepsinnig; grondig.
profuse, mild, kwistig, oordadig; volop.
progeny, nageslag, kroos.
prognostication: voorteken; voorspelling.
programme, program.
progress, n. vooruitgang, vordering.
progress, v. vooruitgang, vorder.
progressive, a. progressief, vooruitstrewend; toenemend.
prohibit, belet, verbied.
project, n. plan, ontwerp, skema.
project, v; beraam, ontwerp, projekteer; uitsteek.
projectile, n. projektiel; bom; gooiing.
projector, planmaker; projeksielamp.
proletariat(e), proletariaat.
prolific, vrugbaar.
prolix, langdradig, wydlopig, uitvoerig.
prologue, voorspel, voorrede, proloog.
prolong, verleng, langer maak, (uit)rek.
promenade, v. op en af kuier, wandel.
prominent, uitstekend, voortreflik, vernaam; in die oog vallend; vooruitstekend.
promiscuous, deurmekaar; gemeng.
promise, n. belofte; jawoord.
promise, v. belowe, toesê, verseker.
promissory: – **note**, promesse, skuldbewys.
promote, bevorder, vooruithelp; promoveer; bespoedig; oprig.
promotion, verhoging, promosie.
prompt, a. vlug, spoedig, onmiddellik, stip, vaardig, fluks.
prompt, v. aanhits, aanspoor; besiel; voorsê.
promulgate, afkondig; proklameer.
prone, vooroor, plat (op die gesig).
prong, n. (hooi)vurk, ystergaffel; tand.
pronoun, voornaamwoord.
pronounce, uitspreek, verklaar.
proof, n. bewys(grond); blyk; proef, toets; (druk)proef; sterktegraad.
prop, n. steun(pilaar), pilaar, stut.
propaganda, propaganda.
propagate, voortplant, versprei, propageer.
propel, (voort)dryf, vooruitstoot.
propeller, drywer; skroef (van stoomboot).
proper, eie; reg, gepas, juis, geskik; eg; welvoeglik, fatsoenlik.
properly, behoorlik, fatsoenlik; eintlik.
property, hoedanigheid; eiendom, besitting.
prophecy, profesie, voorspelling.
prophesy, profeteer, voorspel, voorsê.
prophet, profeet, siener.
propitiate, versoen, bevredig, gunstig stem.
propitious, gunstig, genadig.
prop-jet, skroef-turbinemotor.
proportion, verhouding, proporsie; deel.
proportional, a. eweredig, proporsioneel.
proposal, voorstel, aanbod; aansoek.
propose, voorstel, aanbied; voornemens wees, ('n meisie) vra.
propound, voorstel, aanbied, voorlê.
proprietary, a. eienaars- . . . , eiendoms- . . . besittend.
proprietor, eienaar, besitter.
propriety, juistheid, korrektheid; gepastheid; welvoeglikheid, fatsoenlikheid.
props, toneelbenodigdhede.

prorogue, verdaag, opskort, uitstel.
prose, n. prosa; alledaagsheid.
prosecute, vervolg; voortsit; uitoefen.
prosecutor: public –, publieke aanklaer.
prospect, n. uitsig, vergesig, vooruitsig, hoop, verwagting.
prospect, v. prospekteer, ondersoek.
prospective, te wagte; toekomstige, aanstaande; vooruitsiende.
prospector, prospekteerder, prospektor.
prospectus, prospektus.
prosper, bloei, floreer.
prosperity, voorspoed, bloei, welvaart.
prosperous, voorspoedig, boeiend.
prostrate, v. neerwerp, verneder; neerbuig.
protect, beskerm, bewaar, behoed.
protector, beskermer, beskermheer.
protectorate, protektoraat.
protégé, beskerm(e)ling, protégé.
protein, (proteïne).
protest, n. protes, (teen)verklaring.
protest, v. protesteer; plegtig verklaar.
Protestant, n. Protestant.
prototype, model, prototipe.
protract, rek, verleng, uitstel.
protrude, (voor)uitsteek.
proud, hoogmoedig, verwaand, fier, groots; pragtig.
prove, bewys; toon, wys; blyk; probeer, beproef.
proverb, spreekwoord, spreuk.
provide, voorsien, verskaf; voorsorg maak (vir); bepaal, neerlê.
provided, op voorwaarde dat, mits, as.
providence, voorsiening; Voorsienigheid.
province, provinsie, gewes, afdeling; gebied, sfeer.
pronvincial, provinsiaal; gewestelik.
provision, n. voorsiening, voorsorg; bepaling; –s, lewensmiddels, proviand.
provocation, provokasie; belediging.
provoke, aanhits, prikkel, opwek; uitdaag, tart; uitlok; beledig.
provoking, tartend, prikkelend.
prowl, v. op roof uit wees, rondsluip.
proxy, volmag; gevolmagtigde.
prudent, versigtig, omsigtig; verstandig.
prudish, aanstellerig, preuts, skynsedig.
prune, n. pruimedant.
prune, v. snoei; besnoei, sny.
pruning-shears, snoeiskêr, wingerdskêr.
Prussian, n. Pruis.
prussic acid, blousuur, siaanwaterstof.
pry, nuuskierig kyk na, loer.
psalm, psalm.
pseudo, onreg, vals; sogenaamd.
pseudonym, skuilnaam, pen(ne)naam.
psyche, gees, siel, psige.
psychic, a. psigies, siels . . . , spiritisties.
psychology, psigologie, sielkunde.
ptomaine: – poisoning, ptomaïnevergiftiging.
puberty, puberteit, geslagsrypheid.
public, n. publiek.
public, a. publieke, openbaar, algemeen.
publication, openbaarmaking; uitgawe, publikasie.
publish, rugbaar maak; afkondig; publiseer.
publisher, uitgewer.
pucker, n. rimpel, plooi.
pucker, v. vou, plooi, frons, rimpel.
pudding, poeding.
puddle, n. modderplas, modderpoel.
puerile, kinderagtig; beuselagtig.
puff, n. rukwind; asemstoot; trek, haal; rook-wolkie; poeierkwas; poffertjie.
puff, v. blaas, hyg, trek; opblaas.

puff-adder, pofadder.
pugilist, bokser, bakleier, vuisvegter.
pugnacious, twissoekerig, bakleierig.
pug-nose, stompneus, platneus.
pull, n. ruk, trek; trekstoot; roeitoggie; teug, sluk; voorsprong.
pull, v. ruk, pluk, trek; roei.
pullet, jong hoender, kuiken.
pulley, n. katrol.
pulp, n. vleis (van vrugte), sagte massa, moes, pap.
pulpit, preekstoel, kansel.
pulsate, klop, slaan; tril.
pulse, n. pols, polsslag; trilling.
pulse, v. klop, slaan; tril.
pulverize, fynstamp, fynmaal; vernietig, ver-morsel.
pumice, puimsteen.
pump, n. pomp; dansskoen.
pump, v. pomp, oppomp, uitpomp; uitvra.
pumpkin, pampoen.
pun, n. woordspeling.
punch, n. deurslag; vuisslag, hou; pons.
punch, v. gate inslaan, knip; steek; moker.
punctual, presies, stip, noukeurig; op tyd.
punctuate, interpunkteer; onderbreek; nadruk lê op.
punctuation, leestekens, interpunksie.
puncture, n. prik, gaatjie, lek(plek).
puncture, v. prik, 'n gat insteek.
pungent, skerp, bytend, bitsig, vinnig.
punish, straf, kasty; toetakel.
punishment, straf, boete.
punt, n. pont, platboomskuit.
punt, v. hoog skop; voortstoot.
punt, v. vir geld speel; wed.
puny, klein, swak, tingerig.
pup, n. klein (jong) hondjie.
pupa, papie.
pupil, leerling, skolier; oogappel.
puppet, (draad)pop, marionet; speelbal.
purblind, half-bind, bysiende; bot.
purchase, v. koop, aanskaf; optrek.
pure, rein, suiwer, skoon; eg, vlekloos; louter, puur.
purgative, n. purgeermiddel, purgasie.
purgatory, n. va(g)evuur.
purge, v. skoonmaak, reinig, suiwer.
purify, reinig, suiwer, louter.
Puritan, n. Puritein.
purl, v. borduur; aweregs brei.
purple, a. purper, pers.
purport, n. betekenis, bedoeling, sin.
purpose, n. oogmerk, bedoeling, doel.
purposely, ekspres, opsetlik.
purr, spin, snor, snork.
purse, n. beursie, geldsakkie.
purse, v. plooi, op 'n plooi trek.
purser, betaalmeester, administrateur.
pursue, vervolg; najaag, voortsit; volg; agtervolg.
purveyor, leweransier, verskaffer.
pus, etter.
push, n. stoot, stamp, druk; volharding; moeilik-heid.
push, v. stoot, stamp, druk; aanhelp, voorthelp; deurdryf; bevorder; aandring.
pusillanimous, lafhartig, kleinmoedig; kleinsie-lig.
put, v. sit, stel, plaas; steek; stoot; uitdruk.
putrefy, bederwe, vrot (verrot), sleg word; sweer.
putrid, vrot (verrot), stink; bedorwe.
putt, rolslag (gholf).
putter, rolstok.
putty, stopverf (stokverf).

puzzle, n. verleentheid; raaisel; knoop; sukkel-
spel.
puzzle, v. verwar, in die war bring.
pygmy, n. dwerg, pigmee.

pyjamas, slaapklere, slaappak.
pyramid, piramide.
pyre, brandstapel.
python, luislang.

Q

quack, v. kwaak.
quack, n. kwaksalwer; grootprater.
quadrangle, vierhoek; vierkant; binneplein.
quadrilateral, n. vierhoek.
quadruped, n. viervoetige dier.
quagga, kwagga.
quagmire, moeras, vlei; modderpoel.
quail, n. kwartel.
quail, v. bang word, moedeloos word.
quaint, eienaardig, raar, sonderling.
quake, v. skud, bewe, sidder.
Quaker, Kwaker.
qualification, bevoegdheid; bekwaamheid; voorbehoud; wysiging, beperking; eienskap.
qualified, bekwaam, geskik, bevoeg.
qualify, bekwaam (bevoeg) maak; finale eksamen aflê; kwalifiseer; beperk, wysig, matig;
bepaal.
quality, kwaliteit, gehalte; eienskap; rang, stand.
qualm, beswaar, wroeging.
quandary, moeilikheid, verleentheid.
quantity, hoeveelheid, klomp.
quantity surveyor, bestek-opmaker.
quarantine, v. onder kwarantyn stel.
quarrel, v. twis, rusie maak, skoor.
quarry, n. prooi, slagoffer, wild.
quarry, n. steengroef, klipbreekgat.
quart, kwart, ¼ gelling.
quarter, n. kwart; kwartier; kwartaal; wyk,
buurt; genade.
quarterly, adv. elke drie maande.
quarter-master, kwartiermeester.
quartz, kwarts.
quash, nietig verklaar, verwerp; platdruk.
quaver, v. tril, vibreer, bewe.
quay, kaai, hawehoof.
queen, n. koningin, vrou (in kaartspel).
queer, a. sonderling, snaaks; verdag; naar,
duiselig.
quell, onderdruk, oorrompel.

quench, blus, doodmaak, uitdoof; les; onderdruk, smoor; afkoel.
querulous, klaend, brommerig.
query, v. vra; betwyfel.
quest, n. ondersoek; soek.
question, n. vraag; kwessie, vraagstuk.
question, v. vra; ondervra; betwyfel, beswaar
maak teen.
question-mark, vraagteken.
queue, n. haarvlegsel, stert; tou.
queue, v. toustaan.
quibble, n. woordspeling, spitsvondigheid; ont-
wyking.
quibble, v. haarklowe; uitvlugte soek.
quick, a. lewendig; gou, vinnig, vlug, haastig.
quicklime, ongebluste kalk.
quicksand, wilsand, dryfsand.
quicksilver, kwik(silwer).
quick-tempered, opvlieënd, kortgebakerd.
quick-witted, skerpsinnig, gevat.
quiescent, rustig, stil; sluimerend.
quiet, a. stil, rustig, kalm, vreedsaam, gerus;
bedaard.
quiet, v. stil maak, kalmeer; bedaar.
quill, n. slagveer, skag; veerpen; (ystervark)pen;
spoel.
quilt, n. sprei, deken, veerkombers.
quince, kweper; kweperboom.
quinine, kina.
quip, geestigheid, spitsvondigheid.
quire, boek (24 vel papier).
quit, v. verlaat, opgee; vertrek.
quite, heeltemal, glad, totaal, volkome.
quiver, n. pylkoker.
quiver, v. bewe, tril, sidder.
quorum, kworum.
quota, kwota.
quotation-marks, aanhalingsteken.
quote, aanhaal, siteer; (prys) opgee.
quotient, kwosiënt.

rabbi, rabbi, rabbyn.
rabbit, konyn; beginner.
rabble, gespuis, gepeupel.
rabid, woes, rasend, mal, dol.
rabies, hondsdolheid.
race, n. wedren, wedloop; –s, reisies (resies).
race, v. hardloop, jaag [ja(e)]; reisies (resies) ja; vinnig laat loop.
race, n. ras, geslag, stam, soort; afkoms.
racecourse, renbaan, reisie(s)baan.
race-meeting, wedrenbyeenkoms.
racialist, rassehater.
rack, n. rak, kapstok; pynbank.
racket, n. raket.
racket, n. rumoer, lawaai; plan, doel.
racketeer, afperser.
racy, geurig, sterk, kragtig, pittig, geestig, lewendig.
radar, radar; – control, radarleiding.
radiant, a. (uit)stralend; skitterend.
radiate, v. glinster, skitter; uitstraal; straal; versprei.
radiator, radiator, elektriese stoof; verkoeler (van 'n motorkar).
radical, a. radikaal, fundamenteel, volkome; wortel- . . .
radio, n. radio, radio(toestel); radiodiens; v. uitsend, uitsaai; sein.
radioactive, radioaktief.
radiogram, radiogram (telegr.), gramradio.
radiograph, radiogram.
radish, radys.
radium, radium.
radius, straal.
raffle, n. lotery.
raffle, v. loot; uitloot, verloot.
raft, n. vlot; dryfhout.
rafter, n. dakspar, kapstuk, balk.
rag, n. flenter, vod, lap, vadoek.
rag, n. jool.
rage, n. woede, toorn; begeerte, gier; mode.
rage, v. moed, raas, te kere gaan.
ragged, ru, ongelyk; onreëlmatig; geskeur, verflenter.
raid, n. inval, strooptog.
raid, v. inval, 'n inval doen; roof.
rail, n. dwarshout, dwarspaal; leuning; latwerk; spoorstaaf.
rail, v. spot, smaal, beledig, skel.
railing, traliewerk, leuning, reling.
railway, spoorweg.
railway engine, lokomotief.
railway station, spoorwegstasie.
rain, n. reën (reent).
rain, v. reën (reent); laat reën.
rainbow, reënboog (reentboog).
rainfall, reënval.
rainy, reënagtig, reënerig.
raise, optel, oplig, opwek, oprig; bymekaarmaak; teel, aankweek; veroorsaak; verhoog, verhef.
raisin, rosyntjie.
rake, n. hark.
rake, v. hark, bymekaar skraap; deursnuffel.
rally, n. (motor)byeenkoms, saamtrek.
rally, v. bymekaarmaak; herenig; herstel; moed skep; moed inpraat; bystaan; 'n sarsie maak (tennis).
ram, n. (storm)ram; stamper.
ram, v. (vas)stamp, instamp; inprop.
ramble, ronddwaal, rondswerwe; 'n uitstappie maak; afdwaal; deurmekaar praat.
rambling, omswerwend; onsamehangend; klimmend, rank- . . . , slinger- . . .
ramification, vertakking.

ram-jet, stustraal.
rampage, v. te kere gaan, raas, baljaar.
rampart, n. wal, skans, borswering.
ramrod, laaistok.
ramshackle, bouvallig, lendelam.
rancid, galsterig, suur, sterk.
rancour, vyandskap, bittere haat.
random, n. **at** –, wildweg, blindweg.
range, n. ry, reeks, aaneenskakeling; rigting, lyn; skietveld; omvang, perke, bereik, gebied; afstand, draagkrag; kaggel, stoof.
range, v. (rang)skik; skaar, opstel; uitstrek, loop; varieer; voorkom; dwaal; dra (van 'n geweer).
ranger, veldwagter, boswagter.
rank, n. ry, gelid; stand; graad; staanplek.
rank, v. in gelid stel; klassifiseer; plaas; beskou word.
rank, a. welig, geil; galsterig, suur; onbeskof; flagrant, puur.
rankle, sweer, ontsteek; knaag.
ransack, deursoek, deursnuffel; plunder.
ransom, v. los, vrykoop, bevry; boet.
rant, v. grootpraat; uitbulder.
rap, n. tik, slag, klop; duit, knip.
rap, v. tik, klop.
rapacious, roofgierig, roofsugtig; gierig.
rape, n. ontering.
rape, v. onteer.
rapid, n. stroomversnelling.
rapid, a. vlug, vinnig, snel.
rapier, rapier.
rapture, verrukking, ekstase.
rare, yl, dun; skaars; buitengewoon, seldsaam.
rarefy, verdun, yl maak (word); verfyn.
rarity, rariteit, seldsaamheid.
rascal, n. skurk, rakker, skelm.
rash, n. uitslag.
rash, a. onbesonne, roekeloos, haastig.
rasp, n. rasper.
rasp, v. rasper, skraap; kras, krap.
raspberry, framboos.
rat, 'n rot; oorloper.
ratchet, **ratch**, sperrat, palrat.
rate, n. standaard, maatstaf; skaal, tarief; prys; belasting; tempo, snelheid; koers; graad, klas.
rate, v. skat, waardeer; beskou.
rather, liewer(s), eerder, meer; taamlik, nogal, bietjie, enigsins.
ratify, bekragtig, ratifiseer.
ratio, verhouding, ratio.
ration, n. rantsoen, porsie.
rational, redelik; verstandig.
rat(t)an, rottang, bamboes, spaansriet.
rattle, n. ratel; gerammel; geroggel; geklets.
rattle, v. ratel, rammel; klets; aframmel.
rattlesnake, ratelslang.
rat-trap, rotval.
raucous, hees, skor.
ravage, v. verniel, verwoes, plunder.
rave, v. raas, te kere gaan, yl; uitvaar; dweep (met), in verrukking wees (oor).
raven, a. pikswart.
ravenous, uitgehonger.
ravine, bergkloof, skeur.
ravish, wegvoer, ontroof; onteer.
raw, a. rou; ru, onbewerk; onervare, dom; seer.
ray, n. straal, ligstreep.
raze, **rase**, skawe; vernietig.
razor, n. skeermes.
reach, n. bereik; mag; omvang.
reach, v. uitstrek; bereik, bykom.
react, reageer, terugwerk.
read, lees; uitlê; raai; lui; studeer.

readable, leesbaar; lesenswaardig.
readdress, heradresseer, nastuur.
reader, leser; persleser; lektor; leesboek.
reading-lamp, studeerlamp.
ready, a. klaar, gereed, gewillig; vinnig.
real, a. werklik, waar, eintlik; eg.
realization, verwesenliking; besef.
realize, verwesenlik; besef; tot geld maak, ('n prys) haal, opbring; realiseer.
realism, realisme.
really, werklik, waarlik, regtig.
realm, koninkryk, ryk, gebied, terrein.
ream, n. riem (papier).
reamer, ruimer (boor).
reap, oes, maai; insamel; pluk.
reaper, maaier; snymasjien.
reappear, weer verskyn.
reappoint, weer aanstel, herbenoem.
rear, n. agterhoede; agtergrond.
rear, v. grootmaak; oplei; teel; kweek; steier; opsteek.
rear-admiral, skout-by-nag.
rearguard, agterhoede.
rearrange, omskik, verander.
reason, n. rede, verstand; motief, oorsaak, rede, grond; billikheid.
reason, v. redeneer; beredeneer; bespreek.
reasonable, billik, redelik, verstandig.
reassure, weer verseker, gerusstel.
rebate, n. vermindering, korting, rabat.
rebel, n. rebel, opstandeling.
rebel, v. rebelleer, opstaan (teen).
rebellion, rebellie, opstand, oproer.
rebound, v. terugspring, terugstoot.
rebuff, n. afjak, affrontasie; weiering.
rebuke, v. bestraf, berispe, teregwys.
rebut, afweer, terugslaan; weerlê.
recalcitrant, a. weerspannig, weerbarstig.
recall, v. terugroep; herroep, intrek; onthou.
recapture, v. herneem, herower.
recede, terugtree, terugwyk, terugtrek; sak; verdwyn.
receipt, n. ontvangs; voldaan.
receipt, v. voldaan maak.
receive, kry, ontvang; toelaat; onthaal.
receiver, ontvanger; hoorbuis; heler (van ge-steelde goed).
recent, onlangs, resent, nuut.
reception, resepsie, ontvangs, onthaal.
reception-room, ontvangkamer.
recess, reses; alkoof; skuilplek.
recipe, resep, voorskrif, preskripsie.
reciprocal, a. wederkerig, wedersyds.
recitation, resitasie, voordrag.
recite, opsê, resiteer, voordra.
reckless, roekeloos, onverskillig.
reckon, reken; tel; beskou, meen.
reclaim, terugwin, red, verbeter; mak maak; terugkry; drooglê.
recline, lê, leun, rus, agteroorlê.
recluse, n. kluisenaar.
recognize, herken; besef.
recoil, v. terugslaan, terugspring, skop; terug-tree.
recollect, (sig) herinner, onthou.
recommend, aanbeveel, aanprys; aanraai.
recompense, v. beloon, vergoed, vergeld.
reconcile, versoen; ('n geskil) bylê; verenig (met).
reconnoitre, v. verken, spioen.
reconstruct, rekonstrueer; herbou.
record, n. offisiële afskrif; gedenkskrif, doku-ment; getuienis; verslag; rekord; plaat.
record, v. opteken, opskryf, vermeld; registreer.
recount, verhaal, meedeel, vertel.

recourse, toevlug.
recover, terugkry; herstel; bykom; inhaal; goed maak.
recreation, ontspanning, vermaak.
recruit, n. rekruut; nuweling.
recruit, v. (aan)werf, rekruteer; versterk.
rectangle, reghoek.
rectify, regmaak, herstel; distilleer.
rector, rektor, hoof; predikant.
rectory, pastorie; rektorswoning.
recuperate, herstel, opknap, beter word.
recur, terugkom op; byval; weer voorkom.
red, a. rooi.
redeem, terugkoop; vrykoop; verlos; nakom.
Redeemer, Verlosser, Heiland.
red-handed, op heter daad.
redolent, geurig, welriekend; herinner aan.
redouble, verdubbel, vermeerder.
redskin, Rooihuid, Indiaan.
red-tape, amptelike omslagtigheid.
reduce, terugbring; herlei; verneder, verlaag, onderwerp; verminder.
reduction, vermindering, afslag; beperking; her-leiding.
redundant, oortollig, oorbodig.
re-echo, v. weergalm, weerklink; herhaal.
reed, riet; mondstuk; fluit.
reef, v. die seile inbind, reef.
reef, n. rif; rotsbank, rotslaag.
reek, v., – of, ruik na.
reel, n. rolletjie, tolletjie, klos.
reel, v. wankel, waggel; duiselig word.
reel, n. riel (dans).
re-elect, herkies.
refectory, eetkamer, eetsaal.
refer, refereer, verwys; toeskryf (aan); voorlê; (sig) beroep op; betrekking hê (op); melding maak (van).
referee, skeidsregter.
reference, verwysing; verband, verhouding, betrekking; melding, gewag; bewysplaas; ge-tuigskrif.
referendum, volkstemming, referendum.
refine, suiwer, raffineer; verfyn, veredel.
refinery, suiweringsfabriek, raffinadery.
reflect, weerkaats, weerspieël; nadink.
reflection, weerkaatsing; refleksie; gedagte; verwyt, skimp.
reflex, a. – action, refleksbeweging.
reflexive, wederkerend, refleksief.
reform, v. verbeter, hervorm.
reformatory, n. verbeteringsgestig.
refract, breek (van strale).
refrain, n. refrein.
refrain, v. bedwing, beteuel.
refresh, verkwik, verkoel, verfris.
refreshment, verversing, verkwikking.
refrigerate, v. koud maak, verkoel.
refuge, toevlug, toevlugsoord.
refugee, vlugteling, uitgeweekene.
refund, v. terugbetaal, teruggee.
refuse, n. oorskiet, afval, vuilgoed.
refuse, v. weier, van die hand wys.
refute, weerlê, teëspreek.
regain, terugkry, herwin.
regard, n. agting, eerbied; verband, opsig; aan-dag.
regard, v. bekyk, beskou; in aanmerking neem; ag slaan op; (hoog)ag; aangaan.
regarding, betreffende, wat betref.
regenerate, v. laat herlewe, opwek, hervorm.
regent, n. regent (regentes); bewindhebber.
regime, (regering)stelsel, beheer; instelling; regime.
regiment, regiment.

region, streek, landstreek, gebied.
register, n. register; lys, kieserslys, rol.
register, v. registreer, inskryf; boek, aanteken.
registrar, registrateur.
regret, n. verdriet, teleurstelling; spyt, leedwese.
regret, v. treur oor; betreur.
regrettable, betreurenswaardig.
regular, a. gereeld, reëlmatig; vas.
regulate, reguleer; regsit; reël.
regulation, regulasie, reëling; reglement.
regulator, reëlaar; slinger.
rehabilitate, rehabiliteer, herstel.
rehearse, opsê; herhaal, opsom; repeteer.
reign, v. regeer, heers.
reimburse, terugbetaal, vergoed.
rein, n. leisel, teuel; beheer.
reincarnation, reïnkarnasie.
reindeer, rendier.
reinforce, versterk.
reiterate, herhaal.
reject, verwerp; verstoot; weier, afwys.
rejoice, verbly, bly maak, bly (verheug) wees.
rejoin, antwoord; weer inhaal, weer aansluit.
rejuvenate, verjong, weer jonk maak.
relapse, n. terugval; weerinstorting.
relate, verhaal, vertel.
related, verwant.
relation, betrekking, verhouding; verwantskap;
  bloedverwant.
relative, n. familiebetrekking.
relative, a. betrekking; respektief.
relax, verflou; versag; ontspan.
relay-race, afloswedstryd, afloswedloop.
release, v. loslaat, vrystel, verlos; losmaak; oormaak; onthef.
relent, toegee, week word, bedaar.
relentless, meedoënloos, onverbiddelik.
relevant, toepaslik, vanpas, ter sake.
reliable, vertroubaar, betroubaar.
relic, reliek; oorblyfsel.
relief, n. verligting, versagting; ondersteuning;
  ontset.
relieve, verlig, lenig; ondersteun; bevry: aflos;
  ontset; lug gee aan.
religion, godsdiens, geloof.
religious, godsdienstig, vroom.
relinquish, opgee, laat staan; loslaat.
relish, n. smaak, geur; genot.
relish, v. behae skep in, hou van.
reluctant, teësinnig, huiwerig.
rely, vertrou (op), steun (op), staatmaak (op).
remain, v. oorbly, oorskiet; bly.
remain(s), oorskiet; stoflike oorskot; ruïne.
remainder, res, oorskiet, die orige.
remark, v. opmerk; aanmerk.
remedy, n. geneesmiddel, (hulp)middel.
remember, onthou, (sig) herinner; byval.
remembrance, herinnering, geheue; aandenking;
  gedagtenis.
remind, herinner, help onthou.
reminiscence, herinnering.
remit, vergewe, kwytskel(d); verminder, verflou;
  terugstuur.
remnant, oorblyfsel, oorskiet; stukkie; lap;
  restant.
remonstrate, protesteer, beswaar maak; teregwys.
remorse, berou, gewetenswroeging.
remorseless, meedoënloos, onbarmhartig.
remote, afgeleë, afgesonder, ver (van mekaar);
  gering, min.
remove, verplaas; ontslaan, afdank; wegneem,
  verwyder, verskuiwe; verhuis, oorbring.
remuneration, beloning, betaling.
rend, (stukkend) skeur, losskeur; verdeel.

render, teruggee; oorlewer; oplewer; bewys;
  vertolk; vertaal; uitbraai, suiwer.
renegade, renegaat, afvallige.
renew, vernuwe, hernieu; hervat; verlewendig,
  versterk.
renounce, afstand doen van; verwerp.
renovate, repareer, regmaak, vernuwe.
renowned, beroemd, vermaard.
rent, n. skeur; opening, bars.
rent, n. huur, pag; verhuur, verpag.
reorganize, reorganiseer.
repair, v. repareer, regmaak; vergoed.
reparation, herstel; vergoeding.
repatriate, repatrieer.
repay, terugbetaal; vergeld, beloon.
repeal, v. herroep, intrek; afskaf.
repeat, v. herhaal; nadoen, oordoen; oorvertel.
repel, verslaan, afweer; afstoot.
repent, berou hê; spyt voel.
repercussion, terugslag, skop; reaksie.
replace, terugsit; opvolg; vernuwe, vervang.
replica, kopie; faksimilee, nabootsing.
reply, n. antwoord; repliek.
report, rapporteer; berig, vertel; (sig) aanmeld.
report, n. gerug; rapport; tyding; knal.
reporter, verslaggewer, beriggewer.
reprehensible, berispelik, laakbaar.
represent, voorstel; voorgee; verteenwoordig.
representative, n. verteenwoordiger.
repress, onderdruk, in bedwang hou.
reprieve, v. uitstel, opskort.
reprimand, v. teregwys, bestraf, berispe.
reprint, herdruk.
reprisal, weerwraak, wraakoefening.
reproach, v. beskuldig, verwyt.
reproduce, reproduseer; weergee.
reproduction, reproduksie; kopie; weergawe.
reprove, berispe, bestraf, skrobbeer.
reptile, n. reptiel; wurm.
republic, republiek, gemenebes.
repudiate, verwerp; ontken.
repugnant, teenstrydig; afkerig; walglik, stuitend.
repulse, terugdrywe, verslaan; afskrik.
reputable, fatsoenlik, agtenswaardig.
reputation, goeie naam, reputasie.
repute, v. ag, beskou, reken.
request, v. versoek, vra; verlang.
require, eis, vorder, vereis; begeer; nodig hê.
requirement, vereiste; behoefte; -s, benodigdhede, behoeftes.
requisite, a. nodig, vereis.
requisition, n. aansoek, eis; opeising; oproep,
  rekwisisie.
requite, vergeld, beloon.
reread, oorlees, herlees.
rescind, herroep, nietig verklaar; afskaf.
rescue, v. red, bevry, verlos.
research, n. navorsing, ondersoek(ing).
resemblance, ooreenkoms, gelykenis.
resemble, lyk na, aard na, trek na.
resent, kwalik neem, beledig voel oor.
resentment, gebelgdheid, boosheid; wrok.
reservation, voorbehoud.
reserve, v. terughou, agterhou, bewaar;
  spreek; voorbehou.
reserve, n. reserwe; voorraad; voorbehoud; beskeidenheid.
reserved, bespreekte; ingetoë.
reservoir, dam, reservoir.
reside, woon, bly; berus.
resident, n. inwoner, bewoner.
residue, oorblyfsel, res; besinksel.
resign, bedank; afstand doen van; (sig) onderwerp aan.
resilient, elasties, veerkragtig.

resin, rosin, n. harpuis; gom, hars.
resist, weerstaan, weerstand bied, (sig) verset teen.
resole, versool.
resolute, vasberade, beslis.
resolve, besluit; ontbind, ontleed.
resonant, weerklinkend, weergalmend.
resort, v. toevlug neem (tot).
resort, n. uitvlug, uitweg; sameloop; oord.
resourceful, vindingryk.
respect, n. agting, eerbied; opsig; betrekking.
respect, v. respekteer, ag; ontsien.
respectable, fatsoenlik, agtenswaardig.
respectfully, beleef(d), hoogagtend.
respectively, onderskeidelik.
respiration, asemhaling.
respite, n. uitstel; verposing, rus.
respond, (be)antwoord; regeer (op).
respondent, n. verweerder; verdediger.
response, antwoord.
responsibility, verantwoordelikheid.
responsible, verantwoordelik.
rest, v. rus, uitrus; laat rus, rus gee; leun; steun; berus (op); baseer (op).
rest, n. rus; slaap; kalmte; pouse; bok (by biljart).
rest, n. oorskiet (oorskot), res.
restaurant, restourant, eethuis.
restful, rustig, stil, kalm; rusgewend.
restitution, vergoeding; restitusie.
restive, koppig, eiewys, steeks.
restless, rusteloos, onrustig, woelig.
restore, teruggee; herstel; vernuwe, regmaak; genees; terugbring.
restrain, in toom hou, bedwing.
restraint, dwang, beperking, bedwang.
restrict, beperk, bepaal; inkrimp.
result, v. uitloop (op), lei (tot); volg.
result, n. uitslag; gevolg, uitwerking.
resume, v. terugkry; terugneem; vervolg; weer inneem; opsom.
résumé, n. opsomming, saamvatting.
resumption, hervatting; herneming.
resurrection, herrysenis, opstanding.
resuscitate, laat herlewe, opwek.
retail, n. kleinhandel.
retail dealer, kleinhandelaar.
retain, hou, behou; onthou; terughou; aanhou.
retaining fee, honorarium.
retaliate, terugbetaal, vergeld.
retard, vertraag; uitstel; agteruitsit; belemmer.
retch, kokhals, brul.
reticent, terughoudend, swygsaam, stil.
retinue, stoet, gevolg.
retire, v. terugwyk, vlug, retireer; (sig) terug-trek; (sig) verwyder; aftree, uit diens tree; gaan rentenier.
retort, n. vinnige (gevatte) antwoord.
retort, n. retort, kromhals, kolffles.
retract, intrek; terugtrek; herroep.
retread, v. versool; n. versoolde band.
retreat, v. terugwyk, terugtrek.
retreat, n. terugtog; stil verblyfplek; skuilplek.
retrench, verminder, beperk, besuinig.
retribution, vergelding, beloning.
retrieve, v. terugvind; vergoed; red.
retroactive, terugwerkend.
retrograde, a. agterwaarts, teruggaand(e).
retrospective, terugwerkend; terugblikkend.
return, v. terugkom, teruggaan; teruggee, terug-stuur.
return, n. terugkoms; wins; terugbetaling; (die) terugstuur; verkiesing; verslag, opgawe.
reveal, openbaar; uitbring; verraai.

revel, v. pret maak; drink; – in, (sig) verlustig in.
revenge, n. wraak, wraakneming.
revenue, inkomste.
revere, vereer; eerbiedig, eer.
reverie, mymering, gepeins.
reverse, v. omdraai, omkeer; omsit; agteruitry; herroep.
reverse, n. teenoorgestelde; agterkant; teen-spoed; neerlaag.
revert, terugval; terugkeer, terugkom.
review, v. hersien; terugkyk op; resenseer; in-speksie hou.
revile, beskimp, slegmaak, uitskel.
revise, v. nasien, hersien, verbeter, wysig.
revive, herlewe, weer oplewe; verlewendig, weer aanvuur; weer in die lewe roep.
revoke, herroep, intrek, terugtrek.
revolt, v. rebelleer, opstaan; oproerig word; (sig) verset; walg.
revolt, n. opstand, oproer, rebellie.
revolution, omwenteling; opstand; revolusie.
revolutionize, omwenteling teweegbring.
revolve, draai, omdraai; oordink.
revolver, rewolwer.
revulsion, om(me)keer.
reward, n. beloning, vergelding.
reward, v. beloon, vergoed; vergeld.
rewrite, oorskryf, omwerk.
Reynard, Reinard, Broer Jakkals.
rhapsody, rapsodie.
Rhenish, n. Rynwyn.
rhetorical, retories.
rheumatism, rumatiek.
Rhine, Ryn.
rhinoceros, renoster.
rhombus, rombus, ruit.
rhubarb, rabarber.
rhyme, rime, n. rym; rympie.
rhyme, rime, v. rym; laat rym.
rhythm, maat; ritme.
rib, n. rib(betjie); ribstuk; ribbebeen.
rib, v. riffel.
ribald, liederlik, vuil, smerig.
ribbon, lint, band.
rice, rys.
rich, ryk, vermoënd; vrugbaar; kragtig; klank-vol.
riches, rykdom.
rickets, Engelse siekte.
rickety, swak, lendelam.
ricksha(w), riksja.
ricochet, v. wegskram, opslaan.
rid, bevry, ontslaan, verlos; be – of, ontslae wees van.
riddle, n. raaisel.
ride, v. ry; laat ry.
ride, n. rit, toertjie.
rider, ruiter, ryer; bygevoegde klousule; pro-bleem.
ridge, n. rug, rant, bergrug; rif, kam; vors, nok; maanhaar (in 'n pad).
ridicule, v. belaglik maak, bespot.
rife, heersend, algemeen.
rifle, n. (koeël)geweer.
rifleman, (skerp)skutter.
rifle-range, skietbaan; skietafstand.
rift, n. bars, skeur, kraak.
right, a. reg, billik; waar; regter.
right, v. herstel, regmaak; reg laat wedervaar; regsit.
right, n. reg, aanspraak; regterkant; regterhand.
right, adv. reg; regs; behoorlik; regverdig.
righteous, regverdig, regskape.
rightful, wettig, regmatig; regverdig.
rigid, styf, onbuigsaam; streng; stip.

rigorous, streng, straf, hard.
rim, n. kant, rant; lys; velling.
rind, n. skil; bas; skors; buitenste.
ring, n. ring; kring, sirkel.
ring, v. lui, klink; weerklink; bel.
ringleader, belhamel, voorperd.
ringworm, douwurm, omloop.
rink, n. skaatsbaan, ysbaan.
rink, v. skaats, op (rol)skaats ry.
rinse, uitspoel, afspoel.
riot, n. drinkgelag; oproer, opstand.
rip, v. (oop)skeur, (los)skeur, (af)skeur, (los) torring.
ripe, ryp.
ripen, ryp word; laat ryp word.
ripple, v. kabbel, rimpel, golf.
rip-saw, kloofsaag, treksaag.
rise, v. opstaan; opkom, rys, styg; in opstand kom; toeneem; ontspring; voortspruit, ontstaan.
rise, n. opgang, styging; verhoging, opkoms; hoogte, bult.
risk, n. gevaar, waagstuk.
risk, v. riskeer, waag.
risky, gevaarlik, gewaag.
rissole, frikkadelletjie.
rite, (kerk)gebruik, plegtigheid, ritus.
ritual, n. rituaal, bepaling; ritueel.
rival, n. mededinger.
river, rivier, stroom.
rivet, n. klinknael.
rivet, v. (vas)klink, vasnael.
road, pad, weg; rede.
roam, swerf, ronddool, rondtrek.
roan, a. rooiskimmel.
roar, v. brul; bulder, raas, dreun.
roast, v. braai; rooster, (koffie) brand.
rob, (be)steel, (be)roof, ontroof, plunder.
robber, rower, dief.
robot, robot, verkeerslig.
robust, sterk, kragtig, frisgebou.
rock, n. rots, klip, steen(rots).
rock, v. wieg, skuld; wankel.
rockery, rotstuin(tjie).
rocket, vuurpyl; raket; – **aircraft**, raketvliegtuig.
rock-rabbit, (klip)dassie.
rod, roede; stok, staf, meetroede; stang, trekbout.
rodent, knaagdier.
roe, viskuit, viseiertjies.
rogue, skurk, skelm; vabond.
role, rol.
roll, n. rol; register, naamlys.
roll, v. rol, oprol, platrol; laat rol; draai; slinger.
roll-call, naamaflesing.
roller-skate, rolskaats.
rolling-pin, rolstok.
Roman, a. Romeins; Rooms.
Roman, n. Romein.
Ro(u)manian, n. Roemeniër; Roemeens.
romantic, romanties, avontuurlik.
Rome, Rome.
romp, v. baljaar, stoei, jakker.
roof, n. dak; verhemelte.
rook, n. kasteel (skaakspel).
room, kamer, vertrek; plek, ruimte.
roomy, ruim.
roost, v. gaan slaap.
rooster, haan.
root, n. wortel; oorsprong, oorsaak.
rope, n. tou, lyn.
rosary, roostuin, paternoster.
rose, n. roos; roset; sproeier.
rosetta, roset, kokarde.
rosin, resin, harpuis.

rosy, rooskleurig; blosend, rose- . . .
rot, v. vrot, vergaan, bederwe.
Rotarian, Rotariër.
rotate, draai; laat draai; (af)wissel.
rotation, rotasie; afwisseling.
rotten, vrot; beroerd, sleg; korrup.
rotter, deugniet, niksnuts, vrotterd.
rouge, n. (rooi) blanketsel.
rouge, v. verf.
rough, a. grof, ru, hard; wild, woes; ongelyk; onafgewerk; onstuimig.
rough-cast, v. rofkas; ruwe skets.
roughly, naasteby, min of meer.
round, a. rond.
round, n. kring, bol; omgang, omloop; rondte.
round, prep. (rond)om.
round, adv. om.
roundly, kortaf, ronduit, botweg.
rouse, wakker maak; aanspoor.
rout, v. verslaan, op die vlug ja.
route, weg, pad, koers.
routine, sleur, gewoonte; roetine.
rove, v. (rond)swerf, dwaal.
row, n. ry; reeks.
row, v. roei.
row, n. rusie, twis; rumoer, lawaai.
rowdy, a. luidrugtig, lawaaierig.
royal, koninklik, vorstelik; rojaal.
rub, v. vrywe, skuur; skawe; polys.
rubber, n. rubber, gomlastiek; uitveër.
rubbish, vuilgoed, vullis, afval; rommel; prulwerk; onsin.
rubble, afval; steengruis.
ruby, n. robyn; (rooi) puisie.
ruck, n. trop, hoop, klomp, massa.
rucksack, rugsak, bladsak.
rudder, roer, stuur.
rude, ru, grof; onbeskof; primitief.
rudimentary, rudimentêr, elementêr.
rue, v. betreur, berou hê oor.
ruffian, n. booswig, skurk.
ruffle, v. deurmekaar maak, frommel; rimpel; vererg, verstoor.
rug, reiskombers, reisdeken; vloermatjie.
rugby, (football), rugbyvoetbal.
rugged, ruig, ru; ongelyk, skurf; nors, streng; lomp; kragtig, sterk.
ruin, n. verderf, ondergang; ruïne, puinhoop, bouval, murasie.
ruin, v. ruïneer (rinneweer), tot 'n val bring, bederf; vernietig, verniel.
rule, n. reël, bepaling, reglement; maatstaf, standaard; voorskrif; beheer, gesag, regering, bewind; maatstok.
rule, v. regeer, beheer; vasstel; linieer.
ruler, heerser, vors; duimstok, liniaal.
ruling, n. beslissing, uitspraak.
rumble, v. rommel, dreun; ratel, raas.
ruminate, herkou.
rummage sale, rommelverkoping.
rumour, n. gerug.
rumple, kreukel, vou, verfrommel.
rump steak, biefstuk.
run, v. hardloop; loop; laat loop; laat wei; laat oploop; vloei; traan, drup; lui; smokkel.
run, n. lopie; toeloop; wedren; ritjie; verloop; (hoender)hok; vry gebruik, toegang.
rung, sport.
runner, hardloper; rank, spruit.
rupture, n. breuk; tweespalk.
rural, plattelands, landelik.
ruse, streek, lis.
rush, biesie.
rust, v. hardloop, hol; bestorm, stormloop; jaag.
rush, n. vaart, haas; stormloop; toeloop.

rusk, beskuit.
Russia, Rusland.
Russian, n. Rus; Russies.
rust, n. roes.
rust, v. roes, verroes; laat roes.
rustic, a. landelik; plattelands; lomp.
rustle, v. ritsel, ruis.

rustler, veedief.
rusty, geroes, verroes; stram; krassend, skor
   roeskleurig.
rut, n. wielspoor, moet; roetine.
ruthless, meedoënloos, wreed.
rye, rog.

Sabbath, Sabbat(dag), rusdag.
sable, swart; swartwitpens.
sabotage, sabotasie.
sabre, n. sabel.
sack, n. sak.
sack, v. plunder, verwoes.
sacrament, sakrament.
sacred, heilig, gewyd.
sacrifice, n. offerande; opoffering.
sacrifice, v. offer; opoffer.
sacrilege, heiligskennis, ontheiliging.
sad, treurig, droewig, bedroef.
sadden, bedroef, treurig stem.
saddle, n. saal; bergrug; stut.
saddle, v. opsaal; belas.
saddle-cloth, saalkleedjie.
sadism, sadisme.
safe, n. brandkas; (bewaar)kluis; koskas.
safe, a. veilig, seker; ongedeerd.
safeguard, v. beskerm, beveilig; verseker.
safety, veiligheid, sekerheid.
safety-belt, reddingsgordel, reddingsboei.
safety-pin, haakspeld, knipspeld.
safety razor, veiligheidskeermes.
safety-valve, veiligheidsklep.
sag, v. uitsak, afsak, afhang, skiet, pap (slap) hang.
saga, saga; sage, legende.
sagacious, skerpsinnig, slim, skrander.
sage, a. wys, verstandig.
sago, sago.
Sahara, Sahara.
sail, n. seil.
sail, v. seil, vaar; laat seil; trek.
sailor, seeman, matroos.
saint, n. heilige, vrome.
sake: for the – of, ter wille van; for my –, ter wille van my.
salad, slaai.
salary, n. salaris, loon, besoldiging.
sale, verkoping, (uit)verkoop; vandisie (vendusie).
salesman, verkoper; winkelklerk.
salient, uitspringend; opvallend.
saliva, spoeg (spuug); speeksel.
sallow, bleek, geel, sieklik.
salmon, n. salm.
saloon, salon, saal; drinkplek.
salt, n. sout.
salt, v. sout, insout, pekel.
saltpetre, salpeter.
salutary, heilsaam, voordelig, gesond.
salute, v. groet, begroet, salueer.
salute, n. groet, begroeting; saluut.
salvage, v. red, berg.
salvation, redding, verlossing, heil.
Salvation Army, Heilsleër.
salve, n. salf, smeersel; balsem.
salvo, salvo, sarsie.
sal volatile, vlugsout.
Samaritan, n. Samaritaan.
same, (die)selfde; einste; genoemde.
samp, gestampte mielies.
sample, n. monster, staaltjie; voorbeeld.
sample, v. monsters (staaltjies) neem (uitdeel); probeer, proe.
Samson, Simson.
sanatorium, sanatorium.
sanctify, heilig, heilig maak, wy.
sanction, n. goedkeuring, toestemming, strafmaatreël.
sanction, v. goedkeur, bekragtig.
sanctuary, heiligdom, toevlugsoord.
sand, n. sand.
sandal, sandaal.

sandpaper, n. skuurpapier.
sandwich, n. toebroodjie.
sane, by jou volle verstand; verstandig.
sanguinary, bloedig; moorddadig.
sanguine, optimisties, hoopvol; vurig.
sanitary, gesondheids- . . . , higiënies, sanitêr.
Santa Claus, Sinterklaas.
sap, n. sap, vog; lewenskrag.
sap, v. tap; droog maak; ondermyn.
sapper, myngrawer, sappeur.
sapphire, v. saffier.
sarcastic, sarkasties, bytend, spottend.
sarcophagus, sarkofaag.
sardine, sardientjie.
sardonic, bitter, sinies, spottend.
sash, serp, gord, lyfband.
sash, (skuif)raam.
Satan, Satan.
satellite, satelliet, byplaneet; handlanger.
satiate, v. versadig, bevredig; sat maak.
satin, n. satyn.
satire, satire, spotskrif, hekelskrif.
satisfactory, bevredigend; voldoende.
satisfy, bevredig, voldoen; oortuig; versadig.
saturate, deurweek, deurtrek; versadig.
Saturday, Saterdag.
Saturn, Saturnus.
sauce, n. sous; vrypostigheid.
saucepan, kastrol.
saucer, piering.
saunter, v. slenter, drentel, kuier.
sausage, wors, sosys.
savage, a. wild, woes; wreed, woedend.
savage, n. barbaar; woestaard, wreedaard.
save, v. red, verlos; bewaar; spaar.
savings-bank, spaarbank.
Saviour, Heiland, Verlosser.
savour, v. smaak; ruik.
savoury, a. smaaklik, geurig, lekker.
savoury, n. southappie; sout nagereggie.
saw, n. saag; cross-cut –, treksaag.
saw, v. saag (sae).
sawdust, saagsel.
Saxon, n. Angel-Sakser; Saksies.
saxophone, saxofoon.
say, v. sê, beweer; opsê.
saying, gesegde, spreekwoord.
scab, skurfte, brandsiekte; kors, roof.
scabbard, skede.
scabies, skurfte.
scaffold, n. skavot; steier, stellasie.
scaffolding, steierhout, stellasie.
scald, v. (met kookwater) brand, skroei.
scale, n. skub; skilfer; lagie.
scale, n. (weeg)skaal.
scale, n. skaal; toonskaal; stelsel; maatstaf.
scale, v. beklim, opklouter.
scalp, n. skedel; kopvel.
scalpel, ontleedmes.
scamp, skurk, skelm, vabond.
scamper, v. hardloop, weghol; galop.
scan, skandeer; bekyk, beskou.
scandal, skandaal, skande; skindery.
scandalmonger, kwaadprater, skindertong.
scandalous, skandelik, lasterlik.
scant, a. karig, skraal, gering.
scapegoat, sondebok.
scar, n. merk, litteken.
scarce, skaars; seldsaam.
scarcely, nouliks, ternouernood, skaars.
scare, v. skrik maak, bang maak, afskrik.
scare, n. vrees, skrik.
scarecrow, voëlverskrikker.
scarf, n. serp, halsdoek.

scarlet, a. skarlakenrooi; – fever, skarlaken-
koors.
scathing, vlymend, skerp, verpletterend.
scatter, strooi, verstrooi, versprei; uiteendrywe.
scatter-brained, warhoofdig.
scavenge, straat vee, opruim, skoonmaak.
scene, toneel, tafereel; voorval.
scenery, natuurskoon; toneeldekorasie.
scent, n. ruik (reuk), geur; laventel, ruikgoed;
odeur; spoor.
sceptical, skepties, ongelowig.
sceptre, septer, staf.
schedule, n. lys, opgaaf, staat.
scheme, n. skema, plan, ontwerp, skets.
scheme, v. planne maak (beraam); knoei, konkel.
scholar, skolier, leerling; geleerde.
school, n. skool, skoolgebou; leerskool.
school, n. skool (van visse).
school-board, skoolraad.
sciatica, heupjig.
science, wetenskap; kennis.
scientific, (natuur)wetenskaplik.
scientist, (natuur)wetenskaplike.
scintillate, vonkel, flikker, skitter.
scion, spruit, steggie; afstammeling.
scissors, skêr.
scoff, v. spot, skimp, bespot.
scold, v. uitskel, berispe, inklim.
scone, botterkoekie.
scoop, n. skop, skepper, skeplepel, skepemmer;
wins, slag; nuustreffer.
scoop, v. (uit)skep, uithol; 'n slag slaan.
scope, (speel)ruimte, geleentheid, kans; vryheid;
bestek; gesigskring; doel.
scorch, brand, (ver)skroei, verseng; nael, woes
(wild) ry.
score, n. keep, kerf, snytjie; streep, skraap, merk,
hou; telling; twintigtal.
score, v. kerfies maak; slaan; opskryf, tel, die
telling hou, opteken; (punte) behaal.
scorn, v. verag, versmaad, minag.
scorpion, skerpioen.
Scotchman, Skot, Skotsman.
Scotland, Skotland.
scoundrel, skurk, skobbejak, skelm
scour, v. skuur, vrywe, suiwer.
scour, v. deurkruis, rondsoek.
scourge, v. gesel; kasty, teister.
scout, n. verkenner, spioen; boy –, padvinder.
scout, v. verken, spioen.
scowl, n. frons, suur gesig.
scraggy, maer, skraal.
scramble, v. klouter; spook, woel.
scrap, n. stukkie, brokkie; uitknipsel.
scrap, v. weggooi, afkeur.
scrap-book, snipperboek, uitknipselboek.
scrape, v. skraap, krap; kras; polys.
scrape, n. gekrap; moeilikheid.
scratch, v. krap, skrap, skraap; uithol; terugtrek, skrap.
scratch-race, gelykstaan-wedren.
scrawl, n. gekrap, hanepote.
scream, v. skree(u), gier, gil.
screech, v. gil, skreeu, gier.
screen, n. skerm; beskutting; doek; groot sif.
screen, v. beskerm, beskut, verberg; sif.
screw, n. skroef.
screw, v. (vas)skroewe.
screwdriver, skroewedraaier.
scribble, v. krap, afkrabbel.
script, manuskrip; handskrif; skryfletter.
scripture, die (Heilige) Skrif, die Bybel.
scroll, rol, perkamentrol; lys; krul.
scrub, n. ruigte, struikgewas; armoedige dier.
scrub, v. skrop, skuur; swoeg.

scruff, nek.
scrum, skrum.
scruple, n. beswaar, aarseling, gewetensbeswaar.
scruple, v. aarsel, beswaar maak.
scrupulous, nougeset, sorgvuldig, noukeurig.
scrutinise, noukeurig ondersoek, navors.
scud, v. vlieg, voortsnel, gly.
scuffle, v. worstel, baklei, stoei.
scullery, opwasplek, bykombuis.
sculptor, beeldhouer.
sculpture, v. beeldhou, uithou; graveer.
scum, n. skuim; uitvaagsel, uitskot.
scurrilous, laag, gemeen, vuil, plat, grof.
scurry, v. (weg)hardloop, wegyl.
scuttle, n. koolbak, koolemmer.
scuttle, v. gate inboor, laat sink.
sea, see, oseaan; golf.
sea-gull, seemeeu.
seal, rob, seehond.
seal, n. seël; stempel; bevestiging.
seal, v. seël, verseël, lak.
sea level, seespieël, seevlak.
sealing-wax, lak.
seam, n. naat; litteken; (kool)laag.
sear, v. brand, skroei, verseng.
search, v. soek; ondersoek, naspeur; deursoek,
visenteer; peil.
searching, a. deurdringend; noukeurig.
searchlight, soeklig.
search-warrant, visentasiemagbrief; visenteer-
brief.
season, n. seisoen; jaargety; tyd.
season, v. geskik maak; laat ryp word; (laat)
droog word; kruie (ingooi); temper.
seat, n. sitplek, bank, stoel; setel; sitting; toneel;
landgoed, buiteplaas; sit.
seaweed, seegras, seewier.
secede, afskei, terugtrek, sedeer.
seclusion, afsondering.
second, a. tweede; ander.
second, n. tweede, ander; sekondant, getuie;
sekonde.
secondary, a. sekondêr; ondergeskik.
seconder, sekondant.
second-hand, tweedehands, halfslyt.
secondly, in die tweede plek, ten tweede.
secret, a. geheim; verborge, heimlik.
secret, n. geheim.
secretary, sekretaris; minister.
secretary-bird, sekretarisvoël.
secrete, wegsteek, versteek; afskei.
secretly, stilletjies, in die geheim.
sect, sekte.
sectarian, a. sektaries.
section, verdeling; deel; afdeling; deursnee;
seksie.
sector, sektor.
secular, wêreldlik, tydelik; eeue-oud; blywend.
secure, v. beveilig, beskerm; vasmaak, sluit;
vrywaar, waarborg, verseker, (ver)kry, bereik.
security, sekuriteit, waarborg, borg, pand; veiligheid.
sedan, sedan, toe motor; draagstoel.
sedate, bedaard, stemmig, kalm.
sedative, n. kalmeermiddel.
sediment, afsaksel, besinksel, moer.
sedition, opstand, muitery, sedisie.
seduce, verlei, verlok.
sedulous, ywerig, vlytig, naarstig.
see, v. sien, kyk, aanhou; begryp, insien, verstaan; sorg, oppas; besoek.
see, n. bisdom; pouslike hof.
seed, n. saad; nakomelinge.
seedling, plantjie, saaiplant.
seed-potato, aartappelmoer.

seedy, siekerig, kaduks; oes.
seeing, conj.: – that, aangesien.
seek, v. soek; probeer; verlang, begeer.
seem, lyk, skyn; deurgaan vir.
seemly, betaamlik, welvoeglik, gepas.
seer, siener, profeet.
see-saw, n. wipplank.
seethe, kook, sied.
segment, segment; gedeelte.
segregate, afsonder, isoleer, afskei.
seize, vat, gryp, neem; in beslag (in besit) neem, beslag lê op; konfiskeer.
seldom, selde, min.
select, v. uitsoek, uitkies, kies.
selection, keuse; seleksie; versameling.
self, self, ekheid, eie-ek.
self-assertion, aanmatiging.
self-assurance, selfvertroue.
self-control, selfbeheersing.
self-defence, selfverdediging.
self-esteem, selfagting, selfrespek.
self-importance, verwaandheid, eiedunk.
selfish, selfsug, baatsugtig.
self-possession, selfbeheersing.
self-preservation, selfbehoud.
self-righteous, eiegeregtig.
selfsame, einste, presies, dieselfde.
self-satisfied, selfvoldaan.
self-service, selfbediening; – shop, selfhelpwinkel.
self-starter, aansitter.
self-sufficient, selfgenoegsaam, verwaand.
self-willed, eiegeregtig, koppig, eiewys.
sell, v. verkoop; verraai, bedrieg.
selvage, -edge, selfkant.
semblance, skyn, voorkome.
semi-circle, halwe sirkel (halfsirkel).
semicolon, kommapunt.
seminary, seminarie, kweekskool.
Semitic, Semities.
senate, senaat; Hoërhuis.
senator, senator.
send, stuur, wegstuur, (ver)send.
sender, (af)sender.
senile, ouderdoms- . . . , seniel.
senior, a. senior: ouer, oudste.
sensation, gewaarwording, aandoening; sensasie, opskudding.
sense, n. sin, sintuig; gevoel, gewaarwording; besef, begrip; betekenis.
sense, v. gewaar(word), voel, aanvoel.
sensible, merkbaar; bewus; verstandig.
sensitive, fyngevoelig, liggeraak.
sensual, sinlik, wellustig, vleeslik.
sensuous, sin- . . . , van die sinne, sinnelik.
sentence, n. vonnis, uitspraak; (vol)sin.
sentence, v. veroordeel, vonnis.
sententious, bondig, kernagtig, pittig.
sentiment, gevoel, sentiment; mening.
sentimental, sentimenteel, oorgevoelig.
sentinel, n. wag, brandwag, skildwag.
sentry, wag, brandwag.
separate, a. afsonderlik, apart.
separate, v. skei, afskei, verdeel.
separator, afskeier; roomafskeier.
September, September.
septic, septies.
sepulchre, n. graf.
sequel, gevolg; uitvloeisel, nasleep.
sequence, reeks, opvolging, volgorde.
Serb, n. Serwiër.
serene, helder; kalm, stil; bedaard.
sergeant, sersant.
serial, n. vervolgverhaal.
series, reeks, serie; aaneenskakeling.

serious, ernstig; stemmig; gewigtig; gevaarlik; deeglik.
sermon, preek; vermaning.
serum, serum, entstof.
serval, tierboskat.
servant, bediende, kneg, diensbode; dienaar, dienares; amptenaar.
serve, v. diens, van diens wees, bedien, baat; voldoende wees; uitdien; dek; afslaan (in tennis).
Servia, Serbia, Serwië.
service, diens, diensbaarheid; (kerk)diens stel; (die) afslaan (in tennis).
serviceable, nuttig, bruikbaar, dienlik.
serviette, servet.
servile, slaafs, onderworpe; kruiperig.
session, sitting, sessie.
set, v. sit (set), plaas, stel; aansit; bepaal, reël, skik; spalk; styf word, hard word; ondergaan (van die son).
set, n. stel; servies; groep, klompie, span; kliek; kring; steggie; stel (in tennis).
set, a. vas, bepaal(d) vasgestel.
set-back, teenslag, klap, knou.
set-square, tekendriehoek.
settee, rusbank, sofa, sitbank.
setter, jaghond, patryshond.
setting, raam, omlysting, montering; broeisel eiers; toneelskikking.
settle, v. (sig) vestig; tot bedaring kom, tot bedaring bring; bepaal, vasstel, reël, in orde bring, regmaak, vereffen; gaan sit; afsak, helder word; koloniseer.
settlement, skikking, reëling; volksplanting, betaling; kontrak.
settler, kolonis, nedersetter, setlaar.
seven, sewe.
seventeen, sewentien.
seventy, sewentig.
sever, skei; afskeur, afkap, afsny.
several, a. verskeie; indiwidueel; respektief; eie; afsonderlik.
several, pron. verskeie.
severe, straf, hard, streng; wreed; ernstig, swaar.
sew, naai.
sewer, n. riool (riool).
sewerage, rioolstelsel, riolering.
sewing-machine, naaimasjien.
sex, geslag.
sex appeal, geslagsattraksie.
sextant, sekstant, hoogtemeter.
sexton, koster.
sexual, seksueel, geslags- . . .
shabby, gemeen, veragtelik; armoedig, slordig, verslyt.
shackle, n. boei, skakel, kram.
shackle, v. boei; belemmer, hinder.
shade, n. skaduwee; koelte; kleur(skakering); skerm; kap; skim; tikkie.
shadow, n. skaduwee; gees, spook; bewys, spoor.
shadow, v. oorskadu; stilletjies volg.
shady, skaduryk; oneerlik, verdag.
shaft, spies; pyl; disselboom; steel; skag.
shaggy, harig, wolhaar; ruig.
shake, v. skud, ruk; uitskud; bewe, bibber.
shaky, onvas, wikkelrig; bewerig; swak, onseker.
shale, leiklip.
shall, sal; moet.
shallow, a. vlak, ondiep; oppervlakkig.
sham, v. voorgee, veins, aanstel, maak asof; bedrieg.
sham, n. bedrog; voorwendsel, skyn, bluf.
sham, a. vals, geveins, aanstellerig.
shambles, slagpale, slagplek; bloedbad.
shambling, waggelend, sloffend.

shame, n. skaamte; skande.
shame, v. beskaam, beskaamd maak.
shameful, skandelik.
shameless, onbeskaamd, skaamteloos.
shampoo, v. hare was.
shampoo, n. kopwas-, haarwasmiddel, sjampoe.
shanty, pondok, hutjie; hok.
shape, v. vorm, maak, fatsoeneer, modelleer; uitwerk.
shape, n. fatsoen, vorm, model; gedaante.
share, n. deel, gedeelte, porsie; aandeel.
share, v. deel, verdeel, uitdeel.
share, n. (ploeg)skaar.
shareholder, aandeelhouer.
shark, n. haai; woekeraar, uitsuier.
sharp, a. skerp, spits, puntig; bitsig, venynig; bytend; deurdringend; skerpsinnig, slim, vlug; oulik, geslepe, listig; vinnig, haastig, snel.
sharp, adv. gou; presies.
sharpen, skerp maak, slyp.
sharp-shooter, skerpskutter.
shatter, verpletter, verbrysel, ruïneer; skok; verydel.
shave, v. skeer; skawe; verbyskram.
shaver, skeertoestel, skeerapparaat.
shaving, (die) skeer; krul, skaafsel.
shaving-brush, skeerkwas(sie).
shawl, tjalie, sjaal.
she, sy.
sheaf, n. gerf; bondel.
shear, skeer; knip, sny.
shears, (tuin)skêr, skaapskêr.
sheath, skede, huisie; vlerkskild, dop.
shed, v. stort; verloor; (ver)sprei, werp, uitstraal.
shed, n. skuur, afdak; loods.
sheen, glans, skittering, glinstering.
sheep, skaap, skape.
sheep-dip, skaapdip.
sheep-fold, skaapkraal.
sheer, a. louter, puur, suiwer; loodreg, regaf, steil.
sheet, n. laken; plaat; vlak, oppervlakte; vel (papier).
shelf, rak; plank; laag; sandbank.
shell, n. dop, peul, skil; skulp; geraamte; bom; neutedop; omhulsel.
shell, v. uitdop; beskiet.
shelter, n. beskutting, skuilplek.
shelter, v. beskut, beskerm.
shelve, rakke insit; uitstel.
shelving, n. rakke; rakplanke.
shepherd, n. skaapwagter, herder.
sheriff, balju, skout.
sherry, sjerrie.
shield, n. skild; wapenskild; skerm.
shift, v. versit, verplaas; verander; omruil, vervang; verhuis.
shift, n. verandering, afwisseling; ploeg (werksmense), klompie; skof; uitvlug, lis; hulpmiddel.
shifty, skelm.
shilling, sjieling.
shim, keil, wig; onderlegplaatjie.
shimmer, v. glinster, glans, skemer.
shin, skeen, maermerrie.
shine, v. skyn, blink; blink maak; uitblink.
shine, n. glans, skyn.
shiny, glansend, blink.
ship, n. skip, vaartuig.
ship, v. verskeep; aan boord neem; inskeep.
shipment, lading, besending; verskeping.
shipping-agent, skeepsagent.
shipshape, agtermekaar, in orde.
shipwreck, v. (laat) skipbreuk ly.

shirk, v. ontduik, versuim (werk, plig, ens.), vermy, ontseil.
shirt, hemp.
shiver, v. bewe, ril, sidder, huiwer.
shoal, n. klomp, trop; skool (visse).
shock, n. botsing; skok; slag.
shock, v. skok; 'n skok gee.
shock-absorber, skokdemper, skokbreker.
shoddy, a. nagemaak, prullerig.
shoe, n. skoen; hoefyster.
shoe, v. beslaan; skroei.
shoehorn, skoenlepel.
shoe-lace, skoenveter.
shoemaker, skoenmaker.
shoot, v. skiet, doodskiet; bot, uitloop; steek; vlieg, trek.
shoot, n. spruit, loot; glyplank; jagtog; skietwedstryd.
shop, n. winkel; werkplek.
shop, v. inkopies doen.
shopkeeper, winkelier.
shore, n. kus, strand, oewer.
shore, v. stut.
short, a. kort, klein; kortaf; bros; beknop; skrap.
short, adv. plotseling, skielik.
shortage, tekort.
short circuit, kortsluiting.
shortcoming, tekortkoming.
shorten, verkort, korter maak; korter word.
shorthand, snelskrif, stenografie.
shortly, binnekort, net-nou; kortliks.
shorts, kort broek.
shortsighted, kortsigtig; bysiende.
short-tempered, kortgebonde, opvlieënd.
short-winded, kortasem.
shot, skoot; hael; skutter.
shotgun, haelgeweer.
shoulder, n. skouer; skouerstuk; skof; blad.
shout, v. skree (skreeu), hard roep.
shove, v. stoot, stamp, skuif.
shovel, n. skop, skopgraaf.
show, v. shew, v. wys, toon; vertoon; bewys.
show, n. vertoning, tentoonstelling; voorstelling; skyn; vertoon.
show-case, uitstalkas.
shower, n. (reën)bui; stroom.
show-girl, verhoogmeisie.
show-room, toonkamer, uitstalkamer.
shred, n. flenter, stukkie, repie.
shred, v. stukkend sny (skeur).
shrew, wyf, heks, helleveeg.
shrewd, skrander, slim; lastig, slu.
shriek, v. gil, skree(u).
shriek, n. gil, skree(u).
shrike, janfiskaal, laksman.
shrill, deurdringend, snerpend, skerp.
shrine, altaar; heilige graf; tempel.
shrink, krimp, inkrimp, ineenkrimp.
shrivel, krimp, verskrompel, uitdroë.
shroud, n. omhulsel; kleed; lykkleed.
shrub, struik, bossie.
shrug, v. die skouers ophaal (optrek).
shudder, v. huiwer, sidder, gril, ril, ys.
shuffle, skuif, slof; (deurmekaar) skud, verwar.
shun, vermy, ontwyk.
shunt, v. rangeer, regstoot; uitstel.
shut, v. sluit, toemaak; toegaan.
shut, a. toe, gesluit.
shutter, hortjie, luik, blinding.
shuttle-cock, pluimbal, kuifbal.
shy, a. sku, skaam, beskroomd.
shy, v. skrik, wegvlie(g), wegspring.
Siam, Siam.
Siamese, Siamees.

Siberian, a. Siberies.
sibilant, a. sis . . . , sissend.
sibilant, n. sisklank.
sibilate, sis, sissend uitspreek.
sibyl, sibille, profetes, waarsegster.
sibyline, profetes, sibillyns.
Sicily, Sicilië.
sick, a. siek, ongesteld; naar.
sickle, sekel.
sick-leave, siekteverlof.
sickly, sieklik, swak; walglik.
side, n. sy, kant, rant; helling.
side, v. party trek, party kies.
sideboard, buffet.
side-car, sywaentjie, syspanwaentjie.
side-line, byverdienste; liefhebbery.
side-step, v. verbyspring.
sideward(s), sydelings, sywaarts.
sideways, sydelings, skuins.
siding, (spoorweg)halte; syspoor.
siege, beleg, beleëring.
sieve, n. sif.
sieve, v. sif.
sift, sif; ondersoek, naspeur; uitvra.
sigh, v. sug.
sigh, n. sug.
sight, n. (die) oë; (die) sien; gesig; vertoning;
skouspel; besienswaardigheid; visier, korrel
(van 'n geweer).
sign, n. teken, merk; voorteken; uithangbord.
sign, v. teken, onderteken.
signal, n. teken, sein, sinjaal.
signal, v. sein, sinjaleer; aankondig.
signal-box, -cabin, seinhuisie.
signature, naamtekening.
signet-ring, seëlring.
significance, betekenis, gewig, belang.
signify, aandui; beteken.
signpost, uithangbord; wegwys(t)er.
silence, n. stilte; stilswye.
silence, v. stil maak, die swye oplê.
silencer, knalpot, (knal)demper.
silent, stil.
Silesia, Silesië, Silesiese linne.
silhouette, n. silhoeët, skadubeeld.
silk, n. sy, systof.
silkworm, sywurm.
silky, syagtig, sag; glad, stroperig.
sill, vensterbank; drumpel (drempel).
silly, verspot, laf, stuitig; onnosel, dom.
silo, n. voerkuil.
silt, n. modder, slyk (slik), slib.
silver, n. silwer; silwergeld; silwergoed.
similar, eenders, gelyksoortig; gelykvormig.
similarly, op dieselfde manier, net so.
simile, vergelyking.
simmer, borrel; sing (van ketel); saggies (effentjies) kook.
simple, a. eenvoudig; enkel, skoon, louter;
enkelvoudig; onskuldig; onnosel.
simpleton, lummel, swaap.
simplify, vereenvoudig.
simply, enkel, eenvoudig, louter, puur.
simulate, veins, voorgee; naboots.
simultaneous, gelyktydig.
sin, n. sonde, oortreding.
sin, v. sondig.
since, adv. daarna; gelede.
since, prep. sedert, sinds, van . . . af.
since, conj. sedert, sinds; aangesien, daar.
sincere, openhartig, opreg, eerlik; eg.
sinew, sening, spier.
sing, sing; besing; gons; suis.
singe, skroei, seng, afbrand.
singer, sanger(es).

single, a. enkel; enkelvoudig; ongetroud, alleen;
eenpersoons- . . .
single, n. enkelspel; een lopie (krieket).
single, v. – out, uitkies, uitsoek.
singlet, onderhempie, frokkie.
singular, a. enkelvoudig; buitengewoon; sonderling; seldsaam.
singular, n. enkelvoud.
sinister, onheilspellend, rampspoedig; kwaadaardig; sinister.
sink, v. sink, sak, daal, val, laat sink; laat sak;
laat val; laat hang; swak word, beswyk;
grawe.
sink, n. afwasbak, wasbak.
sinker, dieplood, sinklood.
sinner, sondaar.
sip, v. slurp, insuie.
siphon, v. opsuig, hewel, aftrap, oortrap.
sir, meneer, seur; sir.
siren, verleister; mishoring; sirene.
sirloin, lendestuk (van beesvleis).
sister, suster; non; pleegsuster.
sister-in-law, skoonsuster.
sit, sit; sitting hê (hou); broei; poseer.
site, ligging; (bou)terrein.
sitting, n. sitting; broeisel eiers.
sitting-room, sitkamer, voorkamer; sitplek.
situated, situate, geleë.
situation, ligging; posisie, toestand, situasie;
betrekking.
six, ses.
sixpence, sikspens.
sixteen, sestien.
sixty, sestig.
size, n. grootte, omvang, maat; nommer; formaat.
size, v. lym.
sjambok, sambok.
skate, n. skaats.
skate, v. skaats.
skein, string; knoop, warboel.
skeleton, geraamte, skelet; skets.
skeleton-key, loper, slotoopsteker.
sketch, skets.
skew, skeef, skuins.
skewer, vleispen, sosatiepen.
ski, n. ski, sneeuskaats.
ski, v. ski, sneeuskaatse ry.
skid, v. rem; gly, uitgly, glip, skuiwe.
skill, bekwaamheid, knapheid.
skilled, bekwaam, bedrewe, geskool.
skim, v. afskuim, afskep, afroom; vlugtig deur-
lees (deurkyk); gly oor (deur).
skin, n. vel, huid; skil, vlies.
skin, v. toegroei; afslag.
skinflint, vrek, geldwolf.
skip, v. spring, huppel; riemspring; oorslaan,
uitlaat, oorspring.
skipping-rope, springtou, springriem.
skirmish, n. skermutseling.
skirt, n. rok; kant, rant, soom.
skirt, v. langs die kant gaan, omsoom.
skulk, loer, sluip, skuil; ontwyk.
skull, skedel, kopbeen.
skunk, muishond; smeerlap, vuilgoed.
sky, n. lug, hemel.
skylight, dakvenster, dakraam, vallig.
slab, plat klip, steen, plaat.
slack, a. slap, los; traag, lui.
slack, v. verslap; vertraag; laat skiet.
slake: –d lime, gebluste kalk.
slam, v. toeklap, toeslaan (van 'n deur).
slander, v. (be)laster, (be)skinder.
slang, plat taal; bargoens.
slant, v. skuins (skeef) loop (staan).

slap, v. slaan, klap (gee).
slash, v. sny; slaan, raps.
slate, n. leiklip; lei.
slattern, slonsige (slordige) vrou, slet.
slaughter, v. vermoor; slag.
slave, n. slaaf, slavin.
slave, v. sloof, swoeg.
slaver, v. kwyl, bekwyl.
slavery, slawerny.
slay, doodmaak, vermoor.
sled, sledge, sleigh, slee.
sledge(-hammer), voorhamer.
sleek, a. glad, glansend, blink, sag.
sleep, n. slaap, vaak.
sleep, v. slaap, rus.
sleeper, slaper; dwarslêer.
sleepy, vaak, slaperig; stil.
sleeve, mou.
slender, dun, skraal, maer; gering, min, klein.
slice, n. sny, skyf; vislepel.
slide, v. gly, glip; skuiwe; laat gly.
slide, n. (die) gly (glip); helling; glybaan; plaatjie; knip, skuif; grond-, aardverskuiwing.
slight, a. swak; klein, gering, min, bietjie; oppervlakkig.
slight, v. minag, gering ag, beledig.
slightly, effe(ntjies), bietjie.
slim, dun, skraal, maer, slank.
slime, slym, slyk, modder.
sling, v. swaai; slinger, gooi.
sling, n. slinger; draagband; riem.
slink, v. (weg)sluip.
slip, v. gly, glip; ontglip; 'n fout maak, jou vergis (verspreek); laat glip, laat gly.
slip, n. fout, vergissing; (kussing)sloop; onderlyfie; onderrok; voorskoot; (bad)broekie; ketting (riem) vir honde; stukkie, strokie papier; spruit, steggie.
slipper, n. pantoffel, sloffie.
slipshod, sloffig; slordig.
slit, v. skeur, splits, kloof.
slit, n. sny, skeur, slip; spleet.
slither, gly, glip.
sliver, n. splinter, spaander.
slobber, v. kwyl, bemors; knoei.
slogan, strydkreet; wagwoord, leuse.
sloop, sloep.
slop(s), n. vuil water; sop, slap drank; pap kos.
slop, v. mors, stort.
slope, n. helling, skuinste, afdraand.
sloppy, modderig, morsig; slordig; week, oordrewe.
slot, n. gleuf, sleuf; valdeur.
slouch, v. slap (pap) bang; onmanierlik sit; slof.
slough, v. vervel.
Slovak, n. Slowaak.
Slovakia, Slowakye.
slovenly, slordig, liederlik, morsig.
slow, a. stadig, langsaam; lomerig, traag.
slow, v. die vaart (snelheid) verminder, stadiger gaan (loop).
slowcoach, druiloor, draaikous.
slug, n. slak; loper.
sluggish, traag, lui, langsaam vloeiend.
sluice, n. sluis; sluiswater; watervoor.
slum, agterbuurte; a –, krot(woning), krotbuurt.
slumber, v. sluimer, slaap.
slump, n. slapie, slap tyd; daling.
slur, v. mommel, slordig (onduidelik) uitspreek (skrywe); beklad; sleep, trek, uitrek (van 'n noot).
slur, n. klad, smet, skandvlek; verwyt, blaam; slordige uitspraak.
slush, modder, slyk, nat, sneeu.
slut, slons, slordige vrou, sloerie.

sly, skelm, listig, slu, geslepe.
smack, v. klap (gee), slaan; (met 'n sweep) klap; met die lippe klap.
small, a. klein, gering, weinig, min; niksbeduidend; bekrompe.
smallpox, kinderpokkies.
smart, v. pynig, brand; smart veroorsaak.
smart, a. skerp, vinnig, oulik, geslepe, slim, gevat; fluks, knap; agtermekaar, netjies; modieus, deftig.
smash, v. (flenters, stukkend) breek, stukkend slaan, stukkend gooi, verbrysel; verpletter; totaal verslaan; moker (tennis).
smash, n. vernieling, botsing, ongeluk, ramp; breekspul; mokerhou (tennis)
smear, v. smeer, bestryk; besmeer.
smell, n. ruik, geur.
smell, v. ruik, snuffel.
smelt, v. (metaal) smelt.
smile, n. glimlag.
smile, v. glimlag.
smirch, v. besmeer; bevlek, beklad.
smirk, v. grimlag, onnatuurlike glimlag.
smith, smid (smit).
smithereens, stukkies, flenters, gruis.
smog, rookmis.
smoke, n. rook, damp.
smoke, v. rook, damp uitrook.
smooth, a. glad, sag, gelyk; soetvloeiend; beleef, vleierig.
smooth(e), v. gelykmaak, glad maak; maklik maak; bewimpel.
smother, v. (ver)smoor, (ver)stik; onderdruk.
smoulder, smeul.
smudge, smutch, v. (be)mors, (be)smeer; (be)vlek, (be)klad, besmet.
smudge, n. vuil kol, klad; vlek, smet.
smug, a. burgerlik, selfvoldaan.
smuggle, smokkel.
smuggler, smokkelaar.
smut, n. roetvlek, roet; vuil taal; brand (in koring).
snack, happie, ligte maaltyd.
snaffle, trens(toom).
snag, stomp, punt; moeilikheid; (val)strik.
snail, slak.
snake, slang.
snake-charmer, slang(e)besweerder.
snap, v. hap, snap, gryp; knal; klap; laat klap (knal); toeklap; knip; breek; afneem, kiek; toesnou.
snapdragon, leeubekkie.
snapshot, n. kiekie; blinde skoot.
snare, n. strik, wip, val; valstrik.
snare, v. in 'n strik vang, verstrik.
snarl, v. knor; grom, (toe)snou, afsnou.
snarl, n. knor. snou.
snatch, v. gryp, vat, wegruk.
sneak, v. sluip, kruip; steel; verklik, verklap.
sneer, v. (be)spot, uitlag, die neus optrek.
sneer, v. gryns(lag), spot(lag), hoonlag.
sneeze, v. nies.
sneeze, n. nies.
sniff, v. snuiwe; snuffel.
snigger, v. giggel, grinnik.
snip, v. (af)sny, (af)knip.
sniper, skerpskutter, sluipskutter.
snivel, v. snotter; grens, huil, tjank.
snob, snob, inkruiper, ploert.
snort, v. snork, proes, snuif.
snot, snot; snotneus.
snout, snoet, snuit, neus.
snow, n. sneeu, kapok.
snow, v. sneeu, kapok.
snow-flake, sneeuvlokkie.

snow-white, sneeuwit, spierwit.
snub, v. afsnou, afjak.
snub, a. stomp.
snuff, v. snuit.
snuff, v. snuiwe; snuffel, ruik aan.
snuff, n. snuif; snuf.
snuffle, v. snuiwe; deur die neus praat.
snug, lekker, warm; beskut, toe; aangenaam, gesellig.
snuggle, inkruip; vasdruk teen.
so, so, sodanig; dus.
soak, v. week, deurweek; drink, suip.
soap, n. seep.
soap, v. inseep, seep smeer.
soar, swerwe, hoog vlie(g), opstyg, seil.
sob, v. snik.
sober, a. nugter; matig; verstandig, bedaard, kalm.
so-called, sogenaamd.
soccer, sokker.
sociable, a. gesellig, aangenaam.
social, a. gesellig; maatskaplik, sosiaal.
social, n. gesellige byeenkoms.
socialist, n. sosialis.
society, samelewing, maatskappy, gemeenskap; vereniging, genootskap; geselskap; die deftige kringe.
sociology, sosiologie.
sock, n. sokkie; binnesool; toneelskoen.
socket, holte; kas (van 'n oog); potjie; pyp; kousie (aan 'n waterpyp).
Socrates, Sokrates, Socrates.
sod, n. sooi.
soda, soda.
soda-water, spuitwater, sodawater.
sodden, a. deurweek, papnat; klam.
sofa, sofa, rusbank.
soft, a. sag (saf), pap, week; soetsappig; goedhartig, simpatiek.
soft-hearted, teerhartig.
soil, n. grond, bodem.
soil, v. vlek, vuil maak; besmet.
sojourn, v. vertoef, verbly.
solace, n. troos, vertroosting.
solder, n. soldeersel.
solder, v. soldeer.
soldier, n. soldaat, krygsman.
sole, n. sool; voetsool.
sole, v. versool.
sole, n. tong(vis).
sole, a. enigste, enkel.
solemn, plegtig, ernstig; stadig.
solicit, versoek, vra, smeek.
solicitor, prokureur.
solicitous, verlangend; bekommerd, besorg.
solid, a. vas, solied, sterk, stewig; onverdeeld, eenparig; gegrond, deeglik.
solid, n. vaste liggaam.
solidarity, solidariteit, eenheid.
solidify, verdig, vas (styf) maak (word).
soliloquy, alleenspraak.
solitary, eensaam, verlate, alleenstaande; enkel.
solo, solo.
Solomon, Salomo.
so-long, tot siens.
soluble, oplosbaar.
solution, oplossing; ontbinding.
solve, oplos, verklaar, uitlê, ophelder.
solvent, a. oplossend, oplossings- . . . ; solvent.
sombre, somber, donker, duister.
some, a. sommige, party, enige; een of ander, sowat, ongeveer, omtrent; bietjie.
some, pron. sommige, party; iets; bietjie.
somebody, iemand, een of ander.
somehow, op een of ander manier.

someone, sien somebody,
somersault, v. bolmakiesie slaan.
something, iets, wat.
sometime, voormalig, vorig, vroeër.
sometimes, somtyds, soms, partymaal.
somewhat, enigsins, 'n bietjie.
somewhere, êrens, iewers.
son, seun (soon); S. of God, Soon (Seun) van God.
song, lied, sang, sangstuk; kleinigheid.
son-in-law, skoonseun.
sonnet, sonnet, klinkdig.
sonorous, welluidend, klankryk, sonoor.
soon, gou, spoedig, binnekort.
soot, roet.
soothe, kalmeer, versag, stil; sus.
sophisticated, oulik, ouderwets, gekunsteld.
sophistry, drogredenering, sofistery.
soporific, n. slaapmiddel.
soprano, sopraan.
sorcerer, towenaar.
sordid, laag, gemeen, vuil; vrekkig.
sore, a. seer, pynlik; gevoelig; swaar.
sore, n. seer, wond.
sorrel, n. rooibruin; vosperd.
sorrow, n. smart, droefheid, verdriet.
sorrow, v. treur.
sorrowful, treurig, verdrietig, droewig.
sorry, jammer, spyt; ellendig, treurig.
sort, n. soort, klas.
sort, v. sorteer, uitsoek.
so-so, so-so, so op 'n manier.
sough, v. suis, sug.
soul, siel; wese, skepsel.
sound, a. gesond, gaaf, goed; gegrond, deeglik; vas, solied; gedug.
sound, adv. – asleep, vas aan die slaap.
sound, n. klank, geluid, toon.
sound, v. klink, lui; laat klink; laat hoor, verkondig; toets, ondersoek.
sound, v. (die diepte) peil; ondersoek; pols.
soundly, terdeë, flink, vas; gaaf, goed.
soup, sop (soep).
sour, a. suur; nors, stuurs.
sour, v. suur maak (word); verbitter.
source, oorsprong, bron.
south, adv. suidwaarts.
south, a. suidelik, suid(e)- . . .
south, n. suide.
south-east, suidoos.
south-easter, suidoostewind, Kaapse dokter.
southern, a. suidelik; S. Cross, Suiderkruis.
souvenir, aandenking, gedagtenis.
sovereign, a. soewerein, opper . . . ; voortreflik.
sovereign, n. vors, heerser; pond.
sow, v. saai, strooi; versprei.
sow, n. sog.
space, n. ruimte, spasie, afstand; duur; – -craft, ruimtevaartuig.
space, v. spasieer.
spacious, ruim, groot; uitgestrek.
spade, graaf, skop(graaf).
Spain, Spanje.
span, n. span; spanning (van 'n brug, ens.); kort tyd (duur).
Spaniard, Spanjaard; Spaanse vrou.
spanner, skroefhamer, (skroef)sleutel, moerhamer.
spar, n. spar, paal; rondhout (skip).
spar, v. skerm; redetwis.
spare, a. skraal, maer; vry; orig.
spare, v. spaar, bespaar; klaarkom sonder, mis; ontsien.
spare wheel, noodwiel, orige wiel.
spark, n. vonk; sprankie, greintjie.

spark, v. vonke afgee, vonk.
sparking-plug, vonkprop.
sparkle, v. fonkel, skitter, flikker.
sparkle, n. glans, flonkering, gefonkel.
sparrow, mossie.
sparse, dun, skaars, versprei, yl.
Spartan, a. Spartaans.
spasm, kramp, trekking.
spastic, spastikus; a. spasties.
spate, vloed, oorstroming.
spatter, spat, bespat, bemors.
spawn, v. eiers lê, uitbroei.
speak, praat, spreek; sê.
speaker, spreker; speaker (Volksraad).
spear, n. spies, lans, speer.
special, a. spesiaal, besonder.
specialize, spesialiseer.
specialist, spesialis, spesialiteit.
speciality, specialty, spesialiteit; besonderheid.
specie, spesie, klinkende munt.
species, soort; geslag; spesie(s).
specific, spesifiek, bepaald, soortlik.
specification, spesifikasie; –s, bestek.
specify, spesifiseer.
specimen, monster, proef; staaltjie, voorbeeld;
    eksemplaar.
specious, bevallig; skoonklinkend.
speck, n. stippel, spikkel, kolletjie; stukkie;
    deeltjie; vlekkie.
speckle, v. (be)spikkel; –d, gespikkel(d).
spectacle, skouspel, toneel, spektakel; a pair of
    –s, 'n bril.
spectacular, skitterend; aanskoulik.
spectator, toeskouer, aanskouer.
speculate, bepeins, bereken; spekuleer.
speculator, spekulant.
speech, spraak, taal; toespraak.
speed, n. snelheid, vaart; spoed, haas.
speed-cop, verkeerskonstabel.
speedometer, mylmeter, snelheidsmeter.
speedy, spoedig; vinnig; haastig.
spell, n. towerspreuk; betowering.
spell, v. spel; beteken.
spell, n. tyd(jie), ruk(kie); beurt.
spelling, spelling.
spend, uitgee; bestee; spandeer, verkwis; deur-
    bring.
spendthrift, n. deurbringer, verkwister.
sphere, bol, bal, globe; hemelliggaam; sfeer,
    (werk)kring, omgewing, gebied.
sphinx, sfinks.
spice, n. spesery, kruie; smakie.
spider, spinnekop.
spike, n. skerp punt, lang spyker; aar.
spill, v. stort, mors, uitgooi; afgooi.
spin, v. spin; laat draai, tot (in die rondte); vertel.
spin, n. draai; ritjie, toertjie.
spinach, spinasie.
spindle, n. spoel; spil, as.
spine, ruggraat, rugstring; doring.
spinster, oujongnôi (oujongnooi).
spiral, n. spiraal.
spire, toringspits, top, spits punt.
spirit, n. gees; moed, energie, geesdrif; siel,
    inspirasie.
spirit-level, waterpas.
spiritualism, spiritisme; spiritualisme.
spit, n. braaispit; landtong.
spit, v. spu, spoeg (spuug); blaas.
spit, n. spoeg (spuug).
spite, n. wrok, kwaadaardigheid, nyd.
spite, v. dwarsboom; vererg; vermaak.
spiteful, haatlik, nydig, boosaardig.
spitfire drifkop, heethoof, rissie.
splash, v. plas, spat; bespat, natspat.

splash, n. geplas, plons; spatsel.
spleen, milt; swaarmoedigheid.
splendid, pragtig, skitterend, kostelik, groots,
    luisterryk; uitstekend.
splendour, prag, luister, praal, glans.
splice, v. splits, las.
splint, n. spalk, splinter.
splint, v. spalk.
splinter, n. splinter, splint, spaander.
split, v. splits, splyt, bars, skeur, kloof (klowe);
    verdeel.
split, n. spleet, skeur, bars; skeuring, tweespalk.
splotchy, gevlek, beklad.
spoil, v. bedrewe, verniel; verfoes.
spoke, speek.
spokeshave, skaafmes; speekskaaf.
sponge, n. spons; klaploper.
sponge, v. spons, afspons; afvee, uitvee (met 'n
    spons), uitwis; opsuie; – on, klaploop, op-
    skeploer.
sponger, klaploper, opskeploerder.
spontaneous, spontaan, ongedwonge; instinktief.
spool, spoel, rolletjie, tolletjie.
spoon, n. lepel.
spoonful, lepelvol.
spoor, n. spoor.
spoor, v. die spoor volg, die spoor sny.
sporadic, sporadies, versprei.
spore, spoor; saad, kiem.
sport, n. pret, korswel, vermaak; speletjie, tyd-
    verdryf; sport.
sporting, spelend; sportief, sport- . . .
sports coat, sportbaadjie.
sportsman, sportman, sportliefhebber.
spot, n. plek; plekkie, kolletjie, merkie, vlek;
    klad, smet.
spotted, gespikkel, bont.
spouse, eggenoot, eggenote.
spout, v. spuit; deklameer.
spout, n. tuit, pyp, geut; straal.
sprain, v. verstuit, verswik, verrek.
sprain, n. verstuiting, verrekking.
sprawl, uitrek, uitgestrek lê; spartel; uitsprei.
spray, n. spreiwater, spuitwater, bruiswater,
    stofreën; skuim; sproeier.
spray, v. (be)sproei, spuit.
spread, v. sprei, versprei, uitsprei, uitbrei, rond-
    strooi; uitstrek; ontvou, ooprol, oopgooi;
    smeer.
spread, n. omvang; uitgestrektheid; uitge-
    breidheid; verspreiding; sprei, tafelkleed;
    fees, maaltyd; arches of equal –, boë met
    gelyke spanning.
spree, n. pret, fuif, drinkpartytjie.
sprightly, vrolik, lewendig, opgeruimd.
spring, v. spring, opspring; ontspruit, ontstaan;
    krom trek, bars; veer.
spring, n. spring, sprong; lente; bron, fontein;
    veer; veerkrag, dryfveer.
springbok, springbok.
springtime, lente.
sprinkle, v. sprinkel, strooi; stofreent.
sprint, v. nael, (hard) hardloop, sny.
sprint, n. naelwedloop.
sprinter, naelloper, hardloper.
sprocket, tand.
sprout, v. opkom, uitloop, opskiet; laat groei.
sprout, n. spruit, loot.
spruce, a. netjies, piekfyn, agtermekaar.
spry, lewendig, vlug, wakker, rats.
spume, n. skuim.
spunk, koerasie, moed, vuur, fut.
spur, n. spoor; spoorslag, aansporing; uitloper
    (van 'n berg).
spurious, oneg, vals, vervals.

spurn, v. versmaad, verag, verstoot.
spurt, v. spat, spuit; laat nael.
sputnik, spoetnik.
sputter, v. spat, spu; sputter; babbel.
spy, n. spioen, bespieder.
spy, v. spioen, bespied; afloer.
squabble, v. rusie maak, twis, skoor.
squadron, eskadron (van leër); eskader (van vloot); eskadrielje (van lugmag).
squalid, vuil, liederlik, smerig, morsig.
squall, n. windvlaag, bui; skreeu, gil.
squander, verkwis, deurbring, mors.
square, n. vierkant; plein; winkelhaak; tweede mag.
square, a. vierkantig, reghoekig; eerlik, billik; gelyk.
square, v. vierkantig (reghoekig) maak; tot die tweede mag verhef; vereffen, betaal; omkoop; in orde bring.
squash, v. plat (pap druk), verbrysel, kneus; doodsê.
squash, n. murg-van-groente, skorsie; gedrang; muurbal.
squat, v. (neer)hurk, op die hurke sit.
squat, a. gehurk; kort, dik.
squatter, plakker; neerhurker; kolonis.
squeak, v. piep; skree(u), knars.
squeal, v. gil, skree(u); tjank.
squeeze, v. druk; afpers.
squint, v. skeel kyk, skeel wees.
squirrel, eekhorinkie.
squirt, v. spuit.
stab, v. steek, doodsteek, deursteek.
stable, a. vas, stabiel, duursaam; standvastig.
stable, n. stal, (resies)perde.
stack, n. mied (miet); hoop, stapel.
staff, n. stok, staf, paal; stut, steun; personeel.
stage, n. toneel; steier, stellasie; stadium, fase, punt.
stage, v. opvoer, op die toneel bring.
stage fright, plankekoors.
stage manager, toneeldirekteur, regisseur.
stagger, v. wankel, waggel, slinger; laat wankel (waggel); aarsel; oorbluf.
stagnant, (stil)staand(e), stil; lui.
stagnate, stilstaan; lui (traag) wees.
staid, bedaard, stemmig; solied, nugter.
stain, v. vlek; besoedel, beklad; kleur.
stain, n. vlek; smet, klad, skande, skandvlek; kleur, tint.
stair, trappie, treetjie; –s, trap.
stake, n. paal, stok, brandstapel; wedgeld; aandeel.
stale, a. oud, muf; afgesaag; bevange; verflou.
stalemate, n. pat (in skaak).
stalk, v. deftig stap; kruip, bekruip.
stall, n. stal, hok, vak; stalletjie, toonbank, kiosk, kraam; –s, stalles (in die skouburg).
stallion, hings.
stalwart, a. fris, stoer; standvastig, dapper.
stamen, meeldraad.
stamina, uithouvermoë.
stammer, v. hakkel, stamel, stotter.
stamp, v. tjap, merk; bestempel; frankeer, seël, 'n posseël sit op; fynmaak; stamp, trap.
stamp, n. seël, tjap; posseël; aard, karakter; stamper; stamp, trap.
stampede, v. op loop sit; op loop ja.
stance, houding, posisie.
stanchion, n. pilaar, stut, paal.
stand, v. staan; gaan staan; uithou, verdra; van krag wees (bly); deurstaan; neersit; laat staan.
stand, n. halt; stelling, posisie, staanplek, staand-plaas; weerstand; standertjie; kassie, rak-(kie); stalletjie, kraam; paviljoen, verhoog.

standard, n. vlag; standaard, peil; maatstaf, gehalte; paal.
standardize, standaardiseer, vasstel.
standpoint, standpunt.
staple, kram.
staple, a. vernaamste hoof- . . . , stapel- . . .
stapler, kramhegter.
star, n. ster; sterretjie; kol (voor 'n perd se kop).
starch, n. stysel; formaliteit.
starch, v. stywe.
stare, v. tuur, staar, aangaap.
stark, a. styf, puur, bloot, louter.
starling, blinkvlerkspreeu.
start, v. skrik, opspring; begin (maak); vertrek; aan die gang (loop) sit; op tou sit.
starter, aansitter; deelnemer; seingeër.
startle, skrikmaak, laat skrik, ontstel.
starve, van honger omkom; honger ly; honger wees; uithonger.
state, n. toestand, staat, stemming; staat; waar-digheid, rang; prag.
state, a. staats- . . . ; staatsie- . . . ; gala- . . . hof- . . .
state, v. (ver)meld, verklaar, sê, opgee.
stately, statig, deftig, waardig, groots; luister-ryk.
statement, verklaring; bewering; opgaaf, staat.
state-room, praalkamer; privaatkajuit.
static(al), staties, gewigs- . . .
station, n. standplaas, pos; stasie; status, posisie, stand.
station, v. plaas, stel, stasioneer.
stationary, blywend, vas.
stationery, skryfbehoeftes.
station-master, stasiemeester.
statistical, statisties.
statue, standbeeld.
stature, lengte, gestalte.
status, status, stand, rang, posisie.
statute, wet, statuut, instelling.
staunch, stanch, trou, betroubaar.
stave, n. plankie, houtjie, sport.
stay, v. teëhou, weerhou, stuit; uitstel, opskort; ondersteun, stut; uithou, volhou; bly, loseer; vertoef, wag.
stay, n. verblyf; uitstel, opskorting; hinderpaal; steun, stut.
stead, stede, plaas, plek; diens, nut.
steadfast, standvastig, onwankelbaar.
steady, a. vas; gereeld, gestadig, egalig; besadig.
steady, v. bestendig (besadig), maak (word), tot bedaring bring (kom).
steak, biefstuk, stuk (vleis).
steal, steel, sluip, kruip.
stealthy, skelm, onderduims, slinks.
steam, stoom, wasem, damp.
steamboat, stoomboot.
steam-boiler, stoomketel.
steamship, stoomskip.
steel, n. staal, swaard; slypstaal.
steel, v. staal, verhard.
steep, a. steil; kras, kwaai (van pryse).
steep, v. indoop, week, dompel.
steer, v. stuur, koers vat.
steering-rod, stuurstang.
steering-wheel, stuurrat, stuurwiel.
stem, n. stam, stingel, steel; voorstewe.
stem, v. stuit, teëhou; opdam.
stencil, v. sjabloneer.
stenographer, stenograaf, snelskrywer.
step, v. stap, tree, loop.
step, n. tree, stap, pas; voetstap; trappie; sport.
stepchild, stiefkind.
step-ladder, trapleer.

stereotyped, stereotiep, vas.
sterile, onvrugbaar, steriel; kiemvry.
sterilize, steriliseer, kiemvry maak.
sterling, sterling; eg, suiwer.
stern, a. ernstig, streng, stroef.
stern, n. agterstewe.
stew, v. stowe.
stew, n. gestoofde vleis.
steward, rentmeester; kelner.
stick, v. steek, vassteek; vassit, vasplak; aanhou; getrou bly.
stick, n. stok, wandelstok; droogstoppel.
sticky, klewerig, taai.
stiff, styf, stram; moeilik.
stifle, v. (ver)stik, versmoor; onderdruk.
stigma, brandmerk, skandvlek; stempel.
still, a. stil; kalm.
still, v. stil, stilmaak, kalmeer, bedaar.
still, adv. nog, nog altyd; nogtans.
still, n. distilleerketel.
stilt, n. stelt; on –s, op stelte.
stilted, hoogdrawend.
stimulate, prikkel, aanspoor, stimuleer.
stimulus, prikkel, aansporing, stimulus.
stimy, 'n blinder (gholf).
sting, v. steek, prik; brand; pyn (wroeging, leed) veroorsaak.
sting, n. angel; steek; prikkel; knaging.
stingy, suinig, vrekkig, inhalig, gierig.
stink, v. stink, sleg ruik.
stink, n. stank.
stint, v. beperk; suinig (spaarsaam) wees, skrap uitdeel, afskeep.
stipend, besoldiging, loon, salaris.
stipendiary, a. besoldig, loontrekkend.
stipulate, stipuleer, bepaal, vasstel.
stir, v. roer, verroer, beweeg; omroer,
stir, n. beweging, opskudding, opgewondenheid, drukte, gewoel.
stirrup, stiebeuel.
stitch, steek.
stitch, v. naai, stik; – up, toenaai.
stock, n. stomp, stam; steel, handvatsel; geslag, ras, familie; vee(stapel); voorraad; kapitaal; effekte.
stock, v. in voorraad hou, in voorraad hê, voorsien van.
stockbroker, effektemakelaar.
stock exchange, (effekte)beurs.
stockfish, stokvis.
stocking, kous.
stocky, kort en dik, geset.
stoep, stoep.
stoic, a. stoïsyns.
stoke, stook.
stoker, stoker.
stolid, flegmaties, ongevoelig, bot.
stomach, n. maag, pens (van diere).
stone, n. klip, steen; pit; haelsteen.
stone, v. stenig; pitte uithaal; straat.
Stone Age, Steentydperk.
stone-dead, morsdood.
stone-deaf, stokdoof.
stoney, klipperig, klip- . . . ; ongevoelig.
stool, n. stoeltjie; ontlasting; stoel.
stool, v. stoel.
stoop, v. buk, vooroor buig; jou verlaag.
stop, v. stop, toestop; stelp; vul; verhinder, 'n einde maak aan; keer; laat stilstaan; stopsit; inhou, terughou; ophou; stilhou, gaan staan; bly.
stop, n. end; stilstand; halte; leesteken.
stopcock, kraan.
stopper, prop.
store, n. voorraad; pakhuis, winkel.

store, v. bêre; opgaar; insamel; bevat.
store-room, pakkamer, bêreplek.
storey, verdieping.
stork, ooievaar; groot sprinkaanvoël.
storm, n. storm, stortbui; aanval.
storm, v. woed, hard waai; tier, raas; storm, stormloop.
story, storie, verhaal, sprokie.
stout, a. kragtig, sterk; geset.
stove, n. stoof.
stow, bêre, wegsit.
stowaway, verstekeling.
straggle, afdwaal; versprei raak, streep-streep loop.
straight, a. reguit; opreg, eerlik.
straight, adv. reguit, onmiddellik.
straightforward, eerlik, padlangs.
strain, v. trek, rek, span; ooreis; verrek; filtreer.
strain, n. inspanning; strewe; oorspanning, druk; verrekking; trant, manier.
strainer, sygdoek, deurgooidoek; siffie.
strait, n. seestraat; –s, moeilikheid.
strait-jacket, dwangbuis.
strait-laced, streng, nougeset, bekrompe.
strand, n. strand, kus.
strand, v. strand.
strand, n. string, draad.
strange, vreemd, onbekend; eienaardig, sonderling, snaaks.
stranger, vreemdeling, onbekende.
strangle, (ver)wurg; onderdruk.
strangulate, vasbind, toebind; (ver)wurg.
strap, n. riem, platriem; gord; skeerriem; lis.
strap, v. vasgord, vasmaak, vasbind met 'n riem; aansit, skerp maak; (met 'n riem) slaan, uitlooi.
strapping, groot, sterk, frisgebou.
strategic, strategies; krygskundig.
strategy, strategie, krygskuns.
stratum, laag, stratum.
straw, n. strooi; strooitjie; kleinigheid.
strawberry, aarbei.
stray, v. dwaal, verdwaal, wegraak.
stream, n. stroom; stroming; rivier.
stream, v. stroom, vloei, loop; wapper.
street, n. straat.
strength, sterkte, krag, mag.
strengthen, versterk, sterk maak.
strenuous, energiek, wakker, ywerig, onvermoeid, kragtig; swaar.
stress, n. drang; inspanning; spanning; klem, nadruk; klemtoon.
stress, v. beklem, nadruk lê op, klem lê op, aksentueer.
stretch, v. rek, trek; uitrek; uitstrek, uitsteek; geweld aandoen.
stretcher, rekker; draagbaar; kateltjie.
strict, streng, stip, presies, strik.
stride, v. lang treë gee, stap.
strident, skerp, krassend, deurdringend.
strife, stryd, twis, onenigheid.
strike, v. slaan; stoot, stamp; tref; trek, (die vlag) stryk; lyk, skyn, (werk) staak.
strike, n. (werk)staking.
striker, staker.
striking, treffend, opvallend.
string, n. lyn, tou, riempie; snaar; snoer, string; reeks, streep.
string, v. (in)rye; snare insit; (snare) span; afhaar (van boontjies).
stringent, streng, bindend, nadruklik.
strip, v. uittrek (van klere); afstroop, kaal maak.
strip, strook, streep; (comic) –, prentverhaal.
stripe, streep; slag, striem.
strive, strewe; worstel, sukkel; stry; wedywer.

stroke, n. hou, slag; aanval (van siekte); haal, streep, trek.
stroke, v. streel, liefkoos, stryk.
strong, sterk, kragtig; geweldig; kras.
strong-room, kluis, brandkamer.
strop, n. skeerriem, slypriem.
structure, bou, struktuur; gebou.
struggle, v. worstel, spartel, sukkel.
strut, v. trots en deftig stap, pronk.
strut, n. & v. stut.
stub, n. stomp(ie), entjie.
stub-axle, stomp-as.
stubble, stoppel.
stubborn, hardnekkig, koppig.
stuck-up, verwaand, hoogmoedig, trots.
stud, n. grootkopspyker; knop; nael; hemps-knopie, halsknopie, boordjieknopie.
student, student, leerling; navorser.
studio, atelier (ateljee); klanksaal (radio).
studious, vlytig, leergierig, fluks.
study, n. studie; studeerkamer.
study, v. studeer, bestudeer.
stuff, n. stof, goed, materiaal.
stuff, v. stop, opstop, volstop, volprop.
stuffing, vulsel; opstopsel.
stuffy, bedompig, benoud.
stultify, belaglik maak; tot niet maak.
stumble, v. struikel, strompel.
stumbling-block, struikelblok, hinderpaal.
stump, n. stomp, stompie; paaltjie (krieket).
stump, v. swaar stap, strompel; politieke toe-sprake hou; stonk (krieket).
stun, verdoof; dronkslaan, oorbluf; bedwelm.
stunning, bedwelmend; uitstekend.
stunt, v. die groei belemmer, teëhou, knot.
stunt, n. kordaatstuk, kaskenade (uithaler-)-streek; gier, streek.
stunted, klein, dwergagtig, verpot.
stupefy, bedwelm, verdoof; dronkslaan, bot (suf) maak.
stupendous, ontsaglik, ontsettend, kolossaal.
stupid, a. dom, onnosel, stom, bot.
stupor, bedwelming, verdowing.
sturdy, a. kragtig, stoer, fors, sterk.
stutter, v. hakkel, stotter, stamel.
sty, varkhok.
sty, stye, n. karkatjie.
style, n. skryfstif; styl; skryfwyse; wyse, manier; mode; naam, titel; soort.
style, v. betitel, bestempel, noem.
stylish, deftig, nuwerwets, fyn, agtermekaar.
suave, vriendelik, sag; tegemoetkomend, beleef.
subconscious, halfbewus, onderbewus.
subdivide, onderverdeel.
subdue, ten onder bring, oorwin, onderwerp, be-teuel; tem, versag.
subdued, stil, gelate, onderworpe.
subject, a. onderworpe; onderhorig.
subject, n. onderdaan; onderwerp; vak; tema; voorwerp.
subject, v. onderwerp; – to, blootstel aan.
subject-matter, onderwerp, stof.
subjucate, onderwerp, ten onder bring.
subjunctive, n. aanvoegende wyse.
sub-let, onderverhuur.
sublimate, v. sublimeer; veredel, verfyn.
sublime, a. subliem, hoog-verhewe.
submarine, n. duikboot, onderseeboot.
submerge, onder water sit, onderdompel.
submit, (sig) onderwerp; voorlê, indien; beweer.
subordinate, a. ondergeskik.
subpoena, v. dagvaar.
subscribe, onderteken; onderskrywe; bydra; inteken.
subscriber, intekenaar; ondertekenaar.

subscription, subskripsiegeld; intekening; by-drae.
subsequent, daaropvolgende, volgende.
subside, sak, sink; insak, wegsak; bedaar.
subsidize, subsidieer.
subsidy, subsidie.
subsist, bestaan, lewe.
substance, stof; selfstandigheid; pit, kern; wese; hoofbestanddeel; inhoud; werklikheid; ver-moë; substansie.
substantial, wesenlik; belangrik; aansienlik; vas, sterk, solied; voedsaam; vermoënd.
substitute, n. plaasvervanger, substituut.
substitute, v. in die plek stel, vervang.
subterfuge, uitvlug, voorwendsel.
subterranean, onderaards.
subtle, subtiel, fyn, serp, spitsvondig; slu, ge-slepe, listig.
subtract, aftrek, verminder (met).
suburb, voorstad.
subway, tonnel, duikweg.
succeed, opvolg; volg op; slaag, geluk.
success, sukses, welslae, voorspoed.
successive, agtereenvolgend, na mekaar.
successor, opvolger.
succinct, kort, bondig, pittig.
succulence, sappigheid, sopperigheid.
succulent, sappig, sopperig.
succumb, beswyk; swig.
such, a. sodanig, sulke, so.
such, pron. sulkes, sulke mense (dinge).
suck, v. suig, uitsuig; insuig; drink.
suckle, laat drink, soog.
Sudan, Soedan.
sudden, skie(r)lik, plotseling, onverwags.
suds, seepsop, seepwater, seepskuim.
sue, (geregtelik) vervolg, eis, dagvaar, aanskrywe.
suffer, ly; uithou, dra; boet; toelaat.
suffice, voldoende wees, genoeg wees.
sufficient, a. genoeg, voldoende.
sufficient, n. genoeg.
suffix, n. agtervoegsel, suffiks.
suffocate, (ver)stik, versmoor.
suffrage, stemreg; stem; goedkeuring.
sugar, n. suiker; mooipraatjies.
sugar-basin, suikerpot.
sugar-cane, suikerriet.
sugar-mill, suikerfabriek.
suggest, aan die hand gee, aanraai; opper; sug-gereer; op die gedagte bring.
suggestion, suggestie, ingewing; wenk, raad, plan, voorstel.
suicide, selfmoord; selfmoordenaar.
suit, n. regsgeding, proses; versoek (huweliks-aansoek); kleur (in kaartspel); pak (klere); uit-rusting, stel.
suit, v. pas; voeg; geskik wees; bevredig.
suitable, geskik, geleë; gepas, behoorlik.
suitcase, handkoffer, valies.
suite, gevolg; stel, reeks.
sulk, v. pruil, mok, nukkerig wees.
sulky, a. nukkerig, pruilerig, nors.
sullen, knorrig, stuurs, nors, suur.
sulpha – drug, sulfamiddel.
sulphur, n. swa(w)el.
sulphuric: – acid, swa(w)elsuur.
sultan, sultan.
sultana, sultana(rosyntjie).
sultry, drukkend, bedompig.
sum, n. som; bedrag; totaal.
summarize, opsom, (kort) saamvat.
summary, n. opsomming, samevatting.
summer, somer.
summit, hoogste punt, top, toppunt.

summon, dagvaar; oproep, bymekaar roep, ontbied.
summons, n. dagvaarding; oproep.
summons, v. dagvaar.
sumptuous, weelderig, kosbaar, duur.
sun, n. son; sonlig, sonskyn.
sun-blind, rolgordyn.
Sunday, Sondag; – best, kisklere.
sundowner, aandsopie, skemerkelkie.
sundries, diverse, kleinigheidjies.
sundry, verskillende, diverse, allerhande.
sunflower, sonneblom.
sunken, hol, ingeval.
sunny, sonnig; bly, vrolik, opgewek.
sunrise, sonop.
sunset, sononder.
sunshade, sambreel, sonskerm.
sun-spot, sonvlek.
sunstroke, sonsteek, sonstraal.
superb, pragtig, skitterend.
supercharge, –d engine, aangejaagde motor.
supercharger, (druk)aanjaer.
supercilious, trots, verwaand.
superficial, oppervlakkig; vlak.
superfluous, oortollig, oorbodig.
superhuman, bo(we)menslik.
superintend, toesig hou, toesig hê.
superintendent, superintendent.
superior, a. hoër, beter, superieur; groter, opper; uitstekend.
superior, n. meerdere, superieur.
superlative, a. oortreffend; voortreflik.
supernatural, bo(we)natuurlik.
supersede, vervang; ontslaan; afskaf; die plek inneem van.
superstituous, bygelowig.
supervise, toesig hou (oor).
supper, aandete, soepee.
supple, slap, buigsaam, soepel.
supplement, n. aanhangsel, byvoegsel; byblad, bylae.
supplicate, smeek, bid, soebat.
supplies, benodigdhede; voorraad; toelaag; middele.
supply, v. voorsien, verskaf, vorg vir, lewer, aanvul.
supply, n. leweransie, lewering, verskaffing, voorsiening; voorraad; toevoer.
support, v. steun, ondersteun, help; hou, dra, stut; onderhou; verdra, uithou; bewys; staaf; aanmoedig, versterk, krag gee.
support, n. steun, ondersteuning, hulp, bystand; onderhoud; stut, voetstuk, voet.
suppose, veronderstel; vermoed, meen.
suppress, onderdruk, 'n einde maak aan; bedwing, inkrop; agterhou, terugtrek, verswyg.
suppurate, (ver)sweer, etter.
supreme, hoogste, opperste, uiterste; oppermagtig; grootste; belangrikste; – court, hooggeregshof.
surcharge, v. oorlaai; ekstra laat betaal.
surcingle, (buik)gord.
sure, a. seker, gewis; onfeilbaar.
sure, adv. seker, waarlik.
surely, seker; tog.
surety, borg; waarborg; sekerheid.
surf, branders, branding.
surface, n. oppervlakte; vlak; oppervlak; uiterlike.
surfeit, n. oorversadiging, satheid.
surge, v. golf, dein.
surgeon, snydokter.
surgery, heelkunde; spreekkamer.
surly, nors, stuurs, kortaf.
surmise, v. vermoed, gis, raai.

surmount, te bowe kom, oorwin.
surname, van, familienaam; bynaam.
surpass, oortref, uitblink bo.
surplus, oorskot, orige, surplus.
surprise, n. verrassing; verbasing.
surprise, v. verras; verbaas; oorrompel.
surprise-party, invalparty; verrassingsparty.
surrender, v. oorgee; afstand doen van, laat vaar; uitlewer.
surreptitious, onderduims, slinks.
surround, omgewe, omsingel, insluit.
surroundings, omgewing.
survey, v. bekyk, beskou, besigtig, opneem; opmeet.
surveyor, landmeter.
survive, oorlewe, nog lewe, nog bestaan, langer lewe as.
survivor, langslewende; oorblywende, oorlewende.
susceptible, vatbaar, gevoelig; liggeraak.
suspect, v. vermoed; verdink.
suspend, ophang, hang; uitstel, opskort; suspendeer.
suspense, spanning, onsekerheid, twyfel.
suspension-bridge, hangbrug, swaaibrug.
suspicion, argwaan, verdenking, agterdog, suspisie, vermoede.
suspicious, agterdogtig; verdag.
sustain, dra, steun; help, aanmoedig; verduur; aanhou, volhou; handhaaf; ly; bewys.
suzerainty, susereiniteit.
swab, v. dweil, feil, opvee; opneem.
swaddle, toedraai.
swagger, v. windmaker stap, spog.
swallow, v. sluk, insluk; verswelg.
swallow, n. sluk.
swallow, n. swa(w)el.
swamp, n. vlei, moeras.
swamp, v. in 'n moeras vassit (sink); wegspoel, vol water (laat) loop; oorstelp; oorrompel; insluk, verswelg.
swan, swaan; a black –, 'n wit raaf.
swank, v. spog, windmaker wees.
swarm, n. swerm; menigte.
swarm, v. swerm; krioel, wemel.
swathe, verbind; vasbind; toedraai.
swatter, vlieëslaner, -plakkie.
sway, v. swaai, slinger; hanteer; regeer; heers.
swear, v. sweer, onder 'n eed verklaar (bevestig); beëdig; vloek.
sweat, n. sweet; harde werk.
sweat, v. sweet; uitsweet; laat sweet; swoeg; uitbuit.
sweater, bloedsuier; oortrui; – girl, kleeftruipop.
Swede, Sweed; Sweedse raap.
Swedish, a. Sweeds.
sweep, v. vee, wegvee, uitvee; vinnig verbyvlie(g), storm; meevoer, saamsleep; trek, stryk, gly; vlugtig beskou; bestryk.
sweet, a. soet; aangenaam, lieflik; vars.
sweet, n. soet; lekker; –s, lekkers; nagereg.
sweetheart, liefling, skat; nooi (nôi), kêrel.
sweet-pea, pronk-ertjie, ertjieblom.
sweet-potato, patat.
swell, v. swel, opswel; uitdy; vermeerder, toeneem, groei.
swell, n. (die) swel, swelling, swelsel; styging; deining.
swelling, n. swelsel, geswel.
swelter, v. bedompig (benoud, drukkend) wees; versmoor, verskroei, versmag.
swerve, v. afwyk; opsy spring, padgee, swenk.
swift, a. vlug, gou, rats, vinnig.
swill, v. spoel, uitspoel; suip.
swill, n. skottelwater, vuil water.

swim, v. swem; drywe; draai.
swimming-bath, swembad.
swindle, v. bedrieg, fop, swendel.
swine, vark(e), swyn(e).
swing, v. swaai, slinger, skommel; hang.
swing, n. swaai; gang; skoppelmaai.
swingle, swingel.
swipe, v. hard slaan, vee(g), (tennis).
swirl, v. draai, warrel.
swish, v. ransel; swiets, suis, ruis.
Swiss, n. Switser.
switch, n. loot, lat; wisselskakelaar, stroom-
wisselaar, (elektriese) knoppie.
switch, v. pak gee; wissel, ('n trein) op 'n ander
spoor bring; inskakel, uitskakel.
switch-board, skakelbord.
swivel, draaiskyf, spil.
swoon, v. flou (word), beswym.
swoop, v. neerskiet, neerstryk.
sword, swaard, sabel.
swot, v. blok, pomp.
sycophant, gemene vleier, kruiper.
syllable, lettergreep, sillabe.

syllabus, sillabus, leerplan.
symbol, simbool, sinnebeeld, (ken)teken.
symbolize, simboliseer.
symmetry, simmetrie, eweredigheid.
sympathize, simpatiseer, medelye hê.
sympathy, simpatie, meegevoel, medelyde.
symphony, simfonie.
symptom, simptoom, teken, verskynsel.
synagogue, sinagoge.
synchronize, op dieselfde tyd plaasvind, saamval;
reguleer, regsit; sinchroniseer.
syndicate, sindikaat, kartel.
synod, sinode.
synonym, sinoniem.
syntax, sintaksis, sinsleer.
synthesis, sintese, samevatting.
Syrian, n. Siriër; Siries.
syringe, n. spuit.
syrup, stroop; **golden –,** goue stroop.
system, sisteem, stelsel; metode; gestel, konstitusie; formasie.
systematic, sistematies, stelselmatig.

tab, strokie, stukkie; tongetjie; (oor)klappie.
table, n. tafel; plato, hoogland; tabel, lys, register.
table, v. op die tafel (ter tafel) lê; uitstel; rangskik, tabelleer.
tableau, tablo.
table-cloth, tafellaken, tafeldoek.
table-spoon, eetlepel.
tablet, tablet; steen(tjie).
taboo, a. heilig, verbode; taboe.
tabulate, v. tabelleer.
tacit, stilswy(g)end.
taciturn, stil, onspraaksaam, swygsaam.
tack, n. platkopspykertjie; rygsteek; rigting, pad; kos.
tack, v. vasspyker; vasryg; laveer; van koers verander.
tackle, n. takel; hystoestel; gereedskap.
tackle, v. aanpak; plant, lak.
tact, tak(t), slag.
tactful, tak(t)vol.
tactics, taktiek, krygskunde.
tadpole, paddavis(sie).
tag, n. veterpunt; lissie; etiket; fraiing, rafel; aanhangsel; stertpunt; stokperdjie; refrein.
tail, n. stert; pant, slip; keersy (van muntstuk); –s, swaelstert(pak).
tail-light, agterlamp; remlamp.
tailor, n. kleremaker.
taint, v. bevlek, besoedel; bederwe.
take, v. neem, vat; bemagtig; kry, ontvang; begryp, snap; aanneem; opneem; afneem; betrap.
taking, innemend, bekoorlik; aansteeklik.
takings, ontvangste.
tale, verhaal, storie, sprokie; getal.
talent, talent, gawe, begaafdheid; talent.
talented, begaaf, talentvol.
talk, v. praat, gesels.
talk, n. gesprek; praatjie.
talkative, praatsiek, spraaksaam.
talkie, praatprent, klankfilm.
tall, groot, lang, hoog; kras.
tallow, kersvet, harde vet; talk.
tally, v. ooreenstem, klop, strook (met).
Talmud, Talmoed.
talon, klou.
tame, v. tem, mak maak.
tame, a. mak, getem; gedwee; suf, slap, tam, swak; vervelend.
tamer, temmer.
tamper: – with, knoei aan; peuter aan.
tan, v. looi; verbrand, bruin brand.
tan, a. bruin, taankleurig.
tang, n. smaak, geur; eienaardigheid.
tangent, raaklyn, tangens.
tangible, tasbaar, voelbaar.
tangle, v. deurmekaar maak, knoop; deurmekaar raak, verwar.
tangle, n. verwarring; warboel.
tango, tango.
tank, tenk; reservoir; vegwa.
tannery, looiery.
tannin, looisuur, tannien.
tantalize, tantaliseer, tempteer.
tantamount, dieselfde as, gelykstaande met.
tantrum, slegte luim.
tap, n. kraan, kantien.
tap, v. tik, klop.
tape, n. band, lint; maatband; – recorder, bandopnemer.
taper, v. spits uitloop; spits maak (word).
tapestry, behangsel.
tape-worm, lintwurm.
tappet, klepligter.

tar, n. teer.
tardy, traag, stadig, langsaam; laat.
tare, n. tarra.
target, skyf, teiken; mikpunt.
tariff, tarief.
tarnish, v. dof maak, dof word, aanslaan; besoedel; verbleek.
tarpaulin, teerseil, bokseil.
tarry, v. wag; vertoef, draal, draai.
tart, a. suur; bitsig, skerp.
tart, n. tert(jie); flerrie.
tartar, n. wynsteen; aanpaksel (aan tande); cream of –, kremetart.
Tartar, n. Tartaar; woestaard.
task, n. taak, werk, arbeid.
taskmaster, baas, werkgewer; opsiener.
tassel, n. klossie.
taste, v. proe; smaak; ondervind.
taste, n. smaak; voorliefde; happie, slukkie.
tasteful, smaakvol; smaaklik.
tasty, smaaklik, lekker.
tatter, lap, toiing, flenter, vod.
tattle, v. babbel; kekkel, skinder.
tattoo, n. taptoe.
tattoo, v. tatoeëer.
taunt, v. beskimp, hoon, terg.
taunt, n. belediging, verwyt, spot.
taut, styf, gespanne; in goeie toestand.
tautology, toutologie.
tawdry, opgeskik, uitspattig.
tax, v. belas.
tax, n. belasting; las, proef.
taxi, **(taxi-cab)**, taxi.
taxidermist, diere-opstopper.
taxpayer, belastingbetaler.
tea, tee.
teach, leer, skoolhou.
teacher, onderwyser(es), (skool)meester.
tea-cosy, teemus.
teak, kiaathout.
team, n. span; ploeg.
teapot, teepot.
tear, v. skeur; ruk, losruk; pluk; vlie(g).
tear, n. skeur.
tear, n. traan.
tea-room, kafee, koffiekamer.
tease, v. terg, pla, versondig: uitkam.
tease, n. plaaggees, terggees.
tea-service, **tea-set**, teeservies.
teaspoon, teelepel.
teat, tepel, tiet; speen.
technical, tegnies.
technician, tegnikus.
technique, tegniek.
tee, n. bof (in gholf); pen (in koits).
tee, v. bof; afslaan.
teem, wemel, krioel.
teenager, tienderjarige.
teethe, tande kry.
telegram, telegram, draadberig.
telegraph, n. telegraaf.
telegraph, v. telegrafeer.
telepathy, telepatie.
telephone, n. telefoon.
telephone, v. telefoneer, opbel, oplui.
telescope, n. teleskoop, verkyker.
telex, n. teleks(toestel); v. per teleks stuur.
tell, vertel, verhaal; sê, meld; bepaal; onderskei.
temerity, vermetelheid, roekeloosheid.
temper, v. brei (van klei); hard maak; temper, matig, versag.
temper, n. humeur; stemming; slegte humeur; mengsel; hardheid.
temperament, temperament, geaardheid.
temperamental, temperamenteel.

temperance, matigheid, gematigdheid.
temperate, matig, gematig; bedaard.
temperature, temperatuur, warmtegraad.
tempered, getemper(d); gehumeur(d).
tempest, storm, orkaan.
tempestuous, stormagtig, onstuimig.
temple, tempel.
tempo, tempo, maat.
temporary, tydelik.
temporize, tyd wen, uitstel, draal, sloer.
tempt, verlei, versoek, verlok; beproef.
ten, tien.
tenable, houbaar; verdedigbaar.
tenacious, taai; klewerig; sterk.
tend, gaan, beweeg; geneig wees, dien.
tend, oppas, kyk na, versorg.
tendency, neiging, strekking.
tender, n. koolwa, tender.
tender, v. aanbied; inskrywe.
tender, a. teer, sag; swak, tingerig; teergevoelig.
tendon, sening.
tendril, rank.
tenement, verblyf, woonhuis; huurkamers, pag-grond.
tennis, tennis.
tennis-court, tennisbaan.
tenon, tap, pen.
tenon-saw, rugsaag.
tenor, koors, gang, rigting, loop; strekking; afskrif; tenoor.
tense, n. tyd, tempus.
tense, a. styf; gespanne.
tension, spanning; gespannenheid, spankrag; opgewondenheid.
tent, tent; kap.
tentacle, voelhoring, voelorgaan.
tentative, a. proef . . . tydelik, tentatief.
tenuous, tingerig, dun, klein, fyn.
tenure, besit; – of office, dienstyd.
tepid, lou.
term, n. perk, grens; tydperk, termyn; kwartaal, semester; sitting; uitdrukking; lid; bewoor-ding.
term, v. noem.
termagant, n. kyfagtige vrou, heks.
terminate, v. eindig, ophou; afloop; 'n einde maak aan, afbreek.
terminology, terminologie.
terminus, terminus, eindpunt.
termite, termiet, rysmier.
terrace, n. terras.
terrain, terrein.
terrestial, a. aards, ondermaans, aards- . . .
terrible, vreeslik, verskriklik, yslik.
terrier, terriër.
terrific, verskriklik, skrikwekkend.
terrify, verskrik, bang maak.
territory, grond(gebied), landstreek.
terror, vrees, ontsteltenis; gruwel.
terrorize, skrik aanja, terroriseer.
terse, pittig, kort en bondig, beknop.
test, n. toets, toetssteen; proef; reagens; smelt-kroes; toetswedstryd.
test, v. op die proef stel, toets.
testament, testament.
testify, getuig; getuienis aflê.
testimonial, getuigskrif; huldeblyk.
testimony, getuienis, verklaring.
test-match, toetswedstryd.
test-tube, proefglasie, reageerbuisie.
tetanus, klem, kramp, tetanus.
tether, op lyn sit (slaan).
Teutonic, Teutoons (Teutonies); Germaans.
text, teks; onderwerp.
textbook, handboek, leerboek.

textile, n. weefstof.
texture, weefsel, samestelling, bou.
than, as, dan.
thank, bedank, dank.
thankful, dankbaar.
thanks, dank, dankbetuiging; dankie
that, pron. daardie, dié; wat.
that, adv. so.-
that, conj. dat, sodat, opdat.
that, adj. sodanig, soveel.
thatch, v. dek; –ed roof, strooidak.
thaw, v. smelt, dooi; ontdooi.
the, die.
theatre, teater, skouburg; toneel.
theft, diefstal.
their, hul(le); –s, hulle s'n.
theme, tema, onderwerp; opstel.
themselves, hul(le), hul(le)self.
then, adv. toe; dan; daarna.
then, a. toenmalig, destyds.
then, conj. dus, dan.
thence, vandaar, daaruit, derhalwe.
thenceforth, thenceforward, van toe af, sedert dié tyd.
theodolite, hoogtemeter, teodoliet.
theology, teologie, godgeleerdheid.
theorem, stelling, teorema.
theorize, teoretiseer.
theory, teorie.
therapeutic, terapeuties, geneeskundig.
there, adv. daar, daarso; daarheen, daarnatoe, soontoe (soheentoe)
thereabout(s), daaromtrent, daar iewers, daar rond, daar in die buurt; omtrent, naasteby.
thereafter, daarna; daarvolgens.
thereby, op dié manier, daardeur.
therefor, daarvoor.
therefore, daarom, derhalwe, dus.
therefrom, daarvan.
therein, daarin.
thereof, daarvan, hiervan.
thereto, daartoe; boonop, behalwe.
thereupon, daarna, daarop.
therm, warmte-eenheid, term.
thermometer, termometer.
Thermos, Thermos, warmfles.
these, hierdie, die.
thesis, stelling; tesis, dissertasie.
they, hulle (hul).
thick, a. dik, dig; troebel; dom; intiem.
thicket, ruigte, bossies.
thickset, digbegroei; geset, dik, fris.
thick-skinned, dikhuidig.
thief, dief.
thieve, steel.
thigh, dy.
thimble, vingerhoed.
thin, a. dun; maer, skraal; yl; flou; deursigtig; swak.
thing, ding; iets; saak.
things, goed, goeters.
thingamy, thingumajig, thingumbob, dinges, hoe-se-naam.
think, dink; glo, beskou; van plan wees.
third, n. 'n derde, derde deel.
thirst, n. dors; – after, for, of, dors na.
thirsty, dors, dorstig.
thirteen, dertien.
thirty, dertig.
this, dit; hierdie, dié.
thistle, dissel.
thither, daarheen, daarnatoe, soontoe.
thong, riem; voor-, agterslag.
thorax, bors(stuk), borsharnas; borskas.
thorn, doring; doringbos, doringstruik.

thorny, doringrig, doringagtig, moeilik.
thorough, grondig; volkome, volledig.
thorough-bred, a. volbloed; welopgevoed.
thoroughfare, deurgang; (hoof)straat.
though, ofskoon, alhoewel, al.
thought, gedagte; oorweging; oorpeinsing; idee, inval.
thoughtful, bedagsaam; nadinkend; suggestief.
thousand, duisend.
thrash, (uit)dors; slaan; oortref, kafloop; – out, uitpluis.
thrashing, (die) dors; pak slae, loesing.
thrashing-machine, dorsmasjien, trapmasjien.
thread, n. draad.
thread, v. draad deursteek (insteek); inryg.
threat, dreigement, bedreiging.
threaten, bedreig; dreig (met).
three, drie.
three-ply, driedraads, drielaag . . .
three-quarter, agterspeler; driekwart.
thresh, sien thrash.
threshold, drumpel (drempel); aanvang, begin, ingang.
thrift, spaarsaamheid, suinigheid.
thrill, v. tril, ril, sidder; laat tril (ril), deurdring.
thrilling, trillend, rillend; spannend, opwindend; sensasioneel.
thrive, voorspoedig wees; floreer; goed aard, geil groei.
throat, keel; ingang, uitgang.
throb, v. klop, pols slaan; bewe, ril.
throe(s), wee, (weë); pyn, (doods)angs.
thrombosis, aarverstopping, trombose.
throne, n. troon.
throng, n. gedrang, menigte.
throng, v. toestroom, verdring.
throttle, n. keelgorrel; smoorklep.
throttle, v. verwurg, versmoor, verstik, laat stik; smoor.
through, prep. deur; uit.
through, adv. deur, tot die einde; deur en deur.
through, a. deurgaande, deur- . . .
throughout, adv. dwarsdeur, deurgaans, geheel en al; in alle opsigte.
throughout, prep. dwarsdeur.
throw, v. gooi, werp, smyt; afgooi; ondergooi; sleg.
throw, n. gooi, worp.
thrum, tokkel, trommel, tjingel.
thrush, spru; lyster.
thrust, v. stoot; steek.
thud, n. dowwe slag, plof, bons.
thud, v. neerdoef, neerplof, (neer)bons.
thumb, v. beduimel, vlek; betas.
thumb-tack, drukspyker(tjie).
thump, n. stamp, slag, hou.
thunder, n. donder, donderweer; donderslag.
thunder, v. donder; bulder, brul.
thunder-clap, donderslag.
thunderstorm, donderstorm.
Thursday, Donderdag.
thus, dus, aldus.
thwart, v. dwarsboom, teenwerk.
tick, v. tik; – off, aanstreep, merk.
tick, n. luis, bosluis, skaappluis.
ticket, kaartjie, toegangskaartjie, etiket.
ticket-examiner, kaartjiesondersoeker; kaartjies-kontroleur.
ticket-office, kaartjieskantoor.
tickey, trippens.
tickle, v. kielie; streel.
tide, n. gety, eb en vloed; tyd.
tidings, tyding, nuus, berig.
tidy, a. netjies, sindelik, mooi.
tidy, v. aan kant maak, opruim; opknap.

tie, v. bind, vasmaak; knoop, strik; gelykop speel; ewe veel punte behaal; verbind; beperk.
tie, n. band, knoop; das; verpligting; gelykspel.
tie-beam, dwarsbalk; dwarslêer.
tier, ry, reeks.
tie-rod, (stuur)koppelstang, koggelstok.
tiger, tier; grootprater, twissoeker.
tight, a. styf, vas, stewig; dig; nou; styf(gespan); netjies, agtermekaar; getik; lekker; skaars.
tights, 'n spanbroek; 'n vleispakkie.
tile, n. teël; (dak)pan.
till, v. bewerk, bebou, omploeë.
till, n. geldlaai, toonbanklaai.
till, prep. tot.
till, conj. tot, totdat.
tiller, n. roerpen.
tilt, v. skuins staan, skuins hou, (een kant) oplig; wip, laat wip.
timber, hout, timmerhout; bos, woud.
time, n. tyd; keer, maat.
time, v. reël, reguleer; die tyd bereken; die maat aangee.
timekeeper, tydaangeër, tydopnemer.
timely, tydig, betyds, net op tyd.
time-table, rooster, spoorboek.
timid, skamerig, bedees, bangerig.
timorous, skroomvallig; bangerig.
tin, n. tin; blik.
tin, v. vertin; inmaak; –ned meat, blikkiesvleis.
tincture, n. tinktuur; tikkie; tint.
tinder, tonteldoek, tontel.
tinge, v. tint, kleur; 'n smakie gee.
tingle, v. suis, tuit, jeuk, prikkel.
tinker, v. heelmaak, lap; knoei, konkel.
tinkle, v. klink, tingel; laat klingel.
tin-opener, bliksnyer.
tint, n. tint.
tiny, klein; gering.
tip, n. punt, top, tip.
tip, v. wip, laat wip; skeef (skuins) hou; (laat) omkantel; gooi; 'n fooi gee; 'n wenk gee.
tip, n. fooi(tjie); wenk; stootjie, tikkie; vuil-goedhoop.
tipple, v. dopsteek, die elmboog lig.
tipsy, dronk, lekker, aan, getik.
tip-toe, v. op die tone loop.
tire, moeg word, teë word (van); vermoei.
tire, n. wielband; buiteband; kleding.
tired, moeg, tam.
tireless, onvermoeid.
tiresome, vermoeiend, afmattend.
tiro, tyro, beginner, nuweling, 'n groene.
tissue, weefsel; goudlaken; reeks.
tissue-paper, sypapier, sneespapier.
titanic, titanies, reusagtig, geweldig.
titbit, lekkernytjie.
tithe, tiende, tiende deel.
titivate, tittivate, mooimaak.
title, n. (ere)titel; opskrif; titel; eiendomsbewys.
title-deed, eiendomsbewys; kaart en transport.
title-page, titelblad.
titter, giggel.
to, prep. na, tot, na . . . toe; vir; voor; aan.
to, (+ infinitief) te, om te.
to, adv. toe.
toad, padda.
toadstool, paddastoel.
toady, n. inkruiper, lekker.
toast, n. roosterbrood; heildronk.
toast, v. rooster, braai; warm maak; die heildronk instel.
toastmaster, seremoniemeester.
tobacco, tabak.
tobacconist, tabakhandelaar.
tobacco-pouch, tabaksak (twaksak).

today, vandag; teenswoordig.
toddle, v. waggel.
to-do, ophef, opskudding, gedoente.
toe, n. toon.
together, saam, bymekaar, gelyk.
toil, v. swoeg, sloof, arbei, sukkel.
token, aandenking, gedagtenis; teken.
tolerable, draaglik, redelik, taamlik.
tolerant, verdraagsaam.
tolerate, verdra, duld, toelaat.
toll, n. tol, tolgeld.
toll, v. (stadig) lui, slaan, klepper.
tomahawk, strydbyl.
tomato, tamatie.
tomb, graf, graftombe, grafkelder.
tombstone, grafsteen.
tomcat, mannetjie(s)kat.
tomorrow, môre.
ton, ton.
tone, n. toon, klank; klem; aard; kleur, tint; gees, aard.
tongs, tang(etjie).
tongue, tong; taal, spraak; tongetjie; klepel (van 'n klok); landtong.
tonight, vanaand, vannag.
tonsil, mangel.
too, te, alte, ook.
tool, n. gereedskap; werktuig.
toot, v. blaas, toeter.
tooth, n. tand.
toothache, tandpyn.
tooth-brush, tandeborsel.
tooth-paste, tand(e)pasta.
top, n. top, kruin; hoof, bo-ent (van 'n tafel); kap; hoogtepunt.
top, a. hoogste, boonste, eerste, beste.
top, v. top, snoei; tot bo klim; hoër wees as; oortref, klop.
top-boots, kapstewels.
top-dog, bobaas.
top-dressing, bobemesting.
toper, dronklap, suiplap.
top hat, pluiskeil, hoë hoed.
top-heavy, topswaar.
topic, onderwerp.
topical, plaaslik; aktueel.
topography, topografie.
topple, (laat) omval, omkantel, omtuimel.
topsyturvy, adv. onderstebo, deurmekaar, agterstevoor.
torch, toorts, fakkel; flits(lig).
toreador, toreador.
torment, v. kwel, folter, martel, pla.
tormentor, kwelgees, plaaggees.
tornado, tornado, orkaan.
torpedo, n. torpedo; knalsinjaal.
torpid, slapend; verstyf; stadig, traag; ongevoelig.
torrent, stroom; stortvloed.
torrid, versengend, skroeiwarm.
torsion, draai(ing), kronkeling; torsie.
torso, romp.
tortoise, skilpad.
torture, n. foltering, marteling.
torture, v. martel, pynig, folter.
toss, v. gooi, opgooi, rondgooi; rondrol; hot en haar slinger.
toss, n. loot.
total, a. totaal, (ge)heel.
total, n. totaal, volle som (bedrag).
totter, (wiggel-)waggel, wankel, slinger.
touch, v. (aan)raak, aanroer, voel aan; tik; aanslaan; bykom; tref, aandoen, roer.
touch, n. aanraking; tikkie; gevoel; trek; bietjie,

sweempie, aanslag; styl; buitelyn (voetbal); buiteskop.
touching, a. roerend, aandoenlik.
touching, prep. betreffende.
touch-line, buitelyn.
touchy, fyngevoelig, liggeraak; kort van draad.
tough, taai; hard, styf; koppig; moeilik, lastig.
tour, n. rond(reis), toer.
tour, v. rondreis, deurreis; toer.
tournament, steekspel, toernooi.
tourniquet, aar-afbinder, aarpers.
tousle, rondruk; verfrommel, (hare) deurmekaar maak.
tow, v. trek, sleep.
toward(s), prep. na . . . toe; teenoor; tot; naby.
towel, n. handdoek; roller –, rolhanddoek.
tower, n. toring; kasteel.
tower, v. hoog uitsteek bo; regop vlie.
towering, baie hoog; geweldig, hewig.
town, dorp, stad.
town clerk, stadsklerk.
town council, stadsraad.
town councillor, stadsraadslid.
town hall, stadsaal, stadhuis.
toxic, giftig; gif- . . . ; vergiftigings- . . .
toy, n. speelding(etjie); speelbal.
trace, v. natrek, oortrek; skets, teken; afbaken, neerlê; opspoor, die spoor sny; naspoor, nagaan.
trace, n. spoor, voetspoor; teken.
trace, n. string.
trachea, lugpyp; lugbuis; tragea.
track, n. spoor; weg; spoor(weg), spoor(baan); renbaan, reisiesbaan.
track, v. opspoor, spoor sny; naspoor, nagaan.
tract, traktaatjie; streek.
tractable, geseglik, gedwee, inskiklik.
tractor, straatlokomotief; trekker.
trade, n. handel, bedryf, ambag.
trade, v. handel, handel drywe.
trade mark, handelsmerk.
tradesman, handelaar; werksman.
trade wind, passaatwind.
tradition, tradisie, oorlewering.
traduce, belaster, beskinder.
traffic, n. handel; verkeer; – jam, verkeersknoop.
tragedy, tragedie, treurspel.
tragic, tragies.
trail, n. (na)sleep; streep; stert (van 'n komeet); sleepsel; rank; spoor; pad.
trail, v. sleep; loshang; opspoor; kruip.
trailer, rankplant, sleepkar(retjie), -wa(entjie).
train, v. leer, oplei, oefen, brei; dresseer; dril; snoei, lei; lok.
train, n. sleep; nasleep; stert; gevolg, stoet, reeks, streep, ry, aaneenskakeling; trein.
trainer, afrigter, instrukteur; breier.
training-college, opleidingskool.
trait, (karakter)trek, eienskap; trek.
traitor, verraaier.
traitorous, verraderlik.
trajectory, baan; koeëlbaan.
tram, trem; koolwa.
tramp, v. stamp; stap, loop, rondloop.
tramp, n. getrap, voetstap; hoefslag; wandeltog; rondloper.
trample, v. trap, vertrap.
trance, verrukking; beswyming, skyndood; hipnose.
tranquil, kalm, stil, rustig.
transact, afhandel, verrig, doen.
transcend, oortref, te bo(we) gaan.
transcribe, afskryf, oorskryf, transkribeer.
transfer, v. oordra, transporteer; oorplaas, verplaas; afdruk.

transferable, oordraagbaar, verhandelbaar.
transfigure, van gedaante verander (verwissel), vervorm.
transfix, deursteek, deurboor.
transform, (van vorm) verander, van gedaante wissel, vervorm.
transformer, tranformator (elektr.).
transfuse, oorgiet, oorstort; oortap.
transgress, oortree, sondig.
transient, verbygaand; verganklik.
transistor, transistor, kristalbuis.
transition, oorgang.
transitive, oorganklik, transitief.
translate, vertaal, oorsit; opvat; verplaas.
translucent, deurskynend.
transmigrate, verhuis; oorgaan.
transmit, aanstuur, deurstuur, oorstuur; nalaat; deurlaat; voortplant.
transmitter, aanstuurder; sender; voortplanter.
transmute, verander, omwissel.
transom, latei; dwarshout, dwarsbalk.
transparent, deursigtig, deurskynend.
transpire, uitsweet, uitlek.
transplant, verplant, oorplaas.
transport, v. vervoer, transporteer; wegvoer; in vervoering bring.
trap, n. strik, wip; val, vanggat, vanghok; slagyster; valstrik; lokvoël; lokvink.
trap, v. (in 'n strik) vang; betrap.
trap-door, valdeur.
trapeze, sweefstok.
trapezium, trapesium.
trapper, pelsjagter.
trash, vuilgoed, afval; bog, kaf.
travel, v. (rond)reis; beweeg, loop.
traveller, reisiger.
traverse, n. dwarshout, dwarsbalk; dwarslyn; dwarsgalery; dwarsbeweging, dwarsgang; dwarswal.
traverse, v. aflê, afreis; deurreis; dwarsboom; draai.
travesty, n. parodie.
trawler, treiler; sleepnettrekker.
tray, skinkbord; platkissie (vrugte).
treacherous, verraderlik; vals.
treachery, verraad; trouloosheid.
treacle, stroop.
tread, v. trap, loop, stap; betree.
tread, n. stap, trap; tree, skrede.
treadle, trapper; pedaal.
treason, verraad.
treasure, n. skat; rykdom.
treasurer, penningmeester, tesourier.
treat, v. behandel; onthaal, trakteer.
treatise, verhandeling.
treatment, behandeling.
treaty, verdrag, ooreenkoms.
treble, v. verdrievoudig.
tree, boom; as; swingelhout; lees.
trellis, n. traliewerk, latwerk, prieel.
tremble, v. bewe, sidder, gril.
tremendous, vreeslik, geweldig.
tremor, bewing, trilling, siddering.
trench, n. sloot, voor; loopgraaf.
trenchant, skerp, vlymend, kragtig.
trend, n. loop, neiging, rigting.
trepidation, ontsteltenis, angs; bewerasie.
trespass, v. oortree; inbreuk maak (op); sondig; misbruik maak van.
trestle, bok, stut.
trial, toets, proef, proefneming, eksperiment; verhoor; beproewing.
trial-match, proefwedstryd.
triangle, driehoek.
tribe, stam; geslag, familie.

tribulation, beproewing, verdrukking.
tribune, spreekgestoelte, verhoog.
tributary, n. skatpligtige; takrivier.
tribute, skatpligtigheid; huldeblyk, hulde.
trick, n. skelmstreek; toer, kunsie; gewoonte, manier; poets, streek; slag (kaartspel).
trick, v. fop, bedrieg.
trickle, v. drup, tap; rol.
tricycle, driewieler.
trifle, n. nietigheid, kleinigheid; koekpoeding.
trifle, adv. bietjie; effe.
trifle, v. speel, korswel; verbeusel.
trigger, sneller, trekker.
trigonometry, driehoeksmeting, trigonometrie.
trim, a. netjies, fyn, viets; in orde.
trim, v. in orde bring; regmaak; knop, snoei; mooimaak, opskik, versier.
trinket, sieraad, snuistery.
trip, v. trippel; struikel; pootjie; betrap.
trip, n. uitstappie, toggie, seereis.
tripe, binnegoed; afval; kaf.
triplet, drietal, drieling; triool (musiek).
triplicate, n. triplikaat.
tripod, drievoet.
trite, afgesaag, alledaags, uitgedien.
triumph, n. triomftog; triomf, oorwinning.
triumph, v. seëvier, triomfeer.
trivial, beuselagtig; oppervlakkig.
Trojan, n. Trojaan.
trolley, -ly, trollie; molwa, beuel.
trombone, skuiftrompet.
troopship, transportskip.
trophy, trofee, ereteken, prys; beker.
tropic, n. keerkring; T. of Capricorn, Steenbokskeerkring; T. of Cancer, Kreefskeerkring: the -s, die trope, die keerkringe.
trot, v. draf, laat draf.
trouble, v. kwel; pla; lastig val.
trouble, n. sorg, kwelling, verdriet; moeilikheid, moeite, las, ongerief.
troublesome, lastig, moeilik.
trough, bak, trog, bakkis.
trounce, uitklop; 'n kafferpak gee.
troupe, geselskap, troep.
trouser(s), broek.
trousseau, uitset, uitrusting.
trout, forel (vis).
trowel, troffel.
truant, n. play -, stokkies draai.
truce, wapenstilstand; verposing.
truck, n. ruilhandel; negosiegoed; kaf.
truck, n. trok, goederewa; vragwa; waentjie.
truculent, wild, woes, wreed.
trudge, v. aansukkel, voortstrompel.
true, a. waar; suiwer, eg; opreg, standvastig; juis.
truly, waarlik, regtig, werklik; trou.
trump, v. - up, versin, uit die duim suie.
trump, n. troef(kaart); 'n staatmaker.
trump, v. troef; 'n troefkaart speel.
trumpet, n. trompet.
truncheon, stok, knuppel.
trundle, v. rol.
trunk, stam, stomp; romp (van die liggaam); hooflyn; trommel, koffer; slurp (van olifant).
trunk-call, hooflyngesprek.
truss, v. stut; vasbind, opbind.
truss, n. stut; bondel, tros; breukband.
trust, n. vertroue; geloof; trust, kartel; bewaring.
trust, v. vertrou; toevertrou (aan).
trustee, trustee; kurator.
trustworthy, vertroubaar.
truth, waarheid; eerlikheid.
try, probeer; op die proef stel, toets; ondersoek; suiwer, kook.

try, n. kans, poging; 'n drie (voetbal).
trying, moeilik; afmattend, vermoeiend.
try-square, winkelhaak.
Tsar, Tsaar.
tsetse, tsetsevlieg.
t-square, tekenhaak.
tub, vat, balie, kuip; badkuip.
tube, buis, pyp; binneband; tonneltrein.
tuber, knol; aartappel; knop. geswel.
tuberculosis, tuberkulose; tering.
tuck, v. opnaaisels maak (insit); plooi; omslaan, inslaan, oprol; intrek; lekker toemaak (toe-draai).
tuck, n. opnaaisel, pylnaat; snoepgoed.
tuck-shop, snoepwinkel.
Tuesday, Dinsdag.
tuft, n. bossie; klossie, kwassie; kuif(ie); trossie, graspolletjie.
tug, v. trek, ruk, pluk; sleep.
tug, n. ruk, trek; sleepboot.
tuition, onderwys; skoolgelde, klasgeld.
tulip, tulp.
tumble, v. tuimel, val; rol; val-val loop (hard-loop); onderstebo gooi, rondgooi; neertrek, neerskiet; bolmakiesie slaan.
tumbler, akrobaat; tuimelaar (duif); (water-)glas.
tumour, geswel.
tumult, opskudding, lawaai, rumoer.
tundra, mossteppe, toendra.
tune, n. toon, melodie, deuntjie.
tune, v. stem; (laat) harmonieer (met).
tuneful, melodieus, welluidend.
tungsten, wolfram.
tunnel, n. tonnel; mynskag.
tunny, v. to(r)nyn.
turban, tulband.
turbid, troebel, modderig, vuil.
turbine, turbine.
turbo-jet, turbinestraal.
turbo-prop(eller), turbineskroef.
turbulent, onstuimig; woelig; oproerig.
tureen, so(e)pkom.
turf, n. turf, kweek; grasveld; **the –,** die renbaan, re(i)siesbaan.
turgid, hoogdrawend, opgeswel.
Turk, Turk; harde kop.
Turkey, n. Turkye.
turkey, kalkoen.
turmoil, gewoel, rumoer, verwarring.

turn, v. draai, laat draai; gaan, keer; omdraai; omgaan; omslaan; verander; (aandag) wy, gee; laat weggaan, laat omdraai; omtrek; word; maak; vertaal; suur word, suur maak.
turn, n. draai, bog, kromming; wending, keer-punt; wandelinkie, toertjie; kans, beurt, ge-leentheid; diens, vriendskap; skok.
turning-point, keerpunt.
turnip, raap.
turnstile, draaisport, draaihek.
turpentine, terpentyn.
turret, torinkie; skiettoring.
turtle, n. seeskilpad.
turtle-dove, tortelduif.
tusk, slagtand; tand.
tussle, n. gestoei, worsteling, bakleiery.
tutor, n. privaatonderwyser.
twaddle, n. geklets, gesanik, gebabbel.
twang, n. snaarklank; neusklank.
tweak, v. knyp; draai; ruk, pluk.
tweezers, (haar)tangetjie.
twelve, twaalf.
twenty, twintig.
twice, twee maal, twee keer.
twig, takkie, twyg(ie).
twilight, skemer(lig), skemerte, skemering.
twin, n. (een van 'n) tweeling; ewebeeld; –s, 'n tweeling.
twine, n. tou, seilgare.
twine, n. vleg, draai; strengel.
twinge, n. steek, pyn; kwelling.
twinkle, v. flikker, fonkel: knip(oog).
twirl, v. (in die rondte) draai, swaai.
twist, v. draai, vleg; kronkel, strengel; krul; verdraai; verwring, vertrek, verrek.
twitch, v. trek, ruk; vertrek.
twitter, v. tjilp, tjirp, kwetter; giggel.
two, twee.
type, n. tipe, soort, voorbeeld; sinnebeeld; (druk)letter; setsel.
type, v. tik; tipeer.
typhoid, a. – fever, ingewandskoors.
typhoon, tifoon.
typhus(-fever), tifus(koors), luiskoors.
typist, tikster (tikker), tipis(te).
tyranny, dwingelandy, wreedheid.
tyrant, tiran, dwingeland.
tyre, buiteband.

ubiquitous, alomteenwoordig.
udder, uier.
ugly, a. lelik, naar; haatlik.
ulcer, sweer; verrotte plek, kanker.
ulterior, aan die ander kant; verder, later; geheim.
ultimate, uiteindelik, eind- . . . , uiterste, laaste; fundamenteel, primêr.
ultimatum, ultimatum; grondbeginsel.
ultimo, van die vorige maand.
ultimo, van die vorige maand, laaslede.
ultra-violet, ultraviolet.
umber, n. omber; ombervis.
umbrage, skaduwee; aanstoot, belediging.
umbrella, sambreel.
umpire, n. skeidsregter, arbiter.
umpire, v. as skeidsregter optree.
unabashed, onbeskaam(d); nie verleë nie.
unable, onbekwaam, nie in staat nie.
unaccustomed, ongewoon.
unaffected, natuurlik, ongedwonge, eg.
unaided, sonder hulp, alleen.
unanimous, eenstemmig, eenparig.
unanswered, onbeantwoord.
unarmed, ongewapen(d), ontwapen(d).
unashamed, onbeskaam(d), onbeskof.
unasked, ongevra(ag), ongenooi.
unassailable, onweerlegbaar, onbetwisbaar.
unassuming, beskeie.
unattainable, onbereikbaar.
unauthorized, onwettig, onbevoeg.
unavailing, nutteloos, tevergeefs.
unavoidable, onvermydelik.
unaware, onbewus, onwetend.
unawares, onverwags, onverhoeds; onwetend.
unbalanced, onewewigtig.
unbearable, ondraaglik, onuitstaanbaar.
unbeaten, onoorwonne; ongebaan.
unbend, ontspan; vriendeliker word.
unblemished, onbevlek, onbesmet, skoon.
unblushing, skaamteloos.
unbounded, grensloos, onbegrens.
unbridled, onbeteuel(d), toomloos.
unbroken, onafgebroke; ongestoord; heel; ongetem.
unburden; ontboesem, lug gee aan (die gevoelens); – oneself, jou hart uitstort.
unbutton, losknoop.
uncalled: – for, onvanpas, onnodig.
uncanny, geheimsinnig, onheilspellend, spookagtig.
unceasing, voortdurend, aanhoudend, onafgebroke.
uncertain, onseker, twyfelagtig; veranderlik, ongestadig; onvas.
uncivil, onbeleef, onvriendelik, onbeskof.
uncivilized, onbeskaaf, barbaars.
unclaimed, onopgeëis; nie gelos nie.
uncle, oom.
uncomfortable, ongemaklik, ongerieflik; ontuis, verleë.
uncommon, buitengewoon, ongewoon.
uncompromising, onversetlik, ontoegewend.
unconcerned, onverskillig, onbekommerd.
unconditional, onvoorwaardelik.
unconnected, onsamehangend, los.
unconquerable, onoorwinlik.
unconscious, onbewus; bewusteloos.
unconstitutional, ongrondwettig.
uncontrollable, onbedwingbaar, onbeteuelbaar.
unconventional, vry, natuurlik.
unconverted, onbekeer(d); onvervyf.
uncork, ontkurk, die prop uittrek.
uncouth, lomp, baar; ongepoets.
uncover, oopmaak; ontbloot.

unctuous, salwend; vleiend; vetterig.
uncurbed, onbeteuel(d), ongebreidel(d).
undamaged, onbeskadig.
undated, ongedateer(d), sonder datum.
undaunted, onverskrokke, onversaag; nie afgeskrik nie.
undecided, onbeslis; besluiteloos.
undeniable, onloënbaar.
under, prep. onder, benede.
under, a. onder- . . . , onderste.
underclothes, underclothing, onderklere.
underdone, halfgaar, half-rou.
underestimate, onderskat, te gering ag.
underfed, ondervoed.
underfoot, onder die voete.
undergo, ondergaan; deurstaan, uitstaan.
undergraduate, ongegradueerde.
underground, a. onderaards, ondergronds.
undergrowth, struikgewas, ruigte.
underhand, a. agterbaks, slinks.
underlie, lê onder; ten grondslag lê aan.
underline, onderstreep.
undermine, uitkalwe; ondermyn.
underneath, onder, benede.
underrate, onderskat.
under-secretary, ondersekretaris.
undersell, goedkoper verkoop as.
undersigned, ondergetekende.
understand, begryp, verstaan, vat.
understanding, a. intelligent.
understanding, n. verstand, begrip; verstandhouding.
understood, verstaan; vanselfsprekend.
undertake, onderneem; aanneem; aanpak.
undertaker, lykbesorger.
underwear, onderklere.
underworld, doderyk, onderwêreld; agterbuurte.
underwrite, onderteken; verseker.
undesirable, a. ongewens; ongerieflik.
undeveloped, onontwikkel(d).
undignified, onwaardig, sonder waardigheid.
undisciplined, ongedissiplineer(d), tugloos; ongeoefen.
undisguised, onvermom; openhartig, opreg.
undismayed, onverskrokke, onvervaard.
undisputed, onbetwis, onbestrede.
undivided, onverdeel(d), geheel.
undo, losmaak, oopmaak, tot niet maak.
undoubtedly, ongetwyfeld, sonder twyfel.
undress, v. ontklee, uittrek.
undue, oordrewe, buitensporig; onbehoorlik.
undulating, golwend, wuiwend.
unduly, oormatig, bowemate, te veel.
undying, onsterflik, ewig.
unearth, (wild) opja; op-, uitgrawe, uitspit; aan die lig bring; opspoor.
unearthy, bowenatuurlik; spookagtig, geheimsinnig.
uneasy, ongemaklik; onrustig; ongerus, besorg, beangs; verontrustend; rusteloos.
uneducated, onopgevoed, ongeletterd.
unemployed, werkloos; ongebruik.
unequal, ongelyk, verskillend.
unequivocal, duidelik, onomwonde.
uneven, ongelyk, hobbelagtig, stamperig, skurf; onewe; ongestadig.
uneventful, stil; onbelangrik.
unexpected, onverwag.
unexpectedly, onverwags.
unexpired, onverstreke, nie om nie.
unfailing, onfeilbaar; onuitputlik; getrou, (ge)wis, seker.
unfair, onbillik; oneerlik, partydig.
unfaithful, ontrou, vals.
unfavourable, ongunstig.

unfeeling, gevoelloos, wreed, ongevoelig.
unfeigned, ongeveins, opreg, eg, waar.
unfit, onbekwaam, ongeskik; ongepas.
unfold, oopmaak, oopvou, uitsprei, ontvou; openbaar maak; ontplooi, ontwikkel.
unforeseen, onvoorsien.
unforgettable, onvergeetlik.
unfortunate, a. ongelukkig, rampspoedig.
unfounded, ongegrond; vals.
unfriendly, onvriendelik.
ungainly, lomp, ongemanierd, onhandig.
ungodly, goddeloos, godvergete.
ungovernable, onregeerbaar, wild, woes.
ungrateful, ondankbaar, onerkentlik.
unguarded, onbedagsaam; onbewaak.
unhampered, onbelemmer(d), vry.
unhappy, ongelukkig.
unheard, ongehoor(d).
unheeded, onopgemerk, veronagsaam.
unholy, onheilig, goddeloos.
unhurt, ongekwes, onbeseer(d).
uniform, a. eenvormig, gelykvormig, dieselfde, uniform; eenparig.
uniform, n. uniform.
unify, verenig, tot een maak.
unilateral, eensydig.
unimpaired, onbeskadig, onverswak.
unimpeded, onbelemmer(d), onvertraag.
uniformed, nie op hoogte van sake nie.
unintelligent, dom, bot, onintelligent.
unintelligible, onverstaanbaar, onduidelik.
unintentional, onopsetlik.
uninteresting, oninteressant, droog.
uninterrupted, ongestoor(d), onafgebroke.
union, vereniging, unie; samesmelting; huwelik; eensgesindheid; eenheid; verbond.
unique, a. ongeëwenaard, enig, uniek.
unison, ooreenstemming; eenstemmigheid.
unit, eenheid.
unite, verenig, verbind, saamsmelt; saamwerk; saamvoeg; een word.
unity, eenheid; eensgesindheid, harmonie, ooreenstemming.
universal, universeel, algemeen.
universal joint, kruiskoppelaar.
universe, heelal.
university, n. universiteit.
unjust, onregverdig, onbillik.
unkempt, ongekam; slordig, vuil.
unkept, verwaarloos.
unkind, onvriendelik.
unknown, a. onbekend.
unless, tensy, behalwe, as . . . nie.
unlike, anders, verskillend; ongelyk.
unlikely, onwaarskynlik.
unlimited, onbeperk, onbegrens.
unload, aflaai, ontlaai; die patroon uithaal.
unmanageable, onregeerbaar, onhandelbaar, onbeteuelbaar, lastig.
unmanly, lafhartig, onmanlik.
unmannerly, ongemanierd, onbeskof.
unmistakable, onmiskenbaar.
unmitigated, ongestil, onversag, onverminder; deurtrap.
unmoved, onbewoë, kalm, koel; onbeweeglik, onwrikbaar.
unnatural, onnatuurlik; gemaak.
unnecessary, onnodig, oorbodig.
unnerve, ontsenu, verswak, uitput.
unnoticed, onopgemerk.
unobserved, onopgemerk.
unobtainable, onverkrygbaar.
unoccupied, vry, nie besig nie; leeg, oop.
unofficial, onoffisieel, nie-amptelik.
unopposed, onbestrede; ongehinder.

unpack, uitpak; afpak, aflaai.
unpaid, onbetaal(d).
unpalatable, onsmaaklik; onaangenaam.
unpardonable, onvergeeflik.
unperturbed, onverstoor(d), (hout)gerus.
unpleasant, onaangenaam, onplesierig.
unpopular, ongewild.
unpractical, onprakties, onuitvoerbaar.
unprecedented, ongehoor(d); ongeëwenaard.
unpremiditated, onopsetlik, onvoorberei; spontaan.
unprepared, onvoorberei, onklaar.
unqualified, onbevoeg, onbekwaam; ongekwalifiseer(d), ongesertifiseer(d); onbeperk, algeheel.
unquestioned, onbetwis.
unquestioning, onbeperk, onvoorwaardelik.
unravel, uitrafel, losmaak, ontwar.
unreal, onwerklik, denkbeeldig.
unreasonable, onbillik, onredelik.
unrefined, ongesuiwer(d); onbeskaaf.
unrelenting, onverbiddelik, sonder ophou.
unreliable, onvertroubaar.
unrequited, onbeloon, onbeantwoord.
unreserved, onvoorwaardelik; openhartig, onbespreek.
unresolved, besluiteloos.
unrest, onrus; beroering, oproerigheid.
unrestrained, onbeteuel(d); onbeperk.
unrestricted, vry, onbeperk.
unrighteous, onregverdig, goddeloos.
unrivalled, ongeëwenaard, weergaloos.
unruly, bandeloos; koppig; wild.
unsaddle, afsaal.
unsafe, onveilig, gevaarlik.
unsaid, ongesê.
unsavoury, onsmaaklik, onaangenaam.
unscathed, ongedeer, onbeskadig, veilig.
unscrew, losskroewe, losdraai.
unscrupulous, gewetenloos, beginselloos.
unseat, ontsetel, afgooi.
unseemly, onbetaamlik, onwelvoeglik.
unseen, a. onsigbaar, ongesien.
unseen, n. die onbekende; onvoorbereide werk.
unselfish, onselfsugtig, onbaatsugtig.
unsettle, in die war stuur; van stryk af bring.
unsightly, lelik, mismaak, afsigtelik.
unslaked, ongeblus.
unsound, ongesond; onjuis, vals; swak; sleg.
unspeakable, onuitspreeklik; onuitstaanbaar.
unspoilt, onbedorwe.
unstable, veranderlik, onvas.
unsteady, onvas, los; onbestendig, wisselvallig, onseker.
unstinted, ruim, mild, oorvloedig, rojaal.
unsuccessful, ongelukkig; misluk, vergeefs.
unsuitable, ongeskik.
unsurpassed, onoortroffe.
unsuspecting, argloos, onskuldig.
untamed, ongetem, wild, woes.
untenable, onhoudbaar.
unthinkable, ondenkbaar.
unthinking, onbedagsaam, onnadenkend.
untidy, slordig; deurmekaar.
untie, losmaak, losknoop.
until, sien **till**, totdat.
untimely, ontydig; ongeleë; vroegtydig.
untiring, onvermoeid.
unto, aan, tot, vir.
untold, onvertel; talloos, ongetel; onberekenbaar.
untouched, onaangeroer, onaangeraak.
untrained, ongeoefen; ongeleer(d), baar.
untried, onbeproef; onverhoor(d).
untrodden, ongebaan, onbetree.
untroubled, ongestoord; onbewoë.
untrue, onwaar, vals; ontrou.

untruth, onwaarheid, leuen.
unusual, buitengewoon, ongewoon.
unveil, ontsluier; onthul.
unwarranted, ongewaarborg; ongewettig; onge-
regverdig.
unwary, onversigtig, onbedag.
unwavering, onwankelbaar; standvastig.
unwell, siek(erig), onwel.
unwept, onbetreur, onbeween.
unwholesome, ongesond.
unwieldly, swaar, lastig, lomp.
unwilling, onwillig; ongeneig, ongeneë.
unwind, afdraai, afrol.
unwise, onverstandig, onwys, dom.
unworthy, onwaardig.
unwritten, ongeskryf (ongeskrewe).
up, adv. op, boontoe, na bo, bo.
up, prep. op.
up, n. –s and downs, wisselvallighede.
up-country, na (in) die binneland.
uphill, opdraand; moeilik, swaar.
uphold, hoog hou; handhaaf; verdedig.
upholster, beklee, oortrek; stoffeer.
upkeep, onderhoud, instandhouding.
upland, hoogland.
uplift, v. ophef; oplig.
upon, op, bo-op; by.
upper, n. bo-leer.
uppermost, a. hoogste, boonste.
upright, a. regop; opreg, eerlik.
upright, n. styl, (stut)paal.
uprising, (die) opstaan; rebellie, oproer.
uproar, lawaai, geskreeu.
uproot, ontwortel, uit die grond ruk.
upset, v. omgooi; omval, omslaan; ontstel; in
duie laat val, in die war gooi.
upshot, resultaat, uiteinde, uitslag.
upside-down, onderstebo; deurmekaar.
upstairs, adv. op solder, bo; boontoe.
upward, a. opwaarts.
upward(s), adv. opwaarts, boontoe, na bo.

Ural: – Mountains, Oeralgebergte.
uranium, uraan.
urban, stedelik, stads- . . .
urbane, hoflik, wellewend, fynbeskaaf.
urchin, kleuter; deugniet, kwajong.
urge, aanspoor, aandring; aanja, aandryf;
dwing; nadruk lê op.
urgent, dringend, noodsaaklik.
urinate, urineer.
urn, vaas, kruik; lykbus; koffiekan, teekan.
us, ons.
usage, behandeling; gewoonte; gebruik; usansie.
use, n. gebruik; nut; gewoonte; bekendheid,
voordeel.
use, v. gebruik, gebruik maak van; behandel;
uitoefen, aanwend; verbruik.
used, gewoond (gewend).
useful, nuttig.
useless, nutteloos; vergeefs; nikswerd.
user, gebruiker; right of –, gebruiksreg.
usher, v. binnelei, aankondig, aandien.
usual, gewoon, gebruiklik.
usually, gewoonlik, in die reël.
usufruct, vruggebruik.
usurer, woekeraar.
usurp, wederregtelik (onwettig) in besit neem,
(sig) toeëien, usurpeer.
utensil, gereedskap, werktuig.
utilize, gebruik, aanwend, bestee.
utilitarian, a. nuttigheids- . . . , utiliteits- . . . ,
utilitaristies.
utility, nut, bruikbaarheid, nuttigheid.
utmost, a. uiterste, verste; meeste, grootste.
utmost, n. uiterste (bes).
Utopia, Utopia.
utter, a. totaal, volkome, algeheel.
utter, v. uit(er), uitdruk, uitspreek; (vals geld,
ens.) in omloop bring.
utterly, heeltemal, totaal, volkome.
uttermost, uiterste, verste.
uvula, kleintongetjie, huig.

vacancy, vakature, oop plek; leë ruimte; ledigheid.

vacant, vakant, leeg, oop, onbeset, ledig, vry; lusteloos; ydel; dom.

vacate, uittrek, ontruim; opgee.

vacation, ontruiming; afstand; nietigverklaring; vakansie.

vaccinate, (in)ent.

vaccine, entstof.

vacillate, slinger, swaai; aarsel, weifel.

vacuous, leeg; dom, onnosel, wesenloos.

vacuum, lugleë ruimte, vakuum.

vacuum cleaner, stofsuier.

vagary, gril, gier, luim, nuk, kwint.

vagrant, n. rondloper, (rond)swerwer.

vague, vaag, onduidelik; onseker.

vain, nutteloos; verwaand, ydel; beuselagtig.

valediction, vaarwel, afskeidswoorde.

valet, (lyf)bediende.

valiant, dapper, moedig, onverskrokke.

valid, gegrond, sterk; geldig.

valley, vallei, dal, laagte.

valour, moed, dapperheid.

valuable, kosbaar, waardevol.

valuables, kosbaarhede.

value, n. waarde, prys; betekenis.

value, v. waardeer, op prys stel; waarde heg aan; valueer, skat.

valve, klep; skulp, skaal.

vamp, n. flerrie, koket.

vamp, v. verlok, in haar strik vang.

vampire bat, vampier.

van, n. voorhoede; leiers.

van, n. (vervoer)wa; bagasiewa (van 'n trein), goederewa.

Vandal, Vandaal.

vane, weerhaan, windwys(t)er; wiek.

vanguard, voorhoede; voorpunt.

vanilla, vanielje.

vanish, verdwyn, wegraak; wegsterwe.

vanity, leegheid, holheid, verganklikheid; skyn; ydelheid.

vanquish, verslaan, oorwen (oorwin).

vaporize, (laat) verdamp.

vapour, n. damp, wasem; stroom.

variable, a. veranderlik, wispelturig, ongestadig; wisselbaar, veranderbaar.

variant, n. wisselvorm, variant.

variation, verandering, wysiging, variasie.

varicose: – veins, knopare, spatare.

varied, verskillend; verander; afwisselend; menigvuldig.

variety, verskeidenheid; afwisseling; veelsydigheid; soort.

various, verskillend; verskeie.

varnish, v. vernis; verbloem.

vary, verander, wysig, afwissel; afwyk; varieer; verskil.

vase, vaas; blompot.

vast, geweldig; reusagtig; eindeloos.

vat, vat, kuip.

Vatican, Vatikaan.

vaudeville, vaudeville.

vault, n. gewelf, verwulf; (graf)kelder.

vaulting-horse, bok.

vaunt, v. spog, grootpraat, roem op.

veal, kalfsvleis.

veer, draai, van koers verander; omspring.

vegetable, plant; groentesoort; –s, groente.

vegetarian, n. vegatariër, groente-eter.

vegetation, plantegroei, planteryk.

vehement, geweldig, kragtig; vurig, driftig.

vehicle, rytuig; middel, voertuig.

veil, sluier; gordyn, voorhang(sel); skyn.

vein, n. aar; luim; gees; trant; aard, neiging.

veld, veld.

velocity, snelheid.

velvet, n. ferweel (fluweel).

vender, -or, verkoper; venter.

vendetta, bloedwraak, bloedvete; vendetta.

veneer, n. fineer(hout); vernis(lagie).

venerable, eer(bied)waardig, agbaar.

venerate, vereer, eerbiedig.

venereal, geslags- . . . ; veneries.

vengeance, wraak.

Venice, Venesië.

venison, wild(s)vleis.

venomous, giftig; venynig.

vent, n. gat, luggat, opening; uiting.

ventilate, ventileer, lug; bespreek.

ventilator, luggat, lugrooster.

ventriloquist, buikspreker.

venture, n. waagstuk; risiko; onderneming.

venture, v. wae (waag); durf.

venue, plek (van 'n misdaad); plek waar 'n saak moet voorkom.

Venus, Venus.

veracious, waarheidliewend; waar.

verb, werkwoord, verbum.

verbal, woordelik; mondeling; letterlik; werkwoordelik.

verbatim, woord vir woord, woordelik.

verbose, woorderyk, breedsprakig.

verdant, (gras)groen; grasbedek; baar.

verdict, uitspraak; oordeel, beslissing.

verge, n. kant, rand; grens; roede.

verge, v. grens (aan); naby kom.

verger, koster; stafdraer.

veritable, waar, eg, werklik.

vermicelli, vermicelli.

vermin, ongedierte, goggas; gespuis.

vernacular, n. landstaal, volkstaal.

versatile, veelsydig; veranderlik.

verse, versreël; vers, strofe; poësie; **blank –**, rymlose verse.

versed, bedrewe, ervare; gekonfyt.

version, vertaling; verklaring; voorstelling.

versus, teen, versus.

vertebra, werwel(been), vertebra.

vertex, top, toppunt; kruin.

vertical, a. vertikaal, haaks, loodreg.

verve, geesdrif, entoesiasme, vuur, gloed.

very, a. eg, waar, opreg.

very, adv. baie, erg, uiters, in hoë mate.

vessel, vat; kan, kruik, fles, kom; vaartuig; bloedvat.

vest, n. onderhemp(ie), frok(kie).

vest, v. beklee (met); oordra; berus (by).

vestibule, (voor)portaal, vestibule.

vestige, spoor, teken, bewys.

vestry, konsistorie(kamer); kerkraad.

veteran, a. oud, ervare, beproef.

veteran, n. veteraan.

veterinary, a. – surgeon, veearts.

veto, n. veto(reg); verbod.

veto, v. die veto uitspreek oor; verbied.

vex, vererg, tretter, pla, kwel.

via, oor, langs, via.

vibrate, tril, vibreer; slinger; sidder, beef.

vicar, vikaris; predikant.

vicarage, vikariaat; vikariswoning.

vicarious, plaasvervangend.

vice, n. ondeug; gebrek; onsedelikheid.

vice, n. skroef; bench –, bankskroef.

vice-chairman, vise-voorsitter, ondervoorsitter.

viceroy, onderkoning.

vice versa, omgekeerd.

vicinity, nabyheid, buurte, omtrek.

vicious, sleg, bedorwe; boos(aardig); gebrekkig,

verkeerd; skerp, venynig; vol streke; kwaai, wys.
vicissitude, wisselvalligheid; lotswisseling.
victim, slagoffer, prooi; dupe.
victimize, verongelyk, onreg aandoen.
victor, oorwinnaar.
victorious, oorwinnend, seëvierend.
victory, oorwinning, seëpraal.
vie, wedywer, ding.
Vienna, Wenen.
view, n. uitsig, gesig; kyk, mening; plan, doel; oorsig.
view, v. bekyk, beskou; besigtig.
vigil, (die) waak, wag; –s, nagwaak.
vigilant, waaksaam.
vigorous, kragtig, sterk, fors; lewenskragtig; gespierd.
viking, wiking.
vile, laag, gemeen, vuil; ellendig; sleg.
vilify, beswadder, beskinder.
village, dorp.
villager, dorpenaar, dorpsbewoner.
villain, skurk; skobbejak.
vindicate, verdedig, handhaaf; regverdig.
vindictive, wraakgierig, wraaksugtig.
vine, wingerdstok, wynstok; klimop; rankplant; rank.
vinegar, n. asyn.
vineyard, wingerd.
violate, skend, oortree; ontheilig; onteer.
violence, geweld; hewigheid; skending.
violent, geweldig, onstuimig; driftig, woes; gewelddadig.
violet, n. violetjie (viooltjie); pers.
violet, a. pers, violet.
violin, viool.
violoncello, tjello.
viper, adder.
virago, mannetjie(s)vrou, heks, helleveeg.
virgin, n. maagd.
virgin, a. maagdelik, rein, onbevlek; – soil, onbeboude (rou, ongebraakte) grond.
virile, manlik; kragtig, fors, gespierd.
virtual, eintlik, feitlik.
virtue, deug; reinheid; doeltreffendheid; krag.
virtuous, deugsaam; kuis, rein.
virulent, giftig; kwaadaardig; venynig.
virus, (ver)gif, smetstof; venynigheid.
visa, visum.
viscount, burggraaf.
viscous, klewerig, taai.
visible, sigbaar; duidelik; te sien.
vision, n. gesig, siening; visioen, visie; droomgesig, droombeeld.
visionary, n. siener, dromer, dweper.
visit, v. besoek (aflê by), besoek.
visit, n. besoek, kuier.
visitor, besoeker, kuiergas.
visualize, aanskoulik voorstel, 'n voorstelling maak van.

vital, a. lewens- . . . ; allergrootste.
vitality, lewenskrag, vitaliteit.
vitiate, bederwe, verpes; vernietig.
viticulture, wynbou, wynboerdery.
vitriol, vitrioel.
vituperate, (uit)skel, slegmaak.
vivacious, lewenslustig, vrolik, opgewek.
viva voce, mondeling.
vivid, helder, duidelik; lewendig; skitterend.
vixen, wyfiejakkals; heks, helleveeg.
vocabulary, woordeskat; woordelys.
vocal, stem- . . . , vokaal; mondeling.
vocation, roeping; beroep; ambag, werk.
vociferous, luidrugtig, skreeuend.
vodka, wodka.
vogue, mode; populariteit.
voice, n. stem, spraak; vorm.
voice, v. uiting gee aan.
void, a. leeg; vakant; ongeldig; kragteloos; ontbloot (van); null and –, ongeldig.
void, n. (leë) ruimte; leegte.
volatile, vlugtig, vlug- . . . ; lewendig, vrolik onbestendig.
volcano, vuurspuwende berg, vulkaan.
volley, n. sarsie, salvo; stroom, (stort)vloed, vlughou (tennis).
volt, n. volt (elektr.).
voltage, spanning.
voluble, vlot, glad, woorderyk.
volume, (boek)deel; volume; grootte; omvang massa.
voluntary, a. vrywillig; ongedwonge; opsetlik.
volunteer, n. vrywilliger.
volunteer, v. vrywillig diens neem; vrywillig onderneem; as vrywilliger dien.
voluptuous, wellustig, sinlik.
vomit, v. vomeer (vermeer), (uit)braak.
voracious, gulsig, vraatsugtig.
vortex, maalstroom, draaikolk.
votary, aanbidder, bewonderaar.
vote, n. stem; stemming; stemreg; stembriefie; mosie; begrotingspos.
vote, n. stem; stemming; stemreg; stembriefie; mosie; begrotingspos.
vote, v. stem; voorstel.
voter, kieser, stemgeregtigde; —s' roll, kieserslys.
vouch, bevestig, getuig; instaan (vir).
voucher, bewys(stuk), kwitansie, teenblad.
vow, n. gelofte, eed.
vow, v. 'n gelofte doen; plegtig belowe.
vowl, klinker, vokaal.
voyage, n. (see)reis.
voyage, v. 'n seereis maak, reis, vaar.
vulcanize, vulkaniseer.
vulgar, plat, onbeskof, grof; vulgêr; algemeen.
vulnerable, kwesbaar, wondbaar.
vulture, aasvoël, roofsugtige.

wad, n. prop, stopsel, pluisie; rol.
wadding, watte, kapok, vulsel.
waddle, v. waggel, strompel.
wade, v. deurwaad, deurloop.
waffle, wafel.
waft, v. drywe, waai, swewe.
wag, v. swaai, waai, kwispel, skud.
wag, n. terggees, grappemaker.
wage, n. loon; gasie; besoldiging.
wage, v. voer, maak.
wager, n. weddenskap.
wager, v. wed.
wag(g)on, wa; vragwa.
wagtail, kwikstertjie.
wail, v. weeklaag, huil, kerm.
waist, middel(lyf); lyfie.
waistcoat, onderbaadjie.
wait, v. wag; versuim, vertoef; afwag.
waiter, tafelbediende, kelner.
waive, afsien, van, laat vaar.
wake, v. wakker word (maak); ontwaak, opstaan; opwek; wakker skud, aanvuur.
wake, vaarwater, sog; spoor; jaarfees; lykwaak.
waken, wakker maak (word).
Wales, Wallis.
walk, v. loop, stap, wandel; betree; op 'n stappie
  gaan.
walk, n. gang, pas; wandeling; wandelweg, loop-
  pad, voetpad; beroep; stand.
walkie-talkie, loopprater, geselsradio.
walk-over, maklike oorwinning.
wall, n. muur.
wallaby, kangaroetjie.
wallet, sakkie; portefeulje; knapsak.
walloping, a. tamaai, yslik, frisgeboud.
wallow, v. rol, wentel; swem.
walnut, okkerneut; okkerneutboom; okkerneut-
  hout.
walrus, walrus.
waltz, n. en v. wals.
wan, bleek, asvaal.
wand, staf, towerstaf, stok.
wander, swerwe; wegraak; afdwaal (van die
  onderwerp); yl.
wane, v. taan, verbleek, verswak, afneem.
want, n. gebrek, behoefte, nood, armoede.
want, v. nodig hê, kortkom, makeer, ontbreek;
  gebrek ly; begeer, verlang, wil hê; wil.
wanton, a. dartel, vrolik; veranderlik; weelderig;
  woes; ligsinnig, losbandig.
war, n. oorlog, stryd, kryg.
war, v. oorlog (stryd) voer.
warble, v. sing, kweel.
war-cry, oorlogskreet, strydkreet.
ward, n. bewaking; bewaring; voogdyskap;
  pleegkind; (stads)wyk; afdeling, saal, kamer
  (in 'n hospitaal).
ward, v. bewaar, beskerm.
warden, voog; bewaarder.
warder, bewaarder, sipier.
wardrobe, klerekas; (voorraad) klere.
ware, n. –s, koopware.
warehouse, n. loods, pakhuis; winkel.
warfare, oorlog, kryg, stryd.
warlike, oorlogsugtig, krygshaftig.
warm, a. warm; heet; verhit; hartstogtelik, vurig;
  hartlik, innig; vars (van spoor).
warm, v. warm maak (word), verwarm.
warn, waarsku; verwittig; vermaan.
warning, waarskuwing, vermaning.
warp, v. kromtrek, skeeftrek, krom (skeef) word;
  bederf, (laat) ontaard, versleg; bevooroordeeld maak; verdraai.
warrant, n. volmag; waarborg, magbrief, lasbrief, bevelskrif.

warrant, v. magtig, volmag gee; waarborg, verseker; regverdig.
warranty, n. volmag, waarborg.
warren, konynwerf.
warrior, krygsman, soldaat, kryger.
warship, oorlogskip.
wart, vrat(jie); knoes.
wart-hog, wildevark, vlakvark.
wary, versigtig, behoedsaam.
wash, v. was, afwas, (af)spoel, uitspoel, bespoel.
wash, n. (die) was; wasgoed; spoeling; geklots;
  kielwater; spoelgrond, dryfgrond; skottel-
  (goed)water; flou (slegte) tee (drank); waterverf; vernis, vloeistof, water, wasmiddel.
wash-basin, waskom.
washer, wasser; waster.
washerwoman, wasmeid, wasvrou.
washing, n. wasgoed.
wash-out, misoes, fiasko.
wasp, perdeby, wesp.
waste, a. woes, woestynagtig; verlate; onbewerk; oortollig.
waste, v. verkwis, vermors; verwoes; verminder,
  afneem; wegkwyn; verniel.
waste, n. woesteny, woestyn, wildernis; ver-
  kwisting, verspilling; afval; vermindering, verbruik; slytasie; verwaarlosing; verval.
waste basket, snippermandjie.
wasteful, verkwistend, spandabel.
waste pipe, afvoerpyp, -buis.
waster, deurbringer, verkwister.
watch, n. wag; waak; horlosie.
watch, v. waak; wag hou; bespied, dophou, in
  die oog hou; oplet, afwag.
watchful, waaksaam, op die hoede.
watchman, nagwag; wagter.
watchword, wagwoord; leuse.
water, n. water.
water, v. natmaak, natgooi; verdun; ('n perd,
  ens.) water gee; water inneem; water (mond,
  oë).
water-bailiff, waterfiskaal, waterskout.
water-colour, waterverf; waterverfskildery.
watercourse, waterloop; watervoor.
watercress, bronkors, bronslaai.
waterfall, waterval.
watering-can, gieter.
water-main, hoofwaterpyp.
water-melon, waatlemoen.
watershed, waterskeiding.
watertight, waterdig.
watt, watt (in elektrisiteit).
wattle, vlegwerk; spar; basboom.
wave, v. golf (golwe); kartel; wapper; wuif,
  waai; wink.
wave, n. golf, brander; kartel.
waver, aarsel, weifel; flikker; bewe.
wax, n. was; byewas; lak; oorwas.
way, weg, pad; rigting; manier; gewoonte, gebruik; toestand.
way-bill, vragbrief, geleibrief.
wayward, eiewys, eiesinnig, wispelturig.
we, ons.
weak, swak; tingerig; flou; slap.
weaken, verswak; verslap; flouer maak.
weakling, swakkeling, sukkelaar.
weakness, swakheid; swak, swakte.
weal, welvaart, welsyn, geluk.
wealth, rykdom; oorvloed, weelde.
wean, speen; afleer, afwen.
weapon, wapen.
wear, v. dra; (af)slyt, uitslyt; afmat.
weary, a. vermoeid, moeg; sat; vermoeiend, vervelend.

weary, v. vermoei, moeg maak; verveel; moeg word (van).
weather, n. weer.
weather, v. te bowe kom, veilig deurkom, braveer, trotseer; verweer, verbrokkel, opkrummel.
weathercock, weerhaan.
weave, weef, vleg.
web, web; weefsel; spinnerak.
wed, trou; verenig, verbind.
wedding, bruilof, trouery.
wedding-cake, bruidskoek.
wedge, n. keil, wig.
wedlock, huwelik, eg.
Wednesday, Woensdag.
weed, n. onkruid, gras.
weed, v. skoffel, gras uittrek.
weeds, onkruid, gras.
week, week.
week-end, naweek.
weekly, adv. weekliks, elke week.
weekly, n. weekblad.
weep, huil, ween; drup.
weevil, kalander.
weigh, wee (weeg); oorweeg; opweeg (teen); geld.
weight, n. gewig; las; belang.
weighty, swaar; gewigtig; belangrik; invloedryk; weldeurdag.
weir, dam, dwarsmuur (in 'n rivier), wal.
weird, a. spookagtig, grillerig; raar, vreemd.
welcome, n. welkom, verwelkoming.
welcome, v. welkom heet, verwelkom.
weld, v. sweis; verenig, verbind.
welfare, welvaart, welsyn.
well, n. bron, fontein, put.
well, v. opwel, ontspruit, ontspring.
well, adv. goed, wel; terdeë.
well, interj. wel.
well-balanced, ewewigtig.
well-behaved, soet, goedopgevoed.
well-being, welsyn, welvaart.
well-doer, weldoener.
well-informed, goedingelig; belese.
well-off, welgesteld.
Welshman, Walliser.
welt, rant, strokie (leer); hou.
welter, v. rol, wentel.
welter-weight, weltergewig.
wend, gaan.
Wesleyan, a. Wesleyaans.
west, n. die weste.
west, adv. wes, na die weste(kant).
westward, weswaarts.
wet, v. bevogtig, natmaak.
wether, hamel.
whack, n. slag, harde hou; deel, porsie.
whale, n. walvis.
whale-oil, walvistraan.
whaler, walvisvaarder, walvisvanger.
wharf, n. kaai.
what, a. watter, wat.
what, pron. wat; hoe; hè.
whatever, wat ook al, al wat.
wheat, koring.
wheedle, vlei, flikflooi, mooipraat, lek.
wheel, n. wiel, rat; swenking.
wheel, v. (laat) swenk; krink, draai; rol, stoot; draaie maak.
wheelbarrow, kruiwa.
wheel-chair, rolstoel.
wheeze, n. gehyg, gefluit (van keel).
whelp, n. klein hondjie; welp.
when, adv. wanneer, toe, as; terwyl.
whence, adv. waarvandaan, van waar

whenever, wanneer ook (al); elke keer as.
where, adv. waar; waarheen, waarnatoe.
where, pron. waarvandaan, waarheen.
whereabouts, n. verblyfplek, boerplek.
whereas, aangesien, nademaal, daar.
whereby, waardeur, waarby.
wherefore, waarom, hoekom, daarom.
wherein, waarin.
whereof, waarvan.
whereon, waarop.
whereto, waarnatoe, waartoe; waarom.
whereupon, waarop.
wherever, waar ook (al); oral waar.
wherewith, waarmee.
whet, slyp, skerpmaak; prikkel.
whether, conj. of; ditsy (hetsy).
which, a. watter.
which, pron. watter, wie, wat.
whiff, luggie, geurtjie, trekkie.
while, n. tydjie, rukkie, wyle.
while, conj. terwyl, onderwyl.
whim, gril, nuk, gier, streek.
whimper, v. huil, grens; kreun, kla(e); tjank.
whimsical, vol nukke (grille), wispelturig; vreemd, raar.
whine, v. huil, tjank; kla(e).
whinny, v. runnik.
whip, v. (weg)spring, wip; gryp; piets, slaan; (eiers) klop, klits.
whip, n. sweep, peits, karwarts; katrol.
whip-lash, voorslag.
whipping, pak (slae).
whir(r), v. gons, snor.
whirl, v. draai, (d) warrel, snor.
whirlpool, maalstroom, draaikolk.
whirlwind, (d)warrelwind.
whisk, n. stoffer, besempie; (eier)klopper.
whisk, v. (af)vee, (af)stof; klop, klits; swaai, draai; wip.
whisker(s), wangbaard, bakbaard; snor.
whisky, whisky.
whisper, v. fluister; toefluister; ruis, ritsel.
whistle, v. fluit.
whistle, n. fluit, gefluit; fluitjie.
white, a. wit; blank; bleek; rein.
whitewash, n. witkalk, witklei, witsel.
whitewash, v. wit, afwit; verontskuldig, goedpraat.
whither, waarheen, waarnatoe.
whitlow, fyt.
Whitsuntide, Pinkster, Pinksterdae.
whittle, v. sny, afsny.
whiz(z), v. gons, fluit, sing, sis.
who, wie; wat.
whoever, whosoever, wie ook.
whole, a. heel; veilig; gesond.
whole, n. hele, geheel; alles.
whole-hearted, hartlik; algeheel.
wholesale, n. groothandel.
wholesale, adv. op groot skaal.
wholesome, gesond, heilsaam.
wholly, heeltemal, geheel, volkome.
whom, sien who, wat, vir (aan) wie.
whoop, skreeu, roep, hoe; optrek.
whooping-cough, kinkhoes.
whopper, n. 'n groot leuen; 'n yslike.
whose, van wie, wie se, wie s'n.
why, adv. waarom, hoekom.
wick, pit (van 'n lamp).
wicked, goddeloos, sondig; ondeund.
wicket, hekkie, deurtjie; onderdeur; baan (krieket); paaltjies (krieket).
wicket-keeper, paaltjie(s)wagter.
wide, wyd, breed; ver; uitgestrek.
wide-awake, wakker, uitgeslaap, geslepe.

wide-spread, verbrei, algemeen.
widow, n. weduwee, weduvrou.
widower, wewenaar.
width, wydte, breedte; breedheid, uitgestrektheid.
wield, uitoefen, beheer, bestuur; swaai; hanteer.
wife, vrou, eggenote.
wig, n. pruik.
wild, a. wild; woes, rasend; bang; roekeloos, losbandig; stormagtig, geweldig; verwilderd.
wild, adv. blindweg; los en vas (praat).
wildcat, n. wildekat.
wildcat, a. onbesonne, halsoorkop- . . .
wildebeest, wildebees.
wilderness, wildernis, woesteny.
wile, n. (skelm)streek, lis, geslepenheid.
wilful, moedswillig, opsetlik; eiewys.
will, v. wil, begeer; wens; vermaak.
will, aux. v. sal.
will, n. wil; wilskrag; begeerte; testament.
willing, (ge)willig.
will-o'-the-wisp, dwaallig; blinkwater.
willow, n. wilgerboom (wilg).
will-power, wilskrag.
wily, listig, slu, geslepe, slim, oulik.
win, v. wen (win); behaal; verdien.
win, n. oorwinning; wenslag.
wince, v. (ineen)krimp, terugdeins; gril, huiwer, ys.
winch, slinger, wen, windas.
wind, n. wind; lug; ruik; asem.
wind, v. ruik.
wind, v. slinger, kronkel; draai, rol.
windbreak, windskut, windskerm.
windfall, geluk, meevallertjie.
winding staircase, wenteltrap.
windlass, n. wen, windas.
windmill, windpomp, windmeul.
window, venster, raam.
window-sill, vensterbank.
windpipe, lugpyp.
wind-screen, windskerm; – wiper, ruitveër.
windy, winderig; opgeblaas, windmakerig.
wine, wyn.
wineglass, wynkelkie.
wing, n. vlerk, vleuel; wiek; vlug.
winged, gevleuel.
wink, v. knipoog, wink; flikker.
winner, wenner, oorwinnaar.
winning-post, wenpaal.
winnow, (uit)wan, uitwaai; (uit)sif, skei.
winsome, innemend, bevallig, vriendelik.
winter, n. winter.
winter, v. oorwinter.
wipe, v. (af)vee, afdroë, skoonvee.
wire, n. draad; telegraafdraad; telegram.
wire, v. met draad vasmaak; die drade lê (span); inrye; telegrafeer.
wire-cutter, draadtang, draadskêr.
wire-haired, steekhaar- . . .
wireless, n. radio, draadlose telegrafie.
wire netting, sifdraad.
wiry, draadagtig; gespierd, sterk.
wisdom, wysheid; verstand.
wise, a. verstandig, wys.
wiseacre, alweter, slimprater.
wish, v. wens, begeer, verlang.
wis! , n. wens, begeerte, verlange.
wisp, bossie, toutjie, hopie.
wit, n. vernuf, verstand; geestigheid.
witch, n. (tower)heks, towenares.
witchcraft, toordery, toorkuns.
witch-doctor, toordokter.
with, met, saam met; by; van.
withdraw, wegtrek; herroep; intrek; wegneem; verskuiwe; opsygaan, weggaan.

wither, (laat) verwelk, verlep word; kwyn, vergaan.
withers, skof (van 'n perd).
withhold, weerhou, terughou, weier.
within, adv. binne; van binne.
within, prep. binne, in.
without, adv. buitekant, (van) buite.
without, prep. buite, buitekant, sonder.
withstand, weerstaan.
witness, n. getuie, getuienis.
witness, v. getuig; aanskou, sien; as getuie onderteken.
witness-box, getuiebank.
wittingly, opsetlik, bewus.
witty, geestig.
wizard, towenaar, waarsêer.
wizened, verrimpel, verskrompel.
wobble, v. slinger, waggel; aarsel.
woe, wee, nood, ellende, smart.
woebegone, treurig, armsalig.
woeful, treurig, droewig.
wolf, wolf; vraat, gulsigaard.
wolf-hound, wolfshond.
wolfram, wolfram.
woman, n. vrou.
womanly, vroulik.
wonder, n. wonder; wonderwerk; verbasing.
wonder, v. verwonder, wonder; nuuskierig wees; verbaas wees.
wonderful, wonderlik; merkwaardig.
wont, n. gewoonte, gebruik.
woo, vry na; probeer omhaal (ompraat); flikflooi.
wood, bos, woud; hout.
woodcutter, houtkapper, houthakker.
woodpecker, houtkapper, speg.
woodwork, houtwerk.
woody, bosagtig, bosryk; houtagtig.
wool, wol; wolklere; wolhare.
wool-gathering, n. afgetrokkenheid; verstrooid wees.
word, n. woord; boodskap; wagwoord, bevel.
word, v. uitdruk, stel, formuleer.
wording, bewoording.
work, n. werk, arbei.
work, v. werk, arbei; (laat) bewerk; uitwerking hê; laat werk; beheer, (be)stuur; hanteer; teweegbring, veroorsaak; gis, rys (suurdeeg, ens.); oplos, bereken, uitreken; deurwerk, knie, brei.
workable, bewerkbaar; uitvoerbaar.
workaday, gewoon, alledaags, saai.
workless, werkloos, sonder werk.
workman, werksman.
workmanship, knapheid; afwerking, uitvoering; maaksel; werk.
workshop, werkwinkel, werkplek.
world, wêreld.
wordly, wêrelds, aards; wêreldsgesind.
world-wide, alombekend, wêreld- . . .
worm, n. wurm; skroefdraad.
worm, v. kruip; kronkel.
worn, vermoeid; verslete (verslyt), afgeslyt; oud, afgesaag.
worry, v. lastig val, peuter, pla(e); kwel; karnuffel, byt, hap.
worry, n. moeite, las; plaery; kwelling, kommer, sorg.
worse, a. erger, slegter.
worship, v. aanbid; verafgood.
worst, a. ergste, slegste.
worst, n. ergste.
worth, a. werd.
worth, n. waarde.
worthless, waardeloos, nikswerd.

worthy, a. waardig, werd; agtenswaardig.
wound, v. wond, kwes; seermaak, grief.
wounded, a. gewond, gekwes.
wrangle, v. twis, kyf, rusie maak.
wrap, v. toemaak, toedraai; inpak; hul.
wrapper, omslag; reisdeken.
wrath, toorn, gramskap.
wreak, wreek, wraak uitoefen op.
wreath, krans; kring, ring.
wreck, n. wrak, gestrande skip; skipbreuk, (die)
vergaan (van 'n skip); verwoesting.
wreck, v. (laat) skipbreuk ly (vergaan); (laat)
verongeluk; laat misluk; vernietig, verniel.
wreckage, wrak, wrakhout; oorblyfsels.
wrench, n. ruk, pluk, draai; skroefhamer.
wrench, v. ruk, draai; verdraai, verrek.
wrestle, v. worstel, stoei.
wrestler, stoeier, worstelaar.
wretch, drommel; ellendeling.
wretched, ellendig, miserable, armsalig; ongelukkig; vervlakste.

wriggle, kronkel; kriewel, wriemel, woel, vroetel
wikkel.
wring, v. wring, (om)draai; druk.
wrinkle, n. plooi, rimpel.
wrinkle, v. plooi, rimpel.
wrist, handgewrig, pols.
wrist-drop, voorarmverlamming.
wristlet, armband; – **watch,** polshorlosie.
writ, n. skrif; lasbrief, bevelskrif; dagvaarding.
write, skryf (skrywe).
writhe, (ineen)krimp, draai; verwring.
writing-pad, skryfblok.
written, geskrewe; skriftelik.
wrong, a. verkeerd; nie pluis nie.
wrong, n. kwaad; onreg.
wrong, adv. verkeerd, mis.
wrong, v. onreg aandoen, verongelyk.
wrongdoer, kwaaddoener, oortreder.
wry, skeef.

X-ray, v. met X-strale behandel.
X-rays, X-strale, Röntgen-strale.

xylophone, xilofoon.

Y

yacht, n. (seil)jag.
yap, v. kef, blaf.
yard, n. agterplaas; werf.
yarn, n. garing (gare), draad; storie.
yawn, n. & v. gaap.
year, jaar; leap –, skrikkeljaar.
yearn, smag, hunker (na).
yeast, suurdeeg; gis.
yell, v. gil, skreeu.
yell, n. gil, skreeu, kreet.
yellow, a. geel; lafhartig.
yelp, tjank, kef.
yes, ja.
yesterday, gister.
yet, adv. nog; al; tog, nogtans; tot nog toe.
yet, conj. en tog.

yield, v. oplewer, opbring, produseer, inbring; oorgee; toegee.
yield, n. opbrings; oes; produksie.
yoke, n. juk; skouerstuk.
yoke, v. die juk oplê; (osse) inspan.
yoke-pin, jukskei.
yolk, geel van 'n eier, door (dooier).
yonder, a. daardie, ginds, gunter.
yonder, adv. daar(so), (daar)gunter.
you, jy, jou, julle, u.
young, a. jong; klein.
youngster, kind, seun, snuiter.
yours, joue; van u.
yourself, jouself, self; uself.
youth, jeug, jonkheid; jonkman; jongspan.

Z

zeal, ywer, erns, vuur, geesdrif.
zebra, sebra, kwagga, streepesel.
zenith, senit, toppunt, hoogste punt.
zero, nul; nulpunt; vriespunt; zero (sero).
zest, graagte, gretigheid, lus.
zigzag, v. draai-draai loop, kronkel; sigsag.

zinc, n. sink.
zip-fastener, ritssluiting; ritssluiter.
zone, sone, (aard)gordel, lugstreek; streek.
zoo, dieretuin.
zoology, dierkunde, soölogie.
Zulu, Zoeloe.

Some Common Abbreviations and Symbols

AA Automoblie Association.
acc. account; accusative.
A.D. Anno Domini.
A.D.C. Aide-de-camp.
a(dj). adjective.
ad lib. ad libitum (to the extent desired).
adv. adverb.
alg. algebra.
Adv. Advocate.
Afr. Afrikaans.
alg. algebra.
a.m. ante meidiem (before noon).
anon. anonymous.
appro. approval.
Ass(n). Association.
asst assistant.

b. born; bowled.
B.A. Bachelor of Arts.
Bart Baronet.
BBC British Broadcasting Company.
B.C. before Christ.
B.Comm. Bachelor of Commerce.
B.D. Bachelor of Divinity.
Bros Brothers.
B.Sc. Bachelor of Science.

C Celsius.
c. caught; century; chapter; circa; cubic.
c cent(s).
C.A. Chartered Accountant.
Capt. Captain.
cf. confer (compare).
ch., chap. chapter.
C.I.D. Criminal Investigation Department.
c.i.f. cost, insurance and freight.
circ. circa, circiter.
cm centimetre.
Co. Company.
C.O. Commanding Officer.
c/o care of.
C.O.D. cash on delivery.
Col. Colonel.
col. column
Co-op. Co-operative.
cp. compare.
Cr Creditor.
cm² square centimetre.
cm³ cubic centimetre.
cub cubic.
c. & b. caught and bowled.

d. daughter; denarius (penny); died.
D.D. Doctor of Divinity.
Dec. December.
deg. degree.
Dept. Department.
D.F.C. Distinguished Flying Cross.
dim. diminutive.
div. dividend.
dl decilitre.
D. Lit(t). Doctor of Literature.
do ditto.
doz. dozen.
D.Phil. Doctor of Philosophy.
Dr debtor, doctor.
D.Sc. Doctor of Science.
D.S.O. Distinguished Service Order.
D.V. Deo volente (*God willing*).

E. & O.E. errors and omissions excepted.
esp. especially.
Esq. Esquire.
etc. et cetera.

et seq(q). et sequentia (and what follows)
ex. example.
exam. examination.
Exod. Exodus.

f feminine; franc(s); from.
fc(a)p. foolscap.
Feb. February.
fem. feminine.
fig. figure, figurative(ly).
f.o.b. free on board.
Fo., fol. folio.
f.o.r. free on rail.
Fr. French.
fr. franc(s).
F.R.C.S. Fellow of the Royal College of Surgeons.
fut. future.

g gram(s).
G.B. Great Britain.
GCM greatest common measure.
Gen. General; Genesis.
gen. general, genitive.
geog. geography.
geol. geology.
geom. geometry.
G.P. general practitioner.
GPO General Post Office.
gr. grain(s); grammar.
gym. gymnasium; gymnastic costume.

h hour.
ha hectare.
HCF highest common factor.
H.E. His Excellency.
hg hectogram.
hl hectolitre.
hm hectometre.
H.M. His (Her) Majesty.
HMS His (Her) Majesty's Ship.
Hon. Sec. Honorary Secretary.
h.p. hire purchase

ib(id). ibidem (in the same place).
id. idem (the same).
i.e. id est (that is).
ind(ic). indicative.
inf(in). infinitive.
inst. instant.
int(erj). interjection.
intr(ans). intransitive.
Is. Island (Isle).
Iscor (South African) Iron and Steel Corporation.
I Q intelligence quotient.

Jan. January.
J.P. Justice of the Peace.
Jr. Junior.
jun., junr. junior.

K.C. King's Counsel.
K.C.B. Knight Commander of the Bath.
kg kilogram.
kJ kilojoule (practical unit of energy).
kl kilolitre.
km kilometre.
km/h kilometre per hour.
Kt Knight.

l. left; lira.
ℓ litre (s).

lat. latitude.
l.b.w. leg before wicket.
LCM lowest common multiple.
L.D.S. Licentiate in Dental Surgery.
Lieut. Lieutenant.
Litt. D. Literarum Doctor (Doctor of Letters).
LL.B. Legum Baccalaureus (Bachelor of Laws).
LL.D. Legum Doctor (Doctor of Laws).
loc. cit. loco citato (in the place quoted).
log. logarithm; logic.
long. longitude.
L.P. long-playing (record).
Lt. Lieutenant.

m metre
M. Monsieur.
M.A. Master of Arts.
Maj. Major.
masc. masculine.
matric. matriculation.
M. Comm. Master of Commerce.
M.D. Medicinae Doctor (Doctor of Medicine).
MEC Member of Executive Committee (Council).
memo. memorandum.
Messrs Messieurs.
mg milligram.
min minute(s).
ml millilitre.
Ml megalitre.
Mlle Mademoiselle.
mm millimetre.
Mme Madame.
MOH Medical Officer of Health.
MP Member of Parliament.
MPC Member of Provincial Council.
Mr Mister.
Mrs Mistress.
MS manuscript.
MSS manuscripts.
Mt Mount.

n. neuter; nominative; noon; noun.
n.b. no ball.
N.B. nota bene (note well).
n.d. no date.
nem. con. nemine contradicente (no one objecting).
No numero (number).
nom. nominative.

ob. obiit (died).
obj. object(ive).
OFS Orange Free State.
op. opus (work).
op. cit. opere citato (in the work quoted).

p. page.
par. paragraph.
PAYE pay as you earn.
P.C. Privy Councillor.
p.c. per cent.
pd paid.
per pro. per procurationem (by proxy).
Ph.D. Philosophiae Doctor (Doctor of Philosophy).
pl. plural.
p.m. post meridiem (after noon).
PMG Postmaster General.
P.O. Post Office.
prep. preparation; preposition.
Pres. President.
Prof. Professor.

pron. pronoun.
pro tem. pro tempore (for the time).
Prov. Proverbs.
prox. proximo (next month).
PS postscript.
Ps. Psalm(s).
PTO please turn over.
PWD Public Works Department.

Q.E.D. quod erat demonstrandum (which was to be proved).
Q.E.F. quod erat faciendum (which was to be done).
qr quarter(s).
quot. quotation.
q.v. quod vide (which see).

R rand(s).
R. River.
RAC Royal Automobile Club.
RAF Royal Air Force.
R.C. Roman Catholic.
Rd Road.
recd received.
Ref. Reformed.
ref. reference, referee.
regt. regiment.
Rev. Reverend.
R.I.P. requiescat in pace (rest in peace).
R.M.S. Royal Mail Steamer.
R.S.V.P. repondez s'il vous plait (please reply).
Rt Hon. Right Honourable.
Rt Rev. Right Reverend.

S South.
s second.
SA South Africa(n).
SAR South African Railways/(Republic).
Sec. Secretary.
Sen., Senr. senior.
Sept. September.
S(er)gt Sergeant.
SI Système International d'Unités.
sing. singular.
Soc. Society.
sq. square.
Sr Senior.
SSE south-south-east.
St Saint; Street.
st. stem; stumped.
Supt Superintendent.
SW South West.

TB tuberculosis.
T.O. Turn over.
Toc H Talbot House.
Treas. Treasurer.

US(A) United States (of America).
USSR Union of Soviet Socialist Republics.

v. verb; versus; vide (see); volt.
verb. sap. verbum sapiento (a word to the wise).
viz videlicet (namely).
vol. volume.

w.c. water closet.

YMCA Young Men's Christian Association.
YWCA Young Women's Christian Association.